By Rollin Chambliss
UNIVERSITY OF GEORGIA

SOCIAL THOUGHT

From Hammurabi to Comte

The Dryden Press - New York

Copyright 1954 by

The Dryden Press, Inc., New York 19, N. Y.

MANUFACTURED IN THE U.S.A.

All the selections used in this volume have been reprinted by special permission of their respective copyright owners and may not be reproduced without similar permission from them.

First printing: March 1954

The Dryden Press
Sociology Publications

GENERAL EDITOR
T. LYNN SMITH
UNIVERSITY OF FLORIDA

For AMY

PREFACE

This volume, designed primarily as a textbook, offers a brief survey of social thought from Hammurabi to Comte. The former ruled over Babylonia in the seventeenth century B.C., and the latter attempted in nineteenth-century France to enthrone positivism in the intellectual world.

Hammurabi and Comte were separated by more than 3600 years. During that time many civilizations emerged and developed, and some of them decayed. The Chinese and the Hindus discovered ways of life that have been followed by millions upon millions of people. The Greeks and the Romans stated principles that still guide many other millions in their relations with one another. With a Hebrew heritage, Christians rallied around a faith that sustained medieval Europe and today undergirds life with meaning for a large portion of mankind. The Arabs emerged from their tents, built an empire, which disintegrated, and founded a religion, which endured. Finally, with the tools of science at their disposal, men of diverse nations worked together to fashion the modern world.

It is obvious that a book of ordinary length can contain only a part of the social ideas that appeared during the long period between Hammurabi and Comte. Many of those ideas, however, had little influence on the course of human events. By concentration on ideas that lived and developed, the problem of choice has been considerably reduced. The material for this book, then, has been taken from the solid body of living ideas that constitute an important part of the intellectual heritage of mankind.

In the presentation of the selected ideas, the needs of college students have been kept constantly in mind. Since usually it is more difficult to apprehend than it is to censure, a conscious attempt has been made to enter sympathetically into the ideas expressed. This means that, for the moment, the original writer's point of view is taken. Discussion thrives only when people are talking about the same thing. Therefore, in this book emphasis has been placed upon comprehension, and it is left to the reader to make the critical evaluation so important in the learning process. To have included more would have meant the extension of the book beyond reasonable bounds. Comprehension, furthermore, should precede evaluation. Indeed, the most effective criticism of an idea is often a clear statement of it.

A textbook in social thought should be concerned more with stimulating the intellect than with exercising the memory. For that reason, an attempt has been made here not to catalogue many ideas but rather to summarize and explain a few. These are presented with the various shades of meaning they have had as time passed, so that the development of social thought is disclosed and its unity made apparent.

It is hoped that the readers of this book will be encouraged to turn to the sources upon which it has been based. Although some of them are secondary, most are original. Sufficient documentation has been introduced to locate certain important social ideas in their original setting. Other than that, the appurtenances of scholarship have been kept to a minimum.

The problem of giving credit to those to whom credit is due is always difficult. Certain social scientists set a generation of students to thinking about social origins, social organization, social development, and methods of social inquiry. Other writers have awakened an interest in the ancient civilizations and have attempted to trace the development of social thought. To all those scholars who have blazed this trail, to publishers who have permitted quotations, and to personal friends who have given direct assistance in the writing of this book, grateful thanks are hereby expressed.

Finally, to those who blame me,

> Thinking that merely to touch in brevity
> The topics I dwell on, were unlawful,—
> Or worse, that I trench, with undue levity,
> On the bounds of the holy and the awful . . .

I offer from his "Christmas Eve" Robert Browning's praise and pity. Surely the spirit of sympathy that it has ever been the aim of liberal education to foster will recognize his claim that below the light speech we utter, "the soul's depths boil in earnest!"

R. C.

Athens, Georgia
February 28, 1954

CONTENTS

1. SOCIAL THOUGHT AND SOCIAL HISTORY   1

I. FIVE ANCIENT SOCIETIES

2. BABYLONIA   13
3. ANCIENT EGYPT   42
4. CONFUCIUS AND THE CHINESE CLASSICS   75
5. ANCIENT INDIA   102
6. THE HEBREWS OF THE OLD TESTAMENT   125

II. GREECE, ROME, AND MEDIEVAL CHRISTENDOM

7. PLATO   157
8. ARISTOTLE   179
9. ROME   206
10. AUGUSTINE   233
11. THOMAS AQUINAS   260

III. EARLY MODERN SOCIAL THOUGHT

12. IBN KHALDUN   285
13. RENAISSANCE AND REFORMATION   313
14. JOHN LOCKE   342
15. GIAMBATTISTA VICO   366
16. AUGUSTE COMTE   392
17. SOCIAL PHILOSOPHY AND SOCIAL SCIENCE   426

NOTES   433

BIBLIOGRAPHY   445

INDEX   457

1 · INTRODUCTION

The contemplation of social thought from ancient times to the midnineteenth century demands boldness and inspires humility. Hundreds of books have been written on topics to which this volume allots only a few sentences, and innumerable scholars have devoted their lives to the study of works that are treated here in a single chapter. Nevertheless, the voyage into the deep of man's age-long meditations about social relations and the good life offers the inviting prospect of moments with some of the most profound of men. They have much to say. We can not expect in a brief survey to receive pure and complete the ideas of those whom, more than others, the world has judged wise, but we can learn something from them that will make our lives richer.

One of the great tragedies of our age is that a large number of educated persons attempt to understand the present without concerning themselves about the past. Yet, as Oscar Wilde said, "He to whom the present is the only thing that is present, knows nothing of the age in which he lives." Each of us is a part of all that mankind has met and made. We live, whoever we are and wherever we may be, in one world. The sea of man's timeless speculations is around us, unifying the intellectual world as the physical universe is made one by the waters of the deep.

Some of the wise men of old gave answers not only to their own fundamental questions about man in society but also to ours. Although we may disagree at times with some of their views, these men have won the right to our attention, and any one of them whose social thought is reviewed in this book is entitled to a sympathetic hearing. "It is useful, nay essential," said Thomas Carlyle, "to see his good qualities before pronouncing on his bad." We should seek, therefore, first to apprehend and only then to show just how Plato, for example, missed the mark and Thomas Aquinas foundered. In criticism there are many measures, and we can weigh arguments only on our own scales. But weigh them we must. Else we fall into that irrational acceptance of the old so characteristic of mankind.

> *For of the wholly common is man made,*
> *And custom is his nurse! Woe then to them*
> *That lay irreverent hands upon his old*
> *House furniture, the dear inheritance*
> *From his forefathers! For time consecrates;*
> *And what is gray with age becomes the sacred.*[1] *
>
> — Schiller

As we read old classics, we ought to keep that truth ever before us, because it is only when we realize that "honors with increase of ages grow/As streams roll down, enlarging as they flow," that we are protected against giving easy assent to all the views expressed by famous men. We become aware of the fact that their ideas are not equally excellent. Some are a precious heritage; others have not stood the test of time.

From the *stoa,* Zeno uttered profound truths, and in the dark days of Rome's collapse Augustine showed a way into the mysteries of Christian faith. The *Vedas* of the Hindus and the *Analects* of Confucius have long given, and still offer, inspiration and hope to many millions of people. Our daily lives are shaped by the laws of the ancient Hebrews, and some of our highest aspirations arise from the vision and the eloquence of their prophets. In the presence of Plato, we feel as humble as did his disciples, and in the Golden Mean of Aristotle we discover a way of life which, after all the years that have elapsed since he lectured in his garden in Athens, is still appealing. Ideas from such men as Thomas Aquinas, Ibn Khaldun, Luther, Calvin, Locke, Vico, and Comte are living forces in the world today.

Now that the battle for science has been won, there is little reason to fear that the hand of the past will rest so heavily on our age as to restrain scientific inquiry. There is, however, cause to be alarmed at a present tendency among social scientists to confuse the latest with the best. Taking a cue from some of the natural scientists, they ask whether ancient lore can have other than merely historical interest. "Does the physicist look to Democritus for his science, or the biologist to Aristotle?" the social scientist may well inquire. If no doctor practices medicine by the prescriptions of Galen, why should any person be guided in his conduct by the social ideas of Aristotle?

The answer is clear: the advance in knowledge about the physical universe since Galen is not matched by a corresponding growth in understanding of human behavior since Aristotle. The student today begins his first physics course with knowledge which even Galileo never had; he uses techniques and instruments developed since Galileo's time. He ought soon to learn more science than Galileo ever grasped. The same student is not so fortunate, however, with respect to Shakespeare. He is not likely to read more clearly the human heart, or to set down his observations more lucidly, than did Shakespeare, despite all

---

* Numbered footnotes will be found in the section beginning on page 433.

the writing that has accumulated since Shakespeare died. Similarly, the latest social ideas are not necessarily the best.

In some fields of experience knowledge becomes more adequate as it accumulates, but not in all. Much of Aristotle's science is out of date; most of his analysis of social relations is not. The "Golden Mean" interests us, not because it was suited to the needs of a small nation in an ancient age but because it well defines a way of life that has a universal and a timeless appeal. The "Just Price" of Thomas Aquinas is a noble conception of the price controls without which, in some form, our modern economic order would collapse. Augustine's spiritual insights and Locke's recognition of the rights of the individual are not outmoded. Down through the ages have come the voices of the Hebrew prophets, still ringing strong with their exhortations. It would be foolish to depend wholly on ancient wisdom, regarding as trivial, if not actually useless, the development of social science during the last century and especially the fruits of recent research in comparatively unexplored areas of human experience. Vast strides are being made in the social sciences, and we can hope some day to know far more about human society than we know now. For the present, however, many old ideas have lost none of their vitality, and it may well be that they never will.

SOCIAL THOUGHT AND SOCIAL HISTORY

We are concerned in this book primarily with social thought and only incidentally with social history—that is, we are concerned with ideas rather than with events. Social history is a vast subject. In order to describe accurately the social customs which once prevailed in a specific society, one may either avoid generalizations altogether or qualify those made so as to make clear the period of time in which a certain custom was found, the fluctuations in it that occurred during that period, the social classes that practiced it, and the reliability of the works which describe it. Consequently, the task of portraying Roman society during a given age, for example, is one to challenge the ability and the industry of the ablest scholars. Since the writing of a complete social history of a single society is so difficult a task, it is easy to understand why most social historians have found it necessary to stake out certain small areas of that history as their particular domains if they hoped to discover something not earlier known.

A broad survey of social thought attempts something less ambitious. It is easier to record what Plato said than what the Greeks did. Many volumes are required to give even the outlines of universal history; but the story of social thought can be sketched in a single book through representative samples. Moreover, it is important that this story of ideas be told. We live in an age when facts are highly regarded but it is abstract ideas that make concrete facts comprehensible. Facts no more form a systematic body of knowledge than bricks in a pile form a house. Theory is to the scientist what a plan is to a house-builder. The collection of social facts is a worthy enterprise; the arrangement of these facts so that they form designs and patterns ought to be similarly regarded.

Social thought is not easy to define. All thought is related to social experience in some way. The Egyptians, for example, needing to re-establish the boundaries obliterated by the Nile floods, developed mathematical principles to serve social ends. In their search for the key to individual happiness, the Greeks were led to social ethics. In his brooding over the problem of personal salvation, Augustine wrote about cities. The theological works of Thomas Aquinas are also prescriptions for social order. The natural scientists who first forsook authority and began to experiment were seeking through knowledge to make mankind more at home in the world.

Since thought arises in social experience, finds expression in social symbols, and endures only as it becomes a part of the social heritage, it might be claimed that all thought significant for mankind is social thought. Such a definition is, however, much too broad. It fails to reckon with the division of labor in intellectual pursuits. The humanities, the social sciences, and the natural sciences are all concerned with reality as man can know it through experience, but they do not view reality from the same perspective.

Biology considers man as a creature; psychology, as an individual; sociology, as a part of the social whole. Social thought is concerned with human beings in their relations with their fellows. Man's thoughts about his relations to others, whether expressed in folk literature or in the compositions of individual thinkers, form the object of attention in this survey.

As social science has developed in modern times, the broad field of human relations has been broken up into a number of specialized areas, a separation not found in early social thought. Politics, the oldest of the social sciences, was for many centuries intertwined with theology, and history was written more often to fortify beliefs and prejudices than to record events. Most early social thought was primarily religious in nature, and even early secular thought was usually closely related to religious beliefs. Science has radically modified the character of social thought, but many religious conceptions prominent in earlier thinking are still deeply entrenched in the background. If, therefore, we appear to dwell overmuch on religious matters in this survey of early social thought, it must be remembered that social ideas have usually been, and still are to a considerable extent, framed in the dogmas of religion.

TOPICS

The arrangement of the subjects presented in this book under certain topical headings provides a helpful frame of reference. We must be content to select

HISTORICAL BACKGROUND

Social thought should be studied in the light of historical background. Where abstract formulation of dominant ideas does not appear in written works that have survived, we must attempt to discern these ideas in the customs of the people. Even when we can turn to the expressed theories of a single individual, we must bear in mind the fact that

> ... the form in which men cast their speculations, no less than the ways in which they behave, is the result of the habits of thought and action which they find around them. Great men make, indeed, individual contributions to the knowledge of their times; but they can never transcend the age in which they live. The questions they try to answer will always be those their contemporaries are asking; their statement of fundamental problems will always be relative to the traditional statements that have been handed down to them.[2]

Ideas arise out of a social milieu. As human personality is shaped by the influences to which the individual is subjected, so is human thought a part of a cultural configuration. Genius, nevertheless, is not dated. Only Elizabethan England could have produced Shakespeare, yet he spoke not merely to those few who gathered in the Globe Theatre but to mankind. The genius of Plato may be peculiarly Hellenic, but it embraced the whole field of philosophy. However much the Mona Lisa may reflect the spirit of the Italian Renaissance, there is in the art of Leonardo da Vinci something that is universal and timeless. So it is with the masterworks of social thought.

BIOGRAPHICAL DATA

The influence of personal experience on intellectual activity and general outlook is an intriguing subject, and the private affairs of men undoubtedly help to shape their ideas. It is significant that Aristotle was intimate with kings, that Augustine embraced Christianity only after a long struggle, that Ibn Khaldun took an active part in the affairs of state, and that Comte loved and lost Madame Clotilde de Vaux. For that reason, brief biographical sketches are presented of the writers whose ideas are discussed in this book. Biography, like history, is in itself absorbing, and the temptation to concern ourselves with what men have done rather than with their thoughts is strong. We must, however, hold to our purpose, and this requires that we state only a few pertinent biographical facts that bear upon the social thinking of these men.

SOURCES

One of the main advantages in studying in some detail the social ideas of a few persons rather than attempting to include, in all their variety, those of many persons is that we are thus brought close to primary sources. No one is entirely consistent in all that he says. Let anyone who dares ask what ancient writers believed ask himself the question "What do I believe?" Our thoughts are not the same from day to day; the man is stranger to the boy. The Plato who appears in the *Laws* wears intellectual garments different from those with which he clothes himself in the *Republic*. The older Comte, according to some critics, bears little resemblance to the younger. Every person knows moments of elation, and what is said in happiness may appear discordant with what is said in pain. When we state that anyone believed this or affirmed that, we ought to beware of assuming that his views, once stated, never changed. In short, a certain kind of meticulous scholarship would prohibit our making any general statements at all about the ideas expressed in words or deeds.

A compromise, however, can be made between facile generalizations and the bewildering mass of ideas which confronts the student of social phenomena. If making such a compromise is audacious, our boldness is tempered by the sober realization that anyone may soon discover for himself whether or not we are right. Generalizations cease to be facile when we point and say, "Here it is said!"

METHOD

Ideas and the methods by which they were attained are inseparably linked. Not less important than what is said is how the statement came to be made and how it can be proved. We ask not merely, "What do you know?" but also, "How do you know it?" Thus, most, if not all, real contributions to knowledge add something to the means by which knowledge can be obtained. The modern Western world employs the method of science as medieval Christendom did that of revelation, but neither of these methods is fixed. There is much similarity in the thought of Plato and Aristotle, of Augustine and Aquinas, and of Vico and Comte; yet there are fundamental differences, partly explained by the fact that they followed somewhat different methods. It is well, therefore, to give attention to the methods employed by the various writers whose works we shall examine, not only because of the bearing of their methods on their ideas but also because of their contributions to methodology.

HUMAN NATURE

Another topic that should not be neglected in the study of social thought is the view of human nature taken by a specific writer. Sometimes that view is expressly stated; often it is an unrecognized assumption. The Leviathan state of Hobbes offers a reasonable solution to the problem of order in a society composed of men driven by an insatiable desire for power. The Christian doctrine of salvation grew out of an awareness of the corruption of man's nature, which the disobedience of Adam is revealed in the Old Testament to have caused. The caste system of India is comprehensible only in the light of the doctrines of *karma* and reincarnation, which describe personality rather than society. In social thought it matters tremendously whether men are regarded as evil or as good, as fallen or as naturally base, as creatures of will and power or as pawns of destiny. Consequently, in turning to any system of social ideas, we do well to ask, "What are the characteristics of human nature revealed here?"

SOCIAL INSTITUTIONS

The main body of social thought deals with the social institutions, those patterns of behavior which define expectations and provide order in society. The uniformity in the culture of various peoples is not less apparent than the variability, and a number of common areas of institutional organization are evident. All societies have some means of exercising force on those who do not conform to expectations, and some form of *political* organization, with a body of laws, is always found. The exchange of goods and services is everywhere regulated by some kind of *economic* system, formed by a network of economic institutions. No human society could long endure without *family* institutions of some kind, for the sex drive, the helplessness of infants, and the emotional needs of human beings make necessary an intricate web of behavior patterns designed to preserve the social order and to propagate the kind. Likewise, systems of beliefs about and practices toward sacred objects appear at the dawn of history and have been found in every human society of which we have record. *Religious* institutions change, but they do not disappear. The human need for self-expression requires institutions to channel behavior in *recreation* and *the arts,* and all societies have *educational* institutions of some kind to socialize the individual and to transmit and develop knowledge across the generations. Finally, *language* affords human beings that symbolic expression which gives man his great advantage over the lower animals. Whatever may be the language of a people, and however much that language may change, it is not conceivable that *homo* would long remain *sapiens* without the ability to use words.

SOCIAL ORGANIZATION AND SOCIAL CHANGE

The social institutions form the framework of society. They may be examined separately, but in any society they are all interrelated. Each is sensitive to changes in the others. The arrangement of its various institutional elements constitutes the organization of a society, and social theories seek to explain social organization by showing the relationships that exist among various cultural elements. Social organization is a portrait of society in cross section.

Societies are, however, continually changing, and theories of social change attempt to point out uniformities in the flux of human experience. In terms of long-time trends, three types of theories appear: those that reveal a decline from a Golden Age, those that hold out the promise of infinite or indefinite progress,

8 · Introduction

and those that describe some kind of cyclical movement. Our natural disposition to ponder over the shape of things to come makes social change a topic that we would not care to pass over lightly in our survey of social thought.

VALUES

Finally, the ends which men seek in social life give meaning to their personal acts and make comprehensible various forms of social behavior. Unless we know what men are endeavoring to accomplish, we cannot clearly understand their acts. The way in which they define "good" influences their conduct. Social values constitute an important part of each system of social thought, and since they are varied, they must be found and recognized.

CRITERIA OF SELECTION

There is not likely to be complete agreement about what should be included in a book on social thought from Hammurabi to Comte, but a few simple principles have guided our choice. A statement of these will explain, even though it may not justify, exclusions which might prove annoying to some persons. For example, it may seem strange that Vico is included but not Machiavelli, and Locke but not Hobbes. And what can be said for dealing, in early portions of this book, with whole civilizations, rather than with individuals?

ORIGINAL WORKS

Our first requirement is that there be a substantial body of original writings available in the English language. Societies older than the Babylonian and the Egyptian may have had profound social insights, but we can know little about what men thought before cuneiform script and hieroglyphs were invented. The record of human thought awaited the development of the written word, and wise men with the truth on their lips have died and been forgotten simply because they left nothing tangible that endured. Just as mankind profited little from the wide and dangerous journeys of the Norsemen, simply because they failed to record their experiences, so are unexpressed ideas of little use in the world.

We begin with Babylonia, therefore, because of the firsthand, not hearsay, information about that civilization. Many thousands of clay tablets have survived upon which the Babylonians wrote in a language that we can now read. Likewise, present-day libraries contain Egyptian writings produced more than a thousand years before the Greeks and Romans filled the ears of their hearers with tales about what they had observed on the banks of the Nile.

The Confucian classics preserve the social heritage of the Chinese people from that period in the sixth century when Confucius stated the principles that were to guide Chinese society for at least twenty-five centuries. At about the same time, sacred literatures appeared in India and in Palestine. The Hindu literature was not put into written form until long after the beginning of the Christian era, but it was transmitted orally from generation to generation with such fidelity that we may feel confident that it represents the authentic voice of the ancient Hindus. Of the thoughts of Hebrews in Palestine, the Old Testament gives eloquent expression.

These five ancient civilizations offer, therefore, in contemporary writings that have survived the ravages of time, a sample of social thought at the dawn of history.

In studying the individual theorists, we go to their own writings and to selected secondary sources. This book is itself a compromise with the principle that the place to begin the study of Plato, for example, is with Plato himself. It may often be advisable not to begin with the "master." Sometimes we have to climb by slow degrees to the heights attained by genius, and we need support along the way. Accordingly, both primary and secondary works are used in this book.

A second requirement is that the system offer a coherent body of ideas bearing on a number of aspects of social experience. The development of social thought in specialized fields, especially politics, will be found in numerous books. We are concerned, however, with social thought in all its branches. We should like to have social systems as comprehensive as the philosophical system of Plato; but we do not find many such systems. As nations began to emerge after the breakdown of feudalism and the disintegration of the vast medieval Catholic political organization, social thought was directed primarily toward politics. Not all writers, however, specialized to the same extent. There is a wider range of social thought in Locke than in Hobbes, and in Vico than in Machiavelli. This in itself would not justify our selecting for study the one rather than the other, because variety is but one criterion, and not the most important. Nevertheless, one reason for choosing Augustine rather than Jerome, Aquinas rather than Albertus Magnus, Locke rather than Hobbes, and Comte rather than Montesquieu is that in each instance the former offers a wider range of social thought.

A third requirement is that the thoughts expressed be timely. Of these there is no dearth, for works of genius survive their creators. The sacred literatures of the East and the West, the philosophies of the Greeks and the Romans, the Christian doctrines explained and published by Catholic and Protestant leaders, as well as more recent contributions to knowledge, constitute a heritage of living thought. Whether we know it or not, these are the sources of many of our opinions. We do not all agree as to what is living and what is dead in old ideas. Thought which is alive and full of meaning to one person, simply because it relates to his experience, may be of little interest to another. The ideas presented in this book will have, therefore, a varied appeal, but, with so much from which to choose, there surely will be something for everyone.

Finally, we concern ourselves only with recognized masterpieces. We seek the best that the mind of man has produced in the field of our interest. There are no exact standards by which all writings can be measured. Nevertheless, although some persons delight, for example, in that ancient philosophical song of the Hindus, the *Bhagavad-Gita,* and others prefer John Locke's *Essay Concerning Human Understanding,* most persons will agree that both are masterworks. There is no claim that Ibn Khaldun and Vico, for example, are the intellectual peers of Plato and Thomas Aquinas; what is maintained is that the *Prolegomena* and the *New Science* are works of unusual distinction. Both are instructive and inspiring. The *Confessions* of Augustine has a popular appeal lacking in the *Summa Theologica* of Thomas Aquinas, but most persons who read either will be richly rewarded.

In every culture appear certain works that are clearly greater than others. The beauty in ancient Greek designs does not fade, and the haunting charm of medieval art still captures the thoughtful observer. So it is with ideas. The filial piety of Confucius, the ethics of Aristotle, the eternal city of Augustine, the liberalism of John Locke, the positivism of Auguste Comte—these, among many others, are great ideas from the past. Age adds nothing very important to their value, nor does it take anything away. The measure of their greatness is survival, vitality, and appeal to the common sense and the conscience of mankind. It is important to recognize such ideas, woven as they are into the fabric of the modern mind.

PART ONE

FIVE ANCIENT SOCIETIES

The civilizations of Babylonia and Egypt emerged several thousand years before the beginning of the Christian era. Babylonian civilization attained its highest development between 2000 and 1500 B.C.; Egypt's golden age began in the sixteenth century B.C. and was showing definite signs of decline by the middle of the fourteenth century B.C. We shall focus our attention on each of these civilizations at the peak of its development, referring to earlier and later periods only to point up the major contributions of each of these societies to social thought. A vast body of contemporary literature is available, the Babylonian preserved in tablets of clay, and the Egyptian, on the walls of sepulchers and in papyrus scrolls buried with the dead.

Unlike the ancient river civilizations of the Near East, the Chinese civilization did not decay after it had reached a high level of achievement but has continued to develop to the present time. Its leading figure in the ancient period was Confucius, and in the life and works of this Chinese sage of the sixth century B.C., the early social thought of the Chinese at one of their truly great moments in history is revealed.

No survey of ancient social thought can afford to neglect the profound religious works of the Hindus. This literature began to develop with the entry of the Aryans into India, about 2000 B.C. Even though it was not committed to writing at the time, it probably reflects with unusual fidelity the thought of the period corresponding roughly in time with the Confucian and the ancient Hebrew.

The Hebrews of the Old Testament did not create an independent civilization, but they did establish some of the main foundations of the Judaic-Christian tradition, which has played an important part in the shaping of Western civilization. The Old Testament covers a period in Hebrew history extending from about 1000 to about 400 B.C., and it is to this source that we turn for information about the early social thought of the Hebrews.

In this portion of our study we are often compelled to draw inferences about certain important aspects of social thought from what was said about other matters and from how people lived. With the possible exception of Confucius, no individual in these ancient societies stands out as a spokesman for his people. Furthermore, because people apparently did not then write about many of the matters which now concern us, and because certain types of works have probably survived better than others, there are lacunae in the specific statement about social matters available to us. We are often compelled, therefore, to turn to events, seeking to gain knowledge of what people were thinking by observing what they did.

2 · BABYLONIA

Behold the land of the Chaldéans! ISAIAH 23:13

It is an ancient nation. JEREMIAH 5:15

HISTORICAL SKETCH

On the opposite slopes of a mountain range in Armenia arise two rivers, the Euphrates and the Tigris. The former flows westward as though seeking to enter the Mediterranean, then turns south and east and winds its way to the Persian Gulf almost eighteen hundred miles from its source. The latter pursues a more direct route to the same destination but approaches and runs roughly parallel to the Euphrates after both rivers break out of the mountains onto the Mesopotamian plain, until finally the two rivers lose their distinct identity in the alluvium at the head of the Persian Gulf. The Euphrates receives only minor tributaries after it leaves the mountains, but the Tigris continues to be fed by streams arising in Kurdistan and the mountains of western Iran, hence, as it nears the gulf, the Tigris is a greater river than the Euphrates and has higher banks and a deeper channel. Together the rivers water the land known to various peoples as Chaldea, Mesopotamia (Land between the Rivers), and Babylonia. The land is in reality a gift of the rivers, since they brought down silt and distributed it over the plains in flood seasons, thus forming in ancient times soil of remarkable fertility.

It is difficult to see how Babylonian civilization could have developed without the rich soil and abundant water that the two rivers provided. Nevertheless, it is easy to exaggerate the social importance of the natural environment. Nature's gifts must be seized upon and put to use in order for a civilization to develop; but they must be matched with human ingenuity and social organization. Sometimes a comparatively unfavorable geographical setting acts as a spur to drive men on to great accomplishments, as in the case of the Mayas in Central America and the Incas on the plateaus of the Andes. On the other hand, a favorable climate and fabulous wealth in natural resources may stimulate no sweeping social changes; witness North America before the Europeans came. The success of the Babylonians in developing the first civilization, with the possible exception of the Egyptian, that written history records is not, therefore, attributable wholly to water, climate, and soil. At least as early as the fourth millennium B.C., the dwellers on this rich plain developed an elaborate system of irrigation and learned to control the flood waters with dikes, dams, and canals. Two thousand years before the Christian era, their versatile talents found expression in the arts and sciences of Babylon, that ancient center of civilization, which came to be the symbol for any great and luxurious city, wicked perhaps but magnificent.

Of the earliest inhabitants of Babylonia we know very little except that those with whom history begins were called Sumerians and had developed a non-Semitic written language known to us as *cuneiform,* because of the wedge-shaped symbols it employed. Perhaps the Sumerians came originally from the mountainous regions north and east of Babylonia, but by the time of the earliest written records they had been joined by an undetermined number of Semites from the deserts of Arabia. No natural boundary separates the delta of the two rivers from the steppes of Arabia, which have been from time immemorial the home of nomadic tribes. In ancient times at least four great migrations of these Semitic nomads occurred, the first being that in the fourth millennium B.C., into lower Mesopotamia, where they gave a decidedly Semitic character to the society into which they were assimilated, although many important elements of Sumerian culture survived the invasion.

In the latter part of the third millennium B.C., a second Semitic migration, the "Amorite," seems to have occurred. This flow of Semites led finally to the unity of all Babylonia under a dynasty of kings of Semitic origin and transformed a little village on the Euphrates into mighty Babylon, a fitting abode for the king of the "Four Quarters of the World." Earlier, Babylonia had been divided into two rather distinct parts: Sumer, in the south, and Akkad, in the north; each of these, in turn, was broken up into city-states. The First Dynasty of Babylon, which began about 1900 B.C., was not the first line of rulers to claim wide authority in the land. Extant king-lists account for mythical dynasties extending over hundreds of thousands of years; but Sargon I and Narim-Sin were historical figures who, in the third millennium B.C., claimed dominion over the entire country. Moreover, Babylon was not the first important city to arise on the plains. Of the numerous cities which at some time existed, the ruins of Eridu, Ur, Lagash, Larsa, Erech, Nippur, Borsippa, Kish, Cutha, Agade, Sippar, and Nineveh, together with references to them in contemporary records which have survived, reveal that each of these cities had its moment in the exciting history of Babylonia. Eridu, in the south, and Nippur, in the north, were especially important as great sanctuaries, although apparently they never became the seats of secular kingdoms.

The political extinction of Sumeria, which resulted from the rise of Babylon to supreme power over the city states of Sumer and Akkad, did not lead to the loss of Sumerian culture. On the contrary, the art, science, literature, and legal traditions of ancient Sumeria provided the cultural heritage upon which Babylonian civilization developed, just as, centuries later, Hellenic culture was to be made whole in Athens and find there its full expression. Furthermore, Babylonian kings carried the war to the enemy, and Babylonian merchants traveled afar, so that the prestige of Babylon was established and its influence extended throughout the vast region now known as the Near East. The extent of the indebtedness of Greco-Roman civilization to this ancient people was not known even as recently as a hundred years ago, and perhaps the full story has not yet been told.

TABLETS OF CLAY

For thousands of years the history of ancient Babylonia lay buried in the mounds which mark the ruins of her dead cities. Within those ruins were countless tablets of clay on which were recorded in cuneiform script the life and thought of people who lived several millennia before our era; they lay undisturbed while centuries passed.

> When the city of Nineveh fell, and when Babylon was finally given over to the destroyer, a deep darkness of ignorance settled over their ruins. The very site of Nineveh was forgotten, and, though a tradition lived on which located the spot where Babylon had stood, there was almost as little known of that great capital as of its northern neighbor. In the Middle Ages the world forgot many things, and then with wonderful vigor began to learn them all over again. In the general spell of forgetfulness it cast away all remembrance of these two great cities. Even the monk in his cell, to whose industry as a copyist the world owes a debt that can never be paid, recked little of barbarous cities, whose sins had destroyed them. He knew of Jerusalem and of Bethlehem, for these had imperishable fragrance in his nostrils. They were sacred cities in a sacred land, and he sighed as he thought that they were now in the hand of infidels. But of Nineveh and Babylon, they were mentioned, it is true, in the prophets; but then Nahum had cursed the one and Isaiah predicted the destruction of the other, and they had received their deserts. Where they might be he knew not, nor cared.[1]

The language in which these tablets were written had long ago been forgotten, despite the fact that it was the oldest language in which written records have been preserved and had been known for centuries in many lands.

Perhaps even earlier than the Egyptians, the Sumerians had developed their written language beyond the crude pictures which primitive people use for communication. The recognition of the fact that pictures can convey thought is the first stage in the development of a written language. In time, pictographs are simplified and cursive symbols appear which convey conventional meanings to the initiated. The next step, the communication of abstract ideas by means of ideograms, was a truly remarkable human achievement. However, the ancient Babylonians went even further than that: they discovered that thought is more easily and accurately expressed when written symbols represent sounds instead of distinct ideas. With nothing more than wedge-shaped lines they formed about three hundred and fifty symbols.

At this stage the development of their language stopped, just short of an alphabet; in the third millennium B.C., they did have, however, a formal and conventional written language. With a stylus made usually from reed but sometimes from stone or metal, they inscribed on soft clay the symbols they used. When the clay tablets hardened, they became durable manuscripts, strong enough to withstand fire and water and remain legible even when exposed to the elements or buried in the ground for centuries. Although clay was by far the most commonly used material, the Babylonians sometimes wrote on stone or metal and engraved inscriptions on gems.

The story of the linguistic studies and archaeological explorations that led to the rediscovery of ancient Babylon is an exciting account of the labor of many scholars. Together they succeeded in removing the dust of centuries from hundreds of thousands of Babylonian documents, many of which have been translated into modern languages, and thus saved for posterity the thoughts and emotions of people who lived more than four thousand years ago. Among the types of composition found on the tablets and cylinders that have survived are codes of law, myths, epic tales, historical texts, rituals, songs, letters, lamentations, school exercises, scientific treatises, contracts, property transactions, prayers, proverbs, royal proclamations, administrative instructions, and guides to the interpretation of dreams.

Ancient chronology is an esoteric art, and the date of most old documents can only be approximated. The recently discovered method of dating archaeological objects by means of radioactive carbon may eventually lead to important corrections in chronology, but its value is as yet undetermined. Furthermore, it is much easier to determine when a manuscript was written than when it was originally composed; a legend, ritual, song, or custom may be passed along orally for centuries before it is written down. It is clear that a considerable body of the extant Babylonian literature was written in the first half of the second millennium B.C. Some of it originated obviously at a much earlier date—as, for example, the famous *Epic of Gilgamesh,* and even many of the laws which appear in Hammurabi's code. Nevertheless, the literary revival which seems to have accompanied the political unification of all Babylonia produced a body of writings that possess considerable unity with respect to social thought. In many respects Babylonian culture reached its highest peak in what may be called the Age of Hammurabi, or roughly during the first half of the second millennium B.C. A large body of important Babylonian documents from this period is available; by confining our study to these works we shall have both a focus in time and a degree of unity that would be lacking in a wider selection of Babylonian literature. Obviously, if we would discover what the Babylonians thought about human relations, we must read myths and epics as well as laws.

MYTHS AND EPICS

The term *myth* has various meanings, but most of the ancient myths relate an event in which supernatural powers appear as active agents. When a natural phenomenon, such as a flood, is explained by natural causes, the mythical element, in this meaning of the term, is lacking. Stories nonreligious in character may have some of the characteristics of myths, but these are usually known as *fables* or *folk tales,* the term *myth* being reserved for stories which are a part of religious belief. An *epic* is a narrative poem dealing with some dignified theme, often the exploits of a legendary hero, in noble and exalted style. The epic may serve to relate several myths and fables about a central figure of heroic proportions. For example, *The Epic of Gilgamesh* contains the most complete version of the Babylonian deluge myth yet discovered.

THE DELUGE MYTH

The inundation of the earth by a mighty flood at some earlier time was accepted by the Babylonians as a historical fact. Even Berossus, who lived in the time of Alexander the Great and wrote in Greek as well as in cuneiform script, regarded the Deluge as an important landmark in Babylonian history.

The Babylonian myth is similar in many respects to the account of the Flood found in the Bible. The Sumerian Noah, Utnapishtim,[2] was told by one of the gods that a great flood was to be sent to destroy mankind and that if he would be saved, he must tear down his house and build a boat. Utnapishtim did as he was ordered, building the boat of equal width and length, as he had been told, and coating it with bitumen. Then he loaded aboard all his possessions, his family and kin, "all the craftsmen," and the "beasts of the field." Since he had been ordered to preserve the "seed of all living things," he must have neglected to enumerate, when he told the story long afterward, the entire cargo. No sooner had he closed the door of his boat than the weather became "awesome to behold." Such darkness came upon the land as was terrifying even to the gods. The goddess Ishtar cried out "like a woman in travail." For six days and nights the flood winds blew. Then on the seventh day "the sea grew quiet, the tempest was still, the flood ceased." When Utnapishtim opened a hatch and the light fell upon his face, he sent forth a dove, which found no resting place and returned; likewise a swallow went forth and came back; then a raven loosed to survey the scene did not return and the people on the boat gladly believed that land was near. On Mt. Niser the boat came to a halt and unloaded "to the four winds."

THE EPIC OF GILGAMESH

The Epic of Gilgamesh is one of the great epics of antiquity. It has been found in many versions—Old Babylonian, Assyrian, Hittite, and Hurrian. It records the experiences of the king who "saw everything to the ends of the land" and "all things experienced." In it Gilgamesh, two thirds god and one third human, moves across a shadowy stage on which gods and men played out the drama of history in ages past, as the Babylonians saw it. In combat with the monsters which prey upon his people, he is a hero without peer; the "onslaught of his weapons verily has no equal." With his friend Enkidu, a strange creature who was sent by the gods to bridle Gilgamesh's arrogance but who became instead his devoted companion, he rids his country of the Elamites. In the moment of his triumph he is so majestic a figure that the goddess Ishtar is moved to offer herself to him in matrimony. He spurns her offer, and in retaliation she brings about the death of Enkidu. Haunted by the fear of death, Gilgamesh seeks out Utnapishtim to find the secret of immortality. From this ancient survivor of the Flood, he hears the account of that great event; but the efforts of Utnapishtim to gain for him immortality are not successful, and in the end Gilgamesh is seen awaiting his mortal fate.

> The theme of this epic is essentially a secular one. The poem deals with such earthy things as man and nature, love and adventure, friendship and combat—all masterfully blended into a background for the stark reality of death. . . . For the first time in the history of the world a profound experience on such a heroic scale has found expression in a noble style. The scope and sweep of the epic, and its sheer poetic power, give it a timeless appeal. In antiquity, the influence of the poem spread to various tongues and cultures. Today it captivates student and poet alike.[3]

These two works from this type of Babylonian literature we have summarized briefly because of their intrinsic interest and because they yield important information about Babylonian social thought. Like other Babylonian myths and epics, they deal with creation, paradise, the "nether world," the creation of man, and many other interesting themes only indirectly related to our subject.

LEGAL DOCUMENTS

The most important single source of information about the social thought of Babylonia is the *Code of Hammurabi*. In A.D. 1901, French archaeologists who were making excavations in the ruins of the old Elamite capital of Susa discovered in three fragments a block of black diorite upon which was engraved a code of laws. It proved to be the oldest written code as yet known to man. The stone had been carried from Babylon to Susa by some raider in perhaps the twelfth century B.C. The inscriptions upon it are written in cuneiform script and contain a prologue, an epilogue, and two hundred and eighty-two laws. About thirty-five of the laws (65-100) had, for some reason, been chiseled off; but from other fragmentary copies of the Code these laws are known; thus the complete code, except for a few words, has survived. At the top of the stone in bas-relief King Hammurabi is seen receiving the laws from the Sun-god. The stone is nearly eight feet high and slightly more than seven feet wide, and the writing extends entirely around it. It was carried to Paris, where it now reposes in the Louvre.

Despite the fact that his famous code has been preserved, together with a number of his letters and monuments, not very much is known about Hammurabi himself. Most Bible scholars identify him with the Amraphel mentioned in *Genesis* 14:1 and give him credit for organizing a central government over the city states of Babylonia. It is known that he belonged to the Old Babylonian (Amorite) Dynasty, but until recently that dynasty was believed to have begun in the late third millennium B.C.; consequently the years 2123-2080 B.C. were generally accepted as the approximate period of Hammurabi's reign. Later discoveries, however, have brought about a considerable revision of the earlier chronological tables, and many scholars now believe that Hammurabi ruled during the period 1728-1686 B.C.

Hammurabi had his memoirs written, so that posterity would be well advised regarding the accomplishments for which he wished to be remembered—a practice commonly observed by statesmen and soldiers—but these writings deal largely with the administrative details of government. He was especially proud of a great canal which he had dug as the main artery of an elaborate system of irrigation. Of his accomplishments he says:

> I turned both its banks into cultivated ground, I heaped up mounds of grain and I furnished perpetual water for the people of Sumir [*sic*] and Accad. The country of Sumer and Accad, I gathered together its nations who were scattered, I gave them pasture and drink, I ruled over them in riches and abundance, I caused them to inhabit a peaceful dwelling-place.[4]

Although, in the prologue to the Code, Hammurabi claims divine authority "to cause justice to prevail in the land, to destroy the wicked and the evil, to prevent the strong from oppressing the weak . . . to enlighten the land and to further the welfare of the people," the Code itself is secular throughout. The laws were based upon established customs, and many of them were already in writing long before the reign of Hammurabi. Perhaps the scene in which he is seen receiving the laws from the Sun-god is intended only to represent the authority invested in him to administer the traditional laws, divinely given for the guidance of mankind.

There are many indications that Hammurabi was a capable and successful ruler. The apparent self-esteem which appears in his writing was probably nothing more than a literary fashion of his day. In his statement of the purpose of the code, he discloses a feeling of personal concern for the security and happiness of his subjects.

> Let any oppressed man who has a cause
> come into the presence of my statue as the king of justice,
> and then read my inscribed stela,
> and give heed to my precious words
> and may my stela make the case clear to him;
> may he understand his cause;
> may he set his mind at ease! [5]

OTHER LEGAL DOCUMENTS

The *Code of Hammurabi* is important not for its originality but for its detailed presentation of some of the ideas prevailing in ancient Babylonia. Other codes of law have also survived, among which may be mentioned fragments of the *Lipit-Ishtar Code,* which is probably about a hundred and fifty years older than Hammurabi's code, and the *Laws of Eshnunna,* which also antedates the *Code of Hammurabi.* Contract tablets, deeds, wills, and business correspondence have also been preserved in considerable quantity; and these supply many details about the legal system of ancient Babylonia.

GOVERNMENT AND LAW

Religious beliefs only vaguely related to actual practices gave the Babylonian conception of government, which at the time of Hammurabi was remarkably secular in character, a distinctly theocratic quality. Hammurabi claimed that he had received from the gods the authority which he exercised and that he ruled, therefore, by divine right. As the beloved of the gods, he was able to perform deeds beyond compare, according to his own accounts.

> Hammurabi, the mighty king, the king of Babylon, the king who hath brought to subjection the four quarters of the world, who hath brought

about the triumph of Marduk, the shepherd who delighteth his heart, am I.

When Anu and Bel gave me the land of Sumer and Akkad to rule and entrusted their sceptre to my hands, I dug out the Hammurabi-canal named Nuhus-nisi, which bringeth abundance of water unto the land of Sumer and Akkad. Both the banks thereof I changed to fields for cultivation, and I garnered piles of grain, and I procured unfailing water for the land of Sumer and Akkad.

As for the land of Sumer and Akkad, I collected the scattered peoples thereof, and I procured food and drink for them. In abundance and plenty I pastured them, and I caused them to dwell in a peaceful habitation.

At that time I, Hammurabi, the mighty king, the beloved of the great gods, through the great power which Marduk had bestowed upon me, built a lofty fortress, at the head of the Hammurabi-canal named Nuhus-nisi, with much earth, the top of which reacheth on high like unto a mountain. This fortress I named Dur-Sin-muballit-abim-walidia, and thus did I cause the name of Sin-muballit, the father who begat me, to dwell in the four quarters of the world.[6]

Hammurabi's relations with the priesthood are not entirely clear. That he may have been in some respects high priest as well as king is indicated by several references to his collection of the revenues of the temples. These institutions possessed great wealth in lands and herds, and from the documents that have been preserved it appears that the priests were respected not only because they mediated between man and the gods but also because they engaged in lucrative banking and trade on an extensive scale. They were in the advantageous position of being able both to declare the day propitious for trade and to make a business deal under the favorable portents revealed to them.

It does not appear that the unity of the Babylonian city states under the central control of Hammurabi was matched by a corresponding integration of the temples, with a hierarchy of priests leading up to the pontiff in Babylon. It seems probable, therefore, that Hammurabi did not exercise the same authority over local priests that he did over his administrative officials throughout the kingdom, and that the divine authority which he claimed did not remove him wholly from the thumb of the priests. Their nearness to the people, and their wealth in land, slaves, flocks and herds, industries, and capital gave them advantages which even a king appointed by the gods could not disregard. Nevertheless, if Hammurabi had doubts about his sovereignty, he did not admit them; only to the gods did he bow.

The government of Babylonia was, therefore, a monarchy, with the succession to the throne determined by birth. However, the right to rule was established by divine adoption as well as by human birth. For example, Hammurabi received the kingship from his father and from the god Bel-Merodach (Marduk) in the same moment, and he passed it on to his son, who would likewise become the adopted son of the god when he took over the reins of government. Apparently there were no constitutional bodies which in any way limited the power of the king. That this may not always have been the case is suggested by a very interesting episode in the story of Gilgamesh. A Sumerian epic tale describes a scene in which Gilgamesh, then lord of Erech, appeared before the "convened assembly of the elders" and urged them to reject an ultimatum from a foe to surrender their city. When the elders denied his plea and expressed instead a willingness to submit rather than carry on the struggle, he carried the matter to a convened assembly "of the men of his city." They agreed to resist, and in the end Erech was saved. This casual reference to governing bodies of citizens at an early period in Babylonian history is especially important, not only because it suggests the existence at that time of some kind of constitutional government but also because "it records what are, by all odds, the oldest two political assemblies as yet known to man."[7]

The myth of the adoption of the king by the gods on his succession to the throne must not have been taken very seriously either by the king or by the people. Whatever may have been Hammurabi's duties to his people as their spiritual shepherd, his own writings display a highly practical concern for their material prosperity and for social justice, to the all but complete neglect of concern for their spiritual welfare. Although he acknowledged no earthly restraints upon his authority, Hammurabi ruled in accordance with customs and traditions of long standing. A theocratic despot might have tuned his ear to the voice of the gods and ruled by fiat; Hammurabi heard, instead, the voice of the people and ruled by the common laws which he found and codified.

ADMINISTRATION OF JUSTICE

The laws of a people are not merely a statement of rights but also a declaration of principles. They define both what may be expected and what is just. The law of retaliation (*lex talionis*), which demands an eye for an eye and a tooth for a tooth, for example, provides a suitable penalty for a certain act but at the same time it states a principle of just dealing among men—the principle that justice demands that one suffer in like degree with the suffering one has caused. For that reason the ancient codes of law are documents of inestimable value to those who are seeking to discover ancient conceptions of justice. Among such documents, the *Code of Hammurabi,* virtually intact after almost four thousand years, deserves the closest scrutiny, not only because of its antiquity but also because of its revelation of some attitudes and ideals that have not disappeared with time.

In his prologue to the Code, Hammurabi declared that the gods had made him king so that he might "cause justice to be practiced in the land." He published the laws so that all those who "were oppressed" or were "involved in lawsuits" might read them and discover their rights. There is much evidence to show that he did not rest content with these measures to ensure justice but that he endeavored to see that the laws were understood and obeyed. He insisted that his governors be impartial in the conduct of their offices. He warned administrators against allowing the courts to be used to recruit forced laborers for public projects. He acted personally on appeals from citizens who felt that they had been treated unfairly by his officers. On one occasion Hammurabi directed a governor to repay, with interest, corn which he had borrowed from a merchant. He investigated reports of bribery and brought corrupt officials to justice without delay. In short, he took seriously the laws that he had promulgated and expected his subjects to do likewise. Since laws sometimes bear little relation to the real sentiment of people, as revealed in their conduct, this is an important point.

LEX TALIONIS

The principle of equivalent retaliation, an eye for an eye, is rooted deep in human nature. The most enlightened peoples, no less than savages, take care to see that those who have done wrong atone in suffering for their misdeeds, as though expiation removed the guilt. Our own speech is replete with expressions that reveal a deep-seated satisfaction in this kind of even-handed justice. The refinement of sentiment has, however, demanded the concealment of the grim features of the principle of *Lex talionis;* if we would see it bare, we must turn back to the time when men had not learned to clothe a harsh thought with fine phrases. Hammurabi states the principle this way:

> If a man destroy the eye of another man, they shall destroy his eye.
> If one break a man's bone, they shall break his bone.
> If a man knock out a tooth of a man of his own rank, they shall knock out his tooth. [8]

The man who strikes another man's daughter and causes her death is punished by the execution of his own daughter. The physician who is unsuccessful in an operation loses his fingers. If a builder fails to make firm the construction of a house and it collapses and causes the death of the owner's son, then the builder's son is put to death; if the owner himself is killed, the builder must likewise die.

As with the physician's fingers, symbolic mutilation is prescribed for various offenses. Criminal curiosity may be penalized by the removal of the eye, and ingratitude by cutting off the tongue. If a nurse deceive her master, "they shall cut off her breast." The hand that strikes the blow must pay. If this sounds barbarous, we must remind ourselves that all the influences in our own time which make men sensitive and charitable are not sufficient to drive out the yearning for revenge that sometimes finds expression in the very manner which Hammurabi declared to be appropriate. It should be noted, also, that punishment is prescribed and limited by the *lex talionis*—a tooth for a tooth, and no more than an eye for an eye.

INEQUALITY

The Babylonian conception of justice was not based on the democratic ideal of personal equality before the law; on the contrary, penalties for crimes against the person varied according to the class status both of the offender and of the injured party. If a man struck a superior, he might be given sixty strokes with an ox-tail whip in public, whereas the penalty for an assault on an inferior was a fine scaled according to the status of the victim. It cost considerably more to break the bone of a freeman than of a slave. To knock out the tooth of a man of one's own rank cost a tooth in return, but an aristocrat could knock out the tooth of a commoner for the small sum of twenty shekels.

On the other hand, merchants, officials, and men of wealth were expected to act honorably; if they failed to do so, a much heavier penalty fell on them than upon those of whom less was expected because of their lower social status. A merchant was required to repay an agent sixfold the amount which he had obtained from him unjustly, whereas an agent who attempted to cheat his superior had to return only threefold the amount involved. Patricians were fined sixty shekels of silver for exchanging blows with one another, since they should have exercised more self-control, whereas the fine within the class of commoners was only ten shekels. A governor or magistrate who neglected his official duties received the death penalty, as did a judge who was convicted of accepting a bribe. In various other ways, responsibilities were closely related to rights; those who possessed the greatest rights were subject to the greatest penalties when they failed in their responsibilities.

SEVERITY OF PUNISHMENT

The list of offenses punishable by death was a long one. Conviction of a certain crime, however, did not invariably result in the death penalty; in fact, extenuating circumstances were explicitly recognized in many laws, and deliberate intention was an important consideration. The maximum penalty was, of course, permissive and not mandatory; circumstances determined the seriousness of the crime. Also, since the *Code of Hammurabi* contains no laws against treason, or even against murder, we may assume that the penalty for such crimes was so well known as to require no statement.

Nevertheless, the offenses listed as capital are revealing of the attitudes of the time. Among such offenses are the following: stealing a man's son, helping a slave to escape, harboring an escaped slave, making a breach in a house, brigandage, stealing property from a burning house, neglect of official duties, witchcraft, rape, incest, cheating in the measurement of wine, harboring outlaws, adultery, "gadding about" on the part of a woman and belittling her husband, procuring a husband's death by his wife in order that she might marry another man, building a house so poorly that it collapsed and caused death, and avoidance of military duties. A mother and son involved in incest were burned to death (incest involving a father and daughter was punished only by the banishment of the father from the city), as was a votaress who opened a wine-shop or entered a wine-shop for a drink. A woman who brought about the death of her husband for the sake of another man was impaled.

As has been noted, the law was especially stern with respect to the officers of the king; apparently Hammurabi required his officials to set a pattern of exemplary conduct, and he dealt severely with those who failed to measure up to his expectations.

ENLIGHTENED LEGISLATION

Despite some of the bizarre provisions which it contains, the *Code of Hammurabi* is in most respects a piece of humane and enlightened legislation. Although punishment was severe, guilt had to be clearly established. Hammurabi had no patience with gossip and slander. An accuser who could not substantiate an accusation was guilty of a crime equal in seriousness to that with which the accused was charged. Severe punishments were prescribed for bearers of false witness. A man who pointed an accusing finger at a priestess or the wife of another man and could not prove his charges was brought before the judges and branded on his forehead; false testimony by a witness in court was punishable by death.

A statement made under oath, in the absence of documentary proof, carried great weight. An agent who declared under oath that he had been set upon and robbed of his goods was held blameless. If a man struck another in a quarrel and only wounded him, he could swear, "I struck him without intent" and escape all penalties except the payment of the physician's bill; even if the man died, the oath reduced the penalty that would otherwise have been imposed. Statements under oath that the gods had caused the death of a rented ox, that a certain quantity of corn had been placed in storage, that a boat which had been run down and sunk had contained a certain cargo, that a man had been misinformed when he removed the brand from a slave, and that a charge of adultery was false were accepted without question. It can be seen from these examples that the Babylonians believed that people would tell the truth when they made statements under oath. The oath might be given in the name of one god, of several gods, or of the king.

In many other respects as well, the Code was designed to ensure social justice. Tenants were protected from landlords, borrowers from lenders, and buyers of goods from merchants. Numerous articles restrained the rich and powerful from exploiting the poor and weak. Taking advantage of an individual in distress was forbidden. A man whose fields had been inundated by the gods so that they produced no grain could not be required to pay his debts that year. Private property in lands and goods was fully protected. The rights of women and children could not be arbitrarily disregarded; a son could be disinherited only after the judges were satisfied that he had committed a crime sufficiently grave to justify this action; a wife was allowed to retain possession of her marriage portion. Even a slave might gain a hearing before the judges.

Since irrigation was of vital interest to the entire society, and the maintenance of the intricate system of canals required close supervision, there were, naturally, many laws dealing with the control of the waters. A man who failed to strengthen his dikes lost not only his own possessions when a break occurred but was responsible also for any damage incurred by his neighbor from the overflow. Property rights were carefully defined and protected. A gardener received half interest in an orchard which he had planted and cultivated on another man's land, but any waste space in the orchard which the owner had failed to utilize was assigned to the gardener as an added portion. Carelessness on the part of an agent was not excused; but if an agent met with misfortune over which he had no control, he was not blamed.

There was no compromise with negligence. The builder's house was expected to stand, the gardener's trees to live and produce, the physician's operation to restore the organ, the shepherd's herd to be kept under control, the farmer's dikes to withstand the floods, the merchant's agent to prosper, the herdsman's bull to be dehorned if he was in the habit of goring, and the boatman's calking to last for a year without leaks. The penalties for inattention to duty were severe, but there is no indication that any man was called on for performance beyond human ability or was made to suffer from acts over which he had no control. It was one thing to lose sheep because of neglect; it was quite another to lose sheep as a result of the acts of Providence.

By our standards some of the laws do, however, seem unfair and unduly harsh. For example,

> If a physician operate on a man for a severe wound with a bronze lancet and cause the man's death; or open an abscess in the eye of a man with a bronze lancet and destroy the man's eye, they cut off his fingers.[9]

This law must have discouraged the practice of surgery, but when one recalls how little was then known about antiseptics, one may feel that in requiring the physician to share in the risks of an operation, society gained more than it lost.

An article in the Code dealing with the careless wife is interesting, although it is not in harmony with many of the laws which recognize and protect the inherent dignity of women:

> If she [a wife] was not careful but was a gadabout, thus neglecting her house and humiliating her husband, they shall throw that woman into the water. [This probably meant to execute by drowning.][10]

It should be noted that although citizens were protected against injustice from their fellow men and from the king's ministers, they were nowhere promised protection from the government itself. Hammurabi was sovereign, not the people. He was the servant of the god Marduk but the master, not the slave, of the governed. He chose in the conduct of his office to follow custom and, being a practical man, he undoubtedly chose wisely; but under the Babylonian conceptions of government he might, with equal right, have chosen to disregard custom. He was theoretically under no obligation to give heed to the people when their wishes ran counter to divine commands which he transmitted. Furthermore, the king's justice was but little, if at all, tempered with mercy. The laws specified the rules to be followed, but the king made no promises to law-abiding citizens who found themselves in distress; paternalism in government was yet to come.

ECONOMY

The materialistic character of Babylonian civilization, the preoccupation of the people with trade and possessions, is clearly revealed in the documents which have survived. The British Assyriologist Sidney Smith went so far as to say of the Babylonians: "No other [civilized] people [of antiquity] was so perpetually devoted to the acquisition of shekels, so completely absorbed in the pursuit of prosperity in this life." [11] Whereas other ancient peoples took care to preserve their prayers, the Babylonians appear to have been more concerned with the preservation of their ledgers. Contracts, deeds, wills, laws, and business correspondence make up a large part of the extant Babylonian writings.

Perhaps business affairs were committed to writing to a greater extent than were matters of the spirit. The law required that all contracts, from a marriage agreement to the hire of an ox, be written. If a man could not produce a bill of sale, signed and witnessed, to prove his lawful acquisition of "a slave, a slave girl, an ox, or any other valuable good," he was regarded as a thief. A merchant was required by law to demand a written report from his agent and to give to his agent a "sealed receipt" for any money he received from him. No marriage was legal without a written contract, possibly because the marriage contract recorded the property agreements made at the time of marriage. Signatures were usually affixed to documents by means of a cylinder seal which most Babylonians probably carried tied with a string about their necks. A simple bill of sale might bear the signatures of as many as eleven witnesses. The following deed had about twenty witnesses, who identified themselves by giving, in addition to their own names, the names of their fathers.

> Tappum, son of Iarbi-ilu, "has bought two GAN of field, in the Isle, next to the field of Hasri-kuttim, and the field of Sin-abushu, son of Ubar-

Ishtar, from Salatum, daughter of Apilia, the GI-A-GI [?] and has paid its full price in silver. The business is completed, the contract is valid, his heart is content. In future, man with man, neither shall take exception. By the name of Shamash, Marduk, Sin-mubalit, and the city of Sippara, they swore." [12]

A lively interest in property can be observed in various other types of Babylonian writings. In the lamentation on the destruction of Ur at the hands of her enemies it is the loss not of sons and daughters but of property which evokes anguish unrestrained.[13]

INDUSTRY AND TRADE

The documents from the age of Hammurabi portray a scene of bustling business activity in Babylon—merchants sending out their agents to trade; herdsmen coming in to report on the sheep entrusted to them; scribes busily pressing contracts into wet clay; weavers at their looms producing fabrics which spread afar the fame of Babylonia for rugs and tapestries; moneylenders greedily waiting with the cash; dyers, cobblers, smiths, veterinarians, stonecutters, vintners, and physicians plying their trades. Boats laden with goods moved along the major canals; caravans passed in and out the city gate, where customs officials waited to collect the "gate money." Marketplaces both within and without the city walls were maintained for the exchange or sale of goods; and wineshops, presided over usually if not always by women, provided a place to visit with friends and perhaps to haggle over prices. Of the temples and priests little is said; it is as if the din of bargaining drowned out the call to prayers.

Babylon had at that time no coinage; although silver was often used as a medium of exchange, the *shekel* was really a unit of weight. There were sixty shekels in a *mina* and sixty minas in a *talent*. When silver was used in a trade, its weighing must have been watched closely, and acrimonious disputes must have arisen when a piece of silver had lost weight through wear while in a man's possession so that he was able to get for it less than he had given. It is a simple matter to fix the value of a piece of metal by scratching on it a mark indicating its weight and purity, but this had not been done in Hammurabi's time. Other metals, especially gold, were also used for money, but "shekel" usually meant a shekel-weight of silver. The extent to which silver was used in the ordinary affairs of daily life cannot be determined, but it is probable that simple barter was by far the most common method of trade. Since money is worth only what it will buy in goods and services at any particular time, there is little to be gained by attempting to express the value of a Babylonian shekel in contemporary currency.

Grain as well as silver was legal tender, and the relation between the two was fixed; in fact, the shekel was defined as a weight of one hundred and eighty "grains of wheat." Loans of grain and silver were often made. If interest was charged, the rate, by modern standards, was high: twenty percent is the figure usually found in loan contracts, and this is the rate fixed by law in both the *Laws of Eshnunna* and the *Code of Hammurabi*. The latter code contains a provision that if a higher rate of interest was collected, the lender would forfeit "whatever he lent." In addition to interest-bearing loans, there were some loans made both by individuals and by the temples which for some reason carried no interest charges. If a loan was not paid when due, a heavy penalty might be imposed. In addition to loans, various kinds of advances of goods were also made, to an agent, a laborer, or a tenant. A merchant might furnish an agent with merchandise and share with him the profits from its sale or exchange; a temple might advance the wool or yarn to be worked into cloth; a landowner might furnish a "sharecropper" the supplies needed to produce a crop.

PRICES, WAGES, AND LABOR

This very early society affords an example of an elaborately planned economy; wage and price controls, for example, were extensive. The fixing of wages and prices is all the more remarkable because of the inflexible nature of the established rates; they were written into the laws forever, if we are to take seriously the curses which the lawmakers hurled at anyone who might be disposed to modify the laws set down. Apparently a drought was not supposed to affect the value of grain—nor a large influx of captives in war, the price of slaves. In one of his laws Hammurabi fixed the worth of a slave at twenty shekels, and this seems to have been the average price paid for slaves in his time, although some were, of course, more valuable than others. The wages for labor set by the Code varied between about four and eight shekels per year, six shekels being an average yearly wage. The fee charged for the storage of grain was fixed at one-sixtieth per year of the amount stored.

From evidence contained in the codes of law and from a large number of contracts which have survived, it is clear that not all labor was performed by slaves. It would be interesting to know the extent to which freemen were in competition with slaves, and whether or not certain types of work were usually performed by slaves; but the answers to these important questions are as yet uncertain.

SOCIAL CLASSES

Babylonian society at the time of Hammurabi was divided into three broad classes: patrician, plebeian, and slave. There is considerable ambiguity in the Babylonian term for *man,* and the distinction between patricians and plebeians is not clear. Undoubtedly the class line was drawn roughly between the rich and the poor; it could scarcely have been otherwise in a society in which material possessions were highly regarded and laws protecting private property and the rights of inheritance were an important part of the legal system. It is possible, however, that factors other than wealth entered into the determination of class identity. As King says,

> The highest or upper class embraced all the officers or ministers attached to the court, the higher officials and servants of the state, and the owners of considerable landed property. But wealth or position did not constitute the sole qualification distinguishing the members of the upper class from that immediately below them. In fact, while the majority of its members enjoyed these advantages, it was possible for a man to forfeit them through his own fault or misfortune and yet to retain his social standing and privileges. It would seem therefore that the distinction was based on a racial qualification, and that the upper class, or nobles, as we may perhaps term them, were men of the predominant race, sprung from the West-Semitic or Amorite stock which had given Babylon its first independent dynasty.
> . . . The second class in the population comprised the great body of free men who did not come within the ranks of the nobles; in fact, they formed a middle class between the aristocracy and the slaves. They bore a title which in itself implied a state of inferiority, and though they were not necessarily poor and could possess slaves and property, they did not share the privileges of the upper class.[14]

Although the basis upon which membership in a social class in Babylonia was decided is now a matter for debate, it must have been crystal clear at the time to the Babylonians, since the rights and responsibilities of patricians were different in important respects from those of plebeians. The patrician was required to pay more for medical care than the plebeian paid; his fine was greater if he allowed himself to become involved in an assault; he had to pay more for a divorce. Breach of trust was a much more serious offense for the patrician than for the plebeian, and corruption on the part of a patrician judge was punishable by death. On the other hand, the patrician had not only the natural advantages associated with wealth and power but also some special protection in the law for both his property and his person. There must have been considerable opportunity for a plebeian to rise to a higher class. At the bottom of the social scale was the slave. It would be interesting to know the relative size of these three classes, but there is little accurate information on that subject.

SLAVERY

Slavery was a basic institution in Babylonia, important to the economy of the society, and apparently not at all disturbing to the conscience of the people. Slaves could be branded, pledged for debt, and sold at their master's will. Various laws deal with the escape of slaves, but these laws were designed to protect the slave owner rather than the slave. A purchaser could have his money refunded if a newly acquired slave proved to be defective. A slave could be seized for his master's debts. Insubordination on the part of a slave was a grave offense.

Nevertheless, if one realizes that slavery could not exist without some limitation on the freedom of slaves and some security for the masters in their human property, it is apparent that the Babylonian system of slavery was remarkably humane. A slave was permitted to marry a free woman, and the children were free. A female slave who had borne children to her master could not be sold; her children were free; and she herself gained freedom on the death of her master. A slave could acquire property, engage in trade, enter into a contract with other slaves and under certain conditions with free persons, purchase his own freedom, act as a witness in court, and be a party to a suit. The respect for individual rights which the Babylonians reveal in so many ways would not allow them to regard slaves merely as chattel: slaves were also persons, and as such they possessed certain inalienable rights, including the right to be deprived of life only by due process of law.

Since slaves were often only victims of defeat in war, their inferior status might be a matter of fortune, which could do any man harm, rather than a result of low birth. Some of the slaves were skilled artisans, and others excelled their masters in education and literary accomplishments. Furthermore, there was generally no marked physical difference between masters and slaves—a matter of no little importance in determining their attitude toward one another. Whatever the reason, the Babylonians appear to have been more disposed to deal justly and to show mercy to human beings within their power than many later and more enlightened peoples have been.

AGRICULTURE

If the foodstuffs mentioned in various documents were produced in adequate quantity, it is clear that the Babylonians had a nutritious diet. Meat was furnished by sheep and cattle, and from various references to fishing rights we may assume that the rivers and canals provided a regular supply of fish. Bread made from wheat and barley, and enriched perhaps with oil pressed from sesame seed, was the staple item in the daily fare. Proteins were supplied by cheese and beans. Apples, grapes, apricots, figs, cucumbers, and onions were cultivated, in addition to the ubiquitous date. The date palm, which thrived in the warm, well-watered delta soil, provided a variety of useful products: wine and a flour mix were made from the fruit, the sap yielded sugar, the trunk furnished building material, and the bark provided rope. Consequently, large areas were planted with date palms.

Fields, gardens, and orchards were either cultivated with slaves and hired laborers or rented for a share in the yield. Wages for laborers were fixed by law at about one half a shekel per month, with some seasonal variation; the pay for day labor was slightly higher during the first five months than it was during the remainder of the year. The rental price to be paid for an ox, ass, goat, or wagon was fixed in both the *Code of Eshnunna* and the *Code of Hammurabi*. Where land was rented on shares, the owner received one third or one half of the yield from a field planted to grain, and two thirds of the yield from a garden or an orchard. He was protected against a renter's negligence by a law that gave him the right to expect from his fields a return equal to that obtained from adjacent fields, gardens, and orchards. If a renter failed through neglect to achieve production comparable to that of his neighbors, he had to give up as much of his own share as was required to give the owner a proper return from his property. On the other hand, the tenant was not held liable for losses that resulted from excessive rains, storms, or drought. Also, he had the right to sublet property which he had rented.

The royal estates, temple possessions, and large holdings of the landed patricians probably contained a major part of the productive land of Babylonia, but there are many indications that small holdings were not uncommon. The owners of small estates had all the property rights given the wealthy members of society.

FAMILY

Almost all the available information about the Babylonian family system comes from the *Code of Hammurabi* and from several other codes of laws which have survived in fragmentary form. In letters, contracts, and various other documents are found corroborative facts and additional details about the legal aspects of family relations, but there is little information about the intimate experiences of courtship, marriage, and family life. Babylonian youths were doubtless not lacking in ardor, but apparently they rarely committed their sentiments to writing. Erotic feeling could more appropriately be addressed to the deities, as this sensuous description of the goddess Ishtar well illustrates:

> In lips she is sweet; life is in her mouth.
> At her appearance rejoicing becomes full.
> She is glorious; veils are thrown over her head.
> Her figure is beautiful; her eyes are brilliant.[15]

Restraint seems to have been exercised in the expression of affection for mortals, as this letter, probably addressed to the writer's wife, reveals:

> To Bilbea say, thus saith Gimil-Marduk: May Shamash and Marduk for my sake preserve thy health forever. I have sent for thy health. Tell me how thou art. I went to Babylon and did not see thee. I was greatly disappointed. Send me the reason of thy leaving, and let me be cheered. In Marchesvan do thou come. For my sake keep well always.[16]

Marriage was the custom, and monogamy the most common practice, but celibacy and polygamy were both permitted in certain circumstances. Every boy was expected to be provided from his family's estate with a bride price. With this he declared the seriousness of his intentions and showed that he had his parents' consent to a proposed match; the purchase of a wife was not apparently a Babylonian practice. Every girl was entitled to a dowry, whether she married or entered one of the temples as a votaress. Since this dowry remained her private estate, it constituted her badge of self-respect and independence. In marriage a man acquired a helpmate and not a household drudge; although he was the nominal head of the family, she was protected against abuse and given rights not possessed by women today in many societies.

It is apparent that the individual, not the family, was the unit of Babylonian society. Although some laws were designed to strengthen the family system—as, for example, those dealing with adultery—most legislation which affected family behavior was directed toward the rights of the individual rather than those of the family unit. A man's authority over his children was much greater than that over his wife, but even the legal rights of children were defined in considerable detail. For example, a father could not disinherit a son unless the son had committed a crime which the judges considered "sufficiently grave to cut him off from sonship," and he did not have the power of life or death over his children which the Roman father possessed under *patria potestas*. Most of the laws anticipated a family group composed of husband, wife, and minor children; though a newly married couple might reside for a while with the groom's family, that arrangement apparently was regarded as temporary.

Since a family's possessions seem usually to have been distributed equally among the children upon the death of the parents, the rights of the individual members of the family took precedence over the rights of the family as a whole. Such practices as entail and the common ownership of family property found in many other societies do not appear to have been customary in Babylonia. It is probable, therefore, that there was a good deal of movement of families up and down the social ladder. Low birth may have been, in fact, no bar to the attainment of high social prestige. Centuries before the time of Hammurabi the great king Sargon had boasted:

> My mother was a changeling, my father I knew not.
> The brothers of my father loved the hills.
> My city is Azupiranu, which is situated on the banks
>   of the Euphrates.
> My changeling mother conceived me, in secret she bore me.
> She set me in a basket of rushes, with bitumen she
>   sealed my lid.
> She cast me into the river which rose not over me.[17]

Some scholars believe that in the time of Hammurabi a large part of the plebeian class was composed of the children of slaves. If it were possible for large numbers of people to rise so far in a single generation, might not an ambitious and talented person have climbed even higher up the social ladder?

MARRIAGE

The laws and marriage contracts which have survived give a fairly clear picture of the legal aspects of the Babylonian marriage system. In order to obtain a bride, a man was expected to pay to the girl's parents a small bride price, usually about ten shekels. This was apparently merely a part of the marriage ritual and did not imply wife purchase, since the bride seems generally to have claimed for herself the token payment; in addition, she was given a marriage portion by her own family, and this too remained her property after marriage. The girl from a well-to-do family came to her husband with private wealth in the form of slaves, furniture, money, and other valuable possessions; consequently her dignity and self-respect were well protected. If during the betrothal the man changed his mind, he merely forfeited the sum he had paid; if the bride's father broke off the engagement, the rejected suitor received twice what he had paid. No marriage was recognized without a formal written contract. A man might negotiate for himself, but apparently a girl's first husband was selected by some member of her family. Once married, however, she was no longer under parental control; and if her marriage was terminated by the death of her husband, by separation from him for some reason, or by divorce, she might be granted permission by the judge to choose another mate.

Various references to a "second" wife reveal the legality of polygyny, but a plurality of wives must have been uncommon. The second wife seems usually to have been subordinate to the first. A sterile wife was allowed to select for her husband a slave to bear children in her stead, or her husband might take a concubine for that purpose. Once a slave or a free concubine had borne children, her status was vastly improved, but she remained inferior to a legal wife. Clearly it was to a woman's advantage to be both wife and mother, but in some circumstances she could honorably be one and not the other. It is reasonable to assume that polygyny was permitted only for the sake of children and that a fertile wife had a claim to the undivided attentions of her husband. Polyandry seems not to have been practiced, nor is there any indication of the existence of the levirate.

STATUS OF WOMEN

Babylonian women possessed, two thousand years before the Christian era, many rights which they have gained but recently in some of the more enlightened societies of our own time. In the Age of Hammurabi a woman, whether married or single, could operate an independent business, own slaves, control an estate, buy and sell property in her own name, make a will, carry her grievances to court, retain possession of her legacy, adopt a son or a daughter, and in general enjoy the privileges of men. Her personal integrity and inherent dignity as an individual were fully recognized. Brothers and sisters shared alike in an estate, unless there was some specific provision in the will making an exception. When a girl married, she received a dowry appropriate to her station in life; although she might allow her husband the use of her property, she could retain it as a private possession. If divorced, she kept her dowry; if she died without children, her own property reverted to her paternal family.

A woman's right to be maintained by a husband, if she lacked other means of support, was guaranteed by a law which authorized her to take another mate if her husband was absent for an extended period. Perhaps for the benefit of men made captives in war, the law provided that a husband whose absence had been involuntary could reclaim his wife when he returned; a husband who had simply deserted her could not do so. No blame attached to a woman who entered another man's house in such circumstances and bore him children, unless it could be shown that she had the means to live without remarrying; any children born of such marriages remained with their father. Likewise, a wife was protected in case she lost her health or her appeal to her husband; in sickness she was entitled to be supported in her husband's house as long as she lived. In the event that her husband took a concubine and had children by her, the legal wife was empowered to keep the concubine in a subordinate position.

The education of girls was not neglected, since they were able to read and write and to manage their own business affairs. Long afterwards Herodotus was shocked at the position of Babylonian women in the temples, but the observations of this "father of history" were sometimes colored by an active imagination; the temple morals which he described were probably to some extent an "invention of the Greeks." The use of slaves undoubtedly reduced the domestic duties of women in the wealthier homes. Since the employment of wet nurses was common enough to warrant the regulation of the practice by law, we may assume that even the mothers of young children were able to obtain some relief from the burdens of child-rearing. Women of the upper classes had, therefore, considerable freedom and might engage in business or pursue private interests. It is significant that in the literature of the period women are not described as fragile and men are rarely portrayed as manly; there is a striking absence of those terms which identify women with frailty, and though men boast of their strength, they do not praise the gods that they were born men.

On the other hand, women were at a decided disadvantage in some respects. The bride became a member of her husband's family and might reside for a time in the home of her father-in-law. The father acted as head of the family in the marriage arrangements made for his children; apparently a mother gave a daughter in marriage only when the father was absent. A husband might bind his wife in service to a creditor for three years, provided that the debt was incurred after the marriage took place. All blame for childlessness fell on the woman; if a man's wife had borne him no children, he was permitted to divorce her, saying, "You are not my wife." For other reasons also a man might divorce his wife, but a woman could obtain a divorce only when she could prove to the judges that she had been careful and was not at fault. If a wife neglected her house and humiliated her husband, she could be drowned; if she brought about the death of her husband on account of another man, she could be impaled on stakes; her penalty for adultery was always death.

These opposing attitudes toward women may have resulted from a clash between the matriarchal pattern of the early Sumerians and the patriarchal pattern which the Semites introduced into Babylonia, although in some fragments of pre-Semitic codes of law are found certain marked discriminations against women. For example, Sumerian law required that a woman who repudiated her husband because of hatred for him should be "thrown into the river," whereas a husband was fined only half a mina of silver for a similar repudiation of his wife.[18]

Most of the Babylonian deities were represented as masculine. Furthermore, it is especially noticeable that where goddesses appear they are cast in less noble roles than those of the gods. The awful primeval chaos is personified by the goddess Tiamat. Female vanity is the theme of a touching scene in the *Epic of Gilgamesh,* in which Ishtar, made furious by unrequited love, threatens to raise up the dead so that they shall "outnumber the living" unless Gilgamesh is punished for his scorn of her advances. The satanic god Nergal, lord of the lower world, was really only the consort to the mistress of the nether realm, the goddess Allatu (Erishgal). In religion, therefore, the name of woman was not so much Frailty as it was Evil. Sayce believes that the Semitic influence was responsible for a less elevated position of females among the deities than among mortals.

> For the Semite the woman is the lesser man, formed out of him and dependent upon him. Like the feminine of the noun, she is the colourless reflection of her husband. . . . Wherever the Semitic spirit has prevailed, the woman has been simply the helpmeet and shadow of the man; for the orthodox Mohammedan she hardly possesses a soul. It is only where the Semitic spirit has been met and checked by the influence of another race that this is not the case; the high place retained by the woman in Babylonian society would of itself have been a proof that Semitic culture had here been engrafted on that of an older people, even if the monuments had not revealed to us that such was indeed the fact. It is not surprising, therefore, that the goddesses or female spirits of Sumerian faith faded away as the Semitic element in Babylonian religion became stronger.[19]

RELIGION

It must be remembered that Babylonian civilization was an outgrowth of the fusion of two rather distinct cultures. Some of the elements of Sumerian culture prevailed against the Semitic influences: the cuneiform writing, which clearly antedated the arrival in mass of the Semites, is a good example. On the other hand, some of the beliefs and practices of the Semites triumphed in the clash of cultures: Babylonian religion at the time of Hammurabi was obviously more Semitic than Sumerian. The unification of the two religions was not, however, perfect; two systems of theological concepts, one derived from the Sumerians and the other from the Semites, are found in the religious literature of Babylonia. That may partly explain the failure of the Babylonians to develop a coherent religious system. This difficulty would not have proved insurmountable had the Babylonians possessed the religious enthusiasm of other ancient peoples, such as, for example, the Hebrews. But religion was not the dominant Babylonian institution. Babylonian thought reflects, as we have seen, a decidedly materialistic and secular turn of mind, especially striking because of its appearance in a society standing at the dawn of civilization. People gave a tithe to the priests and observed numerous religious rites and ceremonies, but seemingly they found in the marketplace greater attractions than the temple afforded.

The names of the numerous Babylonian deities and the titles given them on various inscriptions are important only to the specialist. Of wider interest, however, is the matter of how the Babylonians conceived of deity, what they understood death to mean, whether they had visions of heaven and fears of hell, and what inspiration and guidance in the conduct of their lives they derived from the gods whom they worshiped. Accurate and complete answers to these questions are not, of course, available. From the hands of many writers have come the literary myths, heroic tales, rituals, incantations, hymns, prayers, and lamentations in which the religious thoughts of the Babylonians are expressed. The burst of literary activity which occurred in the first half of the second millennium B.C. included reproductions of older compositions as well as original works. The utterances of a writer inevitably represent a restricted point of view, and we may not know with certainty for whom a specific writer spoke. Nevertheless, some very general ideas emerge with a high degree of consistency and clarity, and from these we are able to gain some insight into the religious thought of the Babylonians.

BABYLONIAN GODS

The title of *Bel,* which Marduk received when Babylon rose to power, represented only his claim to precedence over the other gods; their continued existence was not questioned, and a polytheistic conception of deity prevailed in

38 · Five Ancient Societies

Babylonia, no matter how much the hierarchy of gods was changed to accord with the rise and fall of kingdoms. Maspero says that

> Among all the thousands of tablets or inscribed stones on which we find recorded prayers and magical formulas, we have as yet discovered no document treating of the existence of a supreme god, or even containing the faintest allusion to a divine unity. We meet indeed with many passages in which this or that divinity boasts of his power, eloquently depreciating that of his rivals, and ending his discourse with the injunction to worship him alone: "Man who shall come after, trust in Nebo, trust in no other god!" The very expressions which are used, commanding future races to abandon the rest of the immortals in favour of Nebo, prove that even those who prided themselves on being worshippers of one god realized how far they were from believing in the unity of God.[20]

Minor deities sometimes appeared as attributes of major deities, but their distinct identity was not wholly lost. Likewise, the ranking of a god was determined by the political fortune of states. For example, the god of Babylon, Marduk, became the sovereign deity when Babylon became the sovereign state. Monotheism was not, therefore, a Babylonian conception.

Although the gods differed one from the other, they were all like men in appearance and disposition; an anthropomorphic conception of deity is, therefore, a characteristic of Babylonian religion. Marduk was begot of Ea, conceived by Damkina, and suckled like a human infant. He is described in the *Creation Epic* as having a good figure and a lordly gait, although he had four ears and four eyes and was exceedingly tall. The gods had organs and appendages of human beings; they slept and required nourishment; they were capable of the normal human emotions. The human aspect of the gods is made unmistakably clear; the divine and abstract element in them is pushed into the background as though it were of little consequence. The gods were awful in their wrath, and men stood not humbly before them but afraid, expecting justice but not mercy.

HUMAN ENDS

The *Creation Epic* describes the divine origin of the earth and all that it contains. Its theme is the struggle of the hero Marduk against a bestial creature called Tiamat to transform chaos into cosmic order. The monster and her demon brood are finally vanquished, and from her crushed body Marduk fashions the firmament. Then his heart prompts him to declare:

> Blood I will mass and cause bones to be.
> I will establish a savage, "man" shall be his name.
> Verily, savage-man I will create.
> He shall be charged with the service of the gods
>   That they might be at ease![21]

Additional details about the creation of man are found in another epic, in which a man of clay is seen receiving life through blood taken from the vessels of a slain god. "Let him be formed out of clay, be animated with blood!" the gods ordain, and let him thenceforth bear the "burden of creation."[22] Truly man was made to serve the gods.

When that service is ended, it is man's fate to return to the clay of which he is made. Death severs forever his contact with the gods; but in that awful moment when life runs out and the fetters of fear are cast off, man enters upon a joyless existence for all eternity amid shadows and gloom. It is no wonder, therefore, that

> The thoughts of the Babylonian were fixed rather on this world than on the next; his horizon, speaking generally, was bounded by death. It was in this world that he had relations with the gods and duties towards them, and it was here that he was punished or rewarded for the deeds committed in the flesh. The practical character of the Babylonians did not lend itself to dreams and speculations about the future; the elaborate map of the other world, which is drawn in the sacred books of Egypt, would have been impossible for them. They were too much absorbed in commerce and trade and the practical pursuit of wealth, to have leisure for theories that concerned themselves with a doubtful future and an invisible world.[23]

Gilgamesh settled for many centuries in Babylonia the question of immortality. The central theme of the *Epic* is his quest for eternal life. The death of his friend Enkidu inspires him to search for the secret of immortality, even to the Waters of Death, where the deified survivor of the Deluge dwells. After roaming over the steppes and through the shadows he finally learns that

> Only the gods live forever under the sun.
> As for mankind, numbered are their days;
> Whatever they achieve is but the wind.[24]

An ale-wife advised Gilgamesh to seize the day, thus offering at the dawn of history the *carpe diem* escape from a brooding sense of futility.

> The life thou pursuest thou shalt not find.
> When the gods created mankind,
> Death for mankind they set aside,
> Life in their own hands retaining.
> Thou, Gilgamesh, let full be thy belly,
> Make thou merry by day and by night.
> Of each day make thou a feast of rejoicing,
> Day and night dance thou and play . . .
> For this is the task of mankind.[25]

The call to duty that Hammurabi sounds, and the impatience with negligence that speaks out in his laws and letters, may have been a necessary legal antidote

40 · *Five Ancient Societies*

for a religious malady. The virtues without which a society cannot endure must be supported by secular forces where they are not sustained by sacred beliefs. The faith which enabled Job, despite his tribulations, to praise the name of the Lord is lacking in the anguished cry of an Akkadian, who, like Job, was good and righteous and yet afflicted:

> He who was living yesterday has died today;
> Instantly he is made gloomy, suddenly is he crushed.
> One moment he sings a happy song,
> And in an instant he will moan like a mourner.
> Like day and night their mood changes.
> When they are hungry they resemble corpses,
> When they are sated they rival their god;
> In good luck they speak of ascending to heaven,
> When they are afflicted they grumble about going
>   down to the underworld.[26]

These words from a man who claimed that supplication was his concern and sacrifice his rule reveal how futile is the sense of fate when the sense of guilt has not been quickened. The penitent in Babylonian psalms usually asks to be forgiven for sins of which he has no knowledge rather than for sins which he has wilfully committed.

SUMMARY OF RELIGIOUS THOUGHT

In summary, the gods of Babylonia were numerous, and their rank corresponded to that of their respective cities; Marduk was the supreme god because Babylon became the chief city of Babylonia. They were believed to be immortal but like men in appearance and conduct. Men were like gods except for the dagger of mortality ever suspended above their heads; death bore the righteous and the wicked alike into a "prison-house of darkness" forever. The various terms used to describe the hereafter are in themselves revelations of what it was conceived to be: the "nether world," the "land of no return," the "house which none leave who have entered it," the "road from which there is no way back." Since death was the end and not the beginning, there was every reason to make the most of life. A strong sense of the present is reflected in the highly practical and materialistic attitude that prevailed in Babylonia.

BABYLONIAN ACHIEVEMENTS

Babylonian civilization neither began nor ended with Hammurabi, but the numerous extant writings from his age give a more comprehensive account of that period than we have of any other in the long history of Sumer and Akkad. His age also represents a high moment in Babylonian civilization, when natural resources and human institutions were in harmony. Food was varied and usually plentiful, trade thrived, and the arts and sciences flourished.

This happy stiuation did not, however, endure. The Babylonians lacked both the human and the natural resources to create a lasting empire. The Assyrian came down veritably like the wolf on the fold, raiding the towns and temples. From the East came the Kassites mounted on horses, to plunder and subdue. (It is small wonder that an aversion to horses later found expression in the Bible.) The dikes broke and were not repaired, the irrigation systems collapsed, the dispossessed swamps crept back to claim their own. Babylonia belonged to everybody and to nobody, as tides of restless migrants came and departed.

New monarchs appeared to claim the proud title "King of Sumer and Akkad and of the Four Quarters of the World." One of these was Nebuchadnezzar, known today not so much for his victories over the Assyrians, the Persians, and the Egyptians as for his discipline of the Israelites. When, early in the sixth century B.C., they rebelled against his authority, he carried off into captivity in Babylon an untold number of them.

Our knowledge of Babylonia is of recent date and is yet meager. It will, as time passes, undoubtedly be extended. From what we already know, however, the achievements of the ancient Babylonians command our respect.

The Babylonians controlled the water of two great rivers, the Euphrates and the Tigris, and the water gave them food. They created codes of law, and the law gave them social order. They recognized the inherent dignity of the individual, and men and women found the will and the means to develop the arts and sciences. They wrote on clay and built with clay. Their writings did not perish, and their techniques of building approached the skills that enabled the Egyptians to construct the pyramids. They looked up at the heavenly bodies and discovered both science and religion. Thus, in their control over nature, their highly developed social organization, their individualism, their art and knowledge, their materialism, and their religion they displayed thousands of years ago that capacity for thought which has created civilizations.

3 · ANCIENT EGYPT

Be not arrogant because of thy knowledge, and have no confidence in that thou art a learned man. Take counsel with the ignorant as with the wise, for the limits of art cannot be reached, and no artist fully possesseth his skill. A good discourse is more hidden than the precious green stone, and yet it is found with slave-girls over the mill-stones. PTAH-HOTEP

Ancient Egyptian civilization, older perhaps than the Babylonian and more advanced in art, architecture, literature, religion, and ethics, reached the peak of its splendor in the Eighteenth Dynasty (c. 1546-1319 B.C.)[*] and maintained during the two succeeding dynasties a high level of accomplishment. As we turn to the social thought of ancient Egypt, we shall focus our attention, to a considerable extent, on this period. At this time the pyramids had already been built, and some of the finest among them had been standing for more than a thousand years. Likewise, the technical skills that enabled artists and artisans to produce objects both useful and beautiful had already been developed. Some of ancient Egypt's finest sculpture dates from the third millennium, and from the Twelfth Dynasty (c. 2000-1780 B.C.) came much of the best literature produced by the ancient Egyptians. Nevertheless, the Eighteenth Dynasty witnessed the rise of Egypt to dominion over an empire extending from the headwaters of the Nile to the banks of the Euphrates; for more than a century Egypt ruled the East.

The pharaohs who controlled this vast empire had at their command the products of earlier labors in the arts and sciences. The ancient classics were well known, and the use of many of them as school exercises ensured against their

---

[*] Many dates in Egyptian chronology are still debated. Most of the dates given in this chapter are taken from George Steindorff and Keith C. Seele, *When Egypt Ruled the East* (Chicago: University of Chicago Press, 1947), pp. 274-275. An example of minor variations can be seen in Margaret A. Murray, *Egyptian Religious Poetry* (London: John Murray, 1949), p. 24.

neglect. The artistic forms in which the quality of Egyptian thought is so well expressed had already been worked out and were available for use. As Rostovtzeff says: "At this time Egypt was able to make full use of all that the past had attained, and she created immortal monuments of brilliant beauty, strong and graceful, huge and yet shapely, harmonized with nature, and full of enchanting detail."[1] In this short period, the finished products of ancient Egypt's versatile talents were gathered together to a greater extent than at any other time in Egypt's long history.

For a moment Egypt held the torch of civilization but, as the light grew dim, the records of Egypt's golden age were buried in the tombs of the pharaohs. In the fifth century B.C., Herodotus was amazed at the arts and customs that he discovered in Egypt and spread such tales as inspired among the Greeks a reverence for Egyptian culture. The world long viewed ancient Egypt through the eyes of Greek and Roman writers who came upon the scene after Egypt's strength was spent. But men such as Herodotus could not have known that long before Homer lived—in fact, many centuries before Achilles was supposed to have sulked in his tent and Odysseus to have wandered far on his journey home from the Trojan War—the finest products of Egyptian genius had been buried and lost. Not until two thousand years after Herodotus were those tombs and temple ruins to give up their secrets and lay bare the accomplishments of the ancient Egyptians. Since that day when Herodotus stood on the banks of the Nile and was astounded at what he saw, scholars from many lands, working with tools far sharper than those at his disposal, have probed into Egypt's broken and buried past and brought out and fitted together the pieces. Now that the scholars have enabled us to catch a glimpse of Egypt in the days of her glory, we can ill afford to neglect, because of habit, one of the world's great civilizations.

The Egyptian civilization, like the Babylonian, was made possible by water flowing down from the mountains onto a plain that would have been dry and barren without a ceaseless flow and an annual flood. The White Nile arises three degrees south of the equator and is fed by numerous tributaries from the highlands of equatorial Africa. At Khartum, about thirteen hundred and fifty miles from the sea, it is joined by the Blue Nile from the lofty mountains of Abyssinia. The Nile thus formed flows down over the cataracts of Ethiopia (known as Nubia in ancient times) into the valley cut ages ago in the desert plateau of northeast Africa. From the First Cataract, the valley of the Nile is a ribbon of productive soil in a desert waste. The valley varies in width from about ten to thirty miles, until the delta (so-called by the Greeks because of its resemblance to their letter *delta*) is reached. Ancient Memphis stood near the entrance to the delta, and at the other end of the valley was situated the city of Thebes.

In natural environment ancient Egypt had much in common with Babylonia. They produced similar foodstuffs under about the same climatic conditions.

Both had to build dikes, dams, and irrigation ditches to control the water; both depended upon an annual inundation to preserve the fertility of the soil. As a result of these natural conditions, both were compelled to develop a wide variety of cooperative activities and to achieve a high degree of social organization; drainage and irrigation on the extensive scale necessary could not have been left to individual inclinations. Egypt was less exposed to attack than was Babylonia, since only from Nubia to the south and the Sinai region to the northeast could a large-scale invasion come; but the wealth of each was the envy of its neighbors, and each had at times to maintain an army for the defense of its territory. Nevertheless, the basic social institutions of the two peoples differed radically in many respects, as we shall see.

HISTORICAL SKETCH

As early as the fourth millennium B.C., the small provinces (nomes) and city states existing along the valley and in the delta of the Nile appear to have united gradually into two kingdoms, one in the delta and the other in the valley proper. These two states probably lasted for centuries, with now one and then the other claiming supremacy, until Menes, who was said by Herodotus to have been the first mortal king of Egypt, gained control over all Egypt and established a capital at Memphis. Of the first three dynasties in Egyptian history little is known except that the building of pyramids began during this time. The one at Meydum, built in the Third Dynasty, is not a true pyramid but rather three tiers of massive stones; yet it is impressive not only for its age but also for its grandeur.

The Pyramid Age really began with the Fourth Dynasty (2900-2750 B.C.) since the true pyramid form was developed at this time and the first three of the famous pyramids of Giza were built. The Great Pyramid of King Khufu (Cheops) is more than four hundred and eighty feet high, covers thirteen acres, and contains at least two and a half million cubic yards of stone. In addition to its architecture, the Old Kingdom is distinguished for its art, literature, and social organization. The diorite statue of King Khafre, the little ivory statuette of King Khufu, and the wood carving of the Sheik-el-Beled, all from this period, are among the finest examples of Egyptian art. This age produced also the *Pyramid Texts,* the *Teachings of Ptah-hotep,* and an extensive body of religious literature of various kinds. In many fields of endeavor, as Breasted points out, the accomplishments of the Old Kingdom merit recognition:

> To us it has left the imposing line of temples, tombs and pyramids, stretching for many miles along the margin of the western desert, the most eloquent witnesses to the fine intelligence and Titanic energies of the men who made the Old Kingdom what it was; not alone achieving these wonders

of mechanics and internal organization, but building the earliest known sea-going ships and exploring unknown waters, or pushing their commercial enterprises far up the Nile into inner Africa. In plastic art they had reached the highest achievement; in architecture their tireless genius had created the column and originated the colonnade; in government they had elaborated an enlightened and highly developed state, with a large body of just law; in religion they were already dimly conscious of a judgment in the hereafter, and they were thus the first men whose ethical intuitions made happiness in the future life dependent upon character. Everywhere their unspent energies unfolded in a rich and manifold culture which left the world such a priceless heritage as no nation had yet bequeathed it.[2]

Eventually a social revolution occurred, and for about three centuries Egypt was again broken up into small principalities. As a result of civil strife, "the land trembled, all the people were in terror, the villages were in panic, and fear entered into their limbs." The Middle Kingdom, or Feudal Age, which lasted for about four centuries, witnessed the second period of stable government and productive development in Egypt. During the first portion of this age, the provincial rulers (nomarchs) exercised independent control over their kingdoms, but gradually a feudal organization was perfected and Egypt enjoyed again the advantages of an integrated government. In the Twelfth Dynasty (2000-1788 B.C.), Egypt entered upon what is known as the *classic period* of her history. A lively trade developed with Crete, Palestine, and Syria; the copper mines of Sinai were again exploited; large tracts of land were reclaimed by the construction of vast retention walls; numerous temples and tombs were built; and literature flourished to such an extent that the age produced many of the works which later Egyptians regarded as their classics.

Egypt was destined, however, to pass through another period of chaos. As time passed, the hand of the pharaoh was strengthened at the expense of the feudal barons, but the monarchy did not endure. In the convulsions resulting from internal discord, Egypt was an easy prey for a horde of barbarians who swept in about 1700 B.C. and seized control of the government. Little is known of these Hyksos ("shepherd kings"), but the Egyptian historian Manetho (c. 270 B.C.) is quoted by Josephus as saying that they were "a people of ignoble origin from the east [who] had the audacity to invade the country which they mastered by main force without difficulty or even a battle. Having overpowered the chiefs, they then savagely burnt the cities, razed the temples of the gods to the ground, and treated the whole native population with the utmost cruelty."[3]

The empire, which began with the expulsion of the Hyksos about 1546 B.C., is often referred to as Egypt's Golden Age. A capital for all Egypt was established at Thebes, and the pharaohs of the Eighteenth Dynasty succeeded in giving Egypt not only a government able to ensure prosperity at home but also an empire that filled the royal coffers with tribute. Thutmose III (c. 1482-1450 B.C.), known as the "Napoleon of Ancient Egypt," swept all of his country's enemies before him, from the Fourth Cataract of the Nile to northern Syria. Egypt now passed through a period of security and wealth, of which Breasted says:

> The imperial age was now at its full noontide in the Nile valley. The old seclusiveness had totally disappeared, the wall of partition between Asia and Africa, already shaken by the Hyksos, was now completely broken down by the wars of Thutmose III. Traditional limits disappeared, the currents of life eddied no longer within the landmarks of tiny kingdoms, but pulsed from end to end of a great empire, embracing many kingdoms and tongues, from the upper Nile to the upper Euphrates. The wealth of Asiatic trade, circulating through the eastern end of the Mediterranean, which once flowed down the Euphrates to Babylon, was thus diverted to the Nile Delta, now united by canal with the Red Sea. All the world traded in the Delta markets. Assyria was still in her infancy and Babylonia no longer possessed any political influence in the west. The Pharaoh looked forward to an indefinite lease of power throughout the vast empire which he had conquered.[4]

This was the age of Queen Hatshepsut (c. 1504-1482 B.C.), who was not content to be the wife of a king but took in her own hands the reins of government; of Amenhotep III (c. 1412-1375 B.C.), known as "the Magnificent," who sought to make Thebes a city of splendor and gaiety, a fitting abode for the rulers of the East; of Ikhnaton (c. 1387-1366 B.C.), who in his devotion to religion gave little thought to the empire which he inherited; of Tutankh-Amon (c. 1366-1357 B.C.), a weak and undistinguished king who would have passed unnoticed had not chance preserved his tomb intact; of Rameses II (c. 1299-1232 B.C.), who sought unsuccessfully to recapture Egypt's lost power, although he was able during his long reign to give his name to about two hundred children from his harem and to many monuments, some of which had been built by earlier kings.

After about 1150 B.C., the power and prestige of Egypt steadily declined, as the once mighty empire again broke up into small principalities. In the latter part of the eighth century B.C., Egypt was conquered by the Ethiopians. A renaissance in the sixth century proved short-lived, and in 525 B.C., Egypt became a province of Persia. When Alexander evicted the Persians in the fourth century, he put Ptolemy, one of his generals, in charge of the conquered land, and the Ptolemies ruled Egypt from the death of Alexander, in 323 B.C., until Octavius Caesar supplanted Cleopatra, in 30 B.C., and made Egypt a Roman province.

ANCIENT EGYPTIAN DOCUMENTS

The picture script which the Egyptians employed in their earliest writings reveals a "delightful assemblage of birds, snakes, men, tools, stars, and beasts."

It had been used for thousands of years when the Greeks, who could not interpret the signs, attached a mystical meaning to them and called them *hieroglyphs* (sacred signs). When Egyptian civilization died under the Romans, the earliest written language of the Egyptians—and, as an adequate system of written expression of thought, probably the oldest written language known to man—was lost. It was not until Napoleon's engineers found the Rosetta Stone (1799), on which appeared an inscription in hieroglyphics, in popular Egyptian script, and in Greek, that the darkness of thirteen centuries was lifted from the earliest recorded Egyptian thought. Early in the dynastic period, the Egyptian scribes had developed a cursive script, the *hieratic,* which compares with the decorative and often painted hieroglyphs as the handwritten does to the printed character, and from this came the careless *demotic* script found on the Rosetta Stone. Writing in hieratic was common, and most of ancient Egypt's best literature was either originally produced in or translated into hieratic script. The Egyptians were reluctant, however, to give up the ancient signs, partly because of their reverence for the old and partly because of their disinclination to sacrifice beauty for the sake of convenience; and all three systems of symbols were in use until the Egyptians took over the Greek alphabet and developed, with some additions, the *Coptic* system of writing.

The reluctance of the Egyptians to give up anything from the past, so clearly seen in their tenacious hold on the hieroglyphs after their language had developed to the point at which they might easily have had a complete alphabet, is to be observed also in their religion and in their literature. Sayce has pointed out that this "veneration for the past, which preserves without repairing or modifying or even adapting to the surroundings of the present, is a characteristic which is deeply engrained in the mind of the Egyptian." [5] It is important to bear this trait of Egyptian culture in mind, since many of the documents produced in the early dynasties contain ideas that belong to much later periods as well. Portions of the living thought of the Empire came down virtually unchanged from the Old Kingdom. In order, therefore, to understand Egyptian thought in the later period it is necessary to examine not only the contemporary works but also some of the older writings which preserved the old order in the midst of the new.

A vast body of documents from ancient Egypt has survived the ravages of time.

> This happy circumstance is due to the Egyptian climate; for centuries the dry air and the sand have preserved to us even such delicate objects as clothes and papyrus rolls. Moreover, under the influence of their strange religious conceptions the Egyptians paid particular regard to the lasting character and rich adornment of their tombs. Whilst most people of similar standing in civilisation have been content with perishable graves, the Egyptians prepared for their mummies vast enduring monuments, the rich deco-

ration of which gives us full details of their manner of life. Thus in Egypt we learn to know those centuries of the remote past which in other countries are covered with a thick veil.[6]

Many of these early documents are religious in nature. Written on the walls of five of the pyramids from the Fifth and Sixth Dynasties are the hymns and incantations known as the *Pyramid Texts*. With the accompanying pictures in relief, these texts present a view of life and thought about 2800 B.C., or earlier.

Much has been written about the *Book of the Dead*. The practice prevailed from the earliest times to bury with the deceased a written version of the spells and prayers needed in the hereafter. These might be inscribed on the walls of the tomb, as in the case of the *Pyramid Texts,* which E.A.W. Budge calls "the oldest form of the Book of the Dead known to us," or, as was usually done, they might be written on papyrus. Ideas about the efficacy of certain rituals must have differed, since there are many "editions" of the *Book of the Dead*. However, modern scholars have adopted the title given by Lepsius to the vast assortment of instructions furnished the dead, and there is some agreement as to the arrangement and numbering of the "chapters." Only the so-called "negative confessions" (Chapter CXXV) bear directly on life situations; in these the deceased is represented as appearing before a tribunal and denying having committed in life certain acts which were apparently regarded as reprehensible. Many other religious documents have survived, among which may be mentioned Ikhnaton's longer *Hymn to Aton,* the Cairo *Hymn to Amon,* and the *Hymn to the Nile*. These represent Egyptian literature at its best.

Although the religious theme is dominant, by no means all of the extant Egyptian documents are religious in nature. A large number of historical records, lengthy correspondence about the affairs of state, scientific treatises, social tractates, secular songs and poems, didactic works, and narratives of various types have survived. The Egyptians possessed no real epics, but in the *Story of Two Brothers,* the tale of *Sinuhe,* and the remarkably vivid account of a "ship-wrecked sailor," to give only a few examples, they displayed considerable ability in narration. This type of literature is, however, less important for our purposes than the didactic and wisdom writing of the Egyptians. The "wisdom" texts suffer from the fact that they were used as school exercises, and in several instances the only surviving copies were written by youths who obviously did not understand what they were writing. This is especially true of an apparent favorite in the classrooms, the *Teachings of Duauf*. Of this work Erman says:

> The way in which the boys have mangled the text baffles description. There are not many passages in it with regard to which one does not despairingly ask what can have been written there originally; for what the boys have written are too often meaningless words—they simply did not understand what they had to copy out.[7]

Nevertheless, despite the garbled texts, it is in such works as the *Instruction for King Merikare,* the *Instruction for King Amenemhet,* the *Instruction of Ani,* and various other similar texts that the social wisdom of the ancient Egyptians is to be found.

GOVERNMENT AND LAW

THE GOD-KING

The only form of government known to ancient Egypt was monarchy, both when there were many kings and when there was but one. Furthermore, the monarch was no mere mortal but a god; he ruled not only by divine right but also as a divine being. In one of the finest pieces of Egyptian sculpture which has survived, King Khafre, of the Fourth Dynasty, is shown with the god Horus in the form of a falcon sitting with protecting wings outstretched behind the King's head. The representation of the king in works of art as both human and divine continued as long as Egyptian civilization preserved its distinctness. Likewise, in many inscriptions the divine nature of the pharaoh is expressly declared. In one of the documents the god tells Rameses II:

> I am thy father, who begat thee as the gods, all thy limbs are of the gods. . . . I have set thee as everlasting king, ruler established forever. . . . I have given thee the divine office, that thou mayest rule the Two Lands like [as] the King of Upper and Lower Egypt;

and Rameses replies:

> I am thy son whom thou hast placed upon thy throne. Thou hast assigned to me thy kingdom, thou hast fashioned me in thy likeness and thy form, which thou hast assigned to me and hast created. I shall do again every good thing that thou desirest, while I am sole lord, as thou wast, to settle the affairs of the land. I have created Egypt for thee anew, I have made it as at the beginning. . . I have built it up with temples.[8]

So firmly fixed in the minds of the people was the idea of the king's divinity that even the conquering Alexander thought it wise to become a god when he became an Egyptian king, and he performed holy rites by which he was transformed into the son of the supreme god of Egypt. The love of Julius Caesar and of Antony for Cleopatra may well have led to matrimony only because they knew that in the eyes of the Egyptians no one except her lawful husband could be during her life the real pharaoh.

The deification of the king was by no means an empty ritual. By the beginning of the Empire all property belonged in theory to the pharaoh, and although he might allow the people to use his lands and goods, he was entitled to impose such taxes as he saw fit. Wars were fought at the will of the king and for the purpose of extending his power; monuments were erected at enormous public cost to establish his prestige in this world and to ensure his felicity in the life to come. His position as high priest was so firmly established that one sovereign, the idealist Ikhnaton, dared to proclaim a new religion. Although Ikhnaton failed to gain lasting support for the god of his faith, the attempt to make so radical a change, and the partial success which crowned his efforts, are evidence of the awe and reverence which the office of the king inspired.

ADMINISTRATIVE DUTIES

The halo of divinity did not relieve the king from many practical responsibilities of government. Social life in Egypt, where so much depended on use of the Nile, would have been difficult without a highly organized system of agencies regulating and directing the activities of the people. At the head of this vast bureaucracy was the king. As a rule he was active in the administration of the affairs of the state.

> He did, of course, as high priest of the land, participate in the great religious festivals; he personally conducted foundation and dedication ceremonies in the temples which he built for the gods, as well as other priestly functions. These were, nonetheless, not his chief business. There is no doubt that most of his time was devoted, as in the case of rulers in other lands and in other ages, to the transaction of the actual business of ruling and in the administration of the empire. He had to read and dispose of the countless documents and reports which were brought to his court by the high officials, and even if most of the routine duties were performed by clerks and other assistants, there must have been a large amount of work which demanded his personal attention. He was accustomed to give audience and to receive oral reports from the chief dignitaries, who kept him informed, for example, of the condition of the harvest, the amount of tax collections, the height of the Nile inundation, and the like. Moreover, the king was traditionally the chief justice of the nation, with the responsibility of settling all controversies.[9]

In the exercise of his office of chief justice, the king might, in unusual circumstances, remove a case from the jurisdiction of the established courts and appoint a special court to hear the case; this was done, for example, when a conspiracy was discovered in the harem of Rameses III. Apparently any person might carry his grievances direct to the king and expect to receive not an arbitrary ruling from an exalted being who could do no wrong but justice from the individual charged with administering the laws of the land.

THE VIZIER

The chief among the many officials who assisted the king in administrative duties was the *vizier*. From the tomb of Vizier Rekhmire, who held office under

Thutmose III in the Eighteenth Dynasty, has come an inscription that gives a detailed account of the duties of the pharaoh's first minister. Breasted summarizes the inscription as follows:

> After prescribing the external arrangements for the vizier's daily sitting in his "hall," as his office is termed, the document proceeds to the daily conference of the vizier with the king, and, immediately subsequent to this, the daily reports of the chief treasurer and the vizier to each other, and of the chief officials to the vizier. These daily duties are now followed by a long list of exceedingly varied functions to be discharged by the vizier, making in all at least thirty. . . . It will be seen that the vizier is grand steward of all Egypt, and that all the activities of the state are under his control. He has general oversight of the treasury, and the chief treasurer reports to him; he is chief justice, or head of the judiciary; he is chief of police, both for the residence city and the kingdom; he is minister of war, both for army and navy; he is secretary of the interior and of agriculture, while all general executive functions of state, with many that may not be classified, are incumbent upon him. There is, indeed, no prime function of the state which does not operate through his office. He is a veritable Joseph, and it must be this office which the Hebrew writer has in mind in the story of Joseph. The only person other than the king to whom he owes any respect is the chief treasurer, to whom he seems to offer a daily statement that all is well with the royal possessions. Such power is, of course, possible only in a highly centralized state, and Egypt is shown by this inscription to be in the Empire simply a vast estate of the Pharaoh, of which the vizier is chief steward.[10]

PRECEPTS FOR RULERS

Since the government was so important in Egyptian society, it was perhaps fortunate that the kings and their ministers sought to discover and to hand down to their successors the art of governing. Their teachings are contained in compilations of wise sayings which royal fathers and high officials prepared, as a rule, for their sons and heirs. In this "wisdom" literature there are, of course, differences in emphasis, but there is considerable agreement respecting the nature of good government.

In sharp contrast to the practice of *noblesse oblige* among the Babylonians stands the Egyptian doctrine of equality. A proud boast of rulers was that they had given the lowly the same consideration shown those in high position. A feudal noble had engraved on his tomb, "I did not exalt the great man above the small man in anything that I gave." [11] The instructions given Meri-ka-re by his father to prepare him for the throne contained the admonition "Do not distinguish the son of a man [of birth and position] from a poor man, but take to thyself a man because of the work of his hands." [12] The installation ceremony for viziers contained this statement:

> It is an abomination of the god to show partiality. This is the teaching: thou shalt do the like, shalt regard him who is known to thee like him who is unknown to thee, and him who is near like him who is far. . . . an official who does like this, then shall he flourish greatly in the place.[13]

An attitude of charity and humility was also highly recommended for those in high positions. The oft-repeated phrase "I gave bread to the hungry, raiment to the naked, and him who had no boat I ferried over the river" [14] appears to have been more than a bit of pleasing rhetoric: it was an ideal that many Egyptian rulers seem to have taken to heart. At least Egypt was spared during much of her history, if the records do not deceive us, from the cruel despotism to which unlimited authority in the hands of kings has so often led in human history. After the Hyksos were expelled, Egypt was comparatively free from tyranny until the Ptolemies came; and in all ages we find fathers telling their sons to walk humbly and to show mercy. Over and over again we hear the advice repeated: be not arrogant because of thy knowledge, counsel with the ignorant as with the wise, quiet the weeper, give food and clothing to those in need, and remember always that rare good discourse may be found with "slave-girls over the millstones." Even princes were expected to know that though the ears may hear, only the heart can understand,[15] and when the vizier of King Huni was commanded to put into writing the wisdom that he had gained from his life's experiences, he began by saying, "The tent is opened for the humble." [16] These sentiments of humility are all the more remarkable because of the shameless boasting of the pharaohs in the inscriptions on their monuments. Perhaps the contrast was a result of the dual nature of the monarch; as a god he was beyond compare, but as a king he was expected to set an example in charity.

JUSTICE

Since scarcely a trace of Egyptian law has survived, the basis upon which justice was decided by the courts or by individuals in their dealings with one another is a matter of considerable importance. Without a code of laws—nothing corresponding to the Babylonian codes has been found, and it is not certain that the Egyptians ever attempted to codify their laws—what prevented the judges from rendering purely arbitrary decisions? An answer to this question is found in the conception of justice revealed in many of the surviving documents.

Justice was personified by the Egyptians as the goddess *Maat*, the patron saint of all the judges. A small figure of the goddess was worn by the chief justice as a symbol of his authority, and in temple art she is shown presiding over the scales in which justice is being weighed. Justice was thus a deification of law and order in the state, and since the god-king was the lawgiver, justice was one of his divine attributes. The pharaoh Thutmose III leaves no doubt in the mind of Vizier Rekhmire as to what is expected of him in the name of justice. The king tells him to "act in conformance with what I may say! Then Maat will rest in her place."

From this it might appear that the law was what the king declared, but this is too narrow a view of the Egyptian conception. There is nothing unusual about identifying the voice of the king with the voice of God, but there was an added element in the Egyptian conception of this relationship: the idea of order inherent in the nature of things. The faith that there is order in *natural* phenomena did not really take hold of the imaginations of men until the seventeenth century of our own era, but we see here at the very dawn of history the faith that there is order in *social* phenomena. Breasted sees in this belief the emergence of a moral conception of the universe.

> It was this impressive vision of an enduring state and its ever-functioning organization, which contributed substantially to the larger, more comprehensive meaning of the Egyptian word "Maat," till it had come to signify not only "justice," "truth," "righteousness," which the men of the Pyramid Age discerned as something practiced by the individual, but also an existent social and governmental reality, a moral order of the world, identified with the rule of the Pharaoh. . . . Over and over again in the ancient monuments Maat is the thing which the Pharaoh personifies and enforces, as against anarchy, injustice, and deceit practiced by his rivals for the throne, who afflict the people with disorganization. . . . Having arisen as an individual and personal matter, as a designation of right conduct in the family or immediate community, Maat had then gradually passed into a larger arena as the spirit and method of a *national* guidance and control of human affairs, a control in which orderly administration is suffused with moral conviction. There was thus created for the first time a realm of universal values, and in conceiving the divine ruler of such a realm the Egyptians were moving on the road towards monotheism. . . . In the Egyptian conception of a great administrative and moral order, designated by Maat, we must recognise the highest manifestation of ancient oriental civilisation.[17]

The Egyptian conception of justice had an ethical as well as a metaphysical meaning. As an ethical principle, justice seems to have meant nothing more than honest and humane administration. A pharaoh thus advises a son who is to succeed him:

> Do justice whilst thou endurest upon earth. Quiet the weeper; do not oppress the widow; supplant no man in the property of his father; and impair no officials at their posts. Be on thy guard against punishing wrongfully.[18]

This fatherly advice is tempered with a decidedly Machiavellian tone when the old king touches on the proper treatment of rebels:

> If thou findest a man whose adherents are many in total and he is gracious in the sight of his partisans and he is excitable, a talker—remove him, kill

him, wipe out his name, destroy his faction, banish the memory of him and of his adherents who love him.[19]

Even a lowly peasant might expect to be treated justly, and in a story that seems to have been a great favorite among the Egyptians one of them did not hesitate to lecture the king's steward on his obligation to maintain justice in the land by setting a good example.

> Punish those who are deserving of punishment, and then these shall be like unto thee in dispensing justice. Do not the small scales weigh incorrectly? Doth not the large balance incline to one side? [20]

ECONOMY

The economic institutions of the Empire can be sketched only in broad outline, since many important details cannot be supplied from the documents now available. For example, inheritance through the mother rather than the father seems to have been common, but much is obscure about the basis and the actual operation of this practice. Likewise, the status of those members of society who were neither serfs nor officials, the rules and practices in trade relations, and the rights and duties of peasants are by no means clear. Even with respect to slavery, we can be sure only that slave labor was far less important to the Egyptians of this period, as indeed it was generally throughout Egyptian history, than it was to many other ancient peoples; few references to the slave system have survived. Despite these limitations in the data, it is possible, as a result of the labor of numerous Egyptologists, to present a very general view of the economic life and thought of the ancient Egyptians.

PROPERTY

With the consolidation of all Egypt under a single pharaoh in the sixteenth century B.C., after the expulsion of the Hyksos, the feudal system of land tenure which had prevailed during much of the Middle Kingdom did not reappear. On the contrary, the pharaoh claimed actual possession of all landed property, and a vast bureaucracy was created to administer this property in his behalf. Aside from large estates given over to the temples, all the land of Egypt was under the control of officials appointed by the pharaoh. Thus there were limits set to the rights of individuals to create for themselves great fortunes through exploitation of the land.

Likewise, private individuals were unable to acquire great possessions through the control of capital. Egypt lacked a medium of exchange by which financial power could be acquired. Most trade was a matter of simple barter, and even taxes were paid in produce. Copper, silver, gold, and other commodities served as measures of value, but they were not money in the modern sense. This prevented the accumulation of wealth in money, or its equivalent, and deprived the Egyptians of a means of becoming wealthy through private enterprise. Lacking the opportunity to possess great wealth in lands or capital goods, the ambitious Egyptian found the means of improving his social position through service to the king or the temples. There were, of course, social and economic inequalities: the higher officials often possessed fine homes in both town and country and lived in a style befitting their station, whereas the peasants had to content themselves with thin-walled huts and simple fare. Nevertheless, social position was based not on property but on preferment. Perhaps this explains the absence among the Egyptians of that preoccupation with material goods which was so striking a characteristic of the Babylonians.

When one considers that ownership of land is not so important as are the rights which attach to its use, it is conceivable that the peasant fared better under the pharaohs than the landless have often fared under private landlords. Where all are landless and none has capital in money, goods are important for use but not for power. In such a situation those who have prestige may enjoy possessions denied the lowly, but their prestige is not created by their wealth. For that reason the Egyptians probably found acceptable an economic system which other peoples have found intolerable; at least very few revolutions seem to have occurred during the long span of Egypt's history.

Nevertheless, there are many indications that the Egyptians expected their rights to such property as they possessed to be fully respected and protected. Thefts occurred, but thieves were punished; not even the king's agent had the right to plunder the property of a poor man. Soldiers were allowed to keep at least some of the loot which they seized from the enemy. It was against the law to harbor escaped slaves. The peasant drove out his own cattle to pasture and plowed his fields with his own oxen.[21] The property of a foreigner who died in Egypt was expected to be delivered safely to his native country for the benefit of his family.[22] As for the official with "a beautiful villa, a fine carriage, a splendid boat, numerous negroes—as lackeys, servants, and house officials—gardens and cattle, costly food, good wine, and rich clothing," it is obvious that as long as he was in favor with the king, his rights to the property which the king had bestowed upon him were fully protected.

SOCIAL CLASSES

The upper class was composed largely of the higher officials of the king and of the temples. From inscriptions in which persons of apparently high social standing are named without titles, it appears that private individuals sometimes shared the honors given public officers. The number of such persons, however, must have been comparatively small. It is difficult to see how large fortunes could have been acquired by private enterprise. Foreign trade was at times extensive, but much of this trade appears to have been undertaken at royal command by the officers of the king.

A middle class, composed of minor officials, small merchants, foremen, artisans, and the upper ranks of peasants, undoubtedly existed, but little is known about the comparative size of this class, the status of its members, or the role it played in Egyptian society. As a consequence of the prosperity which resulted from the military victories of the Empire, with peace at home and tribute pouring in from the conquered kingdoms, it is probable that this class attained during this period considerable prominence. Studies of the ruins of dwellings support this view; those from the earlier dynasties seem to have been for the most part either mansions or huts, but "when we come to the Eighteenth Dynasty at Amarna, the most usual dwelling is a detached house of a dozen fair-sized rooms surrounded by an enclosure." [23]

At the bottom of the social scale of freemen were the poor laborers, who produced food for themselves and for their superiors. They were subject to levy for work on public projects, but since they had no employment in agriculture during the fall months when the fields were flooded and again in the spring after the crops had been harvested and the earth was parched and cracked, this enforced service may have been no great hardship. Although, as Petrie says, "Much nonsense has been written about the oppression of the people, their tears and groans," [24] it is clear from the sculpture and literature of the time that the upper classes were socially far removed from those who fed them. In a didactic piece which the Egyptians apparently prized, the writer, with obvious and intentional exaggeration, describes the sad plight of the poor peasant in these words:

> The worm has taken the half of the food, the hippopotamus the other half; there were many mice in the fields, the locusts have come down, and the cattle have eaten, and the sparrows have stolen. Poor miserable agriculturist! What was left on the threshing-floor thieves made away with. . . . Then the scribe lands on the bank to receive the harvest, his followers carry sticks and the negroes carry palm rods. They say, "Give up the corn"—there is none there. Then they beat him as he lies stretched out and bound on the ground, they throw him into the canal and he sinks down, head under water. His wife is bound before his eyes and his children are put in fetters. His neighbours run away to escape and to save their corn.[25]

It may be that ambitious fathers painted such dismal prospects in order to goad their sons to give heed to their studies. The practical education which enabled an individual to achieve superior skill in his occupation was highly regarded, and competence was probably important in determining an individual's social standing. One way of climbing the social ladder in Egypt, where the written document was highly regarded, was by becoming a scribe, and learning was justified because it paved the way to fame and fortune. As one father said to his son:

I have compared the people who are artisans and handicraftsmen [with the scribe], and indeed I am convinced that there is nothing superior to letters. Plunge into the study of Egyptian Learning, as thou wouldst plunge into the river, and thou wilt find that this is so. I would that thou wouldst love Learning as thou lovest thy mother. I wish I were able to make thee to see how beautiful Learning is. It is more important than any trade in the world. Learning is not a mere phrase, for the man who devoteth himself thereto from his youth is honoured, and he is despatched on missions.[26]

The reason for the value attached to education is clearly revealed: one should acquire knowledge in order to be honored and to be sent on missions. Although this fatherly advice comes from an earlier period, it is entirely in accord with the Egyptian thought during the Empire. The Egyptians advanced the science of mathematics in order to measure the Nile's inundation and to restore the boundaries which it had obliterated. They displayed in their writings little of that curiosity about the nature of things which fired the imagination of the Greek philosophers of the fifth century B.C. They seem to have little realized that training is only a part of education and that there is a difference between skill and knowledge. It seems probable, therefore, that the competent artisans and administrators gained social recognition which those who were merely wise never shared.

The army afforded another ladder to high social status. One military leader, Harmhab, became Pharaoh and founded a dynasty (the Nineteenth), after rising through the ranks to the position of supreme commander of the Egyptian forces. In the Empire an officer might hope to become the governor of a conquered kingdom; the higher officers were expected to be able to rule as well as to conduct military operations.

AGRICULTURE

Whatever hardships may have attended the cultivation of the soil and the care of the herds, however low the social status of the peasant may have been in the eyes of the scribes, the fact remains that the economy of Egypt was founded on the land and its products and that most of the ancient Egyptians were occupied in agricultural pursuits. The privileged few lived in great luxury, cultivating expensive and sophisticated tastes in art, literature, architecture, and entertainment; but they constituted a thin crust on a mass of humanity that may have numbered from six to ten millions. As for the masses, it was enough if the Nile, from which all alike received nourishment, brought down fresh rich soil in good season and made damp the earth for planting. No faithful scribes recorded in words or temple art their hopes and fears, but an occasional incident or song affords some insight into their daily lives. We hear the plowmen singing as the oxen turn up the earth for planting:

> A good day—it is cool.
> The cattle are pulling,
> And the sky does according to our desire.

Barley and wheat were sown, and sometimes millet; the blades shot up under cloudless skies, and soon the heads were heavy with grain. Then could the reapers say:

> This good day is come forth in the land;
> The north wind is come forth,
> And the sky does according to our desire.

Finally, it was time for threshing, and as the oxen were driven round and round over the strewn harvest to separate the grain, the peasant might relieve the monotony of his task by singing to his dumb creatures:

> Thresh ye for yourselves, thresh ye for yourselves,
>   O cattle!
> Thresh ye for yourselves, thresh ye for yourselves!
> Straw to eat, and barley for your masters—
> Let not your hearts be weary, for it is cool.[27]

There appears to have been an abundance of food except in lean years. A tradition existed that seven good years were followed by a like number of years of want. The following passage gives a somewhat exaggerated picture of the condition that may have come about at any period of Egyptian history as a result of the failure of the Nile to act according to expectations:

> Grain was scant, fruits were dried up, and everything which they [the people] eat was short. Every man robbed his companion. They moved without going ahead. The infant was wailing; the youth was waiting; the heart of the old men was in sorrow, their legs were bent, crouching on the ground, their arms were folded. The courtiers were in need. The temples were shut up; the sanctuaries held nothing but air. Everything was found empty.[28]

In good years, however, bread, meat, wine, oil, honey, figs, fish, and vegetables might be enjoyed every day. The oil came from several sources, among them sesame, linseed, castor-berry, and olives. For vegetables there were onions, cucumbers, peas, beans, lentils, leeks, and garlics. Cattle, sheep, and goats, with some fowl and a great deal of fish, provided the meat supply. Figs and dates were common, and several other fruits were cultivated. Statements about the daily fare differ widely. Certainly the following ration, issued to certain troops in the Nineteenth Dynasty, could hardly have been the normal fare of the average man:

> His majesty, L.P.H. [Life, Prosperity, Health],* increased that which was furnished to the army in ointment, ox-flesh, fish, and plentiful vegeta-

---

* This salutation often accompanies a reference to the pharaoh.

bles without limit. Every man among them had 20 deben [nearly four pounds] of bread daily, 2 bundles of vegetables, a roast of flesh; and 2 linen garments monthly. Thus they worked with a loving heart for his majesty, L.P.H.[29]

Perhaps the peasant's share in the food he produced was small, and he had usually to content himself with a diet of bread, cheese, and fish, washed down with water instead of the beer he would have chosen had it been within his means. Numerous sketches depicting the life of farm laborers and herdsmen have been found on the monuments of the Old Kingdom. The manner of life they portray is so similar to that which Greek visitors observed in Egypt two thousand years later that we may well believe that for those who lived close to the soil there was little change though dynasties passed. Erman interprets an Old Kingdom picture of herdsmen in the marshes with their cows as follows:

> . . . it is evening and the work is at an end; some of the men are squatting round on the low hearth roasting their geese on wooden spits at the fire; one has not got so far and is only plucking his goose. Others are occupying themselves either with plaiting papyrus reeds or cooking dough for the cattle. Another man is comfortably asleep. He sat down on his mat when he came home and fell asleep there with his shepherd's crook still in his hand; his dog with the long ears and the pointed muzzle has followed his master's example and has gone to sleep at his feet. A large jug, a basket with some small vessels, and a few papyrus mats are all the goods required for our herdsman's housekeeping.[30]

The Egyptian's love of nature, his emotional attachment to the good earth, and his pleasure in green and growing things are revealed in numerous ways.

> Everywhere on the monuments we meet with flowers; bouquets of flowers are presented to the gods; the coffins are covered with wreaths of flowers; flowers form the decoration of the houses, and all the capitals of the pillars are painted in imitation of their coloured petals. The Egyptian also loved shady trees. He not only prayed that the "Nile should bestow every flowering plant in their season" upon his departed soul, but also that his soul might sit "on the boughs of the trees that he had planted, and enjoy the cool air in the shade of his sycamore. . . . the gentleman of ancient Egypt talked with pride of his shady trees, his sweet-smelling plants, and his cool tanks. All the sentiment with which we regard the woods and meadows of nature, the Egyptian felt towards his well-kept garden; to him it was the dwelling-place of love, and his trees were the confidantes of lovers." [31]

FAMILY

Much more is known about Egyptian family life in Ptolemaic times, when Greek historians were on the scene, and in the period when Egypt was a Roman province, than in the Golden Age of Egypt's history. The Greeks and Romans, however, not only recorded Egyptian customs as they observed them but also introduced customs which had a demoralizing effect on Egyptian family life. Consequently, to view Egyptian family customs through the eyes of Greek and Roman writers, who knew nothing of documents now available, is to overlook conditions found in the days of Egypt's splendor and to concentrate on those which existed in the days of Egypt's degradation.

The disintegration of Egyptian civilization was a slow process. The decadence, which began in the twelfth century B.C., led to the subjugation and rule of Egypt by Libyan kings. When the Nubians, whom the proud Egyptians had formerly regarded as barbarians and openly despised, conquered Egypt, a Nubian king was able to refuse to receive into his presence some of Egypt's distinguished citizens because, he said in all seriousness, they smelled of fish. The comparatively kindly Ethiopians were succeeded by the Persians, the Greeks, and finally the Romans, all of whom came to exploit and to destroy. By the beginning of the Christian Era, Egypt had suffered every indignity that can be visited upon a conquered people. Naturally, family life was much affected by Egypt's political fortunes but, with that reverence for the old which they displayed in numerous ways, the Egyptians held on to many of their ancient family traditions.

MATRIARCHY

The Egyptian family system was clearly matriarchal, but in ways peculiar to Egyptian culture. Descent was traced through the mother, the name of the father often being omitted in genealogical references. One might imagine that in prehistoric times mating was casual and the mother and child constituted the basic family unit, but proof of this surmise is lacking; we do not know how the Egyptians came to adopt a matrilineal practice. Likewise, no adequate explanation has been found for another matriarchal characteristic of the Egyptian family: the possession by the female of the family's property and the inheritance of it by a daughter rather than by a son.

> The entail in the female line seems to have been fairly strict, and nowhere so strict as in the royal family. The practical result was that the husband enjoyed the property as long as his wife was alive, but on her death her daughter and the daughter's husband came into possession.[32]

These matriarchal customs may have had in actuality little practical significance; they may merely have reflected fictions bound up in the folklore to which the Egyptians so tenaciously clung. The king was the real ruler, even though he did gain the throne by marriage instead of by birth; his son succeeded him, even though convention demanded that the prince establish his claim by marrying the heiress. Fathers willed property to their sons and trained them to meet the responsibilities which they were expected to inherit. The herdsman tended *his* cattle, and the plowman tilled *his* fields. There is little indication that wives generally dominated their husbands. On the contrary, women are often represented as being dependent and much in need of guidance. The advice of Ptah-hotep has a decidedly patronizing tone.

> If thou art a wise man, be master of thy house. Love thy wife absolutely, give her food in abundance and raiment for her back; these are the medicines for her body. Anoint her with unguents, and make her happy as long as thou livest. She is thy field, and she reflecteth credit on her possessor. Be not harsh in thy house, for she will be more easily moved by persuasion than by violence. Satisfy her wish, observe what she expecteth, and take note of that whereon she hath fixed her gaze. This is the treatment that will keep her in her house; if thou repel her advances, it is ruin for thee. Embrace her, call her by fond names, and treat her lovingly. . . . If thou art a wise man, beget a son who shall be pleasing to God.[33]

The statement made by Herodotus that in Egypt the women attended the markets and trade while the men sat at home beside the loom may have been accurate for his time, but it may lead to conclusions that are wholly false. It does not appear that men were in a subordinate position at any time in Egyptian history, and certainly this was not the case during the Empire. Women held a dignified position in society, as we shall see, but Egyptian matriarchy was not a system of female domination of males, either within the household or in social relations outside the home. In temple art, the female companion of a hunter is seen watching with open admiration as her husband or sweetheart snares a bird; women appear as singers and dancers, not as judges and overseers; the master of the house is not less prominent than the mistress when guests are being entertained; women nurse their children with tender devotion, while men bear arms and beat down the foe with mighty blows. Many other examples might be cited to show that, despite certain matriarchal characteristics, ancient Egypt from this distance bears close resemblance to a man's world.

MARRIAGE

The prohibition of marriage between those closely related by blood is all but universal. The fact that marriage of close kin does sometimes take place with social approval is difficult to explain—even more difficult, in fact, than the incest taboo itself. The Egyptian situation presents a particularly thorny problem to those who have probed into this matter. Although in Egypt the practice of close in-breeding may not have been common until after the Greco-Roman conquest, the marriage of a brother and sister was not only permitted but was also considered necessary under certain conditions from the earliest periods of Egypt's history. The actual situation is obscured by the fact that the terms *brother* and *sister* had meanings other than those with which we are familiar, and also by some uncertainty as to what marriage meant to the ancient Egyptians. Nevertheless, marital unions involving parents as well as siblings did actually occur. In order to obtain a share in his mother's property, a son was sometimes obliged to marry his sister, who was legal heir to the property, and, although such marriages probably occurred more often where there was considerable wealth, and especially in the royal family, where at times marriage to the heiress was the only legal means of becoming king, there is reason to believe that close affinity was not regarded as a bar to marriage even among the members of the lower classes.[34]

The marriage rituals of pharaonic Egypt have been the subject of much speculation, since virtually nothing is said about this important subject in the documents that have survived. The customs of the Ptolemaic and Roman periods, about which much has been written, should not be regarded as representative of those prevailing during the Empire. However, through a study of practices found in the Ptolemaic period which were apparently not borrowed from the conquerors and which are in accord with attitudes revealed in the old documents, something can be learned about the marriage system of the earlier periods. A careful study by Edgerton leads to the following conclusions.

> In native Egyptian law, marriage was a private contract; there is no evidence that any civil or religious official participated. No written document was required. The marriage continued during mutual consent; either party could dissolve it at will, and we have no evidence that the law attached any penalty to divorce. Marriage could also be limited in advance to a definite period.[35]

There are many indications that marriage was the custom. "Take for thyself a wife while thou art still a youth," Ani advised his son, as many centuries earlier the wise Ptah-hotep had counseled his son to found a household as soon as he had become a "man of standing." That the sanctity of the home was respected is shown by frequent admonitions to "beware of approaching the women of another household." The *Tale of the Two Brothers* vividly describes a husband's anger at his wife's attempt at infidelity and makes her death appear a fitting penalty for her act. The theme of a fairy tale entitled *The Enchanted Prince* is the love of a wedded princess for her mate and her unsuccessful attempt to prevent his meeting a foreordained fate. Ikhnaton concludes his great religious hymn with a tribute to his "chief royal wife, his beloved Nofretete."

During the Empire, monogamy seems to have been the custom for most of the people. The pharaohs usually had more than one wife, and some of them maintained large harems. A princess married to the pharaoh for political reasons might bring with her a number of handmaidens, and these were probably counted as women of the pharaoh's secluded household. A single bride brought to King Amenhotep III more than three hundred maidens, "the choicest of the secluded." The ruins of some of the ancient dwellings occupied apparently by wealthy families seem to indicate that the maintenance of a group of singers and dancing girls for the pleasure of the master was not confined to the royal household. It is likely that additional mates might have been taken without arousing public indignation by almost anyone able to do so. The practice of monogamy may, therefore, have been dictated by practical rather than by religious or ethical considerations.

STATUS OF WOMEN

The respect for the inherent dignity of the individual is everywhere evident in the Egyptian documents, but it is nowhere more clearly revealed than in the recognition of the rights of women. Extreme views are found, of course, some writers describing women in the likeness of the Mother Goddess Isis and elevating them to a position much nearer heaven than earth, and others portraying them as temptresses and placing on their frail shoulders the burden of human depravity. The *Instruction of Ani* presents both views of the female character:

> Beware of a woman from abroad, who is not known in her city. Look not upon her when she comes, and know her not. She is like the vortex of deep waters, whose whirling is unfathomable. The woman whose husband is far away, she writes to thee every day. If there is no witness with her she arises and spreads her net. Oh, deadly crime if one hearkens! [36]

On the other hand, Ani advises his son to be guided in his treatment of his wife by the memory of the mother who bore and nurtured him:

> When thou art a young man and takest to thee a wife and art settled in thine house, keep before thee how thy mother gave birth to thee, and how she brought thee up further in all manner of ways. . . . Act not the official over thy wife in her house [but] let thine eye observe and be silent, that so thou mayest know her good deeds.[37]

On the whole, however, Egyptian women seem to have suffered neither from too much praise nor from too much blame. Max Müller says, "No people, ancient or modern, has given women so high a legal status as did the inhabitants of the Nile Valley." Maspero believes that this high position was not confined to women of the nobility. He says, "The Egyptian woman of the lower and middle class was more respected, more independent, than any other woman in the world." [38] Murray makes the following general comment on this subject:

> Women's position was high, due perhaps to their economic independence. They went about freely, except of course in time of war; but more than one Pharaoh boasts in his Triumph-Song that he has not only

driven out the invaders but the country is so peaceful that a woman can go where she will without molestation. In ordinary times of peace, the scenes of daily life show the wife accompanying her husband in all his inspections of his estates, she watches the craftsmen at their work, is present at the counting of the cattle, and oversees the harvesters in the fields. In the Eighteenth Dynasty mixed parties of men and women were not uncommon; the guests sat on chairs and were served by young girls, who handed the refreshments and put garlands of scented blossoms round the necks of the guests or anointed them with perfumed ointment. . . . Even in late times, when foreign ideas were beginning to influence Egypt, there is a charming record of a beloved lady. She was "profitable of speech, agreeable in her conversation, a good counsel in her writings, all that passed her lips is like the work of the Goddess of Truth, a perfect woman, greatly praised in her city, giving the hand to all, saying that which is good, repeating what one loves, giving pleasure to all, nothing evil ever passed her lips, most beloved by all." [39]

FAMILY VALUES

In art and literature the love of home and family is vividly expressed. The reliefs found on the walls of temples and tombs often present idyllic pictures of the relations of parents and children in the home. Breasted thus describes some of these reliefs:

> . . . the Egyptian noble is shown accompanied by his wife, and when he enters the gate that leads to the beautiful garden in the midst of which his luxurious villa is embowered, she moves by his side; she shares with him all his life and all his work, and is his hourly companion. Their children are ever with them. One of the most charming scenes among these tomb chapel pictures shows us a little boy trotting about beside his father, clutching in one hand a tiny hoopoe bird. When the lord of the manor hunts in the marshes, which were the ancient Egyptian's hunting preserves, we see his wife and child beside him in the little raft-like reed boat with which he pushes about among the tall papyrus blossoms, where the child leans down and plucks the water lilies. Or when he is shown resting in his garden, we see his children playing at ball or splashing about in the garden pool chasing the fishes.[40]

The responsibility of the father for the guidance of his children, especially his sons, is declared repeatedly. As Ptah-hotep stated the matter: People behave as they are taught; therefore, let a father converse with his children so that they in turn will converse with their own children, and thus will wisdom pass down from generation to generation. One example may be given of the filial piety that must have resulted from the close bond between father and son: "I did this for my father when he journeyed to the west upon the beautiful ways, whereon the revered dead journey." [41]

RELIGION

The complexity of the religious beliefs and practices of the ancient Egyptians becomes immediately evident when one examines only a few of the extant religious documents. Hundreds of deities appear, rituals and incantations express a wide range of attitudes, and myths and tales reveal faiths of bewildering diversity. The orderly Western mind demands that these varied elements be fitted into a system. The Egyptians apparently felt no such necessity, or at least they were willing that primitive animism and monotheism should exist side by side, even in the religious experience of a single individual. In the early days of the discoveries by modern scholars of ancient Egypt, one theologian thus stated the situation:

> When the student turns his attention to the Religion of the Ancient Egyptians, he is at once confronted with the disputed question as to its essential character. . . . When [he] consults the works of the Egyptologists, he finds himself compelled to choose between two diametrically opposite theories. The advocates of the one view see in the Egyptian Religion what amounts to a pure monotheism, exhibiting itself through the manifestly silly or even barbaric forms of a multiform polytheism, with the loftiest ideas hidden like a pure gem in the crude shell of magical arts and symbolical notions. The advocates of the other view see in it a religion which is still really barbaric, animistic, and therianthropic, and to which priests and scribes endeavoured to give a mystical sense—a sense not understood by the people, and one which left the superstitious practices undisturbed.[42]

Since that time, additional discoveries and careful analysis of the documentary evidence have narrowed the gulf between the opposing views described by Tiele; but the religion of the ancient Egyptians still defies systematic presentation. The following discussion should, therefore, be regarded as only an introduction to the religious thought of the Egyptians of the Empire.

POLYTHEISM

The ancient Egyptian seems to have had a peculiar aversion to abstractions. He saw the sun in the sky and felt its warming rays; he witnessed the flight of birds as they rose from the earth and disappeared from view in the skies; he observed that bulls, rams, crocodiles, cats, and all other animals were warm with life; and wherever he turned his gaze in the Valley, the Nile was active—creating, sustaining, destroying. All these observations had for him a religious meaning. In the sun, the falcon, the cat, the river, and other such concrete objects he sensed the presence of something mysterious and wonderful. What the senses so readily grasped was little disturbed by intellectual curiosity. Breasted has described this quality of the Egyptian mind as follows:

66 · *Five Ancient Societies*

  The Egyptian always thought in concrete terms and in graphic forms. He thought not of theft but of a thief, not of love but of a lover, not of poverty but of a poor man: he sees not social corruption but a corrupt society. Hence the Misanthrope, a *man* in whom social injustice found expression in the picture of a despairing soul who tells of his despair and its causes; hence Ipuwer, a *man* in whom dwelt the vision to discern both the deadly corruption of society and the golden dream of an ideal king restoring all; hence the Eloquent Peasant, a *man* suffering official oppression and crying out against it; hence Ptahhotep, a *man* meeting the obligations of office with wholesome faith in righteous conduct and just administration to engender happiness, and passing on this experience to his son; hence the Instruction of Amenemhet, a *king* suffering shameful treachery, losing faith in men and likewise communicating his experience to his son. The result is that the doctrines of these social thinkers were placed in a dramatic setting, and the doctrines themselves find expression in dialogue growing out of experiences and incidents represented as actual.[43]

Although polytheism has appeared among people who dealt freely in abstractions—as, for example, the Greeks—the strong disposition of the Egyptians to think in concrete terms and graphic forms may partially explain the number and nature of their gods. About seventy are identified by name in the *Book of the Dead* alone, and many others appear in other religious writings. In addition to the anthropomorphic gods, a large number of birds and animals appear as deities.

  In one nome or another, in one period or another, Egyptians worshiped the bull, the crocodile, the hawk, the cow, the goose, the goat, the ram, the cat, the dog, the chicken, the swallow, the jackal, the serpent, and allowed some of these creatures to roam in the temples with the same freedom that is accorded to the sacred cow in India today. When the gods became human they still retained animal doubles and symbols: Amon was represented as a goose or a ram, Ra as a grasshopper or a bull, Osiris as a bull or a ram, Sebek as a crocodile, Horus as a hawk or falcon, Hathor as a cow, and Thoth, the god of wisdom, as a baboon.[44]

When to this list are added numerous birds, especially the ibis, and a large number of plants, including the onion, it is clear that the number of Egyptian deities was countless.

  In this multiplicity of gods, several inexact but discernible categories appear, among which the following are the most important: (1) gods of place, (2) the solar gods, and (3) the Osirian gods. Each community had local deities, whose rank in the pantheon of gods corresponded to the rank of the place with which they were identified. Amon was the local god of Thebes, and when Thebes was made the capital of all Egypt by the pharaohs of the Eighteenth Dynasty, Amon became the supreme state god. However, Re, the Sun-god, was widely accepted as the Great God, "who came into being by himself, who made heaven, earth, water, the breath of life, fire, gods, men, small and large cattle, creeping things, birds, and fishes, the king of men and gods at one time." [45] Consequently all local gods were but reincarnations of Re, and the Amon-Re of the Empire was Amon and Re in one.

Finally, there was the family of Osirian deities, among whom Isis, the sister and wife of Osiris, appears as an "embodiment of wifely fidelity and maternal solicitude." Osiris was described by Rameses IV in these words: "Thou art indeed the Nile, great on the fields at the beginning of the seasons; gods and men live by the moisture that is in thee." [46] In addition to being the Nile, the fruitful earth, and, in fact, the spiritual embodiment of fertility, Osiris was lord of the kingdom of the blessed dead. The cult bearing his name developed around the myth of the suffering, death, and resurrection of an ancient king. Of this cult Budge says:

> Osiris was the God-man through whose sufferings and death the Egyptian hoped that he might rise again in a glorified Spirit-body, and to him who had conquered death and had become the king of the Other World the Egyptian appealed in prayer for eternal life through his victory and power. In every funeral inscription known to us, from the Pyramid Texts down to the roughly-written prayers upon coffins of the Roman period, what is done for Osiris is done also for the deceased, the state and condition of Osiris are the state and condition of the deceased; in a word the deceased is identified with Osiris. If Osiris liveth forever, the deceased will live forever; if Osiris dieth, then will the deceased perish.[47]

MONOTHEISM

Our brief comment on Egyptian polytheism presents but one aspect of ancient Egyptian religious thought. There is another, however, about which the Greek and Roman writers knew virtually nothing. For two thousand years the world was willing to accept the word of Herodotus that Egyptian religion made much of the worship of cats, and the opinion of St. Clement of Alexandria that the Egyptian deity was only "a beast that rolls itself on purple coverlet." But now that excavations have stocked many museums with contemporary documents from the ancient Egyptian scene, it is possible to discover in the religious thought of this gifted people a conception of deity far nobler and more important to mankind than the bizarre beliefs and practices about which so much has been written. It could scarcely be expressed more clearly than it was by the Egyptians themselves, in numerous documents of various dates. A few passages which reveal the nature of ancient Egyptian monotheism follow:

> God is One and only, and none other existeth with Him.—God is the One, the One who hath made all things.—God is a spirit, a hidden spirit, the spirit of spirits, the great spirit of the Egyptians, the divine spirit.—God is from the beginning, and He hath been from the beginning. He hath existed from

of old, and was when nothing else had being, He existed when nothing else existed, and what existeth He created after He had come into being. He is the Father of Beginnings.—God is the eternal One, He is eternal and infinite, and endureth for ever and aye.—God is hidden and no man knoweth His form. No man hath been able to seek out His likeness; He is hidden to gods and men, and He is a mystery unto His creatures.—God is Truth, He liveth by Truth, He feedeth thereon, He is the King of Truth, and He hath established the earth thereupon.—God is life, and through Him only man liveth. He giveth life to man, he breatheth the breath of life into his nostrils.—God is father and mother, the father of fathers and the mother of mothers. He begetteth, but was never begotten; He produceth, but was never produced; He begat Himself and produced Himself. God is merciful unto those who reverence Him, and He heareth him that calleth upon Him. God knoweth him that acknowledgeth Him.[48]

It is from Ikhnaton, however, that fourteenth-century pharaoh who defied the priests and neglected the affairs of state in order to worship in undisturbed tranquillity, that the clearest expression of Egyptian monotheism comes. In hymns near in spirit, if not in form, to the Hebrew Psalms, he sang praises to the God of all the Universe, the true and only God. A few lines from his greatest hymn will suffice to show his conception of God.

> How manifold are all Thy works!
> They are hidden from before us,
> O Thou sole God, whose powers no other possesseth.
> Thou didst create the earth according to Thy desire,
> While Thou wast alone:
> Men, all cattle large and small,
> All that are upon the earth,
> That go about upon their feet;
> All that are on high
> That fly with their wings.
> The countries of Syria and Nubia
> The land of Egypt;
> Thou settest every man in his place
> Thou suppliest their necessities.
> Every one has his possessions,
> And his days are reckoned.
> Their tongues are divers in speech,
> Their forms likewise and their skins,
> For Thou, divider, hast divided the peoples.
> . . . How excellent are Thy designs, O Lord of eternity! [49]

IMMORTALITY

The Egyptians had expressed a belief in reincarnation, at least for kings, as early as the Twelfth Dynasty. Although this doctrine is much less important in

Egyptian than in Hindu social thought, it should be noted because of its antiquity. In fact, Herodotus declared:

> The Egyptians were the first who asserted that the soul of man is immortal, and that when the body perishes it enters into some other animal, constantly springing into existence; and when it has passed through the different kinds of terrestrial, marine, and aerial beings, it again enters into the body of a man that is born; and that this revolution is made in three thousand years. Some of the Greeks [Pythagoras?] have adopted this opinion, some earlier, others later, as if it were their own; but although I knew their names I do not mention them.[50]

The faith in immortality, however, whatever the form of life eternal, is one of the most striking characteristics of Egyptian religion. Breasted says, "Among no people, ancient or modern, has the idea of a life beyond the grave held so prominent a place as among the ancient Egyptians." [51] In tombs and temples that faith is everywhere recorded; in fact, much of our knowledge about the ancient Egyptians is derived from documents that were produced and safeguarded for the benefit of the dead. The massive pyramids by which the earlier kings sought to secure for themselves felicity in the afterlife, the practice of mummification, the fitting out of the tombs with all the necessities for comfortable living, the delivery to the dead of a book of instructions for their life in the Abode of the Blessed—all these attest the power of the Egyptian's faith in immortality, despite the diverse forms in which it found expression. As Steindorff and Seele say:

> Rooted deeply in the hearts of the people was at least the belief that death was really not the end of everything but rather that a man would continue to live on exactly as on earth, provided that the conditions necessary for contined existence were fulfilled. First of all, he must be supplied with food and drink; hence the anxious and constantly reiterated desire of the Egyptians to receive "thousands of loaves, geese, oxen, beer, and all the good things by which a god lives" in the life hereafter. To avoid suffering from hunger and thirst after death, each Egyptian provided his tomb with great jars filled with food and drink, or, if he had the means, established endowments the income of which would secure for all time the necessities of life in the netherworld. If he had surviving children or other close relatives, piety demanded that they go forth on the great feast days to the cemetery in order to deposit food and drink offerings at the tomb. Nevertheless, all of these provisions were still insufficient. From the time of the Old Kingdom the walls of the tomb or at least of the coffin were covered with representations of all sorts of objects which by magic could be transformed into the actual products depicted, when they would become available to serve all the physical needs of the dead. . . . how manifold the tomb equipment of the dead became in the golden age of the pharaonic empire is best

illustrated by the treasure from the tomb of Tutankhamun, which contains several thousand objects.[52]

There are many other aspects of Egyptian religious thought that we must pass over. A study of the components of the human being, of which the *ka* (spirit) and *ba* (soul) are rather more important than the body, would be in itself a book. Myths, legends, and rituals describe in varied detail the passage of the dead through the vast and awful Tuat, until they reach at last the nether world and stand in the presence of Osiris; but these are too varied and complex for analysis here. We are more concerned with the bearing of certain religious conceptions on the experiences of life than with the pageant of death presented in the ancient texts.

ETHICS

Religion is concerned with man's relations to the sacred, whereas morality is a matter of his behavior toward his fellow human beings. It is conceivable, therefore, that the two might have no close connection with one another. Such works as the *Book of the Dead* might lead one to believe that this was in fact the case among the ancient Egyptians, since aside from the "negative confessions," this Egyptian religious work has virtually nothing to say about human relationships. But of course no "confession" can be negative, and the *Book of the Dead* was little more than its name implies—namely, a book for the dead, not for the living. Moreover, from numerous other sources it is obvious that the Egyptians possessed strong moral convictions rooted in religious faith. The sense of sin cannot be lacking where the voice of conscience is heard, and Breasted has shown that there developed slowly but steadily among the Egyptians an awareness of the stern call not only to personal piety but also to moral responsibility.

> The impelling voice within, which had originally grown up out of social influences and had since been further developed by many centuries of contemplative reflection, was now unreservedly recognized by the believer to be the mandate of God himself. We have seen that this idea arose . . . at the beginning of the Empire [and developed into] . . . the unmistakable voice of God. Under these circumstances there can of course be no concealment or denial of sin, and the believer, conscious that his whole case is known to his God, places himself without reserve in the hand of God, who guides and controls all his life and fortunes.[53]

There is, however, a note of gladness in Egyptian art and literature that thoughts of transgression and of death did not repress. One gets the impression of an amiable, lighthearted people, fond of music, wine, and food, and little disposed to fight with one another or with other nations. The masses had to contend with the arrogance of petty officials, they undoubtedly suffered from the exercise of too much magic, and occasionally some of them turned to crime; but the general picture is one of kindliness and contentment. A lover endears himself to his beloved by singing of her likeness to the flowers and trees of the garden:

> Come through the garden, Love, to me,
>   My love is like each flower that blows;
> Tall and straight as a young palm-tree,
>   And in each cheek a sweet blush-rose.[54]

Or, if death is the theme, it is described as the sweet odor of myrrh or lotus flowers, and as the feel of a fresh breeze, "when one sitteth under the sail on a windy day." From a fourteenth-century tomb come these verses expressive of the joyous resignation to death so in keeping with the Egyptian belief that death was but an interlude between the good life on this earth and the happy existence in the West, the land of eternity.

> This land which has no opponent—
> All our kinsfolk rest in it since the first day of time.
> They who are to be, for millions and millions,
> Will all have come to it.
> There exists none who may tarry in the land of Egypt.
> There is not one who fails to reach yon place.
>
> As for the duration of what is done on earth,
> It is a kind of dream;
> But they say: "Welcome, safe and sound!"
> To him who reaches the West.[55]

Ideals and practices may have been as far separated in ancient times as they often are in our own day, but it is not without significance that the Egyptians kept repeating through the centuries the phrase: "I gave bread to the hungry, clothing to the naked, and I ferried him who had no boat." The king himself might not walk humbly, but at least he claimed always to deal justly. This statement from Rameses III is in accord with the sentiments expressed by most of the pharaohs.

> I sustained alive the whole land, whether foreigners, common folks, citizens, or people, male or female. I took a man out of his misfortune and I gave him breath; I rescued him from the oppressor, who was of more account than he. I set each man in his security, in their towns. . . . The land was well satisfied in my reign.[56]

Of course there were the misanthropes, the sad fellows brooding over the suffering caused by man's inhumanity to man. One of them disputes with his own soul in these words:

> To whom can I speak today?
> One's fellows are evil;
> The friends of today do not love.
> To whom can I speak today?
> Hearts are rapacious:
> Every man seizes his fellow's goods.
>
> To whom can I speak today?
> The gentle man has perished,
> But the violent man has access to everybody.
> To whom can I speak today?
> Even the calm of face is wicked;
> Goodness is rejected everywhere.[57]

The very fact that some men were able to recognize injustice and were willing to speak out against it is regarded by Breasted as evidence of a crusade for social justice.

> The pessimism with which the men of the early Feudal Age contemplated the hereafter or beheld the desolated cemeteries of the Pyramid Age and the hopelessness with which some of them regarded the earthly life were met by a persistent counter-current in a gospel of righteousness and social justice set forth in the hopeful teachings of the more optimistic social thinkers—men who saw hope in positive effort toward better conditions. We must regard the Admonitions of Ipuwer, the prophecies of Nefer-rohu, and the Tale of the Eloquent Peasant as striking examples of such efforts, and we must recognise in their writings the weapons of the earliest known group of moral and social crusaders.[58]

It would be foolish to assert that the masses of Egyptians were motivated in their behavior by considerations other than those of self-interest. Nor can we say that widespread belief prevailed that a dwelling place in the land of the dead could be purchased by good works in the land of the living, although expressions of such belief are not lacking altogether. Most people probably practiced such virtues as seemed to them useful in this life. Nevertheless, although not all students of history will agree with Breasted that the Egyptian social sages were "the first men to discern the worth of character and the inner values of the human heart," [59] it is easy to understand how some of those who have drawn near to the ancient Egyptian scene have been moved to speak in wonder and in praise. As a single example, that impractical dreamer Ikhnaton has received from Baikie this high praise: "Few men, even among those whom the world counts great, have done as much";[60] and Weigall pays him the following glowing tribute:

> He was the first human being to understand rightly the meaning of divinity. When the world reverberated with the noise of war, he preached the

first known doctrine of peace; when the glory of martial pomp swelled the hearts of his subjects he deliberately turned his back upon heroics. He was the first man to preach simplicity, honesty, frankness, and sincerity; and he preached it from a throne. He was the first Pharaoh to be a humanitarian; the first man in whose heart there was no trace of barbarism. He has given us an example three thousand years ago which might be followed at the present day: an example of what a husband and a father should be, of what an honest man should do, of what a poet should feel, of what a preacher should teach, of what an artist should strive for, of what a scientist should believe, of what a philosopher should think. Like other great teachers he sacrificed all to his principles, and thus his life plainly shows—alas!—the impracticability of his doctrines; yet there can be no question that his ideals will hold good "till the swan turns black and the crow turns white, till the hills rise up to travel, and the deeps rush into the rivers." [61]

ANCIENT EGYPT AND BABYLONIA

Although our knowledge of the social thought of the ancient Near East is at best meager, it has grown astoundingly by virtue of what we have been able to learn in recent years from tablets of clay and from the tombs of the pharaohs. No one knows what yet may be found in the marshes of Mesopotamia and along the Nile to add to our understanding of the thoughts of mankind at the dawn of civilization.

Without the clues found on the Rosetta Stone, which enabled J. F. Champollion, Robert Young, and others to discover a lost language, the science of Egyptology, with all that it has contributed to knowledge, might never have developed. In 1922, Howard Carter opened a door that had been closed, from all accounts, for three thousand years and entered the tomb of Tutankh-Amen. Since the tomb contained no written documents, Carter's discovery added little to knowledge about social thought in ancient Egypt, but the works of art taken from the tomb and now on permanent display in the Cairo Museum furnish visible proof of the artistic achievements of the ancient Egyptians.

Judging from the information now available, and conscious of the risk involved in attempting to describe what can be seen but dimly, we are struck with certain contrasts between Babylonia and ancient Egypt. Egyptian society displayed remarkable vitality. In fact, Toynbee maintains that it produced "the longest lived and most firmly compacted and most organically unified and most individually accentuated civilization that has ever yet been seen." [62]

In comparison, Babylonian civilization matured quickly under the Semites and after a brief period of great achievements entered into a stage of disintegration and decay. The Babylonians loved possessions and feared death; the Egyptians used their material goods to make themselves happy and regarded the abode of the dead as a place even more blessed than the good earth. A somber quality in Babylonian thought contrasts sharply with the gladness expressed in Egyptian art and literature. The Babylonians wrote much about justice; the Egyptians were more likely to write about mercy. Women had a high status in both societies, but the Egyptians gave them not only full rights as persons but also some important advantages as women. Neither the Babylonians nor the Egyptians found the escape from tribalism afforded by the Hebrew conception of the brotherhood of man resulting from the fatherhood of God, but the Egyptian Ikhnaton saw dimly what the Hebrews grasped clearly and proclaimed; the Babylonians produced no corresponding religious insight.

These contrasts are the more remarkable because Babylonia and ancient Egypt had so much in common. Both were river societies, with rich soil and an abundance of water. They had, to a considerable extent, the same domesticated plants and animals. They traded with one another, and they seem to have exchanged ideas and customs. Consequently, the differences we have noted prove that even at the dawn of history civilized people found various ways of satisfying their individual and social needs.

4 · CONFUCIUS AND THE CHINESE CLASSICS

The high mountain, he looked toward it;
The distant road, he walked along it.
                              BOOK OF POETRY

Ancient Babylonian and Egyptian civilizations perished, and their records were buried in crumbled ruins, where they lay until they were literally dug from the earth in modern times. Chinese civilization, on the other hand, has had continuous existence since it first began to develop in the basin of the Yellow River at a time not later perhaps than that at which the river civilizations of the Near East emerged. It has endured, consequently, for a longer period of time than any other civilization in history.

Before the organization of the Shang State in the fourteenth century B.C., Chinese history is a matter of myth and legend, and it was not until the eighth century B.C. that authentic Chinese history can be said to have begun. At that time pottery dishes were in use and the Chinese gentleman dressed for festive occasions in a robe of silk and wore shoes made of leather. While the forebears of some of the most advanced Europeans were gnawing their meat from the bone, the fastidious Chinese required that theirs be served in small pieces. By the sixth century B.C., the Chinese had a written language much like the one now in use. Since perhaps as many as one fourth of the people who have lived on the earth since written history began have been Chinese, or have been directly influenced by the Chinese, the Chinese civilization can claim to be not only the most enduring but also one of the most embracing of world civilizations.

HISTORICAL SKETCH

Like so many other men of great distinction, Confucius lived in an age of crisis. His times were neither better nor worse than those which have often appeared in history, but they were trying enough to distress a sensitive soul like Confucius.

The royal House of Chou, which, since 1122 B.C., had exercised authority over the various states which constituted the Chinese empire of that day, had lost control over the rulers of the several kingdoms. The feudal system which long had formed the basis of social organization was disintegrating, and China was passing through a stage comparable to that brought about by the collapse of feudalism in Europe almost two thousand years later. The disruption of feudal control resulted in political chaos. The conditions which Watters believes drove Laotse into exile faced the young Confucius:

> The whole country was torn up into petty states, which were always warring with each other. Year by year, army after army, with flaunting banners and gay pennons, passed and repassed through the fields of the people, and left desolation and misery in their track. Fathers and husbands, sons and brothers, were taken away from their homes and their work, and kept in long military service far away from their families. Laxity of morals accompanied this state of civil confusion. Chiefs forgot their allegiance to their princes, and wives their duties to their husbands—usurpers were in the state, and usurpers were in the family. Every little chief was striving with his neighbour for the mastery, and the weak and wicked princes of Chou were unable to overcome them and reduce them to peace and obedience. Men of shining abilities and inordinate ambition rose to power in each state, and, wishing to satisfy their ambition, increased the anarchy of their kingdom.[1]

This might have been regarded as a normal state of affairs had not history recorded for the inquiring Chinese scholar a Golden Age in which men had lived happily in perfect innocence. The account was, to be sure, somewhat confused by myths and legends. There was, for example, the fabulous emperor, in appearance part man and part serpent, who had brought order to a savage people by teaching them to live in a wedded state and to produce food by cultivation. He was, according to the accounts, followed by various other rulers who exercised such wisdom in the management of affairs as caused them to be looked upon as perfect emperors. Among them the Emperor Yau (2357-2258 B.C.) may be given as an example:

> He was reverential, intelligent, accomplished and thoughtful—naturally and without effort. He was sincerely courteous, and capable of all complaisance. The bright influence of these qualities was felt through the four

quarters of the land, and reached to heaven above and earth beneath. He made the able and virtuous distinguished, and thence proceeded to the love of all in the nine classes of his kindred, who thus became harmonious. He also regulated and polished the people of his domain, who all became brightly intelligent. Finally, he united and harmonized the myriad states; and so the black-haired people were transformed. The result was universal concord.[2]

This blissful condition did not last, according to the old accounts, and toward the end of the Shang (Yin) Dynasty the quality of emperors had so deteriorated that one of them is portrayed as a wicked and debauched despot. The Emperor Ch'ou-sin (1154-1122 B.C.) was a man of

> quick discernment, gifted with sharp senses, mental ability beyond the ordinary, and physical strength of brutal power. Knowledge enabled him to keep remonstrance at a distance; eloquence enabled him to gloss his vicious acts. Boasting to his subjects of his ability, and exalting his empire by clamoring, was to him the means to make himself prominent. He loved the pleasures of the cup and debauchery, and was infatuated with his consort, the beloved Ta-ki, whose word he obeyed.[3]

Ta-ki was as sadistic and as wicked as any woman in history, if we are to believe the accounts of her which Confucius read as he searched the old records for a solution to the problems which confronted his age.

> Ta-ki was shamefully lustful and cruel. The most licentious songs were composed for her amusement, and the vilest dances exhibited. . . . In the palace there were nine market stands, where they drank all night. The princes began to rebel, when Ta-ki said that the majesty of the throne was not sufficiently maintained; that punishments were too light, and executions too rare. She, therefore, devised two new instruments of torture. One of them was called "The Heater," and consisted of a piece of metal made hot in a fire, which people were obliged to take up in their hands. The other was a copper pillar, greased all over, and laid above a pit of live charcoal. The culprit had to walk across the pillar, and when his feet slipped and he fell down into the fire, Ta-ki was greatly delighted. This was called the punishment of "Roasting." These enormities made the whole empire groan and fume with indignation.[4]

Obviously the time had come for the Shang Dynasty to fall, and the emperor and his consort met a cruel fate at the hands of rebellious tribesmen.

The Chou Dynasty (1122-249 B.C.) which followed, organized, it appears, an integrated feudal empire headed by an emperor. The nobles who administered the fiefs were cooperative and obedient, and for centuries peace and justice prevailed. With the passing of time, however, the feudal lords grew less respectful toward the emperor and began to fight among themselves. Conditions grew steadily worse until finally the government collapsed. In 771 B.C., the disinheritance of the rightful heir in favor of the son of a concubine led to a rebellion, and from that time the actual administration of the government was in the hands of the feudal lords. At times they cooperated in various kinds of leagues and coalitions, but generally they were actively engaged in a struggle with one another for power. Kingdoms were gained and lost, and the boundaries of the empire, which was probably at no time larger than about one sixth the area of modern China, were in a constant state of flux. Intrigue, corruption, and a cynical disregard for treaties characterized the activities of states both large and small. The "logic of the fish" (the big ones eat the little ones) was firmly established in the conduct of politics. Lesser officers in the government aped their superiors and abused those beneath them while they kept an ever watchful eye for the opportunity to usurp the authority of those over them. By the time Confucius was born, conditions in civilized China had reached a point where, as Creel says:

> Not merely in Lu [the home state of Confucius] but in the other states as well, there was almost no basis of authority and order, save the constantly shifting balance of brute force. The forms of religion were widely practiced, as witnessed by the ceremonies with which treaties were constantly being solemnized, but an officer of Ch'u [an adjoining state] struck the keynote of the age when he said, "If we gain the advantage over our enemies, we must advance without any consideration of covenants." Nor was there our concept of the law, which stands over all alike. Human life was cheap. When a ruler of Wu did not wish bad news he had received to spread, he cut, with his own hand, the throats of seven men who happened to be in his tent. Food suspected of being poisoned was tested on a dog and a servant. The ruler of one small state was a collector of swords and tried out new acquisitions on his subjects. Duke Ling of the great state of Chin enjoyed shooting at the passers-by from a tower, to watch them try to dodge his missiles; when his cook did not prepare bears' paws to his taste, he had the cook killed. Such rulers were unusual, but it was not unusual for nobles to threaten subordinates who dared to advise against their conduct and to kill those who continued to remonstrate. Hired murderers were sometimes used. Punishments were severe and common; in Chi mutilation of the feet was so usual that special footgear was sold in the shops for those who had suffered it. Bribery at all levels was common, from the perversion of justice in favor of individuals to bribes demanded and received by ministers of great states, from other states, to insure a favorable foreign policy.[5]

The illiterate masses probably did not brood much over these conditions, however little they may have been directly affected by them. They gave less heed to politics than to food, and they were well content when they had enough to eat. Life stirred and hope revived with the coming of spring. Then the peasants could go out from the villages, in which they had huddled during the cold winter months, into the fields. Autumn harvests brought a feeling of security. Young people married at the proper time under the guidance of their parents and eagerly awaited the arrival of sons, and old people enjoyed in serenity the blessings of filial piety.

Confucius, however, was not a part of this untutored and insensitive mass of humanity. He was able to read and write, and his emotions were aroused by the ancient odes and by the stories he read about a time when order and justice had prevailed in the land of his birth. He who was himself so orderly that he would not sit upon a mat unless it were straight must have found the disorder and the evils of his day oppressive almost beyond endurance.

CONFUCIUS (551–479 B. C.)

So much has been said about Confucius, both in praise and in blame, that it is difficult to know just what sort of person he really was. Laotse, the Taoist philosopher, is supposed to have had a rather low opinion of his youthful contemporary, saying to him on one occasion:

> Those whom you talk about are dead, and their bones are mouldered to dust; only their words remain. . . . Put away your proud air and many desires, your insinuating habit and wild will. These are of no advantage to you. This is all I have to tell you.[6]

It is not certain, however, that Confucius had ever talked with Laotse, and this criticism may be no more than an example of the opposition that the teachings of Confucius created in his own day. Since that time there have been rival philosophies in China, and in recent centuries the sometimes overzealous efforts of Christian missionaries to discredit and uproot Confucianism have resulted in a distorted portrayal of the man and his ideals. It is claimed that he was austere, aloof, and so blindly devoted to the past that he considered whatever was old as excellent. His teaching is said to consist only of platitudes about virtue and some very impractical ideas about government.

On the other hand, it is obvious that the man who, more than any other, has given moral guidance to one of the world's largest societies for almost twenty-five hundred years deserves to be recognized as one of the truly great men of history. Born, as he says of himself, "without rank and in humble circumstances," he held only minor offices in the government and died undoubtedly believing that his life had been a failure. He believed that some persons are born with more insight than others, but he denied that he was one of these. Nor did he claim divine inspiration. "To divine wisdom and perfect virtue I can lay no claim," he said. He regarded himself, therefore, as an ordinary man, possessed of no unusual talents except perhaps the willingness to apply himself to study. He attributed to the love of learning and to hard work any knowledge that he might have gained beyond that possessed by a "dozen honest and conscientious men to be found in any hamlet." He insisted, furthermore, that he was only a transmitter of knowledge, passing on to his generation and to posterity the wisdom of the ancients, and not a creator of knowledge.

Only a few details about the life of Confucius have been recorded, and most of these have been questioned. For all that, he is not less well known than Homer or Shakespeare. He was born, apparently, in 551 B.C., in the state of Lu. Since he was afforded an opportunity to acquire an education and to cultivate a taste for archery and music, we may assume that his father was a man of some standing in the community, perhaps even a minor official, although he seems not to have possessed very much wealth. One account of his father traces his ancestry back to the royal House of Yin and describes him as a man of great physical strength and courage. He is said to have reached the age of seventy with nine daughters but no son to carry on the family name and then to have married a young maiden who bore him his distinguished son. Shortly thereafter he is reported to have died. When Confucius was still a young man, he lost his mother also. We read that as a youth Confucius worked as a keeper of stores and of herds, but he seems to have prospered sufficiently to be able at the age of nineteen to marry. His marriage probably ended in divorce, but not until his wife had borne him a son and perhaps two daughters.

At an early age Confucius gained recognition as a scholar, and his reputation drew pupils to him, many of whom became devoted followers. The number of disciples who at one time or the other surrounded him is not known, but his influence through his teaching even in his own day was probably considerable. Perhaps his pupils were in demand for posts in the government, and there is some indication that government officials sometimes sent their sons to Confucius to be prepared for the positions which they were expected to inherit. The nature of the offices that he himself held is disputed, and the influence that he was able to exert directly as an adviser to high government officials cannot be determined. He may have been unwilling to accept a post as an officer or an adviser in which his services could not be fully utilized, and his failure to gain greater political recognition than he did may have resulted, consequently, from his unwillingness to compromise with his principles. As he neared old age, he left his home and set off in search of a prince who would heed his advice. He wandered for thirteen years, perhaps accompanied by some of his disciples, but he failed in his quest. Creel believes, nevertheless, that his travel was not wholly in vain:

> If Confucius' travels had no outward result, it is nonetheless true that if he had stayed in Lu he would have been a different man. Assuredly his proper realm was that of ideas and of teaching them to others; he was incapable of the compromises necessary to put them into practice. But it was extremely important that he should try. The difference is that which distinguishes an officer who says, "Follow me!" from one who says, "Advance!" If Confucius had stayed in Lu, enjoying a sinecure and strolling

about with his pupils, he would have remained a preacher; by setting off on his hopeless quest he became a prophet. The picture of this venerable gentleman, in some respects still unsophisticated, setting off in his fifties to save the world by persuading the hard-bitten rulers of his day that they should not oppress their subjects, is in some ways ridiculous. But it is a magnificent kind of ridiculousness, found only in the great.[7]

At the age of sixty-eight, Confucius returned home. Legend has him occupied during the last years of his life with the task of editing the classics. His old age was saddened by the death of his son, but he probably rejoiced to know that a grandson would carry on the family, as indeed he did: there is said to be an unbroken line of descendants to this day. The untimely death of his most beloved disciple, a man upon whom he had counted to carry on his work, was a severe blow to the aging sage. Shortly before his death at the age of seventy-three, he was heard crooning one of the odes from *The Book of Poetry* he had long known and loved:

> The great mountain must crumble,
> The strong beam must break;
> And the wise man wither away like a plant.[8]

THE CONFUCIAN CLASSICS

Although there is not universal agreement as to what should be included as a part of the canonical literature of orthodox Confucianism, the following works are generally accepted as the Confucian classics:

> Five Canons:
> *Book of History*
> *Book of Poetry*
> *Book of Changes*
> *Book of Rites*
> *Spring and Autumn Annals*
>
> Four Books:
> *Analects of Confucius*
> *Book of Mencius*
> *The Great Learning*
> *Doctrine of the Mean*

Confucius himself may have written no part of this literature—at least, in the form in which it has survived—although he is sometimes credited with the *Spring and Autumn Annals* and is believed by some scholars to have edited the contents of the other four canons. It is pleasing to imagine that Confucius carefully selected from thousands of old Chinese poems the some three hundred odes contained in the *Book of Poetry*. However, Legge's doubts on this point have been shared by many later scholars, who agree with him also on another point—that, whatever their origin, the poems are genuinely Confucian. As Legge says:

> While we cannot discover, therefore, any peculiar labour of Confucius on the Book of Poetry, and we have it now . . . substantially as he found it directly compiled to his hand, the subsequent preservation of it may reasonably be attributed to the admiration which he expressed for it, and the enthusiasm for it with which he sought to inspire his disciples. It was one of the themes on which he delighted to converse with them. He taught that it is from the poems that the mind receives its best stimulus. A man ignorant of them was, in his opinion, like one who stands with his face toward a wall, limited in his views, and unable to advance. Of the two things which his son could specify as enjoined on him by the sage, the first was that he should learn the odes. In this way Confucius, probably, contributed largely to the subsequent preservation of the Book of Poetry; —the preservation of the tablets on which the odes were inscribed, and the preservation of it in the memory of all who venerated his authority and looked up to him as their master.[9]

The same statement might be made about the *Book of History,* to which Confucius appears to have been almost equally devoted. Whether or not he wrote any part of it, or had any hand in the selection of the matter that it contains, the fact remains that it affords historical examples of the principles by which Confucius believed men should regulate their own conduct and direct the affairs of the state. The other three canons are, for our purposes, less important. The *Book of Changes* is concerned largely with divination, the *Book of Rites* with ritual and ceremony, and the *Spring and Autumn Annals* with events taking place in the state of Lu between the eighth and fifth centuries B.C. It is possible that none of these three works is pre-Confucian.

The four "Books" obviously date from some time during or after the life of Confucius. The *Analects* is believed to have been written by his disciples or—more likely, as Legge believes—by the "disciples of the disciples of the sage." Mencius (372-298 B.C.) was a devout Confucian whose work not only expounded and elaborated the doctrines of the Master but also defended his school from its critics. *The Great Learning* and the *Doctrine of the Mean* are short works of uncertain date and authorship, although they probably came from the hands of followers of Confucius who lived not more than a few centuries at most after his death.

A casual examination of the various translations of the Chinese classics will reveal the differences among scholars as to the meaning of the Chinese ideograms. The problem of putting within the grasp of the general reader in the Occident the thought of the Oriental is not less serious today than it was when Legge explained his method of arriving at a translation:

> How to surmount this difficulty occurred to me after I had found the clue to the interpretation [of a certain work] in a fact which I had unconsciously acted on in all my translations of other classics, namely, that the written characters of the Chinese are not representations of words, but symbols of ideas, and that the combination of them in composition is not a representation of what the writer would say, but of what he thinks. It is vain therefore for a translator to attempt a literal version. When the symbolic characters have brought his mind *en rapport* with that of his author, he is free to render the ideas in his own or any other speech in the best manner that he can attain to.[10]

The results of the freedom which this system allows a translator—and unfortunately no better system has yet been found—are immediately obvious to one who turns to several versions of a text.

SOCIAL ORDER

The society envisaged by Confucius can best be thought of as a large, harmonious family. The members of this society are bound together by numerous ties, and the proper relations among them are those found most commonly in families where the feeling of respect, confidence, loyalty, and mutual responsibility is strong. Such a society was no mere figment of Confucius' imagination: it was described in the history he read and in the poems he learned to recite. The times in which he lived were out of joint, he believed, because the ancient wisdom was neglected. In the old books were to be found, he felt, the inspiration and guidance to right every wrong and to establish social order. The literature to which he so devoutly turned spoke not of war and mighty deeds of valor, as does the earliest literature of most nations, but of peace and good will. The men of old had discovered that the proper study of mankind is man, and that nothing matters so much as the "culture, conduct, conscientiousness, and good faith" of human beings. Let one but attend to the duties arising from the five social relations, said Confucius, and social order will inevitably prevail.

> The duties of universal obligation are five, and the virtues wherewith they are practised are three. The duties are those between sovereign and minister, between father and son, between husband and wife, between elder brother and younger, and those belonging to the intercourse of friends. . . . Knowledge, magnanimity, and energy, these three are the virtues universally binding.[11]

Confucius believed that all men are brothers, but he never claimed that they are equal. The modern idea of individualism, in which each person counts for one and none for more than one, is not found in his teachings. He believed that the individual is the supreme value and that man's chief aim is to complete himself, but he insisted that man can do this only by being faithful to his social obligations. All men are equal in innate goodness, in inherent dignity, and in personal rights. Society exists for the individual, and a government is good when "it makes happy those who live under it." But in many respects men are not equal: they differ in ability and come to have vastly different social responsibilities. The minister advises and serves the king, the son exercises filial piety toward his father, the wife obeys her husband, and the younger brother defers to the elder. Family matters are not decided by debate in which all, young and old alike, freely participate; nor is the business of government conducted amidst the clamor of many voices. Order in society requires that some have rights and duties denied others. Confucius could not conceive of a family without a head or a government without a king any more than we can conceive of an army without a general. The hierarchy of rights and duties found in a modern military organization corresponds closely to his idea of a social system. The similarity, however, is limited to form: his ideal society has none of the other characteristics of a military state.

CONVENTIONAL FORM

The individual is not, according to Confucius, free to do as he pleases in society; he does what is required of him in that station of life in which he is placed. Thence arises the importance of knowing the rules of right behavior for any situation in which he may find himself. Abstract principles must be made specific; the individual must be taught what respect, justice, honesty, and the other virtues require on any specific occasion. There is a proper way to comport oneself in the presence of the king, to take a bride, to recognize a son, to mourn for a departed mother, to receive a message, to appear in public, and to act in the home. A son should feel reverence for his father, but he must be taught the rituals of filial piety. Although the act is not more important than the spirit in which it is performed, unless one acts correctly the intention means very little. The character of a man, consequently, is formed by his observance of the "rules of fitness." These rules distinguish caution from timidity, courage from pugnacity, and forthrightness from brutality. Spontaneous action is guided by impulse; correct behavior demands conformity to established rules.

Even the abstract principle of reciprocity, which is at the base of Confucian ethics, is not sufficient to guide behavior in the various relations of life: it must be defined in specific and detailed rules applicable to concrete experiences. These rules are not mere conventions. As concrete forms of absolute principles they are not less than the principles themselves the "laws of Heaven." The Confucian emphasis on conventional form is easily distorted by the Western mind into empty ceremony. Confucius would agree that intent is the important thing, but he would add that good intentions are not enough: right behavior requires not only the Golden Rule but also the knowledge necessary for its application in specific situations. Confucius believed that the key to personal and social harmony, which modern nations attempt to fashion by laws, was to be found in faithful adherence to the conventional forms of behavior from the sacred past.

GOVERNMENT

We have seen that Confucius regarded the state as a large family. Just as the family is governed without laws, so should the state be governed. He distrusted written laws, saying that if the people were virtuous they would act justly, and if the proprieties were not observed the threat of punishment had little effect. When Confucius was yet a young man, a certain statesman had proposed to publish the criminal laws by which supposedly the rulers were guided. One of Confucius' pupils preserved a letter written at the time, which, although it is not from the hand of the Master, is revealing of his opinion on this subject.

> When the people themselves become cognizant of a written law, they will cease to fear their superiors, and, moreover, they will acquire a contentious spirit. Having [the] book to refer to, they will employ every device to elude the letter of the law. This will not do at all. . . . The Book of Odes says, "King Win . . . took virtue as his guide, and thus gradually pacified the four quarters of the world." It also says: "The methods of King Wu . . . secured the confidence of all the other countries." Where were the written laws in those times? When people begin to get the contentious spirit upon them, they will have done with the principles of propriety.[12]

PENAL JUSTICE

Since there are in society individuals who are either unwilling or unable to acquire understanding, penal justice is necessary. Such persons cannot be expected to rectify their conduct and must be restrained by the fear of punishment. They themselves profit little by this kind of control, however necessary it may be for society as a whole. Although the weaklings may in this way be persuaded to shun crime, they will develop no "sense of shame." Only those who are led by virtue and follow willingly the rules of propriety will "learn shame and become good." As Hsü says:

> Confucius maintains that the rule of virtue is above the rule of law. The latter is passive and negative, preventing the people from doing wrong; while the former is active and positive, encouraging people to do good. Furthermore, moral rule influences conscience and hence its influence is universal and unlimited. Legal rule governs only outward activities. People may attempt to evade law and to escape from punishment. At length they lose self-respect completely. On the other hand, when the people are virtuous and enlightened, law and punishment will become useless.[13]

FAMILISTIC GOVERNMENT

As in a well-governed family sons obey their fathers not because they fear punishment at their hands but because they trust and respect them, so, according to Confucius, will citizens obey their just rulers. The emperor is the father of his people; their welfare is his chief concern. If Confucius had been asked why a ruler might not use his high office to make himself rich and powerful, he probably would have answered, "Has a virtuous father no sense of shame?" A disciple once sought his views on the art of governing:

> Tzŭ Kung asked for a definition of good government. The Master replied: It consists in providing enough food to eat, in keeping enough soldiers to guard the State, and in winning the confidence of the people.— And if one of these three things had to be sacrificed, which should go first?—The Master replied: Sacrifice the soldiers.—And if of the two remaining things one had to be sacrificed, which should it be?—The Master said: Let it be the food. From the beginning, men have always had to die. But without the confidence of the people no government can stand at all.[14]

Government by persuasion rather than by force must extend down through all ranks of officials. Obedience is necessary if order is to prevail, but a virtuous king can ill afford arrogant agents. One king addressed to his administrative officers this warning:

> Oh! All ye men of virtue, my occupiers of office, pay reverent attention to your charges. Be careful in the commands you issue; for once issued, they must be carried into effect, and cannot be retracted. Extinguish all selfish aims by your public feeling, and the people will have confidence in you and be gladly obedient.[15]

PATRIARCHAL GOVERNMENT

The emperor, according to Confucius, has the same absolute authority in the state that the patriarch has in the family. He exercises this authority through ministers, but the responsibility is his.

> When good government prevails in the empire, civil ordinances and punitive expeditions issue from the emperor. When good government fails in the empire, civil ordinances and punitive expeditions issue from the nobles. When they issue from a noble, it is rare if the empire be not lost within ten generations. When they issue from a noble's minister, it is rare if the empire be not lost within five generations. But when a minister's minister holds command in the kingdom, it is rare if it be not lost within three generations.[16]

It seems never to have occurred to Confucius that the people might administer the government, and he would probably have scornfully rejected any such idea.

In fact, he believed that the people ought not even to discuss the government as long as the kingdom is orderly. What if the kingdom is disorderly, as it was in Confucius' own time? His answer to that question is not certain, but clearly he made the right to rule contingent upon the ability of the ruler to fulfill the obligations of his office, and he denied an incapable ruler a legitimate claim to the throne. He does not explicitly state that the people have the right to revolt against an incompetent king, but he does ask, "If a man cannot govern himself, what has he to do with governing others?" He also declared that by winning the support of the people, the kingdom is won, whereas by losing the support of the people, the kingdom is lost.[17] (Mencius developed this idea, declaring that the government exists for the people and that when it fails to promote their welfare it should be overthrown.)

Although the Confucian attitude toward the doctrine of revolution may be disputed, there can be little question about the teaching of the Master as to the proper aim of government: governments exist to promote the welfare of the people. He took to heart this lesson from the *Book of History:*

> It was the lesson of our great ancestor:—
> The people should be cherished and not looked down upon.
> The people are the root of a country;
> The root firm, the country is tranquil.
> When I look at all under heaven,
> Of the simple men and simple women,
> Any one may surpass me (in wisdom and virtue).
> In my dealing with the millions of the people
> I should feel as much anxiety as if I were driving six horses
>   with a rotten rein.[18]

Confucius believed that the ruler can best secure his position of control by taking steps to ensure that every link in the chain of government is strong. He did not minimize the importance of the officers serving under the king. Each of these has responsibilities which he cannot shirk without doing harm to the government. Above all, every officer of the state must set an example for those beneath him.

> When a ruler is right in himself, things will get done without his giving orders. When he is not right in himself, he may give orders, but they will not be obeyed. . . . If those in the higher ranks of society be devoted to ritual, then none of the common people can dare not to venerate them. If they be lovers of justice, then none of the common people can dare not to obey them. If they be worthy of confidence, then none of the common people can dare to prevaricate. If that be the state of affairs in a country, then the common people will come to it from all parts, carrying their babies on their back.[19]

SUMMARY

In summary, Confucius conceived of the state as a benevolent patriarchy. The emperor alone exercises authority over the state, but he employs the services of trained advisers and administrative officials. Governments exist for the benefit of the governed and derive their just powers from their consent. Control is exercised through paternal love and the precepts and examples of virtue. Foreign to Confucius' thought are conceptions of nationalism, militarism, colonial expansion, and democracy in the modern sense. Good government is as simple as this:

> The ancients who wished to illustrate virtue throughout the kingdom first ordered well their own States. Wishing to order well their States, they first regulated their families. Wishing to regulate their families, they first cultivated their persons. Wishing to cultivate their persons, they first rectified their hearts. Wishing to rectify their hearts, they first sought to be sincere in their thoughts. Wishing to be sincere in their thoughts, they first extended to the utmost their knowledge. Such extension of knowledge lay in the investigation of things.
>
> Things being investigated, knowledge became complete. Their knowledge being complete, their thoughts were sincere. Their thoughts being sincere, their hearts were then rectified. Their hearts being rectified, their persons were cultivated. Their persons being cultivated, their families were regulated. Their families being regulated, their States were rightly governed. Their States being rightly governed, the whole kingdom was made tranquil and happy.[20]

FAMILY

In view of the traditional importance of the family group in Chinese society, one might expect to find in the Confucian classics many details about family life. This is not the case. Although much is said about filial piety and the proper relations of the members of the family, little is said about marriage, the management of family property, the division of labor in the home, the education of children, the construction and arrangement of houses, recreation in the home, the status of concubines, and many other matters about which we should like to be informed. Female infanticide may have been common, but the subject is not mentioned by Confucius; nor are sex morals given more than casual mention.

The portrayal of ancient, as well as modern, China as a society organized around the family group and held together by the disciplines of the home is familiar to the Western world. For example, E. R. Hughes says:

> A Westerner will never really come to understand the Chinese traditional approach to the state unless amongst other things he really tries to grasp

how much the approach was conditioned by the exaltation of the family above the state.[21]

Creel goes perhaps even further and says:

> The family has been important in many cultures, but it is doubtful that it has anywhere been more important, for a longer time, than in China. Certain aspects of its importance, especially nepotism, have been deplorable, yet it has probably done more than any other institution to make possible the remarkable survival of Chinese culture. It has dealt with many social problems in their nascent stages. By virtue of it, China has consisted of a vast number of almost self-contained social cells, whose functioning has been little affected even by national catastrophe. It has been the incubator of morality and a microcosm of the state. From one point of view, Confucianism might be defined as the philosophy of the Chinese family system.[22]

This position has been challenged by Granet, who believes that the disciplines of the home, and especially the filial piety which is at the base of domestic and civic morality in China, were, in ancient times, an outgrowth of feudalism and were, consequently, the results rather than the causes of social organization in the society as a whole. After considerable analysis of the situation, he says:

> It is well then to invert the historic postulate which is at the foundation of Chinese theories. Civic morality is not a projection of domestic morality: it is, on the contrary, the law of the feudal citadel which has impregnated domestic life. . . . Hence arises a characteristic trait in the private life of the Chinese. . . . While the domestic order seems to rest entirely upon parental authority, the idea of respect takes absolute precedence of the idea of affection in family relationships. Regulated on the model of court assemblies, domestic life forbids all familiarity. Etiquette rules there and not intimacy.[23]

The question as to whether the family is the basic social unit in the Chinese, or in any other, society is a complex one and lies beyond the scope of this book. Our concern here is with the thoughts about family organization and institutions found in the Confucian classics. That the ancient Chinese attached great importance to family life is immediately obvious. The following ode reveals the characteristic attitude:

> The happy union with wife and child
> Is like the music of lutes and harps.
> When concord grows between brother and brother,
> The harmony is sweet and intimate.
> The ordering of your household!
> Your joy in wife and child![24]

FAMILY ORGANIZATION

The Confucian family system was patriarchal, with the authority of the head absolute and unquestioned. There was no criticism of a plurality of wives, but we must infer from the evidence that a plurality of husbands was most exceptional, if it occurred at all. Divorce was not uncommon, and the practice seems not to have been regarded as a social problem; it is probable that Confucius himself divorced his wife. Wives were expected to be submissive and obedient to their husbands. Little was said about the status of girls in the family, but a bride became a member of her husband's family, and duty to him and to his people took precedence over her duty to her own kin. The husband, however, still remained bound to his own family of birth by the closest ties, and the claims of his wife were subordinate to those of his parents upon him.

MARRIAGE

Marriages were arranged, at the will of the parents, by a "go-between." From various sources Legge has brought together such little information about marriage customs in Confucian China as he could find, which he summarizes as follows:

> Marriages were arranged at the commencement of the year before the ice was melted by the return of the heat; and the ceremony took place at the flowering of the peach tree. . . . When the bride was of a noble family, she was conducted to her husband in a chariot adorned with feathers. . . . Musicians and a numerous suite accompanied her. The husband awaited his future wife at the door of the house. . . . After having sojourned in the house of her husband, the new wife returned to pass two or three months with her parents.[25]

The purpose of the bride's extended visit with her parents is not stated, but it may well have been her last, as long as she remained a member of her husband's family. Should he cast her off, she might return to her parental roof, but in that event she seems to have anticipated no great welcome. There were no priests, of course, and it is doubtful that marriage among the common people was regarded as the business of the state. Many details of the marriage contract are lacking, but Granet gives the vows that may have been commonly pledged:

> In death, in life, in sorrow—I take thee for my partner!—I take thy hands in mine:—I hope to grow old with thee.[26]

The *Book of Poetry* contains much love poetry, some of it descriptive of the passions of lovers but more of it expressive of the solicitude of wives for their absent husbands. There are bridal songs, odes in praise of marriage, and laments of faithful widows.

STATUS OF WOMEN

Whether in China women have been, and still are, regarded as inferior to men depends on how inferiority is defined; certainly Confucius believed that the sexes are psychologically as well as physically different and that they have different roles in society. The weak and passive nature of the female is sharply contrasted with the strong and active nature of the male. There probably had existed before Confucius' time some rather vague conception of a duality in nature revealed everywhere in two principles which might be called the male and the female. The metaphysical expression of these principles in the concepts of *Yang* and *Yin,* which are important in later Chinese thought, was doubtless of little interest to Confucius, if he were acquainted with it at all. He was not concerned with the cosmological speculations out of which these concepts developed. Nevertheless, the contrast between men and women in his thinking finds in Yang and Yin an abstract formulation that might easily develop from his beliefs. At various times in Chinese history, Yang, the male principle, has represented light, activity, hardness, and heat, to mention only a few qualities associated with this concept. Yin, on the contrary, has represented darkness, passivity, softness, and cold. Yang is spirit, Yin is body; Yang is the sun, Yin is the moon; Yang is fire, Yin is water; Yang is heaven, Yin is earth. These terms are introduced here not because they belong to Confucian thought but because they reveal an interesting development in Chinese thought of what may originally have been only an observation of sexual differences. Confucius was not a logician, but implicit in his thought is a differentiation between the sexes expressed in the principles of Yang and Yin.

Ancient China was, in most respects, a man's world. Parents wanted sons, not daughters. Sisters were expected to defer to brothers, and when a girl was mature she was expected to marry, bear sons, and devote herself wholly to the duties of the home. Among the masses this home service probably included a full day's work in the fields, but the odes depict women busy at their looms. Since there were few, if any, slaves in China at this time, it is likely that women of the upper classes were able to employ domestic servants to do the housework, but they nowhere seem to have forsaken the home for the world outside. The contrast between the joy at the birth of a son and the gloom when a girl was born is brought out in this poem about a royal family:

> A son is born.
> He is placed upon a bed,
> And clothed with brilliant stuffs.
> They give him a semi-sceptre.
> His cries are frequent.

> They clothe the lower part of his body with red cloth.
> The master, the chief sovereign, is born, and to him
>   they give the empire.
>
> A daughter is born:—
> They place her on the ground;
> They wrap her in common cloths;
> They place a tile near to her.
> There is not in her either good or evil.
> Let her learn how to prepare the wine and cook the food.
> Above all she should exert herself not to be a charge on
>   her parents.[27]

If a princess newly born found no greater welcome, what must have been the fate of a girl born into a humble home where already there were too many mouths to feed? The announcement that the baby was a girl was an occasion for shame, not rejoicing, and a wife who failed to provide her husband with a son could be divorced.

It is difficult to believe that parents even then were lacking in sheer animal attachment to their young, male or female, but the Chinese were trained to repress the elemental emotions, and outwardly the Chinese family was characterized more by a show of respect than by the display of affection. Girls were born for marriage, and a faithful mother had done her duty by her daughter when she had brought her up prepared for that great event. The sum of all her teaching is contained in this parting word of advice whispered to a daughter leaving to be married: "You are going to your home. You must be respectful. You must be careful. Do not disobey your husband." [28] From birth to death the female was under the authority of some male:

> The woman follows the man. In her youth she follows her father and elder brother; when married, she follows her husband; when her husband is dead, she follows her son.[29]

Confucius himself rarely spoke about women, but this statement in the *Analects* is attributed to him:

> Girls and servants are the most difficult people to handle. If you treat them familiarly, they become disrespectful; if you keep them at a distance, they resent it.[30]

The *Spring and Autumn Annals* specifically condemns the exercise by women of political powers and their participation in political conferences. However, although women were not encouraged to take an active part in government, there is evidence that a woman might occasionally hold public office. After all, women do grow old, and in ancient China, age was more important in many respects than sex.

In summary, it is clear that the Confucian classics reveal an attitude that is opposed to most of the aims for which modern feminism stands. This is not to say that women were not given an honorable, and perhaps even a satisfying, role in society. The odes abound in sentiments of respect and devotion for womankind, and it is not to men but to humanity that Confucius addressed his teachings. Do not unto others that which you would not have others do unto you—this is a universal rule of conduct, binding on men and women alike in all their relations. He probably believed that women are happier, and that society is better served, when women restrict their interests and their activities to the home.

FILIAL PIETY

If the principle of reciprocity (the Golden Rule), so prominent in the thinking of Confucius, is thought of as the cement binding together the Chinese social system, then filial piety is the keystone of that system. Confucius did not originate the idea. In the *Book of History,* an ancient king (King Khang, 1116 B.C.) is quoted as saying to a noble whom he was raising to the rank of high duke:

> Oh! your ancestor, Thang the Successful, was reverent and sage, with a virtue vast and deep. . . . His achievements affected his age, and his virtue was transmitted to his posterity. And you are the one who [doth now] pursue and cultivate his plans;—this praise [has belonged] to you of old. Reverently and carefully you discharged your filial duties, gravely and respectfully you behave to spirits and to men. I admire your virtue, and pronounce it great and not to be forgotten.[31]

The value attached to filial piety at this early date is further shown in a statement in which it is pointed out how much more serious is disobedience to "natural principles" than are such crimes as theft, villainy, treachery, assault, and murder. In the words of the king:

> Fung, such chief criminals are greatly abhorred, and how much more detestable are the unfilial and unbrotherly![32]

The *Analects* virtually begin with the question "Are not filial devotions and respect for elders the very foundations of an unselfish life?" The answer is, of course, implied in the question; but Confucius returns repeatedly to the theme and makes it clear that he regards filial piety as the root of all virtue. Neither he nor his immediate disciples ever attempted, however, an explicit definition of the term; and those who in later times made the meaning of filial piety simple enough to be understood by any schoolboy probably gave it interpretations that Confucius did not intend. A work known as *The Book of Filial Piety* is regarded by some scholars as true to the teachings of Confucius, but this book, a portion of which may have been the work of the Master himself, is not generally regarded as one of the Confucian classics.

The Chinese character *hsiao,* from which the term "filial piety" is derived, consists of symbols signifying an old man being supported by a son. It is clear that Confucius regarded this relationship as not merely a material one. "Mere support of one's parents without reverence is beastly," he said.[33] Naturally, parents are taken care of in their old age by their filial children, but, far more important, they are entitled to expect devotion and willing obedience from their children. Patient service to the aged and self-denial for their sake are easy, said Confucius; the difficulty lies in doing these things gladly, "with filial respect and love." When Confucius was asked what he meant by filial piety, he answered:

> That parents should be served in the proper spirit while living, buried with the proper rites after death, and worshipped thereafter with the proper sacrifices.[34]

This is no matter of mere ceremony: the obligations of filial piety require that children obey their father while he is living and on his death strive not less to follow him than when he was alive. A filial son carries on his father's work. "King Wan is considered blessed," said Confucius, "in having his work founded by his father and carried out by his son."[35] Physical death does not terminate a man's social usefulness; he lives in the memory of his devoted children, who carry on the good work to which his life was dedicated. Thus the good that men do lives after them and only their bones lie buried.

Filial piety requires that a son take care of his body, since that is the gift of his parents; that he remain close to the parental roof and not "wander aimlessly about"; that he rejoice as his parents grow old, and yet feel apprehensive and serve them more diligently; and, above all, that he be obedient. Confucius did not deny the young any voice whatsoever; he insisted only that the decision rest with the old. A filial son might go no further than gently to remonstrate with his parents. "If he sees that they are not inclined to yield," said Confucius, "he should be increasingly respectful but [should] not desist, and though they deal hardly with him, he must not complain."[36]

Because of the importance of filial piety in the social organization of China from the earliest times to the present day, let us attempt to formulate in modern terms the meaning of this concept implicit in the thinking of Confucius, even though he did not thus express it.

1. Filial piety means a backward rather than a forward look and makes sacred that which is gray with age. Progress is a modern faith that the world will become, if men act intelligently, a better place in which to live; filial piety secures one in the possession of the wisdom of the ages and checks what Confucius would have regarded as a childish impulse to remake the world.

2. Filial piety develops an attitude of respect for rightful authority. It begins in the home, but it extends outward to embrace all relations. It imposes upon every individual the duty to direct those below him and the obligation to obey those in authority over him. Where everybody attempts to pass judgment on all matters whatsoever, there is, from this point of view, no possibility of social order. In time the filial son becomes the revered father; only the unfilial son usurps the authority of his father, and evil is the hour in which this occurs.

3. Filial piety brings about continuity in human effort. Action extends across generations, and death is only an episode in an on-going process. The Western mind employs means to achieve an end—a conclusion, a victory; the Chinese mind is conscious of a process in which all ends become means, if indeed the distinction can be made at all; victory is not at the end but in the middle.

4. Filial piety demands that loyalty to the members of one's family take precedence over loyalty to the state or even to the demands of legal justice.

5. Filial piety ensures, in the words of that Duke of Chou whom Confucius venerated, that "the principles of morality given to the people by Heaven will not ignorantly be thrown into rude disorder."

THE SUPERIOR MAN

"One thread," said Confucius when he was once talking to his disciples, "runs through all my teachings." [37] He did not need to explain what he meant, because those close to him knew well the theme of which he never tired: the characteristics of the superior man. Again and again he endeavored to point out the difference between the superior man, who by study has come into his birthright of self-realization, and the ordinary man, who has not achieved real selfhood. He described the superior man in hundreds of ways, showing just how he differs from the ordinary man in numerous traits of character, but his disciples agree that this statement comes close to summing up his definition: a superior man is one who is true to himself and who exercises benevolence toward others. The superior man considers what is right; the ordinary man considers what will pay.

Confucius was a humanist. A Chinese philosopher has recently declared that humanism as a social movement began with Confucius. He says:

> This emphasis on humanism in Confucius is supreme. It underlies all his political, educational, aesthetic, and even his logical doctrines. People are to be ruled by the good examples of the rulers, guided by virtue, and regulated by the principles of propriety, and the object of government is to bring wealth and education to the people and security to the state. Knowledge is to "know men." The superior man "studies in order to apply his moral principles." Poems are "to stimulate your emotions, to broaden

your observation, to enlarge your fellowship, and to express your grievances." . . . This humanism is complete.[38]

Confucius believed that the aim of all knowledge is the good life, that the supreme value is the human individual, and that man is the measure of all things whatsoever. How, then, did he consider man?

HUMAN NATURE

Since Confucius seems never himself to have ventured an opinion as to whether the human being is by nature good or evil, it is possible to attribute to him both views. He was not a logician, and his philosophical system required no premise regarding man's original nature. He was less concerned with man's original state than he was with man's growth in humanity. Mencius, on the other hand, probed more deeply into this matter and was fond of discussing it. He explicitly declared that the nature of man is good.

> From the feelings proper to it, it [mankind] is constituted for the practice of the good. This is what I mean by saying that *the nature* is good. If men do what is not good, the blame cannot be imputed to their natural powers. The feeling of commiseration belongs to all men; so does that of shame and dislike; and that of reverence and respect; and that of approving and disapproving. The feeling of commiseration implies the principle of benevolence; that of shame and dislike, the principle of righteousness; that of reverence and respect, the principle of propriety; and that of approving and disapproving, the principle of knowledge. Benevolence, righteousness, propriety, and knowledge are not infused in us from without. . . . Hence it is said, "Seek and you will find them. Neglect and you will lose them." [39]

Confucius seems to have shared the opinion of Mencius that the capacity for moral growth is a natural attribute of mankind. Man is disposed to strive for moral self-perfection, whatever may be the forces of circumstance or even the other drives of his own nature. Is the capacity for virtue matched by the capacity for vice, so that man is not one but two, a house divided, a focus of struggle between the spirit and the flesh? Confucius did not answer this question, if, indeed, it ever occurred to him. He did point out, however, that he could not trust wholly the dictates of his own heart until he was ripe in wisdom.

> At fifteen I set my mind upon wisdom. At thirty I stood firm. At forty I was free from doubts. At fifty I understood the laws of Heaven. At sixty my ear was docile. At seventy I could follow the desires of my heart without transgressing the right.[40]

Is Confucius saying here that men crave to do wrong? He observed on one occasion that all men desire wealth and high station, a view that might suggest his belief in an inborn impulse to vanity. But is it not possible that men do evil through ingorance rather than because of natural inclinations, and that men are vain only when they have failed to attain humility? This seems to be the Confucian position. Nature does not make man superior; nor does circumstance: man makes himself superior, by study and by thought. Confucius said that he had not himself been able to become a superior man—that is, he had not been able to serve his father, his prince, his elder brother, and his friend as he would have required service from each of these had he been in his place. But he regarded his failure to live as he would have others live as a personal failure; he did not place the blame on forces beyond his control. Furthermore, he believed that every man has the capacity for virtue. "By nature men are nearly alike," he says; "by practice they get to be wide apart." [41] The way of the superior man is, therefore, open to all; but it is not an easy way. Knowledge makes a man superior; ignorance keeps him ordinary. Hence the importance which Confucius attached to education.

EDUCATION

It is not enough to read the heart aright, says Confucius; to become a superior man one must acquire knowledge. To Confucius that knowledge was contained in the books in which the thoughts and experiences of the ancient Chinese were recorded. He did not say that we learn from history; rather he said that we learn from the wisest and best men. He turned for guidance to the ancient kings and the ancient literature, not with blind devotion to the past but with deliberate choice. To the question, What can man do? Confucius gave the answer: Let him follow the king. Rationalism is based on faith in human reason; empiricism, on faith in human senses. The authoritarianism of Confucius is based on faith in the whole man.

Confucius taught that the desire to live a good life, to be a superior man, is universal; what is lacking in the ordinary man is the stern resolution to learn. He had little patience with those people with full hearts and empty heads who at all times have caused so much harm in society by trying to do so much good. Deep love of learning, he insisted, and not shallow sentiment, is the key to all virtue.

> Love of kindness, without a love to learn, finds itself obscured by foolishness. Love of knowledge, without a love to learn, finds itself obscured by loose speculation. Love of honesty, without a love to learn, finds itself obscured by harmful candour. Love of straight-forwardness, without a love to learn, finds itself obscured by misdirected judgment. Love of daring, without a love to learn, finds itself obscured by insubordination. And love for strength of character, without a love to learn, finds itself obscured by intractability.[42]

The kind of education in which Confucius was interested had little to do with such vocational skills as gardening or husbandry, however important such training might be; he demanded of education that it shape the mind and heart. Much depends, he says, on the early training in the home, for it is here that "the son is prepared to secure his wisdom in the future, as if it were decreed to him." He had a high regard for poetry and music in the program of education. He believed that anyone, regardless of his class, should have an opportunity to advance in learning as far as his ability and his will permitted. Of his own teaching he says: "From the man bringing his bundle of dried fish upwards, I have never refused instruction to anyone." [43] He strongly advocated the kind of intellectual democracy that has made China pre-eminent among the nations of the world in recognizing and rewarding intellectual accomplishments without regard to the distinctions of class.

In practical pedagogy, Confucius was indeed the Master. Of one student he said, "He gives me no assistance. There is nothing that I say in which he does not delight." Once he remarked, "Teaching is the half of learning." [44] He believed that the acquisition of wisdom requires both study and thought. "Learning without thought is labour lost," he said; "thought without learning is perilous. . . . I used to spend whole days without food and whole nights without sleep, in order to meditate. But I made no progress. Study, I found, was better." [45]

In short, Confucius had great faith in education. He had no doubt as to its proper aims; he believed that all men are alike entitled to educational opportunity, and he had some views about teaching methods that are as sound today as they were when he expressed them. Above all, he believed that only through education, in the full sense of the term, can one become a superior man.

THE GOLDEN RULE

The truly educated man, said Confucius, is benevolent: he practices the Golden Rule. The principle of reciprocity in the negative form in which Confucius expressed it has sometimes been called the "Silver Rule." There is little reason to make this distinction. The principle is basic in all of the great ethical systems of the world, and nowhere more prominent than in the teachings of Confucius.

> "Is there any one word," asked Tzu Kung, "which could be adopted as a lifelong rule of conduct?" The Master replied: "Is not Sympathy the word? Do not do to others what you would not like yourself." [46]

To say, however, that the way in which the Golden Rule is phrased is of little importance is not at all to say that the principle has everywhere the same meaning. In the actual carrying out of the rule, there are important differences created by the other characteristics of any particular system. Confucian and Christian ethics, despite their common base in the principle of reciprocity, are far from identical. For example, Christ taught that a man should love his enemies and do good to them that hate him. When, however, Confucius was asked what he would say concerning the principle that injury should be recompensed with kindness, he replied, "With what then will you recompense kindness? Recompense injury with justice, and recompense kindness with kindness." [47] Far more important is another fundamental difference between Christian and Confucian ethics: the Christian ethic derives its authority, in the belief of the adherent, from God; the Confucian, on the other hand, lacks a similar supernatural sanction.

THE REWARDS OF VIRTUE

The path that leads up to virtue is difficult to ascend, and only the superior man can reach the top. The "good, careful people of the village" should not be confounded with the virtuous; virtue is made of sterner stuff. Confucius scorns the ruler who in his love of hunting and women "abandons his state to ruin," the scholar who "cherishes the love of comfort." He pities the weakling who in his desire for ease follows the downward path, which, he says, is the way of the ordinary man, although he does not say whither it leads. He probably did not suppose that the ascetic life would have very wide appeal, but he does call it good:

> With coarse food to eat, water for drink, and a bent arm for a pillow, —even in such a state I could be happy, for wealth and honour obtained unworthily are to me as a fleeting cloud.[48]

Men sometimes practice asceticism in order to commune with the Absolute, but Confucius never discussed supernatural matters. When he spoke of the "will of Heaven," he seemed to have in mind something similar to what we loosely call the "law of nature"; he avoided the metaphysical implications of *Tao*. Also, men sometimes practice asceticism for the sake of salvation beyond the grave; but Confucius asked, "What can we who know so little of life know about death?" He did not withdraw from the world, in the fashion of some ascetics who have found it too oppressive to endure; to the end of his life he was active in society.

All this suggests that Confucius was not an ascetic at all. He loved the creature comforts and the warmth of a dram of wine, but more than these he loved the warmth of human fellowship. A modern scholar has said of him, "He trusted the human race." [49] He believed that people need the guidance provided by the precepts and the examples of the superior man. He sought to "enlarge with learning" the minds of those about him, so that they, and through them all mankind, might live happily and in peace.

CONFUCIANISM

The scope of this brief survey of Chinese social thought is obviously restricted, but limitations of space have prevented a larger view. A few writers, such as

Max Weber, Arnold J. Toynbee, Marcel Granet, F. S. C. Northrop, and others, have gone much further. They have attempted, in fact, to plumb the depths of Chinese culture at some point and to grasp the ethos of the Chinese people. Their interpretations of the spirit that has guided Chinese life and thought help to dispel the mist that prevents the Occidental from observing and understanding the workings of the Oriental mind. It is enough here, however, to consider Confucius and the Chinese classics, leaving to others the analysis of the varied and profound civilization of China from ancient to modern times. There is more to Chinese thought than Confucianism embraces, but the Chinese sage is a tall mountain by which all ways leading into that thought must pass.

Early Chinese social thought may seem to the Western reader to lack profundity. It may appear to consist largely of aphorisms extolling virtue and common sense. Such is the difference between Eastern and Western ways of thinking! The fact remains, however, that for twenty-five hundred years Confucianism has given to countless millions of people a way of life which they have found meaningful and good. It has had to compete, in the past, with Taoism, Buddhism, and other Eastern philosophies and has shown a remarkable ability to compromise without sacrificing any of its essential characteristics. Today it is facing the challenge of Western civilization. It is yet too soon to determine the outcome of this new threat to the traditional beliefs and practices of the people of China, but it is not too late to see what Confucianism has offered mankind.

Briefly stated in the words of the Chinese philosopher Lin Yutang,

> Confucianism stood for a rationalized social order through the ethical approach, based on personal cultivation. It aimed at political order by laying the basis for it in a moral order, and it sought political harmony by trying to achieve the moral harmony in man himself. Thus its most curious characteristic was the abolition of the distinction between politics and ethics. Its approach was definitely an ethical approach, differing from the Legalists who tried to bring about a strong nation by a rigid enforcement of the law. It was also a positive point of view, with a keen sense of responsibility toward one's fellow men and the general social order, as distinguished from the negative cynicism of Taoism. Fundamentally, it was a humanist attitude, brushing aside all futile metaphysics and mysticism, interested chiefly in the essential human relationships, and not in the world of spirits or in immortality. The strongest doctrine of this particular type of humanism, which accounts for its great enduring influence, is the doctrine that "the measure of man is man," a doctrine which makes it possible for the common man to begin somewhere as a follower of Confucianism by merely following the highest instincts of his own human nature, and not by looking for perfection in a divine ideal.[50]

Confucius was not a systematic philosopher, but his love of knowledge was no less intense than that which moved the great philosophers of the West in their search for the ultimate nature of beauty, truth, and goodness. But whereas they fashioned their discoveries into intellectual edifices adorned with intricate patterns of speculative thought, Confucius abhorred metaphysics. When asked what knowledge is, he replied, "When you know a thing, to recognize that you know it; and when you do not know a thing, to recognize that you do not know it. That is knowledge." [51]

Confucius is sometimes accused, and the Chinese people with him, of dwelling too much in the past. It cannot be denied that he delighted in describing himself as one who regarded antiquity with "trust and affection." It is equally clear that he found the past a much more admirable object of contemplation than the future. But why? Although he did not himself attempt to answer that question, we may infer his reason from his devotion to Tao.

Confucius was ever striving to identify himself with what he regarded as the only ultimate reality—the way of Heaven. How can that way be known? Only as it is revealed in history. Carefully studied, the lives of men disclose the working out of the laws of Heaven. It is plain to see in human experience, for example, that Heaven wants men to love one another, that the principle of reciprocity—"What you do not wish done to yourself, do not do to others"—is the universal plan and that adherence to this plan results in peace and contentment, whereas departure from it inevitably results in pain and misery. Such truths are not given intuitively, nor are they attained by reason alone. Only in the experience of mankind are they clearly revealed, and their discovery is the fruit of labor devoted to the study of history. Such study meant to Confucius not merely, or even primarily, intellectual grasp of indubitable truths but the permeation of one's being by these truths. In other words, he recognized the distinction between *knowledge how* and *knowledge about,* and he regarded the former type as far more important than the latter.

This subtle conception is not peculiar to the Chinese, as we shall see when we turn to Greek and medieval social thought. Nevertheless, it found in Confucianism a convincing and an enduring expression. Chinese civilization has not escaped the conflict of ideas in the modern world, but by the sheer impact of their number, if in no other way, the Chinese may yet preserve and extend in influence, with incalculable value to mankind, the noblest ideals of Confucianism, while allowing much in the system that can no longer be reconciled with human aspirations to be forgotten.

5 · ANCIENT INDIA

Never was time it was not: End and Beginning are dreams!
BHAGAVAD-GITA, BOOK II

As large as all Europe except Russia, and two thirds the size of the United States, India is a land of contrasts: mountain peaks lost in the mist and sluggish rivers meandering through broad basins barely raised above the sea; eternal snows and sweltering heat; fertile fields sustaining a population of more than three thousand persons per square mile and broad stretches of arid desert; some of the richest people on earth and some of the poorest; a land which has cradled some of the world's greatest poets, philosophers, religious leaders, artists, and scientists, yet a land where even today not one person in ten is literate; home of fierce fighting men, yet throughout history an easy prey for conquerors; a people divided by thousands of castes and hundreds of tongues, yet bound by a tradition of unity which gives white heat to Indian patriotism; a land where life in every form is sacred, yet where death is the highest good; floods and drought, feasts and famine, nonviolence and fanaticism, Hindus and Moslems, Aryans and Dravidians, Brahmans and Pariahs—this is India.

HISTORICAL BACKGROUND

DRAVIDIANS

When the light of history breaks over India, we find widely scattered over the land but more thickly settled in the southern regions, a people with broad noses and dark skins known as the Dravidians. These may have been the aborigines of India, although certain primitive tribes which may claim that title are found today in sections of the country isolated by geographical barriers. Also there is a kinship between the language of the Dravidians and that spoken in certain districts of Baluchistan. This suggests the possibility that the Dravidians may have migrated into India from some place in that vast area to the north which has been called the cradle of mankind. Or perhaps these early Indians may have been at some time in contact with peoples dwelling beyond the present Indian frontiers. In any event, when the Aryans, with sharp noses and light skins, appeared in India, they found the land already occupied.

ARYANS

It is not definitely known who the Aryans were or whence they came. We do know that the Indo-Iranians, who appeared at an early date in India, were related to the Indo-Europeans found in Europe at the same time. Together they formed the Caucasian race. Originally the term *Aryan* was applied to a family of languages—Teutonic, Latin, Greek, Sanskrit, Russian, and others. As a result of the discovery late in the eighteenth century that Sanskrit bears a strong affinity to Greek and Latin, excited scholars undertook numerous comparative philological studies, which revealed a kinship among various language groups. There is no distinct Aryan language but rather a family of languages and dialects giving strong evidence of a remote common ancestry. Likewise, there is no Aryan race. In the scientific use of the term, *race* refers to a physical division of mankind, and is, consequently, only an anthropological abstraction. The most obvious, but not the only, difference between so-called races is in pigmentation of the skin. Thus race is a relative rather than an absolute concept, and Aryan uniqueness is a myth. The Aryans who came to India were probably considerably lighter in color than the Dravidians, but they did not constitute a distinct ethnic stock. Rather they were Aryan-speaking members of the Caucasian race.

Just when the Aryans first appeared on the Indian scene is not definitely known. Perhaps two thousand years before Christ their forebears had begun to drift away from the Caspian regions, which may have been their homeland. They appear to have gone west as far as Ireland at about the same time that they went south into India. They must have been a sturdy stock, strong of body, adventurous in spirit, and able not only to conquer but also to rule. In India the Aryans were probably well established by at least 1500 B.C. Their presence soon resulted in the appearance of the earliest of that body of sacred literature which has colored Hindu life and thought from ancient times to the present day.

SACRED LITERATURE*

VEDAS

The earliest works of Indian literature are the *Vedas*. These were transmitted orally from generation to generation in Sanskrit verse. Although India possessed a script by at least the ninth century B.C., it was not until the eighth or ninth century A.D. that the Vedas were reduced to writing. Most of them were composed, however, much earlier, some of them dating back to at least 1500 B.C. There is no indication that their authors, who were perhaps numerous and are certainly unknown, were familiar with the written word. Yet for two reasons those Vedas which survived underwent few changes during the centuries. The Sanskrit in which they were chanted, though changing slowly through the years, was used only by the priestly classes. Consequently it was not subjected to the corrupting influence of common use on the spoken word. Sir William Jones has said of the Sanskrit that it was "more perfect than the Greek, more copious than the Latin, and more exquisitely refined than either." [1]

Also, because of the sacred nature of the Vedic literature, great care was exercised to commit to memory not only the exact word but also the correct pronunciation of each syllable. Training for the priesthood was long and arduous, but as a consequence of rigorous discipline over the bearers of this early Hindu culture, the ancient literature of India has been preserved with unique fidelity.

Of the numerous Vedas which probably once existed four have survived: *Rig-veda, Sama-veda, Yajur-veda,* and *Atharva-veda*. Of these the *Rig-veda*, composed of more than a thousand hymns expressing the awe and devotion of ancient seers in contemplation of the mysteries of existence, is the earliest. (c. 1400-1000 B.C.) In its tone of homage and devotion to the sacred objects of Hindu religion, it has been compared with the *Psalms* of the Christian Bible. The *Sama-veda* and the *Yajur-veda* are liturgical in nature, designed to guide priests in the exercise of their functions. The *Atharva-veda* is probably later in origin than the other Vedas; it reflects popular concern with magic, incantations, and evil spirits, and contains numerous references to the efficacy of plants and potent brews in curing disease.

UPANISHADS

Although certain philosophical sections of the Vedas were known as the *Upanishads,* as time passed a separate body of work, distinctive in character and

---

* We follow common practice in calling the religious books of the East "sacred." The term "holy" is a more precise description of religious literature, since in modern sociological usage the term "sacred" is not the equivalent of "religious." See Howard Becker, *Through Values to Social Interpretation* (Durham, N.C.: Duke University Press, 1950), pp. 43-45 and 248-280.

independent of the Vedic hymns, appeared. The term *Upanishads* usually refers to this collection. The original Vedas were followed by prose works known as the *Brahmanas,* which explain certain legends and sacrificial rituals. The *Upanishads* are the last of the Vedas and for that reason are sometimes called the *Vedanta,* or end of the Vedas. Composed by various philosophers about whom little is known, the earliest of these discourses certainly antedated Buddha. Some writers place the *Upanishads* between 800 and 500 B.C., whereas others extend the period of their origin from 1000 to 300 B.C. Whatever their actual date of origin, they bring to bear on the religion of the Vedas the questioning attitude of philosophy. As Sen points out:

> In the period of the *Rig-veda,* the emphasis was mainly on the performance of sacrifices for the attainment of quite practical ends—long life, progeny, good crops or wealth of cows. In the period of the *Upanishads,* the emphasis shifts to spiritual knowledge. The Vedic gods are not altogether discarded, but they are growing dim and becoming merged in the idea of one all-comprehensive unity.[2]

The sublimity of the *Upanishads,* and their value even to minds not tuned to ancient Hindu mysticism, has often been recognized. "The unaided mind of man never attained," Epiphanius Wilson declared, "in any literature, to a profounder insight into spiritual things." [3] Schopenhauer was of the opinion that "in the whole world there is no study so beneficial and so elevating as that of the Upanishads." [4]

HINDU EPICS

Following the *Upanishads* in order of time, and drawing on them for philosophical content, are two epics, the *Mahabharata* and the *Ramayana*. Similar to the Greek epics in telling a story in which myth and legend blend with a sober record of the religious, social, and philosophical ideas of the time, they surpass the *Iliad* and the *Odyssey* as pictures of national manners but fall short of these famous works in literary quality. On this point Wilson says:

> The Hindoo poet flounders along, amid a maze of prolix description and wearisome simile. Trifles are amplified and repeated, and the whole poem resembles a wild forest abounding in rich tropical vegetation, palms, and flowers, but without paths, roads, or limits. Or rather, we are reminded of one of the highly painted and richly decorated idols of India, with their many heads and many hands; but when we turn to the Greek epic we stand before a statue of pure outline, flawless proportions, and more than human beauty.[5]

The *Mahabharata* (c. 500 B.C.-400 A.D.) is the longest poem in existence, thirty times as long as *Paradise Lost* and seven times as long as the *Iliad* and the *Odyssey* combined. It probably grew to its present proportions of

100,000 verses by accretions extending over many centuries. The theme story was well known by at least the fifth century B.C., but after that time "a hundred poets wrote it, a thousand singers moulded it, until . . . the Brahmans poured their own religious and moral ideas into a work originally Kshatriyan, and gave the poem the gigantic form in which we find it today." [6] The subject of the poem is the struggle for the throne of India between the descendants of two brothers, but the narrative serves only to bind together a vast body of lore and philosophy. One of its gems is the *Bhagavad-Gita,* or "Song of the Lord." Although some may not share Von Humboldt's conviction that this is "the most beautiful, perhaps the only true, philosophical song existing in any known tongue," few will deny that it eloquently expresses many basic principles of Hindu theism.

The *Ramayana* (c. 500 B.C.) is much shorter than the *Mahabharata* and gives evidence of being largely the work of a single author, although there are obvious additions to the original story. The scene is laid in Ayodhya, a mythical city of great beauty and wealth,

> In by-gone ages built and planned
> By sainted Manu's princely hand.

In the narrative, the heroic Rama is banished, as a result of intrigue, from the kingdom to which he is rightful heir. With him into exile goes his lovely wife Sita. By means of tricks, evil spirits cause them to become separated, and much of the story is concerned with the struggle of Rama against demons to regain his faithful wife. Eventually they are reunited and Rama becomes king. But soon false rumors against Sita make it necessary for the king to choose between his duty to his people and his love for his wife. The sense of duty prevails, and Sita is banished to an asylum. There she bears twin sons to Rama. When they have been reared and recognized by their father, Sita prays that Mother Earth may receive her; and she is seen no more. Despite his loneliness, Rama rules wisely, and Ayodhya enjoys under him, as it had under his father, a golden age.

LAWS OF MANU

One other important source of information about early Indian thought is the code of laws known as the *Laws of Manu* (c. 200 B.C.-200 A.D.). Later in origin—at least in the form in which it has been preserved—than the Vedas and the epics, the *Laws of Manu* (sometimes called *Code of Manu*) is essentially an ethical code. In Vedic mythology, Manu is the father of mankind. Numerous legends are found in Indian literature regarding Manu. In one of these Manu is described as the sole survivor of a great flood which came upon the earth and destroyed all living things save this progenitor of mankind. His prayers for a companion produced a female, Ida, through whom the race of Manu was generated. In another legend he is represented as the son of a god, and generally in the sacred literature he reveals the attributes of divinity. When, therefore, certain wise men approached Manu, who sat with a collected mind, and received from him the laws by which mankind was to be guided, these laws became divine commandments. They cover a wide range of conduct and furnish a guide to behavior in virtually every situation with which the individual is likely to meet. They contain not only ethical and religious precepts but also civil and criminal laws and regulations governing numerous details of daily life.

These sources, the *Vedas, Upanishads, Mahabharata* and *Ramayana,* and *Laws of Manu,* furnish the basis for our analysis of the social thought of ancient India. There are numerous other important works that might have been included, such as the *Brahmanas* (commentaries on the Vedas), certain religious poems known as the *Puranas,* and various other codes of law, but the Indian literature is so vast that some selection must be made. The ideas expressed in these famous works represent the finest products of early Hindu thought.

RELIGION

In one of the *Upanishads* the questions that lie at the heart of all real religious experience burst forth from a group of young devotees gathered to ponder eternal things:

> Is Brahma the cause? Whence are we born?
> Whereby do we live, and whither do we go? O
> ye who know Brahma, tell us at whose command
> we abide, whether in pain or in pleasure? [7]

It is one of the distinguishing characteristics of Brahmanism that it affords a variety of answers to these questions. In its elasticity is found its appeal both to keen minds seeking intellectual as well as spiritual satisfactions and to the untutored asking no more of religion than the solace of rites and ceremonies.

Furthermore, Hinduism has been the source of religions other than Brahmanism. Most important among these is Buddhism, founded in India by Gautama in the sixth century B.C., partly as a protest against the caste system and the formality and ritual aspects of Brahmanism. Although Buddhism is today one of the great religions of the world, it has all but disappeared from India, after centuries of struggle with Brahmanism. Before this powerful religious force departed the Indian scene, however, it incorporated into its body of doctrine some of the most important concepts of Brahmanism and in turn made a lasting impression on Brahmanic beliefs and practices.

JAINISM

Contemporary with Gautama lived Mahavira, the last great prophet if not the founder of *Jainism,* another religion growing out of Hinduism but distinct from Brahmanism in many of its doctrines. Although Jainism has never approached Buddhism in popular appeal, and like Buddhism has for many centuries steadily declined in followers among the Hindus, it has been widely accepted among some of the leaders of Hindu society and has exercised, as a consequence, an important influence in India. The Hindu doctrine on noninjury to living beings finds in Jainism an extreme expression.

SIKHISM

Another religion derived in part from Hinduism, but not until the fifteenth century A.D., should also be noted. *Sikhism* developed out of the impact of Mohammedanism on Hinduism, and appears in modern times to be losing some of its distinctive characteristics and to be drawing close to orthodox Hinduism. Though numerically weak in membership in comparison with Brahmanism, Sikhism claims today many more followers in India than either Buddhism or Jainism.

This very brief discussion of Hindu religions other than Brahmanism suggests the variety in the religious literature of Indian origin. We are concerned here, however, with what may properly be called Brahmanism, or orthodox Hinduism, as that religion is revealed in the writings generally accepted as the main body of sacred ancient Hindu literature.

GOD

Brahmanism presents an all but infinite variety of deities, ranging from household and local gods to universal gods. In the earliest Vedic literature the forces of nature were worshiped as distinct gods. In some Upanishadic thought, Brahma is entirely devoid of anthropomorphic characteristics, but in some of the later *Upanishads,* and more especially in the famous philosophical song the *Bhagavad-Gita* of the *Mahabharata,* personalized conceptions of Brahma appear. In later times, orthodox Hinduism made certain qualities of the Supreme Spirit the objects of worship, and especially around the gods Vishnu and Shiva distinct church groups were formed. But despite the various polytheistic patterns which Brahmanism has at times assumed, the dominant note is the unity of ultimate reality. God finds expression in devious ways, but the *Rig-Veda* declares: "That which exists is one; sages call it variously."

All natural forces such as fire and wind, all natural objects such as mountains and rivers, all living things—these all reveal God. The life-force flows through countless living forms, both animal and plant; this force is God.

Furthermore, living matter is not the only manifestation of divine energy; the storm clouds, rain, fire, the earth, the rivers which flow without rest— these too are formed of God's essence. But God is not contained in the universe. The universe is not merely the essence of God; it is also the creation of God.

> As the threads from the spider, the tree from the seed, the fire from the coal, the stream from the fountain, the waves from the sea, so is the world produced out of Brahma. . . . He is the creator.[8]

Pantheism may be defined as the doctrine that God and Nature are one. In that sense it is not entirely accurate to describe Brahmanism as pantheistic. In the ancient Hindu literature, God is portrayed as formless spirit as well as formed entity. There is no real distinction between the *Creator* and the *Created,* but even the infinitude of creations does not contain wholly God's Self. God is both immanent in the universe and transcends the universe. God is more than existence. In his poem *Brahma,* Emerson has beautifully expressed this conception of limitless spiritual reality:

> If the red slayer thinks he slays,
> Or if the slain thinks he is slain,
> They know not well the subtle ways
> I keep, and pass, and turn again.
>
> Far or forgot to me is near;
> Shadow and sunlight are the same;
> The vanished gods to me appear;
> And one to me are shame and fame.
>
> They reckon ill who leave me out;
> When me they fly I am the wings;
> I am the doubter and the doubt,
> And I the hymn the Brahman sings.

KARMA

In the doctrine of *karma,* a concept which may be defined, though not wholly accurately, as "retributive justice," Brahmanism achieves a moral view of the universe. Of this basic doctrine, Durant says:

> Life can be understood . . . only on the assumption that each existence is bearing the penalty or enjoying the fruits of vice or virtue in some antecedent life. No deed small or great, good or bad, can be without effect; everything will out. This is the Law of *Karma*—the Law of the Deed —the law of causality in the spiritual world; and it is the highest and most terrible law of all. If a man does justice and kindness without sin his reward cannot come in one mortal span; it is stretched over other lives in which, if his virtue persists, he will be reborn into loftier place and larger

good fortune; but if he lives evilly he will be reborn an Outcaste, or a weasel, or a dog. . . . But *Karma* is not Fate; Fate implies the helplessness of man to determine his own lot; Karma makes him (taking all his lives as a whole) the creator of his own destiny.[9]

The soul is immortal and passes from one reincarnation to another. "This body indeed withers and dies when the living Self has left it; the living Self dies not." [10] No man escapes the consequences of his conduct in earlier births. In the Ramayana, Dasa-ratha speaks out of the sad memories of his own past when he says:

> Deeds we do in life, Kausalya, be they bitter, be they sweet,
> Bring their fruit and retribution, rich reward or suffering meet.
> Heedless child is he, Kausalya, in his fate who doth not scan
> Retribution of his *karma,* sequence of a mighty plan.[11]

Karma is to the moral universe what uniformity is to the physical universe. As matter cannot be destroyed but can only be transformed, so is it with morality. Sin has somewhere its wages, and virtue somewhere its rewards.

Although the soul never dies, it may lose its individuality. The final goal of man, the ultimate end, is the extinction of self, the cessation of reincarnations, the complete absorption of the human self into God.

> As the flowing rivers disappear in the sea, losing their name and their form, thus a wise man, freed from name and form, goes to the divine Person, who is greater than the great.[12]

ETHICS

In any single existence an individual is chained to his past. Consequently he is not free. He is what he is as a result of earlier conduct.

> Those whose conduct has been good, will quickly attain some good birth, the birth of a Brahman, or a Kshatriya, or a Vaisya. But those whose conduct has been evil, will quickly attain an evil birth, the birth of a dog, or a hog, or a Kandala.[13]

Every man, therefore, is born into that station of life for which he has prepared himself. But he cannot climb to salvation upon a ladder constructed of his own good deeds. No merit attaches to virtue prompted by fear of punishment or hope of reward. In a footnote to his translation of one of the *Upanishads,* Müller says:

> . . . the Upanishad wishes to teach the uselessness by themselves of all good works, whether we call them sacrificial, legal, or moral, and yet,

at the same time, to recognize, if not the necessity, at least the harmlessness of good works, provided they are performed without any selfish motives, without any desire of reward, but simply as a preparation for higher knowledge, as a means, in fact, of subduing all passions, and producing that serenity of mind without which man is incapable of receiving the highest knowledge.[14]

This idea of conduct explains and justifies Hindu charity. The gentleness, patience, and perseverance which have characterized so many of India's illustrious leaders are the ideals set forth in the ancient writings.

> Single is each being born: single it dies; single it enjoys the reward of its virtue; single it suffers the punishment of its sin. Leaving the dead body on the ground like a log of wood, or a clod of earth, the relatives depart with averted faces; but the spiritual merit follows the soul.[15]

Manu prescribes kindness and compassion toward all living creatures. The *Mahabharata* states thus the Golden Rule:

> This is the sum of duty: do naught to others which if done to thee, would cause thee pain.[16]

Virtue is extolled not because it pays but because it is right. Salvation is not the reward of virtue: it is the attainment of virtue.

Hindu ethical doctrines are directed primarily toward self-discipline. Serenity, detachment, and self-control are necessary to the attainment of the supreme felicity of liberation. Social welfare is by no means neglected in the sacred literature, but social ends are subordinated to individual ends or, rather, they are best served when they are not specifically sought as such. The good society is that society in which every man does his duty—that is, when he conforms to the demands of his own nature to do what is required of him in any specific situation. For example, when, in the *Bhagavad-Gita,* the warrior Arjuna, sick at heart at the sight of bloodshed, let fall his bow and arrows, Krishna (God) thus sternly spoke:

> Do thy part!
> Be mindful of thy name, and tremble not!
> Nought better can betide a martial soul
> Than lawful war; happy the warrior
> To whom comes joy of battle—comes, as now,
> Glorious and fair, unsought; opening for him
> A gateway unto Heav'n.[17]

HUMAN NATURE

What is man? The answer found in the ancient Hindu literature to this eternal question well illustrates the profound and timeless quality of early Indian thought. Man is body, whence springs desire; he is mind, and thus able to choose; he is spirit, seeking union with God. These three qualities of the self are reflected in the dark passions that result from ignorance, the activity that produces the mixed pains and satisfactions of daily life, and the goodness to which knowledge leads.

> The craving after sensual pleasures is declared to be the mark of Darkness, the pursuit of wealth the mark of Activity, the desire to gain spiritual merit the mark of Goodness.[18]

Man is a creature of mixed desires, capable of giving full expression to those impulses that he shares with beasts. His elemental self is

> Bound by the fetters of the fruits of good and evil, like a cripple; without freedom, like a man in prison; beset by many fears, like one standing before Yama (the judge of the dead); intoxicated by the wine of illusion, like one intoxicated by wine; rushing about, like one possessed by an evil spirit; bitten by the world, like one bitten by a great serpent; darkened by passion, like the night; illusory, like magic; false, like a dream; pithless, like the inside of the Kadali; changing its dress in a moment, like an actor; fair in appearance, like a painted wall.[19]

But man is able to obtain release from the constricting bonds of the elemental self. Through knowledge of the Vedas and through the performance of his duties, he may realize a higher self, and come at last to union with God. When the self is merged with the universal whole, then comes the joyous escape from individuality. Some of the Upanishads declare the possibility of achieving this goal in life, but in the earlier Vedas the escape from the fetters of egoism is offered only in death.

The attainment of real selfhood is not the reward of virtuous conduct but rather the result of purging the self of all impurities. Only the pure can know God. Knowing God involves the whole self, not merely the intellect. Mind cannot grasp, nor words express, the eternal verities. The intellect is not the only avenue to understanding; faith is a condition of all knowledge. Through divine insight one is prepared for understanding; only then can one lay hold, with heart as well as mind, upon Truth. "When one believes, then one perceives. One who does not believe, does not perceive. Only he who believes, perceives." [20] In such words as these the ancient Hindu mystics declared that knowledge is of the whole self and not of the mind alone, that the heart discloses what never can be told.

Although perfect knowledge is for all men the final goal, the way is hard and the masses have far to go. Men struggle with themselves and with their fellows, and in their frailties need to be governed. Manu assumes that the king will be an absolute monarch, a Kshatriya charged with the responsibility of maintaining order at home and leading his people to victory in wars, able to inspire fear and obedience.

> ... As the weeder plucks up the weeds and preserves the corn, even so let the king protect his kingdom and destroy his opponents. ... Of him who is ready to strike the whole world stands in awe.[21]

CASTE

Social classes are found in most human societies; caste as described in the sacred writings of the ancient Indians, however, is peculiar to Hinduism. The relations of Negroes and whites in the United States have some of the characteristics of caste relationships, but Negroes and whites in the United States do not constitute castes in the Hindu meaning of the term. The word *caste* is sometimes used to describe a scheme of social organization in which status is wholly ascribed: one is born into a station in life, and there is no escape from that station into another. At the other pole is the open-class system, in which status is wholly achieved: one comes by effort and demonstrated ability to the appropriate social level. The caste system means lack of any opportunity whatsoever to climb above one's station in life, whereas the open-class system means complete freedom of opportunity. Obviously both are polar types, representing highly abstract extremes in patterns of social mobility. The Hindu caste system does not fit neatly into this typological scheme. Caste, to the Hindu, is not an abstract conception; it is the most important factor in the concrete experiences of his daily life.

Caste is peculiarly a product of the Hindu mind. It is elaborately described and supported in the ancient sacred literature. It has provided, in the political turmoil created by numerous conquests of India, a stable base for social order. The light-skinned Aryans and the dark-skinned Sudras found in their mutual acceptance of the principles of the caste system a means of adjustment to each other. Because of caste, a degree of amity among classes widely separated in prestige and power has prevailed. The United States affords a good example of the social consequences of an opposing ideal: whereas caste in India has encouraged the acceptance by every individual of the station of life into which he was born, the American dream has fired the individual with the ambition to rise above his station. The racial dilemma in the United States results from the inevitable clash between the deeply rooted American ideal of equality and the discrimination which denies Negroes the opportunity to obtain what are declared to be the rights of all men. For that reason the term *caste* is misleading when applied to the American situation; the dilemma in the United States results not only from racial discrimination but also from the rejection of the caste principle. In a sense, the caste system has solved the race problem in India.

It developed under a complex of conditions—racial, religious, geographical, economic—found nowhere else in the world.

The origin of the caste system has been the subject of much debate. It has been maintained that the system was a cunning contrivance of the Aryan priests to insure their control over Hindu society. But it is difficult to reconcile the lofty idealism of the Brahmans with lust for material power. The prestige and authority of the Brahmans have been preserved for at least a score of centuries without any of the usual accompaniments of power, such as a formal organization, a hierarchy of officials, a police force, and the control of capital. Originally certain favored groups may have sought deliberately to preserve their social distance from the masses by religious rites and doctrines. Their success in gaining acceptance of the caste system among the lower classes may have prevented the development of a strong political power. Thus no opposing group came into existence to question their claims to authority. Nevertheless, the arbitrary pretensions of priests are not adequate to explain the origin and development of the caste system in India.

In his analysis of the origin of the system, Radhakrishnan, the Indian philosopher, attaches considerable importance to the racial conditions resulting from the Aryan invasion of India:

> The system of caste is in reality neither Aryan nor Dravidian, but was introduced to meet the needs of the time when the different racial types had to live together in amity. It was then the salvation of the country. . . . The only way of conserving the culture of a race which ran the great risk of being absorbed by the superstitions of the large numbers of native inhabitants, was to pin down rigidly by iron bonds the existing differences of culture and race. . . . Only caste made it possible for a number of races to live together side by side without fighting each other. India solved peaceably the interracial problem which other people did by a decree of death. When European races conquered others, they took care to efface their human dignity and annihilate their self-respect. Caste enabled the Vedic Indian to preserve the integrity and independence of the conquering as well as the conquered races and promote mutual confidence and harmony.[22]

BRAHMANS

In the ancient Hindu literature, four castes are named: Brahman, Kshatriya, Vaisya, and Sudra.* In addition there are occasional references to the Out-

---

* No attempt is made in this survey of the Hindu caste system to describe any actual conditions ever found in India. It is possible that the four castes were never demarcated to the extent indicated in the ancient literature. Likewise, it is a well-known fact that there have existed in India hundreds, perhaps thousands, of castes and subcastes. But the caste system found in India today, however different it may be from that described in these pages, is rooted in the teachings of the sacred literature of the Hindu people.

castes—*i.e.,* to those who do not belong to any one of the four recognized castes. At the top of the hierarchy are the Brahmans. From the earliest times to the present, this caste has been closely identified with the sacerdotal classes, although originally any Aryan might become a priest and throughout Indian history many Brahmans have not been priests. Manu declares that for a Brahman the most commendable occupation is that of teaching the Vedas.[23] To prepare for that service he must leave his home at an early age and live for many years the hard life of an anchorite under his *Guru,* or teacher. When he has learned the Vedas and proved himself capable of meeting with fortitude all the vicissitudes of life, he is required to marry and rear a family. During this period of his life he participates actively in worldly affairs and assumes fully the responsibilities of father and citizen. Only when these parental and civic obligations have been met does he withdraw from worldly concerns. Then must he subsist by means of alms, live austerely, and seek by ascetic penance to achieve union with God. If he is able wholly to free himself from the senses of the body, he may break forever the chain of reincarnations and come at last to the imperishable bliss of pure spirit. As he stands at the threshold of salvation,

> Alone let him constantly meditate in solitude on that which is salutary for his soul; for he who meditates in solitude attains supreme bliss.[24]

The Brahman's position is at the apex of the hierarchy of all created things. His very birth is the eternal incarnation of sacred law.

> Of created beings the most excellent are said to be those which are animated; of the animated, those which subsist by intelligence; of the intelligent, mankind; and of men, the Brahmans.[25]

Kings pay him homage. Courts recognize his superior status and give him preferential treatment. To him belongs in reality all property, so that in asking alms he only claims a small part of his own goods. Whether he is ignorant or learned, he is entitled to the respect accorded a great divinity. Whatever his occupation, he must be honored.

> On account of his pre-eminence, on account of the superiority of his origin, on account of his observances of particular restrictive rules, and on account of his particular sanctification, the Brahman is the lord of all castes.[26]

KSHATRIYA

Next to the Brahmans in rank are the *Kshatriyas,* who constitute the caste of warriors, nobles, and kings. In the *Ramayana* King Dasa-ratha is a Kshatriya, as are the other rulers mentioned in the Vedic literature. The rise of the Brahmans to a position of superiority may have occurred only after a long struggle between the nobles and the priests, but the sacred writings have come down to us through the priests and leave no grounds for doubting the relative rank of the two castes.

> To Kshatriya he [Manu] commanded to protect the people, to bestow gifts, to offer sacrifices, to study the *Veda,* and to abstain from attaching himself to sensual pleasures.[27]

The Kshatriya stands in relation to the Brahman as son to father; his inferior status should never be questioned.

> When the Kshatriyas become in any way overbearing towards the Brahmans, the Brahmans themselves shall duly restrain them; for the Kshatriyas sprang from the Brahmans.[28]

In court proceedings the word of the Brahman is his bond, but the Kshatriya must be admonished to speak the truth. A crime committed against a Brahman is a much more serious matter than one committed against a Kshatriya. But neither caste can prosper without the other; their unequal status in no way bemeans the Kshatriya in order to exalt the Brahman. Subordination of one caste to another no more means humiliation for the lower caste than does the respect and obedience which a son accords his father mean that the son sacrifices his own dignity through recognition of his father's superior status. Hence in ancient India it did not appear strange that kings should belong to the second class of men rather than to the highest class.

VAISYA

Lowest among the twice-born castes are the *Vaisyas,* the artisans, agriculturists, merchants, and clerical workers.

> Vaisya [Manu commanded] to tend cattle, to bestow gifts, to offer sacrifices, to study the Veda, to trade, to lend money, and to cultivate land.[29]

A Vaisya must be at all times attentive to business affairs. He needs to be familiar with the quality and value of the articles sought in trade. The good and bad qualities of fields and the manner of sowing seed are matters to which he should give attention. He is commanded to be diligent and industrious.

> Let him exert himself to the utmost in order to increase his property in a righteous manner, and let him zealously give food to all created beings.[30]

Since the Vaisya is occupied with the mundane affairs of daily life, with production and trade, not so much can be expected from him in regard to self-discipline and initiative as from the two higher castes. Where economic motivation is not sufficient to spur him on, he must be compelled by the king to perform his assigned work. The threat of penalties by the courts may be necessary to keep him from misconduct; especially effective as a means of social control is the prospect that the penalty for his misdeeds will be the loss of his goods. He can be expected to act from self-interest rather than from devotion to the common good. In short, it seems reasonable to assume that the Vaisya caste was intended to include virtually all Aryans except the two small select groups of priests and nobles. The Vaisyas, therefore, constituted the bulk of the Aryan population of India and exhibited in their conduct the frailties of self-centered human beings. The ascetic ideals set forth in the ancient Hindu literature for those drawing near to salvation were not expected to appeal to the masses of people still occupied with material things. Realistically, the Hindu mind grasped the distinction between the motivation of the Brahman, standing at the threshold of Eternal Bliss, and that of the Vaisya, who was nearer the beginning than the end of his journey.

SUDRA

At the bottom of the caste system are the *Sudras,* the hewers of wood and the drawers of water.

> The Brahman, the Kshatriya, and the Vaisya castes are the twice-born ones, but the fourth, the Sudra, has one birth only; there is no fifth caste.[31]

One occupation only is prescribed for the Sudra, that of serving meekly the other three castes. He may not receive the sacraments, or hear, learn, recite, or teach the Vedas. Only when he is unable to find service with the twice-born is he permitted to maintain himself by handicrafts. If he attempts arrogantly to teach a Brahman his duty, "the king shall cause hot oil to be poured into his mouth and into his ears." He may not acquire wealth, and such goods as may come into his hands are the property of his master. He is, in fact, a slave.

> Though emancipated by his master, [he] is not released from servitude; since that is innate in him, who can set him free from it?[32]

The explanation for the extremely low status of the Sudra is perhaps found in the history of the Aryan invasion of India. It will be recalled that the Aryans found the land possessed by the dark-skinned Dravidians, whom they placed under subjection. As conquerors they held themselves far removed from the "once-born" natives. Most of these natives came to have a recognized status in Hindu society as menials serving the needs of their masters. These were the Sudras.

OUTCASTES

Another group is occasionally mentioned in the sacred literature—the *Outcastes*. These were individuals who had no caste identification. Some of the natives in India, when the Aryans came, fled into remote and inaccessible regions and held themselves for a time aloof from the invaders. Eventually they were bound to make some contact with the Aryan culture, and it may have been then that they were first recognized as not belonging to the existing social system. Sen has described them as follows:

> They hung on the outskirts of the mixed Aryan and Sudra villages and timidly offered for barter their humble wicker baskets, their clay pottery or their jungle produce. They even began to perform the most degraded of the village services, such as scavenging, skinning the dead cattle or burning the bodies of the dead, but they remained entirely beyond the pale of Aryan society.[33]

It is not surprising, therefore, that they should appear in the early Hindu literature as mortal sinners whose fall from grace had removed them from human society and made their very presence an anathema.

> He who associates with an outcast, himself becomes an outcast after a year, not by sacrificing for him, teaching him, or forming a matrimonial alliance with him, but by using the same carriage or seat, or by eating with him.[34]

Where Outcastes were involved, therefore, the use of common buildings, the contacts normal in common economic activities, and the communications required in social life were prohibited by stern injunctions. A caste Hindu who happened to touch an Outcaste could be made pure only by bathing. In no other society has social distance comparable to that separating the Outcaste from caste Hindus been found. The dedication of the saintly Gandhi to the task of bridging the gulf vastly improved the condition of the Outcastes, but even today their lot is hard.

CASTE AND PERSONALITY

Caste is not merely a matter of position in the social order; it is also a revelation of personality. The Brahman, for example, not only holds a high position in society but also possesses those personal qualities identified with his status. These qualities are inherited, just as is his position on the social scale. In the *Bhagavad-Gita,* Krishna tells the battle-weary Kshatriyan prince:

> The work of Brahmans, Kshatriyas, Vaisyas,
> And Sudras, O thou Slayer of thy Foes!
> Is fixed by reason of the Qualities
> Planted in each:
>
> A Brahman's virtues, Prince!
> Born of his nature, are serenity,
> Self-mastery, religion, purity,
> Patience, uprightness, learning, and to know
> The truth of things which be. A Kshatriya's pride,
> Born of his nature, lives in valour, fire,

Constancy, skilfulness, spirit in fight,
And open-handedness and noble mien,
As of a lord of men. A Vaisya's task,
Born with his nature, is to till the ground,
Tend cattle, venture trade. A Sudra's state,
Suiting his nature, is to minister.

Whoso performeth—diligent, content—
The work allotted him, whate'er it be,
Lays hold of perfectness! [35]

FAMILY LIFE

Many contradictions appear in the ideas about marriage, family life, and the status of women expressed in the early Hindu literature. Some of these reflect changes that took place over the centuries during which this literature was taking the form in which it has come down to us. For example, the *Rig-Veda* and the epics portray a family relationship of striking gentleness and deep affections. The position of women was one of dignity and honor. The practice of suttee* was rare, and the faithful wife was not then, as she became later, under any religious obligation to end her life on the death of her husband. In the earliest Vedic period there was no prohibition against the remarriage of widows, even though this injunction does appear in the later sacred literature. Some preference was expressed by parents for boys rather than girls, but the latter were treated generally with tenderness, were given educational advantages appropriate to their needs, and were provided with husbands as soon as they reached maturity. With the passing years the tone of the sacred literature reflects a marked decline in the status of wives and daughters. Manu severely admonishes women to obey their husbands. He warns men, though not with the ardor of St. Paul, to beware of the seductive charms of women. The representation of woman as the temptress appears, although, it must be noted, with nothing approaching the vituperation which women received from Tertullian, the Latin theologian.

MARRIAGE

Marriage was to the ancient Hindus not merely a custom: it was a religious obligation. Failure to marry was regarded as a mortal sin. Even the Brahman priest was required, after he had received his initial religious training, to marry and beget children.

---

* The word actually means a chaste and virtuous woman but came to apply to a widow's self-annihilation on the funeral pyre of her deceased husband. The practice became common after the Moslem conquest and was not legally prohibited until 1829.

> To be mothers were women created, and to be fathers men; religious rites, therefore, are ordained in the Veda to be performed by the husband together with the wife.[36]

Perhaps a partial explanation of the failure of Buddhism in India to compete successfully with Brahmanism is found in the fact that Buddhism exalted celibacy over marriage and thus struck at one of the most deeply rooted attitudes in Hindu society.

Marriage might be entered into by mutual consent, but since girls were expected to marry as soon as they were physically mature, and were often plighted even earlier, marriage was normally a family matter. The acceptance of a bride price by the father was forbidden, since that would make the father a seller of his offspring; nevertheless, numerous references to wife purchase suggest that the custom existed and was under some conditions condoned. Manu prescribed different marriage rites for the various castes. In the Brahman rite, the father presents his daughter, after decking her with costly garments, to a man of her choosing. At the other extreme is the base and sinful Pisakas rite, in which a man by stealth seduces a girl who is sleeping, intoxicated, or disordered in intellect.[37]

In the *Ramayana* the marriage of Rama and Sita is described by Dutt as follows:

> Janak placed his beauteous daughter facing Dasa-ratha's son,
> Spake with father's fond emotion and the holy rite was done:
>
> *This is Sita child of Janak, dearer unto him than life,*
> *Henceforth sharer of thy virtue, be she, prince, thy faithful wife.*
>
> *Of thy weal and woe partaker, be she thine in every land,*
> *Cherish her in joy and sorrow, clasp her hand within thy hand.*
>
> *As the shadow to the substance, to her lord is faithful wife,*
> *And my Sita best of women follows thee in death or life.*
>
> Tears bedew his ancient bosom, gods and men his wishes share,
> And he sprinkles holy water on the blest and wedded pair.[38]

Since a man might have several wives, it was important to specify the conditions under which polygyny was permissible. The first wife of a man of the upper three castes must be from the same caste as his own. A limited number of wives of lower castes might then be taken by those who desired them. For example, a Brahman might have, in addition to his Brahman wife, one Kshatriya, one Vaisya, and one Sudra wife. The status of children born of mixed castes was defined as follows:

> In all castes those children only which are begotten in the direct order on wedded wives, equal in caste and married as virgins, are to be considered as belonging to the same caste as their fathers.[39]

There is no reference in the early sacred literature to a woman's having more than one husband. In view of the fact that polyandry, the sharing of a common wife by several husbands, is sometimes practiced even today by members of the hill tribes of the Himalayas, it is interesting to note that the ancient literature does not sanction this practice. A single legend in the *Mahabharata* does record, to be sure, the marriage of five brothers to one woman, but this instance is unique in the history and literature of the Aryan Hindus. Polygamy meant to the ancient Hindus, as to the modern, a plurality of wives.

STATUS OF WOMEN

In Rabindranath Tagore's play *Chitra,* the remark is made:

> When a woman is merely a woman—when she winds herself round and round men's hearts with her smiles and sobs and services and caressing endearments—then she is happy. Of what use to her are learning and great achievements? [40]

This attitude toward women found in the work of a contemporary Indian writer is not exactly that found in the early Hindu literature. A wife is there portrayed, it is true, as the shadow of her husband. She is incapable of independent action. Even as was the case with Milton's Eve in *Paradise Lost,* she may not safely be left to her own devices. She must be kept occupied in useful household activities. She is required to be faithful to the religious duties of her sex, but she may not become an ascetic. Mothers are required to prepare their daughters for marriage, both by setting them a good example and by giving them proper instructions, but the education of boys is a man's responsibility. At no time in her life does the female stand alone.

> Her father protects her in childhood, her husband protects her in youth and her sons protect her in old age; a woman is never fit for independence. [41]

Even though her husband be destitute of virtue, even though he seek pleasure elsewhere, yet must the good wife remain faithful to him and adore him. A widower may, after he has given the sacred fires to his deceased wife, marry again and rekindle the fires. As for the widow, Manu says:

> In the sacred texts which refer to marriage the appointment of widows is nowhere mentioned, nor is the re-marriage of widows prescribed in the rules concerning marriage. [42]

We have seen that in the earliest Vedic period women as well as men might remarry; nevertheless, it was the harsh dictum of Manu which was to prevail in India. If the widow has a son, she becomes subject to him on the death of her husband; without a male to whom she can cling, her existence is joyless and apart from the creative activity of her fellow human beings; she is socially dead.

It would be a mistake, however, to give an interpretation to these views which neglects the context in which they are set. Such attitudes in our society would indeed reflect a callous indifference to the human aspirations of women, and a lack of respect for their dignity and self-respect. But in the early Hindu literature there is little trace of mere masculine arrogance. There is a difference between social subordination and personal degradation. In the ancient Hindu literature, women were considered to be different from men in mind and character as well as in body. They were not accorded the privileges of men, but they were not mocked. The derisive tone of Tagore's lines about women, quoted above, is foreign to the sacred writings of the Hindus. On the contrary, the belief in the equality of men and women finds expression in many forms. The story of woman's creation affords a good example:

> In the beginning this was Self alone, in the shape of a person. . . . But he felt no delight. . . . He wished for a second. He was so large as man and wife together. He then made this his Self to fall in two and thence arose husband and wife. . . . [He] said: "We two are thus each of us like half a shell." [43]

As their bodies differ, so do men and women perform different functions in life; but the two sexes complement one another. Each alone is but half a person, male no less than female. Happiness in the home depends upon both.

> In that family where the husband is pleased with his wife and the wife with her husband, happiness will assuredly be lasting . . . if the wife is radiant with beauty, the whole house is bright.[44]

Romantic love as we know it is new; the deep and abiding satisfactions of mutual respect and confidence between men and women are as old as history. Far deeper than the pleasantries and sentimental gestures which are often accepted in our time as evidence of affection was the devotion of Sita, who recognized that the measure of love is sacrifice. When her husband was banished into exile, her fate was determined.

> For the faithful woman follows where her wedded lord may lead,
> In the banishment of Rama, Sita's exile is decreed.
> Sire nor son nor loving brother rules the wedded woman's state,
> With her lord she falls or rises, with her consort courts
>   her fate.[45]

It is not easy to reconcile the frequent exhortations to honor women with other statements, which seem to degrade womankind. But those able wholly to enter into the spirit of ancient Hindu thought perhaps may find that in a society where all life, even the lowly worm, was sacred, woman, who bears life, attained her highest adoration.

INDIAN AND CHINESE SOCIAL THOUGHT

The gulf between the early social thought of India and that of China is wide. Chinese thought is practical and down to earth, whereas Hindu thought soars on wings of speculation far beyond earthly existence. Confucian humanism puts so much emphasis on man's relation to his fellows, and so little on his relation to anything supernatural, that some persons insist that Confucianism is not a religion but rather a philosophy. On the other hand, the religious overtones are so pronounced and the spiritual motive so pervading in Indian thought that ancient Hindu philosophy would be meager indeed without the religious concepts that give it form—Brahma, Karma, Nirvana, transmigration, and others.

Confucian thought expresses the optimism of people who have found the way and need only to hold to it. Hindu thought is pervaded by a dark pessimism relieved only by the hope that life's seemingly endless turnings will lead finally to Nirvana. Perhaps the Hindus asked questions that cannot be answered and reached for something that lies beyond human grasp. The mysticism in Indian thought, with its ceaseless searching for ways of drawing near to the Absolute (as, for example, in the various systems of Yoga), stands in sharp contrast to the preoccupation with traditional propriety in Confucian thought.

There is another important difference between Indian and Chinese thought: Confucius spoke to every man; the ancient Hindu sages addressed themselves to a select few. The teaching of Confucius was simple enough to be apprehended, each in his own fashion, by the learned and untutored alike. There is nothing esoteric about the Middle Way. On the contrary, the wise men of ancient India probed into the enigmas of life and the mysteries of the universe and talked about matters which the masses could not understand. In fact, the very language in which they expressed their ideas was kept a close-guarded secret, and only those who had undergone severe preliminary discipline were permitted to sit at the feet of a guru.

> "Give it to none that is not tranquil," says one Upanishad, for it was feared that an indiscriminate broadcasting of the truth that all is one might lead to its distortion and bring it into discredit. . . . The necessary pre-condition for starting on the course of Vedantic life is detachment. In other words, no one that has not undergone a course of ethical training calculated to kill all egoistic impulses is qualified for a serious study of the Upanishads.[46]

Despite these differences, and many others, the Confucian and the ancient Hindu writings are alike in their focus on man rather than on nature. They fall far short as regards the scientific interest in the material universe so clearly manifested by certain of the ancient Greek philosophers. The failure of materialism to take root in the East, as it did in the West, is not easily explained. The fact remains, nevertheless, that even today the treasure of the Orient consists not only, or mainly, of material things for the human body but of myths and symbols which nourish the human mind and sometimes fortify the human spirit. The physical and biological sciences, which have had such influence upon the Western world, are bound to transform radically many ideas which have molded thought in the East for centuries. At the same time, in that worldwide exchange of ideas which seems inevitable in the years to come, people of the West may gain, in the wisdom of the East, a profit not less generous than that which they once received in spices, jewels, and other precious goods.

6 · THE HEBREWS OF THE OLD TESTAMENT

By the waters of Babylon there we sat and wept, when we remembered Zion.

PSALM 137

The Jordan River rises near Mount Hermon in what is now the republic of Lebanon and, after flowing through the Sea of Galilee, pursues a winding and precipitous course down to a lifeless sea. The Dead Sea is thirteen hundred feet below the level of the Mediterranean and, since it has no outlet, its water is brine.

The narrow valley along the Jordan, ranging from three to fourteen miles in width, is drained rather than irrigated by the river. Crossing over the Jordan —in the dry season, at least—has never been more than a simple matter of fording a shallow stream. The Jordan, unlike the Nile, the Yellow, the Indus, and the rivers of Babylonia, is not one of the large rivers of the world, but it has an enduring claim to the affections of men: the plateau through which it flows, and the country along it between the desert and the sea form what has long been called the "Holy Land."

The Old Testament calls this land Canaan, but the Greeks named it Palestine after the Philistines, and the Greek name has been commonly accepted. Ancient Palestine, or Canaan, which was about the size of the state of Vermont, lay at the western end of a fertile crescent which borders with a fringe of green the northwest portion of the great Arabian Desert.

The vast expanse of Arabia to the east contains not only burning sand but also land suitable for human habitation, as its prodigious fecundity through the ages bears evidence; but the sun beats fiercely upon it, and water is scarce. In comparison with the Arabian peninsula, Palestine was indeed a "good land, a land of brooks of water, of fountains and springs, flowing forth in valleys and hills, a land of wheat and barley, of vines and fig trees and pomegranates, a land of olive trees and honey" (Deut. 8:7-8). It had precious water not only as a "gift from Heaven" in the form of rain but also in springs and wells, and even in the rainless season there was dew to cool the earth.

We cannot know how much natural conditions have changed in this region since Old Testament times, although it is obvious that—until recently, at least—the country has suffered greatly at man's hands. Hills on which shepherds once grazed their herds are now bare and eroded, and in places where the pharaohs once found timbers for their palaces only bushes and stunted trees now grow. The Dead Sea loses by evaporation half an inch of water daily, and the Jordan valley receives only about four inches of rainfall a year! From the fact that the Hebrews regarded a gift of water as a token of generous hospitality, a refreshment beyond compare, and alluded to water so frequently in figurative speech, we may assume that even in ancient times water was none too plentiful in Palestine. Life could not have been easy, but the industrious and the frugal were probably able to live comfortably. A shepherd like David found good grazing for his herds, and Boaz was rich from his fields. The Plain of Sharon was perhaps far from being as fertile as the Plain of Shinar, as the Hebrews called Babylonia, but it produced crops that aroused envy. In short, though the Promised Land was no place for the carefree and indolent, it offered much to a people from whom much was required.

Except for the plains along the coast, ancient Palestine was a land of hills and mountains. The rugged terrain served to shut communities off from one another and thus encouraged a tribal type of organization rather than a unified kingdom. It provided also haunts for robber bands and lairs for dangerous animals. We read of bears, wolves, leopards, and lions. They raided the herds, and a child might be snatched away or a grown man attacked by beasts. The dread of lions is shown by more than a hundred references in the Old Testament to this animal. As if marauding beasts were not enough, the people were frequently plagued with locusts and hail, and occasionally an earthquake destroyed a city and made the people tremble.

Shut in by the natural barriers of mountains, deserts, and the sea, Palestine might have afforded a refuge where a weary people could have lived in undisturbed peace, had it not been situated on the only land route between the continents of Asia and Africa. As it was, an endless stream of caravans and armies passed by, and since the Israelites who lived there had not the means to defend themselves against strong forces, their property was seized, their homes were destroyed, and their people were often slaughtered. The clash of arms was a familiar sound in Palestine; the fear of violent death or servitude was ever present. From the north came at various times, to pillage and slay and to use the pasture lands of the Israelites for battlefields, the Babylonians, Hittites, Aramaeans, Hyksos, Assyrians, and Persians; from the south the armies of the pharaohs came up, and out of the desert came the Midianites, Kenites, Amalekites, and Ishmaelites. Even the Greeks and the Romans trampled on little Palestine, and of wars and rumors of wars there was no end.

The exact date at which the Israelites first settled in the land of Canaan is not known, nor is it known how certain of them came to be in Egypt. This much, however, is clear: the Israelites who came up out of Egypt and crossed the desert about 1450 B.C.* believed that they were returning home. Furthermore, they firmly declared that their right to do so was established by a solemn covenant into which they had entered with their God.

In the beginning the Israelites had to fight for possession of the land which they regarded as rightfully theirs. Finally, on the plains of Esdraelon, they made good their claim to the "Land of Israel" by defeating the Canaanites, but they had then to struggle wth their kinsmen, the Moabites, Ammonites, and Edomites, over its distribution. Nor were they able to avoid civil strife.

After the death of Saul, the Hebrew nation was divided into the kingdoms of Israel and Judah. Israel, the northern kingdom, was the larger of the two and contained better land, but Judah was more compact and easier to defend. Israel was made up of ten tribes, which were often at war with one another; Judah was closely bound to the house of David and was better united. At the time of the division, Jerusalem lay on the border between the two kingdoms, and this may have led to its becoming the capital of all Palestine. David's efforts to make Jerusalem a religious center were successful, and it soon became a sacred city, a symbol to the Hebrews of their unity under their God. It has continued to be, in the thoughts of countless millions, Christians, Moslems, and Jews alike, a holy place.

This brief sketch of ancient Palestine and of the conditions which confronted the Hebrews as they endeavored to make a home there raises the question "Who were these Hebrews?"

THE OLD TESTAMENT HEBREWS

We may begin by noting that the ancient Hebrews were a Semitic people. The original home of this great family of nations is not known. In the table of nations (Gen. 10) the Semites are described as the descendants of Noah's son Shem, but how they came to settle in Arabia and in the countries adjoining is not

---

* Some scholars put this date about two centuries later, but there is considerable traditional and archaeological support for the earlier date. For the early history of the Hebrews, see Abram L. Sachar, *A History of the Jews* (New York: Alfred A. Knopf, 1930).

clear. Some scholars believe that originally they came up out of Africa, others that they came from the north or east, and still others that they were born of the desert. In any event, at the time written history begins, they were spread over the Near East. Certain similarities can be observed in the languages of ancient Babylonia, Syria, Palestine, Arabia, and northern Africa. Comparative studies of these languages suggest the likelihood of waves of migration at various times. These migrations not only dispersed the Semites but also resulted in considerable mixture of blood. Physically the Semites belong now, as they appear to have belonged in Old Testament times, to the family of Caucasians. Certain physical traits are commonly found among the Semites today, especially in Arabia, where there has probably been less mixture than elsewhere, but these traits are neither exclusive to the Semites nor uniform among them. In fact, most scholars of the present day regard the Semites as a language, rather than a biological, group. Furthermore, they believe that many of the psychological and social characteristics attributed to the Semites are probably the results of social experience rather than manifestations of physical peculiarities.

In saying that the Hebrews of the Old Testament were Semites, and thus kinsmen of the Babylonians, Assyrians, Amorites, Canaanites, Arameans, Moabites, and many other peoples of the ancient Near East, as they undoubtedly were, we do not mean that they were not a distinct and unique group. As Caucasians, they were probably distantly related to the Indo-Europeans, and, for that matter, to all mankind. All men are brothers, even in a physical sense, if we go back far enough; but all men are not alike, and they have not been for a very long time. Certainly the Hebrews of the Old Testament were different from other groups and were so recognized. Hammurabi is called a Semite, not a Hebrew. We are told that the Hebrews, not merely some Semites, were enslaved in Egypt and carried away by Nebuchadnezzar into captivity in Babylonia. In the cruel wars of the time many people other than the Hebrews were captured and enslaved, but the descendants of Abraham were a marked people. The judges and prophets of the Old Testament were called not Semites but Hebrews. Palestine became the Holy Land not through the presence of the Semitic Canaanites but through the presence of the Hebrews. Judaism is a Hebraic, not a Semitic, faith. Mary, the mother of Jesus of Nazareth, was descended from the Hebrew David (Rom. 1:3; 2 Tim. 2:8; Acts 2:30).

Thus we see that the Hebrews of the Old Testament were clearly distinguished from their kinsmen. They were known in ancient times, as now, not only as Hebrews but also as Israelites and as Jews. In places in the Old Testament only the members of the ten tribes of Israel were called Israelites, but the Old Testament commonly refers to all the Hebrews by this term; before the formation of the kingdom of Judah, the Hebrew tribes were collectively called by the name of Israel. It was not until the exile that the Hebrews or Israelites were called Jews in the Old Testament. The word *Jew* was probably derived from the house of

David, Judah, but this name is used in the New Testament to designate all the members of the Hebrew nation, whether collected in a common state or scattered throughout the world (Mt. 2:2). Although the three terms have today slightly different connotations, they refer to the same people. The Old Testament reveals a preference for *Israelite* or *Hebrew,* whereas *Jew* is more commonly used in the modern world; but the terms are virtually interchangeable.

Many details about the history and customs of the Hebrews before their entry into Palestine are not known. We do not know, for example, the name of the pharaoh "who knew not Joseph," or why the Hebrews in Egypt were persecuted. Nor do we know what occupations other than herding they had pursued, what matriarchal practices, if any, they had followed, and what blood vengeance their system of justice had required. We do not know why, with their strong sense of social solidarity, they should have waited so long to organize a political state. Hundreds of books about the ancient Hebrews have attempted to answer these questions, but there is little agreement among them on many important points. If, however, much about the early Hebrews is obscure, this, at least, is clear: in the eloquent and beautiful language of the Old Testament their thoughts and emotions stand revealed.

THE OLD TESTAMENT

The Old Testament is the most important, though not the only, source of historical information about the ancient Hebrews. References to them are found in the literature of contemporary Egyptians and Babylonians, as well as in the writings of Greeks and Romans of a later period. Archaeological explorations in the Holy Land and in the adjoining countries, especially in Egypt, Babylonia, and Assyria, have led to discoveries of incalculable value. A history of the ancient Hebrews cannot afford to neglect these sources, but we are concerned here with thoughts rather than events. Of early writings other than the Old Testament which reveal Hebrew social ideas, the most important are the New Testament, Apocrypha, and Pseudepigrapha. The New Testament covers historically a span of about seventy years, beginning shortly before the birth of Christ and extending to about the time of Paul's death in A.D. 61. Since the historical period covered by the Old Testament ends about 400 B.C., there is a lapse of about four centuries between the two parts of the Bible. Moreover, the New Testament is the story of Jesus and His teachings. For these reasons it seems advisable not to include the New Testament in our survey.

The *Apocrypha* is the name given usually to the sixteen books or parts of books (fourteen if III and IV Maccabees are omitted) that have survived from the period extending from about 250 B.C., to the early Christian centuries. Some of these books have been accepted as canonical by the Roman Catholic

Church since the Council of Trent in 1546, but they are not included in the Hebrew canon. Protestant churches have generally adopted the view taken by the Westminster Confession of 1643, which held that "the books, commonly called Apocrypha, not being of divine inspiration, are no part of the canon of Scripture, and therefore are of no authority in the Church of God, or to be any otherwise approved or made use of than other human writings." The Apocrypha contains much social thought, especially the book commonly called Ecclesiasticus, but the comparatively late origin and the nature of some of the books make the inclusion of the Apocrypha in this survey inadvisable. The same may be said of the Pseudepigrapha, a number of books written apparently under assumed names but associated with Moses, Enoch, Isaiah, Solomon, and other Old Testament characters. The Old Testament refers (Num. 21:14; 1 Sam. 10:25; 2 Sam. 1:18) to various other books that have not survived.

The most important later works of the Hebrews are the *Mishna* and the *Talmud*. These books establish the basic doctrines of Judaism and reveal much about earlier conditions prevailing among the Hebrews, but they took form many centuries after Old Testament times. They may be omitted from our survey, therefore, for the same reasons that led to our not including the New Testament and other sources of information about the ancient Hebrews.

The manner of life and the ideas of the Hebrews undoubtedly changed as centuries passed, and lapses of time may explain some apparent contradictions in their social thought. It is generally believed that the writing of the Old Testament itself covered a period of about a thousand years, extending roughly from 1200 to 200 B.C. On the whole, however, there is remarkable unity and coherence in ancient Hebrew thought, and especially is this true of the social ideas revealed in the Old Testament.

The first complete English translation of the Old Testament appeared in manuscript in the year 1382, under the direction of John Wycliffe. From the Hebrew in which the book was originally written, except for a few portions in Aramaic, a Greek version, the *Septuagint,* written between the third and second centuries B.C., and a Latin version, the *Vulgate,* completed by Jerome under commission of the Pope in A.D. 385, had long provided theologians with a text of the Old Testament. Wycliffe and his associates were striving, against considerable opposition, to offer a readable version of the Bible to any person able to read the English language. Their translation was based on the Vulgate, which had been the source of translations into the vernacular of various parts of the Bible since as early as the seventh century. Numerous English translations of the Scriptures, in whole or in part, followed the Wycliffe Bible, and the fears of the established Church that the text might easily become corrupted proved to have been justified. Variations in accuracy and in style among the various versions invited controversy and confusion.

In order to obtain a translation "aunswerable to the truth of the Originall,"

King James I of Great Britain (1603-1625) assembled a group of the most eminent scholars in the land (forty-seven names appear in the list) for the purpose of issuing a new and authorized translation. They proceeded with the utmost care and with great diligence to translate, "out of the original tongues and with the former translations diligently compared and revised," the book now known as the King James Bible. It appeared in 1611, and although minor corrections have been made in succeeding editions, and spelling and punctuation have been modernized, it remains for many English-speaking people *the* Bible, although various other English translations and versions are now available. In an essay on its literary qualities John Livingston Lowes calls it "the noblest monument of English prose," and says:

> Of its unique significance in the field of English letters there can be no doubt. Its phraseology has become part and parcel of our common tongue—bone of its bone and flesh of its flesh. Its rhythms and cadences, its turns of speech, its familiar imagery, its very words, are woven into the texture of our literature, prose and poetry alike. For the Biblical style is characterized not merely by homely vigour and pithiness of phrase, but also by a singular nobility of diction and by a rhythmic quality which is, I think, unrivaled in its beauty.[1]

The Revised Standard Version of 1952, from which the quotations in this chapter are taken, replaces words in the earlier Bible which have lost the meaning there intended and contains other minor changes designed to enhance the clarity and yet preserve the beauty of the King James Bible.

We shall be concerned in this book with the Old Testament as it portrays human beings capable of suffering and of remorse. But they were inspired as well as troubled, and above the tumult of their struggles sound continually these comforting words, which give to the Old Testament a sublime unity and which reverberate and echo and never die:

> Comfort, comfort my people,
>   says your God.
> Speak tenderly to Jerusalem,
>   and cry to her
> that her warfare is ended,
>   that her iniquity is pardoned,
> that she has received from the Lord's hand
>   double for all her sins.
>
> A voice cries:
> "In the wilderness prepare the way of the Lord,
>   make straight in the desert a highway for our God.
> Every valley shall be lifted up,
>   and every mountain and hill be made low;

> the uneven ground shall become level,
>   and the rough places a plain.
> And the glory of the Lord shall be revealed,
>   and all flesh shall see it together,
>   for the mouth of the Lord has spoken."
>
> (Is. 40:1-5)

HUMAN NATURE

The men and women of the Old Testament are human beings of flesh and bone, possessed of all the weaknesses to which the flesh is heir, weighted down with the burdens of their sins, in bondage to their passions, uncertain of their fate, and often in despair that they will live to see a better day; yet daring still to hope, and rising on the wings of faith to ecstasy and exaltation. None of them is perfect, and some of them are rude and wicked. Elijah slew the prophets of Baal (1 Kings 18:40) as gladly as Ruth followed after Naomi (Ruth 1:16-17), and Cain killed his brother Abel without remorse (Gen. 4:8-9). Most of them have both good and evil qualities. David, "the sweet singer of Israel," was at times beside himself with passion and committed a crime in order to avoid a scandal. Samson, the man of strength, could not avoid playing boyish pranks, as his cruel acts were probably then regarded, and was a dupe in the hands of the wily Delilah. Far from being pale saints, the people of the Old Testament are moved by pride and wrath as well as by humility and compassion. Under chastisement, they confess their faults, but when they are rescued, as Augustine says, "their tears are quickly dried." The faith of Job is matched by the doubt of the writer of the book of Ecclesiastes; the quietude of the twenty-third Psalm, by the passionate outbursts of Jeremiah. Hope and despair, courage and fear, exaltation and despondency, charity and hate, wisdom and foolishness, godly strength and satanic weakness—these are the human traits that the men and women of the Old Testament reveal.

The Book of Genesis begins with that sublime scene of Creation in which God made man in His own image, to have dominion over all the earth and over every living thing that moves upon the earth. Then God looked upon His handiwork and saw that it was good. Man was made a little lower than the angels and crowned with glory and honor (Ps. 8:5-8). He alone of all the creatures was made upright (Eccles. 7:29), and in the beginning he was blameless in his ways (Ezek. 28:15). In the sixth chapter of that first book, however, we read:

> The Lord saw that the wickedness of man was great in the earth, and that every imagination of the thoughts of his heart was only evil continually. And the Lord was sorry that he had made man on the earth, and it grieved him to his heart. (Gen. 6:5-6)

Thus, quickly, does the Old Testament get to one of its central themes; man's disobedience and the fruits of his sin. This theme builds up until it becomes in the words of the prophets the thunder of impending doom. Isaiah thus sternly speaks:

> For your hands are defiled with blood
>   and your fingers with iniquity;
> your lips have spoken lies,
>   your tongue mutters wickedness.
> No one enters suit justly,
>   no one goes to law honestly;
> they rely on empty pleas, they speak lies,
>   they conceive mischief and bring forth
>   iniquity.
>
> (Is. 59:3-4)

Jeremiah challenges anyone to run through the streets of Jerusalem and find one man "who does justice and seeks truth" (Jer. 5:1) and warns that the Lord will pass judgment on the people for their sins (Jer. 19:15). In an oft-quoted passage, Micah raises a question which is its own answer:

> . . . and what does the Lord require of you but to do justice, and to love kindness, and to walk humbly with your God? (Mic. 6:8)

In sad and prophetic words, Micah reveals his sickness of heart at man's failure to meet these requirements:

> The godly man has perished from the earth,
>   and there is none upright among men;
> they all lie in wait for blood,
>   and each hunts his brother with a net.
> Their hands are upon what is evil, to do
>   it diligently;
>   the prince and the judge ask for a bribe,
> and the great man utters the evil desire
>   of his soul;
>   thus they weave it together.
>
> (Mic. 7:2-3)

Yet David, adulterer though he was, was capable of compassion and was a devoted and a forgiving father. He cried out in anguish when news was brought to him that his treacherous and rebellious son was dead, saying:

> O my son Absalom, my son, my son Absalom! would I had died instead of you, O Absalom, my son, my son! (2 Sam. 18:33)

Humanity cannot be wicked beyond redemption where there is place in the human heart for devotion like that of Ruth:

> Entreat me not to leave you or to return from following you; for where you go I will go, and where you lodge I will lodge; your people shall be my people, and your God my God; where you die I will die, and there will I be buried: May the Lord do so to me and more also if even death parts me from you. (Ruth 1:16-17)

Amos, who talked about the emptiness of ritual without morality, was a good man; if his words seem trite today, it must be remembered that they were not so in his own day and that his message is still vital. Isaiah, who burned in indignation at injustice and poured out a flame of protest against avarice and greed, was a good man; he took the hard way when he spoke out against love of luxury and absorption in material things. Micah, man of the people, protested in outbursts of passionate eloquence against exploitation; and Jeremiah, man of sorrow, kept faith with God and man, even in moments of dark despair. Job, a righteous man who suffered and never learned why, repented of his doubts and in peace praised the name of the Lord. In the lives of these people, and many others, it can be seen that man, though fallen, may yet rise in his best moments to a position only a little lower than that of angels.

These ancient Hebrews were not concerned with the innate drives which motivate human action. They observed that man is torn by conflicts, but they made no attempt to reduce these inner struggles to instincts or to inquire whether they are inborn or acquired. It is enough to realize, they believed, that man does not possess within himself the means of achieving the good life. He is not self-sufficient, he must be restrained by law, and he must be guided by faith. He must look beyond himself for strength which he does not possess. Only when he acknowledges his weakness and turns with humble and contrite heart to God can he know the peace of which the Psalmist spoke.

> The Lord is my shepherd, I shall not want;
>   he makes me lie down in green pastures.
> He leads me beside still waters;
>   he restores my soul.
> He leads me in paths of righteousness
>   for his name's sake.
>
> Even though I walk through the valley
>   of the shadow of death,
> I fear no evil;
> for thou art with me;
>   thy rod and thy staff,
>   they comfort me.

> Thou preparest a table before me
>   in the presence of my enemies;
> thou anointest my head with oil,
>   my cup overflows.
> Surely goodness and mercy shall follow me
>   all the days of my life;
> and I shall dwell in the house of the Lord
>   forever.
>
> (Ps. 23)

GOVERNMENT

Among the ancient Hebrews kinship ties were strong, and intense loyalty to the tribe made difficult the organization of a united kingdom. In primitive times the clan, even more than the family, was the social unit; as tribal organization developed, the bond of blood remained strong. The kinship terms often used in describing the Hebrews are not mere figures of speech; the concepts "father," "children," and "family" actually describe the pattern of personal relationships within the Hebrew nation. Israel never became an absolute monarchy in any sense other than as a family may be thought of as an absolute patriarchy. Only for a short time under Solomon did all the Hebrews ever yield entirely to the authority of any one monarch except in the presence of great danger. The delegation which pleaded with Jephthah to become their head was seeking a leader for the fight against the Ammonites (Judg. 11:6). Saul, the first king of all Israel, was selected by Samuel, perhaps reluctantly, to lead the Israelites in the war against the Ammonites and the Philistines, by whom they were sorely pressed. Fear of the enemy, not love of monarchy, forced the people to beg Samuel to give them a king. Samuel lived to grieve that the throne had been given to Saul (1 Sam. 15:35), and the king over Israel wore indeed an uneasy crown. The reproach of women came to him in a song:

> Saul has slain his thousands,
> And David his ten thousands.
>
> (1 Sam. 18:7)

The king's business was with the enemy, not with his own people, and only the man who succeeded in war deserved to be king.

David's succession to the throne upon the death of Saul was decided by the elders of the tribes of Israel, who made a covenant with him and anointed him king (II Sam. 5:3). A people at war needed a common leader; allegiance to him was dictated by necessity. The right to rebel was recognized, and David, who exercised that right against Saul, lived to see his own son raise an army of the people against him. Carried to an extreme, this right can lead to anarchy, and anarchy was in fact invited in David's reign by a certain "base fellow" who blew a trumpet and said:

> We have no portion in David,
> and we have no inheritance in the son of Jesse;
> every man to his tents, O Israel!
> (2 Sam. 20:1)

Every man can be a law unto himself, the Hebrews believed, only in a peaceful society in which there is neither threat from the outside nor cause for dissension within; David's Israel was faced with an ever-present danger from abroad and with seething discontent within the nation. Consequently, united action was necessary for survival.

Under Solomon the people were discontented but helpless. The enemy was kept at bay, and Solomon stripped the tribal elders of some of their powers by dividing the land into administrative districts which cut across tribal boundaries (1 Kings 4:7). Nevertheless, the storm clouds were gathering during his reign, and with his death came the deluge: Israel broke apart, never since to be wholly reunited as an independent state, even though in recent years a new Israel of hope and promise has risen on portions of the ancient homeland of the Israelites.

THE HEBREW NATION

The failure of the Hebrews to develop an effective and enduring political organization raises the question "What was their conception of a nation?" The Hebrews believed that Israel came into existence as a result of a covenant between the Lord and His chosen people. They wanted, of course, to have peace and security, but they believed that these could be obtained only through obedience to the Lord and through fidelity to the sacred covenant. It is remarkable how seldom the Hebrews blamed someone else for their troubles: they blamed themselves. We hear little about the wicked and perfidious enemy; always it is Israel that hath sinned (Josh. 7:11), and suffering is a just penalty (Num. 32:13). Jeremiah never doubted that the destruction of Jerusalem by the northern armies and the captivity of Judah in Babylonia were penalties imposed upon the Hebrews for forsaking the Lord (Jer. 32:28-36). Amos went even further and declared that the Lord would not have punished Israel so severely had not the Israelites been His chosen people (Amos 3:2); from those to whom much is given, much is expected, and, as the Book of Hebrews puts it, the Lord disciplines him whom he loves. (Heb. 12:6.)

SOCIAL ORDER

What is the basis of social order in a nation so conceived? This question invites attention to the extent to which Hebrew thought is directed toward the group rather than toward the individual. The Lord is the God not of this or that Israelite but of all the *families* of Israel, and they are His *people* (Jer. 31:1). This emphasis on the group is evident throughout the Old Testament. The Lord's anger was kindled against Israel and He made *them w*ander in the wilderness (Deut. 1:37-40); the *house* of Israel rebelled and was punished (Ezek. 20:13); the *children* of Israel were taken by the Lord for a *people* (Ex. 6:7). The suffering of Job is a rare exception to the rule that the Israelites share a common lot of good fortune or adversity. The offender brings shame and punishment not on himself alone but on his people.

Personal responsibility is clearly recognized (Deut. 24:16; Num. 16:22; Is. 55:7; Ps. 32:5); but far more frequently the people are collectively held responsible for whatever happens among them. Surely all are not equally guilty in that city which the Lord will destroy with "all that is therein" (Amos 6:8); nor do all equally deserve the blessings which reward the labors of the righteous. Nevertheless, when Amos pleads that justice may "roll down like waters" (Amos 5:24), he is speaking not for the faithful alone but for all Israel. As a family suffers through the misdeeds of any one of its members, and the honors attained by one individual bring recognition to the entire family, so was it with Israel.

The problem of social order involves something more, however, than personal conformity to social norms: it involves the nature of the norms themselves. The Old Testament Hebrews believed that a nation devoted to Baal will not have order, regardless of the pious faithfulness of the people to their god, because there is not in devotion to tribe or race the principle of order. Good and kindly men cannot with the best of intentions and with the utmost diligence in the promotion of their plans create an orderly society, because there is not such power in unaided human reason. The individual conscience can be trusted only when it accords with God's will; human reason is useful only when it implements God's plan. Divine law is the only answer to the problem of social order.

> Behold, I set before you this day a blessing and a curse: the blessing, if you obey the commandments of the Lord your God, which I command you this day, and the curse, if you do not obey the commandments of the Lord your God, but turn aside from the way which I command you this day, to go after other gods, which you have not known.
>
> (Deut. 11:26-28)

THE IDEAL GOVERNMENT

Where God reigns supreme, the Hebrews believed, obedience to His laws requires no effort, no choice, no act of will; in doing what seems natural, one does what is right. The ideal government is a pure theocracy; monarchy is a compromise. "I have given you kings in my anger," said the Lord (Hosea

13:11). So surely must law have been a compromise, given to people who though chosen were not saved, and knew not of themselves the way.

The attainment of social order through perfect obedience to Divine Law was recognized as an ideal. The Hebrews believed that perfect government could come only with the Perfect Prince. The Messianic hope was not, however, a pious wish but a conviction that the time would surely come when the nations of the earth would "beat their swords into plowshares, and their spears into pruning hooks" (Is. 2:4). In the glowing words of Isaiah, the promise is made:

> For every boot of the tramping warrior in
>   battle tumult
> and every garment rolled in blood
> will be burned as fuel for the fire.
> For to us a child is born, to us a son is given;
>   and the government will be upon his shoulder,
>   and his name will be called
> "Wonderful Counselor, Mighty God,
>   Everlasting Father, Prince of Peace."
> Of the increase of his government and of peace
>   there will be no end,
>   upon the throne of David, and over his
>   kingdom,
>   to establish it, and to uphold it
>   with justice and with righteousness
>   from this time forth and for evermore.
>   (Is. 9:5-7)

When that far-off Divine Event takes place, mankind will no longer require the coercion and restraint of law. Meanwhile, in a state of affairs among men which is far from ideal, laws are necessary. They prevent chaos and promote peace. It is not enough to tell man to walk humbly and to show mercy: he must be told *how* to do these things. Thus the elaborate detail in which the laws are declared. They provide norms for conduct here and now by means of which men may achieve a measure of peace while they await redemption. Although we shall be concerned, in the remaining portions of this chapter, only with these laws, it is important to bear in mind that the Old Testament contains the promise of perfect peace in an ideal kingdom as well as the means to a measure of peace among men unredeemed.

OLD TESTAMENT LAW

The first five books of the Old Testament—Genesis, Exodus, Leviticus, Numbers, and Deuteronomy—were known to the Israelites as the "Law of Moses."

The Jews have retained the Hebrew word *Torah* for these books, but the Greek term *Pentateuch* (the five books) is also in common use. They contain the Ten Commandments, both in Exodus (20:2-17) and in Deuteronomy (5:6-21), as well as many other laws regulating the relations of men with one another and with God. The Mosaic Code is not, however, the whole "law" of the Old Testament, in the sense of its statement of a system of morality and of faith; the entire book is both a guide to right relations among men and a manual of devotion to God. We must turn, therefore, to the "prophets" and the "writings" as well as to the "law" for the commandments regarding social relations.

CRIMINAL JUSTICE

The law of retaliation (*lex talionis*) is clearly stated: life for life, eye for eye, tooth for tooth, hand for hand, foot for foot, burn for burn, wound for wound, stripe for stripe (Ex. 21:23-25; Lev. 24:17-20; Deut. 19:21; 25:11; Job 2:4). There are, however, some objections to assuming that this was the basic principle of Mosaic criminal justice. In the first place, although the Old Testament affords many historical details about social customs, it does not appear that the Hebrews practiced this system of justice in Old Testament times except in the case of the death penalty. Moreover, the code leaves to the judges the determination of the penalty in some matters (Ex. 21:22) and provides for the payment of fines and also for exile in lieu of physical punishment (Ex. 21:18; 21:30). Blood vengeance, the duty of the clan to take revenge in blood for harm done to a member, was a principle well established among the Semitic people of the ancient world, although it is not specifically mentioned in the famous code of Hammurabi. It is conceivable, therefore, that the Mosaic statement of *lex talionis* was designed to point out, in terms which the people could understand, the seriousness of criminal acts and the obligation to make appropriate compensations for injuries done to others.

Intent was not always regarded as a necessary element in a criminal act, but it was an important one (Num. 35:6-24; Deut. 19:5-6). The group as a whole might be penalized, as we have seen, for acts committed by certain individuals in which other members of the group did not participate, yet individual responsibility was recognized:

> The fathers shall not be put to death for the children, nor shall the children be put to death for the fathers; every man shall be put to death for his own sin.
>
> (Deut. 24:16)

When Moses was in doubt as to how the system of justice of the Israelites applied to a stranger, the Lord spoke to him saying:

> You shall have one law, for the sojourner and for the native.
>
> (Lev. 24:22)

It should be noted, however, that exceptions were made to this general rule—as, for example, the prohibition against taking interest on a loan from an Israelite, although interest could be charged all others. The importance of obedience to rightful authority is brought out in many places. In the following passage the penalty for disobedience is dramatically stated:

> If a man has a stubborn and rebellious son, who will not obey the voice of his father or the voice of his mother, and, though they chastise him, will not give heed to them, then his father and his mother shall take hold of him and bring him out to the elders of his city at the gate of the place where he lives, and they shall say to the elders of his city, 'This our son is stubborn and rebellious, he will not obey our voice; he is a glutton and a drunkard.' Then all the men of the city shall stone him to death with stones.
> (Deut. 21:18-21)

ADMINISTRATION OF JUSTICE

A person convicted of crime might be sent into exile, but confinement does not seem to have been one of the penalties imposed by the judges. A man might pay for crime with his goods, but sometimes he paid with his person, as references to lashing show (Deut. 25:1-3). It is interesting to observe that excessive beating was prohibited as degrading and that once a man had been lashed for a crime, he was considered to have paid the full penalty for that crime and was restored to good fellowship in his society.

The judges were upheld in the exercise of their judicial functions by the sternest injunctions to the people to obey their rulings:

> ... according to the instructions which they give you, and according to the decision which they pronounce to you, you shall do; you shall not turn aside from the verdict which they declare to you, either to the right hand or to the left. The man who acts presumptuously, by not obeying the priest who stands to minister there before the Lord your God, or the judge, that man shall die; so you shall purge the evil from Israel.
> (Deut. 17:11-12)

On the other hand, the judges were expected to maintain a high standard of behavior in the exercise of their official duties. The judge is told:

> You shall do no injustice in judgment; you shall not be partial to the poor or defer to the great, but in righteousness shall you judge your neighbor.
> (Lev. 19:15)

> You shall not pervert justice; you shall not show partiality; and you shall not take a bribe, for a bribe blinds the eyes of the wise and subverts the cause of the righteous.
> (Deut. 16:19)

The Hebrews of the Old Testament · 141

Among the rules of trial was the provision that the testimony of at least two witnesses was required to substantiate the charges against the accused. (Deut. 19:15). The accused was further protected against slander and false testimony by the seriousness with which these acts were regarded. Capital punishment was authorized for about thirty crimes. (In Blackstone's England no fewer than one hundred and sixty offenses were punishable by death.)

ECONOMY

When the Israelites were not at war, they appear to have been engaged primarily in herding and in agriculture. When one considers the favorable location of Palestine for a nation of traders at a time when there was a considerable exchange of goods between Egypt and the people of northwest Asia and the Mediterranean area, the failure of the Israelites to establish great markets and to act as commercial agents for their rich neighbors is not easy to understand. The fact remains, nevertheless, that the Phoenicians, the Babylonians, and even the Egyptians appear to have been far more interested in trade than were the Israelites, although the latter seem to have had no objections to such activities (Ezek. 27:33; Ps. 107:23; Prov. 31:14).

The Northern Kingdom was much more commercial than the Southern, and the tribe of Dan even engaged in maritime expeditions. Solomon had copper mines, and there are references to the extraction of other ores. For the most part, however, the Israelites remained close to the soil.

OCCUPATIONS

Furthermore, the Israelites appear to have had little aptitude for the industrial arts. There were carpenters and masons among them (Is. 28:17; 2 Kings 21:13), but when Solomon required skilled labor for his grand buildings, he sought aid from the king of Tyre, saying, "you know that there is no one among us who knows how to cut timber like the Sidonians" (1 Kings 5:6). The Philistines attempted to monopolize the arts of working metals, but there were among the Hebrews various kinds of smiths, some manufacturing weapons and tools (1 Sam. 13:19; 2 Kings 24:14), and others apparently working with bronze, silver, and gold (1 Kings 10:21). Whether few or many (2 Kings 24:14-16), however, they seem never to have gained distinction through display of artistic skills. There were enough potters to form organizations (1 Chron. 4:23), and since carts, wagons, harness, and similar equipment were in daily use, it is probable that there was some specialization in the manufacture of such things. Barbers (Ezek. 5:1), perfumers (Neh. 3:8), jewelers (Jer. 17:1), apothecaries (Jer. 8:22), midwives (Exod. 1:15), and physicians (2 Chron. 16:12) are also mentioned, as well as a number of other occupational groups. Not very much is said about the healing arts, but this statement from Ben Sira may well have expressed the popular feeling about physicians among the earlier as well as among the later Hebrews:

> He that sinneth before his Maker—let him fall into the hands of the physician. (Ecclesiasticus 38:15)

Interest in sculpture and in painting was definitely discouraged because of the association of these arts in the minds of the Israelites with idols. Only in music and in literature did the Israelites display unusual artistic ability. Their religious insight requires no comment, but their failure to exhibit in other fields the genius that Jews have later displayed should be noted.

Despite their religious devotion to the good earth, the Israelites must have found the growing of crops no easy task. With rude plows drawn usually by oxen, although asses were also used in cultivation (Is. 30:24), they prepared the ground. Wheat and barley were the major crops, but lentils, millet, spelt, and beans were also grown. Reaping was done with a sickle, which sometimes left something for the gleaners. Threshing was accomplished with a flail or with stones or iron teeth fastened to a sledge, which was pulled around over the strewn harvest, or sometimes cattle were driven around on it to separate the grain. Olives were extensively produced for their oil, but their cultivation seems to have required less attention than did the vineyards. The labor and risks involved in the culture of grapes, urgently needed for wine, is indicated in a song in which Isaiah describes his neighbor's vineyard:

> He digged it and cleared it of stones,
> and planted it with choice vines;
> he built a watchtower in the midst of it,
> and hewed out a wine vat in it;
> and he looked for it to yield grapes,
> but it yielded wild grapes.
>
> (Is. 5:2)

Isaiah points a moral from this experience, but the episode reveals as well some of the problems encountered in the culture of the vine. From a tower the keeper could overlook the vineyard and protect it from man and beast, but even then the vines might yield inferior fruit.

Likewise, herding was dangerous and tedious, an occupation suitable only for men. The use of dogs to help control the herd and to give warning of the approach of marauders did not appear until a comparatively late period and was probably not common at any time, since the Israelites expressed little fondness for dogs (Is. 56:10; Job 30); more frequently mentioned are watchtowers, from which the shepherd could keep his grazing herd under close surveillance. It is no idyllic picture of a carefree shepherd's life which Jacob gives in his complaint to Laban:

> These twenty years I have been with you; your ewes and your she-goats have not miscarried, and I have not eaten the rams of your flocks. That which was torn by wild beasts I did not bring to you; I bore the loss of it myself; of my hand you required it, whether stolen by day or stolen by night. Thus I was; by day the heat consumed me, and the cold by night, and my sleep fled from my eyes.
>
> (Gen. 31:38-40)

ATTITUDE TOWARD LABOR

Although the Israelites seem to have derived little pleasure from most of the labor in which they engaged, even the rich and mighty among them were willing to share the burdens of useful toil. Saul was seen in the field behind the oxen after he had been anointed king (1 Sam. 11:5), and men of wealth like Boaz (Ruth 2:14), the rich farmer of Shunem (2 Kings 4:18), and Elisha, whose father possessed many oxen, went to the fields with their workers. Nevertheless, although no stigma seems to have been attached to useful labor as such, occupation had some bearing on social status. Vine-dressers and plowmen are referred to as "the poorest of the land" (2 Kings 25:12). Isaiah probably was sensitive to the fondest hopes of the afflicted Israelites when he held before them this prospect:

> Aliens shall stand and feed your flocks, foreigners shall be your plowmen and vine-dressers.
>
> (Is. 61:5)

SLAVERY

The ancient Hebrews probably never held slaves in large numbers, but the Old Testament contains many references to the treatment of slaves. Like wives and children, they were regarded both as property and as members of the family (Ex. 21:7-20). A slave was entitled to rest on the Sabbath (Deut. 5:14); if he escaped, the man into whose hands he fell was required to protect him (Deut. 23:15); if he was injured at his master's hands, he was set free (Ex. 21:26); a master who struck a slave, male or female, with a rod so that death resulted was severely punished (Ex. 21:20); the native slave (but not the foreign-born) could be kept in slavery for only six years, after which he was set free (Ex. 21:2). These and many other laws which regulated the handling of slaves and provided protection for them reveal the comparatively humane treatment that slaves received at the hands of the Hebrews. In fact, female slaves differed very little in status from wives or daughters and their sons shared in the estate of their fathers (Deut. 21:10-15; Ex. 21:9).

PROPERTY

Most property belonged to families or to tribes. The wealthy families were distinguished from the poor by greater holdings of cattle, sheep, goats, camels, grain, oil, wine, and similar goods. The system of land tenure probably underwent some changes in Hebrew history, but in the early period at least the individual landholder seems to have been a tenant of the tribe (Num. 26:52-55). After careful study of the Old Testament, Kennett believes that the Hebrews probably had a system of land tenure, found in various other places in ancient times, under which land was apportioned to individuals by the community for use during a limited period of time. He says:

> The facts mentioned above make it extremely probable that there once existed in ancient Palestine a system of land-tenure similar to that which once prevailed in regions as widely separated as India and Britain. . . . If, then, we may assume that the village communities of ancient Palestine formerly held land in common like the former village communities of Western Europe, we may be pretty sure that such land was *periodically* divided into set portions and allocated to those freemen of the village who possessed the right to cultivate it and enjoy its fruits; and the guess may be hazarded that the re-allotment took effect after the septennial year of fallow.[2]

The ownership of orchards and vineyards raises a question for which there is no satisfactory answer, but it does not seem likely that these could have been periodically redistributed as other cultivated lands may have been.

ATTITUDE TOWARD WEALTH

The possession of some property in common may have influenced the attitude of the Hebrews toward wealth. Certainly they believed that it was good to be rich and to have the material comforts and the security afforded by large herds and abundant harvests (Prov. 10:15). Wealth was recognized as one of the blessings that the Lord bestows upon the faithful and was a proof of standing in His grace (1 Kings 3:13; Prov. 3:10).

> Blessed is the man who fears the Lord,
> Who greatly delights in his commandments!
> His descendants will be mighty in the land;
> The generation of the upright will be blessed.
> Wealth and riches are in his house.
> (Ps. 112:1-3)

> The reward for humility and fear of the Lord
> is riches and honor and life.
> (Prov. 22:4)

Likewise, poverty was regarded as evidence of lack of favor with the Lord:

> Poverty and disgrace come to him who ignores instruction,
> but he who heeds reproof is honored.
>
> (Prov. 13:18)

On the other hand, the Hebrews regarded the desire for possessions with great distrust and sternly warned against the greed through which men become wicked and detestable. The man who takes advantage of a shortage of grain for his own gain is cursed (Prov. 11:26); the house of a man grown rich is said to be full of treachery (Jer. 5:27); we read of the arrogance of the rich (Prov. 18:23) and are told that for the sake of "a bribe from the bosom" justice is perverted (Prov. 17:23). Riches have wings, we are told in the Proverbs (23:5), and Jeremiah (17:11) says that the man who acquires undeserved riches shall in the end lose them. The sum of the matter is contained in this verse from one of the Psalms:

> If riches increase, set not your heart on them.
>
> (Ps. 62:10)

USURY

The prohibition against interest-taking affords a good example of the Hebrew attitude toward the accumulation of wealth. A good harvest is a blessing, but to take advantage of a brother's distress for private gain is wicked.

> You shall not lend upon interest to your brother, interest on money, interest on victuals, interest on anything that is lent for interest.
>
> (Deut. 23:19; Ex. 22:25; Lev. 25:36)

The prohibition applies only to taking interest from a *brother;* it was not considered reprehensible to lend on interest to a stranger (Deut. 23:20). The distinction made between the two situations is not difficult to understand when we recall how strong was the feeling of unity among the Israelites. That feeling is most often found in our own society in a well-integrated family. The members of a good family do not take advantage of one another; a brother has a claim which can in no way be denied and should not be abused.

FAMILY

The family institutions of the ancient Hebrews have had a profound influence for twenty-five centuries on family life among a large portion of the world's people. In the lives of the Israelites, family ideals were intimately bound with religious beliefs, but family behavior was influenced also by personal inclinations and by material conditions. The fact that adultery and concubinage are in evidence in the Old Testament is no proof, therefore, that they were regarded as ideals. Since both ideals and practices are reported, the distinction between the two is sometimes difficult to make; but it is no more reasonable to assume that seven wives are to be regarded as an ideal number because David had seven wives than to assume that adultery is an ideal because David committed adultery, or fratricide an ideal because Cain slew Abel. The distinction between ideals and practices should be kept in mind, therefore, in studying the Hebrew family.

POLYGYNY

There can be no doubt that polygyny occurred among the Israelites and there is much to indicate that the taking of several wives was not regarded as reprehensible. David had seven wedded wives whose names are known (1 Sam. 18:27; 2 Sam. 3:2-5), and Solomon had dozens, perhaps hundreds of wives and concubines (Song of Solomon 6:8; 1 Kings 11:3). That is not, however, to say that polygyny was the usual custom or that it was exalted above monogamy. There are only about thirteen men in the Old Testament who are specifically described as having had two or more wives at the same time, and nine of these were kings. Although polygyny is not censured, neither is it anywhere declared to be an ideal. The term "wife" is used, and not "wives," in referring to marriage and family life, except in the case of those few men known to have several wives. For example,

> Therefore a man leaves his father and his mother and cleaves to his wife, and they become one flesh. (Gen. 2:24)

Other passages clearly presuppose monogamy (Prov. 5:18; 12:22; Ex. 21:4), and there is nothing to indicate that polygyny was common. It may have occurred more frequently in the earlier periods than the later, and it certainly was a practice in which only men of some wealth could indulge: brides were purchased from their fathers. Also, the plurality was always in wives; apparently it was not conceivable that a woman should have more than one wedded husband at the same time.

MARRIAGE

A wife was usually acquired by payment to her father of such a marriage price as might be agreed upon (Gen. 29:20; 31:15; 34:12; Ex. 21:7; 22:16-17). The value of Rachel was reckoned at seven years of service from Jacob to her father Laban (Gen. 29:18), and Saul required of David the slaughter of a hundred Philistines in lieu of a bride price (1 Sam. 18:25). Fifty shekels (about twenty dollars) is a figure named in one place (Deut. 22:29) as a fair price, but Hosea paid less (Hos. 3:2). This payment appears to have been an actual purchase, although not in a strictly commercial sense, and was not a mere ritual. The daughter of a wealthy family might bring to her husband a dowry (Gen. 31:15; I Kings 9:16), and apparently the bride was sometimes provided by her father with a slave for her personal use (Gen. 16:1-2; 24:59; 29:29, 30:3-9), but in Old Testament times this practice was probably limited to the rich. It may be observed that in later periods of Hebrew history the dowry became an important consideration. The bride seems usually to have gone to the home of her husband. It is difficult to reconcile wife purchase with the continued residence of the bride with her own people, although Laban did insist that Jacob had no right to take Leah and Rachel away from him (Gen. 31:43), and Samson's wife did not immediately go away with him when they were married (Judges 14 and 15).

Few details of the marriage ceremony are known, but there are indications that the Israelites observed three practices that are all but universal: a contract (Ezek. 16:8), a public procession, and a sharing of food. At Jacob's marriage all the men of the place were gathered for a feast (Gen. 29:22), and Samson's wedding banquet appears to have been an elaborate affair (Judges 14:10). The Song of Solomon portrays a marriage procession in which the bridegroom, escorted by armed friends, publicly brings the bride to his home (3:7-10).

Marriage was a joyous occasion, in which expressions of parental solicitude are found along with the unashamed declarations of affection by the bride and groom. In His wisdom had not the Lord declared, "It is not good that the man should be alone" (Gen. 2:18)? One of the Proverbs puts the matter succinctly:

> He who finds a wife finds a good thing,
> and obtains favor from the Lord.
> (Prov. 18:22)

CHILDREN

Rachel's poignant cry, "Give me children or I shall die," (Gen. 30:1) sums up the Hebrew wife's conviction about her chief function in life. The mother of children praises the name of Jehovah in her song of joy (Ps. 113:9), and the glad tidings that "A son is born to you" (Jer. 20:15) makes a father glad, because

> . . . sons are a heritage from the Lord,
> the fruit of the womb a reward.
> Like arrows in the hand of a warrior
> are the sons of one's youth.
> Happy is the man who has
> his quiver full of them!
> (Ps. 127)

Kennett is of the opinion that "seven children were commonly regarded as the maximum number that a woman might be expected to bear."[3] On the basis of statements made in a number of passages in the Old Testament (1 Sam. 1:22-24; 2:21; 2:5; Hos. 1:8; Jer. 15:9), he suggests that family size may have been limited by the practice of husband and wife's living apart during the period of about three years during which the infant was suckled.

The training of their children was an important function of parents, and for the sake of discipline a wise use of the rod was recommended. Kennett summarizes his study of the training of children as follows:

> At an early age both boys and girls appear to have taken their part in the various activities connected with their homes, such as gathering fuel, overlooking sheep and cattle, driving them to the watering place, and fetching water.
>
> General education, as we understand the term, was almost non-existent in the days of the Hebrew monarchy, and probably to a much later period. Children, however, received not only moral instruction from their parents, but were also taught historical ballads, such as the song of Deborah, and the poems in which the prophets set forth their teaching. Reading and writing were not, however, universal accomplishments, and the metaphorical statement that the trees of the Assyrian forest would be so few that a child could write down the number of them, is no proof that most children learned to write.[4]

The status of children within the family varied with birth order and with sex. A first-born son had rights of inheritance and authority not possessed by his younger brothers (Deut. 21:17), and boys had rights not possessed by their sisters (Num. 36). Sons were allowed considerable freedom, but daughters were sheltered and carefully protected from criticism (Deut. 22:13-21).

The Hebrew father did not have the arbitrary power of life and death over his children (Deut. 21:18), but that was virtually the only limitation to his authority. He might sell a child into slavery (Exod. 21:7; Neh. 5:2-5), and in one instance a father's permission was required before a son could take service even with the king (I Sam. 16:22). At the age of forty, Esau married boldly with little concern for his parents (Gen. 26:34), but that must have been most unusual in the case of a son and virtually unknown in the case of a daughter. Children were exhorted to honor the aged (Lev. 19:32), and striking or cursing a father or a mother was punishable by death (Ex. 21:15-17).

ENDOGAMY

Marriage between the Israelites and other peoples seems to have occurred at all periods of Hebrew history, although it was, of course, more common at some times than at others. We read in the Book of Judges that

> ... the people of Israel dwelt among the Canaanites, the Hittites, the Amorites, the Perizzites, the Hivites, and the Jebusites: and they took their daughters to themselves for wives, and their own daughters they gave to their sons; and they served their gods.
>
> (Judg. 3:5-6)

There are many examples of mixed marriages—as, for example, the marriage of Joseph to the Egyptian Asenath (Gen. 41-45), of Judah to a Canaanite (Gen. 38:2), of Samson to a woman of the Philistines (Judges 14:2), and of Solomon to women of many nations. Marriage to non-Israelites was, in fact, specifically authorized under some conditions (Deut. 21:10-14).

Nevertheless, there was a strong and continuous effort to discourage, if not to forbid, the marriage of Israelites to other peoples. Joshua declared that such unions were scourges in the flesh and thorns in the eyes of Israel (Josh. 23:12-13), and Ezra rent his garments and plucked the hair of his head at the thought. He warned the people to heed the words of the Lord:

> Therefore give not your daughters to their sons, neither take their daughters for your sons, and never seek their peace or prosperity, that you may be strong, and eat the good of the land, and leave it for an inheritance to your children for ever.
>
> (Ezra 9:12)

He went even further and required "the leading priests and Levites" and all "Israel" to take an oath to put away non-Jewish wives taken when Israel was disorganized by the Babylonian exile (Ezra 10:2-4). Solomon's sins were attributed to the influence on him of "outlandish women." Nehemiah said, in speaking of Solomon, that marrying "strange women" was a great evil (Neh. 13:23-28). Malachi declared that Judah had profaned the sanctuary of the Lord in marrying the daughter of a foreign god (Mal. 2:11). Such warnings, threats, and promises did not prevent intermarriage altogether, but they did keep alive the thought that it was wrong.

EXOGAMY

Chapter 18 of the Book of Leviticus contains the laws stating the degrees of relationship within which marriage is forbidden. They have become a part of the common law of many nations and constitute in principle the incest laws of the United States. There is not complete agreement in the courts, however, as to their interpretation, and some states have added by statute additional prohibitions. The Levitical code applies to both consanguinal and affinal types of kinship and does not distinguish between them: marriage is forbidden between certain relatives, whether their bond be a physical one of blood or a social one of propinquity. They contain some prohibitions which are expressly stated and others which are obviously implied. For example, the marriage between a mother and a son is expressly forbidden; that between a father and a daughter is forbidden by implication. Marriage is expressly forbidden with a granddaughter, and by implication with a grandmother. It is reasonable to assume that the laws refer to closeness of relationship and must be interpreted in that light.

The following table summarizes the Levitical code. Italics are used to denote prohibitions by implication.

LAWS OF INCEST [5]

A WOMAN MAY NOT MARRY HER	A MAN MAY NOT MARRY HIS
Grandfather	*Grandmother*
Grandmother's husband	*Grandfather's wife*
Husband's grandfather	Wife's grandmother
Father	Mother
Stepfather	Stepmother
Husband's father	Wife's mother
Son	*Daughter*
Daughter's husband	Son's wife
Stepson	Stepdaughter
Grandson	Granddaughter
Granddaughter's husband	*Grandson's wife*
Husband's grandson	Wife's granddaughter
Brother	Sister
(Sister's husband) (?)	Brother's wife
Husband's brother	*(Wife's sister)* (?)
Uncle	Aunt
Aunt's husband	Uncle's wife
Husband's uncle	*Wife's aunt*
Nephew	Niece
Niece's husband	*Nephew's wife*
Husband's nephew	Wife's niece

It will be seen from this table that marriage is forbidden between those related by consanguinity or affinity, either lineally (*e.g.*, parent-child) or collaterally (*e.g.*, brother-sister), within the first two degrees of kinship. Marriage is not prohibited between those related in the third degree—as, for example, first cousins, who are collaterally so related.

Also, it should be noted that a question is raised in the table about the marriage to a wife's sister or to a husband's brother. This is an important question, since the *sororate* (marriage to women who are sisters) and the *levirate* (marriage to men who are brothers) are practices that have been found in many societies, including the ancient Hebrew. The verse in Leviticus containing the law on this point states:

> And you shall not take a woman as a rival wife to her sister, uncovering her nakedness while her sister is yet alive. (Lev. 18:18)

The phrase "while her sister is yet alive" may indicate that this law was intended to apply only to a polygamous union, and that the marriages of a widow to her husband's brother and of a widower to his wife's sister were not regarded as incestuous. If this is the correct interpretation of this verse, then it was introduced to provide an exception to the general rule, since a husband's brother (brother-in-law) and a wife's sister (sister-in-law) are collateral relatives of the first degree by affinity, and marriage between persons so related is in all other instances forbidden.

THE IDEAL WIFE

This brief discussion of the ancient Hebrew family may well end with the well-known passage from the Book of Proverbs which sets forth the characteristics of the ideal wife. Since Old Testament times, ways of life have changed in much of the world, and a complex money economy has replaced the simple domestic economy that prevailed long ago in Palestine. Nevertheless, whatever the changes in forms of expression, the ideals of character and conduct portrayed in the following lines are deeply embedded in the living Judaic-Christian tradition.

> A good wife who can find?
>   She is far more precious than jewels.
> The heart of her husband trusts in her,
>   and he will have no lack of gain.
> She does him good, and not harm,
>   all the days of her life.
> She seeks wool and flax,
>   and works with willing hands.
> She is like the ships of the merchant,
>   she brings her food from afar.
> She rises while it is yet night
>   and provides food for her household
>   and tasks for her maidens.
> She considers a field and buys it;
>   with the fruit of her hands she
>   plants a vineyard.
> She girds her loins with strength
>   and makes her arms strong.
> She perceives that her merchandise
>   is profitable.
>   Her lamp does not go out at night.
> She puts her hands to the distaff,
>   and her hands hold the spindle.

> She opens her hand to the poor,
> and reaches out her hands to the needy.
> She is not afraid of snow for her household,
> for all her household are clothed in scarlet.
> She makes herself coverings;
> her clothing is fine linen and purple.
> Her husband is known in the gates,
> when he sits among the elders of the land.
> She makes linen garments and sells them;
> she delivers girdles to the merchant.
> Strength and dignity are her clothing,
> and she laughs at the time to come.
> She opens her mouth with wisdom,
> and the teaching of kindness is on her tongue.
> She looks well to the ways of her household,
> and does not eat the bread of idleness.
> Her children rise up and call her blessed;
> her husband also, and he praises her:
> "Many women have done excellently,
> but you surpass them all."
> Charm is deceitful, and beauty is vain,
> but a woman who fears the Lord is to be praised.
> Give her of the fruit of her hands,
> and let her works praise her in the gates.
>
> (Prov. 31:10-31)

THE HEBRAIC HERITAGE

People often speak of Western civilization as "Greco-Roman," unmindful of a third pillar, the Hebrew, which supports that vast structure. Later chapters in this book will deal with certain contributions of the Greeks and Romans, but before we leave the ancient Hebrews, a brief survey of some of their achievements may serve to remind us that Western society has been inspired not alone by the art and philosophy of the Greeks and the law and politics of the Romans but also by the religion and ethics of the Hebrews.

The Hebrews gave the world the conception of one God—omnipotent, omniscient, eternal, creator of the earth and all that dwells therein and of the heavens, the ruler and the father of mankind. They were not the first to accept monotheism. The Egyptians who followed Ikhnaton had no other god but the Sun-god, and the Hindus learned from the Rig-Veda that, however variously sages may call it, "That which exists is one." Nevertheless, by their eloquence and piety, the Hebrews were able to loose, as none before them had done, the shackles of polytheism, which held the ancient world in superstitious fear.

In a brutish age when men were often hard and cruel in their dealings with one another, the Hebrews fought as others did against their enemies and kept alive with songs and prayers a martial spirit; nevertheless, they held up a high ideal of justice. Protests against oppression were heard in all the civilized societies of antiquity, but nowhere were they louder and more persistent than among the Hebrews. The appeal of Amos that justice might "roll down like waters, and righteousness like a mighty stream" was made by the Hebrew prophets with such effect that a thunderous echo now resounds from voices once crying in a wilderness. Where devout Jews and Christians fail to practice social justice in the world today, they are tortured by an uneasy conscience because of a commandment to do justice which they can evade only by repudiating their religious faiths.

The ancient Hebrews demonstrated the value of critical self-analysis and of deliberate collective action. One of the striking characteristics of Jews in the modern world is their ability to suffer calamity without loss to personal pride or ethnic solidarity. Under persecution most groups protest bitterly at first; then they become apathetic when their wails go unheard, and finally they disintegrate. Throughout history the Jews have shown a remarkable ability to forego the indulgence of futile regrets, and this may explain in part their survival as a strong ethnic group. They have depended upon rational judgment and united effort to solve their common problems. We have seen these traits in the Hebrews of the Old Testament, where emphasis was always placed on the group rather than on the individual and where suffering was regarded as chastisement.

Finally, the Hebraic heritage has enriched mankind in ways other than those here explored. Woodrow Wilson once said that

> . . . if we could but have the eyes to see the subtle elements of thought which constitute the gross substance of our present habit, both as regards the sphere of private life and as regards the action of the state, we should easily discover how very much besides religion we owe to the Jew.[6]

PART TWO

GREECE, ROME, AND MEDIEVAL CHRISTENDOM

The following five chapters deal with the social thought of Western society from the golden age of Greece to near the end of the Middle Ages. Plato and Aristotle represent Greek thought at its best; because so many social ideas in the modern world can be traced to them, a chapter is devoted to each. The works of Polybius, Lucretius, Cicero, and Seneca, together with Rome's ancient code of laws, the *Twelve Tables,* are examined in the chapter on Rome. A chapter on Augustine and one on Thomas Aquinas present the social thought of Christendom.

Plato was born in 427 B.C., and Thomas Aquinas died in A.D. 1274. The seventeen centuries between these dates witnessed events and social changes of great complexity and import. The Age of Pericles was short-lived; soon Greece fell so low that, figuratively at least, wild boars rooted in Plato's garden. Rome's grandeur persisted, and indeed it appeared that it might endure forever. The Catholic Church pushed religion into the brilliant foreground while science lurked behind in dark shadows. The Western world passed through its feudal age. The bodies of the Greek philosophers lay buried, but in the thirteenth century of the Christian Era their ideas were again on the lips of men. Rome declined and fell, but not before Roman law and politics had been woven into the fabric of Western civilization.

Of all the Church fathers, Augustine is by far the most interesting, as he may well have been the most influential. He lived when the Catholic Church was establishing its dogmas and perfecting its organization. He, and those who worked with him, laid foundations so solid that the power and the prestige of the Church were secure for nine centuries. By the thirteenth century a new age was slowly dawning, and Christendom was threatened. Then Thomas Aquinas appeared, to bridge the old and the new orders and to revive in a rapidly changing world the appeal of the old drama of salvation.

It is no simple task to survey in five chapters the social thought of Plato, Aristotle, the Romans, Augustine, and Thomas Aquinas. Seventeen hundred years is a long time in human history, and the works we shall study are products of some of the greatest intellects the human race produced during those years or has produced since. These men said much that is vital today, and they fashioned many of the molds in which our own thought is set. For that reason, we are encouraged to look into their lives and social ideas, somewhat comforted by the fact that they are all in the stream of Western thought.

7 · PLATO

(427-347 B.C.)

> *Writing, Phaedrus, has this strange quality, and is very like painting; for the creatures of painting stand like living beings, but if one asks them a question, they preserve a solemn silence. And so it is with written words; you might think they spoke as if they had intelligence, but if you question them, wishing to know about their sayings, they always say one and the same thing.*
>
> PHAEDRUS, 275

The achievements of the Greeks in the Hellenic period continue to amaze and to inspire mankind. What age in all history can match such names as these: in literature, Sappho of Lesbos, Aeschylus, Sophocles, Euripides, Aristophanes; in philosophy, Socrates, Plato, Aristotle; in government, Solon and Pericles; in sculpture and architecture, the unknown creators of those designs still widely copied; in science, Heraclitus the dynamist, Democritus the atomist, and Hippocrates the father of medicine? It is futile to ask whether these, and hundreds of other illustrious men and women living in that momentous period, were creators of Western culture or were merely among the first, and therefore the most noticeable, products of that culture. Personality and culture are intertwined; they cannot be separated. Suffice it, therefore, to recognize the enduring quality of the accomplishments of these early Greeks.

SOCIAL BACKGROUND

The year 776 B.C. has come to mark the beginning of the Hellenic Period. That year is by tradition identified with the founding of the Olympic games, which brought all the Hellenes together as one people. Originally the name *Hellenes* was applied only to a tribe in Thessaly, but by the eighth century B.C. the Greek city states, not only in Greece proper but also on the adjacent islands and coastal regions of the Mediterranean, had come to feel through common language and customs that they were united. Likewise, the year 338 B.C. is commonly accepted as marking the end of the Hellenic Period, since on this date, as a result of military defeat at the hands of Philip of Macedonia, Greece lost true independence and became merged with the empire of Alxander the Great.

The cause of the decline of Greece is not clear. Perhaps she wasted her strength in military undertakings.

> The Peloponnesian War was a catastrophe for Athens and Greece. The Athenians had had it in their means with wise management to build up a lasting power, the strongest in Hellas, to win recognition of their political leadership from many or all the other Greeks, and to lift their race to a political destiny worthy of its civilization. All these possibilities they sacrificed. They persisted in the War, the Sicilian expedition was a scheme of conquest ill-conceived and conducted with obstinate folly, and they mismanaged their Empire. Never again was Athens a first-rate power, although she remained the cultural leader of Hellas.[1]

Toynbee believes that the Greek city states never really solved the problems arising from rapid growth of population. Expansion into colonies made it necessary for the various states to cooperate in order to maintain order over the far-flung colonial possessions. But within Greece the growth and economic changes taking place led, at the moment when a united effort was most important, to the enfranchisement of new classes, who exercised their newly won political power to block creation of an effective league. As Toynbee says,

> From the opening of the fifth century B.C. onwards the whole of the rest of Hellenic political history can be formulated in terms of an endeavour to transcend city-state sovereignty and of the resistance which this endeavour evoked.[2]

SOCRATES (469-399 B.C.)

The social ideas of Socrates are difficult to distinguish from those of Plato; for whereas Plato left to posterity a solid body of writing in which Socrates is the main character, not a line from Socrates himself has been found. It is probable that he made no attempt to commit his thoughts to written form. Content to push in with disturbing questions wherever groups gathered for serious discussion in the streets, gardens, or homes of Athens, he may have felt no urge to write anything. He is, however, the spokesman for Plato in all of the dialogues except the *Laws*, where his place is taken by an Athenian Stranger. His thought can, therefore, be identified with that of Plato.

As to Socrates' life and character, we have more definite information, much of it from Plato himself, his most distinguished pupil. His father was Sophroniscus, a stonecutter; and his mother, Phaenarete, a midwife. Little is known about his education in youth or his means of livelihood in maturity. He tells us with waggish satire that from his earliest youth he wanted to learn from the professors of moral improvement, the Sophists, how to become a teacher of the art of virtue, but that he lacked means for such instruction.[3] His education in dancing seems to have been neglected in youth, since he received instruction in this accomplishment at an advanced age. Either in the gymnasia or elsewhere he acquired the physical strength and the courage to conduct himself creditably in several military campaigns. In the battle of Delium he is reported to have saved the life of Xenophon.[4] There are numerous references in the dialogues to his courage in battle and his marvelous endurance, not only in military campaigns but also under the strains of disputation. He probably adopted his father's occupation and may even have become a sculptor. He boasted that his needs were simple.

> The purple robe and silver's shine
> More fits an actor's need than mine.[5]

At the tables of some of his friends, he seems often to have exchanged good conversation for food.

His wife Xanthippe, like most other Athenian women in her day, was not encouraged to join in manly discussions of philosophy; and although she remained faithful to him, bore him three children, and was so taken with grief at the prospect of his untimely end that she had to be dismissed from his presence—yet, for all that, Socrates often complained to his hearers that she nagged him about money for marketing. If we are to take Diogenes Laertius seriously, no less an authority than Aristotle reported that Socrates charitably took a second wife, Myrto, when men became scarce in Athens as a result of the wars. Such are the details recorded about the life of the man who gave the name *Socratic* to a method still widely used in probing into ultimate matters.

In the sublime prose of Plato, a record of Socrates' last hours on earth has been preserved. He had been brought to trial before a jury of five hundred members, charged with religious heresy and false teaching. It was claimed that he had asserted that there was one God, when in reality there were many; and that he had corrupted the morals of young people by asking them to think about the meaning of virtue. He might have saved his life had he been willing to recant, but instead of promising to mend his ways, Socrates dared to assert to the court:

> I shall repeat the same words to every one whom I meet, young and old, citizen and alien. . . . For know that this is the command of God; and I

believe that no greater good has ever happened in the state than my service to the God. For I do nothing but go about persuading you all, old and young alike, not to take thought for your persons or for your properties, but first and chiefly to care about the greatest improvement of the soul. . . . This is my teaching, and if this is the doctrine which corrupts the youth, I am a mischievous person . . . understand that I shall never alter my ways, not even if I have to die many times.[6]

The court decreed that he should die, and he was sent away to wait in prison until the hemlock should be brought for his self-destruction. There in the prison his friends came, begging him to let them arrange for his escape; but at seventy Socrates had no inclination to deny the principles by which he had lived. As he said, they who buried Socrates buried his body only.

When he had spoken these words, he arose and went into a chamber to bathe; Crito followed him and told us to wait. So we remained behind, talking and thinking of the subject of discourse, and also of the greatness of our sorrow; he was like a father of whom we were being bereaved, and we were about to pass the rest of our lives as orphans. When he had taken the bath his children were brought to him—(he had two young sons and an elder one); and the women of his family also came, and he talked to them and gave them a few directions in the presence of Crito; then he dismissed them and returned to us.

Now the hour of sunset was near, for a good deal of time had passed while he was within. When he came out, he sat down with us again after his bath, but not much was said. Soon the jailer, who was the servant of the Eleven, entered and stood by him, saying:—To you, Socrates, whom I know to be the noblest and gentlest and best of all who ever came to this place, I will not impute the angry feelings of other men, who rage and swear at me, when, in obedience to the authorities, I bid them drink the poison —indeed, I am sure that you will not be angry with me; for others, as you are aware, and not I, are to blame. And so fare you well, and try to bear lightly what must needs be—you know my errand. Then bursting into tears he turned away and went out.

Socrates looked at him and said: I return your good wishes, and will do as you bid. Then turning to us, he said, How charming the man is: since I have been in prison he has always been coming to see me, and at times he would talk to me, and was as good to me as could be, and now see how generously he sorrows on my account. We must do as he says, Crito; and therefore let the cup be brought, if the poison is prepared: if not, let the attendant prepare some.

Yet, said Crito, the sun is still upon the hill-tops, and I know that many a one has taken the draught late, and after the announcement has been made to him, he has eaten and drunk, and enjoyed the society of his beloved; do not hurry—there is time enough.

Socrates said: Yes, Crito, and they of whom you speak are right in so acting, for they think that they will be gainers by the delay; but I am right in not following their example, for I do not think that I should gain anything by drinking the poison a little later; I should only be ridiculous in my own eyes for sparing and saving a life which is already forfeit. Please then to do as I say, and not to refuse me.

Crito made a sign to the servant, who was standing by; and he went out, and having been absent for some time, returned with the jailer carrying the cup of poison. Socrates said: You, my good friend, who are experienced in these matters, shall give me directions how I am to proceed. The man answered: You have only to walk about until your legs are heavy, and then to lie down, and the poison will act. At the same time he handed the cup to Socrates, who in the easiest and gentlest manner, without the least fear or change of colour or feature, looking at the man with all his eyes, Echecrates, as his manner was, took the cup and said: What do you say about making a libation out of this cup to any god? May I, or not? The man answered: We only prepare, Socrates, just so much as we deem enough. I understand, he said: but I may and must ask the gods to prosper my journey from this to the other world—even so—and so be it according to my prayer. Then raising the cup to his lips, quite readily and cheerfully he drank off the poison. And hitherto most of us had been able to control our sorrow; but now when we saw him drinking, and saw too that he had finished the draught, we could no longer forbear, and in spite of myself my own tears were flowing fast; so that I covered my face and wept, not for him, but at the thought of my own calamity in having to part from such a friend. . . . Socrates alone retained his calmness: What is this strange outcry? he said. I sent away the women mainly in order that they might not misbehave in this way, for I have been told that a man should die in peace. Be quiet then, and have patience. When we heard his words we were ashamed, and refrained our tears; and he walked about until, as he said, his legs began to fail, and then he lay on his back, according to the directions, and the man who gave him the poison now and then looked at his feet and legs; and after a while he pressed his foot hard, and asked him if he could feel; and he said, No; and then his leg, and so upwards and upwards, and showed us that he was cold and stiff. And he felt them himself, and said: When the poison reaches the heart, that will be the end. He was beginning to grow cold about the groin, when he uncovered his face, for he had covered himself up, and said—they were his last words—he said: Crito, I owe a cock to Asclepius; will you remember to pay the debt? The debt shall be paid, said Crito; is there anything else? There was no answer to this question; but in a minute or two a movement was heard, and the attendants uncovered him; his eyes were set, and Crito closed his eyes and mouth.

Such was the end, Echecrates, of our friend; concerning whom I may truly say, that of all the men of his time whom I have known, he was the wisest and justest and best.[7]

PLATO

Plato was twenty-eight years old when his teacher and friend met the fate which has just been described. He had known Socrates, and had been his ardent disciple, for at least eight years. At the trial he is said to have attempted to intercede for Socrates but was shouted down by the judges. Certainly the man who was later to make the search for justice the theme of one of his greatest works must have been deeply moved by the injustice of the accusations and the trial.

After the death of Socrates, Plato left Athens, to be gone for twelve years. How far he traveled and how he spent his time are not known. It seems fairly certain that he went to Italy, Sicily, and Egypt. He may have gone to Palestine, Babylonia, Persia, or even deeper into the continent of Asia. But, in any event, in 387 B.C., he returned, now a man of forty, to establish a residence in Athens that, save for a short time spent at Syracuse, was unbroken for the remainder of his life. In his private garden, named for the legendary hero Academus, he established the school which came later to be called the Academy. Here, forty years later, he died and was buried.

In his writings Plato laid bare his most intimate thoughts; but as successfully as did Shakespeare two thousand years later, he threw a blanket about his private life. It is thought that he was a native Athenian, son of Ariston. His mother, Perictoine, was said to trace her descent from Solon. His real name was Aristocles, but because of his broad brow, or perhaps his broad shoulders, he came to be called Plato.

As a youth Plato seems to have tried his hand at poetry, writing thousands of verses, a few tragedies, and a portion of an epic, which he destroyed when he felt that it did not compare favorably with the *Iliad*. We hear of two brothers and a sister, but nowhere is there reference to a wife or children. He mentions himself only twice in the dialogues, once in the *Phaedo* and again in the *Apology*. When he died, he was buried in the garden of the Academy. Of the epitaphs that are said to have been inscribed at various times on his tomb, none is more fitting than this:

> Here lies the god-like man Aristocles, eminent among men for temperance and the justice of his character. And he, if ever anyone, had the fullest meed of praise for wisdom, and was too great for envy.[8]

PLATO'S APPROACH TO KNOWLEDGE

The social ideas of Plato afford an excellent illustration of the way in which genius derives from a culture and pushes beyond that particular culture. Shakespeare, for example, is a product of Elizabethan England and Goethe is first a

German. So Plato is as surely classic Greek as is the Parthenon. But although Plato gives explicit formulation to the ideals and values of the Greek civilization of his time and reflects in his thought the harmony and balance of an Athenian temple of the fifth century B.C., he belongs not to Greece alone but to the world. No one more than he has felt the need of finding ideals and values which transcend time and place. If on the one hand he reflects the simplicity and restraint of Greek art, on the other he reveals in myth and allegory the turbulent struggle of the human spirit to escape the bondage of ignorance.

Some men claim that might makes right, that knowledge is but opinion, that one man's judgment is as good as another's, that virtue is merely a convention, that there is no distinction between appearance and reality. Some even take a darkly pessimistic and fatalistic view:

> There is no Good, there is no Bad;
> These be the whims of mortal will:
> What works me weal that call I "good."
> What harms and hurts I hold as "ill":
>
> They change with place, they shift with race;
> And, in the veriest span of Time,
> Each Vice has worn a Virtue's crown;
> All Good was banned as Sin or Crime.[9]

But Plato vigorously condemned such reasoning. To be sure, what is considered right opinion today may be regarded tomorrow as wrong opinion; yet when right opinion is chained by reason, it remains fixed. There was to Plato a realm of perfect order beyond this labyrinth of endless turnings. Human thought reaches beyond the senses to grasp the eternal and changeless. Man alone of all the creatures is capable of wisdom, of justice, of reverence. The uniqueness of mankind, the humanity of human beings, arises in thought. It is the power of mind which exalts and glorifies *Homo sapiens*. Knowledge is virtue. Knowledge ennobles. It is good to know. Socrates says to Protagoras:

> Uncover your mind to me, Protagoras, and reveal your opinion about knowledge, that I may know whether you agree with the rest of the world. Now the rest of the world are of opinion that knowledge is a principle not of strength, or of rule, or of command: their notion is that a man may have knowledge, and yet that the knowledge which is in him may be overmastered by anger, or pleasure, or pain, or love, or perhaps by fear,—just as if knowledge were a slave, and might be dragged about anyhow. Now is that your view? Or do you think that knowledge is a noble and commanding thing, which cannot be overcome, and will not allow a man, if he only knows the difference of good and evil, to do anything which is contrary to knowledge, but that wisdom will have strength to help him?[10]

But Plato was not merely rationalistic. Knowledge begins with sensory observations and is extended through reason, which discloses relations. It is made perfect by faith, which transforms knowledge into meaning and purpose. Plato insists that thought is both necessary and inadequate—necessary to show the way to faith, inadequate because the deeper insights are felt as well as understood. Thought depends on words, and the eternal truths cannot be grasped by the conventional symbols of language. The forceps of the mind are, indeed, crude, and they crush the truth in seizing it.

THE SOCRATIC METHOD

In prose which is often more moving than poetry, Plato employed what has come to be called the "Socratic method" of inquiry. The dialogues are discussions. In a group a question is raised—*e.g.*, the question of justice. What is justice? Plato might have defined justice, but definition was not his method. He saw that a definition is only a statement that one word, or a group of words, is the equivalent of another. All definitions are tautological. Every word in the dictionary is defined by some other word in the dictionary. Words in themselves are merely symbols: they are shadows of the reality which they represent. Hence only shadows are held fast in the words: substance is free. Justice is immutable, eternal, universal; interpretations of justice necessarily reflect the experience of the speaker or the writer. For that reason, Plato preferred the spoken language, which is alive, to the written, which is forever fixed.

So the queston with which the *Republic* opens is never definitely answered. Justice is not defined. Socrates says that it is easier to see justice on a large scale in the state than on a small one in the lives of individuals. Consequently, an ideal commonwealth is created in imagination, a society in which men live justly with one another. But even this conception is no mere intellectual exercise. Justice is not something to be examined; rather it is something to be known. The Sophists could examine justice; Plato wanted to quicken a sense of justice. The Sophists claimed to be teachers—that is, persons who could draw from their large store of learning small bits for the enlightenment of those less well informed; Socrates vigorously denied being a teacher in this sense. To his judges he said:

> For if you kill me, you will not easily find a successor to me, who, if I may use such a ludicrous figure of speech, am a sort of gadfly, given to the state by God; and the state is a great and noble steed who is tardy in his motions owing to his very size, and requires to be stirred into life. I am that gadfly which God has attached to the state, and all day long and in all places am always fastening upon you, arousing and persuading and reproaching you.[11]

He is a midwife helping to give birth to conviction. Even if sometimes he engages in logic-chopping, that is not his only method. Never pedestrian, he is ever ready when the time is ripe to employ myth and allegory to stir the emotions as well as the rational faculties.

There was in Plato no separation of knowing from doing, no justification of knowledge for its own sake. With apparently innocent questions about the meaning of their terms, Socrates sought to shock those whom he queried into a consciousness of their ignorance. Plato implied that learning thrives on humility and a felt need and withers in an atmosphere of intellectual conceit. He insisted, however, that skepticism is the beginning of wisdom, not the end. Knowledge begins with doubt but leads to confident action. At one pole in the scale of attitudes is naïveté, and at the other, cynicism. Both are sterile. Knowledge means the displacement of the false by the true, the abandonment of the worse for the sake of the better. As Raphael Demos has said, "In the Socratic method we encounter a technique analogous to that of religious salvation; questioning results in a conviction of intellectual sin and learning is self-purification." [12]

HUMAN NATURE

In his discussion of human nature in various dialogues Plato took a view that reflects his customary avoidance of extremes. He did not believe, as some have claimed, that man is by nature evil, loving himself and hating his fellow man and yearning for death more than for life. And he did not share the conviction of others that man is born good and becomes evil only as a result of corrupting influences to which he is subjected in society. But although Plato believed that man shares with other animals the appetites essential to survival, he was more concerned with man's peculiar gifts, his uniqueness among living forms. For man alone of all creation is endowed with the capacity for wisdom and justice and with a sense of reverence.[13] Man is, therefore, pulled two ways: by appetite, toward bestiality; by reason, toward the good. He is not one, but two—a house divided. The beast in him craves pleasure, the indulgence of appetite; the soul seeks release from the bondage of the flesh. In Christian theology this basic duality in human nature is represented by the struggle between good and evil, or God and Satan, for the soul of man. But Plato did not identify appetite with evil or reason with good. Both appetite and reason are natural.

> For I maintain that the true life should neither seek for pleasures, nor, on the other hand, entirely avoid pains, but should embrace the middle state, which I just spoke of as gentle and benign, and is a state which we by some divine presage and inspiration rightly acribe to God.[14]

The "middle state" is not, however, a compromise. Reason is higher in the hierarchy of human qualities than appetite, and in the struggle of man with himself reason should prevail over appetite.* If men act like beasts, it is because they are ignorant. Men would do good if they but knew the good. No man chooses injustice in preference to justice, or the base when he might have the noble, or the lesser of two goods when he might possess the greater. Lacking understanding, he merely mistakes the one for the other. Hence the importance of education.

In the most famous of his myths Plato portrays man in the darkness of the cave, chained there by appetite, and, in his ignorance, seeing only shadows. Then, somehow, the chains break, and he is able to escape from the dim, weird images in the cave. At first he is confused and frightened. He would turn back if he were not aided in his climb up the steep and rugged ascent. But finally he reaches a height from which the wonder of light is revealed, the joyous experience of understanding is achieved.[15]

It is characteristic of Plato that he did not in this myth permit the individual who has just gained his freedom from the cave to bask in the sunlight. The first thoughts of such a person must be of his fellow prisoners. He must return to the cave, where, as a result of the light he has experienced, he will now see "ten thousand times better than the inhabitants of the den." His eyes having been opened, he will know that "God created him for the whole, not the whole for the sake of him." [16] To Plato, therefore, it appeared that only in society does man achieve full stature as a human being.

This does not mean, according to some Platonists, the subordination of the individual to society in the sense in which totalitarian regimes have regarded the individual as a tool of the state. On the other hand, Plato did not go to the other extreme of regarding the state (society) as an instrument designed to serve private ends and justified only to the extent to which it contributes to personal happiness. In his thinking, private good is not opposed to public good.

This idea was expressed long before Plato lived and has appeared, in various forms, many times since his death. But no one has stated more clearly than did Plato the delicate nature of the balance between freedom and order. They were to him not mutually antagonistic but complementary. There can be no freedom, for the individual or for the group, he believed, without order. The individual who allows free rein to his appetites is enslaved to his passions; the society which fosters, in the name of liberty, an excessive individualism invites chaos. On the other hand, the imposition from above, for the sake of order, of artificial restraints denies the individual an opportunity to develop and enjoy his natural abilities. Plato's insistence on the harmony of the whole, whether individual or social, is the key to his conception of morality.

* Plato actually divides human nature into three parts: the appetitive, the spirited, and the rational. But the spirited, out of which arise enthusiasm, intensity, and especially assertiveness, is more closely identified with appetite than with reason.

SOCIAL STRATIFICATION

In his portrait of the democratic man, Plato sketched the outcome of unbridled freedom. The democratic man is characterized by excesses of all kinds.

> . . . he lives from day to day indulging the appetite of the hour; and sometimes he is lapped in drink and strains of the flute; then he becomes a water-drinker, and tries to get thin; then he takes a turn at gymnastics; sometimes idling and neglecting everything, then once more living the life of a philosopher; often he is busy with politics, and starts to his feet and says and does whatever comes into his head; and, if he is emulous of any one who is a warrior, off he is in that direction, or of men of business, once more in that. His life has neither law nor order; and this distracted existence he terms joy and bliss and freedom; and so he goes on.[17]

The democratic man is a product of a democratic society and reflects in his life and conduct the weaknesses of a social system based upon an assumed equality of men. Plato believed that men are not equal—in physical strength, in spirit, in mental ability. He was convinced that any society which fails to reckon with individual differences, and neglects to afford an opportunity to every individual to develop those talents natural to him, will surely come to anarchy. So men should strive not to be as alike as peas in a pod but to be themselves, finding in the full development of their own potentialities their highest good. We should say to our children:

> . . . you are brothers, yet God has framed you differently. Some of you have the power of command, and in the composition of these he has mingled gold, wherefore also they have the greatest honour; others he has made of silver, to be auxiliaries; others again who are to be husbandmen and craftsmen he has composed of brass and iron.[18]

Although Plato thought that parents usually produce offspring like themselves, he was opposed to a rigid class structure based on birth. "A golden parent will sometimes have a silver son, or a silver parent a golden son." Every individual should have the status for which he is fitted and not necessarily that of his parents. On this point, Plato's insistence on equality of opportunity brings him close in spirit to one of the basic ideals of democracy, despite the fact that he lacked confidence in democracy and described in the *Republic* a state more totalitarian than democratic in nature. Plato's practice of exploring a subject from many different points of view has made it possible for communists, fascists, socialists, monarchists, and virtually all other kinds of political bodies to claim him on their side. Plato's approval of many democratic ideals is obvious, just as is his opposition to the kind of government he believed democracy is likely to create.

To Plato the whole is greater than the parts. Society is an organism, characterized by differentiation, by subordination, and, above all, by integration. Some organs of the body are more important than others; most of the organs are indispensable. People form societies because of mutual needs arising from specialization and a division of labor. Some members of society have positions of greater responsibility, and consequently of greater prestige, than others. But all are necessary to the whole society, the artisans not less than the rulers. Unity grows out of diversity, or, in the language of Spencer, out of heterogeneity rather than homogeneity. But unlikeness will result in disunity if organization is lacking. A healthy society is one in which each organ performs its proper function and in so doing promotes the harmony of the whole.

Like most other Greeks of his day, Plato classified all those who were not Hellenes as barbarians. Obviously these outsiders were identified with a lower social stratum. They were not entitled to citizenship; they were employed only as hirelings and traders. For each class there was suitable employment. Citizens should not engage in the handicrafts or in retail trade, since public service "does not admit of being made a secondary occupation." Apparently Plato looked upon slavery, universally practiced in the world known to the Hellenic Greeks, as natural and right, although he did not, like Aristotle, attempt to justify the practice.

THE FAMILY

In his anaysis of ideal family institutions, Plato gave full play to the imagination. It must be remembered that he did not attempt, in the *Republic,* to describe the Athens of his day or any community likely to be found upon the earth. He pushed on where logic led, fully conscious that in so doing his reach exceeded the grasp of mankind. He merely asked, "If there were an ideal republic, as most certainly there is not, would it not be characterized by common wives and children in the guardian class?" Plato was suggesting that the small group charged with the responsibility of administering the affairs of the state might find family ties an encumbrance. It seemed to him that these select few, at least, should abandon all private ends if they were faithfully to serve the whole society with undivided loyalty. Although he sometimes suggested that this arrangement should extend to the artisan classes as well, usually he was careful to emphasize that it was only the guardian class to which he referred, as when he said that "the wives of our guardians are to be common, and their children are to be common, and no parent is to know his own child, nor any child his parent." [19]

Some religious bodies protect themselves against divided loyalties in their servants by requiring celibacy in their priesthood. But Plato was persuaded that a society would deteriorate if the wisest and best of its citizens produced no progeny. He felt that children were needed from the guardians even more than from the population at large and outlined the rules of marriage. The brides and bridegrooms must be in their prime. For the women this means ages twenty to forty; for the men, ages twenty-five to fifty-five. The rulers contrive that by a system of lots the brave and fair are mated—eugenics is no modern concept! Brides and bridegrooms are brought together at state-arranged marriage festivals. Sacrifices are offered and suitable hymeneal songs are composed by the poets of the realm. The offspring of superior parents are carried to an enclosure in a certain part of the city, where they are attended by suitable nurses. After this no mother knows her own child.

Plato was not unmindful of the possibility of incest where family identification was so completely obscured, and offered the following solution to that problem:

> . . . dating from the day of the hymeneal, the bridegroom who was then married will call all the male children who are born in the seventh and the tenth month afterwards his sons, and the female children his daughters, and they will call him father. . . . All who were begotten at the time when their fathers and mothers came together will be called brothers and sisters . . . and these . . . will be forbidden to intermarry.[20]

He was conscious also of the necessity of exercising control over the number of births in the state in order to prevent the population from becoming too large or too small. This was to be accomplished by eliminating badly deformed children, and by putting away in "some mysterious, unknown place" the offspring of inferior parents.[21]

In an age when the status of women had reached one of the lowest points recorded in the history of Western civilization, it is a tribute to Plato's independence of thought that he would offer educational and occupational equality to women. He qualified this position by voicing the assumption that women are by nature generally inferior to men. But since no two people are identical in abilities, some must be more capable than others. Therefore, it is likely that occasionally women will appear who are qualified to become guardians. Wherever ability is discovered, the sex of the person should be no deterrent to its utilization by the state. In the distribution of other labors, the only difference between the duties of males and those of females is that the lighter work should be assigned to women, whereas men should be given the more strenuous tasks.

Since their duties are similar, males and females receive the same nurture and education.

> You will admit that the same education which makes a man a good guardian will make a woman a good guardian; for their original nature is the same.[22]

Both are taught music for the soul and gymnastics for the body. In addition, both are instructed in the art of warfare and are expected equally to participate in the defense of the state. Women need to share equally with men the fortunes of life; otherwise they will "live softly and waste money and have no order of life." [23] Lacking order in their lives, they will be unhappy; and the state will suffer as a consequence.

The selection of a mate should not be a purely private matter, even for the masses. Beauty and amorous desire are not sufficient guides to marriage. The young must be taught how "to seek after what is suitable and appropriate." [24] The newly married couple should without delay set up a home apart from their parents. If they find that they cannot agree, or if after ten years they are without children, divorce should be permitted them for their mutual benefit.

Despite his numerous comments on family organization, it is clear that Plato did not regard the family as the basic social unit. When the family was not altogether eliminated, as with the guardians, it was regarded primarily as an instrument of procreation for the state rather than as a means to personal happiness. Others have claimed that the moral consciousness of mankind is rooted in the discipline of the home, but Plato looked beyond the private family to the larger society for the forces that shape personality.

EDUCATION

That Plato, the aristocrat, chose to build a school and devote his life to teaching is proof of the importance that he attached to education. His statements regarding the meaning and purpose of education are practical, and they have endured.

In the *Republic*, and again in the *Laws*, Plato writes about many technical matters: the sequence of courses, the subjects to be taught at various grades and to various classes of students, the gymnastic program, the regulation of musical instruction. Some of this discussion is dated and has only historical interest. On the other hand, many of Plato's insights into the real meaning of education are timeless. His philosophy of education is still a beacon light.

It is difficult to express this philosophy in a single statement. Perhaps Livingstone has grasped the essence of Plato's thought when he says:

> In fine, for Plato the supreme aim of education is human goodness, but goodness of a far wider kind than our normal use of the word suggests. Conduct in the narrower sense is only a part of the natural habit of a mind attuned to ultimate reality "intimate with the eternal order of things and the music of the spheres." Nothing matters compared with this. For, as Plato says, the ignorance most fatal to states and individuals is not ignorance in the field of technology or of the professions, but spiritual ignorance. So he conceives education essentially as a training in values. This seems to me the most important truth that we can learn from Plato.[25]

The aim of education is not knowledge but being, not information but wisdom. Knowledge is virtue, and ignorance is vice, only because there is no real distinction between knowing and doing. The individual who has not discovered that knowledge is for use, who fails to be guided in his actions by the best knowledge at his command, who allows, in other words, a schism in his own soul to develop as a result of a breach between ideals and behavior, reveals the worst kind of ignorance.

> . . . the greatest ignorance is when a man hates that which he nevertheless thinks to be good and noble, and loves and embraces that which he knows to be unrighteous and evil.[26]

Thus, the function of education is, above all else, moral. Information may be used for evil as well as for good, and "there is far greater peril in buying knowledge than in buying meat and drink," since the former you receive "into the soul and go your way, either greatly harmed or greatly benefited." [27] Through education we learn to discriminate.

> Now I mean by education that training which is given by suitable habits to the first instincts of virtue in children;—when pleasure, and friendship, and pain, and hatred, are rightly implanted in souls not yet capable of understanding the nature of them, and who find them, after they have attained reason, to be in harmony with her. . . . [Education means] the particular training in respect of pleasure and pain, which leads you always to hate what you ought to hate, and love what you ought to love from the beginning of life to the end.[28]

Education is not indoctrination; it is discovery. The teacher does not implant ideas into the minds of his pupils; he merely helps to give birth to ideas already there. Education is growth from within, not accretions from without. If education were a matter merely of maturation, then it might come easily and naturally. But the cultivation of mind and character is an arduous undertaking. It cannot be left to nature. The moral virtues thrive only with care. Hence education should begin early.

> . . . of all animals the boy is the most unmanageable, inasmuch as he has the fountain of reason in him not yet regulated; he is the most insidious, sharp-witted, and insubordinate of animals. Wherefore he must be bound with many bridles.[29]

Education means, therefore, discipline and control, especially as these are self-administered. It means the development in the individual of those qualities of mind and heart that make for good citizenship. But it is not mere preparation for life; it is the active process of growth and development. Consequently, it continues throughout life. Ideas appropriate to the adult are ill-suited to the child. Plato was opposed to the attempt to teach philosophy to the young. He regarded the subjection of the immature to dialectics as likely to lead only to their lack of respect for moral principles. The youth crawls before he walks. Soft diets precede meat, and inappropriate thoughts result in intellectual indigestion. This is, indeed, to corrupt the morals of the young and is in itself evidence of the worst kind of instruction. The teacher who does not elicit right conduct in the child fails in his primary duty; not, to be sure, that virtue can be taught for a fee, as the Sophist claimed, but that education is directed toward the soul rather than toward the memory.

Even though knowledge is recollection, *what* is recollected is determined by education. Good teaching serves to quicken those moral laws of which Sophocles said:

> They were born where Heaven is.
> Mortal parent have they none,
> Nor shall man's forgetfulness ever make them sleep.
> A god in them is great. He grows not old.[30]

THE STATE

The *Republic,* Plato's most important political work, is intended more as an essay on justice than as a description of a political state. Plato is careful to observe that this republic is "founded in words" and exists nowhere on earth. He does not expect philosophers to become kings; he says only that in his opinion it would be better for all if the wisest men headed the government.

> Until philosophers are kings, or the kings and princes of this world have the spirit and power of philosophy, and political greatness and wisdom meet in one . . . cities will never have rest from their evils,—no, nor the human race.[31]

In the *Laws,* written in his declining years, Plato abandons some of the utopian conceptions found in the *Republic,* but even in this later work he is concerned more with personal relations than with political organization.

In none of his writing is the state distinguished from the community or from society. When he speaks of the *state,* Plato is thinking of the Greek *polis,* an organization unlike anything in the modern world but corresponding more closely to our local community than to a political subdivision in our society. A true state is, therefore, a small body, large enough to provide for the division of labor that Plato believes necessary if individuals are to develop their peculiar talents, and for military security, and yet not so large as to prevent intimate contact and general discussion among the heads of households. In fact, Plato determines by some rather intricate mathematical calculations the exact size of the ideal city-state.

The territory must be sufficient to maintain a certain number of inhabitants in a moderate way of life—more than this is not required; and the number of citizens should be sufficient to defend themselves against the injustice of their neighbours, and also to give them the power of rendering efficient aid to their neighbours when they are wronged. . . . The number of our citizens shall be 5040—this will be a convenient number . . . [because it] can be divided by exactly fifty-nine divisors.³²

Plato means, as he makes clear in his discussion, 5040 households, each with a citizen head. Since each household may be assumed to contain several members of the family, as well as a number of slaves, it follows that the actual population of the *polis* is much greater than the figure stated by Plato. In fact, when account is taken of the large foreign population in Greece, as well as of slaves and members of the household other than the head, it is possible that Plato had in mind a city state of several hundred thousand persons. Since Athens is believed to have contained, in the fourth century B.C., at least 300,000 persons, Plato may have made his native city the measure of the population of an ideal community.³³ His reference to the number 5040 probably reflects the influence of Pythagorean mysticism, in which 7 is a holy number. The product of $1 \times 2 \times 3 \times 4 \times 5 \times 6 \times 7$ is 5040.

The state is but an enlargement of the characters of the men who dwell therein, no better and no worse than the people who compose it. As the individual is characterized by appetite, spirit, and reason, so the state is composed of three classes of men: artisans, soldiers, and rulers. They are graded from bottom to top exactly as human qualities are graded. At the bottom are the artisans, the hewers of wood and drawers of water. At the top are the rulers, or philosopher-kings. These are called guardians. Plato usually includes the soldiers among the guardians, but sometimes he speaks of these as auxiliaries.

The guardians are few in number, fewer even than the blacksmiths, and their lives are dedicated wholly to the service of the community, even at the price of personal satisfactions.

> . . . we were fashioning the state with a view to the whole . . . if any of our guardians shall try to be happy in such a manner that he will cease to be a guardian, then he will have to learn how wisely Hesiod spoke when he said, 'half is more than the whole.' ³⁴

Among the guardians, therefore, but not among the masses, private property as well as private families must be denied. Plato is fully conscious of the radical nature of these proposals.

> The first and highest form of the state and of the government and of the law is that in which there prevails most widely the ancient saying that 'Friends have all things in common.' Whether there is anywhere now, or will ever be, this communion of women and children and of property, in

which the private and individual is altogether vanished from life, and things which are by nature private, such as eyes, and ears and hands, have become common, and in some way see and hear and act in common, and all men express praise and blame and feel joy and sorrow on the same occasions. . . . Whether all this is possible or not, I say that no man, acting upon any other principle, will ever constitute a state which will be truer or better or more exalted in virtue.[35]

Although some of Plato's conceptions of ideal social organization are similar to those found in Marxian communism, it should be noted that whereas Marx looked toward the elimination of classes and the ultimate development of a classless society, Plato envisaged no such prospect. Indeed, using his analogy of the individual, Plato might have asked, "Is appetite to rule reason until the soul is made formless?" To Plato, the very form of human nature and of human society, as of truth, beauty, and goodness, is determined by a hierarchy ranging from the least to the greatest.

As to the form of government, Plato saw the weaknesses of each type. He believed that no one form could long survive. Aristocracy, timocracy, oligarchy, democracy, and tyranny rise and fall in eternal succession. In the *Republic* he preferred the rule of a philosopher-king, which he did not distinguish from an aristocracy, but he was convinced that all we can hope for is a second-best state. Timocracy, a government in which honor and glory are pre-eminent, develops an excess of ambition. It is well suited to a military state but little serves the ends of peace. Oligarchy, a government by the wealthy, leads to an extreme division of the social classes into the opulent and the starving. With the increase in wealth of the ruling class comes easy living and a decline of virtue. As for democracy, Plato could say no more in its favor than that it is the "best of the lawless" and the "worst of the lawful" governments.[36]

Perhaps the memory of Socrates, whose trial and sentence to death well illustrated the fickleness of people in mass, prompted Plato to resort to invective in his criticism of democracy. It is a bazaar, he says, at which everyone finds whatever he seeks. Full of variety and disorder, of excesses, of uninhibited freedoms, democracy attempts impossible aims and neglects those which are attainable. It seeks to dispense a sort of equality to all alike, without regard to individual differences. This is absurd, Plato asserts. On the contrary we should give "to the greater more, and to the inferior less, and in proportion to the nature of each. . . . this is justice, and is ever the true principle of states at which we ought to aim." [37] In a democracy the strong wine of freedom intoxicates, and liberty knows no limit.

. . . the father grows accustomed to descend to the level of his sons and to fear them, and the son is on a level with his father, he having no respect or reverence for either of his parents; and this is his freedom, and the metic is equal with the citizen and the citizen with the metic, and the stranger is quite as good as either. . . .

In such a state of society the master fears and flatters his scholars, and the scholars despise their masters and tutors; young and old are all alike.

. . . see how sensitive the citizens become; they chafe impatiently at the least touch of authority and at length, as you know, they cease to care even for the laws, written or unwritten; they will have no one over them.[38]

So democracy falls and is succeeded by tyranny, the worst form of government. The tyrant emerges as a protector, promising to bring order out of the chaos to which an excess of freedom has led.

At first, in the early days of his power he is full of smiles, and he salutes every one whom he meets. . . . But when he has disposed of foreign enemies by conquest or treaty and there is nothing to fear from them, he is always stirring up some war or other, in order that the people may require a leader . . . as the saying is, the people who would escape the smoke which is the slavery of freemen, has fallen into the fire which is the tyranny of slaves. Thus liberty, getting out of all order and reason, passes into the harshest and bitterest form of slavery.[39]

Fortunately, the tyrant has the heel of Achilles. Some of those about him are high-minded; they rise against him and are purged. But the blood of martyrs generates a host of opponents. The tyrant becomes "more faithless, more unjust, more friendless, more impious, than he was at first." As he becomes miserable himself, he makes everyone else miserable. The situation can be no longer tolerated; the tyrant is overthrown.

SOCIAL CHANGE

If progress means change in a definite and desirable direction, then Plato saw no evidence of progress in the world. He saw, instead, a constant state of flux. It was clear to him that everything which has a beginning has also an end. Death follows life; cities flourish and decay; no form of government endures. There is nothing lasting under the sun.

But Plato was familiar not only with the dictum of the dynamists, that everything flows, but also with the belief of the Eleatics, that being is ultimately one —eternal, immutable, immovable, indivisible, sovereign. This ceaseless change is not wholly random and unpredictable: it is ordered. Motion does not merely happen: it is caused. Only the world of appearances given to the senses lacks form, meaning, and purpose. Reason apprehends a reality which transcends appearance and orders change. Plato was not able wholly to accept an ever present unity.

> There is a time when God himself guides and helps to roll the world in its course; and there is a time, on the completion of a certain cycle, when he lets go, and the world being a living creature, and having originally received intelligence from its author and creator, turns about and by an inherent necessity revolves in the opposite direction.[40]

God's hand in the shaping of events was more evident in a Golden Age long past than now.

> . . . that blessed and spontaneous life does not belong to the present cycle of the world but to the previous one, in which God superintended the whole revolution of the universe. . . . In those days God himself was their shepherd and ruled over them, just as man, who is by comparison a divine being, still rules over the lower animals.[41]

The best-ordered of existing states is a copy of that blessed condition in which men once lived under the rule of God, when all things were spontaneous and abundant.[42] In such phrases Plato deplored the fall from a state of goodness and suggested that change has resulted in retrogression rather than in progress. But generally he takes a cyclical view of change. Day follows night, the seasons repeat themselves, cities rise and fall, organisms are generated and perish, now love, now hate, are in abeyance in the affairs of men.

Plato believed that all change is directed toward the attainment of the good, however far short of its goal it may fall. He deplored change because it reveals an imperfection in whatever is changing; it involves a struggle to attain in one kingdom the goods which can be had only in another. Plato's metaphysical speculations about transcendent Ideas clarify his views on this subject, but his doctrine of two worlds, the one of sense and the other of intellect, the one of particulars and the other of forms, the one of appearance and the other of reality, cannot be stated simply.

Moreover, the good toward which all change is directed is not so much a metaphysical idea as it is a religious insight. Demos has stated the bearing of Plato's idea of God on his theory of social change as follows:

> There is order in the world: the rhythm of the seasons, the revolutions of the stars, the cycle of generation and decay, and the like, which cannot be explained by chance, as the atomists claim; these facts presuppose the operation of intelligence. . . . God is the efficient cause of creation. He is the cause both of the happening of the world and of its order; he is a maker and a designer; he is a creative intelligence. We may say of him either that he is an intelligence which is creative, or a creator who is intelligent; in short . . . he is a purposive cause. And as the creator of the temporal world, he is timeless and ungenerated.[43]

But even though God "guides and helps to roll the world in its course," Plato is far from taking the fatalistic position that all is in God's hand. He dared believe that the world could be remade by human thought and effort. He claimed for reason dominion over appetite and spirit in the life of the individual. He wanted in society the wisest men in the seats of government. If he had moments of pessimism, he at least accepted the efficacy of knowledge. Men are foolish, he believed, only because they are ignorant. He devoted his life to the task of freeing his fellow man from the cave of superstition and fear. Even his utopian dreams of an ideal society are clearly recognized as such, and hence have the highly practical value of revealing goals attainable to a regenerated mankind.

Knowing, as he did, the disturbing effects of war, it is a little surprising that Plato referred so rarely to the prospects for peace. Not that he favored war. "The truth is," says Plato, "there neither is, nor has been, nor ever will be, either amusement or instruction in any degree worth speaking of in war." [44] But there is in war the hope of gain, and so long as men are motivated by desire for gain, wars must be prepared for. Apparently, in the fourth century B.C., the prospect of peace was dim even for Utopia.

PLATO AND PLATONISM

About twenty-five centuries have passed since Plato lectured and wrote in the Academy. He did not address himself to the masses, and he even doubted that persons too much occupied with earning a living should concern themselves about the matters he discussed. Yet Plato's influence throughout the years among people in all walks of life gives eloquent testimony to his universal appeal. In addition to being a system of thought, Platonism is a philosophy of life.

Plato raised all the basic philosophical questions, and in his analysis of ethics, politics, education, religion, art, literature, recreation, human nature, social organization, human relations, and many other topics, he touched the experience of every man. It is helpful when reading him to be familiar with the doctrines of ultimate reality against which all his speculations are set, but much of his social philosophy is easily grasped by those not versed in his metaphysics.

Plato believed that life is worthy of examination, that social participation is natural for man and necessary for his attainment of the good life, that by putting first things first it is possible to create the kind of society most congenial to man, that wrongdoing is due to ignorance, that right conduct is more satisfying than indulgence, and that moral distinctions are securely rooted in rational principles.

Plato's political theory was but part of his ethical system. The *Republic* inquired into the nature of justice and sought to discover how the state should be organized to serve moral ends. Plato clearly recognized that the ideal political organization which he envisaged was unattainable and showed in the *Laws* his ability to take a practical point of view toward politics. Despite the popularity of the *Republic,* Plato's later political work probably has had greater direct influence on society. The *Laws* helped to shape Greek jurisprudence and, through the codes of the Hellenistic Age, the great legal system of Rome.

Although the Academy endured until the Emperor Justinian closed all the schools of Athens in the sixth century A.D., no worthy successor appeared, after Aristotle went his own way, to carry on and develop Plato's ideas. Plotinus, the great exponent of Neoplatonism in the third century A.D., emphasized the mystical strains in Platonic thought and helped to bring Plato's philosophy into the stream of Christian theology. Augustine was for a time a Neoplatonist, and the Church fathers absorbed Plato as the medieval Scholastics absorbed Aristotle. When in the thirteenth century there seemed to be no place for both in Christian theology, Plato was rejected. He was considered a heathen, whereas Aristotle was clothed in Christian garments. Nevertheless, the appeal of Plato, even among good Christians, has continued to this day, and those who follow Augustine rather than Thomas Aquinas are led back to the Academy.

Platonism has experienced an occasional revival—as, for example, at Cambridge in the seventeenth century under the influence of Cudworth and Henry More. Although such organized movements mirror Platonic ideals to the modern world, many of Plato's thoughts, no longer associated with his name, have become part of the world's heritage of ideas. His influence on philosophy has been so pronounced that Alfred North Whitehead's somewhat jocular remark that European philosophy consists of "a series of footnotes to Plato" seems scarcely exaggerated.

8 · ARISTOTLE

(384-322 B.C.)

. . . for as it is not one swallow or one fine day that makes a spring, so it is not one day or a short time that makes a man blessed and happy!
                                                                              ETHICS

THE LIFE OF REASON

Plato once remarked that the Greeks loved knowledge as the Phoenicians loved money. Certainly the world has never known a greater devotion to knowledge in and for itself than that revealed in the Greek philosophy of the fifth and fourth centuries B.C. Whereas ancient Chinese philosophy was chained to morality, and ancient Hindu philosophy, like that of medieval Christendom, was a handmaiden of religion, Greek speculative thought was independent and free. To the Greek philosophers, thought was not a necessary evil but a positive good, not a means but an end, not a mere inclination but an imperative. They gave little heed to the fact that thought is destructive as well as creative, that it plays havoc with old beliefs and customs, that it is a foe to complacency and comfort, that it destroys before it rebuilds, and that it foments an inner turmoil of spirit that is not easily stilled. Instead, they declared that reason exalts and glorifies mankind, and that through its exercise the divine element in man's nature is developed. Aristotle asserts that self-realization demands nothing less than the full exercise of reason:

> If reason is divine, then, in comparison with man, the life according to it is divine in comparison with human life . . . that which is proper to each thing is by nature best and most pleasant for each thing; for man, therefore, the life according to reason is best and pleasantest, since reason more than anything else *is* man.[1]

GREEK HUMANISM

Humanism places man at the center, makes him the measure, seeks for the means of enhancing his dignity and worth, and demands that he prove all things and hold only to the good. The varieties of humanism are many, ranging from excessive individualism to the submergence of the individual in the social whole. In our own day humanism is supported by the faith that man is able to create for himself the kind of social order he chooses. The classic Greeks lacked that faith; they saw no more reason to anticipate social progress in this life than to hope for blessed personal experience beyond the grave. In their literature they often depicted human beings as puppets in the hands of fate, and they sometimes lamented that they had been born to suffer from the jealousy of fickle gods. Yet their faith in human reason, and in the ability of man to attain through reason the good life, reveals a humanism not less elevated than our own.

In their discovery of the power of the human intellect, the Greeks were saved from vanity by their awareness of man's obligation to measure up to the demands, both human and divine, of his nature. Consequently there is little evidence in their writings of the boasting which resulted from the rediscovery of man's distinctive and marvelous mental powers in a much later age, as can be seen in the assertion of Campanella, the seventeenth-century Italian philosopher, that man is

> a second god, the first God's own miracle, for man commands the depths, mounts to heaven without wings, counts its moving bodies and measures their nature. . . . He knows the nature of the stars . . . and determines their laws, like a god. He has given to paper the art of speech, and to brass he has given a tongue to tell time.[2]

Greek thought lacks this self-adulation of man gazing down from an awful height on his vast domain. Greek poetry, art, and philosophy are pervaded by a sense of humility, as these vivid lines from Empedocles well illustrate:

> Straitened are the powers that are shed through the limbs of men; many the strange accidents that befall them, and blunt the edge of thought; brief is the span of that life in death which they behold—swift death to which they are doomed; then are they whirled away, and like a vapour fly aloft, each persuaded only of that on which he has himself chanced to light, driven this way and that. But the whole—man boasts that he has found it: all idly; for these things no eye hath seen, nor ear heard, neither may they be grasped by the mind.[3]

Fatalism is only a partial explanation of this humility; more important is the knowledge that even the best men fall short of perfection. Ideals serve not only to inspire but also to chastise, and the Greeks were chastened by their steadfast devotion to ideals—in art, architecture, politics, literature, and ethics.

In Aristotle, known to the Middle Ages as *the* philosopher and called by Dante "the master of those that know," the peculiarly Greek conception of the life of reason found its full expression.

BIOGRAPHICAL SKETCH

In the twilight of his life, the German poet Goethe paid this tribute to Aristotle:

> If, now in my quiet days, I had youthful faculties at my command, I should devote myself to Greek, in spite of all the difficulties I know. Nature and Aristotle should be my sole study. It is beyond all conception what that man espied, saw, beheld, remarked, observed. To be sure he was sometimes hasty in his explanations; but are we not so, even to the present day?[4]

When a man of genius could hold so high an opinion of a Greek philosopher who died more than three centuries before the beginning of the Christian era as to declare him of all mortals the greatest master, it behooves us to ask who Aristotle was that he should deserve such praise.

The few established facts about his life can be told quickly. He was born in 384 B.C., at Stagira (whence came the name "Stagirite," by which he is sometimes known), a Macedonian city about two hundred miles from Athens. His father, Nicomachus, was court physician to Amyntas II, king of Macedonia and grandfather of Alexander the Great. Except for the fact that Aristotle was thus favored by birth, we know little of his early youth. Durant says:

> We have a choice of stories for his youth. One narrative represents him as squandering his patrimony in riotous living, joining the army to avoid starvation, returning to Stagira to practice medicine, and going to Athens at the age of thirty to study philosophy under Plato. A more dignified story takes him to Athens at the age of eighteen, and puts him at once under the tutelage of the great Master; but even in this likelier account there is sufficient echo of a reckless and irregular youth, living rapidly. The scandalized reader may console himself by observing that in either story our philosopher anchors at last in the quiet groves of the Academy.[5]

Perhaps at eighteen, Aristotle arrived in Athens and entered the Academy. Plato was then ripe in wisdom, and his influence on Aristotle during the twenty years of their close relationship must have been profound. The extent of the agreement between the master of the Academy and his ablest pupil over this long period has been debated, but there is much evidence to show that there existed between them mutual admiration and respect. Aristotle became a severe critic of some of Plato's ideas, but some scholars maintain that much of Aristotle's philosophy had its roots in the teachings of the Academy and represents a growth and logical development of some of Plato's basic ideas.[6]

Aristotle may well have hoped to succeed Plato in the Academy, but when Plato died and a nephew of his was named head, Aristotle left Athens and went to Asia Minor. There he continued his studies, and some of his most important investigations in the field of biology may have been made at this time. He was close to the court, and soon married Pythias, a princess about twenty years his junior. Shortly afterwards he was invited by Philip of Macedonia to become the tutor of Alexander, then a youth of thirteen. For about three years the future master of many peoples studied under the master of ideas, and they seem to have formed an abiding affection for each other. When in later years Alexander traveled far in his conquest of the world, he sent back to his former teacher many manuscripts and specimens of plant and animal life.

In 335 B.C., Aristotle returned to Athens, where he established a school known as the Lyceum. Here for the next twelve or thirteen years he studied, taught, and composed most of his extant writings. When Alexander died, in 323 B.C., the anti-Macedonian party in Athens began demanding the death of Aristotle, but the now aged philosopher, mindful of the fate of Socrates, took advantage of an Athenian law and departed from Greece, saying that he would not voluntarily allow Athens to sin a second time against philosophy. At his country place in Chalcis in Euboea he died a year later, at the age of sixty-two, from a disorder of the stomach.

If the will which Diogenes Laertius quotes is authentic, Aristotle seems to have been a devoted husband, an affectionate father, and a kind master in his own household: he gave instructions that the bones of Pythias should lie beside his own, that his children "be taken in charge" and given generous settlements when they married, and that none of the servants who had waited upon him should be sold but that instead they be given their freedom.

MAJOR WORKS

Since Aristotle is believed to have lectured as he strolled through the gardens of the Lyceum attended by his pupils, his school is sometimes called the Peripatetic (walking about) School. The morning lectures, intended especially for members of the school, were more technical and advanced than those given in the afternoon to the general public. The manner in which his lectures were preserved is much debated. We do not know how much, if any, of the vast body of literature attributed to Aristotle actually came from his own hand. Consequently a number of theories regarding his "writings" have developed, among which the following are the most prominent: (*a*) Aristotle's books represent for the most part a compilation of notes taken by members of his audience; (*b*) they are lecture notes used by Aristotle in his discourses, and although they may have been revised at some later date, they were not prepared by him for publication; and (*c*) Aristotle's original manuscripts underwent considerable change and emendation at the hands of copyists, and spurious works were included in his collection. These theories may help to explain the unfinished nature of much of Aristotle's work, because it is obvious that his thought oftentimes has not come down to us in a form which does justice to his genius.

Diogenes Laertius, who probably lived in the third century A.D., gives a catalogue of Aristotle's works with one hundred and fifty-six titles, many of them comprising several books. Apparently only a fragment of Aristotle's written work remains, but even then the body of extant literature identified with him is vast. It includes treatises on logic, metaphysics, psychology, natural science, ethics, politics, rhetoric, and poetry. Whether or not Aristotle was, as many scholars have believed, "the best educated man that ever walked on the surface of this earth," it is clear that he took all knowledge to be his province and established in every major division of inquiry his right of suzerainty.

A collection of his logical treatises, which came to be known as the *Organon,* contains his analysis of the criteria of proof. This work includes his detailed explanation of the syllogism, and although his invention of this logical tool may be disputed, it cannot be denied that he did more than anyone else before him to perfect it as an instrument of thought. His inquiry into natural phenomena, in which he is said to have been aided by a large staff of assistants and by the generosity of Alexander in providing him with specimens of plants and animals from many lands, resulted in numerous works in the physical and biological sciences, such as his treatises on meteorology, astronomy, growth and decay, the parts of animals, the generation of animals, and many other subjects. In these writings Aristotle developed and applied an inductive method which has developed into the *scientific* method of investigation. The term *metaphysics* (after or beyond physics) was not used by Aristotle, but it has been applied to a considerable body of his work concerned primarily with first principles, or ultimate reality. His treatises on rhetoric and poetry have tremendously influenced literary criticism down to our own day, and they constitute even today major contributions to the field of esthetics.

Such versatility staggers the imagination, but Aristotle would undoubtedly have been numbered among the greatest thinkers of all time even had he contributed nothing in the fields of knowledge mentioned above; his *Ethics* and his *Politics,* together with such portions of other works as deal with man in society, entitle him to that honor. In fact, it is mainly for his insight into the true nature of the good life in society and the means by which it may be achieved that we read Aristotle today. In natural science, the latest ought to be the best; but in the field of human behavior, the wise observations of the ancients remain vital and fresh for all their antiquity, and the voices of men long dead still speak with unmistakable authority.

ETHICS

The *Nicomachean Ethics* (usually abbreviated as *Ethics,* as in this book) is Aristotle's main contribution to the theory of conduct, although it is not his only work in this field. The *Eudemian Ethics* is regarded by most scholars as another authentic statement of Aristotle's ethical doctrine, although it may date from an earlier period in his life than his more famous work. Werner Jaeger believes that a development of Aristotle's moral philosophy can be traced from the *Protrepticus,* dating from the time when Aristotle was very much under the influence of Plato, through the *Eudemian Ethics,* in which the break with Plato is evident, until his theory matured and found complete and final expression in the *Nicomachean Ethics.* In this book Aristotle raises the question of the nature of the good life and gives an answer so convincing that it has been widely accepted for more than twenty-three centuries.

POLITICS

Since Aristotle assumed that the individual could live well only in an organized society, the *Politics* is a companion piece to the *Ethics.* He considered that he was dealing in these two works not with separate subjects but rather with the same subject from different points of view. The state came into being, he says, for the sake of life, but it exists for the sake of the good life. In the *Politics* he repeatedly returns to ethical considerations, and he begins the *Ethics* with the statement that it is preliminary to his study of politics. As Barker points out:

> In the life of the Greek city-state, which drew little distinction between what was private and what was public, and included in its scope the area of social life and moral conduct as well as that of political action, ethics could be regarded as a part or branch of politics. This is the view which Aristotle adopts in many parts of the *Politics.* But his general view of the relation in which ethics stands to politics can hardly be said to be constant; and the very fact that he wrote a separate work on ethics would suggest that he assigned to it a relative independence. In any case, however, the two subjects are closely connected; and the student of the *Politics* who wishes to grasp the whole of Aristotle's political theory is bound to consider the references to politics which are also to be found in the *Ethics.*[7]

Aristotle's education for politics was thorough. In boyhood he was close to the court of Philip of Macedonia. In the Academy he studied politics with the ablest statesmen in Greece, and as a result of his long association with Plato, he was able to build upon the political insights of the *Republic* and the *Laws.* He was an intimate friend of Hermias, the tyrant of Atarneus. He was tutor to Alexander the Great and wrote for him at least two treatises on politics, one on kingship and the other on the administration of colonies. When Greece lost her independence at Chaeronea, and Antipater was directed by Alexander to supervise Greek affairs, Aristotle renewed his acquaintance with his old friend and the two remained on intimate terms. Aristotle was close to the statesman Lycurgus. In addition to these practical experiences, he collected and studied the constitutions of one hundred and fifty-eight states and wrote, according to most scholars, the extant Constitution of Athens.

The practical philosophy of the *Ethics* and *Politics* is, therefore, an outgrowth of experience as well as of thought. Endowed with genius and with worldly goods sufficient for his needs, Aristotle was able to take full advantage of his superior opportunities; by rare good fortune he was able to witness at close hand events of a scope and magnitude commensurate with his ability to comprehend. Aristotle's ethics and politics are, of course, grounded in his metaphysics and supported by his logic, but his living thought on these two subjects can be grasped without probing too deeply into his basic philosophy. Accordingly, the *Ethics* and the *Politics* will form the basis of our analysis of Aristotle's social ideas, although for the sake of convenience and clarity other sources will be used occasionally. First, however, a brief survey of Aristotle's method is necessary, since his logic has framed the thought of thousands of scholars and his inductive science, had it taken hold, might have brought the modern world into existence two thousand years ago.

METHOD

In his search for uniformity by means of inductions from experience, Aristotle was a true scientist. The significance of his accomplishments in the natural sciences can be appreciated only when we realize how meager were the means at his disposal for extending and refining observation. As Zeller points out, Aristotle was compelled

> to fix time without a watch, to compare degrees of heat without a thermometer, to observe the heavens without a telescope, and the weather without a barometer. . . . Of all our mathematical, optical and physical instruments he possessed only the rule and the compass, together with the most imperfect substitutes for some few others. Chemical analysis, correct measurements and weights, and a thorough application of mathematics to physics, were unknown. The attractive force of matter, the law of gravitation, electrical phenomena, the conditions of chemical combination, pressure of air and its effects, the nature of light, heat, combustion, etc., in short, all the facts on which the physical theories of modern science are based were wholly, or almost wholly, undiscovered.[8]

We may well wonder what Aristotle might have contributed to the physical and the biological sciences had he had only a few of the instruments now available to any scientist.

In the social sciences Aristotle's handicap was less serious. To be sure, the tools of social analysis have been sharpened since his time; but they are blunt and crude still in comparison with the sharp instruments employed in the study of natural phenomena. As a consequence, despite Aristotle's all but complete lack of that substantial body of empirical data now available, his failure to possess the aids to observation and analysis now used by social scientists may have been no great handicap to him in his exploration of those areas of human experience to which he gave his attention. For that reason his ethics and politics possess a vitality and timeliness lacking in his physics and biology. Whatever the limitations of his contributions to factual knowledge in some fields, his use and development of induction and logic as means of inquiry constitute a monumental triumph of the human mind.

SYLLOGISM

His main contribution to logic was the syllogism, which he received in a crude state from the hands of his predecessors and developed into a remarkable instrument of exposition. The syllogism does not discover truth; it merely clarifies, extends, and gives precision to ideas accepted as true. It is, according to Aristotle, "a mental process in which certain facts being assumed something else differing from these facts results in virtue of them." Thus, if every man is mortal (major premise), and if Socrates is a man (minor premise), it follows that Socrates is mortal (conclusion). The major premise states a general rule of which the minor premise is a specific instance; the conclusion results from an elimination of the common term (in this case, *man*). Critics have pointed out that the major premise takes for granted what is most in need of proof; for, in the example given above, if death overtakes all men without exception, it is tautologous to say that Socrates is not an exception. The syllogism affords, therefore, a test of consistency rather than of truth, since the conclusion will be true only if the premises are true. Nevertheless, as Benn declares in *The Greek Philosophers:*

> Aristotle has discovered and formulated every canon of theoretical consistency, and every artifice of dialectical debate, with an industry and acuteness which cannot be too highly extolled; and his labors in this direction have perhaps contributed more than any other single writer to the intellectual stimulation of after ages.[9]

We may put the matter thus: if the syllogism does not tell us what we may accept as true, it does show the way to certain conclusions to which we are committed once we have made certain assumptions.

INDUCTION

If thought alone cannot give us truth, how then are we to gain truth? Aristotle's answer to that question is: by sensation and by thought. Aristotle was aware that sensory experience does not give us knowledge in the full sense of the term. According to him, scientific knowledge requires an insight into the causes of phenomena, and causes are grasped not by the senses but by the mind.

Knowledge begins with experience, but it is made perfect by induction, of which man alone is capable.

> Now art arises when from many notions gained by experience one universal judgement about a class of objects is produced. For to have a judgement that when Callias was ill of this disease this did him good, and similarly in the case of Socrates and in many individual cases, is a matter of experience; but to judge that it has done good to all persons of a certain constitution, marked off in one class, when they were ill of this disease, e.g. to phlegmatic or bilious people when burning with fever—this is a matter of art.[10]

If Aristotle had recognized the importance of verifying an induction, he would have described in every essential respect the method of modern positive science, but he did not see with sufficient clarity that an insight is a hypothesis, which must be rigorously tested before it can be accepted. His faith in reason led him to exaggerate the power of the human mind to apprehend universals directly, immediately, and with certainty. He saw clearly that the syllogism assumes "an audience that accepts its premises," but in asserting that induction exhibits "the universal as implicit in the clearly known particular," [11] he failed to attach sufficient importance to the means by which the validity of an induction is established. Consequently he himself often indulged in overhasty generalizations, which, even with the limited data at his command, careful scrutiny would have shown to be untenable. It should be noted, however, that Aristotle was well aware of the imperfections in his method. Of his great work in logic he says:

> We have had no works of predecessors to assist us in this attempt to construct a science of Reasoning; our own labors have done it all. If, therefore, the work appears to you not too inferior to the works on other sciences which have been formed with the assistance of successive laborers in the same department, you will show some indulgence for the imperfections of our work, and some gratitude for the discoveries it contains.[12]

DOCTRINE OF CAUSES

One other characteristic of Aristotle's approach to knowledge, as natural to the Greeks as it is foreign to our own age, is seen in his doctrine of causes. Modern science seeks uniformities and causal relationships; Aristotle demanded more. The fall of a bridge may be explained by excessive strain at some point in its structure; this is the kind of explanation which science can give. But where loss of life results from the collapse, we may want to know just what circumstances brought together at that moment the specific individuals who were killed. Thus the inquiry moves from one level of causal analysis to a higher, and soon reaches a rare atmosphere into which the scientist dare not venture. In his *Bridge of San Luis Rey* the novelist Thornton Wilder probes into causes in the spirit, though not in the form, of Aristotelian philosophy.

According to Aristotle, four causes or principles inhere in the existence or the cognition of anything: the material, formal, efficient, and final. Take, for example, a pottery bowl. It is clay (material), formed in a certain shape (formal), at the hands of a potter (efficient), for a certain purpose (final). Modern science is concerned with material and efficient causes, but Aristotle believed that formal and final causes are more important. To return to the illustration of the falling bridge, Aristotle was willing to look for the design in this particular event and the purpose which lay behind it. In practice he usually confined himself to the simpler forms of causal analysis, but the fact that he regarded inquiry into ends and purposes as the most important part of scientific analysis is highly significant. The admission of design and purpose into the realm of science prepares the way not merely for faith in a mysterious divine power but for the positive knowledge of God. It is easy to see why the medieval Church came near to making Aristotle a saint.

HUMAN NATURE

An analysis of Aristotle's conception of human nature must reckon with a doctrine of human inequality as basic to ancient Greek thought as the idea of equality is to modern thought. Aristotle frankly admitted his social and intellectual detachment from the masses. He showed little compassion for those who toil, either as freemen or as slaves, to provide goods and services for themselves and for their masters. He realized that husbandmen, seamen, tradesmen, and artisans perform services necessary to the state, but he was persuaded that speculative philosophy has little to offer them and that from them should be expected only that degree of virtue "proper to the part they have to play." The kind of work in which they engage deforms the body and degrades the mind, and their way of life is "ignoble and inimical to virtue." Those in authority act wisely with respect to the toiling masses when they keep them in a state of contented submission.

Such sentiments are repugnant to minds tuned to the ideals of human brotherhood. But it may be noted that the charity of which we boast in our day, the faith that we profess in human equality, and the declaration of equal rights that we inscribe in our laws establish only a principle; they do not always describe a practice. We may deplore the failure of Aristotle to recognize the inherent dignity of every human being and the inalienable rights of which no man may be justly deprived; but as long as the weak are exploited and the hungry turned away from the full table, it behooves us to beware of condescending criticism of him.

Aristotle, furthermore, did not know that the good life which he envisaged for the few might eventually be within reach of the many. He did not know that some day single machines would do the work of thousands of men, and that laborers would have time to spend as they please. He happened to live at a time when only the privileged classes were able to take advantage of leisure, but leisure may be worthily used by the many as well as by the few, and Aristotle's prescription for the good life is as effective for a large number of people as for a small. Likewise, in his analysis of human nature, Aristotle probed into the characteristics and possibilities of the men of his own class, but what he actually described is universal man as he saw him. However large may be the proportion of people who are prevented by circumstances from realizing their potentialities, the man whose nature Aristotle described is every man. What, then, did Aristotle believe to be the nature of man?

MAN AS AN ANIMAL

As a student of biology, Aristotle saw that man belongs to the animal kingdom, but he also recognized in man such distinctive characteristics as the hand, the organs which make articulate speech possible, the large brain, the upright posture, and, above all, the power of reasoning which memory and speech enable him to exercise. Man is not by nature virtuous, and where virtue has not developed by teaching and by habit, "no animal is so unscrupulous, or savage, none so sensual, none so gluttonous," as man.

> Neither by nature, then, nor contrary to nature do the virtues arise in us; rather we are adapted by nature to receive them, and are made perfect by habit . . . the virtues we get by first exercising them, as also happens in the case of the arts as well. For the things we have to learn before we can do them, we learn by doing them, e.g., men become builders by building and lyre-players by playing the lyre; so too we become just by doing just acts, temperate by doing temperate acts, brave by doing brave acts.[13]

Like other animals, man seeks pleasure through the satisfaction of his desires, but those men who make the satisfaction of desire their sole object are described by Aristotle "as not appreciably superior to the lower animals." Man's reason enables him to see, as no other animal can, that "desire is in its nature limitless" and consequently enables him to moderate some of his natural inclinations and live as a human being rather than as a beast. Aristotle was aware that society sometimes contains the "tribeless, lawless, heartless" persons denounced by Homer, but he declared that a man who "by nature and not by mere accident is without a state is either above humanity or below it."

MAN AS A SOCIAL ANIMAL

If man were not also by nature a social animal (Aristotle says "political"), he might not develop and use his powers of speech, through which he acquires the human virtues, but he has a natural inclination to seek the company of his kind.

> ... for no one would choose the whole world on condition of being alone, since man is a political creature and one whose nature is to live with others. Therefore even the happy man lives with others; for he has the things that are by nature good. And plainly it is better to spend his days with friends and good men than with strangers or any chance persons. Therefore the happy man needs friends.[14]

The practical advantages of community life, such as security and mutual aid in meeting household needs, form a motive for the union and add to its attractiveness, but "even where there is no need of mutual service, men are none the less anxious to live together." This view of human nature is an important element in Aristotle's theory of political organization. It should be noted, however, that he accepted it as self-evident and did not seek to prove it. He observed community life and assumed that it was natural, just as today we sometimes observe certain behavior and explain it as instinctive without realizing that the "instinct" is not a cause but only another name for the action we have observed.

HEREDITY AND ENVIRONMENT

Aristotle fully appreciated the effects both of heredity and of environment in shaping human nature.

> Some hold that men become good by nature, others by training, others by instruction. The part that is due to nature obviously does not depend upon us, but is imparted through certain divine causes to the truly fortunate.[15]

He declared that some men are by nature slaves, and he justified slavery as a natural institution arising out of differences in the native endowments of men. The weak deserve to be slaves, and they are better off and the whole society prospers when they are enslaved. His recognition of the importance of heredity led to his advocacy of a eugenics program in the state. He said little about its positive aspects—*i.e.*, the means by which the people considered to be the fittest to bear children should be encouraged or required to perform this civic duty. He had much to say, however, about negative eugenics—*i.e.*, about the elimination of the physically unfit. The limits to which he was prepared to go to ensure the preservation of a sound physical stock are, by modern standards, so extreme that one could hardly accuse Aristotle of underestimating the importance of heredity. For example, he sanctioned abortion as a means of relieving society of unwanted children and desired that laws be passed requiring the destruction of children born defective.

Nevertheless, he obviously regarded experience as a more important influence than birth in shaping the nature of the individual. He maintained that human action is voluntary, and that volition is desire guided by reason. Without imagination, there would be no desire, but although man shares with lower animals the capacity for sensuous imagination, he alone is able through his imagination to form rational desires. Nothing in his nature compels him to choose the good; custom and reason enable him to make that choice, and he may choose the bad instead of the good if he has not learned from experience how to choose the good.

> Now each man judges well the things he knows, and of these he is a good judge. And so the man who has been educated in a subject is a good judge of that subject, and the man who has received an all-round education is a good judge in general.[16]

Hence the importance which Aristotle attaches to education, in the sense of the total life experiences of the individual as they shape reason and are in turn mediated by reason. Fools learn nothing from life, but those capable of learning have the wisdom of others to guide them until they are strong enough to think things out for themselves. Thus, man is what he has learned to be, and personality is formed by experience in organized society. Only in its developed form is human nature fully revealed.

ETHICS

The ethical doctrine of Aristotle is not based on a transcendental principle; it derives from the nature of man and is directed toward happiness in this life. Right conduct is defined not in terms of a divine imperative but as that activity which human reason reveals to be most satisfying. As Aristotle denied individual immortality, at least to the extent of disregarding the prospect of salvation beyond the grave as an element in conduct, he was required to exclude the hope of eternal reward, as well as the inspiration of a sense of duty to God, from his ethical theory. It rests, therefore, on self-interest or self-love, which, as Wallace observes, Aristotle believed

> to be the highest law of morals, because while such self love may be understood as the selfishness which gratifies a man's lower nature, it may also be, and is rightly, the love of that higher and rational nature which constitutes each man's true self.[17]

Self-love, however, may be interpreted in many ways, as a few illustrations will show: Shakespeare's Polonius tells his son that good faith among men requires only that each be true to himself; the flesh calls with imperious voice, say the hedonists; and the Golden Rule requires of each that he love his neighbor as himself. It is important, therefore, to see what Aristotle meant by self-interest and self-love.

HAPPINESS

There is nothing unusual about regarding happiness as the highest human good and the measure of self-realization. In regarding happiness "not merely as one among other good things" but as "the most desirable of all things," Aristotle was saying only what many people believe. Yet, although they agree that happiness is the highest good, they differ as to its meaning and the means by which it may be attained. Aristotle's views on these all-important points can best be given in his own words.

> Perhaps, however, it seems a truth which is generally admitted, that happiness is the supreme good; what is wanted is to define its nature a little more clearly. The best way of arriving at such a definition will probably be to ascertain the function of Man. . . . What, then, can this function be? It is not life; for life is apparently something which man shares with the plants; and it is something peculiar to him that we are looking for. We must exclude therefore the life of nutrition and increase. There is next what may be called the life of sensation. But this too, is apparently shared by Man with horses, cattle, and all other animals. There remains what I may call the practical life of the rational part *of Man's being*. But the rational part is twofold; it is rational partly in the sense of being obedient to reason, and partly in the sense of possessing reason and intelligence. The practical life too may be conceived of in two ways, *viz., either as a moral state, or as a moral activity;* but we must understand by it the life of activity, as this seems to be the truer form of the conception.
>
> The function of Man then is an activity of soul in accordance with reason, or not independently of reason. Again the functions of a person of a certain kind, and of such a person who is good of his kind, e.g., of a harpist and a good harpist, are in our view generically the same, and this view is true of people of all kinds without exception, the superior excellence being only an addition to the function; for it is the function of the harpist to play the harp, and of a good harpist to play the harp well. This being so, if we define the function of Man as a kind of life, and this life as an activity of soul, or a course of action in conformity with reason, if the function of a good man is such activity or action of a good and noble kind, and if everything is successfully performed when it is performed in accordance with its proper excellence, it follows that the good of Man is an activity of soul in accordance with virtue, or, if there are more virtues than one, in accordance with the best and most complete virtue.[18]

The *Nicomachean Ethics* is devoted to an analysis of the implications and various shades of meaning of this definition of happiness. Since at the end of the book Aristotle himself makes a recapitulation of his main ideas on the subject, his conclusions are available in concise form in his own words.

We said that happiness is not a moral state; for, if it were, it would be predictable of one who spends his whole life in sleep, living the life of a vegetable, or of one who is utterly miserable. If then we cannot accept this view, if we must rather define happiness as an activity of some kind, as has been said before, and if activities are either necessary and desirable as a means to something else or desirable in themselves, it is clear that we must define happiness as belonging to the class of activities which are desirable in themselves, and not desirable as means to something else; for happiness has no want, it is self-sufficient.

Again, activities are desirable in themselves, if nothing is expected from them beyond the activity. This seems to be the case with virtuous actions, as the practice of what is noble and virtuous is a thing desirable in itself. It seems to be the case also with such amusements as are pleasant, we do not desire them as means to other things; for they often do us harm rather than good by making us careless about our persons and our property. Such pastimes are generally the resources of those whom the world calls happy. Accordingly people who are clever at such pastimes are generally popular in the courts of despots, as they make themselves pleasant to the despot in the matters which are the objects of his desire. . . .

The reason why these things are regarded as elements of happiness is that people who occupy high positions devote their leisure to them. But such people are not, I think, a criterion. For a high position is no guarantee of virtue or intellect, which are the sources on which virtuous activities depend. And if these people, who have never tasted a pure and liberal pleasure, have recourse to the pleasures of the body, it must not be inferred that these pleasures are preferable; for even children suppose that such things as are valued or honoured among them are best. It is only reasonable then that, as men and children differ in their estimate of what is honourable, so should good and bad people. . . .

Happiness then does not consist in amusement. It would be paradoxical to hold that the end of human life is amusement and that we should toil and suffer all our life for the sake of amusing ourselves. . . . [Neither does happiness consist of relaxation or of any other bodily pleasure.] Anybody can enjoy bodily pleasures, a slave can enjoy them as much as the best of men; but nobody would allow that a slave is capable of happiness unless he is capable of life [i.e., the life of a free Athenian citizen]; for happiness consists not in such pastimes as I have been speaking of, but in virtuous activities, as has been already said.[19]

Some definitions of happiness which Aristotle examined and rejected may be noted. According to him, happiness is not a moral state, since a state of character remains unchanged in sleep and one is not happy when asleep; it is not a matter of wealth, for "to say that goods make happiness is like saying that a lyre makes music"; it is not power or honor, since we seek such ends not for themselves but with a view to happiness; it is not bodily pleasure or the avoidance of pain, for then a contented beast would be the happiest of creatures; it is not characteristic of life, because such living things as plants lack the capacity for happiness; it does not consist in pleasant pastimes or in freedom from the risks of life, for that would bemean its nature; it is not a gift of Heaven but rather an achievement of man—in short, it is nothing that lacks self-sufficiency. After showing that these and other interpretations of the nature of happiness are unacceptable, Aristotle is prepared to give his own. Happiness, he says, is conduct in accordance with virtue.

VIRTUE

But what is virtue? Since Aristotle believed that happiness means activity and not a state of character, and that only virtuous activity affords man real happiness, it is clear that his conception of the nature of virtue is the key to his ethical theory.

Unfortunately, the Greek *areté,* usually translated as "virtue," has in English no exact equivalent; perhaps "excellence" is today a close approximation. Even in Greek thought the meaning of the term varied in accordance with changing conceptions of ideal conduct. Jaeger says that in Homeric times the term meant "a combination of proud and courtly morality with warlike valour," and declares:

> The Greeks felt that areté was above everything else a *power,* an *ability to do something.* . . . It is true that areté often contains an element of social recognition . . . its meaning then alters to "esteem," "respect." But that is a secondary sense, created by the highly social character of all human values in early times. The word must originally have been an objective description of the worth of its possessor. It means a power which is peculiar to himself, which makes him a complete man.[20]

Since, according to Aristotle, man's distinctive characteristic is his power of reason, it follows that contemplation is the most virtuous, or most excellent, activity in which he may engage. In pure speculative thought, therefore, man expresses his essential nature, exercises his highest function, and achieves his greatest virtue. Since virtue is not something which one merely possesses but something which one expresses in conduct, it follows that virtuous activity is the life of reason.

DOCTRINE OF THE MEAN

Only God, however, is able to enjoy the perfect happiness of pure contemplation; mortals are incapable of perfection. Aristotle well knew that godlike man has feet of clay, and he refused to allow his vision of perfect bliss in an ideal man to divert his attention from the struggles of his fellow mortals to achieve with imperfect virtues a measure of happiness. He saw that mortality implies imperfection and that however high the spirit may rise in its heavenward flight, the earth still claims mankind for its own. Man's need for some material comforts proves that the sublime happiness which pure contemplation affords lies just beyond his reach.

> Man, as being human, will require external prosperity. His nature is not of itself sufficient for speculation; it needs bodily health, food, and care of every kind. It must not, however, be supposed that because it is impossible to be fortunate without external goods a great variety of such goods will be necessary to happiness . . . it is possible to do noble deeds without being lord of land and sea, as moderate means will enable a person to act in accordance with virtue. . . . Solon was right perhaps in his description of the happy man as one "who is moderately supplied with external goods, and yet has performed the noblest actions,"—such was his opinion—"and had lived a temperate life," for it is possible to do one's duty with only moderate means.[21]

Practical virtue means, therefore, the moderate and harmonious expression of the various impulses, both intellectual and appetitive, of man's nature and their symmetrical development. Aristotle emphatically declared that virtue is not a midpoint between the indulgence of the flesh and the exercise of reason, and pointed out that "such actions or emotions as malice, shamelessness, envy, adultery, theft, murder" are altogether incompatible with virtue. Far from being a mere compromise of opposing impulses, virtue means the guidance of all impulses by reason in order to attain through self-control and the exercise of will as much harmony as possible.

> . . . it is possible to go too far, or not to go far enough, in respect of fear, courage, desire, anger, pity, and pleasure and pain generally, and the excess and the deficiency are alike wrong; but to experience these emotions at the right times and on the right occasions and toward the right persons and for the right causes and in the right manner is the mean or the supreme good, which is characteristic of virtue. . . . It appears then that virtue is a mean state, so far at least as it aims at the mean.[22]

Aristotle did not oppose virtue to vice; he maintained instead that moderation is the key to harmony in life.

> The first point to be observed then is that in such matters as we are considering deficiency and excess are equally fatal. It is so, as we observe, in regard to health and strength; for we must judge of what we cannot see by the evidence of what we do see. Excess or deficiency of gymnastic exercise is fatal to strength. Similarly, an excess or deficiency of meat and drink is fatal to health, whereas a suitable amount produces, augments and sustains it. It is the same, then with temperance, courage, and the other virtues. A person who avoids and is afraid of everything and faces nothing,

becomes a coward; a person who is not afraid of anything, but is ready to face everything, becomes foolhardy. Similarly he who enjoys every pleasure, and never abstains from any pleasure is licentious; he who eschews all pleasures like a boor is an insensible sort of person.[23]

This does not mean that virtue is an uneasy truce between conflicting impulses, or that it is mere prudence. The avoidance of extremes may be nothing more than a cautious effort to gain respectability, but this is not what Aristotle had in mind. He was seeking the *right* course of action, not the easy. Rogers explains this view as follows:

> Put in a somewhat less mechanical way, moral virtue is the sort of action which *adequately* meets the situation that confronts us. It consists in accepting the conditions of life, not resting content, on the one hand, with less than the full possibilities, nor on the other, neglecting the possible for unattainable ideals.[24]

Furthermore, said Aristotle, virtue is not the same for all men. It is not absolute but relative to the life experiences of each individual. Understood as harmony of the whole, the virtue of a simple man is of a different order from that of an educated man, and what would be excess or deficiency for one person might not be so for another.

> Thus if ten be too much and two too little, we take six as a mean in respect of the thing itself; for six is as much greater than two as it is less than ten, and this is a mean in arithmetical proportion. But the mean considered relatively to ourselves must not be ascertained in this way. It does not follow that if ten pounds of meat be too much and two be too little for a man to eat, a trainer will order him six pounds, as this may itself be too much or too little for the person who is to take it; it will be too little for Milo [the famous Crotoniate wrestler] but too much for a beginner in gymnastics. It will be the same with running and wrestling; the right amount will vary with the individual. This being so, everybody who understands his business avoids alike excess and deficiency; he seeks and chooses the mean, not the absolute mean, but the mean considered relatively to ourselves.[25]

By identifying conduct with happiness and recognizing degrees of happiness, Aristotle avoided making right conduct a purely personal matter, relative to time, place, circumstance, and the whole life history of the individual. Brutes are incapable of happiness, and only the truly gifted of men come near to its full enjoyment. From him to whom much is given much is required. Slavish and brutish men find happiness in sensual indulgence, but the needs of intelligent men for self-expression are both more demanding and more rewarding. Between lack and plentitude men struggle to achieve such happiness as they can get, and the range in capacity for happiness is vast. Each enjoys that degree of happiness to which he is entitled. Aristotle saw the wisdom in the remark made by Heraclitus that a donkey will choose, in preference to other goods, a bundle of hay.

POLITICS

Like most other Greeks of his time, Aristotle regarded politics not merely as a science seeking to discover the means by which political ends are gained but also as an art defining the good life and guiding the individual toward it. In fact, he begins the *Ethics* with the statement that this work is preliminary to a study of politics, and declares politics to be the supreme art or science. Politics, he says,

> . . . determines what sciences are necessary in states, and what kind of sciences should be learned, and how far they should be learned by particular people. . . . as it makes use of the other practical sciences, and also legislates upon the things to be done and the things to be left undone, it follows that its end will comprehend the ends of all the other sciences, and will therefore be the true good of mankind. . . . For while in an individual by himself [good] is something to be thankful for, it is nobler and more divine in a nation or state.[26]

ORIGIN AND PURPOSE OF THE STATE

In the order of time, the household is prior to the state. Hesiod was right, says Aristotle, when he sang:

> First a house, then a wife, then an ox for the plough.

Family life is nature's way of ensuring the survival of human kind, and the household comes naturally into existence to provide for the individual's material needs. Only in a temporal sense, however, is the family prior to the state. In a natural sense the state is prior to the individual, the family, and the village; because "the whole is necessarily prior to the part." According to Aristotle, the state is not merely, or primarily, a political organization. Its moral ends are far more important than its services in protecting property and providing security; it exists to make life good.

It is not difficult for us today to grasp this idea, because we have a somewhat similar conception of the nature of the state. We regard democracy not only as a system of government but also as an ethical premise. We say that democracy defines ends which people ought to pursue in communal life, and that the democratic state makes secure the means for attaining those ends. Thus, in a sense, the state is a physical embodiment of a moral ideal. That is the essence of Aristotle's position. There is, however, an important difference between his conception and that now prevailing in the United States: Aristotle exalted the state and subordinated to it other agencies in society which also define, and serve to make attainable, the good life. We should note, however, that the Greeks had not then learned to distinguish between the state and society, and that Aristotle's state should be thought of as something similar to our "community" or "society."

THE POLIS

The Greek *polis* (usually translated "city state") was a form of political organization which had its brief moment in the Hellenic World, went into decline after the Peloponnesian War, and perished with the society which had created it. Although such terms as "community" and "society" describe some of its characteristics, nothing very similar to the *polis* exists in the modern world. Barker says of it:

> The assumption of Aristotle, as of Greek thought generally down to the days of Zeno and the Stoic doctrine of the *cosmopolis,* is that of the small state or civic republic whose citizens know one another personally, and which can be addressed by a single herald and persuaded by a single orator when it is assembled in its "town meeting." It is a small and intimate society: it is a church as well as a state: it makes no distinction between the province of the state and that of society; it is, in a word, an integrated system of social ethics, which realizes to the full the capacity of its members, and therefore claims their full allegiance. A limit of size is imposed upon it by its very nature and purpose (as, conversely, the limit of its size has helped to produce its nature and purpose): being a church and a system of social ethics, it cannot be a Babylon. Small as it is, it is complete in itself: it is "self-sufficient," in the sense that it meets from its own resources—its own accumulated moral tradition and the physical yield of its own soil and waters—all the moral and material needs of its members; and as it does not draw upon others, so it is not conceived as giving, or as bound to give, to others, or as making its own contribution to the general development of Hellas. Whole and complete, with a rounded life of its own, the *polis* rises to a still higher dignity than that of self-sufficiency. It is conceived as "natural"—as a scheme of life which, granted the nature of man, is inevitable and indefeasible.[27]

Aristotle describes in some detail the size, arrangement, and physical setting which he considered to be most desirable for a *polis*. It should be large enough to be self-sufficient but small enough to be "comprehended in a single view." The arrangement of private houses in straight lines is both convenient and pleasant to the eye, but for the sake of security, beauty must be sacrificed in certain portions of the *polis* by some disorder, so that it will be "difficult for strangers to get out of a town and for assailants to find their way in." The ideal geographical location is one open both to the land and to the sea, with exposure to the east, whence come healthful breezes and with protection from the north winds. The climate should be temperate, since too much cold makes men bold but stupid, and too much warmth makes them intellectual but effeminate.

CITIZENSHIP

In Aristotle's opinion, citizenship should be granted only to those residents of the *polis* who have the education, the freedom, and the inclination to participate in government. Those engaged in productive labor of any kind are disqualified, both by the demands of various occupations and by lack of training. Citizenship means "the privilege of participation in deliberative or judicial office." Naturally the *polis* will require a large number of free husbandmen, artisans, tradesmen, and other productive workers, as well as many slaves, but such persons have neither the leisure nor the capacity to share in the responsibilities of government and consequently should not be regarded as citizens.

The distinction that Aristotle makes, however, between citizens and noncitizens is neither sharp nor consistent. He speaks of different classes of citizens, the noble being citizens in a truer sense than the ignoble. He admits that the proportion of citizens in a *polis* will depend on the form of government, there being, for example, many citizens in a democracy and few in an oligarchy. In his ideal state each man does not count as one and no man as more than one, as modern democracy requires; but, at the same time, noncitizens have rights which must be respected. Aristotle shows regard for the collective power of the masses, as well as respect for their collective judgment. He defines a citizen as "one who shares in governing and being governed"; thus, the citizen shares with the noncitizen the obligation to recognize the authority of the state. Furthermore, the kind of citizen Aristotle has in mind is as much a servant of the people as he is their master. He requires wealth and freedom, but justice and valor are required of him. For, as Aristotle says, "without the former qualities a state cannot exist at all, without the latter not well." [28]

Such a doctrine of citizenship is incompatible, of course, with the modern democratic ideal of equality. But Aristotle did not believe that men are equal. Some are stronger than others, as an old fable well illustrates. Antisthenes says that at a council of the beasts the hares began haranguing the lions and claiming equality; but the lions replied, "Where, then, are your claws?" Aristotle denied that men are equal in virtue and insisted that justice demands only that equal things be rendered those who are equal. Laws may not be administered uniformly, since only that behavior may be required of an individual which is appropriate to his station in life. The law is sovereign, but it must be adapted to circumstances; Aristotle even declared that men of pre-eminent virtue are themselves a law. His defense of slavery is based on a denial of equality. Slavery is just, he says, where those enslaved are natural slaves and not merely victims of circumstance.

For that some should rule, and others be ruled is a thing, not only necessary, but expedient; from the hour of their birth some are marked out for subjection, others for rule. . . . It is clear, then, that some men are by nature free and others slaves, and that for these latter slavery is both expedient and right.[29]

THE INDIVIDUAL AND THE STATE

It is easy to accuse Aristotle of maintaining that the individual exists for the sake of the state, since much that he says does seem to give support to that view. This interpretation, however, results from confusing modern conceptions of the nature of the state with those prevailing in ancient Greece. Thomas Woody has well described the Greek point of view:

> As the city-state became progressively the instrument of the good life for a greater number of men, it took on an ever larger significance, required more service, and a sort of loyalty hitherto unknown. Indeed, as the state became thoroughly a part of Hellenic consciousness, service to it became the most vital religion of the citizen. "Man versus the State" was a concept unknown to the Greek. In the state he was complete, was enabled to enjoy a rational existence. Plato, logically enough to men of his generation, regarded "service of the laws" as "also the service to the Gods. . . ." To defend the city and preserve the vineyards was synonymous with religion itself. Man losing his identity in the state was no more difficult for Greeks than losing one's self in God was to the early Christians. Aristotle declared: ". . . men should not think it slavery to live according to the rule of the constitution; for it is their salvation." [30]

According to Aristotle, the state is by nature prior to the individual; it affords the scene of his birth, makes possible his survival, and provides his security; it forms his aspirations and makes possible their realization; it prescribes his special virtue and maintains the conditions which permit its exercise—in short, the state makes it possible for the individual through losing himself to find himself and enjoy the happiness he deserves.

> No citizen has a right to consider himself as belonging to himself; but all ought to regard themselves as belonging to the state, inasmuch as each is a part of the state; and care for the part naturally looks to care for the whole.[31]

For the sake of order, Plato had advocated an unconditional submission of the individual to the state. Aristotle's political utopia requires no less of the individual, but it bases its claim on the inherent needs of man's nature.

> For man, when perfected, is the best of animals, but, when separated from law and justice, he is the worst of all; since armed injustice is the more dangerous, and he is equipped at birth with arms, meant to be used

by intelligence and virtue, which he may use for the worst of ends. Wherefore, if he have not virtue, he is the most unholy and the most savage of animals, and the most full of lust and gluttony. But justice is the bond of men in states, for the administration of justice, which is the determination of what is just, is the principle of order in political society.[32]

For one who was himself stateless and a sojourner among an alien people, this view may be colored by personal experience, and it is not surprising that Aristotle should have left the way open for a few gifted individuals to rise above this need and view with calm detachment the ebb and flow of political tides.

FORMS OF GOVERNMENT

In the *Republic,* Plato gave free rein to his imagination and created an ideal state. Aristotle, on the other hand, constantly shifted in his discussion of politics from the ideal to the practical, from the kind of state that he would like to see to the kinds that he actually observed. A good government is a well-administered government, whatever its form. He declared, however, that there are three natural forms of government and that which of these is best depends at any specific time on the character of the people. These forms are monarchy, aristocracy, and constitutional republic (or timocracy). Each of these forms has an unnatural or corrupt variation: tyranny, oligarchy, and democracy.

Aristotle called monarchy "the best form of government," but he was quick to admit that the conditions which enable it to exist—high authority based on goodness in the king and voluntary obedience in the subjects—occur but rarely and never endure. He declared that even should a monarchy be established it will soon degenerate into a tyranny, which he called the worst form of government. Kingship fails because the people expect too much of the king, and tyranny fails because the tyrant requires from the people too much for his own sake.

A government of aristocrats, with the best of men wisely directing the affairs of state for the common good, must certainly have appealed to Aristotle. But his realism would not permit him to close his eyes to the hard facts of human experience, and he asserted, consequently, that aristocracies are beyond the reach of ordinary states and within the grasp of exceptional states only "in a limited sense of the term." An aristocracy is easily converted into an oligarchy because of the "inordinate value" which ruling classes set on wealth. As the rich become richer, the social distance between them and the poor increases.

> Thus arises a city, not of freemen, but of masters and slaves, the one despising, the other envying; and nothing can be more fatal to friendship and good fellowship in states than this: for good fellowship springs from friendship; when men are at enmity with one another, they would rather not even share the same path.[33]

Therefore the constitutional republic must be regarded as the best attainable form of government for most states. Aristotle called democracy, or the rule of the many, a perverted form of constitutional government but maintained that there are many kinds of democratic governments and that generally democracy is the best of the unnatural forms of government. If it attempts to establish absolute equality of political privilege, demagogues arise and destroy it; its security depends upon the support of a large middle class.

> Thus it is manifest that the best political community is formed by citizens of the middle class, and that those states are likely to be well-administered, in which the middle class is large, and stronger if possible than both the other classes, or at any rate than either singly; for the addition of the middle class turns the scale, and prevents either of the extremes from being dominant. Great then is the good fortune of a state in which the citizens have a moderate and sufficient property; for where some possess much, and the others nothing, there may arise an extreme democracy, or a pure oligarchy; or a tyranny may grow out of either extreme—either out of the most rampant democracy, or out of an oligarchy; but it is not so likely to arise out of the middle constitutions and those akin to them.[34]

In pointing out the characteristics of the various forms of government, Aristotle kept an open mind. He set forth ideals which any government might strive to attain, but he was also willing to consider

> the best constitution for most states, and the best life for most men, neither assuming a standard of virtue which is above ordinary persons, nor an education which is exceptionally favoured by nature and circumstances, nor yet an ideal state which is an aspiration only, but having regard to the life in which the majority are able to share, and to the form of government which states in general can attain.[35]

POLITICAL CHANGE

Aristotle maintained that all forms of government are sooner or later overthrown "either from within or from without." He saw some sequence in political change, as, for example, the degeneration of each of the natural forms into its unnatural variation, but apparently he did not believe in a fixed cycle of change in the forms of government.

With characteristic Greek distaste for change, he sought for means by which change might be moderated and offered some suggestions that are still sound. The spirit of obedience to the law, he says, must be jealously maintained and not allowed to weaken through disregard of small offenses. Movements should be checked before they gather momentum. Care should always be taken "never to wrong the ambitious in a matter of honor, or the common people in a matter of money." It is sometimes wise "to invent terrors and bring distant dangers near, in order that the citizens may be on their guard, and, like sentinels in a night-watch, never relax their attention." No one should be permitted to profit financially from a government office. The most important means of maintaining power, however, is through the political indoctrination of the young; whatever the form of government, it is the business of the state to instill in the minds of young people their duty to support it.

Aristotle was persuaded, nevertheless, that no form of government endures forever. The measures we have described, and others, may delay the collapse of a government, but they cannot prevent its eventual succession by another form.

THE FAMILY

In general, Aristotle adopted the prevailing views of his day regarding marriage and family life. He sharply criticized Plato for advocating, in the *Republic* at least, reforms which were repugnant to the Greek mind of that time. As Davidson says:

> . . . the Greek in marrying looked above all things to the chances of worthy offspring. Indeed, it may be fairly said that the purpose of the Greek in marriage was, not so much to secure a helpmeet for himself as to find a worthy mother for his children. . . . The romantic, pathological love-element, which plays so important a part in modern match-making, was almost entirely absent among the Greeks.[36]

The state was the unit of social organization among the Greeks, not the family. Aristotle regarded marriage and childbearing as public rather than private matters and maintained that they ought to be controlled by the state. In other respects as well, he definitely subordinated the family to the state.

MARRIAGE AND CHILDBEARING

Since Aristotle believed that the age of parents affects the inherited characteristics of their offspring, he would have the state fix the ages at which marriage might occur. In order to ensure the birth of children to parents in their prime, he held that women ought to marry at eighteen and men at thirty-seven (he followed this rule himself); procreation would then begin as parents were entering the years of their greatest intellectual strength. The number of children allowed any married couple should be fixed according to the needs of the state; any others begotten should be destroyed either before or after birth, preferably before they had seen "the light of day." Aristotle regarded this method of controlling the size of the population as entirely natural. Indeed, says Lecky,

> The practice of abortion was one to which few persons in antiquity attached any deep feeling of condemnation. The physiological theory that the foetus did not become a living creature till the hour of birth had

some influence on the judgments passed upon this practice. . . . Aristotle not only countenanced the practice, but even desired that it should be enforced by law, when population had exceeded assigned limits. No law in Greece, or in the Roman Republic, or during the greater part of the Empire, condemned it. . . . The language of the Christians from the very beginning was very different. With unwavering consistency and with the strongest emphasis, they denounced the practice, not simply as inhuman, but as definitely murder.[37]

The preservation of a sound physical stock appeared so important a matter to Aristotle that he would have laws prohibiting the rearing of deformed children and denying any man over fifty-five the right to become a father.

FAMILY RELATIONS

According to Aristotle, the relations in the home are comparable to, and take their pattern from, those found in the state.

> The association of a father with his sons takes the form of a kingship, as a father cares for his children. . . . The association of husband and wife seems to be aristocratical; for the husband's rule depends upon merit, and is confined to its proper sphere. He assigns to the wife all that suitably belongs to her. . . . The association of brothers resembles a timocracy; for they are equals except so far as they differ in years; hence if the difference of years is very great, the friendship ceases to be fraternal.[38]

Aristotle regarded the subordination of women to men as natural, and therefore proper. "Silence is a woman's crown," Sophocles had said; and Aristotle shared his conviction. He claimed that males are by nature superior and better qualified to command than females, and that nothing could be worse than a household without a head. Apparently with an eye to the experience of Sparta, he declared that political power in the hands of women seems always to create a certain indecorum and to encourage the growth of avarice in the state.

If we are inclined to accuse Aristotle of masculine arrogance, we must again take care not to intrude the sentiments of our own age into his. Apparently he simply believed that women are better off, and that the whole state prospers, when they exercise their chief functions of bearing children and caring for their families "free from anxiety and in comparative indolence."

ARISTOTLE AND ARISTOTELIANISM

Although Plato and Aristotle worked together in the Academy for twenty years, fundamental differences existed between them. Plato expressed himself in the language of poetry; Aristotle preferred the tight logic of the syllogism.

Plato might have rested content with the Chinese saying, "The Tao that can be expressed in words is not the eternal Tao"; Aristotle would probably have struggled to make the matter plainer. Plato distrusted the senses; Aristotle made himself the master of all the sciences of his time. Plato used the deductive method of mathematics, descending from principles to particulars; Aristotle employed the inductive method of biology, ascending from phenomena to generalizations. Plato's *Republic* expresses social ideals and inspires social reconstruction; Aristotle's *Politics* is a scientific analysis of various forms of political organization. Plato provided the philosophical basis of the theology of Augustine and other Church fathers; Aristotle, that of Thomas Aquinas and other Scholastics. To this day the "tender-minded," in the language of William James, prefer Plato, and the "tough-minded" choose Aristotle.

Aristotle's thought found expression after his death in the works of such philosophers as Theophrastus, Eudemus, and Strato, but it gradually receded to the background. By the sixth century A.D., it was virtually lost to all save a few Arabian and Assyrian scholars. In the twelfth and thirteenth centuries, as we shall see, it was revived to afford a framework for Thomistic theology. During several succeeding centuries Aristotle's prestige was so great that Dante's famous tribute expressed what many scholars believed. To most of the educated people of that period, Aristotle was in fact the master of those that know.

The popularity of Aristotle waned with the rise of Cartesian rationalism and even more with the growth of the scientific spirit. His identification with Scholasticism made him an easy target for those who sought to discredit the learning of the monks, and the fact that he had himself been a scientist was at first overlooked by many of those who sought to establish the scientific method. After his own writings became generally known, he inspired the scientists as he had formerly served the Scholastics.

Like Plato, Aristotle will not lie buried. The numerous references to him in contemporary social and philosophical writings are proof of his secure position in the realm of ideas. As perhaps no other had done, or has done since, he made all knowledge his province. Many of the concepts now used in science and philosophy have come from him. He divided philosophy into the branches still recognized. He found his way into all the dark places where the human spirit dwells; wherever he turned, he usually shed light on human experience. He has inspired men and women of diverse interest and religions. If, as he believed, the good for man consists in man's use of his peculiarly human faculties, then Aristotle might well be called, in that sense, one of the best of men.

In the nineteenth century Pope Leo XIII encouraged the study of Aristotle, and the revival of Thomism in modern times has increased interest in his writings. The emotional stimulation of Plato is not found in Aristotle, but as long as people delight in hard, clear thought, shorn of rhetorical flourishes, Aristotle is likely to be read.

9 · ROME

The commonwealth of Rome was founded firm
On ancient customs and on men of might.
                                    ENNIUS—*Annales*

In the early history of Rome, myth is so entwined with fact that it is impossible to say precisely how Roman civilization began or to determine the exact date on which Rome began to take shape as a political society. Certainly the Republic had existed for several centuries before the Romans met the Macedonian forces in 168 B.C. and forced the Grecian peoples to acknowledge Rome's military superiority. On that date Rome assumed political control over the Greco-Roman world. The Republic lasted until 31 B.C., when Imperator Caesar Octavius, known as Augustus, obtained supreme command over Roman troops and assumed kingly powers; that year marks the beginning of the Empire.

Augustus is credited with having ushered in the Golden Age of Roman civilization. He brought to an end the civil strife which had characterized much of Rome's history during the Republic, and he extended and consolidated the Empire. Perhaps the century just preceding the birth of Christ and the first century of the Christian era witnessed Rome's greatest achievements. Although for a century more Rome's domain continue to expand, her Golden Age barely survived Augustus.

THE RISE OF ROME

Much has been said about the decline and fall of Rome but very little about the rise of Rome—Rome the city, which more than any other city in history constituted the heart of a civilization and furnished the life blood which sustained it; and Rome the civilization, which encompassed in the day of its glory the Mediterranean world. Thousands of historians, poets, and moralists, including some who talked with the Caesars and counseled with the Antonines, have traced out in lurid detail a picture of Rome grown wicked and feeble; few have been able to discover what made possible her rise to power.

If history is made by great men, then we should find among the Romans some of the greatest personalities the world has yet produced. But who? There is, to be sure, Julius Caesar, the military genius. On the other hand, it may be questioned whether Caesar, in all his campaigns, made a contribution to military science equal to that of Hannibal at Cannae. The literary accomplishments of Lucretius, Virgil, Horace, Ovid, Juvenal, and many other Latin writers were truly magnificent, but many of their best works are often crowded out of a collection of the masterpieces of world literature. Cicero and Seneca preserved Greek philosophy, but they added little to it. Rome produced no Archimedes, and Greek science withered when transplanted in Roman soil. Over the long centuries of Rome's power and prestige one looks in vain for Romans who have among men the eminence which Rome has among civilizations.

The city of Rome did not possess advantages of geographical location so conspicuous as to set her apart from other cities. The seven or more hills on which ancient Rome was situated were fourteen miles from the sea, along a river serving but poorly the needs of agriculture and trade. Nearby were marshes from which came the malaria plagues against which Rome often struggled. The protection which the site afforded from attack, either by land or by sea, might have been important when Rome was a village, but throughout most of her history Rome carried the fight to the enemy. The hinterland was the most fertile and productive in Italy, but from ancient times to the present Italy has had to import food. Rome was located near the center of the Mediterranean area, but other cities of antiquity—Athens, Syracuse, Carthage, Alexandria—were also favorably situated from the point of view of easy access to the lands lapped by that inland sea. Any advantage that Rome might have had as a result of her proximity to northwest Europe was lessened by the formidable barriers of the Alps. Hispania and Gallia were by no means the brightest jewels in Rome's imperial crown, and Roman strength was dissipated against Germania. One physical asset Rome had, and still has, abundantly—a setting of great natural beauty. But this might be expected to develop gaiety and joy in life rather than greed for power, a Renaissance rather than an Empire.

Furthermore, Rome failed to develop any of those great ideas which serve to fire the imagination and bring people together in unity of purpose and in hope. She conquered without a theory of conquest; she ruled by practices dictated by expediency; she lacked the sustaining force of religion; she found no answer to the problem of class conflict; she caught no vision of a goal toward which the united efforts of her people could be directed. In the fifth century

B.C., Rome was an agrarian society, with a stern code of laws and a family system designed for discipline. By the third century B.C., the strength of the peasants had been organized under urban leadership, and Roman society had achieved political solidarity within the framework of democracy. From the point of view of public morality and private self-respect, this was the high point in Roman civilization. But the Empire had not then been born, and by the time Rome had come to maturity, the independence and the homely virtues of peasants had been supplanted among the masses by vices which only a highly sophisticated urban people can fully develop. The Romans did not, therefore, gain strength from ideals; they did not in practice dedicate themselves to noble causes. The *Pax Romana* was not achieved in the name of justice. Even that supreme achievement, Roman law, which the Byzantine Emperor Justin had codified (A.D. 528-534), was forged from the hard facts of experience as an instrument of power.

The claim sometimes made that the Romans were a superior racial stock is an assumption, not a verifiable fact. The Romans were Indo-Europeans, kinsmen to the Greeks whom they conquered and racially close to some of the barbarians whom they scorned. Even in the days of the Republic, the blood of all those peoples with whom Rome had made contact flowed freely in Roman veins.

The search for a simple explanation of Rome's rise leads to the conclusion that no single cause can be found. Rather must we recognize the fact that many conditions made Roman civilization possible, some obscure and the others impossible to weigh accurately. Although Roman generals lost battles, they were collectively able to win wars. Roman eloquence was adequate for the demands of patriotism; Roman verse kept aglow the flame. The Roman ship of state might shift her course, but in so doing she was able to ride out the storms. A better geographical location might have been found, but the one which came to constitute the hub of the Roman world had some natural advantages. If Rome lacked a mission, at least she was able to envisage aims within human grasp and to achieve those aims. The Roman breed, if not superior, was tough. Collectively these are the factors which explain the rise of Rome. Social causation is always complex. Causes lead to causes, as from single drops of water come the streams from which broad rivers flow.

REPRESENTATIVE ROMANS AND SELECTED WORKS

The task of deciding which extant works best describe Roman social thought is a formidable one. Writing was fashionable in Rome, and the leisure afforded by the extensive use of slaves made it possible for many to follow the fashion. A considerable body of correspondence developed from the dispersion of Romans over the Empire. Commentaries, orations, epistles, histories, treatises, laws, and public and private records have all been preserved in considerable number, to say nothing of a vast body of creative literature of miscellaneous character. Caesar, Cicero, Seneca, Livy, Cato, Lucretius, Virgil, Horace, Ovid, Tacitus, Juvenal, Petronius, Martial, Plutarch, Pliny, Apuleius, Aurelius—these are only a few of the gifted Romans whose works have survived. This is a deep well into which to let down the bucket, but those whose thirst is only whetted by a sample can go to the well from which we have drawn and drink deeply.

THE TWELVE TABLES

In Cicero's day students were required to memorize an ancient code of laws known as the *Twelve Tables*. As a result of that academic requirement, fragments of Roman law in the fifth century B.C. have been preserved in the writings of Romans who lived centuries later. If it were not for these scattered fragments, we would today know little about Rome's first code of laws, since neither the original tablets nor copies made from them have survived.

According to tradition, the patricians and the plebeians were in early Roman history at odds with each other over economic and social matters, and one source of grievance to the plebeians was the ignorance in which they were kept respecting the law. At that time the patricians may have exercised priestly as well as secular functions of authority; in any case, they kept secret the basis upon which they administered justice, and the plebeians demanded a written statement of the laws by which they were judged. Finally it was decided that the consuls and tribunes should resign their offices in order that an elected body of ten citizens could exercise supreme executive power and thus have complete freedom of action for two years, during which time they were charged with the responsibility of drawing up a code of laws for the Roman people. A delegation may have been sent to Athens to study the laws of Solon, but the code that was offered to the people in 451 B.C. was distinctly Roman. Ten tables of laws were approved by the Assembly and were displayed on bronze tablets in the Forum for the information and guidance of all. Two years later another board of ten citizens, elected to complete the work, produced two additional tables; and when these had been approved by the Assembly, the whole body of laws was adopted as the *Laws of the Twelve Tables*.

Livy says that this code was for the Romans the "source of all law, both public and private." Certainly it established early in Roman history a basis for constitutional government. In a society which centuries later was to discover what despotism can mean, it stirred a desire for government under law that laid Julius Caesar low in the day of his triumph and forced Nero finally to take his own life. Furthermore, since the code claimed to be based on customs, it established Roman law on a secular basis. With their basic laws codified and openly displayed, the Romans did not need to look to the priests for definitions of social justice; this may have been an important reason why the priesthood did not become in Roman society an important center of power. Despite the fragmentary form in which the code is available, the *Twelve Tables* is a valuable source of information about early Roman social thought.

POLYBIUS (204-122 B.C.)

Polybius, a Greek, resided in Rome at various times in his life and there had access to official Roman documents. He knew intimately some of Rome's most distinguished citizens, including Scipio Africanus, with whom he witnessed the destruction of Carthage. Early in life he recognized the supremacy of Rome and urged the Greeks to submit to Rome's authority. His *Universal History,* in which he attempted to show why "all the known regions of the civilized world had fallen under the sway of Rome," was a monumental undertaking to which he devoted the best years of his life. Of the forty books in this history, only the first five have been preserved in complete form, but fragments from the others have been collected from various sources. There is, consequently, a body of work extant from which the thinking of Polybius on at least three important social topics can be learned: (1) social change, (2) the structure and function of political institutions, and (3) the forces which shape human behavior. It is impossible to estimate the extent to which he reflects the social ideas of the Roman society he came to know so well; but he was more Roman than Greek, more Roman even than many of those in Rome who were first introduced to serious thought by Greek teachers and who frankly admitted Greek superiority in intellectual matters. Polybius lived to the age of eighty-two, meeting death as a result of an accidental fall from his horse.

LUCRETIUS (c. 98-55 B.C.)

Little is known about the author of the greatest philosophical poem that Rome produced. Lucretius left but a single work, *De Rerum Natura,* which is both an exposition in verse of some of the main principles of Epicurean philosophy and also a sermon on human happiness. The purpose of the poem is ethical rather than speculative. Lucretius preaches the doctrine of salvation according to Epicurus—that is, the attainment of happiness through avoidance of pain. Since, according to Epicurus, the greatest source of pain is fear of the gods and of punishment after death, Lucretius vigorously attacks belief in the gods. It should be noted, however, that the gods he rejects are the cruel, capricious Greek deities who could look down from Mount Olympus with favor on the sacrifice of Iphigenia by her father when his ships were becalmed. Although Lucretius insists that this world is but one of many worlds, that it was not purposely created and is not divinely guided, that the soul disintegrates with the flesh; yet he maintains that substance is eternal and motion incessant, and that Natural Law pervades the universe. Thus Lucretius is much nearer to the spirit of modern theism than he is to atheism. Cicero saw in Lucretius "high lights of genius," and later critics have declared that, for depth of feeling and vividness of expression, he is the equal, if not the superior, of Virgil.

CICERO (106-43 B.C.)

In the year 80 B.C., a certain Sextus Roscius was on trial in Rome, charged with the crime of parricide. His advocate was a young man of twenty-six, whose eloquence and skill carried the day and gave notice to Roman society that a new leader had arrived. His success in defending the accused was no accident. Born in 106 B.C., the son of an equestrian,* Marcus Tullius Cicero had studied rhetoric under the ablest masters to be found, not only in Rome but also in Athens and in Rhodes. He sat at the feet of the most famous philosophers of his time; it is said that Diodorus the Stoic and Philo the Academician were among his teachers. He attended lectures, traveled widely, tried his hand at poetry, and read law under the most distinguished jurisconsults in Rome.

When his talent was ripe, Cicero married into a wealthy and distinguished family and began the literary and political activities for which he had labored to prepare himself. His ability as an advocate was soon recognized, and his services were in great demand. What he had not learned about the fine points of law from the Scaevolas he more than compensated for by his mastery of invective and pathos. In 76 B.C., he became a quaestor, within ten years he was praetor, and in 63 B.C., he was elected consul; he had reached the top of the political ladder at the age of forty-three.

At various times in his life Cicero held administrative posts in the provinces. As a youth he bore arms under Strabo and Sulla; as governor of Cilicia he conducted successful military operations, and in the struggle between Caesar and Pompey he was offered military commands by both sides. His literary accomplishments were prodigious. Poetry, political and philosophical treatises, orations, and letters literally poured from his facile pen. Among his political works are the *Republic* and the *Laws,* both written in imitation of Plato. In *De Finibus,* he criticizes the Stoic and Epicurean philosophies which Rome had inherited from Greece. Fifty-eight of his orations have survived, most of them adapted by Cicero himself for publication. His letters, of which more than nine hundred have been preserved, are often frank and intimate; especially in the letters to Atticus, his "second self," he drops the mask he wears in his formal writings.

Cicero was not a lovable character. He has been accused of insincerity, lack of integrity, and even dishonesty. It is unfortunate for our purposes that his education should have fitted him so admirably for sophistry; he does not hesitate to make the worse appear the better cause. His training prepared him to support with the same air of sincerity either side of an issue, as school debaters in our

---

* The equestrian order was a wealthy citizen class of knights formed originally of soldiers with the means to serve in the cavalry.

own day are sometimes taught to give an honest ring to a false sentiment. Many inconsistencies in his utterances are in part explained by his desire to gain a specific effect rather than to communicate a genuine conviction.

Although Cicero gained wealth and fame, he was never able to rest on his laurels; to the day of his death he was active in politics. The sharp tongue that won him so many victories over his opponents finally cost him his life. Antony writhed under his philippics and persuaded Octavius to turn against him. On the 7th of December, 43 B.C., he was killed. The statement attributed to him when he saw that death was near reflects not only his vanity but also his courage and his patriotism: "Let me die for the country which I have so often saved."

SENECA (c. 3 B.C.–A.D. 65)

Lucius Annaeus Seneca was the son of a wealthy and distinguished equestrian. In youth he studied rhetoric, with parental approval, and philosophy, against his father's wishes. His delicate constitution did not prevent his preparation for a senatorial career, and at the age of thirty-five he became a quaestor. His advancement in politics was rudely checked by Messalina, who in A.D. 41 succeeded in having him banished. After eight years, however, Seneca was recalled by Agrippina as a tutor for her son, Nero, then eleven years old. He was advanced to a praetorship within a short time, and six years later was made consul. At the age of sixty he was politically powerful and rich. Perhaps he was too rich, because Nero turned against his former teacher and forced him to retire from public life. For the sake of peace in his old age, Seneca was willing to give up his fortune; but, stripped of political power, he was at the mercy of men who felt no compassion for the weak. He was accused of taking part in Piso's conspiracy and forced in A.D. 65 to commit suicide.

There are contradictions in the life and character of Seneca. He claimed to despise wealth, yet he amassed one of the largest fortunes of his day. He preached noble indifference to circumstance, yet he displayed a lively concern for his own practical affairs. His moral courage failed when he was called upon to help Nero prepare a justification for the murder of Agrippina. Perhaps he was born into an age in which no sensitive soul could thrive. As Dill says:

> He was continually torn by the contrast between the ideal of a lofty Stoic creed and the facts of human life around him, between his own spiritual cravings and the temptations or the necessities of the opportunist statesman. He was imbued with principles of life which could be fully realised only in some Platonic Utopia; he had to deal with men as they were in the reign of Nero, as they are painted by Tacitus and Petronius. If he failed in the impossible task of such a reconciliation, let us do him the justice of recognising that he kept his vision clear, and that he has expounded a gospel of the higher life, which, with all its limitations from temperament

or tradition, will be true for our remotest posterity, that he had a vision of the City of God.[1]

His extant works are numerous, but they constitute only a part of his prodigious literary accomplishment in the form of essays, plays, poetry, letters, treatises, orations, and scientific studies. His main interest was in conduct, which he said was "three-fourths of life," and his point of view was essentially that of Stoicism.

HUMAN NATURE AND ETHICAL BEHAVIOR

Although many schools of philosophy had adherents in Rome, only two flourished there; it is significant that both were concerned primarily with ethics. The Romans cared little for the theoretical problems of knowledge, but they were much interested in the practical problems of conduct. Consequently they neglected Plato and Aristotle in favor of two Greek philosophers who had concentrated on the problem of human happiness. Epicurus (342-270 B.C.) had taught that men find happiness by seeking out and avoiding the causes of pain; Zeno (350-260 B.C.), that they find happiness when they live in harmony with nature. Since so many Romans preferred Epicureanism and Stoicism to the more comprehensive philosophical systems with which they were acquainted, we must ask what there was in these philosophies of happiness that appealed to the Roman mind.

Little of Epicurus' writing has been preserved, and it is fortunate, therefore, that Epicureanism should have had so able and devoted an exponent as Lucretius, whose *De Rerum Natura* is generally regarded as an orthodox statement of some of the most important doctrines of Epicurus. Although Epicureanism is easily corrupted into a justification of sensuality, the gentle Epicurus taught those who assembled in his gardens in Athens, both by precept and by example, that real happiness is found in the peace of mind which comes when foolish fears are banished. It is this conception of happiness which Lucretius espoused rather than a narrowly defined hedonism into which many Romans, even including Cicero, were inclined to corrupt the teachings of the founder of Epicureanism.

The attitude toward life of Zeno the Stoic is reflected in the writings of Seneca, even though he often quotes Epicurus with approval and denies that he accepts wholly the teachings of the Stoics. He did not attempt a theoretical analysis of Stoicism, as did Cicero, nor did he develop the system as fully as did Epictetus or the Emperor Marcus Aurelius; but for the most part his comments on human nature and ethical behavior present the Stoic point of view. Stoicism is similar to Epicureanism in its focus on ethics and its emphasis on the sublime happiness achieved through victory over the passions to which flesh is heir. Both maintain that man is happiest not when he possesses riches but when he lacks desires. To both, happiness is the highest human good, and tranquillity of soul the means by which happiness is attained. But whereas Epicureanism encourages man to resign himself to Fate and drift serenely with the eternal tide, Stoicism requires that he assume the obligations of stewardship.

> In the morning when thou risest unwillingly, let this thought be present —I am rising to the work of a human being. Why then am I dissatisfied if I am going to do the things for which I exist and for which I was brought into the world? Or have I been made for this, to lie in the bedclothes and keep myself warm?—But this is more pleasant—Dost thou exist then to take thy pleasure, and not at all for action or exertion? Dost thou not see the little plants, the little birds, the ants, the spiders, the bees working together to put in order their several parts of the universe? And art thou unwilling to do the work of a human being, and dost thou not make haste to do that which is according to thy nature? [2]

Both Epicureanism and Stoicism declare the price of personal peace to be submission to Nature, but the Stoics make of that resignation not merely a truce with Fate but also an alliance with Providence. In Stoicism duty takes precedence over ease, and only through dedication to divine ends can harmony with Nature be achieved.

In his *De Finibus*, written shortly before his death, Cicero sets forth the basic doctrines of Epicureanism and Stoicism. He criticizes both and declares the ethical philosophy of a contemporary, Antiochus, to be more acceptable than either. But since Antiochus had merely compromised some of the prevailing systems by sacrificing both precision and logical consistency, it is likely that Cicero found that system congenial because he himself lacked conviction. He probably remained to the end undecided about ethical values. Nevertheless he was deeply interested in the problems of conduct.

Sensitive Romans had cause to be concerned about human behavior. The athletic games which had satisfied the people during the early period of the Republic had been replaced in Cicero's time by cruel, barbaric contests. Caesar offered the populace the spectacle of ten thousand gladiators in combat on a single day, and Nero gave a show in which four hundred tigers were engaged in mortal struggle with elephants and bulls. Gladiatorial schools were established to train men not so much how to fight as how to kill without mercy and to die for the amusement of the spectators. Men fought to the death against men and against beasts. The Colosseum was dedicated in a series of gory contests in which five thousand animals perished. Lack of honor, debauchery, licentiousness, infidelity in marriage, indolence, contempt for those of lower status, and a fawning attitude toward those with money or power were everywhere to be observed. The proof of man's depravity was convincing. Votes were openly bought and juries bribed, and greed for power stifled sentiments of love or pity. Small wonder that a deep pessimism about human conduct pervades Roman thought.

It is impossible to say whether Rome was more or less wicked than other societies have been. Seneca himself tells us:

> The complaint our ancestors made, the complaint we make, the complaint our posterity will make, is that morality is overturned, that wickedness holds sway, and that human affairs and every sin are tending toward the worse. Yet these things remain and will continue to remain in the same position with only slight movement now in this direction, now in that, like that of the waves, which a rising tide carries far inland, and a receding tide restrains within the limits of the shoreline.[3]

Despite such apologies, however, most of the Romans who wrote about human conduct admitted that Rome was wicked. Juvenal declared, "We are arrived at the zenith of vice, and posterity will never be able to surpass us." In one of his letters to Atticus, Cicero complained about political corruption and trials "venally managed" and exclaimed: "If I were to give you a brief summary of what has happened since you left, you would certainly exclaim that Rome cannot possibly stand any longer."[4] Even the uninhibited Ovid congratulated himself on being born into an age whose morals were so congenial to his own. Cato believed that the affairs of mankind were beyond human hope. Perhaps if Seneca had found life more attractive, he would not have been so preoccupied with suicide. When death finally drew near, he said: "Nor do I shrink from changing into another state, because I shall, under no conditions, be as cramped as I am now."[5] These dim views about human society invite attention to the beliefs most commonly expressed about man himself. What is man?

HUMAN NATURE

To the Roman writers whose works are being analyzed, man is one of Nature's creatures, an animal. Lucretius, believing that nothing exists in the universe except atoms and a void, went further and declared that ultimately man is one with earth and air. It follows, therefore, that "living things are born of elements insensate" and that man is a material and not a spiritual entity. Cicero and Seneca lacked Lucretius' interest in substance, but they shared his conviction about man's membership in the animal kingdom.

All agreed that man is exalted above other creatures by his unique attribute of reason; he alone is able to comprehend the nature of things; he alone possesses the means of self-control. Consequently, by the exercise of his reason man can regulate his natural inclinations so as to live well.

> Those vestiges of natures left behind
> Which reason cannot quite expel from us

> Are still so slight that naught prevents a man
> From living a life even worthy of the gods.[6]

Cicero speaks of "that animal which we call man, endowed with foresight and quick intelligence," and says that "man is the only one among so many different kinds and varieties of living beings who has a share in reason and thought."[7] Seneca declares:

> For man is a reasoning animal. Therefore, man's highest good is attained, if he has fulfilled the good for which nature designed him at birth. And what is it which reason demands of him? The easiest thing in the world—to live in accordance with his own nature.[8]

But man is not only a reasoning animal, he is also a social animal. He is endowed by nature with a desire for the company of his fellows; he is, in Aristotle's words, a "political animal." Many other animals are disposed to herd together, but man's superior intelligence enables him to profit from social experience as no other animal can. Lucretius gives a glowing account of the gradual development of man's humanity under the softening influences of home and society. Cicero denies that the human virtues, such as "respect for truth" and "fidelity to promises," without which there could be no social justice, are inborn; rather they are acquired and developed through social participation.

> [The affection] which, coming into existence immediately upon birth, owing to the fact that children are loved by their parents and the family as a whole is bound together by the ties of marriage and parenthood, gradually spreads its influence beyond the home, first by blood relationships, then by connections through marriage, later by friendships, afterwards by the bonds of neighbourhood, then to fellow-citizens and political allies and friends, and lastly by embracing the whole of the human race.[9]

Although nature fits man for social life, the quality of his life in society is determined by his social experience. Polybius insists that no beast is more cruel or wicked than man when he is subjected to wrong training and exposed to bad examples. Seneca is persuaded that nobility of character is attained through deliberate effort at self-improvement. He recommends to Lucilius the advice of Epicurus: "Cherish some man of high character, and keep him ever before your eyes, living as if he were watching you and ordering all your actions as if he beheld them."[10]

In summary we may say that man was regarded as a reasoning animal, disposed by nature to seek the company of his fellows, and deriving from social participation his essentially human characteristics.

HAPPINESS

These Roman writers agreed that the chief aim of life is happiness; they differed only with respect to the means of its attainment. The good life is the happy life, but happiness must be earned; it is not, like reason and gregariousness, a part of man's native endowments. Man is born for happiness, but he comes into possession of his birthright only through the exercise of right reason. Of that, the Romans were certain.

Reason has been regarded both as a creative force able to remake the world and as a means of personal adjustment to the existing social order; in ancient Rome the latter view is more commonly found. Rome founded no enduring religion, inspired no great social movement, created no distinctive philosophy. The reason is not far to seek. Men of genius in many societies have been driven by thought, and by the discontent which thought arouses, to attempt to make the world a more suitable abode for mankind. The Romans whose works we are examining protested against the state of affairs, but not violently. This is well illustrated in Seneca's comments on slavery. As a sensitive soul, he can feel the hurt of the slave; his heart bleeds; he implores compassion; but he does not seek the extirpation of the institution of slavery. He probably would have called absurd any attempt to uproot a custom so long and so firmly established.

To the Romans life could not be good, unless it was happy. Cicero was constantly perplexed at his own desire to live, repeatedly he contemplated suicide, and finally he declared in a letter to Terentia that had it not been for his eagerness to live he would have suffered in life "no sorrow, or not much of it." [11] Seneca repeatedly returns to the theme of suicide. Men should neither love life nor hate it, he tells us, but should seek to live well, which is possible only when they throw off all fears, even the fear of death. It is life here and now which matters, as Seneca declares, quoting an old proverb, "The fool's life is empty of gratitude and full of fears; its course lies wholly toward the future." [12] The *carpe diem* attitude, expressed in such statements as "My friends, while we live, let us live," and "Eat, drink, disport thyself, and then join us," is, as has been stated already, a corruption of the teachings of Epicurus. Yet the stoical Seneca, even when he is advocating fixed standards toward which to strive, declares that man passes his days in indecision, knowing his wants only "at the moment of wishing," and a moment later wishing for the exact opposite. He maintains that only those are greedy for the future who have not learned to enjoy the present. Polybius sought to justify history as a guide to the future, but he also noted that history serves to make men stronger by showing them that others have faced difficulties with fortitude. From the historical references in the works of Cicero and Seneca, it appears that they looked to history more for courage with which to meet adversity than for knowledge with which to read the future. Lucretius has little to say about the future. To him virtue is good because it pays off in peace of mind; religion is evil because it disturbs. In the long sweep of time man's days are few; let him enjoy them here and now.

IMMORTALITY

Perhaps these writers would not have been so preoccupied with present happiness had they regarded life on this earth as preparation for life beyond the grave. That they were little concerned with eschatological salvation is made clear in their writings. It is likely that in their lack of faith in immortality they represented the views of most educated Romans in their day.

> The philosophy of Greece came to the cultivated Roman world with many different voices on the greatest problem of human destiny. And the greatest minds, from Cicero to M. Aurelius, reflect the discordance of philosophy. . . . The prevailing philosophy in the last generation of the Republic, demoralized by internecine strife, was that of Epicurus. It harmonised with the decay of old Roman religion, and with the more disastrous moral deterioration in the upper cultivated class. The cultivated patrician, enervated by vice and luxury, or intoxicated with the excitement of civil war and the dreams of disordered ambition, flung off all spiritual idealism, and accepted frankly a lawless universe and a life of pleasure or power, to be ended by death.[13]

Lucretius vigorously attacked the belief in immortality as the main source of those fears which prevent men from being happy. Polybius believed that such religious superstition helps the statesmen control the masses but serves little purpose among the educated classes. Cicero and Seneca were inconsistent in their statements about religious belief. Cicero posed the question as to the "final and ultimate aim, which gives the standard for all principles of well-being and right conduct," [14] but he did not answer it. He declared that the voice of human reason is the voice of God, but, on the other hand, he said:

> For whence comes our sense of duty? From whom do we obtain the principles of religion? Whence comes the law of nations, or even that law of ours which is called "civil"? Whence justice, honour, fair-dealing? Whence decency, self-restraint, fear of disgrace, eagerness for praise and honour? Whence comes endurance amid toils and dangers? I say, from those men who, when these things have been inculcated by a system of training, either confirmed them by custom or else enforced them by statutes.[15]

Seneca came close to religious conviction in his faith in the on-going processes of Nature which shape man's destiny, but the fervor of his crusade for personal morality lacks the fortifying and sustaining power of belief in immortality. Man's best hope is that he may come to the end of his life only a little worse than he was at the beginning, lest Nature scold him, saying:

> What does this mean? I brought you into the world without desires or fears, free from superstition, treachery and other curses. Go forth as you were when you entered! [16]

Rome · 219

It may be, as Dill believes, that Seneca caught the vision of the City of God, but there is much in his writing to indicate that he never quite succeeded in deciding whether or not it was a mirage.[17]

GOVERNMENT

A nation able not only to conquer but also to rule is rare in history. Since Rome did both, scholars have for centuries probed for the sources of her strength. They have found that Rome possessed able leaders and intelligent citizens; that she was able in crises to achieve unity at home while her enemies abroad were divided; that her administration of conquered peoples was sagacious; that, at least in the days of her rise to power, she had a remarkably adaptable form of government. Polybius, to whom Rome's system of government appeared far superior to anything in his native Greece, did not hesitate to declare that it was Rome's political organization and the peculiar virtues of her constitution which enabled her to gain and hold ascendancy over other peoples.[18] His close view of Rome is no proof of the accuracy of his judgment, but we ought not to neglect the opinions about government expressed by those who were witness to Rome's rise to domination over the Mediterranean world.

TYPES OF GOVERNMENT

The Romans followed the Greeks in recognizing three general types of government: (1) a kingship, in which the supreme authority is in the hands of one person; (2) an aristocracy, in which a group of selected citizens exercise this authority; and (3) a democracy, in which the power of the state is in the hands of the people. Any one of these types may be superior, but, as Cicero says, "Before each of them lies a slippery and precipitous path leading to a certain depraved form that is a close neighbour to it." Kingship degenerates into tyranny, aristocracy into timocracy, and democracy into mob rule.

Polybius observed that the Romans had reached, "not by any process of reasoning but by the discipline of many struggles and troubles," a form of government superior to any of the three types mentioned above: a combination of all three varieties. Cicero adopted this point of view and said:

> Therefore I consider a fourth form of government the most commendable—that form which is a well-regulated mixture of the three, which I mentioned at first. . . . For there should be a supreme and royal element in the State, some power also ought to be granted to the leading citizens, and certain matters should be left to the judgment and desire of the masses.[19]

Polybius became enthusiastic as he contemplated the strength of this kind of government, declaring that "it is impossible to find a better political system," as it possesses "an irresistible power of attaining every object upon which it is resolved." [20]

But even this form of government is not free from dangers. Its strength, Cicero believed, lies in the checks and balances which preserve in the state a balance of rights, duties, and functions; so that "the magistrates have enough power, the counsels of eminent citizens enough influence, and the people enough liberty." [21] The maintenance of this delicate balance of power is difficult and uncertain; hence it is important that the rights and responsibilities of each branch of government be carefully defined. Cicero feared especially that the balance might be upset by the demands of the people for greater freedom. He shared Plato's distrust of democracy.

> There is no government to which I should more quickly deny the title of commonwealth than one in which everything is subject to the power of the multitude. . . . I prefer even a kingship to a free popular government, for that . . . is the worst of all governments.[22]

One interesting example of Cicero's opposition to too much power in the hands of the masses is found in his proposal that votes in the assembly be open rather than secret, so that "the people may enjoy liberty also in this very privilege of honourably winning the favour of the aristocracy." [23] Apparently Cicero believed that the average man could not be counted on to vote discreetly unless he were watched by the aristocrats. Keyes suggests that this provision contains the key to Cicero's idea of a balanced constitution:

> Absolute power is given to the People, but as many opportunities as possible are provided for the play of senatorial influence upon this all-powerful democracy. . . . If he thinks of the common people as entirely lacking in political wisdom, why has he given them the supreme power in the State? Simply because he recognizes the great fact that, in any form of the state, they actually possess the supreme power. . . . Only the aristocracy can govern the state wisely, but it cannot govern the state at all, except with the full approval of the People. This approval is in general gained by persuasion; but when this is found impossible, by trickery based on popular superstition.[24]

Cicero observed that in times of trouble the people will prefer to extend the power of the rulers. He was careful to point out that his constitution was an idealized conception better suited to the early days of the Republic than to his own, troubled age. He witnessed apparently undisturbed the growth in power of the privileged few at the expense of the masses. Although the balance of power was not in his day ideal, it appeared to Cicero to be adequate for the needs of the hour.

ORIGIN OF GOVERNMENT

When Cicero set for himself the task of exhibiting Rome's political constitution "in its infancy, progress, and maturity," out of which came his *De Re Publica,* he declared that the Roman government was "not the work of one man, but of many" and that it was founded "not in one generation, but in a long period of several centuries and many ages of men." In other words, it was an outgrowth of the experiences which Rome had had. He did not neglect the influence of "men of might," but he attached even more importance to the fortuitous events in Rome's history. Polybius also declared that the Romans gained their form of government not by reasoning but "by the discipline of many struggles and troubles, and always choosing the best by the light of the experience gained in disaster." [25]

Cicero observed that the first written laws which Rome possessed, the *Twelve Tables,* were based on prevailing customs. So it seemed to him that Rome's laws, like her government, grew up without any particular plan or purpose. In the Epicurean doctrine of conscious self-interest as a basis for society, accepted by Lucretius, is found an idea that was to germinate many centuries later into the social-contract theory of the origin of government. After speaking of a primitive state in which each man sought for himself "dominion and supremacy" and there was war of each against all, Lucretius observed that then:

> Some wiser heads instructed men to found
> The magisterial office, and did frame
> Codes that they might consent to follow laws.
> For humankind, o'er wearied with a life
> Fostered by force, was ailing from its feuds;
> And so the sooner of its own free will
> Yielded to laws and strictest codes.[26]

But the Epicureans did not develop this idea; and they, no less than the Stoics, believed that man is a political animal by nature rather than by choice. Men are not driven for the sake of peace into an uneasy truce, a mutual agreement to exercise self-restraint; rather, they cannot live well except in society. Cicero declared:

> The first cause of such an association is not so much the weakness of the individual as a certain social spirit which nature has implanted in man. For man is not a solitary or unsocial creature, but born with such a nature that not even under conditions of great prosperity of every sort is he willing to be isolated from his fellow man.[27]

This line of reasoning leads logically to a conception of a universal state. In fact, Cicero often writes as though he were thinking of government not for Rome but for all mankind; and of a universal society in which every man gains his natural heritage of justice under law. On the other hand, he sometimes sounds a strong nationalistic note.

> But when with a rational spirit you have surveyed the whole field, there is no social relation among them all more close, none more dear than that which links each one of us with our country. Parents are dear; dear are children, relatives, friends; but one native land embraces all our loves; and who that is true would hesitate to give his life for her, if by his death he could render her a service? [28]

The clash between nationalism and universal brotherhood as social ideals can be reconciled by the assumption that men are not created equal. This leads to a theory of the natural right of the strong to dominate the weak, and hence to the view that government originates in conquest. The Romans did not overlook this conception. Cicero declared that Nature "forbids that anything shall belong to any man save to him that knows how to employ and use it." [29] "Do we not observe," he says, "that dominion has been granted by Nature to everything that is best, to the great advantage of what is weak?" [30] The strong and not the meek will inherit the earth, according to Cicero, when government develops in accordance with Nature's laws. Seneca likewise rejected the idea that Nature has created men equal.

> But the first men and those who sprang from them, still unspoiled, followed nature, having one man as both their leader and their law, entrusting themselves to the control of one better than themselves. For nature has the habit of subjecting the weaker to the stronger. Even among the dumb animals those which are either biggest or fiercest hold sway.[31]

FAMILY

The Roman *familia* was a household, consisting of those related to the head of the household by blood, marriage, or adoption, and also of all slaves and "clients" attached to the household. In the early Republic, the head of the family had supreme legal authority over the household. His *patria potestas* over his children gave him the right to decide whether an infant should be reared or killed, as well as the right later to condemn to death a child spared at birth. The *manus* (that is, the power of a husband over a wife and her belongings) gave him, in reality, the same authority over his wife that he had over his children, the only difference being that *manus* was theoretically established by consent rather than by birth. He was in complete control of all property possessed by the family, including such chattels as slaves, over whom he also exercised the power of life or death.

It is doubtful that extensive use was ever made of these extreme powers, and certainly they were restricted as time passed. By the first century B.C., the *manus* relationship was rarely entered into by women of the aristocracy. Also the Julian Law and the Poppaean Law, enacted under the influence of the Emperor Augustus, limited still further the exercise of *manus*. These laws were directed against the deterioration of the family as reflected in adultery, illegitimacy, celibacy, and childlessness. They placed the sanctity of the home under the protection of the courts.

MARRIAGE

Marriages were usually arranged by the families involved. Although the consent of both parties to the marriage seems to have been required, it is probable that the wisdom of a parental choice was not often questioned. The Roman jurist Ulpian observed, "The daughter who does not object is regarded as consenting. She has, moreover, no right to resist her father, unless he tries to give her a dishonored or deformed husband." Betrothals might be arranged at any ages, but the minimum ages for marriage were those now established in our own society for marriage under common law, namely twelve for girls and fourteen for boys. Likewise, marriage by *usus,* which required no more than that a man and a woman live together as husband and wife for one year without interruption in order to be recognized as legally married, has come down to our own time as a form of marriage under common law. This form of marriage may have been at certain times widely practiced by the plebeians, but by the time of Cicero it seems largely to have disappeared. Marriages were civil, not religious, affairs, with the exception of the *confarreatio,* an exclusively patrician ceremony.

There must have been from earliest times some objection to the absolute control of the wife by the husband. The *Twelve Tables* contained, according to Gaius, the following provision:

> . . . any woman who did not wish to be subjected in this manner to the hand of her husband should be absent for three nights in succession every year, and so interrupt the usucapio of each year.[32]

This is obviously a fiction by means of which a woman, who was required to be under some man's authority, could retain her father's protection while enjoying her husband's company.

Another article in the *Twelve Tables* forbade the marriage of patricians with plebeians. Cicero, who was an equestrian and not a patrician, had this to say about that law:

> When the Board of Ten had put into writing, using the greatest fairness and wisdom, ten tables of laws, they caused to be elected in their stead, for the next year, another Board of Ten, whose good faith and justice have not been praised to a like extent. . . . When they had added two tables of unfair laws, they ordained, by a very inhuman law, that intermarriage,

which is usually permitted even between peoples of separate States, should not take place between our plebeians and our patricians.[33]

This law created such protest as to suggest that it was not, as the *Twelve Tables* are said generally to have been, based on custom but was deliberately intended to make secure the prestige of the patrician class. In any event, the law was repealed in 445 B.C., after being in effect for only about five years.

STATUS OF WOMEN

A Roman woman of the upper classes possessed many privileges. Within the home the wife was in fact as well in name the mistress. Gide has described her condition as follows:

> The atrium was not, like the gynaeceum in a Greek house, a secluded apartment, an upper floor, a hidden and inaccessible retreat. It was the very center of the Roman house, the common hall where the whole family assembled, where friends and strangers were received. There near the hearth was the altar of Lares, and around this sanctuary were gathered all the most precious and sacred possessions of the family, the nuptial bed, the images of the ancestors, the web and spindle of the mother, the chest containing the family records and the money. All these treasures were placed under the guard of the wife. She, as head of the family, offered herself the sacrifices to the Lares. She presided over the domestic labors of the slaves. She directed the education of the children, who even after they passed out of childhood continued to submit to her authority. In short, she shared with her husband the administration of the property and the rule of the house.[34]

She sat at the table—literally, since men followed the Greek custom of reclining —even when there were guests in the house, and she accompanied her husband when he was invited to dinner. She adorned herself with raiment and jewels and used cosmetics to enhance her attractiveness. Having received in childhood the same basic education given boys, she was able to read philosophy, to write poetry, and to participate in the discussion of art and music. Although barred from active participation in politics and business, she exercised indirectly a tremendous influence in both fields. The practice of medicine was open to her, but she seems to have been denied the opportunity to practice law except in unusual circumstances.

A woman's rights to inheritance varied from equality with those of men, under the *Twelve Tables,* to considerable inequality, under the Voconian Law of the second century B.C. Cicero, who was no feminist, declared the latter law to be "full of injustice to women." Cato warned that if women achieved equality they would turn it into mastery, but he protested in vain. Women did, in fact, achieve equality with men in many important respects; and when Cornelia asked that she be remembered only as the mother of the Gracchi, she had already earned the right to be remembered for her other accomplishments.

In view of the actual equality of women in many respects, it is interesting to observe that the Roman writers almost universally rejected their equality as a principle. The code of the *Twelve Tables* not only recognizes a laudable preference for male children but also declares:

> Our ancestors have seen fit that females, by reason of levity of disposition, should remain in guardianship even when they have attained their majority.[35]

Polybius said that a woman's "natural shortness of view" renders her unfit for the management of the affairs of the state.[36] Lucretius believed that men had originally to develop and then to teach women even the simplest skills.

> And nature forced the men,
> Before the woman kind, to work the wool:
> For all the male kind far excels in skill,
> And cleverer is by much—until at last
> The rugged farmer folk jeered at such tasks,
> And so were eager soon to give them o'er
> To women's hands, and in more hardy toil
> To harden arms and hands.[37]

Although Cicero supported the right of women to have "money of their own," he believed that "there should be a censor to teach men to rule their wives." [38] He doubted that women could be trusted to act decorously when their conduct was concealed by darkness, and he approved of the ancient decree of the Senate against nocturnal assemblies attended by both men and women.

> Assuredly we must make most careful provisions that the reputation of our women be guarded by the clear light of day, when they are observed by many eyes.[39]

Seneca, who had a good wife, was of the opinion that "the wise man will do well not to marry," since marriage is so often "the beginning of sorrow to come." [40] He was ready to admit that a woman has aptitude for virtue and culture, but he was mindful of her close natural affinity to lower forms. "She is just the same unthinking creature—wild, and unrestrained in her passions—unless she has gained knowledge and had much instruction." [41]

Martial, who wanted only a "kind but simple" wife, never married; and Cicero, who married twice, failed to find a congenial mate, although he lived with his first wife, Terentia, for thirty years.

FAMILY VALUES

Polybius noted the important social role the family plays in developing good citizens.[42] He placed great emphasis on the political function of family institutions. Lucretius attributed to the softening influences of shared affections in the family the development of those human sentiments that made organized society possible and enabled kings to found cities and establish citadels. He valued compassion not because it is good for the individual but because it is good for society.[43] Cicero, with more oratorical zeal than logic, declared:

> For since the reproductive instinct is by Nature's gift the common possession of all living creatures, the first bond of union is that between husband and wife; the next, that between parents and children; then we find one home, with everything in common. And this is the foundation of civil government, the nursery, as it were, of the state.[44]

It has been observed that when family institutions are justified only in terms of their value to the state, they develop a degree of instability comparable to that of the political system to which they are bound; they lose in like degree their basic function of conserving values and moderating social change. One evidence of such instability is divorce. During a good part of Roman history divorce among the upper classes seems to have been regarded as a casual matter. The Senate passed laws designed to discourage divorce, but they had little effect. Catullus, famous for his marriage songs, never married; but many of Rome's most distinguished citizens did not hesitate to use marriage as a means of furthering their ambitions. Cicero and Seneca each married twice; Ovid, Octavian, and Pliny the Younger had three wives; Caesar had four; Pompey and Sulla had five. Although polygamy was never practiced in Rome, a system of successive monogamy developed as a result of easy divorce and remarriage. This system bore little resemblance to the enduring marital pattern of the early Republic.

Since a situation becomes a problem only when there exists a desire to change it, divorce was not in Rome a major problem. In the hands of the satirists, divorce practices were held up for ridicule, as when Juvenal offered "Eight husbands in five years" as a suitable inscription for one woman's sepulcher. But even Seneca directed his caustic satire on the subject not against divorce but against divorced women.

> Is there any woman that blushes at divorce now that certain illustrious and noble ladies reckon their years, not by the number of consuls, but by the number of their husbands, and leave home in order to marry, and marry in order to be divorced? They shrank from this scandal as long as it was rare; now since every gazette has a divorce case, they have learned to do what they used to hear so much about. Is there any shame at all for adultery now that matters have come to such a pass that no woman has any use for a husband except to inflame her paramour?[45]

SOCIAL CHANGE

As long as men speculate about the rise and fall of civilizations, the causes of the collapse of Rome will be debated. Most of those who venture opinions about this matter in our own day recognize several important factors but regard them as symptoms rather than as causes. For example, Rostovtzeff says:

> None of the existing theories fully explains the problem of the decay of ancient civilization. . . . Each of them, however, has contributed much to the clearing of the ground.[46]

It is quite evident that Rome lost the ability to rise to crises. Long before Alaric came, in A.D. 410, with his plundering horde, her strength was spent. It is also true, as Rostovtzeff points out, that the educated classes had gradually been absorbed by the masses, with the resulting "barbarization of the ancient world." Rome lacked leaders in the hour of her greatest need; the great Empire slowly disintegrated because of internal weakness. Historians have traced that weakness to its sources; and although they do not agree as to the relative importance of the various factors, they are far better able to evaluate the significance of what happened than were the Romans themselves. For history, therefore, rather than social ideas, we must go to those who with great diligence have raised Roman civilization from the dust.

But we should not overlook the thoughts of those who walked the streets of ancient Rome. How did they regard the events which they witnessed? How did they interpret the changes which they observed? What visions did they see as they meditated about the future?

PROGRESS

In the fifth book of his *De Rerum Natura,* Lucretius traced the slow development of man and his institutions. Since Lucretius introduced the idea of progress to our own society, it is important to analyze the meaning of this concept to him.

He believed that the universe is composed of indestructible atoms, which form and reform in the void. In the beginning, there was no earth, or ocean, or air, or sun, but only a "prodigious hurly-burly mass." Then,

> Portions began to fly asunder, and like
> With like to join, and to block out a world,
> And to divide its members and dispose
> Its mightier parts—that is, to set secure
> The lofty heavens from the lands, and cause
> The sea to spread with waters separate,
> And fires of ether separate and pure
> Likewise to congregate apart. . . .
>
> . . .
>
> They pressed from out their mass those particles
> Which were to form the sea, the stars, the sun,
> And moon, and ramparts of the mighty world.[47]

The sun wheeled in the sky, clouds formed, the earth stood firm, and the sea flowed forth "with fixed tides."

> In the beginning, earth gave forth, around
> The hills and over all the length of plains,
> The race of grasses and the shining green.
>
> . . .
>
> How true remains
> How merited is that adopted name
> Of earth—"The Mother!"—since from out the earth
> Are all begotten. And even now arise
> From out the loams how many living things—.[48]

Of the innumerable living forms which came from the earth, many have already perished, wrote Lucretius, and the remainder must ultimately vanish. Long ago Mother Earth became too old to bear new forms. Since no form evolves into another, the species was fixed at the moment of creation. Man first appeared as mortal man, tough but ignorant of fire and of clothes. Like other animals, he ate what nature provided and sought protection under nature's cover from the lashings of the wind.

> Afterwards,
> When huts they had procured and pelts and fire
> And when the woman, joined unto the man,
> Withdrew with him into one dwelling place,
>   . . . then first the human race
> Began to soften. For 'twas now that fire
> Rendered their shivering frames less staunch to bear,
> Under the canopy of the sky, the cold;
> And Love reduced their shaggy hardiness;
> And children, with the prattle and the kiss,
> Soon broke the parents' haughty temper down.
> Then, too, did neighbors 'gin to league as friends,
> Eager to wrong no more or suffer wrong.[49]

Urged on by nature, men fashioned speech; cities were formed; rivalry led to war; laws were framed to save man from the ills of feuding; but still war's grim business was carried on with every kind of weapon human ingenuity could invent and with beasts to assist in giving the enemy a "goodly cause of woe."

This, in brief, is Lucretius' idea of progress. He explicitly denied that there is a teleological principle in the universe, a "far-off divine event toward which the whole creation moves." According to him, in time the whole earth will disintegrate into the atoms of which it is composed. Worlds come and go without plan in a universe in which ultimate matter is indestructible and restless. Lucretius did not recognize the possibility of organic evolution; man is Earth's supreme, and perhaps final, creation. As for the social evolution which might be brought about by intelligence, he declared that man had already reached the "supreme pinnacle" in all those arts learned by "practice and the mind's experience." As he wrote of the "vain futilities" in which man wastes his years, and the "mighty waves of war" that inevitably result from his desire for "better and for more," he came very close to the unrestrained pessimism of Seneca regarding the future of mankind. Lucretius was the historian rather than the missionary of progress. He lacked the faith in mankind which supports the modern idea of progress.[50]

CYCLICAL CHANGE

In Polybius' analysis of changes in the forms of government we find a clear statement of the cyclical theory of change which most Romans, and especially the Stoics, accepted. He claimed that each of the three main types of government has a counterpart into which it degenerates.

> We should therefore assert that there are six kinds of governments, the three above mentioned which are in everyone's mouth and the three which are naturally allied to them, I mean monarchy, oligarchy, and mob-rule. Now the first of these to come into being is monarchy, its growth being natural and unaided; and next arises kingship derived from monarchy by the aid of art and by the correction of defects. Monarchy first changes into its vicious allied form, tyranny; and next, the abolishment of both gives birth to aristocracy. Aristocracy by its very nature degenerates into oligarchy; and when the commons inflamed by anger take vengeance on this government for its unjust rule, democracy comes into being; and in due course the licence and lawlessness of this form of government produces mob-rule to complete the series. The truth of what I have just said will be quite clear to anyone who pays due attention to such beginnings, origins, and changes as are in each case natural. For he alone who has seen how each form naturally arises and develops, will be able to see when, how, and where the growth, perfection, change and end of each are likely to occur again.[51]

Polybius believed that this cyclical pattern of change in government is natural and inevitable. One might be wrong as to the time the process will take, but one need have no doubt as to the sequence. Rome was fortunate, according to Polybius, in having a government in which the three main forms were balanced in relation to one another. But he did not believe that this balance could be preserved.

> For, as I said, this state, more than any other, has been formed and has grown naturally, and will undergo a natural decline and change to its contrary.[52]

He did not find it necessary to posit Fate to account for this natural decline and change. Instead, he claimed that the cycle was caused by such factors as war, education, morality, occupation, and the distribution of wealth.

It is easy to understand why the cyclical theory of change appealed to the ancient world. The heavenly bodies appeared to wheel around the earth and return to their starting place; dawn, noonday light, and dusk followed one another in inevitable sequence; birth, maturity, and death characterized every living thing. So it was easy to imagine that society is an organism.

> If any one, then, contemplates the Roman people as he would contemplate a man, and considers its whole age, how it had its origin, how it grew up, how it arrived at a certain vigour of manhood, and how it has since, as it were, grown old, he will observe four degrees and stages of its existence.[53]

DECLINE FROM A GOLDEN AGE

A third theory of change—that of social deterioration from a Golden Age—is reflected in the writings of Seneca. This theory assumes the existence of an orginal state of innocence in which man lived happily in harmony with Nature. But for some cause man forsook this earthly paradise and set out upon a course which has carried him ever deeper into the gloom. This theory of change was elaborated by the Greek Hesiod (about 800 B.C.), who regretted that he had been born in a day when "men never rest from labour and sorrow by day, and from perishing by night." It is found in much of the ancient Oriental literature, including that of Persia, India, China, and Babylonia. Usually those who have accepted this theory have taken the pessimistic view of the future which characterizes much of the social thought of Seneca. A few excerpts from his *Epistolae Morales* will serve to present his view of social retrogression.

He speaks of the Golden Age, in which men lived without avarice under the jurisdiction of the wisest among them and in harmony with Nature.

> Nature was not so hostile to man that, when she gave all the other animals an easy role in life, she made it impossible for him alone to live without all these artifices. . . . Luxury has turned her back upon nature; each day she expands herself, in all the ages she has been gathering strength, and by her wit promoting the vices. At first luxury began to lust for what nature regarded as superfluous, then for that which was contrary to nature; and finally she made the soul a bondsman to the body, and bade it be an utter slave to the body's lusts.[54]

Seneca declared that in the early state of innocence man was happy and without guile, but he was not virtuous. He alone of all the animals is capable of virtue, and he cannot be true to himself unless he seeks to acquire such virtues as self-control, justice, and bravery. These are acquired only through knowledge, and they are brought to perfection only through unremitting practice. Thus the pessimism deepens: innocence is the bliss of ignorance; man's nature requires that he seek knowledge; the price of knowledge is that very innocence which enables him to live happily. Seneca found a solution to the dilemma only in the utter destruction of all human life in one vast and final catastrophe.

> Therefore, there will one day come an end to all human life and interests. The elements of the earth must all be dissolved or utterly destroyed in order that they all may be created anew in innocence, and that no remnant may be left to tutor men in vice. . . . A single day will see the burial of all mankind. All that the long forbearance of fortune has produced, all that has been reared to eminence, all that is famous and all that is beautiful, great thrones, great nations—all will descend into the one abyss, will be overthrown in one hour.[55]

It is impossible to say which of these theories of social change was dominant in the thought of the period.

DECLINE AND FALL OF ROME

Many factors—military, political, biological, economic, and religious—contributed to the decline and fall of Rome. The most important military factors were incessant wars, the employment of mercenaries when the supply of native soldiers became inadequate, the superior fighting ability of the barbarians, and the boldness and strength of Rome's adversaries. Government in the Empire was weakened by centuries of despotic rule, which stripped political office of prestige and destroyed civic pride. Able men were discouraged from taking part in politics; the offices of the state were filled by greedy and unscrupulous men. The measure of power in government was the strength of the army at one's command, and colonial despots struggled with one another for supremacy, until finally, in A.D. 395, the Empire was divided.

Some writers claim that a gradual biological deterioration resulted from the fusion of various racial stocks in the Empire, but this hypothesis lacks convincing proof. What is more evident is that in many parts of the Empire, the population declined as a result of deliberate family limitation. Infanticide was not uncommonly practiced when various methods of birth control proved ineffective. Epidemics were frequent and severe, and the mosquitoes of the Pontine marshes took heavy toll from a population weakened by malnutrition.

The economic conditions which contributed to Rome's collapse were numerous and varied, but it is difficult to determine whether they were causes or effects. Private enterprise was checked by confiscatory taxation and by the excessive risks involved in commerce and trade. Despite doles and public works, the labor supply, both of slaves and of freemen, was inadequate for the needs of agriculture and industry. The sources of the bread supply dried up. The fingers of bureaucracy slowly clutched every vital business enterprise and strangled the economic life of the nation.

To these various factors in Rome's decline must be added another: the conflict among rival religions and philosophies, with resulting moral chaos. The old order was clearly drawing to an end, and the time was ripe for a new order to begin.

10 · AUGUSTINE

(A.D. 354-430)

> *For what is faith unless it is to believe what you do not see?*
> AUGUSTINE—*Joannis Evangelical Tract*

When Augustine went to Rome in A.D. 384, he found a city that, for all the splendor of its gilded roofs and marble columns, was dying. For centuries Rome had ruled the civilized world, and now Rome's strength was spent. The ascetic Jerome, sickened by the sight of a population so jaded and satiated that it found amusement in the barbaric contests at the Colosseum, poured out his feelings in these touching words:

> No doubt all things born are doomed to die, and that which hath grown to maturity must grow old. Every work of man is attacked by decay, and destroyed by age. But who would have believed that Rome, victorious so oft over the universe, would at length crumble in pieces, the mother at once and the grave of her children? She who made slaves of the East has herself become a slave, and nobles once laden with riches come to little Bethlehem to beg. In vain I try to draw myself away from the sight by turning to my books. I am unable to heed them.[1]

The conflicts in religion and in philosophy were greatly disturbing to the people. Hundreds of temples honored the pagan (non-Christian) deities, and marble statues of many gods and goddesses were to be seen in public places. The Persian cult of Mithraism had an active following among the patricians. The Manichaean sect was strong in North Africa and had many devotees even in Rome, where the followers of Mani were subjected to persecution. The confusion created by philosophers is described by Augustine in these words:

> Indeed, in the conspicuous and well-known porch, in gymnasia, in gardens, in places public and private, they openly strove in bands each for his own opinion, some asserting there was one world, others innumerable

worlds; some that this world had a beginning, others that it had not; some that it would perish, others that it would exist always; some that it was governed by the divine mind, others by chance and accident; some that souls are immortal, others that they are mortal—and of those who asserted their immortality, some said they transmigrated through beasts, others that it was by no means so, while of those who asserted their mortality, some said they perished immediately after the body, others that they survived either a little while or a longer time, but not always; some fixing supreme good in the body, some in the mind, some in both; others adding to the mind and body external good things; some thinking that the bodily senses ought to be trusted always, some not always, others never. Now what people, senate, power, or public dignity of the impious city has ever taken care to judge between all these and other well-nigh innumerable dissensions of the philosophers, approving and accepting some, and disapproving and rejecting others? . . . For Babylon means confusion, as we remember we have already explained. Nor does it matter to the devil, its king, how they wrangle among themselves in contradictory errors, since all alike deservedly belong to him on account of their great and varied impiety.[2]

Out of this disorder Christianity, emerging as a social movement, brought together the dispersed bands of Christians and gave to much of the decaying Empire a new ideal and a Church. With the collapse of the authority of Rome, it was inevitable that some new source of social order should develop. The Christians, hitherto unorganized and oppressed, took up the reins of social control. The Catholic Church assumed the responsibility of guiding the thoughts and behavior of mankind, in so far as its influence could be pushed. Among the early "Church fathers," Jerome, Ambrose, Gregory the Great, and Augustine are usually recognized as the most influential. Of these, Augustine, although he was but one of hundreds of bishops, in an African diocese of the Church, was by far the most important. His piety and eloquence helped to build the foundations of the Church so securely that its pre-eminence in the Western world was undisputed for a thousand years.

BIOGRAPHICAL SKETCH

Augustine, who as Bishop of Hippo and eminent Doctor of the Church was destined to influence profoundly the life and thought of a large part of the civilized world for at least seven centuries, was born at Tagaste in Numidia (Algeria) in A.D. 354. His father, Patricius, was a pagan until the year of his death, but his mother, Monica, was a devout Christian. The family, though not rich, was able to give Augustine a good education; and, as he gave promise of literary ability, he was sent at the age of sixteen to Carthage to prepare for a career as a rhetorician. In that gay city the young scholar enjoyed not only the excitement of intellectual pursuits but also the opportunity to indulge in the vices which flourished there. From his own account of his experiences we are led to believe that his impulses were uninhibited. His devotion to learning did not prevent his taking a concubine, who bore him, when he was eighteen, a son, whom he named Adeodatus ("by God given").

For about eleven years (372-383) Augustine studied and taught, at Tagaste and at Carthage, seeking all the while a way of escape from the restlessness and discontentment that possessed him. He rejected the prayers of his mother that he become a Christian and instead embraced Manichaeism, a materialistic philosophy based upon an assumed conflict in nature between the two principles of Good and Evil. Apparently he never wholly accepted the Manichaean solution of the problem of evil; but he was to pass through a stage of extreme skepticism before his philosophical path to Christianity was cleared by the Neo-Platonic view of the nature of evil—the view that evil is nothing positive but only a lack, nothing substantial and existential but only a privation.

In 383 Augustine went to Rome and opened a school of rhetoric. His venture was not a happy one. He complained that his pupils tricked him out of tuition fees, and he expressed pleasure in leaving Rome in order to accept a teaching position in an established school in Milan. There his mother, whom he had left behind in North Africa, joined him. She persuaded him to put aside the woman with whom he had long lived in order that he might take a bride suitable to his station in life. Finding himself lonely after the departure of his companion of so many years, he took another concubine while he was waiting for his bethrothed to reach marriage age. As he was converted shortly afterwards, he never married, and we hear nothing more about the two women who shared his love in the unhappy days of his youth.

These details of his private life are told by Augustine himself. In his *Confessions,* written after he had become Bishop of Hippo, he probably exaggerated the wildness of his youth. The theft of a few pears can hardly be regarded as proof of debauchery, and the sensual indulgences of which he became so much ashamed probably did not violate the mores of his time. His story of personal storm and stress, of sin and its consequences, of doubt, confusion, and despair, and finally of salvation, is one, therefore, which reveals the spiritual progress of a sensitive youth living in a troubled age. The theme is worthy of a master of rhetoric, and the *Confessions* has long been recognized as one of the masterworks of literature.

Augustine was thirty-three years of age when he finally accepted Christianity and resolved to devote the remainder of his life to its service. He gave up his post in Milan and, after a period of preparation, was baptized by Ambrose on Easter in the year 387. A few months later, as he was preparing to sail for Africa, his mother died. Those passages in the *Confessions* which deal with the saintly life of Monica and with her passing reveal in Augustine a devotion for his mother too deep for words to express; his feelings overflow as he seeks to describe a life which was benediction and a death which was peace. A short time afterward his son, Adeodatus, seems also to have died, and thus Augustine was severed from his last remaining tie with private home and family.

Back in Africa, he disposed of his possessions and devoted his time to study and to prayer. In a short time, however, his superior abilities led to his ordination as a priest and, a few years later, to his becoming Bishop of Hippo. As the first half of his life had been occupied in a struggle with himself, so was the last half devoted to a fight against the enemies of the Church. His first serious encounter after he entered the Church was with the Manichaeans. He was not long in proving the Manichaean doctrines to be false and in discrediting the faith which he had once himself embraced. The power of his pen and tongue was then successfully hurled against the Donatists, who claimed that the efficacy of the sacraments depended upon the state of grace of the priest administering them. Augustine saw that if this principle were recognized, the Church could no longer claim to possess the keys to the Kingdom of God A third controversy arose regarding the Church's doctrine of original sin and the means of salvation. The Pelagians (followers of the British monk Pelagius, who went to Rome about A.D. 400) denied that all mankind sinned in Adam and claimed that salvation is gained not by grace but by innocence or good works. In his old age Augustine engaged in a struggle against the Arians (a fourth-century group especially prominent in the Eastern churches), who denied the doctrine of the Trinity and maintained that God is apart from all created things and is unknowable.

It is easy to see that Augustine's life was not an easy one. He was witness to the burial of Roman civilization by the barbarians. Even as he lay dying in August, 430, at the age of seventy-five, the Vandals had crossed the sea to North Africa and were storming the gates of Hippo. We are not told what thoughts passed through his mind in that hour, but perhaps he was not unaware of the fact that he had helped to preserve, in the mold of Christianity, some of the best fruits of Greek philosophical thought. He contributed no small part to that vast synthesis of Christian theology which has survived the death of many nations. Windelband, the German philosopher, says that he was "the real teacher of the Middle Ages," and the Protestant Harnack asks, "Where in all the history of the Western Church do we encounter a man whose influence is comparable to the influence of Augustine?"

Augustine gave vigorous leadership to the Church at a crucial moment. His intellect was quick to discover the weak spot in heresies. His eloquence humiliated his adversaries and gained for him so much fame that he felt it necessary to confess his human frailty in his most popular work. His genius shines forth in the works to which we shall now turn, works that state the fundamentals of his Christian faith and the nature of his Christian experience. Because he lived at a time when the foundations of Catholicism were being laid, he built his faith and his experience into that vast edifice which dominated the medieval scene, the Church.

MAJOR WORKS

The writings of Augustine fill sixteen volumes in the Migne Edition of the works of the Church fathers, and much of his work has perished. His extant writings date from the years when, as Bishop of Hippo, he was engaged in refuting the arguments of unbelievers and heretics and in clarifying and systematizing the theological doctrines of the Catholic Church; no clearly genuine works written before his conversion have survived. Once he was launched on his ecclesiastical career, however, a stream of letters, polemics, sermons, treatises, commentaries on the Scriptures, and books on a wide variety of subjects poured forth in a flow that ended only with his death. This prodigious literary performance was made possible by the assistance of scribes, who seem to have been always at hand to receive his dictation, sometimes in shorthand, and to record sermons and discussions which he later revised and preserved. His correspondence was voluminous, and he kept copies of many of his letters. The Benedictine collection contains two hundred and seventy that are recognized as authentic; a few additional letters have been discovered since the Benedictine edition was published. The Benedictines classify three hundred and sixty-three sermons as authentic, thirty-one as doubtful, and three hundred and seventeen, sometimes attributed to Augustine, as apocryphal.

Doctrinal themes predominate in Augustine's sermons and, although these works reveal more of the theologian than of the man, he was able to suffuse profound intellectual conceptions with the inspiring warmth of his own feeling. His letters consist largely of the official correspondence of a busy bishop. In the disorganized condition of the Church, which was served in Africa alone by perhaps five hundred bishops in Augustine's time, the dangers and difficulties of travel made necessary extensive correspondence by Church officials. Augustine's prestige invited questions from far and near regarding Church doctrines and policies, and his letters served to develop unity of teaching among the servants of the Church. Some of his letters deal with paganism and heresy; others are concerned with the administrative problems of the Church; a few afford a picture of some of the social customs of the day and give Augustine's views on matters secular as well as sacred. A letter written probably in the last year of his life reveals his truce with age. He had been asked to attend the dedication of a church and he excused himself, saying:

> I might have come, had it not been winter; I might have scorned the winter, had I been young; for either the glow of youth would have endured the rigour of the season, or else the glow of summer would have allayed the

chill of age. As it is . . . in winter I cannot bear so lengthy a journey since I must bear with me the frigidity of great age.³

CONFESSIONS

The *Confessions,* which Augustine wrote about the year 400, and thus many years after his conversion, has long been the most popular of his works. It is not an autobiography of the usual type but a statement of the author's anguish resulting from his sins, indecisions, and errors, and of his conversion and the gladness which it brought. The book is really a prayer of praise and gratitude addressed to God, but in it Augustine expressed the hope that it would find an audience among men and give pleasure and guidance to those who read it.

The narrative begins with Augustine's infancy and ends with his conversion. He passes quickly over his earliest years to come to his bondage in youth to concupiscence. He relates how the reading of Cicero's *Hortensius** inspired him at nineteen to study philosophy, how he looked into the Bible and was repelled because he took literally what was intended to be understood allegorically, how he found the ideas of the Manichaeans so intellectually satisfying that he embraced Manichaeism devoutly for nine years, how he wearied of Manichaeism because of its materialism and its unsatisfactory solution of the problem of evil, how he went first to Rome and then to Milan, how he became acquainted with Neo-Platonism and found an answer to some of the philosophical problems which had troubled him, and how finally he came to accept Christianity and was baptized.

His own account of the slow and painful stages of his growth is a moving story. The anguish of the lack of meaning in his life before he came at last to the certitude of God's existence and grace is seen years later through the remorseful eyes of the Bishop, but the agony of doubt and despair in this unhappy period of his life is vividly described. Augustine tells how in his restlessness he sought diversion with friends, in "talking and jesting together" with them, and in "doing kind offices by turn." But such experiences were not satisfying. The reason is not far to seek: he was trembling on the verge of conversion.

> For I bore about a shattered and bleeding soul, impatient of being borne by me, yet where to repose it I found not. Not in calm groves, not in games and music, nor in fragrant spots, nor in curious banquettings, nor in the pleasures of the bed and couch; nor (finally) in books or poesy, found it repose. All things looked ghastly, yea, the very light.⁴

> And behold, Thou wert within, and I abroad, and there I searched for Thee; deformed I, plunging amid those fair forms, which Thou hadst made. Thou wert with me, but I was not with Thee. . . . Thou touchedst me, and I burned for Thy peace.⁵

---
* Now lost.

And when, at last, Augustine entered with his "whole self" into perfect union with God and gained that peace for which he yearned, he found not only peace but also understanding of the nature of God.

> What art Thou then, my God? What, but the Lord God? For who is Lord but the Lord? or who is God save our God? Most highest, most good, most potent, most omnipotent; most merciful, yet most just; most hidden, yet most present; most beautiful, yet most strong; stable, yet incomprehensible; unchangeable, yet all-changing; never new, never old; all-renewing, and bringing age upon the proud, and they know it not; ever working, ever at rest; still gathering, yet nothing lacking; supporting, filling, and over-spreading, creating, nourishing, and maturing; seeking, yet having all things. . . . Great art Thou, O Lord, and greatly to be praised; great is Thy power, and Thy wisdom infinite.[6]

The last three chapters of the *Confessions* are devoted largely to Biblical exegesis and, except as they reveal Augustine's mysticism, are of little biographical interest. The period between his conversion and the writing of the *Confessions* was undoubtedly an important one, but the *Confessions* contains no account of Augustine's activities or of his development during this time.

CITY OF GOD

The sack of Rome in the year 410 by the Goths under Alaric probably stimulated Augustine to begin, three years later, his monumental *City of God*. The Christians were blamed by the pagans for the fall of the "eternal" city, and Augustine undertook to refute the accusation that the Christians had destroyed Rome by undermining Rome's ancient religion. In the first ten books of this great work he maintains that the pagan gods neither founded Rome nor were ever able to protect her. He then turns to a higher task than that of controversy with heathens: the task of revealing Divine Purpose in history. Rome fell, he claims, because she was a "terrestrial city"; the City of God alone endures.

> What an occasion and what a theme [says Paul Janet]! Rome taken, paganism imputing to the new faith this last downfall, this irreparable overthrow of all the grandeur of the past; in its turn, Christianity throwing back these misfortunes upon the entire ancient civilization, and to that frail city which had been vaunted as eternal opposing another city which was really eternal and could only accomplish her destiny in the bosom of God, but which was beginning already in the souls of those who believe and pray.[7]

In the struggle between these two cities Augustine found an explanation of all historical events.

The work required at least thirteen years to complete. It was written by a busy man who turned to it only as he found time. Yet a central theme—the guiding hand of God in human history—gives unity to the essays on a wide variety of topics contained in it. Gibbon says that it has "the merit of a magnificent design, vigorously and not unskilfully executed." Cunningham, who does not hesitate to criticize Augustine, says that "the historical system of the ancient father is more perfect and complete [than that of Hegel]; inasmuch as he had a clearer conception of the beginning, and a more definite perception of the final end towards which the whole Creation moves." [8]

What did Augustine mean by "city"? He himself attempted no definition of this important concept, perhaps because he preferred to leave its meaning somewhat indistinct. Plato, the Stoics, Seneca, Philo, Plotinus, and other writers had used the term earlier without giving it a precise meaning, and the Bible contains numerous references to an indeterminate "city" of God (Ps. 86:3; 47:2, 3, 9; Heb. 11:10, 16). A "city" was to Augustine both a body of human beings and a way of life. Babylon, the terrestrial city, is made up of people who follow after the flesh; Jerusalem, the heavenly city, is represented on earth by those whose spirits have been made pure by God's grace. Thus the symbolic and the ideal elements in the concept "city" blend and become confused with the concrete and real. A fairly small community may contain both the saved and the damned; likewise all mankind is so divided.

> [The human race] we have distributed into two parts, the one consisting of those who live according to man, the other of those who live according to God. And these we also mystically call the two cities, or the two communities of men, of which the one is predestined to reign eternally with God, and the other to suffer eternal punishment with the devil.[9]

Consequently, the City of God is found on earth as well as in Heaven. The earthly city begets citizens "in whom the city of saints above sojourns till the time of its reign arrives."

Beginning with the mixture and the confusion of two cities as a result of the sin of Adam, Augustine traced from Biblical sources their separate ends. As long as earth endures, their struggle with each other marks the course of history, but Augustine promises an end to this struggle. In eternity each of the cities will then come into its own.

> Yet both alike either enjoy temporal good things, or are afflicted with temporal evils, but with diverse faith, diverse hope, and diverse love, until they must be separated by the last judgment, and each must receive her own end, of which there is no end.[10]

RETRACTIONS

One other work deserves especial mention. During the last three or four years of his life, Augustine undertook the task of revising all his major works. He succeeded in correcting, or bringing into line with his later doctrines, more than two hundred passages from his earlier writings. The *Retractations* is concerned largely with theological matters and, when read in connection with his earlier works, reveals the unity in his theological system in its finally developed form.

METHOD

Empiricism is a method of inquiry which seeks for knowledge through the senses. It endeavors to discover through reason the relevant connections in sensory impressions. To the empiricist ideas begin with the raw material of sensation and are formed by rational inductions into empirical knowledge. The knowledge based upon the senses is, therefore, merely the association of ideas gathered from experience, and is relative rather than absolute. The empiricists do not deny the importance of the human mind in fashioning knowledge, but their insistence on empirical verification does limit severely the freedom of the intellect.

Rationalism assumes that the human mind is able to discover truth independently. To the rationalists the mind is not the passive recipient of sensation, a blank tablet upon which experience writes, as the earlier empiricists claimed; it is rather the active agent in knowledge. The earlier rationalists believed that the mind, acting in accordance with its own principles, was able to reach truth without the aid of the senses, but the philosopher Kant proved that sense experience provides the content without which thought is empty. The emphasis in rationalism, nevertheless, is on the part the mind plays in creating or illuminating truth.

In addition to the approach to truth through the senses and through reason, there is a third basis of knowledge—faith. Sorokin has shown in considerable detail that the truth of faith has been widely accepted in history and is today one of the three pillars of wisdom. He concludes a discussion of this topic with the statement:

> The foregoing discussion affords unequivocal proof that all three systems —the sensory, the rational, and the intuitional—are sources of valid cognition; that each of them, when adequately used, gives us knowledge of one of the important aspects of true reality; and that none of them, accordingly, is wholly false. On the other hand, each taken separately, not supplemented by the others, may prove misleading. The history of human thought is a graveyard filled with wrong observations and observational conclusions, with misleading reasoning and speculation, and with false intuitional conclusions. In this respect the position of intuition is in no way worse than that of sensation or dialecticism. None of them in itself, as has been said, can embrace the whole of truth. In the three dimensional aspect of faith, reason, and sensation, integral truth is nearer to absolute truth than that furnished by any one of these three forms.[11]

This brief discussion of three major systems of truth is intended to serve as an introduction to Augustine's theory of knowledge. Although he recognized that sensation and reason are both important to knowledge, he maintained that the highest level of truth is reached through intuition and faith.

REASON AND FAITH

Augustine did not make a clear distinction between reason and faith. He anticipated Cartesian rationalism by deriving the certain knowledge of self-existence from doubt itself—*si fallor sum*—and in assuming that similar knowledge of unquestionable certainty is within human grasp.

> . . . without any delusive representation of images or phantasms, I am most certain that I am, and that I know and delight in this. In respect of these truths, I am not at all afraid of the arguments of the Academicians, who say, What if you are deceived? For if I am deceived, I am. For he who is not, cannot be deceived; and if I am deceived, by this same token I am.[12]

Thus Augustine was able by intuition and reason to escape from the skepticism of his age. The certainty of self-existence paved the way for equally certain knowledge of God. There is little evidence that Augustine ever really doubted the existence of God, even when he was a Manichaean, but his nature demanded positive knowledge rather than pious belief, and this he was able to obtain only by a mental process similar in many respects to that of Descartes.

Once having reached, however, a criterion of truth, Augustine proceeded along entirely different lines from those followed by the seventeenth-century rationalist. Although logic had led him to God, at the same time faith in God had made it possible for Augustine to exercise the full powers of his reason, "since God alone is the truth and the light of the rational soul." With his faith in reason established, Descartes turned the light of the mind outward and set modern science on its way; with a similar faith, Augustine turned toward the source of that light and discovered intellectual justification for faith in God.

Augustine observed that all men have faith in something. Of himself he says:

> . . . what innumerable things I believed, which I saw not, nor was present while they were done, as so many things in secular history, so many reports of places and of cities, which I had not seen; so many of friends, so many of physicians, so many continually of other men, which unless we should believe, we should do nothing at all in this life; lastly, with how unshaken an assurance I believed, of what parents I was born, which I could not know, had I not believed upon hearsay.[13]

Faith is not, therefore, something man needs to get; it is something he already has. The question is one of deciding where to repose it. In putting his in God, Augustine believed that he had found the source of the light of all understanding.

"He that knows the Truth, knows what that Light is," says Augustine, "and he that knows it knows eternity." [14]

Augustine saw that reason and faith complement each other, but he never succeeded in deciding which comes first, as a few quotations will show:

> Faith is understanding's step, and understanding is faith's reward. . . . If a man says to me, I would understand in order that I may believe, I answer, Believe, that you may understand. . . . We believe that we might know; for if we wished first to know and then to believe, we should not be able either to know or to believe.
>
> In certain matters pertaining to the doctrine of salvation, which we cannot yet understand but which some day we shall be able to do, it is right that faith should precede reason. Faith thus purifies the heart, rendering it capable of receiving and enduring the great light of reason. . . . [With respect to other matters] far be it that we should have faith without accepting or demanding reason for our faith.[15]

Perhaps Augustine's own life experience is his best answer to this question of the relationship between faith and reason. That God informs his mind is obvious, but he finds God through the exercise of his highest mental faculties. Only rational beings are capable of faith, and from Augustine's point of view man is less than man if he does not exercise both reason and faith.

MYSTICISM

The belief in the attainment of knowledge through faith, spiritual insight, or mysterious illumination of the mind has been widespread both in time and in place. It has been held not only, or especially, by the ignorant but also by many of the best-informed men in every field of creative activity. The sudden burst of understanding that has come to men of genius in all ages, like light flooding in an instant the whole vast darkness, is disclosed in the biographies of many of the greatest personages in history. The scientist gropes blindly with a problem; suddenly he exclaims, "Eureka!" He knows that he has found the solution, but he is not able to explain how light dawned and made clear what had been dark. The poet fixes fast with words a profound insight from some mysterious source. The musician hears a melody and records it quickly with his symbols before it is lost. The artist catches a glimpse of beauty and his brush preserves it, but he has no answer to Augustine's question, "In what bodily sense is beauty perceived?"

In the field of religion the belief in the attainment through intuition of Truth and Ultimate Reality is especially prominent. Sorokin says:

> All great religions explicitly declare that they are revealed through the grace of the Absolute to charismatically gifted persons—prophets, saints, mystics, oracles, and other instruments of the Absolute. And mystic experi-

ence, which reveals the truth of faith, has little, if anything, to do with ordinary cognition attained through the sense organs or rational discourse. Without mystic intuition, mankind could hardly have possessed any religion worthy of the name. Since religion in general and the world religions in particular constitute one of the foremost achievements of human culture, they testify to the significance of the role played by intuition—especially by mystic intuition—in the history of human thought and civilization.[16]

Augustine did not call himself a mystic but his mysticism* is obvious from a most casual examination of his works. When he spoke of arriving in "the flash of one trembling glance" at "That Which Is," [17] he was clearly asserting his belief in direct and intimate knowledge of God. In his *De Quantitate Animae*, Augustine stated his theory of this experience, through the degrees of growth of the soul from vegetative life to its full realization in union with God. Papini has summarized this theory as follows:

> According to Augustine these degrees are seven in number: the first is the vegetative soul of *vivification*, which we share with plants; the second is the sensible soul or *sensation*, which we share with animals; the third is practical life or *art* which comprehends all of our activities from agriculture to poetry and is of man alone; the fourth is merit or *virtue*, conceded only to those who prefer the soul to the body and the things of the spirit to those of the world; the fifth is permanence in purity, *gladness* or *peace of mind*; the sixth is the *entrance* or *vision* which signifies the complete transference of self into the sphere of eternal light, the final bridling of all trace of concupiscence; the seventh and last is not a degree, but the maintaining of self on the heights attained to, that is to say, in the contemplation and pure enjoyment of God.[18]

This union with God brings perfect understanding. The "far superior sense belonging to the inner man" through which God reveals Himself is not a function of the intellect alone. Knowledge involves the whole physical and incorporeal nature of man, the body and the soul, the intellect and the will. It also brings rapturous joy, like unto the joy of Heaven. The moment of supreme exaltation is brief, and Augustine tells us that soon he falls back and is "absorbed" again in his normal state. But the experience endures in the invigoration and the clearer perception which result from it.

NATURE

A striking characteristic of Augustine's thought is his relative indifference to the natural order in comparison with his consuming interest in the inner man. In regarding inquiry into Nature as an inferior activity of the mind, he was following the example of the Roman moralists and the Neo-Platonists; but he car-

---

* Augustine uses the word "contemplation" to describe what has come to be known as the mystical experience.

ried further the subordination of science to theology, not by depreciating science but by exalting theology. His interest in astronomy and physiology, as well as in other natural phenomena, is evident in his writings. If he was critical of the "curious desire, veiled under the name of knowledge," which induces men to concern themselves with temporal rather than eternal things, it was because he believed that the truth which men can love and live by is more important than that which merely satisfies intellectual curiosity. He warned Christians not to make themselves ridiculous by disregarding, because of erroneous interpretations of the Scriptures, empirical facts established by observation and reason.

> It frequently happens that there is some question about the earth, or the sky, or the other elements of this world, the movement, revolutions, or even the size and distance of the stars, the regular eclipses of the sun and the moon, the course of the years and seasons; the nature of the animals, vegetables, and minerals, and other things of the same kind, respecting which one who is not a Christian has knowledge derived from most certain reasoning or observation. And it is highly deplorable and mischievous and a thing especially to be guarded against that he should hear a Christian speaking of such matters in accordance with Christian writings and uttering such nonsense that, knowing him to be as wide of the mark as, to use the common expression, east is from west, the unbeliever can scarcely restrain himself from laughing.[19]

The knowledge of temporal things should even serve to amplify wisdom, but the latter is achieved only through contemplation of eternal things.

> If therefore this is the right distinction between wisdom and knowledge, that the intellectual cognition of eternal things pertains to wisdom, but the rational cognition of temporal things to knowledge, it is not difficult to judge which is to be esteemed more and which less.[20]

SUMMARY

Augustine helped to turn interest away from the things of the senses to those of the mind and spirit. The trend toward concern with the inner nature of man rather than with the world of nature had developed before Augustine, but he undoubtedly gave impetus to the movement away from science toward religion. Windelband says:

> Under the influence of the ethical and religious interest, metaphysical interest had become gradually and almost imperceptibly shifted from the sphere of the outer to that of the inner life. Psychical conceptions had taken the place of physical, as fundamental factors in the conception of the world. It was reserved for Augustine to bring into full and conscious use, this, which had already become an accomplished fact in Origen and Plotinus.[21]

Augustine does not depreciate reason in order to make a place for authority and faith. "No one believes anything," he says, "unless he has before thought it worthy of belief."[22] He saw that faith and reason work together for understanding, and that it is not less true that faith presupposes reason than that all knowledge rests ultimately on faith in something—in God, says Augustine. He well understood that a faith not founded on reasonable authority, demanding acceptance on reasonable grounds, is no faith at all but mere credulity.

Augustine was a Christian mystic. He believed that insights received by grace, after purgation and holy activities have prepared the recipient for contemplation, are made meaningful to others through dogmas which have to be accepted on authority. He repeatedly declared that truth "unveils itself to him who lives well, prays well, and studies well" the Scriptures. He maintained that the revelation on which all knowledge ultimately rests is brought within the grasp of the ordinary mortal by the Scriptures. They show that prayer derives its efficacy through the blood of the Redeemer, and discloses both the nature of the good life and the means by which it may be attained.

Unfortunately, mysticism suffers from its company, and offers refuge to the mentally indolent and the psychopathic. However, it does not for that reason lose its claim to validity. The life and thought of Augustine reveal both the incomparable meaning of mystic experience and its mystery.

HUMAN NATURE

Since Augustine influenced the interpretation of orthodox Christian doctrine on the subject of human nature and vigorously combated the heresies which threatened its acceptance, his conception of the nature of man is an important part of his social thought. His views on original sin and predestination did not go unchallenged in his own day, as the Pelagian controversy well illustrates, but had he not prevailed against the heretics, the course of Christianity for a thousand years might have been vastly different from that which it followed.

ADAM'S SIN

Augustine believed that Adam began life with a pure and uncorrupted nature, as did Eve, whom God, "working in a divine manner," formed from a bone in his side "to aid him in the work of generating his kind." He was endowed with reason and a free will; otherwise he would have been imperfect. Of his own free will he disobeyed God, and in his sin all his seed were damned.

> For God, the author of natures, not of vices, created man upright; but man, being of his own will corrupted, and justly condemned, begot corrupted and condemned children. For we all were in that one man, since we all were that one man who fell into sin by the woman who was made from him before the sin. For not yet was the particular form created and distributed to us, in which we as individuals were to live, but already the

seminal nature was there from which we were to be propagated; and this being vitiated by sin, and bound by the chain of death, and justly condemned, man could not be borne of man in any other state. And thus, from the bad use of free will, there originated the whole train of evil, which, with its concatenation of miseries, convoys the human race from its depraved origin, as from a corrupt root, on to the destruction of the second death, which has no end, those only being excepted who are freed by the grace of God.[23]

SPIRIT AND FLESH

All men since Adam have been born evil, and for man to live according to his nature is for him "to live like the devil." He does not have within himself any means of escape from that sad state which Augustine likes to describe in the language of Virgil.

> Hence wild desires and groveling fears,
> And human laughter, human tears,
> Immured in dungeon-seeming night,
> They look abroad, yet see no light.[24]

Augustine goes on to say, however, that Virgil was mistaken in the view that the body is the origin of sin. On the contrary,

> . . . the corruption of the body, which weighs down the soul, is not the cause but the punishment of the first sin; and it was not the corruptible flesh that made the soul sinful, but the sinful soul that made the flesh corruptible.[25]

This harsh view of inherent human depravity is not mitigated by a belief in man's possession of a spirit that stands opposed to his flesh: his spirit, too, is corrupted.* From Augustine's point of view, man wholly lacks within himself the means of living well or of finding in death any relief from the torment which through the sin of Adam he justly deserves.

DOCTRINE OF GRACE

Nevertheless, some men obviously live better lives than others, and Augustine was persuaded that some also escape eternal damnation. The grace of God makes this redemption possible. Windelband explains Augustine's doctrine of grace as follows:

> One as little as another deserves to receive this grace; therefore, thinks Augustine, no injustice can be seen in the fact that God bestows this grace,

* However, cf. his statement: "Nor did He take away His whole nature from him, but left him part, whereby to bewail the loss of the rest: which lamentation testifies both what he had and what he has: for had he not some good left, he could not lament for what he had lost" (City of God, XIX, 13).

to which no one has any claim, not upon all, but only upon some; and it is never known upon whom. But, on the other hand, the divine justice demands that, at least in the case of some men, the punishment for Adam's fall should be permanently maintained, that these men, therefore, should remain excluded from the working of grace and from redemption. Since, finally, in consequence of their corrupted nature, all are alike sinful and incapable of any improvement of themselves, it follows that the choice of the favoured ones takes place not according to their worthiness (for there are none worthy before the working of grace), but according to an unsearchable decree of God. Upon him whom he will redeem he bestows his revelation with its irresistible power: he whom he does not choose,—he can in no wise be redeemed. Man in his own strength cannot make even a beginning toward the good: all good comes from God and only from him.[26]

What then, may be expected of man, seeing that he is born of Adam, through whom he is eternally damned unless he is saved by a grace which he can in no way influence? Augustine says that he can at least face the fact that he cannot save himself, that he has nothing within himself better than reason, and that reason is inadequate for salvation. He who would live blessedly must look beyond himself for light and power; he must lose himself in order that he may find himself. He must acknowledge his weakness and seek guidance, saying,

> Narrow is the mansion of my soul; enlarge Thou it, that Thou mayest enter in. It is ruinous, repair Thou it. It has that within which must offend Thine eyes; I confess and know it. But who shall cleanse it? or to whom should I cry, save Thee? [27]

Augustine did not promise that all prayers would be answered; he did not guarantee that humility and contrition would be rewarded. In His Wisdom God may punish a guileless infant and bless a wicked man despite his evil deeds. But Augustine did insist that the humble and contrite heart alone is prepared to receive the Divine Light without which there can be only darkness.

FREEDOM OF THE WILL

According to Augustine, man's true freedom and his greatest happiness are found not in the exercise of his will, for that too is tainted, but in the submission of his will to the Will of God. The price of escape from human bondage is complete submission to the Divine Will, and the reward is perfect freedom. A nineteenth-century English poet, brooding over this matter, came to a similar conclusion when he said:

> Our wills are ours, we know not how;
> Our wills are ours, to make them thine.[28]

POLITICS

The first Christian Emperor had been dead for more than a century when Augustine was born. At Nicaea, in the year 325, Constantine had pledged the support of the Roman Empire to the Christian Church. The Church, meanwhile, had grown in strength, and the Empire had slowly disintegrated. Consequently, when Augustine began his life's work, one of the main tasks confronting him was to fill through the Church the void in organized social control created by the collapse of Rome. The institutional Church, as the strongest organization surviving the old Empire, was faced with temporal as well as with spiritual responsibilities. Political leadership was urgently required, not so much at the administrative level, where force held sway, as at the theoretical level, where intellectual guidance was demanded. The confusion created by the fall of Rome could be relieved only by those able to reorganize society around new ideals and principles. The Church fathers alone possessed the ability to exercise this authority, and men like Ambrose and Augustine superseded the Roman jurists in defining the basis of law, the nature and function of the state, and the rights of temporal rulers, and in molding attitudes toward such matters as equality, slavery, and property. They were too much occupied with matters of the spirit to formulate a systematic theory of politics, but their influence on the political organization of Europe during the Middle Ages was tremendous. Even today, the political thought of the Church fathers is an important part of the cultural heritage of the Western World.

THE STATE

Augustine's theory of the origin of the state is similar to that of the Stoics—that government became necessary only after man's nature became corrupt. But whereas Stoicism assumed that man enjoyed a happy and an innocent existence in a Golden Age, it failed to give an adequate explanation of his degeneration. Augustine accepted the Stoic view of a primitive state in which man was able to live well by the laws of his own nature, but he was not content to leave unexplained the cause of man's corruption. He found the answer in Biblical history. Adam was perfect; he possessed in his God-given nature all that was required for the good life; he lived in a Golden Age. In his sin, all humanity became sinful, and the natural light originally in man grew dim.

Cicero's conception of natural law was well known to Augustine. He shared Cicero's conviction that all laws rests ultimately on divine justice, but he could not agree with Cicero that the state exists only to serve the ends of justice. Since no earthly states can achieve justice, man being what he is, people can live justly with one another only if they are without sin, and the earthly state can be a moral community of people guided by divine justice only if the will of God is revealed to every man. But in that case—that is, if the laws of God were written plainly on the fleshy tablets of every human heart so that justice prevailed—there would be no need for any form of coercive government. Augustine did not deny the theory of natural law. He insisted, however, that it applies in the absolute sense only to the state of nature from which Adam had removed himself and all mankind. He claimed that justice is made of sterner stuff than the state can provide through the dictates of corrupted human reason. True justice is found only in God's kingdom, says Augustine, and the earthly state is best defined as "an assemblage of reasonable beings bound together by a common agreement as to the objects of their love." [29]

Augustine's definition of the state is thus vastly different from that of Cicero. He reduced the state's scope and function in order to make place in society for the Church, which is separate from, and superior to, the state. The Church serves more directly the City of God, whereas the state is primarily concerned with the affairs of the terrestrial city. The Church is charged with the responsibility of serving the spiritual needs of living men and of creating an earthly counterpart of the heavenly City of God. The state, on the other hand, serves man's temporal needs. Its functions are, therefore, not only different from those of the Church but inferior to them, since matters of the flesh are less important than those of the spirit. The king's claim to his proper authority is not to be questioned, but that authority is severely limited in scope by a no less indisputable claim of the Church to sovereignty in its own sphere of responsibility.

This doctrine of two spheres of authority in society explains Augustine's apparent compromise with respect to such practical social matters as equality, slavery, and property. The state must deal with men as they are—men who are unequal, who take advantage of the weakness of others, and who are greedy for possessions. It cannot apply absolute standards to such men. Cicero would make the state responsible for the maintenance of justice; Augustine realistically recognized the inability of the state to create a moral society. He believed that people form the kind of state, and live under the kind of earthly government, that they deserve to have. Augustine never claimed that it is right for man to exploit his fellows; he simply believed that exploitation is a characteristic of the earthly city which human law can direct but cannot transform into the City of God.

SLAVERY

Slavery was certainly incompatible with Augustine's ideals of human equality. He declared that "All mankind is in Christ one man" and preached the Golden Rule. His failure, therefore, to denounce the ancient institution of slavery and to use the force of the Church against it has been claimed by some writers to be an example of the compromise which the Church made with the evils of the day.[30] This criticism fails, however, to reckon with the sharp distinction which

Augustine made between the two cities. Obviously slavery has no place in the City of God; nor has any other form of injustice. But in the earthly city slavery, like war, is fitting, even though it is not good.

> He did not intend that His rational creature, who was made in His image, should have dominion over anything but the irrational creation—not man over man, but man over the beasts. And hence the righteous men in primitive times were made shepherds of cattle rather than kings of men, God intending thus to teach us what the relative position of the creatures is, and what the desert of sin; for it is with justice, we believe, that the condition of slavery is the result of sin.[31]

Augustine did not mean that only the wicked are enslaved; men of charity and good will are as likely to be in a state of captivity as are doers of evil. There is no more reason to expect good men in the earthly city to be free than to expect them to be prosperous. What Augustine did mean is that men get collectively, not individually, what they deserve. Since slavery is the fruit of sin and can be extirpated from society only by cleansing human nature of its corruptions, it follows that mankind should make the best of a bad situation.

> And therefore the apostle admonishes slaves to be subject to their masters, and to serve them heartily and with good-will, so that, if they cannot be freed by their masters, they may themselves make their slavery in some sort free, by serving not in crafty fear, but in faithful love, until all unrighteousness pass away, and all principality and every human power be brought to nothing, and God be all in all.[32]

PROPERTY

Likewise, Augustine accepted the institution of private property as necessary in the earthly city, and therefore lawful. It affords, like slavery and even government itself, a hard discipline without which there would be anarchy. This discipline would not be necessary if men lived by the spirit of God's love. The renunciation of worldly possessions, required both by unselfishness and by complete absorption in spiritual goods, demands, however, a degree of charity of which only the pure in heart are capable. Despite the fact that he regarded interest in private property as in itself evidence of a corrupted nature, Augustine recognized this interest as both real and necessary in the world of men. His casual remarks on this subject are widely scattered through his works, but in general they are similar to those of the other early Christians, whose views are summarized by Doyle as follows:

> The early Christians had vaguely suggested that all things should be held in common amongst the faithful. . . . All goods were originally given to man for the common use; private property was a right to acquire sufficient for one's personal wants; but private property was always limited by the

recognition of the responsibility to use all goods for the common benefit. An absolute right to private property as understood by the Roman jurists was vigorously denied by the Christians. Private property like government and slavery, were conventional institutions superimposed by man or God for the benefit of humanity, after the collapse of the original perfect state of nature occasioned by the fall.[33]

PEACE

The peace with which Augustine was primarily concerned is the perfect peace of Paradise, but he did not neglect the problem of attaining a measure of peace on earth.

> The earthly city, which does not live by faith, seeks an earthly peace, and the end it proposes, in the well-ordered concord of civic obedience and rule, is the combination of men's wills to attain the things which are helpful to this life. . . .
>
> The good of peace is generally the greatest wish of the world, and the most welcome when it comes.[34]

Man is a social animal, disposed to seek the company of his fellows and to live peacefully with them. The natural inclination to accord within the species is found throughout the animal kingdom.

> For the most savage animals . . . encompass their own species with a ring of protecting peace. They cohabit, beget, produce, suckle, and bring up their young, though very many of them are not gregarious, but solitary—not like sheep, deer, pigeons, starlings, bees, but such as lions, foxes, eagles, bats. For what tigress does not gently purr over her cubs, and lay aside her ferocity to fondle them? What kite, solitary as he is when circling over his prey, does not seek a mate, build a nest, hatch the eggs, bring up the young birds, and maintain with the mother of his family as peaceful a domestic alliance as he can? How much more powerfully do the laws of man's nature move him to hold fellowship and maintain peace with all men so far as in him lies, since even wicked men wage war to maintain the peace of their own circle, and wish that, if possible, all men belonged to them, that all men and things might serve but one head, and might, either through love or fear, yield themselves to peace with him![35]

However, despite a universal protestation of love of peace, Augustine saw little hope for a lasting peace in the city of men. Often, it seemed to him, the only way to attain peace is through war. The "godly" peace must be distinguished from the "wicked" peace; while wicked men look upon waging war "and the augmentation of dominions by conquest as a great felicity, the good must needs hold it as a mere necessity." Peace terminates one war, but in the city of men new wars are constantly brewing, and no military victory can "keep a sovereignty forever."

Augustine (A.D. 354–430) • 253

Furthermore, war may be not only necessary but also useful: it may serve to strengthen and to extend God's kingdom on earth. The proper relation of the constitutive parts of a society requires obedience to the lawful commands of a theocratic state. Augustine did not justify the "holy" war, but he did leave the way open for its justification. He did not himself advocate the creation of a universal state. He recognized the risks of tyranny in large states formed through conquests and favored the political organization of the world into small states living in harmony with one another. Nevertheless, in speaking of "one fellowship of government and laws," he may have had in mind some kind of union of the nations.

SUMMARY

Augustine believed that coercive government and such social institutions as slavery, private property, and war are the fruits of sin. They characterize the city of men, and exercise in that city a harsh discipline over unruly natures. The pure in heart do not require this control; but until the whole world is redeemed, it is necessary. A distinction was made between the Kingdom of God and that of man, but Augustine's separation of the two kingdoms was not complete; something of the heavenly city is found on earth. A strong state is needed to maintain civil order, and it is, if not the greatest earthly good, at least the condition for all earthly goods, provided it is dedicated to the service of true religion. The power that the king exercises over temporal matters is not absolute; it is limited by the authority of God. Although the king rules by divine right, a Nero no less than an Augustus, the exercise of his rights is at every point checked by his responsibility to serve God, the source of his authority. Augustine did not create the Holy Roman Empire, but he helped to establish the foundations upon which it developed.

FAMILY

Since religious beliefs and practices are intimately related to family life, the early Church was confronted with the necessity of stating clearly its ideals of family life and of uprooting those pagan practices supported by customs and by law which opposed them. The struggle between Christianity and paganism for control of the family began with the introduction of Christianity into the pagan world, and it was carried on by the Church with unyielding determination. During the first three centuries of the Christian era, celibacy was not required of priests; but restrictions on their enjoyment of private family life became increasingly severe, until, in 387, priests were prohibited from marrying or from living with wives taken before their entry into the priesthood. That issue was settled, therefore, before Augustine appeared on the scene, and he and the other Church fathers probably had less to do with developing the ideal of celibacy among the servants of the Church than with promoting the ideals of Christian marriage among the laity, although they did help to establish monasticism.

Troeltsch describes the general teaching of the Church on family matters as follows:

> From the very beginning the Church set before its members a high and strict ideal; it required them to observe the ideal of monogamy, of chastity before marriage (for both husband and wife), of conjugal fidelity, to exercise an ethical and religious discipline in the care of children, [and] to reject all regulation of the birth-rate by the exposure of children or by artificial sterilization. . . . There was a "perpetual struggle between the highest ideals of Christianity—permission only of complete marriage and that only as an indissoluble union—and the motives of the secular legal system, which, indeed, was interested in the stabilization of the family, but which had also to take into account the ingrained habits of the socially dominant classes." Among these customs was the Roman habit of concubinage, which was always monogamous and quite public, and the contract character of a legitimate marriage, which also implied that it could be easily dissolved. Constantine forbade married men to have extra-matrimonial connections, and made concubinage difficult by making invalid all gifts and legacies from the man to his companion and to his children. His Christian successors attempted now and again to make it more difficult to dissolve a marriage by limiting the reasons for divorce, and by confining women more closely to their homes they tried to ensure the greater purity of marriage.[36]

Augustine's comments on marriage and family relations lack the caustic satire of the utterances of men like Tertullian and Jerome on these subjects, but they express the teachings of the early Church on family matters.

MARRIAGE

Augustine regarded marriage as having been divinely instituted to ensure mutual help and comfort and to provide for procreation. Adam and Eve loved one another "out of a pure heart, and a good conscience, and faith unfeigned." Before the original sin there was no lust in their affection, nor sadness of any kind in their relations, nor foolish joy. Adam's sin corrupted marriage, as it corrupted mankind, and introduced into marital relations an element of lustfulness from which man can escape only by devotion to chastity. That devotion requires supreme dedication and greater powers of self-control than most men can command. Besides, has not God commanded man to increase and multiply and replenish the earth? Marriage is, therefore, both natural and proper for most men and women in the earthly city, and the most that can be expected of them is a proper restraint of their lustful desires.

Betrothal at an early age seems to have been regarded by Augustine as natural. The girl to whom he was betrothed must have been about twelve years of age at the time his mother arranged the match. Apparently Augustine expected that a bride would be bestowed in marriage by her parents or guardians. On one occasion at least he suggested that some time ought to elapse between bethrothal and marriage. "The affianced bride," he says, "should not at once be given, lest as a husband he should hold cheap whom, as betrothed, he sighed not after." [37] He was not unmindful of the material considerations in marriage. Just before his baptism he took a long look backwards and asked whether he should deny himself "a fair and modest woman, one who was cultured or who would at least profit readily by instruction and also bring with her a sufficient dower." [38]

Augustine's opposition to marriage outside the Church was strongly stated on several occasions. He sternly reproved a fellow bishop for suggesting the marriage of a ward to a man who, though a Christian, was not a Catholic. From a study of Augustine's letters, Keenan observes:

> The allusions to mixed marriages occur chiefly in connection with the Saint's account of the evils of Donatism. In two letters he deplores the unhappiness of those homes wherein husband and wife are divided at the altar of Christ. Writing to his friend, Antonius, Augustine recommends that he foster the growth of the true faith in his wife's heart by holy reading and serious conversation.[39]

FAMILY RELATIONS

Augustine pictures a family in which the husband and father is in control. Peace in the household demands nothing less.

> For they who care for the best rule—the husband the wife, the parents the children, the masters the servants; and they who are cared for obey—the women their husbands, the children their parents, the servants their masters. But in the family of the just man who lives by faith and is as yet a pilgrim journeying on to the celestial city, even those who rule serve those whom they seem to command; for they rule not from a love of power, but from a sense of the duty they owe to others—not because they are proud of authority, but because they love mercy.[40]

He speaks with approval of his mother's advice to wives who complained that they were mistreated by their husbands, quoting her as declaring

> that from the time they heard the marriage writings read to them, they should account them as indentures, whereby they were made servants; and so, remembering their condition, ought not to set themselves up against their lords.[41]

In Augustine's teaching, divorce is forbidden, as is the remarriage of widows. Continence in married life is commendable, but mutual consent is required for its practice. Augustine sternly reproved a woman who was led by pious enthusiasm to adopt the practice of continence without the consent of her husband. He reluctantly consented to the wearing of ornaments by women interested in marriage but positively prohibited their uncovering their hair or painting their faces.

Augustine's comments on the relations between parents and children are casual, but his glowing tribute to his mother gives eloquent testimony of the importance he attached to parental guidance. He was moved by an expression of filial devotion in a son. He fully recognized the need for parents to pay close attention to the Christian training of their children. But he forbade a father from using violence against a daughter who, against his will, had become a heretic.

Augustine was also mindful of the duty of parents to fit their children for life in civil society. If any in the household be disobedient and offend the just peace, let him be corrected, he said, "with strokes, or some other convenient punishment," since the discipline in the larger society depends on that in the home. For "obedience in the family has real reference to the orderly rule and subjection in the city." Authority is always from above, and home discipline should serve state ends. The father should "fetch his instructions from the city's government," so that home training may afford a proper preparation for the assumption of civic duties. For the sake of social order, habits of loyalty, respect for rightful authority, and recognition of the rights of others must be developed in the young under the watchful care of their parents.

Most of Augustine's views on marriage and family relations are so similar to those prevailing in our own day that we may easily overlook his influence, and that of other early Churchmen, in establishing the family ideals of the Christian world. In his emphasis on monogamy, conjugal fidelity, the sacramental nature of marriage, the dangers of mixed marriages, the dominance of the husband and father in family organization, the prohibition of divorce, and the proper exercise of parental authority, he helped to restore the family unit, which had disintegrated in the late Roman period, to an important position in the organization of society.

SOCIAL CHANGE

Augustine's theory of social change is both simple and profound. It is as simple as the Bible story of the creation, fall, and redemption of mankind. Its profundity lies in its awful realization of the vast eternity out of which all created things emerged and into which they will disappear. In the moment of creation, time began with movement and transition. In God's eternity, there is no change, but He saw fit to create the heavens and the earth, in which nothing abides. For a moment all creation moves; then again all creation will be at rest. The history of every man, and of mankind, is portrayed against a background of timeless and motionless eternity.

Furthermore, everything that happens is foreordained. A God mindful of every falling leaf will not leave to chance the course of nations. Men are free, but God knows what every man will do. All that happens is a part of God's plan. Thus, history has a discernible meaning. Augustine interpreted history as a great poem, with a beginning, a middle, and an end. Cunningham credits him with presenting in his *City of God* a philosophy of history.

> And so he sets before us a philosophy of History,—the continuous evolution of the Divine Purpose in human society: he contrasts the earthly polities which change and pass with the eternal City of God which is being manifested in the world: he shows how these two are intermingled, interacting now, but how different they are in their real nature; one is of the earth, centered only in earthly things, while the other, because it has its chief regard fixed on that which is Eternal, gives us the best rule for the things of time. The earthly city which aimed only at early prosperity failed to attain even that, while the Heavenly City, aiming at an Eternal Peace, supplies the best conditions for earthly good as well. It is in the hope of the final triumph of the City of God, that the course of the world becomes intelligible, for then we may see that the rise and fall of earthly empires, the glories of ancient civilization, the sufferings of men in their ruin, have not been unmeaning or in vain; for they have served to prepare for the coming of the kingdom of God.[42]

LINEAR CHANGE

That all Creation is moving toward a final end Augustine did not doubt. He rejected as "fantastic" the theories of cyclical social change advanced by some "deceiving and deceived sages." The Bible plainly teaches it, he says, "For once Christ died for our sins; and, rising from the dead, He dieth no more." When we read in the Book of Ecclesiastes that there is "no new thing under the sun," we are to understand that the sun turns in its orbit, that rivers follow their courses to the sea, and that generations follow in succession—not that one Academy in Athens with the philosopher Plato at its head is followed after a long but certain interval by the same school, the same disciples, and the same head.

Augustine did not attempt to penetrate the mystery of Creation.

> Who can search out the unsearchable depth of this purpose, who can scrutinize the inscrutable wisdom, wherewith God, without change of will, created man, who had never before been, and gave him an existence in time, and increased the human race from one individual?[43]

The light of reason and the authority of the Scriptures were Augustine's sufficient justification for accepting the doctrine that all Creation has moved from the moment of its origin in a fixed direction toward a determined and final end.

The close parallel which Augustine portrayed between the development of an individual and that of society has continued to appear under various guises down to our own time. Men are born, they develop, and they come to their appointed ends; so is it with all created things. In the *Retractations* Augustine stated that his purpose in writing the *City of God* had been to describe the birth, progress, and final ends of the two cities. "Our whole life," says Augustine, "is nothing but a race toward death, in which no one is allowed to stand still for a little space, or to go somewhat more slowly, but all are driven forward with an impartial movement, and with equal rapidity." [44] This is equally true of the whole of creation. Augustine felt that the end of the world was near, but he was certain that, whether soon or late, the end would come, just as surely as death claims every person born.

He regarded death as not only the final earthly end, for the individual and for the universe, but as also, for the saved among mankind, the highest good. Death breaks the bonds of mortality and brings peace, order, and everlasting life to all those who are taken up into the eternal City of God. Similarly, in a moment the universe will be no more, the movement which stirred in the deep will be stilled, time will run out, and all change will cease.

THE INFLUENCE OF AUGUSTINE

The collapse of Roman supremacy in Africa led to the disorganization of the African Church, which Augustine had labored hard to establish. Arianism revived, and an Arian bishop helped the Vandals to persecute and scatter the Catholic leaders, many of whom fled to Europe and established new Christian communities. In the Church of Rome, Augustine's influence, which had already become pronounced, was thereby strengthened. He was by far the outstanding figure in Catholicism before Thomas Aquinas appeared.

Augustine's manner of expression, vivid with the symbolism of poetry, has enabled groups of followers to claim his authority for widely divergent points of view. The beauty of his language warms the feelings and captures the imagination. Such poignant utterances as "Late I have loved thee, O Ancient Beauty!" stir the emotions. There is in his writings, nevertheless, a remarkable unity, which in many respects is like that found in Plato's philosophy. What the doctrine of Ideas was to the Greek philosopher, the doctrine of Divine Wisdom was to the Catholic theologian. A tinge of mysticism dispels that unity in neither.

Out of the mist which shrouds his age, Augustine emerges as a giant bestriding two cities—the pagan city which had been inherited from the Caesars and the divine city which Augustine envisaged as a gift from God. He is near enough to the earthly city to be aware of the perils which confront those who dwell there, but his eyes are turned toward the heavenly city of eternal life.

Augustine lacked the ability of his great thirteenth-century successor in the Church to knit the loose ends of thought into a consistent whole and to push through with ruthless logic to final conclusions. Some of his ideas—*e.g.,* his doctrine of grace—have been severely criticized by other Christians. Certain of his teachings were used by the leaders of the Eastern Church to provoke the schism which finally, in 1472, after a number of short breaks, definitely separated that body from the Church of Rome. The Protestants were even able during the Reformation to use Augustine to their own advantage in their struggle against the Church. Nevertheless, Augustine laid many of the theological foundations of Catholicism, and he enunciated social teachings to which the Catholic Church has consistently adhered.

Most Catholic theologians today, whatever their personal stand on doctrines, seem generally to incline toward the view that the warm heart of Augustine complements the cool head of Thomas Aquinas, and that together Augustinism and Thomism work for the greater glory of the Christian faith.

11 · THOMAS AQUINAS

(1225-1274)

The study of philosophy does not aim merely to find out what others have thought, but what the truth of the matter is.
AQUINAS—De Caelo et Mundo

Augustine died almost eight hundred years before Aquinas was born. Until recently the modern world has known little, and cared less, about the lives and thought of the men and women who lived during these centuries. The name given to their period, the Dark Ages, in itself implies that little took place then that was worth investigating. Modern historical research has, however, pulled back the curtain that obscured from view the stirring scenes of the Middle Ages, and we are beginning to discover that medieval society played an important part in the development of Western civilization.

Surely an age was not wholly dark which produced the Emperor Charlemagne (768-814), who was crowned temporal leader of the Roman Catholic world by the Pope; the Anglo-Saxons, who laid the foundations for a strong new nation in the north (577-1066); the institutions of European feudalism (tenth to thirteenth centuries), that unique system of social organization which not only held society together for three centuries but also influenced modern conceptions of land tenure and personal relations; and the Crusades (1095-1291), the long struggle between Christians and Arabs for the sake of religion, adventure, and material gain.

A few names will suggest the variety and the splendor of our medieval heritage: the Babylonian Talmud, Alfred the Great, *Beowulf,* Maimonides, St. Francis, William the Conqueror, the Magna Carta, St. Dominic, Scotus Erigena, Anselm, Abelard, Joachim of Floris, the University of Paris, Byzantium, St. Sofia, Chartres, and, certainly not least among these, the *Summa Theologica.*

The development of civilization in the West was affected, to be sure, by the monopoly of learning by the clergy, who had little occasion to examine the dogmas of the Church. After Christian theology had been set by the Church fathers in a Platonic mold, it required no philosophical support that could not be provided by an occasional reference to the few known works of Plato or his followers. Thus the Christian mind was little troubled during the early Middle Ages by the exciting ideas which certain Greek philosophers had long before embraced with eager anticipation. In 529 the Emperor Justinian closed the pagan schools, and although Greek philosophy survived in Persia, Syria, and especially in Byzantium and other centers of Arabian culture, the Roman Catholics were protected by their intellectual isolation from its disturbing influence.

Although a few outstanding theologians appeared during the long centuries, they found the prevailing climate of thought in most respects congenial. Scotus Erigena (810-880) took the trouble to learn Greek at a time when the language was practically lost to western Christendom, but he employed his knowledge only to use Plato in the Church's struggle with nominalism—the theory that universals are fictions and not, as the Church claimed, ideal types created by Divine Will. In the eleventh century nominalism was revived under the leadership of the canon Roscellinus, and Plato's realism was again brought forth, this time by Anselm (1033-1109). Abelard (1079-1142) confessed an enthusiastic admiration for Greek philosophy but admitted that his knowledge of the subject was derived from the works of Augustine. For a long time the Christian world remained in tranquil isolation. Aristotle, the philosopher who was later to affect profoundly the theology of the Catholic Church, was for many centuries known only through a few treatises on logic, and his influence on Churchmen during this period was negligible.

Then came the Crusades, bringing Arabian versions of Greek philosophy to Europe. Among the Arabs learning had not been confined to the clergy, as it had been generally in the West. Arab scientists, and scattered groups of Jewish scholars residing in Arab lands, had maintained a lively interest in the world of nature. They had also preserved a vast body of ancient writings, especially works of Greek philosophers, which otherwise might have been lost forever. The capture of Constantinople by the Crusaders in 1204 gave Europe many old manuscripts and brought Greek philosophy, above all the philosophy of Aristotle, back into the European arena of ideas. Arab philosophers, who had long been familiar with some of Aristotle's works and had many of them available in their own language, had a great advantage over the Churchmen, and the influence of such men as Avicenna in Persia and Averroës in Spain became widely felt in the Christian world. The harmony in the Church was threatened as it had not been since Augustine. As Carré says:

> During the thirteenth century the philosophical thought of Europe was transformed. The chief factor in this new development was the rediscovery of some of the cardinal works of ancient reflection. From the middle of the twelfth century in Sicily and in the Spanish peninsula numerous translators

were engaged in producing Latin versions from the Arabic records of Greek science and philosophy. A generation earlier Abelard . . . was acquainted with but a few of the minor logical works of Aristotle. Now not only the major logical treatises but the *Physics* and *Metaphysics* were for the first time made available for study. The impact was disturbing, for it was revealed that on many vital points of Christian thought Aristotle's views were at variance with the teaching of the Church. The disparity was exaggerated by the way in which the philosopher's thought was interpreted by Avicenna and Averroës, the great Arab scholars through whom Aristotle's writings were first transmitted to Christian students. Aristotle was presented as maintaining views on providence, on the eternity of the world, on the reality of individuals, on freedom, and on immortality, which were in direct contradiction with Christian beliefs. Repeatedly throughout the thirteenth century masters were forbidden to instruct their students in the doctrines of the philosopher who was soon to become the standard authority of medieval reflection.[1]

The attempt on the part of some Churchmen to close the door to new and disturbing ideas had little success; once its cloisters had been entered, the Church was confronted with a challenge it could not refuse to accept. Fortunately a champion was at hand. Although not alone in facing the challenge to Christian theology resulting from the influx into the Christian world of new and conflicting ideas, the man most responsible for restoring the medieval synthesis of Christian theology and for fortifying it with a vast body of new material incorporated into its conceptual framework was Thomas Aquinas, sometimes called the "Angelic Doctor."

BIOGRAPHICAL SKETCH

In the castle of his family at Roccasecca, near the little village of Aquino not far from Naples, Thomas Aquinas was born about the year 1225. His father, a Lombard noble, was a nephew of Frederick Barbarossa, and his mother traced her lineage to a noble Norman stock. Since two older sons were being trained for a military life, it was early decided by the family that young Thomas should enter the priesthood. Accordingly, he was turned over at the age of five to the Benedictine monks at Monte Cassino, so that he might be prepared to become in time an abbot and uphold the prestige of the family as a high official in the Church and master of some of its vast estates.

The monks could not have hoped for a better or more promising pupil. Thomas was sensitive, serious, and diligent. He loved solitude; he throve on discipline; the quiet atmosphere of the abbey afforded him an opportunity for meditation. Thus his early youth was spent under benign influences that stimulated the development of his precocious talents and caused him to shun the carefree, noisy play of youth. When he was fourteen or fifteen, his father thought it advisable to remove him from Monte Cassino, and he was sent to Naples to continue his studies. At the University of Naples his instruction was not limited to theology, but his interest even then in the work of the Church was so evident, and his ability so pronounced, that his future as an abbot seemed assured. His family had every reason to be well pleased in him.

Then, suddenly, without consulting his family and for reasons which are not certain, Thomas joined the Dominicans. This order of mendicant friars was highly respected for faith and learning, but its complete lack of possessions and the coarse attire and hard life of its members did not commend it to the noble family of Aquinas. His mother went at once to plead with him to reconsider his choice. When he gently refused her request, she asked the Pope to intercede. The Pope, eager to make peace in the family as well as to use most effectively the services of a promising young priest, promised Aquinas that he might become a Benedictine abbot without giving up his Dominican habit. But Thomas remained firm in his resolution to follow the hard way of life of the Dominicans.

The members of his family believed, however, that he might yet be persuaded to change his mind. Accordingly, when he was ordered to Paris, his brothers intercepted him after he had gone a short distance and made him prisoner. He was confined for more than a year, during which time his mother and his sisters pleaded with him, and his brothers threatened him. The story is told that finally in desperation a woman was hired to seduce him. He is said to have chased her shrieking from his cell with a burning brand, with which he thereupon made a cross upon the door. Only then was he given his freedom and allowed to resume his journey. In the end, it may be noted, his influence on the members of his family was far greater than theirs on him: his mother became an ascetic, one of his sisters entered a nunnery, and it appears that one of his brothers died a martyr.

In Paris, Aquinas met Albert the Great, one of the most learned men of the age, and began to study and to work under his guidance. When Albert was ordered to Cologne, Aquinas accompanied him and continued for four more years his intimate relation with the great scholar. Among Albert's many accomplishments was a knowledge of Aristotle's philosophy, and he introduced his young pupil and friend to the works of the Stagirite. Aquinas read, perhaps in Latin translation, all of Aristotle's works that he could find. He soon discovered that Aristotle was a congenial mind, and he grew in intellectual strength through the absorption of the philosophy of the great Greek philosopher.

When Aquinas returned to Paris, he was not long in gaining recognition. He met in public debate, as was the custom of the day, any heretic or unbeliever who dared to raise his voice against the dogmas of the Church, and such were his dialectical skills and his knowledge that no man could stand against him. His advancement was rapid: in 1254 he became a licentiate (bachelor) at the University of Paris, the intellectual center of the Western world, and within three years he was a professor of theology. Thus, at thirty-one, Aquinas stood on the topmost rung of the ladder leading up to fame as a scholar. He had climbed rapidly, but his footing had been sure. His competence established, he was in a position to render that service to the Church for which his talents fitted him.

Aquinas had no time, and certainly no inclination, to bask in the approval of his fellows. Kings sought his advice about governing, theologians turned to him with their problems, novices wrote asking for personal guidance, popes sent him on missions and assigned to him special duties, and his order made heavy demands upon his time and energy. Despite these various activities and a comparatively short life, however, Aquinas was able to produce writings that fill, in the popular Vives Edition of his works, thirty-five large volumes. His powers of memory and orderly thought enabled him, it is said, to dictate to several scribes at the same time on different subjects, and one may judge from his accomplishments that he was seldom idle.

Although Aquinas was busy and his mental powers were strong until the hour of his death, he sensed that he would not live to do all that he had hoped to do. The time came when even his great *Summa,* which he left unfinished, seemed to him to fall far short of saying what he knew. On one occasion he exclaimed sadly, "All I have written appears to me as so much rubbish, compared with what I have seen and what has been revealed to me." His last important fight against the enemies of the Church occurred between 1270 and 1272, when he defended Church orthodoxy so successfully against the attacks of certain followers of Averroës that Christian theology was completely freed of any taint of Averroism.

In 1274, while in Italy, Aquinas received a summons from Pope Gregory X to attend a council in Lyons. Accompanied by a single companion he began by mule the long trip up through Italy. Between Naples and Rome he became ill and stopped in a Benedictine abbey for rest. He failed to recover, and as he grew weaker he realized that his end was near. "This is the place where I shall find repose," he told his companion; "this is my rest for ever and ever; here will I dwell, for I have chosen it." Vaughan makes this touching comment on his passing:

> He was taken from exile on the early morning of the 7th of March, in the year 1274, in the prime of manly life, being scarcely eight-and-forty years of age. It is but natural, it is but beautiful, that he, who in early boyhood had been stamped with the signet of S. Benedict, should return to S. Benedict to die. He had gone forth to his work and to his labour in the morning, and he returned home to his brethren in the evening-tide.[2]

THE WORKS OF AQUINAS

The list of the published works of Aquinas is a long one. As it is readily available in a number of standard reference books, no purpose would be served by reproducing it here.

Aquinas wrote to be studied and not merely to be read. His books are more like modern encyclopedias, to which one turns for answers to particular questions, than like modern nonfiction. The *Summa Theologica,* for example, may well be more inspiring than a medieval cathedral, but although a single glance at the cathedral is enough to elicit a response, an exclamation of wonder or delight, long and hard study is required to seek out the thought in Aquinas' masterpiece. This is true, of course, of all great writing, but the contrast between the visual arts and literature is especially striking in medieval works. The massiveness so awe-inspiring in the cathedral is in a book a forbidding quality; and Aquinas' tomes are massive.

Aquinas addressed himself to the initiated, and a thorough knowledge of Aristotle is, if not absolutely required, at least extremely helpful in following his thought. He does not solicit the reader's interest. He does not even put into his work the warmth of self-revelation. As D'Arcy says:

> The writings of St. Thomas tell us little or nothing of the private history of their author. They are as anonymous as the architecture of the period. One carries away, nevertheless, an impression of serenity and spaciousness and cannot fail to mark the absence of self-advertisement, of envy and rancour. He seems always to be willing to learn and quote from others; he is generous even in his criticisms; he is at peace with himself and with all who seek the truth. It must be confessed that this extreme modesty makes him dull reading. To meet a quotation from St. Augustine, for instance, is like the sight of a silver trout in a clear stream. He could never have imitated the *Confessions* or written the diary of Marcus Aurelius. His psychology is not drawn from personal observation and he has little to say on aesthetic emotion. Even the mystical life of contemplation is treated metaphysically, and what from other sources we know must have been his personal experience is kept in the background or hidden away in dissertations on grace, the state of Adam, and on the prophets or his favourites the angels.[3]

Furthermore, even in his discussion of worldly matters, Aquinas preferred to confine his remarks almost entirely to abstract considerations. His social theories are not explicitly formulated and developed; they must be drawn out in pieces from the vast body of his work and put together. Those who write about his views on such social matters as political organization, social order, property, family relations, slavery, social change, and similar subjects are usually careful to point out that he himself wrote no distinct tracts on these special topics. For example, Benkert's analysis of Thomistic internationalism[4] is admittedly derived "from the fundamental principles of the moral, social, and political philosophy of St. Thomas Aquinas," and not from "a complete and fully developed outline" contained in his writings.

The devotion of Aquinas to principles securely rooted in a logically consistent metaphysical system partly explains the enduring quality of his thought. Thomistic social ideas live today because they afford solutions to social problems vastly different from those which faced Aquinas. Fortunately, the application of Thomistic principles to changing social situations is being continuously made by scholars who believe that Aquinas spoke not to his age alone but to us and to generations yet unborn. Their arduous labor has brought his social ideas within reach of anyone interested in discovering them.

Although Aquinas was primarily a theologian addressing himself to a select body of fellow workers in the Church, his works contain much that is of general interest. To understand his social thought it might be well to master his theology, but it is not necessary to make that effort in order to learn something from him. We may, therefore, turn to the matter of the social and intellectual problems which confronted him and examine the methods he followed in dealing with these problems. His views on politics, economics, and the family are of particular interest to students of society.

PROBLEMS AND METHODS

One of the major tasks confronting Aquinas was the suppression of heretical ideas which had developed under the guise of Aristotelian principles. The Arab interpretations of Aristotle's philosophy disclosed a pantheism which denied God's transcendency, a doctrine of twofold truth which completely separated theology, based on faith, from philosophy, based on reason, and a psychology which rejected the immortality of the individual soul. At first the Church had met these heresies by burning heretics at the stake, and by anathematizing Aristotle, but it soon became clear that even such harsh measures could not end the revolt against the Church's authority. Instead of avoiding Aristotle, the intellectual leaders of the time began to read him avidly, taking advantage of the Latin translations of his works which the controversy regarding him produced. Then, rather suddenly, the theologians discovered that Aristotle did not need to be banished. On the contrary, his original works, untainted by Arab interpretations, provided exactly the rational support which the Church required to make its revealed truths impregnable to attacks from reason. The threatened divorce of reason and faith ended when the Church found Aristotle good and embraced him.

SCHOLASTICISM

What exactly did this acceptance of Aristotle mean to the Church? Aristotle was a pagan, and surely the Church's infallibility did not need to be established on the authority of an unbeliever. It meant that faith and reason were integrated as they had not been before. When it was shown that the greatest master of rational thought which the world had known supported at every crucial point the revealed truths of Christian theology, the Church knew that never again need it fear thought.

Aquinas' commentaries on virtually every one of Aristotle's major works all proved that true faith has nothing to fear from right reason. Christian revelation, wrote Aquinas, affords the truths required for the good life; men can live by these truths without reasoning about them. But rational thought does not disturb Christian faith; it fortifies it. Aquinas insisted that unaided human reason is able to discover absolute standards. He declared that the human conscience is not Divine Illumination, as Augustine had believed, but is the voice of reason.

To be sure, Aquinas admitted, there are revealed truths beyond the range of human reason—such as the Trinity, Incarnation, and Redemption. Rational thought can add nothing to these truths, but on the other hand it can take nothing from them; it simply does not reach that high. Faith is not logically prior to reason; it is rather a more ultimate principle.

Reason and faith blend and harmonize in Aquinas' thought, each supplementing the other. He declares, "Nothing may be asserted as true that is opposed to the truth of faith, to revealed dogma." But he goes on to add—and this is a most important clarification of his statement—that "neither is it permissible to take whatever we hold as true and present it as an article of faith." D'Arcy believes that "St. Thomas would prefer to be read as a Christian philosopher, but he is prepared to stand the test on his philosophy alone." [5]

Scholasticism, the name commonly given to the Christian philosophy of the Middle Ages, took on many meanings in its development from Erigena to Duns Scotus, but it stood consistently for an alliance between faith and reason, theology and philosophy, revealed truth and rational knowledge. It was the task of Aquinas to strengthen this alliance. In the Aristotelian conception of a hierarchical organization of all existence he found rational means of performing this task. As matter is subordinate to form, and body to soul, so is reason subordinate to faith—but, Aquinas emphatically insists, reason suffers no loss from this relationship. There is no question of two truths to be weighed against each other. Faith and reason work together to grasp identical truths to a certain point; then, when reason can go no further, faith leads the way. It is in that sense only that reason is subordinate to faith.

LITERARY FORM

In his major works Aquinas employed a form of writing which grew out of a system of education based on lectures. The technique was as follows: a text was taken, usually from the Scriptures but sometimes from a philosopher, especially Aristotle; then followed a disputation, which might involve two or more persons in debate or might consist only of the weighing by the lecturer of the arguments for and against the proposition stated in the text. Thus the meaning of the text was elaborated and clarified.

Aquinas adopted a literary form that follows this general method of instruction. He divides a stated subject into a number of articles in the form of questions. The discussion begins with objections (often three but sometimes more or fewer) to the position or view implied in the question. This constitutes what might be called an argument for the negative. Then follows a statement of his own answer to the question. Finally, as an argument for the affirmative, the fallacy in each of the objections is shown. Intellectual honesty requires the lecturer to make a good case for the opposition, and Aquinas endeavors to state clearly and forcefully views with which he does *not* agree. Consequently, his statements must always be read in their context. Even then, in some of his commentaries, it is sometimes difficult to determine whether he is explaining a view with which he may not agree or is stating his own. For this reason, and also because he addressed himself to those familiar with his frame of reference, it is difficult to express the social thought of Aquinas in short quotations from his writings.

Aquinas usually writes with complete control of his emotions and with machinelike precision. His prayers and hymns reveal, however, a lyrical quality in his nature, and occasionally his disputations glow with a warmth of feeling—as, for example, when he boasts of his triumph over the Averroists.

> Behold our refutation of these errors. It is based not on documents of faith but on the reasons and statements of the philosophers themselves. If, then, there be anyone who, boastfully taking pride in his supposed wisdom, wishes to challenge what we have written, let him not do it in some corner, nor before children who are powerless to decide on such difficult matters. Let him reply openly if he dare. He shall find me here confronting him, and not only my negligible self, but many another whose study is truth. We shall do battle with his errors, and bring a cure to his ignorance.[6]

POLITICS

The political theory of Aquinas is both broad and deep—broad because it does not divorce politics from ethics, and deep because it relates politics to man's ultimate end. The highest function of political organization, according to

Aquinas, is to maintain justice and promote righteousness. The state shares this function with other forms of social organization, but it employs means which are peculiar to it. The state is not entirely distinct from society: it is merely a kind of natural, permanent, and public society.

SOCIETY

But what is a society? To Aquinas, it was "a union of men acting for a common purpose." In other words, a society is a system of personal relationships arising out of common action for common ends. People form a society only when they are so related, and the common actions and ends which bind together the members of a society are necessary to its existence. All kinds of societies, such as the family, the village, and the state, are alike in that they are formed of persons together engaged in action directed toward common ends.

All societies have the same ultimate purpose: the attainment of the Beatific Vision. They differ only in their immediate ends and in the means which they employ for achieving them. The measure of a society's perfection is its adequacy. It should have just that size and that degree of durability required for the realization of its ends.

> Now, since men must live in a group, because they are not sufficient unto themselves to procure the necessities of life were they to remain solitary, it follows that a society will be the more perfect the more it is sufficient unto itself to procure the necessities of life. There is, indeed, to some extent sufficiency for life in one family of one household, namely in so far as pertains to the natural acts of nourishment and the begetting of offspring and other things of this kind; it exists, furthermore, in one village with regard to those things which belong to one trade; but it exists in a city, which is a perfect community, with regard to all the necessities of life; but still more in a province because of the need of fighting together and of mutual help against enemies.[7]

All societies have a number of ends, and some of these are higher than others. The achievement of ends low in the hierarchical scale strengthens the society only if the society is moving at the same time toward its higher ends. For example, procreation is an end in marriage, but if that were the only end, marriage might be as casual as the mating of lower forms. The human family has a meaningful unity because it has lasting psychological and social ends. These give it a greater degree of stability than business or friendship groups usually have. Furthermore, private families share common ends served by the whole society.

The mating of husband and wife produces children, but the care of children and the bonds of mutual love and helpfulness in the home not only hold the family together but also bring it into participation with other families in a larger society. A political society is made up of a number of families acting for common purposes which can be adequately achieved only in the larger body.

THE STATE

According to Aquinas, the state, like the family, arises naturally. Man is a "social animal." His material and spiritual needs force him to seek the company of his fellows and to form with them whatever kind of society the satisfaction of his needs may require. His personality can develop fully only through participation in a society composed of many households. A state is, therefore, a family of families; it is a comparatively large group of people working together to realize those purposes which define their unity. Obviously this unity is psychological, but it may be, and usually is, territorial as well.

What are the ends of the state? Aquinas was certain that they are not different from the ends of the individuals who make up the state. He denies that the state has ends of its own. There is a strong note of liberalism in his insistence that the state exists only for the welfare of its members. Since the highest good of man is a moral good, it follows that ultimately the ends of the state are moral ends. Aquinas did not neglect the utilitarian ends which are realized in the state, such as security against enemies, the maintenance of internal order, and the satisfaction of material needs; but he declared that self-perfection is for a man a higher goal than self-protection, and that consequently, as Allen has said, the highest end of the state is

> . . . the purpose of life for all humanity. To this end all politics, all law and government, must necessarily be referred. For if there be such an end and purpose of life for all men, it follows that all government must have this end in view constantly . . . [and] that failure to recognise such a meaning and purpose in life leaves all government purposeless, and means for society friction, waste, and chaos.[8]

Aquinas followed Aristotle in regarding man as a social animal whose nature demands for its highest development the existence of the state, but he went beyond Aristotle in showing that only a good citizen can be a good man, that there can be no private good apart from the good of all, and that only as the state makes whole its citizens can its existence be justified.

NATURAL LAW

The natural law, says Aquinas, "is nothing else than the rational creature's participation in the eternal law of God." He maintains that immutable moral axioms can be known and that, when conscience speaks through right reason, they will be known. They constitute a universal ethic, which is nothing human but is, rather, a divine imperative. The natural law is God's law as man can know it. It is above the state, defining the ends which the state should pursue. It is sovereign, above the people and their customs, above kings and prelates, who may proclaim it but who can in no way change it.

This conception of natural law did not originate with Aquinas. The idea of moral law governing the universe, which no man and no group of men can defy with impunity, is as old as abstract human thought. But Aquinas established this idea in thirteenth-century political thought and projected it into the future with the full force of theology and philosophy. Although it may be disputed just how much we owe Aquinas for the view that the state really exists only to the extent to which it expresses the moral consciousness of mankind, the conception undoubtedly gained life and vigor because of him. In our own day it finds expression in these words of Nicholas Murray Butler:

> Moral law is sovereign, and the government of no people can refuse to accept that sovereignty without invoking the animal in man and turning back to the rule of force. When nations are collectively organized as human beings are collectively organized, and when the sovereignty of moral principles can be not only taught but, if need be, enforced by collective action, then and then only will the present reactionary, destructive and really terrifying chaos be brought to an end.[9]

GOVERNMENT

Aquinas clearly saw that natural law is not enough: men require positive human law; they require government. The people are sovereign in the sense that they participate in "the eternal law of God," but Aquinas realized, as F. Aveling has pointed out, that for practical reasons they must

> . . . entrust their sovereignty to a king or monarch, to an aristocracy, or to a republican form of government. His own personal choice, based upon psychological reasons, is a compromise. He prefers a state or kingdom in which the power is given to one president, who has under him others also possessing powers of government. And he shows that a government such as this is in reality one shared by all the people, since all are eligible to govern, and since the rulers are chosen by them all. This, he says, is the best form of polity: partly kingdom, in so far as there is one president; partly aristocracy, in so far as many have authority; and partly democracy or popular government, for the rulers can be elected from the people, and to the people belongs the choice of their rulers. The conception is that of a limited monarchy, in which both the ruler and his subordinates are chosen by the people. The principle involved is one of solidarity and unity, in which all the individual citizens, from the supreme ruler downward, each according to his office, conspire together toward a single end, which is the greatest absolute natural good of each one of them.[10]

In order to develop their natural aptitude for virtue, all men require guidance from others, some more and some less. Aquinas says that "men who are well disposed are led willingly to virtue by being admonished better than by coercion; but men who are evilly disposed are not led to virtue unless they are compelled."

Compulsion is, therefore, a proper function of government, but laws are not binding unless they serve the common good.

> "Law must be enacted," says Aquinas, "for the common welfare of men, and failing this it has no binding power." If a ruler, he goes on to say, makes, or rather tries to make, law "for the gratification of his own cupidity or vain-glory," his enactments must be regarded as acts of violence rather than as laws. But he insists that if law be ordained for the common welfare and be consistent with the moral consciousness, it creates obligation and is binding absolutely. . . . There can, in fact, exist no binding law which is not an expression of man's sense of right.[11]

Who is to determine what laws serve the common good? Since Aquinas upheld the rights of the individual conscience and justified revolution under some circumstances—for example, in order to depose a tyrant—it might appear that every member of society may consider himself a proper judge. But Aquinas limited individual rights. He saw that if every man is free to decide whether or not he will obey the laws, chaos in civil society is invited. Obedience to rightful authority is required of all, especially those whose natures are most imperfect. Coercion is the rule at the bottom of the social scale; it becomes increasingly less necessary as men acquire rational competence. The sovereign is exempt from the coercive power of the positive law which he imposes on his people, since obviously no man may be coerced by himself. But the sovereign does not decide what laws best serve the common good; he prescribes well only as he recognizes the laws of God. To rule well, he must rule according to the laws of God, as he is himself ruled by them. For guidance he must turn to the Scriptures and the faithful servants of the Church whose business it is to discover God's will.

Aquinas never really faced the problem of the relation between church and state, since he assumed that the natural superiority of spiritual values over all others would find expression in ultimate but indirect rule by the spiritual powers.

ECONOMICS

Feudalism, that complex system of personal relationships and property rights which provided for three centuries the social structure of Europe, was by the thirteenth century rapidly disintegrating. Serfs were gaining their freedom in large numbers, and tenants were demanding fixed-term leases. Protection could be secured by means other than vassalage, and wealth in forms other than property became increasingly important in economic life. The Crusades failed in their professed purpose of wresting the Holy Land from the infidels, but they did encourage trade, open up new markets, break down some of the old restraints of commerce, develop new instruments of banking and credit, and stimulate industry.

The Church had not been indifferent to wealth-getting and wealth-using activities, but the rapidly changing social conditions of the thirteenth century revived discussion in the Church about economic matters. The growth and concentration of wealth was disturbing, but the Church itself was rich in worldly goods. Since wealth could not be attacked without disregarding both the existing state of affairs and traditional Christian conceptions, the problem confronting the Church was that of adapting the old principles to the new conditions. The Scholastics proceeded, therefore, to show that with respect to ownership and use, property in money was identical with property in land; that the old arguments for private ownership were still valid; that a legitimate gain from the use of capital should not be confused with usury; that private ownership could not be morally justified apart from public use; and that only a just price could be demanded for goods. Aquinas wrote no tracts specifically on these subjects, but certain rather definite economic ideas can be found in his works.

PROPERTY

As a result of the rise of industry and commerce, money became an important form of property which Aquinas could not ignore. The right to acquire from the land the necessities of life and to accumulate temporal goods for worthy purposes had long been recognized. Had not God given man dominion over all created things? The exercise of that high authority, human reason and will being what they are, leads to the production and use of goods. Property rights are established by laws enacted by legislative bodies (positive laws) rather than by the fundamental laws dictated by nature and disclosed to reason (natural laws), but the moral justification of these rights under positive law is absolute. Are these rights the same for artificial as for natural goods? Aquinas believed that they are. Money, although it is artificial wealth and valued not for itself but as a medium of exchange, facilitates man's use of nature for the common good and is, therefore, not to be condemned. Man's dominion over nature could mean nothing less than his right to employ whatever means he could devise to make his control more effective. Respect for useful property, whatever its form, is, therefore, entirely consistent with Christian principles, and property rights are natural, absolute, and moral.

PRIVATE OWNERSHIP

One important property right is that of private ownership. Aquinas added little to the arguments for private property. He followed Aristotle and many others in the oft-repeated assertions that man is solicitous regarding that which belongs to him, that private ownership fixes responsibility for property, and that the contentment which results from the ownership of goods promotes peace in society.

Augustine's idea that private property came into existence because of human greed was not abandoned, but Aquinas had little interest in the origin of social institutions. He said, in effect, that as long as men remain as they are, private property is both necessary and lawful. Jarrett points out that "he did not, however, base this assertion on the ground that the exercise of the right was a revealed truth connected with the Faith, but only on the ground that it was an experienced truth connected with the art of living." [12]

PUBLIC USE OF PROPERTY

As for the use of property, Aquinas followed the ancient doctrine that private property must be used for the public good. Property must be shared, not equally because human needs are not all the same, but in such a way as to meet as nearly as possible the needs of every person. The Old Testament prescribes definite rules to be followed in certain situations:

> When you go into your neighbor's vineyard, you may eat your fill of grapes, as many as you wish, but you shall not put any in your vessel.
> When you go into your neighbor's standing grain, you may pluck the ears with your hand, but you shall not put a sickle to your neighbor's standing grain. (Deut. xxiii, 24-25)
>
> When you reap the harvest of your land, you shall not reap your field to its very border, neither shall you gather the gleanings after your harvest.
> And you shall not strip your vineyard bare, neither shall you gather the fallen grapes of your vineyard; you shall leave them for the poor and for the sojourner: (Lev. xix, 9-10)

Aquinas interpreted this principle to mean that the right to own private goods is qualified by the duty to share such goods with those who need them. It means that the right of all men to what they need takes precedence over the right of any man to possess goods which he does not need. Aquinas did not believe that property should be equally divided among all the people. His theory of the organic unity of society assumes a hierarchy of social classes. The needs of all classes of people are not the same, and an individual is entitled only to that property required by him for the exercise of his proper functions. Those from whom much is required for the common good need larger possessions than those from whom little is expected.

In other words, Aquinas was less interested in how much a man owns than in how he uses whatever wealth he may possess. He regarded property as a means to an end. He believed that if the acquisition of property is made an end in itself, life is robbed of meaning and purpose. He maintained that the pursuit of wealth must be ordered by ends that transcend wealth. He speaks across the centuries to the modern world when he says:

The art of acquiring money is subordinate to the art of using money. . . . For money and every kind of wealth are merely economic tools.[13]

Mindful of the possibility that some wealthy individuals will not voluntarily give their superfluous property to the poor, Aquinas went so far as to declare that it is not dishonest for a man to take, secretly or openly, another man's property in order to give it to those in need.* But apparently he believed that thoughtful men would see that "the individual good is impossible without the common good of the family, state, or kingdom." Whatever may be the ethical difference between taxation and charity, they serve a common purpose—the public use of private property. Aquinas preferred charity, but he was willing to take stern measures with those who would not voluntarily use their means for the common good.

USURY AND INTEREST

"To accept usury for a loan of money," says Aquinas, "is by its nature unjust." His opposition to usury is unequivocal. In support of his position he quoted Aristotle—"Usury is most reasonably hated"—and the Old Testament—"Thou shalt not lend to thy brother money to usury" (Deut. xxiv, 6) —but he appealed to logic and morality as well as to authority. He maintained that logically money must be viewed with regard to its nature and purpose. It is properly used, he says, to facilitate the exchange of goods and services. It is naturally sterile. Unlike labor, which produces much, money produces nothing. Consequently, the breeding of money from money is unnatural. Properly used, money is an aid in securing the necessities of life; improperly used, it leads to "greed for gain which knows no limit and tends to infinity." His moral arguments against usury were less explicitly stated, but they may be summarized as follows: one who lends money, grain, or any other form of worldly goods to his neighbor cannot claim as his reward the exercise of charity when he receives in return more than he gave.

But although he regarded usury as wrong, Aquinas believed the taking of interest to be natural and moral. The difference is this: usury is gain from a loan; interest is compensation for a risk or an inconvenience. A man who entrusts money to a merchant or craftsman enters, under certain circumstances, into a business enterprise with him. This venture involves risk—for example, the possibility that a cargo may be lost at sea. If the business prospers, the money increases; otherwise, it diminishes. In either case its ownership remains unchanged. Likewise, in putting a portion of his money to a legitimate use, a man may impose upon himself some discomfort or inconvenience. In this case, as where risk is involved, he is entitled to interest on his investment.

* Many centuries later William Graham Sumner was to challenge this conception with his plea for the "forgotten man," whom he described as a worthy citizen whose industry and frugality are rewarded by the seizure of his goods by those in public office for the benefit of the prodigal and indolent.

This distinction between usury and interest did not appear to Aquinas to be trivial. In his discussion of the various means by which attempts to evade the prohibition against usury may be made, he showed that a distinction can and should be made. In his thinking, it rests ultimately on the ends or purposes involved. He saw nothing wrong with trading at a profit for the sake of a livelihood, but he did object to trading for the sake of profit. He denied that trading *at* a profit is the same as trading *for* a profit. Why and under what conditions does a person act in a certain way? If his purpose is that of charity, then he may rejoice in his benevolence. If he seeks material gain, although he may outwardly conform to the Golden Rule, he has no claim to the consolations of virtue. In short, it is wrong to sell the use of one's money for the sake of gain; it is just and right to receive compensation for the use of one's money.

JUST PRICE

The right to take some compensation does not imply the right to as much compensation as one can get. If goods and services are worth whatever price they will bring, then it would be just to take advantage of the needs of others; but this is clearly unjust. Since the exploitation of others is immoral, how is it to be decided where just compensation ends and unjust exploitation begins? Aquinas found the answer to this question in his concept of the "just price."

According to Aquinas, the value of an article is determined by the needs of those who have produced and made it available. The artisan and the merchant serve the common good and have a right to compensation commensurate with their services. But what is the measure of these services? Aquinas frankly admitted that this is a difficult question. "Sometimes the just price cannot be determined absolutely," he says, "but consists rather in a common estimation, in such a way that a slight addition or diminution of price cannot be thought to destroy justice." In other words, in determining a just price, *something* is left to the individual conscience.

But Aquinas knew that the average man could not be trusted to set a just price on his own goods and services. Subjective factors are bound to influence his judgment, so as to prevent in some degree the price he sets from corresponding objectively to the value of the article. He speaks of "moderate gain," and of the gain which a man requires "for the upkeep of his household or for the assistance of the needy." He declares that this matter must be settled by "the judgment of an honest man." Troeltsch believes that this amounts to acknowledging the necessity of government regulation of prices.

> The whole spirit of this way of thinking on economic matters may be summed up thus: property and gain are based upon the personal performance of work; goods are exchanged only when necessary, and then only according to the principles of a just price, which does not give an undue advantage to anyone; (this "just price" is best regulated by the Govern-

ment), consumption is regulated (*a*) in accordance with the principle of moderation, which only permits the natural purpose of the maintenance of existence to be fulfilled, and (*b*) which makes room for a generosity which takes the needs of others into account; at the same time great differences in social position and in fortune, and therefore in the exercise of liberality, are fully recognized.[14]

In summary, Aquinas' "just price" has the following characteristics: (*a*) it is based on the absolute principles of justice; (*b*) it is a price which enables an artisan or merchant to live in a style befitting his station in life; (*c*) it must be set and regulated by common knowledge exercised usually through the government; and (*d*) it must recognize at every point the ends which prices serve. This last point is perhaps the key idea in the whole conception: no price which stimulates greed, rewards exploitation, and provokes ill will can be just.

FAMILY

Despite the fact that in his discussion of family matters Aquinas addressed himself to those educated few in his day who knew well the teachings of the Church fathers and were able to converse in Aristotelian terms, and especially to priests obligated to support monastic vows and practices, he was clearly concerned primarily with the principles required by the masses for the regulation of their private lives. Unlike many of the earlier churchmen, he did not look down on family matters from the lofty heights of righteous celibacy. His devotion to the ideals of asceticism and monasticism did not blind him to the needs of the men and women who perpetuate mankind by marrying and begetting children, and it is *for* these that he wrote. He attempted no description of family life in Europe in the thirteenth century; for that one must turn to the social history of the period. He aimed at something more profound: the establishment of the enduring principles of Christian marriage and family relations.

NATURE AND FUNCTION

The organismic view of society held by Aquinas led naturally to his regarding the family as a social cell. Following Aristotle, he defines a family as "a group of persons, established according to nature, for daily mutual support, making common the daily needs of life, eating at the same table, warming themselves at the same fireside." In other words, the family is a household. By nature man is not only a social animal, he is also a family animal. In infancy he needs parents ever near to minister to his needs; in maturity he needs a wife and children to complete his personal well-being. For most men self-perfection is attained only through marrying and begetting children. Husband and wife complement each other and form a perfect whole of two imperfect halves, and children make rich their lives with meaning and purpose. Aquinas added a third element to the perfect household, the servant, and declared that the mutual aid of masters and servants facilitates the attainment by both of important material and spiritual ends.

The family has, according to Aquinas, two basic functions: the begetting and rearing of offspring, and the rendering by its members of aid and comfort to one another. Although Aquinas emphasized the former, he did not neglect the latter. Even though he did speak of motherhood as a "woman's sole purpose in marrying," he clearly recognized, as many churchmen had failed to do, the other important end of the family: the full development of personality through love and mutual aid in the home.

MARRIAGE

After careful study of Aquinas, Ostheimer believes that his definition of marriage may be accurately stated as follows:

> Marriage is the permanent union of one man and one woman, legitimately formed under contract, with a view to a common life and the procreation of offspring.[15]

Aquinas specifically declared that marriage has three blessings or goods: the good of offspring, the good of fidelity, and the good of sacrament. The good of offspring is the blessing of bearing and rearing children; the good of fidelity is the blessing of that intimate relationship into which husbands and wives enter through marriage; and the good of sacrament is that divine element which makes the marriage bond indissoluble. Thus marriage gives the individual increased responsibility, faith, and security.

Aquinas referred to the first of these goods as the *primary* purpose of marriage; the others he called *secondary* purposes, but he made it clear that they too are basic, natural, and right. The importance he attached to these secondary ends is brought out in Ostheimer's summary of his various statements on this subject:

> Marriage provides for the mutual supply of those things in which the sexes naturally supplement each other, both on the physical and psychical side of their respective natures. In the physical order each requires the other as a help and support in life, for each is peculiarly fitted by nature for the performance of certain tasks. In the mental and moral sphere their need of each other is even greater. The perfections, virtues, refinements, affection, and even sympathies of womankind are not those of men. Marriage provides for the perfect blending of these two sets of tendencies and capacities in one full life.
>
> . . . Additional secondary ends might be multiplied indefinitely from the writings of Thomas. He argues for the indissolubility of marriage that children might properly receive inheritance from parents; that the dignity of womanhood, and justice and equity toward women might be maintained;

that the friendship and mutual love begotten by married life be sustained and strengthened; that discord and enmities between relatives be avoided. In arguing for the unity of marriage, he stresses the necessary equality of husband and wife as human individuals, and the protection of public morality, which marriage unity will afford. Similar reasons are advanced against marriage among close relatives, which would preclude the proper extension of social friendship and well-being.[16]

FAMILY RELATIONS

Relations in the family are regulated at every point, according to Aquinas, by the principle of subordination. Wives are subject to their husbands, children to their parents, and servants to their masters. While recognizing the spiritual equality of all human beings in Christ, Aquinas was ever mindful of their inequality in this world. They share a common nature and are created for a common purpose, but they differ in beauty and strength, in knowledge and virtue, in aptitude and diligence. These differences determine their proper roles and create an ordered hierarchy in society which is both just and natural. Aquinas declares that inequality makes the beauty of order even more manifest.

The subjection of women to men, and consequently of wives to their husbands, is not merely accepted by Aquinas—it is demanded in no uncertain terms. A few quotations will serve to make clear his position.

> The image of God in its principal signification—namely, the intellectual nature—is found both in man and in woman. . . . But in a secondary sense the image of God is found in man and not in woman: for man is the beginning and end of woman, as God is the beginning and end of every creature.
> . . . For good order would have been wanting in the human family if some were not governed by others wiser than themselves. So by such a kind of subjection woman is naturally subject to man, because in man the discretion of reason predominates.
> . . . Woman is subject to man on account of the frailty of nature as regards both vigour of soul and strength of body.
> . . . Woman was created as a helpmate for man, not indeed as a helpmate in other works, as some maintain, since man can be more efficiently helped by other men in other works, but as a helpmate in generation.[17]

Aquinas spoke of woman as "defective and misbegotten" in her individual nature, but he went on to show that this imperfection is necessary for "the work of generation" and does not mean that she is defective "as regards universal human nature." This view can be illustrated by reference to organic life: the unicellular organism is complete but low in the scale of living things; in the multicellular organism the specialized cell lacks independence but it shares in a higher form of life than it could attain alone. As Aquinas saw it, men and women are in a complementary relationship in which men have the dominant role but in which they share equally the advantages resulting from the exercise of their specific roles. The submission of wives to their husbands is not, therefore, in any sense degrading; it involves no loss of dignity; it implies no abrogation of those inalienable rights which all human beings possess. It means only, as Pope Pius XI has declared:

> The sexes, in keeping with the wonderful designs of the Creator, are destined to complement each other, in the family, and in society, precisely because of their differences, which therefore ought to be maintained and encouraged.[18]

Parents are responsible for the education and discipline of their children. To meet this responsibility, Aquinas declared that "parents will not only make use of precepts and admonitions, nor will they achieve it by exhorting and by teaching only, but by correcting and punishing, and especially by the force of good example." [19] Their obligation to instruct their children in the faith and to teach them the rules of right conduct implies the duty of children to give heed and to obey. Aquinas departed from Aristotle in setting limits to the exercise of parental authority. He maintained that a father may admonish a stubborn son but he may neither administer severe punishment nor prescribe death. He declared that children may not be required to marry against their wills, "since consent in marriage must be free." Mindful, perhaps, of his own experience, he granted the right of entering the priesthood to a son whose parents are not in need, even contrary to their wishes.

Ostheimer believes that Aquinas made education the core of the parent-child relationship. He says:

> Such education does not mean physical education alone, but the child's mental, moral, and religious training as well. It is common duty, incumbent on both parents. This education would be impossible without parental authority, and this demands obedience on the part of the child. Such authority is not absolute but is limited by the scope of this education and the needs of domestic life, under the determinations of the natural and the divine law. These obligations of parents find their counterpart in obligations incumbent upon the child. Some of these are temporary, as obedience; others are permanent, such as love and honor to parents, and practical service. The basis of these filial duties is found in the virtue of piety, a potential part of justice. Piety, in turn, is based on the fact that children owe their parents a great debt, for all their parents have done for them; this debt can never be fully paid.[20]

The subordination of servants in the household, whether slaves or free persons, follows from Aquinas' belief that all societies are arranged in ranks or grades. Those individuals at the bottom have a just claim on the superior talents of those at the top. The members of a family, as of any other society, form a single group, and they prosper or suffer together. The head of the household must be free to devote his time and thought to duties which he alone can perform. The servant, on the other hand, fares better under wise direction than he would were he left to his own devices. As a member of the family, his rights are protected and he loses no dignity in accepting servitude.

DIVORCE

Aquinas gave the following arguments against divorce: (1) children need both parents for their proper education; (2) only in an enduring marriage can the material goods required for the preservation of life be conserved across generations; (3) the woman bears more than her share of the penalty imposed by society on the divorced pair; (4) the human personality thrives on love and is irreparably damaged by making counterfeit the vows given in marriage; and, finally, (5) the solemn realization that marriage endures until death fosters a tranquil mind and a steadfast purpose.

THOMISM

The system of philosophy and theology held by Thomas Aquinas is known as Thomism. Its distinctive character is the absence of any formal distinction between rational and revealed truth. It declares that the findings of philosophy and theology are ultimately the same, and that reason and faith complement one another. Thomism makes a metaphysical distinction, however, between "potentiality" (lack of perfection) and "act" (perfection), and this difference provides the principle that gives the system its unity and perfect harmony.

Thomism continued to thrive for some time after the death of Aquinas, especially through the work and influence of the Dominicans, but during the fourteenth and fifteenth centuries it suffered from the general eclipse that occurred in philosophy and theology. The canonization of Thomas Aquinas in 1323 securely established his authority in the Church, and his stature and influence have increased with the passing of time. In 1879, Pope Leo XIII directed that Aquinas' teachings be made the basis of Catholic philosophy and theology, and in the present century Pope Pius XI declared: "In the study of rational philosophy and theology and in the instruction of students the professor should follow entirely the method, doctrine and principles of the Angelic Doctor, and hold them religiously." [21]

Thomism appeals not only to Catholics but also to many non-Catholics who find inspiring the philosophical and religious system which Aquinas founded. By transplanting Aristotle "to a new climate," as Jacques Maritain has described the bringing of the Greek philosopher into the Christian intellectual fold, Aquinas demonstrated that faith and reason can be harmonized and showed that, far from being impious and destructive, human reason guided by revelation partakes of the nature of divinity. He saw the dangers in unbridled reason, but he found a way of liberating the human intellect as no one else in his age was able or dared to do. He was the champion of reason teamed with faith. One great appeal of Thomism to many people is the belief that it does not need to be supported by the authority of Aquinas or of the Catholic Church.

The social thought of Thomas Aquinas is deeply embedded in his metaphysics. He formulated no separate and complete theories of politics, economics, social organization, social change, and other aspects of human relations. That is not to say that he did not express himself about such matters. On the contrary, as we have seen, his thought penetrated every area of human experience, and turned continually toward society. But he did not view social relations as mere human affairs. He directed attention to the religious implications of conduct, and in so doing was able to fit the fragments of experience into a perfect whole.

It is possible to search the writings of Thomas Aquinas for social ideas and to organize these ideas into distinct theories, as numerous monographs give evidence, but the labor involved reduces considerably the number of persons who can afford to go directly to Aquinas, disregarding secondary sources. Since a number of good studies of various aspects of his social thought have been, and are being, published, usually as dissertations in Catholic universities, there is no reason to neglect the greatest of the Scholastics merely because, in an age when few people could read, he addressed himself to educated priests who were prepared to hear him.

PART THREE

EARLY MODERN SOCIAL THOUGHT

The determination of what is modern is arbitrary. History is like a river. As the passing waters have come from somewhere and do not cease to be when they are no longer in sight, so it is with events. The modern world is to a large extent the medieval and the ancient worlds. The languages we speak, the institutions to which we adhere, and the values we cherish are for the most part not modern at all. Nevertheless, just as the waters of a river change in appearance and motion, as crystal-clear streams receive discoloring tributaries or are broken up by cataracts, so do patterns of human behavior and thought undergo transformations. Religion brought about such a change in the Western world in the third and fourth centuries of our era. A thousand years passed before another change of such magnitude occurred. Then science appeared, and men faced with astonished eyes a new and inviting prospect. Of all the forces which shape life in the modern world, science may well be the greatest.

As we turn to what may properly be called the early modern period, we shall observe the impact on social thought of the method and the spirit of science. Ibn Khaldun, the writers of the Renaissance and the Reformation, John Locke, Giambattista Vico, and Auguste Comte have been selected to represent social thought between the fourteenth and nineteenth centuries.

Ibn Khaldun was a fourteenth-century Arab. Although the scientific revolution was not actually accomplished in Europe until the sixteenth and seventeenth centuries, the Arabs had cherished Greek science during the time when most Christian leaders had eyes only for salvation. Consequently, it is not altogether surprising to find Ibn Khaldun taking a scientific point of view toward social phenomena. In fact, in his objectivity and in his regard for empirical fact, he is nearer to the twentieth century than to the fourteenth. The fact that for about five centuries he remained virtually unknown to the Western world is no reflection on the quality of his thought.

Among the writers of the Renaissance and Reformation period, no individual stands out above all others. Martin Luther and John Calvin were the key figures in the Reformation, whereas Erasmus, Machiavelli, Sir Thomas More, Bodin, and Montaigne represent, each in his own way, the daring thought of the Renaissance. Giordano Bruno was burned at the stake and Galileo was intimidated, but finally natural scientists were able to carry on their investigations without excessive interference. Social scientists were, as they have always been, saddled with traditional beliefs which impeded their progress. Nevertheless, the social thought of the period shows the effects of the scientific revolution.

In John Locke the spirit of the modern age is clearly revealed. Locke initiated in England a wave of liberal opinion that ultimately swept over Europe and reached across the Atlantic to the new world. The opposition that he provoked helped in the end to increase his influence, since criticism made his ideas better known. The British colonists in America had from Locke all that was required to justify their revolution, and when they had gained independence they found in Locke a formula for the constitution that they drew up and adopted. Wherever toleration is regarded as a virtue, Locke's ideas appear practical and sensible.

The Italian philosopher Giambattista Vico was little honored in life and has been sadly neglected since he died. His great work, *The New Science,* has been translated into English only recently, and although translations in both German and French have been available since early in the nineteenth century, Vico has never received outside Italy the attention that most of those familiar with his work believe that he deserves. The chapter devoted to him in this survey may help the reader to discover that many social ideas bearing the likeness of Vico have after two centuries come down to us without his name.

Auguste Comte bridges the old order of speculative social philosophy and the new order of empirical social science. Although he was not actually the founder of sociology, he gave this science a name and correctly described its basic characteristics. If empirical data which have been assembled since his day had been available to him, and if he had refrained from the attempt to make positivism a religion, he might have been the Newton of social science. Whatever his shortcomings, however, the genius of Auguste Comte is unmistakable and his contributions to social thought merit well the attention they have received.

12 · IBN KHALDUN

(1332-1406)

Know then—may God guide us and you—that there is no end to the wonders of the world.

—Prolegomena

MOSLEM CIVILIZATION

Between the eighth and the twelfth centuries, while most of Europe was in the throes of barbarism, the Arabs kept alight the flame of Western civilization. To them belongs the unique distinction of having embraced the culture of the East as well as that of the West, conserving from both a precious heritage and injecting into each some enduring elements derived from the other. They formed a theocratic state and created an empire more extensive than that of Rome at the zenith of her power. In the early part of the eighth century, Spain was added to that empire, which then stretched from the Indus to the Pyrenees. Indeed, all Europe appeared to be in danger of succumbing to the power of the Arabs until, in 732, Charles Martel stopped their advance into France in a decisive engagement, which took place between Tours and Poitiers. However, the Arabs occupied Sicily and Sardinia, and centuries later the court in Sicily of Frederick II of Hohenstaufen (1215-50), emperor of the Holy Roman Empire, king of Jerusalem, and ruler of Germany as well as of Sicily, became especially important as a meeting point for Christian, Judaic, and Moslem cultures. Arab navigators were at home on eastern seas as well as on the Mediterranean; they linked India, China, Ceylon, and the East Indies with the Middle East and with Europe in one vast network of trade.

Through certain Chinese papermakers whom they had captured, the Arabs introduced paper to the West. They furnished the language of science, created an improved system of numerals, and developed the mathematical use of the zero. They made important contributions to the sciences of astronomy, cartography, and geography. They classified many human diseases, discovered the pulmonary circulation of blood, and found the curative uses of many drugs. They learned to dissolve metals with sulfuric and nitric acid, and developed improved methods for evaporation and distillation. Although they fell short of the Greeks in scientific theory, they went beyond them in practical use of scientific knowledge.

The Arabs also made enduring contributions to art, literature, architecture, and philosophy. They exercised as conquerors the rare good judgment of building upon what they found instead of destroying whatever they encountered. In this way Arabic culture spread, not by replacing other cultures but by being grafted upon them. The Arabs did not originate arabesque art, but the fact that this form of art bears their name is evidence of their influence upon it. They preserved many ancient manuscripts which, except for them, would probably have perished. As a consequence, their scholars were well versed in Aristotle three centuries before the churchmen became acquainted with most of his books. The Arabs created intricate forms of versification and wrote poems of exquisite beauty. They produced numerous works of literary criticism, wrote voluminous histories, and made innumerable translations.

Above all, they established one of the great religions of the world. Its unifying power is attested by the fact that, although scattered and separated by allegiance to various political states, the more than 250,000,000 Moslems in the world today are in a very real sense one nation in Islam.

THE ARABS

The Arabs, like the Jews, are Semites—that is to say, their language belongs to the Semitic family of languages. Their home, at the dawn of history, was Arabia, cradle also of such other Semitic peoples as the Aramaeans, Edomites, Moabites, Ammonites, and Israelites. That there has been much intermixture of these peoples is obvious, but the Arabs have always been set apart from their linguistic kinsmen by peculiar ethnic and religious characteristics. The term *Arab* applied, as early as the ninth century B.C., to the Bedouin tribes which roamed over the steppes and deserts of Northern Arabia, and served to distinguish these nomads from other inhabitants of Arabia who resided in towns and lived by trade or agriculture. The Koran uses the term in this limited sense, and as late as the fourteenth century we find Ibn Khaldun adopting this usage, although not consistently.

In pre-Islamic times the Bedouins recognized no authority save that of their own tribal chiefs and no bond with others save that of blood. It was not until the rise of Islam brought all Moslems together in one spiritual community that they formed a true nation in the ethnic sense. In some regions of the Near East the distinction between the nomads of the desert and the sedentary people of the towns and agricultural regions is still made by using the term *Arab* to refer only to the former, but this restricted meaning is not common at the present time. There is a bond among all those who follow Mohammed, whatever their political state or manner of existence. They form a body quite distinct in character from that created by the brotherhood of Christian peoples. The Arabs are united not only by religion but also by the pride they take in their common heritage and the faith they share in their common future. As H. A. R. Gibb says, "All those are Arabs for whom the central fact of history is the mission of Muhammad and the memory of the Arab Empire and who in addition cherish the Arabic tongue and its cultural heritage as their common possession." [1]

MOHAMMED

Mohammed (Muhammad), prophet of Allah, was born about 570 A.D. in Mecca. This holy city of Islam is located approximately midway down the Arabian peninsula approximately forty-five miles inland from the Red Sea. At the time of the prophet's birth it was a busy commercial center on the caravan routes that linked the lowlands with inner Arabia. There are many legends about the early life of Mohammed, but most of them are disputed. Apparently he became in infancy an orphan and was brought up by relatives who lacked the means to give him an education—at least he seems not to have learned to read or to write. Since at the time he had need of such unusual accomplishments he was able to secure the services of readers and scribes, this weakness in his education was of no great importance. At twenty-five he married a rich widow and probably became a merchant.

Mohammed's religious experience came rather suddenly, when he was about forty years of age. He relates that he had visions of a voice saying, "O Mohammed! thou art the messenger of Allah," whereupon he began to devote his time to meditation, fasting, and prayer. He publicly announced his divine mission to lead the Arabs to the one and true God, and soon gathered around himself a small band of adherents. The new faith made little headway against the established polytheism in Mecca, and in the year 622 Mohammed moved with his followers to Medina, 280 miles northeast of Mecca. This *Hegira* (flight) is the first certain date in Moslem history and marks the beginning of the Moslem era.

Mohammed lived only ten years after the Hegira, but long enough to return in triumph to Mecca and proclaim it the Holy City of Islam. In the brief space of a decade he led the Moslems to numerous military victories, proved himself an able diplomat, married at least ten wives, dictated the Koran, and founded a religion which served as the basis of a strong theocratic state. As Durant says:

> When he began, Arabia was a desert flotsam of idolatrous tribes; when he died it was a nation. He restrained fanaticism and superstition, but he used them. Upon Judaism, Zoroastrianism, and his native creed he built a religion simple and clear and strong, and a morality of ruthless courage

and racial pride, which in a generation marched to a hundred victories, in a century to empire, and remains to this day a virile force through half the world.[2]

MOHAMMEDANISM

Mohammedanism, or Islam, is the faith of Mohammed, and those who accept this faith are Moslems. Islam means "to surrender," and the Moslems are "the surrendering ones." Mohammedanism rests on belief in Allah and the inspiration of his prophet Mohammed. The holy book of Islam is the Koran, through which the Moslems believe God has declared himself to man. Like both Christianity and Judaism, it is monotheistic—"There is no God but Allah, and Mohammed is the messenger of Allah"—but, unlike Christianity, it does not accept the doctrine of the Trinity. Its creed may be stated as follows: "I believe in God, His Angels, His Books and His messengers, the Last Day, the Resurrection from the dead, predestination by God, Good and Evil, the Judgment, the Balance, Paradise and Hell-fire."[3] It reveals the Divine Creation of the universe, the compassionate and merciful nature of God, and the certainty that a day will come, when "the heavens will be rent, the earth will quake, the stars will be scattered, the seas will boil up, the mountains will soften and move." On that Judgment Day God will reward the righteous in Heaven and punish the wicked in Hell forever.

Mohammed probably had no access to any considerable portion of the sacred writings of the Jews and Christians—in fact, it is unlikely that an Arabic translation of most of the books of the Old Testament or the New Testament existed while he lived. There is only one passage in the Koran (Sura xxi, 105) which quotes directly from the Bible (Ps. 37:29): "And now, since the Law was given have we written in the Psalms that *my servants, the righteous, shall inherit the earth.*" He was, however, in close contact with Jews and Christians, and this may account for some similarities between the Bible and the Koran. In fact, Mohammedanism accepts Moses and Jesus, along with numerous others, as major prophets, but maintains that God's revelation to man was made complete and final through Mohammed, the "seal of the Prophet." Consequently, the head of the holy Moslem state was called after Mohammed's death a *caliph* (successor) and not a prophet.

Mohammedanism has no special priesthood, but various rituals provide common actions which bind together its adherents. The most important of these are the four duties required of all Moslems: prayer, almsgiving, fasting, and pilgrimage. Privately, or in company with others, in response to the voice of the muezzin from the minaret calling, "Come to prayer! Come to prayer!" the orthodox Moslem observes five times daily the prescribed rituals of prayer. Almsgiving on an extensive scale is required: "They who give away their substance in alms, by night and day, in private and in public, shall have their reward with their Lord;

no fear shall come on them, neither shall they be put to grief." The most important of the fasts is that of Ramadan, which lasts a month and permits eating and drinking only at night. All Moslems who can afford to do so are expected to make at least one pilgrimage to Mecca. We shall see that Ibn Khaldun, the fourteenth-century statesman and scholar whose life and work we shall examine, did not neglect this sacred duty.

SUFISM

The development within Mohammedanism of the movement known as *Sufism* should be noted, since it may have had a definite influence on Ibn Khaldun. Sufism emerged in the eighth century as an emphasis on the mystical elements in Mohammedanism. Its foremost exponent was Islam's greatest scholastic theologian, Al-Gazzali (1058-1111). He believed that through prayer, fasting, and asceticism the individual might gain an immediate awareness of God and an intuitive insight into reality which reason could not give.

> The Sufi movement exercised a profound influence over the spiritual and artistic evolution of Islam. Muslim theology, with its innumerable prescriptions of ritual and law, was already well nigh sterile when the spiritual reaction set in. Islam as a faith to live, as well as to practise—this was the fundamental meaning of Sufism. The Sufi, in his contemplation of the divine attributes, discovered beauty anew, and this discovery, as vitalizing as Platonic idealism itself, acted as a powerful stimulus to literary and artistic achievement. A vast proportion of Persian and Turkish literature, and especially poetry, is mystical, while the very romances of the epic writers are treated from a spiritual angle; in Arabic, too, much fine mystical poetry has been written, while numerous treatises . . . bear witness to the fertility and profundity of mystical thought in Islam.[4]

BIOGRAPHICAL SKETCH

The social ideas of Ibn Khaldun are firmly set in the experience of the Arabs. The fact that he was born much too late to share in the highest achievements in political power of his people detracts nothing from his observations. In fact, from the vantage point of a historical perspective he was able to observe the course of events that led to the rise and fall of the Moslem Empire as no contemporary witness could have done. When, late in the twelfth century, Saladin drove the Christians from Jerusalem and rebuilt this vast empire from Syria to Egypt, one might have supposed that the star of the Arabs was yet in the ascendancy. But this was not the case. The Christian states of Europe were beginning to display remarkable vitality. In 1221, Jenghiz Khan seized Persia and made it the center of a Mongol state carved out of the Arabic empire. At about the same time, the Turkish sultans took over most of the empire remaining and mocked the high office of the Caliph. The only Arabs able to retain their independence were those protected by the desert. By the fourteenth century, Arabic civilization was definitely in eclipse. At this opportune moment a man appeared on the scene who possessed the genius to examine its rise and fall and to derive from his analysis a science of society.

Ibn Khaldun was born in Tunis in 1332. His father was a distinguished scholar, administrator, and soldier; his grandfather had served as Minister of Finance in Tunis. Earlier his ancestors had resided in Seville and had held prominent positions in the government of Spain. Ibn Khaldun was, thus, the scion of a distinguished family. At eighteen he was orphaned as a result of a great plague that swept over North Africa and much of Europe. He writes of this calamity: "It folded the carpet with all there was on it; . . . the notables, the leaders, and all the learned died, as well as my parents, on whom be God's mercy." Despite this loss, however, he continued his studies and received an education appropriate to a young man of rank. After learning the religious traditions of the Arabs through careful study of the Koran and the ancient literature, he passed on to grammar, logic, jurisprudence, mathematics, and philosophy. At the age of twenty he was prepared to begin his public career and became a Seal Bearer (secretary) to the Sultan of Tunis. From that time until death claimed him he lived close to the center of politics in Spain and North Africa and had a prominent part in shaping many important affairs of state.

About five years after his entry into politics, Ibn Khaldun became the victim of jealousy among certain political factions and was imprisoned for two years. After his restoration to favor, he went, in 1362, to Spain, where he soon was honored with an important political post. Three years later he returned to Africa and became a prime minister. During the next ten years he saw political intrigue at close hand and seems himself to have stooped sometimes to the unethical means that Machiavelli regarded as necessary in politics. By his early forties he was equipped not only with a sound academic education but also with a wealth of practical experience. Consequently, when he retired from active life in the year 1375 and took up residence in a secluded castle near Oran, he was well prepared to use for scholarly pursuits the brief time which the fortunes of politics had placed at his disposal. It was then that he produced the literary works that have preserved his memory.

After an interlude of about four years devoted wholly to scholarship, he returned to a life of action as a diplomat, judge, and teacher. At the age of fifty, he set out on a pilgrimage to Mecca. Upon his arrival in Cairo he discovered that no caravans were leaving that year for the holy city; so he accepted a professorship and sent for his family. The ship bringing them from Tunis was wrecked, and, as he himself sadly relates, in one stroke he lost his "riches, happiness, and children." This calamity so overwhelmed him that he withdrew from public life and sought consolation in prayer. After completing the pilgrimage to Mecca, he returned to Egypt.

During the remaining years of his life he wrote his autobiography, rendered important diplomatic service on a military expedition into Syria, served as a lecturer and as a judge, and reaped some of the honors as a scholar and a statesman that he so well deserved. The twenty-three years he spent among the Egyptians were comparatively unproductive. He revised and brought up to date his earlier works but found little to add to his basic theories of society. He died in Cairo in 1406, at the age of seventy-four.

> . . . Ibn Khaldun must have been an altogether remarkable man. Living amidst circumstances the most complicated, combinations shifting from day to day, plots and intrigues, despotic arbitrariness and mean jealousies, he played an active and prominent part in many situations. Although often cast down, he as often rose speedily up again; and he remained from youth to age, through all the vicissitudes of a difficult and eventful career, distinguished and influential, courted or persecuted, dreaded or admired. He was a skilful politician, an accomplished courtier, a brilliant member of society, a man subtle in counsel, persuasive in speech, pliant in adapting himself to circumstances, qualified for the most diverse offices, a proficient in almost every liberal art and every department of science cultivated by his Mohammedan contemporaries. He was, perhaps, not wholly devoid of the spirit of intrigue, somewhat too conscious of his own superiority, and inclined to exercise power with rather high a hand. Obviously he was ambitious of eminence and fame both in politics and literature; but he cannot be charged with disregard of moral principles or indulgence in vicious habits. He was a devout and strict Mussulman.[5]

And Nathaniel Schmidt writes, from his careful study of the life and career of this famous Arab, the following comment:

> [The journey of his life] had brought him in touch with Pedro the Cruel in the West and Timur the Lame in the East. It had taken him into the huts of savages and into the palaces of kings, into the dungeons with criminals and into the highest courts of justice, into the companionship of the illiterate and into the academies of scholars, into the treasure-houses of the past and into the activities of the present, into deprivation and sorrow and into affluence and joy. It had led him into the depths where the spirit broods over the meaning of life.
>
> . . . He had his faults, and some of them are serious blemishes on his character. He was without question proud, perhaps inordinately so, of his family, his achievements, and his resourcefulness. . . . [But] he has never been charged with want of sobriety, industry, conjugal fidelity, justice, or humanity. . . . He was a realist; but it is an exaggeration to declare that he was entirely lacking in idealism. . . . His nature is reflected in his observations on human society, his rigorous demand that it be stud-

ied comprehensively and with scientific accuracy, and his faithfulness, so far as time and circumstances permitted, in meeting this requirement. He is a solitary figure, towering above his age, yet to be explained in the way he himself regarded as proper in the interpretation of every historic phenomenon. The law of growth and decay of social groups which he discerned cast him into oblivion; the same law has led to his discovery and the recognition of his genius.[6]

REPUTATION AND MAJOR WORKS

What claim has Ibn Khaldun, who until recently was little known to social scientists, to a place among the masters of social thought? There are some scholars who would give him a very high place indeed. Toynbee describes him as

> . . . an Arabic genius who achieved in a single 'acquiescence' of less than four years' length, out of a fifty-four years' span of adult working life, a life-work in the shape of a piece of literature which can bear comparison with the work of a Thucydides or the work of a Machiavelli for both breadth and profundity of vision as well as for sheer intellectual power. Ibn Khaldun's star shines the more brightly by contrast with the foil of darkness against which it flashes out; for while Thucydides and Machiavelli and Clarendon are all brilliant representatives of brilliant times and places, Ibn Khaldun is the sole point of light in his quarter of the firmament. . . . In his chosen field of intellectual activity he appears to have been inspired by no predecessors and to have found no kindred souls among his contemporaries and to have kindled no answering spark of inspiration in any successors; and yet . . . he conceived and formulated a philosophy of history which is undoubtedly the greatest work of its kind that has ever yet been created by any mind in any time or place.[7]

Sorokin, Zimmerman, and Galpin say that he is, "as much as any one man, entitled to be called the 'founder of sociology,' and possibly more than anybody else is he entitled to be regarded as the 'founder of rural-urban sociology.' "[8] Flint declares that "as a theorist on history he had no equal in any age or country until Vico appeared, more than three hundred years later. Plato, Aristotle, and Augustine were not his peers, and all others were unworthy of being mentioned along with him."[9] Bernard Lewis says that "Ibn Khaldun stands alone as the greatest historical genius of Islam and the first to produce a philosophic and sociological conception of history,"[10] and George Sarton asserts that "Not only is he the greatest historian of the Middle Ages, towering like a giant over a tribe of pygmies, but one of the first philosophers of history, a forerunner of Machiavelli, Bodin, Vico, Comte, and Curnot."[11]

Such praise of the Arab scholar seems strange in view of his neglect by men of letters for almost six centuries. But it must be remembered that he was born too late to have his works translated into Latin by medieval scholars and thus made a part of the medieval literature of the West. Moreover, he wrote in the language of a dying civilization. The new, strong nations in the West had no inclination to study Arabic and little reason to suspect that in it lay buried one of the world's masterpieces.

THE PROLEGOMENA

The reputation of Ibn Khaldun rests almost entirely on a single work—the *Prolegomena* to his *Universal History*. His *History* is not universal, as the title suggests, but it is an ambitious undertaking, containing a survey of the history not only of the Arabs but also of the Greeks, Romans, Israelites, Copts, Syrians, Persians, Turks, and Franks. With respect to peoples other than the Arabs, however, Ibn Khaldun makes little contribution to historical knowledge, and even his history of the Arabs has been adversely criticised by a number of scholars. His *Autobiography*, which he first published about 1395 but later completed to give the story of his life up to the year of his death, is a fascinating story of the man and gives much information about the times in which he lived; but it pales into insignificance in comparison with his *Prolegomena*, which he wrote during a period of about five months of intense concentration.

The circumstances under which Ibn Khaldun wrote his masterpiece were favorable. At forty-five he was rich in experience and mature in judgment. His literary powers were fully developed. He had stored his mind with information gained from wide reading. The solitude of the lonely castle to which he had retired inspired profound thought. He had seen, in his busy life, the trees; now he wanted to see the forest. He had read history and had helped to make it; now the time had come to ask whether there were patterns in the flux of experience. He felt that no one else had ever really asked, "What can we learn from history?" and he believed that he was equal to the task of finding the answer to that question. Accordingly, he began with high hope and was soon trembling with excitement as patterns in history took shape in his thoughts. "I achieved the Prolegomena," he says, "in this wonderful manner, inspired to me in my solitude, ideas and expressions flowing on my mind till they formed a mature and systematic matter." [12]

Manuscript copies of the *Prolegomena* have been preserved, and between 1863 and 1868 Edward de Slane published in French a three-volume translation.[13] An English translation of a considerable part of the *Prolegomena* was made by Charles Issawi in 1950,[14] and scholarly articles and books in various European languages contain excerpts from it.[15]

Ibn Khaldun has himself given a brief and concise statement of the contents of his *Prolegomena*. After a preface to this work in which he declares his intention to raise history to the rank of a science, and an introduction in which he deals with the sources of error in historical writing, he states:

The contents of this book fall into six sections: the first deals with human society in general, its kind and its geographical distribution; the second, with nomadic societies, tribes and savage peoples; the third, with States, the spiritual and temporal powers, and political ranks; the fourth, with sedentary societies, cities, and provinces; the fifth, with crafts, means of livelihood, and economic activity; the sixth and last, with learning and the ways in which it is acquired.[16]

In other words, the *Prolegomena* deals with the influence on human societies of various biological and geographical factors, with the characteristics of certain types of primitive and civilized groups, with the nature and functions of political, economic, and religious institutions, and with the sources of knowledge. This is the subject matter of Ibn Khaldun's "new science" of history.

THE NEW SCIENCE OF HISTORY

HISTORICAL CRITICISM

The historian, says Ibn Khaldun, should first of all distinguish the false from the true. The factors which make for error in writing history are these: "partisanship towards a creed or opinion . . . over-confidence in one's sources . . . failure to understand what is intended . . . mistaken belief in the truth . . . the inability rightly to place an event in its real context . . . the very common desire to gain the favour of those of high rank . . . ignorance of the laws governing the transformations of human society . . . and exaggeration."

Although Ibn Khaldun described and illustrated these various types of error and sought in his own writing to avoid bias, his recognition of the fact that knowledge is conditioned by experience suggests his belief that historical writing cannot be wholly objective. If the basis of all knowledge is sensation, as he believed, and man gains greater knowledge than that afforded by the five senses only if he can grasp the concepts abstracted from percepts, it follows that all knowledge, and especially that of history, is relative to the experience of the one who possesses it. Nevertheless, to recognize some of the important sources of error often made in writing history was an important step in the direction of that objectivity which Ibn Khaldun endeavored to attain.

THE FUTURE REVEALED IN THE PAST

An accurate account of events is, however, not enough for the science of history envisaged by Ibn Khaldun. There remains the even more important task of discovering in unique events the general conditions of human society. In other words, Ibn Khaldun's history is a generalizing science and not merely a record of events. He was searching for uniformities in social phenomena comparable to the laws of nature. "The past and the future resemble each other," he says, "as two drops of water." He was persuaded that the discovery in historical events of patterns, sequences, and uniformities would make possible the prediction of the future of any society. He declared that he was creating a new science with "strange orientation and immense interest." The subject of this science is human society, and not the individual or any one area of social activity, and its aim is to discover in social phenomena "the transformations that succeed each other." Such is the nature of Ibn Khaldun's science of society.*

Ibn Khaldun's reading of the future of mankind from the history with which he was familiar is open to criticism regarding some points and clearly inaccurate regarding others. Apparently he knew no language except Arabic. His knowledge of the ancient nations, even of Greece and Rome, was meager; and he failed to observe many stirring events taking place in Europe during his lifetime. His field of special competence was North African history, and not universal history. Some of the generalizations that he derived from his observation and study of the Arabs are clearly not applicable to other times and places. For example, it is not true, as Ibn Khaldun maintained, that all states have a life span of three generations of men. Nevertheless, there is in his works a solid body of timeless and universal social theory. He was not merely the first to discover certain uniformities in history; he saw and described some causal relationships in social phenomena not less meaningful to our age than to his own.

SCIENCE AND RELIGION

Although he was a devout Moslem, Ibn Khaldun did not seek to explain history by theology.† He quoted frequently from the Koran, but the holy verses scattered through his writings usually have no connection with his argument at the moment. He seems at times to draw back, as though reason were overreaching itself, terminating a discussion by saying, "Only Allah knows."

In his ability to keep his religion separate from his science, so that neither intrudes on the other, one of Ibn Khaldun's most striking traits of character is revealed. That he accepted the revelations of the Koran is obvious. From his discussion of mysticism in the *Prolegomena* and from his poems, it appears that he was also deeply influenced by Sufism. Regardless, however, of the extent to which he adhered to the orthodox Moslem faith or accepted Sufi mysticism, it is evident that he took religion seriously. He even declared it to be far more important than science. He believed, however, that religion lies outside of, and be-

---

* Although it was not until 1838 that Auguste Comte coined the word *sociology*, Ibn Khaldun's science of society is, in many respects, a sociological work. The term *Al-Umran*, which Ibn Khaldun uses to designate his "new science," is usually translated as *sociology*, and many scholars regard Ibn Khaldun as the founder of sociology as a distinct science.

† Since he made no attempt to give his science of history a metaphysical setting, some writers have maintained that he was not a philosopher of history. Others, including Schmidt, Flint, Issawi, and Toynbee, have accorded him this title.

yond science. He repeatedly warned against overconfidence in human reason, and consequently in science, as, for example, when he said:

> The mind is an accurate scale, whose recordings are certain and reliable; but to use it to weigh questions relating to the Unity of God, or the after life, or the nature of prophecy or of the divine qualities, or other such subjects falling outside its range, is like trying to use a goldsmith's scale to weigh mountains. This does not mean that the scale is in itself inaccurate.
>
> The truth of the matter is that the mind has limits within which it is rigidly confined; it cannot therefore hope to comprehend God and His qualities, itself being only one of the many atoms created by God.[17]

There are, to be sure, some traces of Moslem theology in Ibn Khaldun's scientific work, but his new science is not a theological history of mankind. His faith in the orderliness of the social universe, without which obviously there can be no social science, must certainly have had religious roots; but he does not enlighten us as to the source of this faith. What he seems to say about the relation between science and religion is that where science ends, there religion begins.

SOCIETY

Ibn Khaldun was concerned, as we have seen, with the structure of human society and with the nature and the causes of its various transformations. He made society rather than the individual the focus of his attention. But he did not wholly neglect the individual, and some of his assumptions regarding human nature form the base upon which his theory of society rests.

HUMAN NATURE

Ibn Khaldun assumed basic drives in human nature for gain and for power, but he was also well aware of the influence on personality of the physical and social environment. He declared that

> . . . man is the creature of his habits and customs, not of his inborn nature and temperament; for that to which men are accustomed soon becomes to them a second nature or deep-rooted inclination, replacing their original nature and impulses.[18]

Man is distinguished from other animals, says Ibn Khaldun, by his ability to think, and thought enables him to see the personal advantages of collective action. He is a social animal because of his needs. His cooperation with others is motivated by necessity and by self-interest. He must unite with his fellows for purposes of defense. Mankind could not survive without weapons and food, and these can be effectively provided only where there is some division of labor. The whole society must provide for its members "a restraining force to keep men off each other in view of their animal propensities for aggressiveness and oppression of others." Reason shows that the restraints which society imposes upon the individual are necessary and must be endured.

Although Ibn Khaldun had less to say about the psychological needs of man than the physical, he believed that at least some men have within their natures a divine element that makes for morality, and consequently for fellowship and order in society. He speaks of a faith that "guards its possessor against the commission of any sin, whether great or small," and of "instincts of rectitude" implanted by God in some natures. But either because he was dealing with men generally and not with some few individuals whom he believed still able in a hard world to receive divine guidance, or because he considered that religious conceptions have no place in his science, he portrayed man as guided only by self-interest.

SOCIAL SOLIDARITY

The nature of social solidarity, or *esprit de corps*,* is one of Ibn Khaldun's most important contributions to social thought. He anticipated Hobbes in the view that society is possible only where certain natural human inclinations are restrained. But he recognized degrees in self-restraint, and consequently gradations in society which make possible a form of political organization vastly different from Hobbes' Leviathan state. God has given some men superiority and domination over others, he says, because some members of society will not of their own free will cooperate with others for the common good. Only such recalcitrants require the control which Hobbes believed to be necessary for all. Furthermore, Ibn Khaldun went far beyond Hobbes in seeing that the restraint imposed by a sovereign is only one means of preserving social order, and not the most effective.

Social solidarity is a feeling of identity with others. That feeling causes an individual to conform to the expectations of the other members of his group, and thus provides a type of discipline far more effective, Ibn Khaldun believed, than fines and bodily punishments. In small groups, such as the family or the tribe, this unity is created by blood ties. "Men resent the oppression of their relatives," says Ibn Khaldun, "and the impulse to ward off any harm that may befall those relatives is natural and deep rooted in men." But social solidarity is not limited to kinsmen. Those who live in close proximity to one another, confronted with common dangers, sharing the work of common enterprises, and faced with a common fate are closely bound together. The mutual dependence of patrons and clients, as of masters and slaves, creates a bond almost as strong as that

* The Arabic term *asabiyah* or *asabia* has no exact English equivalent and has been translated variously. Toynbee calls it "the *esprit de corps* which expresses itself in effective social action"; Rosenthal, the "corporate will of the group"; Enan, the "vitality of the state or dynasty"; Issawi, "nationalism in its broadest sense, or social solidarity."

formed by kinship. The division of labor compels cooperation and creates an awareness of mutual dependence. A common religion is a "powerful cement." Thus there are various factors responsible for that feeling of unity with others which constrains the individual in his behavior. This *esprit de corps* is a far more effective instrument of social control than the authority of a ruler.

According to Ibn Khaldun, social solidarity is strong among nomads and weak among sedentary peoples. He pointed out that the kinship ties among nomads and their common life in a "hard and hungry home" develop in them a keen awareness of their membership in a tribe, and a willingness to make personal sacrifices for the common good: survival in the desert demands nothing less. In fact, he identified social solidarity with the ethos of "savage peoples living in a wilderness" and denied that it can exist in like degree among civilized peoples. Toynbee rejects this conclusion as much too sweeping and points out that a strong feeling of solidarity is not a "monoploy of Nomadism." But he then goes on to say:

> In offering these criticisms, however, we must not forget that our ability to make them does not arise from any inherent superiority of our intellectual powers, but simply from the external accident that we happen to have at our disposal a wider field of historical evidence to work upon. [9]

Ibn Khaldun maintained that Moslem civilization arose when the strong *esprit de corps* native to the nomads was fortified with religious enthusiasm and the scattered tribes were welded by the force of Islam into one nation. The Arabs were then indeed irresistible.

THE PHYSICAL ENVIRONMENT

In his recognition of the importance that such geographic factors as climate, soil, and precipitation play in determining the forms of human society, Ibn Khaldun was far in advance of his age. In fact, except for some mistakes in his geography and some views on psychology that are not now generally accepted, his observations on this important subject are sound today. He saw that the physical environment sets limits to social development. Where the heat or cold is extreme, human societies are not able to rise much above the level of sheer animal existence. Civilizations develop only in the temperate zones, where the challenge of the climate is not too severe, and where the air is salubrious, the soil productive, and the food varied and plentiful.

Ibn Khaldun's criticism of civilization, which he regarded both as the highest development of society and as an artificial way of life which inevitably destroys the society in which it develops, is clearly shown in his discussion of food habits. He maintained that a rich diet makes the body rough and the mind dull. For that reason, civilized sedentary people grow weak and impotent from indulgence and are easily overcome. On the other hand, where food is too scarce there is little social growth. Only barbarians can initiate a civilization, and their meager diet is an important source of their strength. On the other hand, no sedentary people can long preserve a civilization, partly because they eat too much. The ideal situation is one in which food is neither too plentiful nor too scarce.

Ibn Khaldun maintained also that climate has a marked effect on the physical and psychological characteristics of people. He declared that those who live in cold regions are usually light of color and somber of temperament, whereas those who live in the tropics are dark-skinned and gay. "To attribute the black color of Negroes to Ham," he says, "shows complete ignorance of the nature of heat and cold and of their effect on the air and the animals that live therein." Because the Egyptians live in a warm latitude, they are "so merry, light-headed, and heedless of consequences that they do not store enough food to last them a year, or even a month, but buy their needs from the market."

THE SOCIAL ENVIRONMENT

Although the physical environment has an important influence on people, social forces are not less evident and powerful in shaping individuals and their various societies. In the same place different types of societies emerge and succeed one another without any marked change having taken place in the natural setting. Over the ruins of one great city either the sands may settle or an even mightier city may rise. The sun, the wind, the rain, and even the soil are more constant than the shifting seats of culture. To a considerable extent, therefore, societies are made by men.

> Civilized townsmen follow certain codes in matters of living, dwelling, and building, in religious and worldly affairs, and, in general, in all their customs and transactions. These codes, which regulate all their behaviour and their actions, seem to constitute impassable limits. Yet, in fact, they are conventional things, made by man and learned by each generation from the preceding one.[20]

The kind of work in which men engage has an especially important influence on the nature of their society. Ibn Khaldun believed that trade leads to "a decrease and weakening in virtue and manliness," whereas nomadic life develops a coarse but hardy character. The distinction between the types of societies that develop from two distinct ways of life is a key idea in Ibn Khaldun's thought.

NOMADIC AND SEDENTARY SOCIETIES

Ibn Khaldun observed that the way of life of nomads is quite different from that of sedentary people, and he developed from this observation a theory of two polar types of society. Nomads, he says, are coarse and hard; they are brave, resourceful, and independent; their *esprit de corps* is strong; their family and tribal mores are well defined and strictly enforced; they are healthy, frugal, and prolific. In contrast, sedentary people are refined and soft; they make poor soldiers; they seek pleasure instead of necessities, crave luxuries, and are given to ostentation; their *esprit de corps* is weak; they practice vice rather than virtue, prodigality rather than frugality; and they employ ruses rather than force. The two types of society that result from these differences correspond closely, although not exactly, to the types defined by Becker as sacred and secular, by Tönnies as *Gemeinschaft* and *Gesellschaft*, by Sorokin as familistic and contractual, and by many sociologists as rural and urban.

The contrast is roughly that between barbaric and civilized people. Ibn Khaldun seems to show a marked preference for the nomads, but that is because he saw in them a brute strength which provides the creative force in society, just as he saw in sedentary people the weakness which he believed inevitably results from easy living. The nomads are the roots of society; the sedentary people are the flowers. Roots are gross, but they reach into the earth and draw forth the sustenance for hardy growth; flowers are lovely, but they fade. Yet, despite his praise of nomadic life, Ibn Khaldun wrote what Toynbee has called "perhaps the most crushing indictment of Nomad rule over sedentary populations that has ever been delivered from the mouth of a first-hand witness." [21] Ibn Khaldun's condemnation of the Arabs is so severe that some writers believe that he identified himself with the Berbers rather than the Arabs. Yet he boasted of his Arab ancestry. A few quotations from his discussion of the faults of the Arabs will show his frankness at whatever cost to pride.

> The habits and practices of nomadic life have made the Arabs a rude and savage people. . . . Let the Arabs require stones to place under their cooking-vessels, and they will not hesitate to spoil a house in order to procure them; let them want wood for the stakes or poles of their tents, and in order to get it they will strip from an edifice its roof. . . . Whenever they cast their eyes on a fine flock, or an article of furniture, or a useful instrument, they carry it off by force if they can. . . . Further, the Arabs neglect all the functions of government; they are not anxious to prevent crime or watchful in preserving the public safety.[22]

These remarks should be read, however, in the frame of reference which Ibn Khaldun employs for his study of society. He was not personally attracted to barbarism and to the inevitable triumph of the strong over the weak, but he saw the debility of civilization. He liked neither war nor slavery, and he declared, "God has not ordered some to command and others to obey"; but, as Schmidt says, "he probably considered them [war and slavery] inevitable and did not think that it was his business to justify as well as to explain the course of history, or to attempt to change what is crooked and cannot be made straight." [23] Ibn Khaldun repeatedly asserted that "nomadic life is as contrary to the progress of civilization as the sedentary life is favourable to it"; but he went on to ask why civilizations decay. His heart bled when he contemplated the frailty of the sedentary society to which he himself belonged, but his emotions did not shut out from him the vision of a raw force, wonderful and terrifying, within the tents of the Arabs.

POLITICS

Ibn Khaldun did not attempt to make a sharp distinction between society and the state. He says that the two are inseparable, the state being to society "as form is to matter," and he declares that the whole society and not some particular aspect of it is the subject of his science. Consequently, he did not attempt to formulate a separate science of politics; instead, he augmented his general theory of society with data derived from political history and from his own experience in political life and left somewhat blurred the line between the social and the political. Nevertheless, his analysis of the nature of the state is an important part of his science of history.

RISE AND DEVELOPMENT OF THE STATE

In defining the state as "a human community, established through the force of circumstances and arising with natural necessity as a consequence of ambition to rule and love of power," Ibn Khaldun made it clear that he regarded political organization as both natural and necessary. It is natural because "the state follows its own laws," and necessary because of "the aggressive propensities of men." A society must have some means of restraining its members. Where there is a strong sense of social solidarity, the individual is kept in line by the knowledge that the eyes of his fellows are upon him and that any deviation on his part from the conduct expected of him will meet with stern censure. Among the nomads the tribal chief shares the authority which must be exercised for the common good with all the members of the tribe. Sovereignty, therefore, is vested in all rather than in one.

It is natural, however, for authority to concentrate, sooner or later, in one person.

> This is because . . . a state is founded upon solidarity. Now solidarity is formed by the union of many groups, one of which, being more powerful than the rest, dominates and directs the others and finally absorbs them, thus forming an association which ensures victory over other peoples and states. . . . This wider union and solidarity will be achieved by some group belonging to a leading family; and within that family there is bound to be some prominent individual who leads and dominates the rest. That person will therefore be appointed as leader of the wider group, because of the domination enjoyed by his house over the others.

> And once this leader is so appointed, his animal nature is bound to breed in him feelings of pride and haughtiness. He will then disdain to share with any one his rule over his followers; nay, he will soon think himself a God, as human beings are wont to do. Add to this the fact that sound politics demands undivided rule, for where there are many leaders the result is confusion. . . .
>
> Steps are therefore taken to curb the power and to clip the wings and weaken the solidarity of the other groups, so that they shall not aspire to dispute the power of the ruler. The ruler monopolizes all power, leaving nothing to others, and enjoys alone the glory derived therefrom.[24]

In other words, although the state comes into existence through solidarity, the "end of solidarity is sovereignty." As the state grows in power, the feeling of solidarity becomes weaker and individual liberty is sacrificed to collective strength. When the ruler has absolute authority, the state no longer needs solidarity; it has force.

> Once kingship has been established . . . and inherited by successive generations or dynasties, the people forget their original condition, the rulers are invested with the aura of leadership, and the subjects obey them almost as they obey the precepts of their religion, and fight for them as they would fight for their faith.[25]

THE STATE AND RELIGION

What part does religion play in the rise and development of the state? The answer that Ibn Khaldun gave to this important question is not clear and has, consequently, been much disputed. He said that religion provided the Arabs with "the foundation for the state in the form of a Canon Law." [26] He declared also that "vast and powerful" empires are founded on a religion, because a religion provides unity of purpose and fortifies the *esprit de corps* that is necessary for victory. On the other hand, he observed that a strong *esprit de corps* has enabled some states to become powerful without a Divine Law. Since he believed that "no religious movement can succeed unless based on solidarity," it would seem that in his opinion solidarity is prior to and more nearly basic than religion in the establishment of the state.

Although the force of the collective will for power alone may create a state, Ibn Khaldun declared: "The state whose law is based upon violence and superior force and giving full play to the irascible nature is tyranny and injustice and in the eyes of the Law blameworthy. . . ." [27] Rosenthal believes that Ibn Khaldun's views on the comparative influence of solidarity and religion on the state may be stated as follows:

> As a student of reality, Ibn Khaldun saw that either can exist without the other. But he also saw that a lasting political order is unthinkable with-

out the co-operation of the two. Only if [*esprit de corps*] is transformed by religious zeal and higher aim into a spiritual, formative ideal, only then enduring results of a character far exceeding sheer force and lust for power will be achieved. On the other hand, no religious ideal will see its realisation without that corporate will and enthusiasm behind it. It needs always a party to realise in actual life the message of an ideal. No wonder, therefore, that Ibn Khaldun clung to Islam as the superior State, as the ideal society of men striving for dominion and power, not for their own sake but in order to enforce the ideal of human perfection and happiness in this world and in the world to come.[28]

DECLINE AND FALL OF THE STATE

Ibn Khaldun believed that the state follows an invariable pattern in its development. First, a strong *esprit de corps,* usually fortified by religion, gives it a start. It exists to protect men and to enable them to exercise their collective power. With the growth of the state, the *esprit de corps* weakens, and authority comes increasingly to be assumed by the ruler. Then, says Ibn Khaldun,

> Once the concentration of power in one person has been achieved and luxury and inaction have spread, the state approaches its decay. This is due to several causes:
> *First* because of the concentration of power. For to the extent that glory is equally shared by all the members of a group, they all strive equally for it and make great efforts to overcome others and to defend what they have, spurred on by a collective ambition and force. They all aim at power and find death sweet in the pursuit of glory, and in truth would rather face annihilation than the disruption of their group. When, however, one man concentrates power in his hands, he tries to curb the wills of the others and destroy their feeling of solidarity. . . . As a result they become lazy and unwilling to conquer, and soon get accustomed to humiliation and slavery. . . .
> The *second* reason is that the establishment of a state leads to luxury . . . with an increase in wants and a resulting excess of expenditures over receipts. . . . When the kings demand that their subjects reduce their expenditure, in times of wars and invasions, the latter are no longer able to do so; whereupon the kings punish them and confiscate the wealth of many of them, keeping it for themselves or giving it to their own families or officials. All this weakens [the ruling group] and consequently the power of the ruler himself. . . . Moreover, luxury corrupts morals, by inducing evil and depraved habits. . . . The good qualities of the people, which were a sign of domination, now disappear and are replaced by contrary qualities of evil, which herald decay. . . .
> The *third* reason is that the nature of the state demands docility. . . . Now once men have accustomed themselves to docility and inaction, these qualities develop into a second nature, as with all habits. . . . And it may

well happen, when this luxury and inaction and decay have come about, that the ruler of the state may seek the support of hardy foreign soldiers, who can show themselves more enduring in wartime and better able to bear hunger and rough living. This may preserve the state from decay for a further period of time, until God finally dooms it to extinction.[29]

POLITICAL INSIGHTS

Scattered through Ibn Khaldun's work are many casual observations which reveal the political wisdom of this fourteenth-century historian and statesman. For example, he observed that rulers spend money "without too nice a calculation" and that consequently those having goods to dispose of will do well to sell to the state; that scholars make poor politicians, not because they lack foresight, but because they see too much; that the greater the power of the ruler, the more extensive is the bureaucracy through which he rules; that the state is "stronger at the center than at the periphery" and its optimum size is determined by the strength of the armed forces at its command; and that "the state soon comes to belong to others than those who founded it, and power passes to others than those who first grasped it."

ECONOMICS

In contrast to the other theorists whose works we have examined, Ibn Khaldun dealt usually with economic matters without regard to ethical considerations. He did not say that ethics have nothing to do with business—in fact there is, for example, a decidedly moral note in his discussion of public finance—but he endeavored to describe things as they are rather than as they ought to be. He passed lightly over some of the difficult economic questions that had disturbed the churchmen and attempted to make a strictly empirical analysis of economic phenomena. Although much that he says is of only historical interest, he made some observations that are as revealing of the modern world as they were of fourteenth-century North Africa. Especially timely is his discussion of the profit motive, the influence of various types of occupation on the individual and on society, and the integration of society with particular attention to the way in which economic institutions affect and are affected by the other institutions of the society.

THE PROFIT MOTIVE

As we have seen, Ibn Khaldun maintained that the desire for gain, like the thirst for power, is a basic human characteristic. The insatiable craving for more goods and services is the strong and persistent motivating force in economic activity. Once men have secured for themselves the necessities of life, they seek with unabated zeal the amenities and the luxuries. As their conditions improve, shelter and simple foods no longer satisfy; they build finer houses, even "lofty mansions and castles," and they develop tastes which require "extreme refinement in cooking and the preparation of food." Agriculture, industry, and trade thrive because of the profit motive, and in all walks of life men are driven to effort by the incentive to gain wealth.

The loss of this incentive as a result of arbitrary appropriation of property by the government through seizure or excessive taxation leads to a slackening in enterprise and eventually to economic stagnation and social decay. In speaking of the increase in taxes which inevitably takes place in the state "as time passes and kings succeed each other," Ibn Khaldun says:

> These increases grow with the spread of luxurious habits in the state, and the consequent growth in needs and public expenditure, until taxation burdens the subjects and deprives them of their gains. People get accustomed to this high level of taxation, because the increases have come about gradually, without anyone's being aware of who exactly it was who raised the rates of the old taxes or imposed the new ones.
>
> But the effects on business of this rise in taxation make themselves felt. For business men are soon discouraged by the comparison of their profits with the burden of their taxes, and between their output and their net profits. Consequently production falls off, and with it the yield of taxation.
>
> The rulers may, mistakenly, try to remedy this decrease in the yield of taxation by raising the rate of the taxes; hence taxes and imposts reach a level which leaves no profits to business men, owing to high costs of production, heavy burden of taxation, and inadequate net profits. This process of higher tax rates and lower yields (caused by the government's belief that higher rates result in higher returns) may go on until production begins to decline owing to the despair of business men, and to affect population. The main injury of this process is felt by the state, just as the main benefit of better business conditions is enjoyed by it.
>
> From this you must understand that the most important factor making for business prosperity is to lighten as much as possible the burden of taxation on business men, in order to encourage enterprise by giving assurance of greater profits.[30]

OCCUPATIONS

Ibn Khaldun declared that a man's character is influenced by the way in which he earns a living and that, consequently, society is profoundly affected by the predominant occupations of its members. "The differences between different peoples," he says, "arise out of the differences in their occupations." There are, he stated, four main types of occupations: rulership, trade, agriculture, and industry. He dismissed rulership as an "unnatural means of livelihood," although he showed that men gladly choose it above others wherever and whenever taxes put large revenues at the disposal of the rulers. He observed also that a bureaucracy affords a good and easy living not only to those engaged directly in the public service but also to those who attend and serve public officials. However unnatural it may be, therefore, rulership is an important and a popular occupation in sedentary societies.

Trade was considered by Ibn Khaldun to be a productive and a natural means of livelihood, but he found little in this occupation to praise. The aim of trade, he says, is to "buy cheap and sell dear." He observed that trade becomes increasingly more important as a society advances in civilization. Nevertheless, he insisted that this form of occupation is suited only to the clever, unscrupulous, and daring man, since "most of the methods it employs are tricks aimed at making a profit."

> If [the trader] is known to be bold in entering law suits, careful in keeping accounts, stubborn in defending his point of view, firm in his attitude towards magistrates, he stands a good chance of getting his due. . . . Should a person, however, be lacking in boldness and the spirit of enterprise and at the same time have no protector to back him up, he had better avoid trade altogether, as he risks losing his capital and becoming a prey of other merchants. The fact of the matter is that most people, especially the mob and trading classes, covet the goods of others; and but for the restraint imposed by the magistrates all goods would have been taken away from their owners.[31]

According to Ibn Khaldun, industry, or craftsmanship, becomes increasingly necessary as people develop sedentary habits. Among the craftsmen he included not only those who convert raw materials into finished products, such as carpenters, tailors, and weavers, but also doctors, scribes, librarians, singers, artists, and others who provide desired services. He points out that those crafts that "lead their practitioners into the presence of great kings . . . enjoy a prestige not given to other crafts." He observes that popular demand determines what industries will thrive—*i.e.*, that craftsmen are willing to sell their services to the highest bidder. The explanation, he says, is clear.

> . . . the individual does not allow his labour to go gratuitously because it is his means of living and he will employ it in what has a value in his town, so as to profit from it; if the industry is demanded and prospers, it enjoys the position of a commodity much asked for, which is brought to market in order to be sold; individuals try to learn this industry and to acquire it as a means of living; if the industry is not demanded and does not prosper no attention is directed to learning it and it is abandoned and neglected.[32]

Industry ranks higher on Ibn Khaldun's scale of occupations than trade, but he reserved his praise for agriculture. Although he declared that only "men of small importance and needy countrymen" make a living by agriculture, and even these are ever seeking an opportunity to move to town and share in the conveniences and luxuries of townsmen, he goes on to say:

> As for Agriculture, it is essentially prior to all the others, for it is simple, natural, and instinctive, not requiring much wisdom or learning. This is why men attribute it to Adam, the father of mankind, declaring that he founded and taught it; by this they mean to show that it is the oldest occupation and the one most in conformity with nature.[33]

He recognized three agricultural types: the cultivators, the herders, and the desert nomads. Although noting that these types differ in degree, he sometimes treated them as a single class of rural people who, because they pursue means of livelihood that are natural and wholesome, are superior in most respects to urban people, who are engaged in artificial and corrupting occupations.

INTEGRATION OF SOCIAL INSTITUTIONS

Ibn Khaldun portrayed society as a web formed with interdependent strands. He showed that religious, political, educational, family, and economic activities are all closely related. Any change taking place in any one of these important areas of behavior requires a compensatory change in all the others. Although this conception runs through his treatment of various topics, it is cogently stated in his discussion of economics. As Rosenthal says:

> He perceived that the economic sphere cannot without serious consequences for the machinery of society be looked upon as segregated from finance, army, spiritual culture. They are all interconnected, and only when they are in perfect equilibrium on the basis of a mutual give-and-take is the State at its best and [functioning] normally and effectively. . . . His empiric nature made him see the effect which a disturbance in one sphere had on the other spheres of life, and he discovered the law of causality at the root of this mutual influence. This is something quite new and revolutionary and, indeed, far advancing into the modern age. Nowhere can this be seen better than in his plea for sound finance, moderate taxation and free economy.[34]

OTHER ECONOMIC IDEAS

A brief statement of a number of other ideas found in Ibn Khaldun's works will show the breadth and the keenness of his insights in the field of economics. He noted that production and not trade creates new wealth, that labor expended in the services may be productive, that the value of money depends upon what it will buy, that where hopes are high as a result of increased prosperity, procreation is stimulated, that those with prestige acquire wealth more easily than those who lack it, that those who get their living from industry or trade have greater wealth usually than those who depend on agriculture or animal husbandry, that demand determines what will be produced, that prices vary with supply and cost of production, that wealth in real estate is a social product, that natural resources are valuable only when they have been or can be converted by labor into useful goods, that "all, or most, incomes and profits represent the value of human labour," that heavy purchasing by the state will destroy the delicate balance in the market, and that state controls over the economy are more easily imposed than released.

SOCIAL CHANGE

From his study of history Ibn Khaldun deduced a fatalistic view of the course of states. In the ceaseless change in society there are forces at work which lie beyond human control. If the course of events could be radically changed by the actions of strong men, then there could be no science of society, since the whims of leaders are unpredictable. But it is precisely because the forces that control social change are immanent and are not subject to capricious modification by leaders that the laws of social change can be discovered. Great men make ripples on the surface of the sea of society, but strong currents flow in the deep with unbroken regularity. Ibn Khaldun believed, therefore, that as certainly as tides ebb and flow, states rise and fall. Who can hold back the tide? Who can prevent the decay?

THEORY OF CONFLICT

As Ibn Khaldun read history, war between nomads and sedentary people—*i.e.*, between barbarian and civilized societies—is natural and inevitable. The barbarians yearn for what the civilized possess; they watch and wait and bide their time; at an opportune moment the hard men of the desert strike and conquer the soft men of the cities. "Civilization," says Ibn Khaldun, "is the object which primitive people have in view and their efforts converge on its attainment." He did not show why civilization could not be attained in peaceful toil rather than through the force of arms; he merely concluded from his historical studies and personal experience that group conflict is the basic factor in social change. It is not surprising, therefore, that Ludwik Gumplowicz (1838-1910), a modern exponent of this theory, should have paid Ibn Khaldun this tribute:

> Long before Auguste Comte, even before Vico, whom the Italians regard as the first European sociologist, an Islamic scholar studied, with accurate good sense and moderation, the social phenomena and advanced highly valuable views on the matter.[35]

Although Ibn Khaldun made no attempt to develop a conflict theory, his distrust of monopoly, his belief that competition enables men to "arrive at the maximum satisfaction" of their wants, his analysis of trade, his assumption that greed for power is a basic human characteristic, and various other aspects of his thought reveal the importance he attached to conflict as a factor in social change.

CYCLICAL THEORY

Unlike many modern exponents of conflict theory, however, Ibn Khaldun denied that conflict leads to continuous progress. He saw no far-off event toward which creation moves. On the contrary, in his opinion the end of victory is defeat, and states rise and fall in endless cycles. The conquest of soft, civilized people by hard, primitive people sets in motion destructive forces which sap the strength of the conquerors, who do not stop with seizing the possessions of those they have overcome but begin to imitate their tastes and manners. They cease to be content with necessities and demand the amenities of civilization: rich and varied foods, clothes made of silk, houses and many servants, beauty, intellectual excitement, and freedom. Soon they become weak from easy living, and another civilized society awaits its Nemesis. Ibn Khaldun is even willing to fix the time span required for a state to emerge, mature, and decay.

> . . . generally speaking, it is rare that the age of the state should exceed three generations, a generation being the average age of an individual, that is forty years or the time necessary for full growth and development. . . .
> We [say] that the age of the state rarely exceeds three generations because the first generation still retains its nomadic roughness and savagery, and such nomadic characteristics as a hard life, courage, predatoriness, and the desire to share glory. All this means that the strength of the solidarity uniting the people is still firm, which makes that people feared and powerful and able to dominate others.
> The second generation, however, have already passed from the nomadic to the sedentary way of life, owing to the power they wield and the luxury they enjoy. They have abandoned their rough life for an easy and luxurious one. Instead of all sharing in the power and glory of the state, one wields it alone, the rest being too indolent to claim their part. Instead of aggressiveness and the desire for conquest we see in them contentment with what they have. All this relaxes the ties of solidarity, to a certain extent, and humility and submissiveness begin to appear in them. . . .
> As for the third generation, they have completely forgotten the nomadic and rough stage, as though it had never existed. They have also lost their love of power and their social solidarity through having been accustomed to being ruled. Luxury corrupts them, because of the pleasant and easy way of living in which they have been brought up. . . . They deceive people by their insignia, dress, horse-riding and culture; yet all the while they are more cowardly than women. If then a claimant or aggressor appear, they are incapable of pushing him back.[36]

CIVILIZATION AND DECAY

Ibn Khaldun was not unmindful of the attractions of civilization. Civilization was to him like a flower, which in its full bloom is a thing of infinite sensuous enjoyment. Just as the flower is the supreme achievement of the plant that bears it, so does the fashionable capital of a civilized state exhibit the highest development of the arts and sciences of which the society is capable.

> ... the more prominent the civilization and luxury, the more the arts develop and multiply. This occurs because the culture of the arts begins after the subsistence of the people is assured. When men who are established in a society have been able to procure by their labors more than is required for them to live, they direct their attentions to a more distant end, occupy themselves with matters such as sciences and arts, which pertain more intimately to human nature. ... Thus it is necessary to repair to a great city in order to learn.[37]

But also, just as the flower will surely wither, so will the civilization decay.

> The reader who will have understood and appreciated what we have just said will recognize that civilization is sedentary life and luxury, that it indicates the last stage of the progress of a society, and that, from this time on, the nation commences to decline, to become corrupted, and to fall into a state of decrepitude. ... We will even go so far as to state that the character of men formed under the influence of sedentary life and luxury is in itself the personification of evil. A man is not a man unless he is able to procure by his own efforts that which will be useful to him and is able to reject that which would be harmful; it is for this purpose that he has received such a perfectly organized body. The resident of the city is incapable of providing his prime needs. Slothfulness contracted from living in ease hinders him in this attempt; or it may even be the pride resulting from an education acquired in the midst of well-being and luxury. ... When a man has lost the force of acting according to his good qualities and his piety, he has lost the character of a man and falls to the level of the beasts. ... It is thus evident that civilization marks the point of arrest in the development of a people or of an empire.[38]

Ibn Khaldun maintained that the state is held together by solidarity and a sound economy and that civilization destroys both. The Arabs rose to greatness, he claimed, when the entire Moslem world was united under Islam. The Caliphate was held together by the strong solidarity that was natural to nomads within their own tribes. Thus religion and solidarity worked together to create an empire. In the first stage of Moslem history, says Ibn Khaldun, "the Caliphate existed alone, without any monarchy; later on Caliphate and monarchy were intertwined and intermixed: finally monarchy stood out independently of the Caliphate, because it could lean on a power and solidarity distinct from that of the Caliphate." Even then, with moral law sacrificed to luxury and solidarity growing steadily weaker, the state appeared to have achieved its greatest strength. But, deep within, the forces of its destruction were working, through weakening of *esprit de corps,* the concentration of authority, unsound fiscal policies of the state, and the moral degeneration of the people.

EVALUATION OF SOCIAL CHANGE

We have seen that Ibn Khaldun set out to describe, and not to evaluate, the course of social change. He had faith that there is, as Schmidt says, "an intelligible sequence, a causal connection, an ascertainable order of development, a course of human events following observable tendencies, in accordance with definite laws." We have seen also that he achieved for his time a truly remarkable degree of objectivity in his observations. But occasionally the devout Moslem rather than the scientific observer speaks forth in his works. It is then that a note of pessimism pervades his thought. Pessimism is an outgrowth of evaluation: one wishes that things were different. Ibn Khaldun was saddened by the eternal cyclical movement in society, the rise and fall of states, and he believed that this occurs only because people will not hold steadfastly to moral law. As Gibb says:

> The careful reader will note how he drives home the lesson, over and over again, that the course of history is what it is because of the infraction of the [moral law]* by the sin of pride, the sin of luxury, the sin of greed. Even in economic life it is only when the ordinances of the [moral law] are observed that prosperity follows. Since mankind will not follow the [moral law] it is condemned to an empty and unending cycle of rise and fall, conditioned by the "natural" and inevitable consequences of the predominance of its animal instincts. In this sense Ibn Khaldun may be a "pessimist" or "determinist," but his pessimism has a moral and religious, not a sociological, basis.[39]

This subjective aspect of Ibn Khaldun's thought detracts in no way from his genius. It only bears out Toynbee's contention that "all historical thought is inevitably relative to the particular circumstances of the thinker's own time and place. This is a law of human nature from which no human genius can be exempt." [40] The wonder is that this Moslem of the fourteenth century could have set a standard of objective analysis of history which may well be the envy of a twentieth-century social scientist.

IBN KHALDUN'S SCIENCE

Ibn Khaldun sought to create a science that would describe the transformations which succeed each other in social phenomena. He stated modestly, "It seems to be a new science which has sprung up spontaneously, for I do not

---

* Ibn Khaldun means actually the revealed canon law of Islam.

recollect having read anything about it by any previous writers." In the light of knowledge which Ibn Khaldun did not possess, his claim to originality appears somewhat exaggerated; nevertheless, he developed, as no one had done before, the science now called sociology.

Ibn Khaldun believed that uniformities exist in social phenomena, and that history provides data which make it possible to prove or disprove hypotheses about social organization and social change. He recognized that the first prerequisite for social science is an objective attitude, and he made a conscious effort to state the facts, avoiding wishful thinking and deliberately disregarding his own preferences. He realized that partisanship distorts social inquiry, that an event must be examined in its context, that all the facts bearing on a condition must be assembled and sifted before a conclusion is reached, and that the findings must be stated without the distortions sometimes dictated by a prudent regard for self-interest.

Ibn Khaldun was convinced that the social forces at work are ultimately those generated by human nature. Deep within men is the desire for things that are destructive. Men want power, so they form a state; they want freedom, so they give up solidarity; they want comfort, so they leave the land and build cities; they want civilization, so they give up security and the peace of simple living. Because of these imperious yearnings that drive mankind onward, groups struggle without end against groups, and states are formed, made hard, and eventually destroyed in the crucible of conflict.

A major theme in Ibn Khaldun's writings is the contrast between nomadic and sedentary peoples. He discovered that the psychological differences which exist between people engaged in different types of work are reflected in distinctive forms of social organization. The concepts *Gemeinschaft* and *Gesellschaft,* developed by Ferdinand Tönnies late in the nineteenth century to describe polar types of social solidarity, represent a good example of a later attempt to analyse the same basic situation that claimed the attention of Ibn Khaldun more than five centuries ago.

Perhaps Ibn Khaldun had too much faith in natural laws governing human conduct and too little faith in human volition. He observed a cyclical pattern in social change, but it is conceivable that those who believe in human progress may be right. From his historical studies Ibn Khaldun was impressed with the elemental strength inherent in the order and stability found where people live close to the soil, but there is also historical support for the view that the division of labor in highly developed civilizations creates mutual needs that can be satisfied only by the practice, even if under the pressure of necessity, of the Golden Rule. Those who believe that the exercise of human reason can create a social order in which rude strength will count for less and the advantages of civilized life can be enjoyed without social degeneration need not, therefore, accept Ibn Khaldun's answer to the problem of social change as final.

13 · RENAISSANCE AND REFORMATION

In rivers the water that you touch is the last of what has passed, and the first of that which cometh; so with time present.
—Leonardo da Vinci

There are periods in history when change is in the air. During such exciting times, society seems to rouse itself as from a lethargy and move with giant strides. Then is human genius unleashed, to crush with destructive force the old forms of life and to build a new order. In Europe, the fourteenth century witnessed the beginning of such an awakening, and within three centuries a marvelous new age, the Age of Science, had been ushered in. We have already seen that Europe had not slept during the Middle Ages, but as we turn to a vastly different social order, it is well to remind ourselves of the fact that

> . . . the Middle Ages were by no means wholly dark or dead. It is true that they saw a decline in science, a decadence in art, a dearth in literature, accompanied by an invasion of barbarism, a recrudescence of superstition, a cessation of peace, a disappearance of comfort, a chronic prevalence of plague, pestilence, and famine, a deplorable falling away from the culture and humanity of the pagan world at its best. But, to set over against this, it is equally true that they saw, particularly in their central period (A.D. 604-1303), a vast elevation and purification of religion, an incalculably great exaltation and extension of morality, an immense advance in politics. They saw a pure and spiritual faith exorcise the demons which, under the names of divinities, the pagan masses had adored; they saw the gentler virtues of brotherly kindness and love prevail over the sterner and more limited virilities called forth by sanguinary games and merciless war; they saw the diminution of slavery, the mitigation of serfdom, the spread of freedom, the re-emergence of the individual, the growth of representative institutions, the development of government by debate, the gradual formation of national states dominated increasingly by an ever more articulate

public opinion. Such was the by no means contemptible heritage which the Middle Ages handed down to the modern world.[1]

If during the Middle Ages men and women lived out their days comparatively free from the disturbing influence of new ideas, they perhaps found the old ideas, for all their focus on life beyond the grave, reasonably satisfying. Life for them may not have been especially exciting, but the Church offered hope to those whose hearts were heavy and reward to those who bore their burdens patiently for Christ's sake. The medieval age was characterized by a truce with necessity, which in an individual Thomas Carlyle regarded as evidence of maturity. The age that followed was, to use the same figure, an adolescent age. The lusty, reckless, and bold forces of youth are plainly visible in the rebellion against authority, the daring adventures that led to the exploration of the world, and the craving to know and see and do everything.

THE RENAISSANCE

The term *Renaissance* implies that something lifeless has been born again. As a description of a movement in the age of transition between the medieval and the modern world, it points a contrast between the darkness of the Middle Ages and the wonder and the glory of the golden ages at the dawn of Western civilization. It suggests that the concern of the churchmen with things eternal lacked the vitality of the interest in man and his natural environment shown by the ancient Greeks and Romans. In calling attention to the fact that there came at the end of the medieval period a shift in the direction of human strivings, it appears to deny the no less obvious fact of continuity in the development of Western civilization. The churchmen were, to be sure, concerned primarily with salvation, but their otherworldliness did not efface regard for the good life on earth.

Interpretations of the Renaissance as an escape of the human spirit from the fetters of medieval eschatology have not been lacking. The following passage presents that view.

> Michael Angelo's great painting of the newly created Adam on the ceiling of the Sistine Chapel might be taken as a symbol of the Renaissance, of the time when man was, as it were, recreated more glorious than before, with a body naked and unashamed, and a strong arm, unimpaired by fasting, outstretched toward life and light. Definitions are generally misleading, and it is easier to represent the Renaissance by a symbol than to define it. It was a movement, a revival of man's powers, a reawakening of the consciousness of himself and of the universe.[2]

But, although the Renaissance was certainly a revival of interest in matters which the Middle Ages had neglected, the term "rebirth" has misleading connotations. By the fifteenth and sixteenth centuries a remarkable change had taken place, to be sure, in Europe; nevertheless, the modern world represents a growth and not a sudden creation.

Most writers agree that the Renaissance began in Italy, and that initially it was a revival of interest in the ancient writers. The art, literature, and philosophy of Greece and Rome had been neglected in Christendom for more than a thousand years. Christian people thirsting for salvation required nothing from pagans. Ancient manuscripts had lain undisturbed and forgotten, partly because those who might have read them were not interested in their contents. The Crusades, and finally the fall of Constantinople to the Turks in 1453, brought these old works to light just when Western scholars were beginning to turn their attention to the subjects with which they dealt. Petrarch (1304-1374) and Boccaccio (1313-1375) were entranced with the ancient writers. Many other scholars found them inspiring, and imitation of the old Greek and Roman masters began on an extensive scale. Greek was studied, an attempt was made to purify Latin, and the literary patterns of the classical writers were adopted. In architecture, classical forms were combined with, or entirely replaced, the Gothic designs of the Middle Ages. Sculptors sought to capture the perfect beauty of the classical statues, and artists breathed pagan life into their pictures of good Christians to create works of art that have never been surpassed.

The Renaissance was not, however, confined to Italy or to imitation of the ancient Greeks and Romans. All the countries of central and western Europe had a renaissance, and the revival of classical learning, stimulated by a dispersion of Byzantine scholars with their Greek manuscripts when Constantinople fell to the Turks in 1453, was only one of the many forces that brought this about. The rise of the secular state, the growth of trade and industry, and, above all, the emergence of a spirit of daring which the Middle Ages had lacked were both causes and effects of the social upheaval which took place. Once the revolt from tradition had begun, men struck out in every direction to discover whatever they might find—on earth, in the heavens, and within the depths of the human spirit. The audacity that enabled Leonardo da Vinci to paint the Mona Lisa led mariners to brave the dangers of the deep. Pushing down the west coast of Africa, the Portuguese reached the Gulf of Guinea in 1460 and brought back slaves; in 1486 Bartholomew Diaz rounded the Cape of Good Hope. In 1492 a Genoese sailor who had settled in Portugal obtained money from a Spanish queen for an expedition to Asia by a new route leading due westward. His name, Columbus, might have been given to the continents he discovered across the Atlantic had not a printer named Walzmüller called them America (1507) for an obscure tradesman (Americo Vespucci) who happened to write an account of his travels along tropical coasts beyond the West Indies. Although Columbus failed to reach the East, Vasco da Gama inaugurated a trade route by sea between Europe and the Orient by sailing from Portugal to India (1497-1498) in only ten months and twelve days. In 1496, Henry VII sent John Cabot, a Venetian, to stake out England's claim to any new lands he might reach across the Atlantic above the southern seas. Cabot's report on Newfoundland, Labrador, and Cape Cod was discouraging, and English hopes of profitable trade with the new world faded. In 1519, Hernán Cortés landed in Mexico with four hundred white men and seized the wealth of the Aztecs. Twelve years later the Spaniard Pizarro, with fewer than two hundred soldiers, played both lion and fox to destroy the mighty Incan Empire and confiscate gold worth more than a hundred million dollars. In 1519, a fleet set sail under Magellan; three years later eighteen members of his crew, originally numbering about 275 men, returned home after having circumnavigated the globe. Francis Drake repeated this feat about sixty years later, after he had learned seamanship by tracking down on the high seas the treasure fleets of Spain. A world which had been known only in parts was now clearly seen as a whole.

During the Renaissance, the spirit of adventure rose high, and courage was little daunted by the tears of the bereaved for those who failed to return from expeditions. In the Renaissance there was the exuberance of youth, the boldness to attempt what never before had been done, the curiosity about everything, the self-confidence that created a current of revolt against tradition and authority which the prospect of torture or of sudden death could not hold back. The man who most nearly reflects in his life and work the spirit of the age is Leonardo da Vinci, of whom Preserved Smith says:

> To him the miracle of the world was in the mystery of knowledge—and he took all nature as his province. He gave his life and his soul for the mastery of science; he observed, he studied, he pondered everything. From the sun in the heavens to the insect on the ground, nothing was so large as to impose upon him, nothing too small to escape him. Weighing, measuring, experimenting, he dug deep for the inner reality of things; he spent years drawing the internal organs of the body, and other years making plans for engineers.
>
> When he painted, there was but one thing that fascinated him: the soul. To lay bare the mind as he had dissected the brain; to take man or woman at some self-revealing pose, to surprise the hidden secret of personality, all this was his passion, and in all this he excelled as no one had ever done, before or since.
>
> . . . It is difficult to appraise his work accurately because it is not yet fully known, and still more because of its extraordinary form. He left thousands of pages of notes on everything and hardly one complete treatise on anything. He began a hundred studies and finished none of them. He had a queer twist to his mind that made him, with all his power, seek byways. The monstrous, the uncouth, fascinated him; he saw a Medusa in a spider and the universe in a drop of water. He wrote his notes in mirror-writing, from right to left; he illustrated them with a thousand fragments of exqui-

site drawing, all unfinished and tantalizing alike to the artist and to the scientist. His mind roamed to flying machines and submarines, but he never made one; the reason given by him in the latter case being his fear that it would be put to piratical use.[3]

THE REFORMATION

The Renaissance and the Reformation, although separate and distinct movements, were not unrelated. On the contrary, both developed from an awakened curiosity about nature, man, and God, and represent certain of its various expressions. The former is sometimes referred to as a revival of letters, and the latter as a revival of religion; but, as the *Cambridge Modern History* points out,

> the distinction is neither formally correct nor materially exact. The Renaissance was not necessarily secular and classical—it might be, and often was, both religious and Christian; nor was the Reformation essentially religious and moral—it might be, and often was, political and secular.[4]

The Renaissance preceded the Reformation in time, but the spirit of reform was one of the influences that created the Renaissance. Schismatic movements within the Church were nothing new. The Waldensians in the twelfth century and the Lollards in the fourteenth had rebelled against the authority of the Pope. In Renaissance Italy, Savonarola was imprisoned, tortured, and executed for heresy. Nevertheless, the Reformation derives its name from an attempt to bring about certain reforms in the Catholic Church. The two movements are closely related; the Reformation, in a sense, completed the Renaissance to make clean the break with tradition and authority in matters sacred as well as secular.

As a Protestant revolt, the Reformation started when Martin Luther, a German monk who had become a Professor of Theology at the University of Wittenberg, nailed to the door of the church, as was the custom when debate was invited regarding theological matters, some arguments against the sale of indulgences. Pope Leo X had authorized the sale of indulgence tickets to raise money for building the new cathedral of St. Peter at Rome. This means of securing funds for Church purposes had been abused by misleading claims regarding the efficacy of the tickets and had been criticized by others, but Luther brought the matter to a head.

Intending at first only to correct what he regarded as certain abuses within the Church—the sale of indulgences, the corruption and wickedness of the Papal Court, the filling of German ecclesiastical offices with unworthy bishops, and other acts and conditions of a similar nature—Luther soon found himself leading a revolt against the Papacy. Having come to the conclusion that faith alone is sufficient for salvation, Luther saw no need for priests. When he took this position, he was excommunicated.

318 · Early Modern Social Thought

The Protestant movement spread as new translations of the Bible gave the word of God to anyone able to read, and as men of strong mind and iron determination shared Luther's doctrine of justification by faith. Among these were Ulrich Zwingli and John Calvin. The former led the German-speaking Swiss in setting up the Reformed, as distinct from the Lutheran, Protestant churches. Calvin was French, but he took refuge in Switzerland and carried on from Geneva the work of Protestantism. In 1536 he published *The Institutes of Christian Religion,* a systematic treatise which clearly stated the opposition to Rome. Calvinism spread rapidly to France, Germany, Holland, England, and Scotland; and when Calvin died, in 1564, a host of his followers were active in carrying on his work.

The Reformation was an economic and a political as well as a religious movement. The collapse of feudal organization had aroused the lower classes to demand equality. In the fourteenth century John Ball was hanged for asking

> When Adam dolve and Eve span,
> Who was then the gentleman?

But the masses now dared to raise the question anew. Luther's teaching helped, despite his intentions, to promote the Peasants' War of 1524-1525, a rebellion of German peasants against their landlords; and Calvin's doctrines encouraged, according to Max Weber, the rise of modern capitalism (see p. 334). Zwingli was a political as well as a religious leader; he met death in a civil war provoked by his efforts to reorganize the Swiss government. Calvin helped to arouse national self-consciousness, and his doctrine of ecclesiastical government aided the growth of the idea of popular sovereignty. The Reformation, therefore, far from being merely a Protestant revolt against Catholicism, was a "re-forming" of society. Its influence penetrated every important area of life and helped to bring about the radical social changes that took place during the transition from the medieval to the modern world.

AUTHORITY, REASON, AND EXPERIENCE

AUTHORITY

The revolt from the medieval order resulted initially not so much in the rejection of authority as in the substitution of one kind of authority for another. The men of the Renaissance adored and followed the pagan writers just as Christians had long adored and followed the saints, and the Reformation leaders rejected only the authority of the Church, not that of the Scriptures. Petrarch took Cicero as his idol and Rome's golden age as his ivory tower. "I dwelt especially upon antiquity," he says, "for our own age has always repelled me, so that, had it not been for the love of those dear to me, I should have preferred to have been born in any other period than our own. In order to forget my own time, I have constantly striven to place myself in spirit in other ages, and consequently I delighted in history." The impiety of Boccaccio was clothed in classical garb. The Protestants attacked the Pope by appeals to the authority of the Holy Scriptures, and both Luther and Calvin declared that it was a religious duty to accept the authority of the temporal ruler.

The leaders of the Reformation denied the authority of the individual conscience as vigorously as did the Catholics. The fires kindled at the Pope's command for heretics like Savonarola blazed afresh from fagots laid on by Calvin to burn the Spanish physician Michael Servetus.* As for civil government, the question for debate was who should hold the reins, not whether the reins might be dropped. Even the humanism of the age stifled, by its narrow focus on man's immediate well-being, general and theoretical interest in natural science, thus retarding the development of a truly scientific spirit of free inquiry.

REASON

A general distrust of human reason was at least partly responsible for the dependence upon authority during the Age of the Renaissance and the Reformation. The Catechism of the Council of Trent declares:

> He who is gifted with the heavenly knowledge of faith is free from an inquisitive curiosity; for when God commands us to believe, he does not propose to have us search into his divine judgments, nor to inquire their reasons and causes, but demands an immutable faith. . . . Faith, therefore, excludes not only all doubt, but even the desire of subjecting its truth to demonstration.[5]

Luther feared and detested "that silly little fool, that Devil's bride, Dame Reason, God's worst enemy."

> We know that reason is the Devil's harlot, and can do nothing but slander and harm all that God says and does. If, outside of Christ, you wish by your own thoughts to know your relation to God, you will break your neck. Thunder strikes him who examines. It is Satan's wisdom to tell what God is, and by doing so he will draw you into the abyss. Therefore keep to revelation and do not try to understand.[6]

Calvin likewise strongly opposed general discussion of the religious dogmas that he had helped to establish. What both the Catholics and the Protestants were objecting to, of course, was the intrusion of human reason into areas of experience where they believed religious faith should hold sway. However, to shut reason out of an important part of life was to discredit it as a tool of knowledge.

---

* Although Calvin personally preferred a less painful form of execution, Servetus was slowly burned to death.

Erasmus was not quite sure how the claims of reason and of faith could be reconciled. He says:

> Paul knew what Faith was, and yet when he saith, "Faith is the Substance of things hop'd for, and the Evidence of things not seen," he did not define it Doctor-like.[7]

Also, Erasmus was certain that reason could not override passion in human experience. Reason may shout her prohibitions until she is hoarse, he said, but the passions make such a hideous clamor until at last being wearied the man suffers himself "to be carried whither they please to hurry him." [8]

Francis Bacon, who belonged in spirit to the emerging scientific age, looked back and scowled at the old scholasticism based on unaided reason:

> This kind of degenerate learning did chiefly reign among the schoolmen, who, having sharp and strong wits, and abundance of leisure, and small variety of reading, but their wits being shut up in the cells of a few authors, chiefly Aristotle their dictator, as their persons were shut up in the cells of monasteries and colleges; and knowing little history, either of nature or time, did out of no great quantity of matter, and infinite agitation of wit, spin out unto us those laborious webs of learning which are extant in their books. For the wit and mind of man, if it work upon matter, which is the contemplation of the creatures of God, worketh according to the stuff and is limited thereby; but if it work upon itself, as the spider worketh its web, then it is endless, and brings forth indeed cobwebs of learning, admirable for the fineness of thread and work, but of no substance or profit.[9]

Bacon went even further in his criticism of unaided reason. In his emphasis on empirical observation and induction he neglected the part that creative intelligence plays in science.

> Our method of discovering the sciences is such as to leave little to the acuteness and strength of wit, and, indeed, rather to level wit and intellect. For as in the drawing of a straight line or accurate circle by the hand, much depends upon its steadiness and practice, but if a ruler or compass be employed there is little occasion for either, so it is with our method.[10]

Bacon himself accepted the principle of two truths, one for science, based on experience and induction, and the other for religion, based on faith. He died without knowing that Descartes was about to crown reason with sovereign powers in both fields of knowledge.

EXPERIENCE

Preserved Smith says of the sixteenth century:

> It was an "experiencing" age. It loved sensation with the greediness of childhood; it intoxicated itself with Rabelais and Titian, with the gold of

> Peru and with the spices and vestments of the Orient. It was a daring age. Men stood bravely with Luther for spiritual liberty, or they gave their lives with Magellan to compass the earth or with Bruno to span the heavens. It was an age of aspiration. It dreamed with Erasmus of the time when men should be Christ-like, or with More of the place where they should be just; or with Michelangelo it pondered the meaning of sorrow, or with Montaigne it stored up daily wisdom. . . . Truly such a generation was not a poor, nor a backward one. Rather it was great in what it achieved, sublime in what it dreamed; abounding in ripe wisdom and in heroic deeds; full of light and of beauty and of life.[11]

This craving for experience led eventually not only to increased knowledge but also to a realization of the value of experience as a means of acquiring knowledge.

The monk Roger Bacon had argued in the thirteenth century in favor of experimental science, but he was so far in advance of his time that he suffered imprisonment for his efforts. During the next three centuries, scientific knowledge of the earth and the heavens increased enormously, but there was surprisingly little interest in the methods by which this knowledge was gained. Science is more than knowledge itself; it is a way of acquiring knowledge; but during the Age of the Renaissance and the Reformation interest lay primarily in the matter of science rather than in the method. The empirical method is consciously employed when men turn to experience for answers to certain questions they have raised. Only when they say, "Let us determine from experience what is true," is the method of science recognized. When Bacon said that the natural scientist must "put Nature to the question," he stated the basic principle of experimental natural science. Columbus was attempting to find a new route to India, not to verify a hypothesis, when he discovered the New World. Vasco da Gama, Diaz, and Magellan were explorers, not scientists in the sense of seekers after truth; the earth was circumnavigated for the sake of adventure and trade. The final empirical proof of the roundness of the earth, earlier discovered by the Greek mathematician Thales, probably aroused little general interest, even among those who established it.

Although the value of experience in establishing knowledge was not generally understood, there was growth in the methods of science as well as in the accumulation of empirical facts. In seeking in nature answers to the questions that the heliocentric theory of Copernicus had raised, such men as Tycho Brahe, Kepler, and Galileo belong in spirit to the succeeding age, as does the physician Vesalius, who learned anatomy from observation. In asking what might be learned about human nature and social relationships from experience, Montaigne was following, though unknowingly, the method of empirical science. Bacon was inspired by Montaigne to become a scientist, but he failed, as we have seen, to understand the whole nature of science. Smith's description of the period as an "ex-

322 · Early Modern Social Thought

periencing age" is, therefore, an apt one. Experience is necessary to science, but it is not sufficient.

In summary, we may observe that the age presents a confusion of methods. Authority was questioned, especially that of the Pope, but not all authority. Reason was distrusted, but men dared to think for themselves. Explorers reached across the seas and into the heavens for new experience, and realists looked at princes and described them as they saw them. Twilight was setting over an age of faith. An age of reason was beginning to show dimly, as if illuminated only by the clear, cool light of the moon. But the dawn of a new age, the dazzling age of science, was not far off.

HUMAN NATURE

The discovery of the vast physical world aroused interest, of course, in natural phenomena; but it did not cause scholars to abandon interest in man, his ideas, and his institutions. On the contrary, the liberation of human thought from the narrow confines of scholasticism led to persistent speculation about social phenomena. The extent to which the ever-present vision of Judgment Day had inhibited man's thought about himself during the Middle Ages is well revealed in an old hymn:

> Day of wrath, that day when the world shall fall into ashes, witness David and the Sibyl.
>
> How great a trembling will there be, when the judge shall come, to examine closely all our deeds.
>
> What shall I, wretch, say then, what protector shall I invoke, when even a good man shall scarcely be safe? [12]

In these verses, says Tillyard, from whose work this hymn is quoted, "you see the negation of humanism, of any human virtue, in man's own right, especially in the last line. Mankind is lost and wicked; and even a good man . . . is in a precarious position." [13] The revival of humanism was as important a characteristic of the new age as was the discovery of the physical universe.

RENAISSANCE HUMANISM

The humanism which began in Italy during the Renaissance as a conscious imitation of the spirit of classical Rome meant that

> . . . now the barriers so long imposed on the exercise of the reason were broken down; not all at once, but by degrees. It was recognized that there had been a time when men had used all their faculties of mind and imagination without fear or reproof; not restricted to certain paths or

bound by formulas, but freely seeking for knowledge in every field of speculation, and for beauty in all the realms of fancy. Those men had bequeathed to posterity a literature different in quality and range from anything that had been written for a thousand years. They had left, too, works of architecture such that even the mutilated remains had been regarded by legend as the work of supernatural beings whom heathen poets had constrained by spells. The pagan view was now once more proclaimed, that man was made, not only to toil and suffer, but to enjoy. And naturally enough, in the first reaction from a more ascetic ideal, the lower side of ancient life obscured, with many men, its better aspects. It was thus that Humanism first appeared, bringing a claim for the mental freedom of man, and for the full development of his being.[14]

The lust for living was strong. Men found life good here and now, and warmed their hands before its fires. Erasmus laughed and wrote of folly and of marriage, and More gleefully created Utopia to provide a more fitting abode for mankind. Montaigne regarded all things human as worthy of observation and proudly announced that he would show himself in his "simple, natural, and everyday dress, without artifice or constraint." Rabelais said of himself, "You never saw a man who would more love to be a king or to be rich than I would, so that I could live richly and not work and not worry, and that I might enrich all my friends and all good, wise people." A drinking song in *Gammer Gurton's Needle* is expressive of the reckless mood of men impious and intoxicated from deep draughts of freedom:

> I cannot eat but little meat,
>   My stomach is not good;
> But sure I think that I can drink
>   With him that wears a hood.
> Tho' I go bare, take ye no care,
>   I nothing am a-cold,
> I stuff my skin so full within
>   Of jolly good ale and old,
>
> Back and side, go bare, go bare,
>   Both foot and hand go cold;
> But, belly, God send thee good ale enough,
>   Whether it be new or old.

Love of knowledge was matched by fear of it, and an itinerant charlatan by the name of Faust came to be a symbol for knowledge bought at any price. Marlowe pointed the moral in the Faust legend when he quoted Faustus as saying:

> Philosophy is odious and obscure;
> Both law and physics are for petty wits;

> Divinity is the basest of the three. . . .
> 'Tis magic, magic, that hath ravished me.

Nevertheless, from a surfeit of morality which the Middle Ages had imposed upon them, men turned gladly to new sources of stimulation and suddenly discovered that they were not afraid. The open seas beckoned; the starry skies invited observation as well as awe; men became conscious of powers that they had not known they possessed; as hopes ran high, utopia and universal peace seemed near at hand; the urge to strive, to seek, and to know drove men on to explore the vast spaces of the earth and probe the innermost recesses of human nature.

THE NATURE OF MAN

The picture of man that emerges from this probing is as perplexing as the smile of Mona Lisa. There is not lacking the adoration of man which later found such eloquent expression in *Hamlet*:

> What a piece of work is a man! How noble in reason, how infinite in faculty, in form and moving how express and admirable, in action how like an angel, in apprehension how like a god! the beauty of the world, the paragon of animals.

Yet kindly, gentle Erasmus, who wrote with his tongue in his cheek so that we cannot quite understand him, called woman "a stupid animal, God wot, and a giddy one, yet funny and sweet," and observed that most men play the fool and that there is not one who does not "dote in many ways."

Montaigne, whom Emerson called "the frankest and honestest" of all writers, found in human nature little of the warmth of fellow-feeling; his apparent callousness toward his own children seems strangely fitting. He gloried in his body and claimed to have no fears for his soul. He called philosophy "sophisticated poetry" and declared that all men strive "to plaster up and corroborate their accepted beliefs with all the power of their reason, which is a supple tool, pliant and adaptable to any figure." [15]

Machiavelli gave his Prince this cynical advice:

> A prince being . . . obliged to know well how to act as a beast must imitate the fox and the lion, for the lion cannot protect himself from traps, and the fox cannot defend himself from wolves. One must therefore be a fox to recognise traps, and a lion to frighten wolves. Those that wish to be only lions do not understand this. Therefore, a prudent ruler ought not to keep faith when by so doing it would be against his interest, and when the reasons which made him bind himself no longer exist. If men were all good, this precept would not be a good one; but as they are bad, and would not observe their faith with you, so you are not bound to keep faith with them.[16]

In numerous other passages Machiavelli reveals his convictions about human nature:

> Men never behave well unless they are obliged; wherever a choice is open to them and they are free to do as they like, everything is immediately filled with confusion and disorder. . . . Whoever organises a State, or lays down laws in it, must necessarily assume that all men are bad, and that they will follow the wickedness of their own hearts, whenever they have free opportunity to do so; and, supposing any wickedness to be temporarily hidden, it is due to a secret cause of which, having seen no experience to the contrary, men are ignorant; but time, which they say is the father of all truth, reveals it at last.[17]

Although such statements plucked from Machiavelli's work without regard to context do injustice to the man himself, they do afford an insight into a view of human nature that appears to have been widely held in his day. We must recall that his was not a saintly age. Cust says:

> At the beginning of the sixteenth century Italy was rotten to the core. In the close competition of great wickedness the Vicar of Christ easily carried off the palm, and the court of Alexander VI was probably the wickedest meeting place of men that has ever existed upon earth. No virtue, Christian or Pagan, was there to be found: little art that was not sensuous or sensual. It seemed as if Bacchus and Venus and Priapus had come to their own again, and yet Rome had not ceased to call herself Christian.[18]

When worldly men like Montaigne and Machiavelli could hold such harsh views regarding man's nature, the anguished outpourings of the moralist Calvin are easily understood. He says:

> The mind of man is so entirely alienated from the righteousness of God that he cannot conceive, desire, or design anything but what is wicked, distorted, impure, and iniquitous; that his heart is so thoroughly envenomed by sin, that it can breathe out nothing but corruption and rottenness; that if some men occasionally make a show of goodness, their mind is ever interwoven with hypocrisy and deceit, their soul inwardly bound with the fetters of wickedness.[19]

Luther's conception of grace denies man's ability to rise above his sinful nature by any means within his own control. His emphasis on the authority of the minister of true religion shows lack of confidence in the ability of the individual to regulate his own life. Luther accepts the principle of a duality in human nature, with the spirit ever at war with the flesh, but he declares that the human spirit is not able without grace even to love God. "The greater number of men," he says, "are, and always will be, unchristian, whether they be baptised or not." Especially did he distrust the common man. He took the side of authority when the peasants revolted, saying, "The donkey needs a thrashing, and the brute populace must be governed by brute force."

Thus, in an age when the spirit of adventure and daring ran high, when the old ideas and institutions were no longer regarded as eternal, when the natural order was being discovered and the social order transformed, when there seemed to be every reason for men to feel confidence in themselves, there was widespread lack of faith in mankind. Swinburne's impudent boast, "Glory to Man in the highest! for Man is the master of things," may have quivered on their lips, but it was not in their hearts. The leaders of the age saw to that. From Machiavelli to John Calvin, they proclaimed with one voice the depravity of human nature.

POLITICS

Two very closely related problems, political unity and the reconciliation of freedom with authority, dominated political thinking in the Age of the Renaissance and the Reformation. Political disunity resulted more particularly from the breakdown of feudalism and from Renaissance morality; the conflict between freedom and authority stemmed from the loss of faith in a universal empire and from Reformation individualism. The prevalent opinion during the Middle Ages was that governments exist to help the individual attain salvation. Machiavelli is censured today because he attempted to show how governments attain strength. Disregarding ethics and religion in his analysis of politics, he stated in bold language some effective tricks of governing. He saw Italy torn apart by political disunity and, casting aside scruples, he declared: "Where the safety of one's country is at stake there must be no consideration of what is just or unjust, merciful or cruel, glorious or shameful; on the contrary, everything must be disregarded save that course which will save her life and maintain her independence." [20]

With regard to the second problem, the leaders of the Reformation had to discover how men free to worship God according to the dictates of their own consciences could accommodate themselves to the absolute authority of an earthly king. It was clear that freedom from the control of the church would lead to anarchy unless some other authority were recognized. Luther, who had not at first intended to rebel against the Pope but had sought only to bring about certain reforms in the church, witnessed the spread of revolt against established authority with alarm and sought to stem it by supporting the development of a strong secular power able to check the excesses of the "unchristian" masses. Calvin declared that, without the restraint imposed by government, men live "pell-mell like rats in the straw." Thus, the Protestant leaders shared Machiavelli's conviction that the selfish impulses of "ungrateful, fickle, deceitful, cowardly, and avaricious" men must be held firmly in check by the leaders responsible for the welfare of the state. Furthermore, as Luther and Calvin were quick to point out, the Scriptures require absolute obedience to the temporal ruler.

This line of reasoning supported the claims of earthly kings to sovereign powers, and there the matter might have rested, with a general acceptance of totalitarian forms of government, had not the Scriptures also commanded obedience to God rather than to man. Good Christians had to decide what to do when the king issued commands which they believed to be contrary to the will of God. The Scriptures also contain, to be sure, an answer to that question, but although it is easy to render unto Caesar the things that are Caesar's so long as Caesar does not demand what rightfully belongs to God, how is one to know where Caesar's domain ends? A dilemma arises when a legitimate civil authority attempts to deny the individual the right to follow the dictates of his own conscience. This problem had been of only minor importance during the Middle Ages, when the Pope was the highest authority both secular and spiritual. But when a king speaks only as man, and the voice of God is heard in the individual conscience, there is likely to arise among serious and devout persons a conflict of loyalties. The Age of the Renaissance and the Reformation did not find a satisfactory solution to this problem, nor has any other age, but it is enlightening to review the efforts made at that time to cope with it.

ROOTS OF NATIONALISM

Nationalism flowered in the eighteenth century, but its roots took hold during the Renaissance and the Reformation. The emergence of strong states in England, France, Germany, and Spain as a result of various social conditions created a feeling of unity and aroused sentiments of national self-consciousness. The blind loyalty to country which was to give the modern state a halo of divinity was less intense then than it has been in later times, but patriotism was not lacking. Although the following lines come from Shakespeare, they express a pride in country felt by Machiavelli, Sir Thomas More, and many others who lived before the Elizabethan Age:

> This royal throne of Kings, this sceptered isle,
> This earth of majesty, this seat of Mars,
> This other Eden, demi-paradise,
> This fortress built by Nature for herself
> Against infection and the hand of war,
> This happy breed of men, this little world,
> This precious stone set in the silver sea,
> Which serves it in the office of a wall
> Or as a moat defensive to a house,
> Against the envy of less happier lands,
> This blessed plot, this earth, this realm, this England.[21]

Boastful pride and humble submission go hand in hand, and it was a simple matter for the masses of people to transfer an allegiance which they had given fully to feudal nobles and bishops to the community as a whole; the habit of obedience was established before the state emerged. The sovereign authority in control of the government, whether a single person or a body of men, came to be recognized as the symbol of the community's solidarity and the bearer of its hopes for security and prosperity. The sacred duty to the church was transformed by the Reformation into the sacred duty to the king, who had assumed divine prerogatives.

The medieval idea of political organization for moral ends still persisted, but an acute awareness of the value of political organization for material ends began to develop. Collective action in war and in trade built up a feeling of solidarity within the community and established its territorial boundaries. People organized under a single government and occupying a limited geographical area form a state, in the modern sense of the term; and, although the nature of a state was at that time not fully understood, it seems clear that states bearing close resemblance to modern forms did actually come into existence during the fifteenth and sixteenth centuries, and that some of the modern conceptions of the state began to form during those centuries.

The medieval idea that civil government exists to facilitate personal salvation was not entirely rejected, but it ceased to claim universal acceptance. Machiavelli saw that the power structure of the state exists apart from any direct or necessary connection with the will of God. Luther attributed the existence of the state to God's command to wicked men to obey their rulers, thus opening the way for the creation of as many states as there were strong men able to form them. Calvinism, despite its teaching of obedience to established authority, fostered a spirit of political self-determination. Erasmus, who hoped to see Latin become a universal language and who was equally at home in Holland, France, England, Italy, Germany, and Switzerland, pleaded in vain for a united rather than a divided world. He himself loved moderation and hated excess in any form, including that of patriotism. He wished that states might not be called by separate names. "The entire world is one fatherland," he declared; "why do foolish names still exist to keep us sundered, since we are united in the name of Christ?" Nevertheless, the rising tide of nationalism swept over him, drowning out his pleas for peace.

AUTHORITY OF TEMPORAL RULERS

The right of the duly constituted head of the state, whether a single person or a body of citizens, to exercise almost unlimited authority over secular matters was widely accepted. Luther, Calvin, Melanchthon, Tyndale, and many other Protestant leaders were in complete accord on this point. They agreed, furthermore, that the personal character of the ruler did not affect the obligation to obey him;

wicked monarchs were entitled to the same submission accorded good monarchs. Luther was contemptuous of princes, calling them "the biggest fools or the worst knaves on earth," but he strongly supported their claim to obedience from their subjects. Calvin said:

> Even an individual of the worst character, one most unworthy of all honour, if invested with public authority, receives that illustrious divine power which the Lord has by his Word devolved on the ministers of his justice and judgment, and accordingly . . . in so far as public obedience is concerned, he is to be held in the same honour and reverence as the best of kings.[22]

There are several explanations of this doctrine of virtually unqualified obedience to any ruler who happened to be in office: (1) the Scriptures make obedience to civil magistrates a religious duty; (2) the struggling Protestant bodies needed at that time the support of local princes; and (3) the people were not trusted. On this last point Luther shared Calvin's pessimism about the fate of society when the masses try to govern themselves, and bluntly said:

> The princes of this world are gods, the common people are Satan, through whom God sometimes does what at other times he does directly through Satan, that is, makes rebellion as a punishment for the people's sins. . . . I would rather suffer a prince doing wrong than a people doing right.[23]

Jean Bodin, the sixteenth-century French political writer whose principal work, *The Six Books of the Republic,* is an early example of the application of the method of science to political analysis, saw that the existence of the state, whether it be a monarchy, an aristocracy, a democracy, or any other form, depends upon the possession by its highest authority of the right to make laws and impose them on all its members. He saw that sovereignty means being above all human law, including that of the sovereign, since the monarch is not bound by the laws he makes.

The right forcibly to resist rulers being denied because, as Luther said, if men had this right "there would remain neither authority nor obedience anywhere in the world," there would seem to be no escape from tyranny. In fact, Calvin declared that God chastens sinners with despotic princes and gives men the kind of government they deserve:

> Wherefore, if we are cruelly vexed by an inhuman Prince or robbed and plundered by one prodigal or avaricious or despised and left without protection by one negligent; or even if we are afflicted for the Name of God by one sacriligious and unbelieving, let us first of all remember those our own offences against God which doubtless are chastised by these plagues. And secondly let us consider that it is not for us to remedy these evils; for

us it remains only to implore the aid of God, in whose hand are the hearts of Kings and the changes of kingdoms.²⁴

But although it is for God and not man to punish wicked princes, the doctrine of passive submission does not relieve the individual from the duty to obey God rather than men. "If they command anything against God," says Calvin, "it ought not to have the least attention, nor in this case ought we to pay any regard to the dignity attached to magistrates."

It seems clear, therefore, that despite numerous references in the writings of the age to the absolute authority of rulers, the Christian leaders at least never acknowledged the claim of civil magistrates to completely arbitrary powers. They made passive disobedience a sacred duty whenever a ruler issued commands contrary to the laws of God, claiming that in such instances the ruler was acting without legitimate authority and did not have to be obeyed because it was not really the ruler who spoke. This is subtle reasoning, but it did produce a claim to religious freedom in a state in which all other freedoms were denied.

RELATIONS BETWEEN CHURCH AND STATE

If, as Calvin believed, it is the first duty of secular leaders to ensure that citizens are guided in their private and public activities by true religion, the complete separation of church and state is impossible. More wanted to see the secular and the ecclesiastical organizations united, whereas Luther sought in his earliest writings to make a sharp distinction between their spheres of authority, even to the extent of relieving secular officers from the obligation of maintaining true religion. "Heresy," he said, "can never be contained by force. . . . God's word must do the fighting here; and if that avail not, then will it remain unchecked by temporal authorities though they fill the world with blood." Luther was not able, however, to hold to this unequivocal position. In fact he came finally to the view that where social order is threatened, the temporal authorities should employ force to maintain true religion.

Luther's position in this matter sheds light on his views regarding absolutism. If the secular ruler is free to decide what he will do about supporting religion in the state, it is difficult to see how he is limited by any power above him. The British historian, J. W. Allen, is certain that Luther never went this far:

> I wish to emphasise the point that, whatever his view at the moment, there is just one thing that Luther never says. He says that religious persecution is futile, he even says it is unjust; he says it is necessary, and he says it is a duty. But never for a moment did he admit that it was for the secular sovereign to decide for himself whether or no to tolerate heresy. To him persecution was either altogether wrong or it was a sheer duty. He never quite knew which it was. But in this as in other matters Luther's view was never reconcilable with any theory of absolutism in the state.²⁵

Calvin's position is less confusing: he emphatically stated that magistrates are subordinate to a higher law. They are foolish, he says, who "would wish the magistrates to neglect all thoughts of God, and to confine themselves entirely to the administration of justice among men; as though God appointed governors in His name to decide secular controversies and disregarded what is of far greater importance, the pure worship of Himself according to the rule of His law." [26] In so far as the relations of church and state are concerned, the crux of the matter is the question of who is to interpret that rule. The doctrine of obedience becomes confused when the right of godly people to rebel against an ungodly ruler is recognized. As W. R. Matthews says:

> The reservation which Calvin made to his doctrine of obedience, that we must obey God rather than man, cannot easily be confined, as he confined it, to the question of worship. It may be that God has commands other than those concerning cult and Church, and that in the State itself the maxim applies. If we had to sum up Calvin's influence in a phrase we could not find a better one than this: he taught his disciples that we must obey God rather than men. His weaknesses arise from the fact that he was too positive that he knew always what God commanded.[27]

POLITICS AND ETHICS

To Machiavelli belongs the credit, or the blame, for the discovery that the state can be examined as a power structure without regard to its ultimate moral ends. He neither denied nor affirmed the doctrine that the state is a moral institution; he simply avoided passing moral judgment on the way in which states appeared to him to operate most efficiently. The task of the prince, as he saw it, is to maintain order and to increase the power of his state, since without order and power the state cannot endure. Since religion helps him to achieve both of these objectives, the prince ought to encourage religion in the state. Whether or not the prince himself believes in the religion he supports is a matter of little importance, as is the question of its truth or falsity. Machiavelli felt that something like the old Roman religion, which inspired citizens to serve the state, might well prove to be more useful to the prince than Christianity.

In private advice, intended for the guidance of his prince and not for publication, Machiavelli formulated certain principles of governing that have been publicly denounced by almost everyone who has expressed an opinion on the subject, and privately practiced by many dictators since Machiavelli's time. The prince, he says, "should look mainly to the successful maintenance of his state. The means which he employs for this will always be accounted honorable"—if he succeeds. He should appear "all sincerity, all uprightness, all humanity, all religion," so that he may be loved as well as feared. If he must give up love or fear, it is better to be feared. In his political realism Machiavelli is brutally frank.

> How laudable it is for a prince to keep good faith and live with integrity, and not with astuteness, every one knows. Still the experience of our times shows those princes to have done great things who have had little regard for good faith, and have been able by astuteness to confuse men's brains, and who have ultimately overcome those who have made loyalty their foundation.[28]
>
> . . . Where the deliberation is wholly touching the safety of the fatherland there ought to be no consideration of just or unjust, pitiful or cruel, honourable or dishonourable, but rather, all other respect being laid aside, that course ought to be taken which may preserve the life and maintain the liberty thereof.[29]

For expressing such opinions Machiavelli has been repeatedly and vigorously denounced. It is not quite accurate to say, however, that he completely divorced politics from ethics. What he did was to look at politics empirically rather than ethically, and to take an extremely narrow view. He observed that states need order and power in order to exist, and he endeavored to point out to his prince the means which had been effectively used to gain these ends. Success in achieving a desired end proves that the means employed were good—that is, they were effective—and that is what Machiavelli means by "good" in this context. Machiavelli did not ask whether a state ought to pursue the ends of order and power, just as today we do not as a rule ask whether a state ought to manufacture deadly instruments of war. His science had about as little to do with ultimate ends as does our own and was concerned, as is ours, with practical, commonsense means.

Machiavelli has been called both "immoral" and "unmoral." Perhaps "relentless empiricism" accurately describes his politics. Certainly, in his preoccupation with material prosperity, order, and power, he had little in common with the Greeks, who conceived of the state as an instrument of man's self-realization, or with the churchmen, who saw the state dimly as a part of the great drama of salvation, or, finally, with the religiously minded of his day, who believed that the state exists to promote piety and morality.

ECONOMICS

During the Age of the Renaissance and the Reformation the economic institutions of Europe were changing rapidly. The old social order, in which wealth was in land, and production was largely for local consumption, was giving way to a new social order, in which a considerable amount of wealth was in money. By the seventeenth century some modern economic institutions which had earlier been seen only in rudimentary form began to crystallize.

One striking change was a trend toward control of the economy by the state rather than by small groups within the state or by the church. During the fourteenth century the medieval idea of the "just price" was yet in evidence. Change of residence or occupation was still hampered or prevented by numerous regulations. Merchants were permitted to use only the trade routes assigned to them and were allowed to offer their goods only in certain markets. The guilds still controlled their members, and the freedom of the individual craftsman was severely limited for the sake of the corporate whole. But economic forces which no regulatory bodies then in existence could control were working to transform a natural economy, based on the actual exchange of goods and services and fettered by morality and custom, to a money economy, based on payment for goods and services in gold and silver and comparatively free. In short, the rise of capitalism had begun.

CAPITALISM

The crude systems of barter used in the Middle Ages had sufficed for virtually self-contained communities whose members shared much in common. When, however, gold and silver began to pour in from mines at home and abroad in sufficient quantities to afford a money basis for exchanging goods, the simple primitive systems of local exchange and sharing gave way. Wealth in money meant that economic power could be concentrated and used to stimulate trade, establish industry, exploit natural resources, and create new wealth.

> In competition with capital the medieval communism succumbed in one line of business after another—in banking, in trade, in mining, in industry and finally in agriculture—because it was unable to produce the results that capital produced. By the vast reward that the newer system gave to individual enterprise, to technical improvement and to investment, capitalism proved the aptest tool for the creation and preservation of wealth ever devised.[30]

The rise of capitalism was accompanied by a vast increase of interest in worldly activity. The otherworldly orientation of the Middle Ages has been much exaggerated, but the fact remains that the current of belief that this world is wicked and permanently lost to Satan ran deep for many centuries in medieval Christendom. The command "Love not the world" was interpreted literally and obeyed by untold numbers of people who fixed their gaze longingly on the eternal Kingdom of God. Even Thomas Aquinas regarded worldly activity as a necessary evil. The Renaissance encouraged men to withdraw their fixed gaze from the heavens, and the Reformation rebuilt on earth a City of God. Luther never broke completely with the traditional view that God rules the world and assigns men their places in it. Too much worldly activity seemed to him to indicate a belief in salvation through good works, and he held to the doctrine of salvation by faith alone.

But where Luther stopped short, Calvin plunged ahead to make sober activity in this world a sacred duty. The world in which we live, said Calvin, is God's world, and we are his stewards. All is, to be sure, in God's hand, and we can save neither ourselves nor the world by our efforts, but it is our duty to work hard and try to get ahead; if we prosper, we prove to ourselves and to our fellows that we are among God's elect.

Max Weber has shown that through this line of reasoning Calvin created an attitude toward life which favored the rise of "modern" capitalism. He points out that Calvinism gave the West "a doctrine of rational mastery over the world" and he shows that the failure of the great nations of the East to derive from their religions a corresponding incentive to produce explains in part their servitude to tradition.* The contrast between the East and the West in this respect is illuminating.

> The notable feature of the Chinese social structure is not only its complete failure to root out traditionalism but a sanctification of tradition, second only to that of India. The attitude that the classics, which were the subject of education of every scholar, could never be improved upon is to be contrasted with the inherently dynamic character of Western science. In addition, in China there is a notable absence of any sanction for impersonal specialized functions. The educated man is never the technical specialist but rather the well-rounded cultivated gentleman. Finally, there is also a notable absence of universalism in Confucian ethics. Loyalty to one's own kinship group and one's own particular friends and associates supersedes all generalized obligations as to honesty, truth, and so on.[31]

According to Weber, Calvinism gave "modern" capitalism the following religious foundations: (1) a gospel of work that exalts sober worldly activity to a "calling"; and (2) a doctrine of asceticism based on the belief that since "man is only a trustee of the goods which have come to him through God's grace," he must avoid conspicuous consumption and every form of extravagance.

MERCANTILISM

Capitalism and nationalism united in a policy which came to be known as *mercantilism*. This policy did not develop fully until the seventeenth century, but some of the principles that gave it support can be found in the works of writers of earlier centuries. Before the state could set itself up as a business enterprise and engage in trade with other states similarly organized, the medieval beliefs that money was sterile and foreign trade deplorable had to give way. A number of Renaissance and Reformation leaders helped to undermine the old convictions about money and foreign trade. Thomas More saw the advantages of having gold and silver brought into a country, and for that reason he permitted

---

* See Max Weber, *The Protestant Ethic and The Spirit of Capitalism,* trans. Talcott Parsons (London: George Allen and Unwin, 1930).

the citizens of Utopia to engage in foreign trade. In his dictum "Money is the nerve of the commonwealth," Bodin expressed the growing awareness that money is an important form of wealth. He also realized that a favorable balance of trade enables a nation to accumulate money. Thus he grasped the essential character of mercantilist policy—increase the wealth of the state by selling abroad more goods than are purchased and thus gaining gold and silver.

The esteem in which money was held appeared to be justified by the uses to which it could be put. The ruler with money could hire mercenaries and in other ways build up the military strength of his nation. Rich nations had a great advantage over poor nations in the rivalry for possession of newly discovered natural resources, and money was far superior to other forms of wealth as an instrument for use in economic warfare. But gold and silver were believed to be even more important for domestic uses than for foreign: money stimulated commercial and industrial activity within a nation as apparently nothing else could. "If there be money in the country," said Colbert, a seventeenth-century mercantilist, "the universal desire to turn it to advantage makes people set it in motion, and the public funds benefit thereby." The prosperity of individual citizens, as well as that of the state, was generally regarded as desirable, despite Machiavelli's assertion that the prince ought to make himself rich and keep the people poor.

Since money and power appeared to go hand in hand, the new states struggling for power looked to gold and silver for strength, as the ancient and medieval kingdoms had looked to God. Money, long condemned as a chief source of evil, was made respectable, and the hard labor by which it is acquired was even exalted by Calvinism to the position of man's supreme form of activity on earth. Mercantilist policy has undergone many changes over the years, but the responsibility of the state for the material prosperity of its members which this policy helped to establish is one of the guiding principles of political activity in the modern world. Since the sixteenth century, politics has been concerned less with the moral ends of the state, in the sense in which ancient and medieval theorists discussed the aims of political organization, than with more immediate and practical ends, such as wealth and power.

USURY

One moral issue that might have blocked the advance of capitalism was the ancient prohibition against usury. Capitalism means, among other things, making money with money. As good Christians saw money being loaned out for capitalistic enterprises, they could not avoid asking themselves if interest-taking were compatible with brotherly love. Luther and Melanchthon simply brushed the matter aside by declaring that the ancient Deuteronomic commandment to Jews was not applicable to sixteenth-century Christians. Zwingli shared this opinion, saying that only "by torturing the texts" could an absolute prohibition against taking interest on money loaned to a fellow Christian be supported by the Scriptures. Luther disliked the practice of usury, but he saw no reason to forbid it, provided the interest charged was not excessive.

Calvin went much further: he maintained that the Scriptures actually justify usury. The Mosaic law on this subject, he says, was intended only to ensure that "mutual and brotherly affection should prevail amongst the Israelites." Since it did not deny Jews the right to take interest on money loaned to Christians, God clearly did not intend to forbid usury altogether. "If we wholly condemn usury," Calvin declares, "we impose tighter fetters on the conscience than God himself." To denounce usury, as Calvin did, only "in so far as it contravenes equity and brotherly union" was to open the way to all sorts of profitable uses of capital. By taking his position, good Protestants were able to engage in making money with money without troubled consciences.

The opposition to usury did not end with the sixteenth century, but even at that time Bodin offered economic rather than religious objections to the practice. It leads to speculation, he said, and to gross inequalities in wealth. He claimed that wherever a low rate of interest is permitted, an exorbitant rate is likely soon to follow. In these and other objections which he raised, the significant thing is that he did not rely upon the authority of the Scriptures to support his position. Once the pressure of that authority had been relieved, the way was open for devout Christians to engage in money-making activities even where exploitation of the needs of others was involved.

Calvin's pronouncement gave pious businessmen all the freedom they needed. The friendship morality of Judaism and medieval Christianity, which made every man his brother's keeper and thus denied any man the right to take advantage of his brother's need, gave way to an individualistic morality that did not distinguish between brother and alien. Where business is business, the sentiments of brotherhood are out of place. The universal business ethics, without which capitalism as we know it could not have developed, represent the substitution of rational rules of conduct for the emotional bonds of brotherhood.

FAMILY

The emergence of the national state did not immediately lessen the importance of the family or limit the exercise by it of those functions with which it had long been associated. A domestic economy still prevailed; children received their education, religious guidance, and discipline in the family; love and affection found their richest expression in the relationships of the home; and generally the family still served as the basic unit of society. Some claimed that family life is a gift of God to man, and others that the disciplines of the home are natural and necessary; but all agreed that the state is composed of family cells. More's Utopia was a society formed by discrete patriarchal family groups. Luther declared that the family is a divine institution founded by God and maintained at his command for the procreation of children and the control of lust. Bodin believed that the family is an inevitable form of human association, arising out of individual needs and serving to protect common property.

Despite a high regard for the family generally, the various family institutions were made matters of heated dispute. Monogamy was the custom, but polygamy was recognized as permissible. The Catholics said that marriage was sacred and forbade divorce absolutely, but Protestants such as Luther said that marriage was only "something extrinsic like any other worldly affair" and permitted divorce under certain circumstances. Both groups of Christian leaders condemned adultery, but adultery was common. The Protestants said that the married state was higher than the state of virginity, but the Council of Trent said the opposite. As if to prove to all mankind that the old system had gone forever, Luther, a monk, married a nun who bore him six children.

Since many of the thorny family problems with which we still have to contend developed at that time, it should prove profitable to examine some of the main issues of dispute. The position of women in society, the nature of marriage, and the proper relationships in the home were matters of great interest to the men and women of the Renaissance and the Reformation, and the echoes of what they said on these important subjects can still be heard.

ATTITUDE TOWARD WOMEN

The Middle Ages presented two attitudes toward women: adoration in the abstract and scorn in the concrete experiences of daily life. The Renaissance intensified both of these attitudes, and the Reformation projected them into the future with such force that they have endured to our own day. In the early fourteenth century, the Medical Faculty at Paris considered the question of allowing women to take medical degrees, whereas in the late sixteenth century certain learned men of Wittenberg doubted publicly that women should be regarded as human beings. This proves not that the position of women deteriorated during the time that elapsed between these interesting debates but only that the age failed to clarify thought about women and left to later centuries the question of deciding what the proper attitude toward them should be.

Montaigne's opinions probably reflect an attitude not uncommon in his day. In an introduction to an edition of Montaigne's *Essays,* André Gide says: "I have noted all the passages in the *Essays* in which he speaks of them [women]; there is not one that is not insulting." [32] Erasmus never wished to insult anyone, least of all women, but when he asked himself why women should be educated, the answer he gave was that if they were taught to read, they ought then to give "more diligent heed to the sermons preached in the church." An "amusing but significant picture" that Erasmus gives us of the marital experience of his good friend Sir Thomas More is most revealing.

> A young gentleman [More] married a maiden [Jane Colt] of seventeen years who had been educated in the country and who, being inexperienced, he trusted to form easily in manners to his own humour. He began to instruct her in literature and music, and by degrees to repeat the heads of sermons which she heard, and generally to acquire the accomplishments he wished her to possess. Used at home to nothing but gossip and play she at length refused to submit to further training and when pressed about it threw herself down and beat her head on the ground as though she wished for death. Her husband concealed his resentment and carried her off for a holiday to her home. Out hunting with his father-in-law he told his troubles and was urged to use his authority and beat her. He replied that he knew his power but had much rather that she were persuaded than come to these extremities. The father seized a proper moment and looking severely on the girl told her how homely she was, how disagreeable, and how lucky to have a husband at all; yet he had found her the best-natured man in the world, and she disobeyed him. She returned to her husband and threw herself on the ground saying, "From this time forward you shall find me another sort of person." She kept her resolution, and to her dying day went readily and cheerfully about any duty, however simple, if her husband would have it so.[33]

Apparently this sensible resignation warmed More's feelings toward women, because when Jane quietly passed away, he took a second wife within a month after her death.

Luther, a kind husband, a loving father, and a man of deep compassion, firmly believed that a woman's place is in the home.

> Men have broad and large chests, and small narrow hips, and more understanding than the women, who have but small and narrow breasts, and broad hips, to the end they should remain at home, sit still, keep house, and bear and bring up children.[34]

Calvin thought that female modesty requires that women be "shamefaced and shy," and, according to Allen,

> Bodin asserts that it is not woman's physical weakness but her moral and intellectual inferiority that makes of her the natural subject of man. It is a primary law of nature, he declares, that reason should rule appetite. Man in relation to woman represents reason. To emancipate her can but be disastrous since to do so is to disregard unescapable facts that cannot be altered.[35]

MARRIAGE AND DIVORCE

The nature of marriage was much disputed, as might be expected from the conflict of moral and social ideas during the age. Both Catholics and Protestants believed that the married state, although it represents something of a compromise with concupiscence, is a natural one for most people. But the Catholic Church required monks and nuns to take vows of celibacy and regarded the virgin state as higher than the married state. The Council of Trent (1558) ruled:

> If any one saith, that the married state is to be placed above the state of virginity, or of celibacy, and that it is not better and more blessed to remain in virginity, or in celibacy, than to be united in matrimony; let him be anathema.[36]

The Protestants, on the other hand, maintained that the Scriptures nowhere prescribe one set of laws for ecclesiastical officials and another for the laity. They were not unmindful of the Apostle Paul's advice, but they insisted that when he said, "If thou marry thou hast not sinned," he was speaking to everybody.

A controversy arose also respecting the exact meaning of the marriage vows. In 1164 the Catholic Church had officially recognized marriage as a sacrament. In practical, rather than theological, terms this came to mean that marriage vows once taken by competent parties are irrevocable, and that the breaking of these vows is sacrilege. This position was reaffirmed by the Council of Trent, and the Catholic Church has to the present day continued to forbid absolute divorce. The Protestant leaders did not accept the Catholic interpretation of the Apostle's statement that marriage is a "great sacrament." They did not approve of divorce, of course, but they accepted it under some conditions. In his *Babylonian Captivity of the Church,* Luther made it clear that although he did not sanction polygamy, he considered it less wrong than divorce, which he detested.

The view that polygamy is preferable to divorce was not confined to Luther. Smith says that

> . . . beginning with Luther, many of the Reformers thought polygamy less wrong than divorce, on the biblical ground that whereas the former had been practised in the Old Testament, divorce was prohibited save for adultery. Luther advanced this thesis as early as 1520, when it was purely theoretical, but he did not shrink from applying it on occasion. It is extraordinary what a large body of reputable opinion was prepared to tolerate polygamy, at least in exceptional cases. Popes, theologians, humanists like Erasmus, and philosophers like Bruno, all thought a plurality of wives a natural condition.[37]

FAMILY RELATIONSHIPS

Luther once said, " 'Tis a grand thing for a married pair to live in perfect union, but the devil rarely permits this." This statement probably describes the usual attitude in his day. Marriage was more often entered into for practical reasons rather than for love, and the sensible domination of the husband over the wife was regarded as natural and fitting. "The husband should manage so that he always maintains his authority over his wife," says Erasmus, "but without making it felt too strongly. He should show her kindness and not cruelty." [38]

Apparently most parents were pleased to be blessed with many children, although protests against large families were not lacking. For example, Montaigne says, "The generality of men, and the sanest of them, hold an abundance of children to be a piece of great good fortune; I and some others regard the want of them as equally fortunate." Smith calls attention to a number of families with twenty or more children and states that in the sixteenth century "a brood of six to twelve was a very common occurrence." He continues:

> The *patria potestas* was supposed to extend, as it did in Rome, during the adult as during the callow years. Especially did public opinion insist on children marrying according to the wishes of their parents. Among the nobility child-marriage was common, a mere form, of course, not at once followed by cohabitation. A betrothal was a very solemn thing, amounting to a definite contract.[39]

THE SCIENTIFIC REVOLUTION

By the seventeenth century the outcome of the scientific revolution was certain, and such men as Galileo and Newton were building on foundations laid by Copernicus and Cardan a scientific structure able to withstand any assault. Earlier than this, however, the spirit of scientific inquiry had swept over the Western world, and men of learning had begun to take increased interest in natural phenomena. The men of genius who carried science through to victory were able to succeed because the time had come for a change, and because courageous men had prepared the way for them by revolting against tradition. These predecessors, often in anguish and sometimes at the risk of their lives, had created an intellectual atmosphere in which human curiosity, the spirit of science, could thrive.

We have seen that during the Renaissance and Reformation thought was liberated—and that the price of free thought was confusion. Men dared to think for themselves, but they distrusted reason; they craved new experience but desired, too, the security of established beliefs and customs; they questioned authority but were unwilling to live in doubt. States were formed, the roots of nationalism took hold, and numerous questions about the nature and function of government arose. Growth in industry and trade created perplexing economic and ethical problems. Family ideals were disputed, and troubled efforts were made to understand human nature and to discover man's proper place in the scheme of things. All this resulted in a conflict of ideas such as the world had never before known. It was not confined to academies and cloisters but took place in the public arena, where people from all walks of life met.

The great discoveries in the physical sciences were not at first matched by corresponding advances in the social sciences. Luther and Calvin were moralists and theologians, not scientists. They did not make the clean break with tradition which science demanded. They had no intention of being radical; they wanted only to reform. Erasmus drew back when dangerous ideas loomed ahead. Machiavelli and Montaigne reflect the cynical mood of the age, not the objectivity of scientists. No Ibn Khaldun appeared to give scientific order to social ideas. Perhaps the nearest approach to a social scientist during the age was Jean Bodin, and even he, says Bury, was "safe and dull."

Nevertheless, the stage was being set during the Renaissance and the Reformation for the appearance of such men as Locke, Vico, and Comte. The scientific revolution began in curiosity, gained momentum through free inquiry, produced its first fruits in knowledge of the material universe, and led finally to the empirical observation of society.

14 · JOHN LOCKE

(1632-1704)

Brought up among letters he advanced just so far as to make an acceptable offering to truth alone.
—Epitaph written by himself

THE SEVENTEENTH CENTURY

Many of the ideas by which we live today took root and began to thrive in the seventeenth century. The scientific attitude was not universally accepted during that century, but such men as Bacon, Galileo, Descartes, Harvey, Kepler, Pascal, Locke, Spinoza, and Leibnitz helped to establish the scientific point of view so securely that none other has since been able to challenge its hold on Western thought. Science was regarded by many scholars as the sovereign mistress of the world of mind before Sir Isaac Newton published his *Principia Mathematica*, in 1687, but that great work set a brilliant crown upon her head. Before the seventeenth century, the light of scientific knowledge might conceivably have flickered after its first brilliance and then died out, as it had done in ancient Greece; after that century it could not be extinguished.

The seventeenth century, furthermore, gave Great Britain, at least, a solution to an old political problem, the right of kings, and saw finally the triumph of Protestantism in that country. After Parliament had shown that it could depose a king (1649) and replace him by one of its own choosing (1688), no British monarch could claim, as Louis XIV is said to have done, "I am the state." As for the religious question, late in the century, in Great Britain and on the continent of Europe, the revival of Catholicism as a political force appeared to be entirely possible. James II was a Catholic; Louis XIV revoked the Edict of Nantes, which had given the Huguenots the legal privileges of other Frenchmen; the Duke of Savoy decided that the time had come to end the toleration of Protestants; and a Catholic family gained control in the Palatinate. Nevertheless, although the dispute regarding religious toleration was not entirely settled during the seventeenth century, men dared to speak their minds on the subject. By the end of the century Great Britain was definitely Protestant, and freedom of worship was gaining recognition as an inalienable human right. In fact, in the claims of the individual to freedom from all arbitrary authority, liberalism was emerging as a political ideal.

It is doubtful that the world has ever known social upheavals more fateful than two which occurred during the seventeenth century. The emergence of the age of science and the political revolution in Great Britain are landmarks in history.

EMERGENCE OF THE AGE OF SCIENCE

The separation of history into ages, with fixed dates for the beginning and the end of each, is a convenient practice that does no harm if the arbitrary nature of the divisions is recognized. One age does not succeed another in exactly the same way that a new king occupies a vacant throne—"The King is dead! Long live the King!" Science rules the modern Western world, as scholasticism did the medieval; but medieval thought lives today and scientific thought antedates the modern age. That the modern world is vastly different from the medieval world in many important respects, few will deny. There is less agreement as to the date at which the Middle Ages ended and the Age of Science began. We have noted in the preceding chapter that a period which we called the Age of Transition, extending over about three centuries, witnessed the gradual emergence of the scientific spirit. By the middle of the sixteenth century momentous works of science had been published by Copernicus, Vesalius, and Cardan; but since the revolutionary nature of these works was not appreciated until another generation of scientists had been able to verify and extend the discoveries of their distinguished predecessors, we may regard the seventeenth century as the date when the Age of Science definitely began.

> If one asks why it was that science should, just at this time, have taken so sudden and so vast a growth, the question, though infinitely intricate, can be partially answered. One must assume, as almost constant, the presence in Europe for many thousand years of a race gifted with intellectual curiosity and power. The genius of the Greeks in antiquity and the expanding mental capacities of the European races as a whole, may explain part, but only the smallest part, of the growth of science for a few centuries in ancient times, and again for the last few centuries. Changing conditions account for far more than do slow biological processes. The condition most favorable to the growth of science in the sixteenth and seventeenth centuries was the increasing number of men who were drawn into intellectual pursuits. Genius is like a fire; a single burning log will smoulder or go out; a heap of logs piled loosely together will flame fiercely. So it was that

during the Middle Ages when anarchy prevailed, when communications were poor, and when books, the chief means of learning, were few, comparatively little was added to the sum of human knowledge. . . .

But the establishment of strong governments, insuring at least domestic peace, the accumulation of wealth followed by the growth of a leisure class, the development of a secular, sanguine culture more eager to improve this world than anxious about the next, and above all, the invention of printing, making easier the storing, communication, and dissemination of knowledge, led naturally to the cultivation and hence to the advancement of science. The Renaissance and the Reformation at first retarded and finally helped the revolution. They harmed it provisionally by turning men's thought and effort backward, to the classics or to theology; they helped it, indirectly and finally, by breaking up many of the medieval standards. Cloyed with barren imitations of antiquity, sated with religious strife, men turned eagerly to the new, fruitful, and generally safe paths of experiment and of mathematics.[1]

THE POLITICAL REVOLUTION IN GREAT BRITAIN

When Elizabeth, the last of the Tudors, died in 1603, the British throne was occupied by a line of kings, the Stuarts, who lacked the political astuteness of the Virgin Queen. She had been willing to leave somewhat ambiguous the exact nature of the authority of the reigning monarch and, although the metaphysical principle of the divine right of kings was well established, she had depended on Parliament for revenue with which to run the government.

Elizabeth's successor, James I (1603-1625), believed that his powers were absolute, and he saw no reason to compromise. He had grown up in Scotland and did not understand the English, least of all the "country gentlemen" who sat in Parliament and claimed the right to meddle with his conduct of the government. "Kings," he said, "are rightly called gods, for that they exercise a manner or resemblance of divine power on earth. . . . God hath power to create or destroy . . . and like power have kings: they make and unmake their subjects; they have power of . . . life and death . . . and yet are accountable to none but God only."

James imposed taxes on the people without the consent of Parliament, and thus unwittingly kindled fires of revolution. The Anglican Church, of which the king was the supreme head, was the dominant religious organization in England, and through the bishops, whom he appointed, the king was able to exercise strong political pressure on the people. As James I believed that control over church leaders was a necessary, and a legitimate, power of the king, he had no sympathy with noncomformist groups, such as the Puritans, and refused to grant them freedom of worship. He declared even that he would "harrry" them out of the land. Consequently, the nonconformists writhed under his dictatorial policies, just as Parliament did, and the flame of revolt burned fiercely from this added fuel. James died before the revolution came, but it was not far off.

Charles I (1625-1649) inherited not only the throne but also, in his claim to absolute powers, the bitter opposition of Parliament and of the nonconformists. Instead of withdrawing that claim, Charles sought to settle the quarrel with Parliament by dissolving that body, and that with the noncomformists by bringing even the strong Scotch Presbyterian group under his direct control. The Scots rose in revolt, and when the revolt was successful, Parliament had the king beheaded. Then followed Oliver Cromwell's military dictatorship, which brought many social changes but provided no real answer to the questions of sovereignty and religious toleration. Tiring of Puritan leadership and of soldiers, the British gave the throne back to the Stuarts, and in 1660 Charles II was crowned king. He ruled for twenty-five years and died with the two major political problems of the century still unsolved.

James II (1685-1688), who succeeded him, sought openly to make Great Britain Catholic, as Charles II had tried to do secretly. This gave Parliament all the justification it required to depose him, and again the British demonstrated that the people, and not the king, were sovereign in Great Britain. Since William and Mary, in 1688, received from the people the right to occupy the British throne, no British king has dared to claim absolute powers derived from a divine source. The question of religious toleration remained somewhat undecided, but as the century drew to a close it had lost much of its political importance. The Whigs and Tories had replaced the religious bodies as leading actors in the drama of British politics.

This brief sketch of the rise of the scientific spirit and of the political revolution which occurred in Great Britain during the seventeenth century shows the situation into which John Locke, whose social ideas we shall examine in this chapter, was born. He was a true product of his age, and since he was a practical man and no ivory-tower theorist, he took an active part in that conflict of ideas which makes the seventeenth century so interesting and important a period in the history of Western civilization.

LIFE AND MAJOR WORKS

John Locke, now renowned as a philosopher but celebrated during his lifetime as a physician, theologian, statesman, financier, and natural scientist, was born in England in 1632. His father, a country lawyer and a Puritan, appears to have been in comfortable circumstances but was neither distinguished nor wealthy. Since he spoke out on political matters and commanded a troop of cavalry during the Civil Wars, we may assume that he was not lacking in courage. Little is known about Locke's mother except that she seems to have been a pious woman ten years older than her husband. Both of Locke's parents and an only brother, Thomas, died during the time that he was finishing his formal education, or shortly afterwards; and since John Locke never married, he spent the productive years of his life without any immediate family ties.

At the age of fourteen Locke entered Westminster School, where he was subjected for about six years to stern discipline and the classics. We do not know that he actually witnessed the execution of Charles I in near-by Whitehall Palace Yard on January 30, 1649, but he certainly must have been much impressed by the incident. In 1652 he went up to Christ Church College, Oxford, thus forming a connection with that institution which lasted until 1684, when Charles II ordered that he be expelled. After taking the bachelor's and the master's degrees, he remained as tutor or censor in Greek, Rhetoric, Moral Philosophy, Natural Philosophy, and various other subjects. His residence at Oxford was not continuous, and when he finally abandoned the idea of taking holy orders, he was free to travel and to accept other employment.

The scholastic philosophy that he learned at Oxford led Locke naturally to Descartes, and although he never became a Cartesian, he was much influenced by the great French rationalist. Even more important in his development was the influence of the natural scientists. He formed at Oxford an intimate friendship with Robert Boyle, one of the founders of the Royal Society. For several years he seems to have studied medicine, and although he never became a practicing physician, he did acquire the skill to perform in 1668 a difficult operation on his friend and benefactor, Lord Ashley, afterwards Earl of Shaftesbury; eventually Oxford awarded him a medical degree.

When Lord Ashley became Earl of Shaftesbury and was made Lord High Chancellor, he gave Locke an important post in the government; Locke was thus able to participate in important affairs of state and to observe the machinery of government in actual operation. When Shaftesbury was out of favor, Locke was able to retire to Oxford until that retreat was finally closed to him. Then he fled to Holland, where he remained until he was able to return to England with the royal party of Queen Mary, wife of William of Orange. Locke was offered an important post in the government of the new king, but he refused it on the ground of poor health. Instead he took up residence with Sir Francis and Lady Masham, whose devotion to him eased his declining years and provided an atmosphere in which he was able to bring to completion a number of the works on which his reputation rests.

Until about two years before he moved to the Mashams' manorhouse at Oates, in the spring of 1691, Locke had published nothing except a few poems and an occasional minor essay. In 1669 he had helped to draw up a constitution for the colony of Carolina. He kept a journal, wrote letters, and, from drafts found among his papers after his death, it is obvious that his pen had been active long before his books appeared in print. During his forced exile in Holland, he began to prepare for publication some of the works on which he had labored for many years. In 1689 appeared, anonymously and in Latin, his *Letter Concerning Toleration,* the first of his major works to be given to the public. Within the next few years he wrote two added treatises on the same subject.

In 1690 his two most important works, the *Two Treatises of Government* and the *Essay Concerning Human Understanding,* were published; in 1692, *The Consequences of the Lowering of Interest and the Raising of the Value of Money;* in 1693, *Some Thoughts Concerning Education. The Reasonableness of Christianity,* published in 1695, concluded Locke's major writings. During the remaining years of his life Locke was occupied with theological studies and with replies to some of his critics. After 1700 he paraphrased some of the epistles of St. Paul and made extensive comments on them. He died in 1704, alert and active to the end. "His death was like his life," said Lady Masham, "truly pious, yet natural, easy and unaffected."

CARTESIAN RATIONALISM

Descartes' *Discourse on Method* was published when Locke was five years of age, and Cartesian rationalism soon became the dominant school of philosophy in Great Britain as well as on the Continent. Although the "father of British empiricism" was first a rationalist and never really ceased being one, he did attack some of the principles of the Cartesian system. A brief review of this system will make clear his point of departure in his search for a scientific method.

THE WORLD MACHINE

Scientific inquiry rests upon two assumptions: (1) that there is order in the phenomena which are being investigated, and (2) that the methods employed are adequate for the apprehension of that order. The scientists of the seventeenth century had every reason to feel that their faith in these assumptions was fully justified. It was clear to them that nature is not the confusion it appears to be but rather that it operates according to certain mathematical laws. Working on this theory, Copernicus arrived at his revolutionary heliocentric theory of the universe. Galileo was certain that the book of nature was written in mathematical symbols.* His painful experience with the Church may have caused him to confine his observations as much as possible to physical phenomena. Descartes, however, had no such limitations. He sought to see life clearly and see it whole. He dared to hope that all the secrets of nature might be opened by the keys provided by mathematical laws.

* See Randall, *Making of the Modern Mind,* Chaps. 10 and 11, for a vivid description of this development of thought.

Accepting the mathematical method as the most powerful instrument of knowledge given to man, Descartes proceeded to give to the science of mathematics the principles of analytical geometry, through which he demonstrated the correspondence between algebra and physical space in the universe. He did even more than that: by his application of the methods of mathematics to all inquiry he set rationalistic philosophy on its way. Here was the way to absolute certainty. No longer need men despair of their own powers to attain ultimate truths. No longer need they turn to revelation and authority. In his pride Descartes boasted, "Give me extension and motion, and I will construct the universe." Hobbes joined in the refrain, describing the understanding which was now open to man through mathematics as "the perfect knowledge of the truth in all matters whatsoever."

Men could know that the new discoveries in mathematics disclosed the plan of the universe, because any competent scientist was able by means of mathematical principles to compute the attraction of bodies, to weigh the atmosphere, to determine the laws of pressure in liquids and gases, and to measure the speed of light. In his *Principia Mathematica,* Sir Isaac Newton reduced the apparent confusion in nature to an orderly mathematical system and expressed in a single brilliant synthesis the mechanistic conception of the universe that, since Archimedes in the third century B.C., had been dimly seen by others.[2]

Spinoza agreed with Newton, saying, "Nothing in the universe is contingent, but all things are conditioned to exist and operate in a particular manner."[3] In his portrayal of the universe as a great mechanism, Spinoza pushed on to an extreme determinism. He declared that everything in life, including the work and thought of man, was determined in the beginning. All that is *must* be. It could not possibly be otherwise. Even "God does not act according to the freedom of the will."[4] God and the processes of nature are one. The laws of natural science are the decrees of fate.

Most of the scientists of the seventeenth century were men of deep religious convictions. They believed that their discoveries were in full accord with the teachings of Scripture and Christian theology, that their eyes saw and their ears heard what they had long known in their hearts about ultimate things but had not earlier been able to demonstrate. In 1671 the English Royal Society declared that the new philosophy was "so old as to have been the discipline in paradise."

At the same time certain liberal Christian leaders embraced eagerly the new scientific discoveries and argued that religion was in no way hostile to science. In 1662 Simon Patrick, Bishop of Ely, wrote: "True philosophy can never hurt sound divinity."

Such, in brief, were the views with which Locke became acquainted at Oxford. Their immense popularity can be explained in two ways: (1) the facts discovered about nature could be demonstrated to any competent observer; and

(2) the new ideas were reconciled with the old so that devout Christians did not have to choose between science and religion—they could have both.

LOCKE'S METHOD

At Oxford, however, Locke came into contact not only with Cartesian rationalism but also with experimental science. He became acquainted with the empirical investigations of natural phenomena in which Robert Boyle and some of the other founders of the Royal Society were engaged. Although he did not himself make any important empirical discoveries, he helped to turn science away from mathematical deduction toward empirical observation and induction. He saw that if, as Descartes had claimed, knowledge originates in innate ideas, then the search for truth by observing and experimenting with natural phenomena would be wasteful of time if not actually futile. He observed, however, that men actually were adding to knowledge in this way. Consequently, if the doctrine of innate ideas means, as he believed, that we can add nothing to knowledge by empirical inquiry, but can only find confirmation in nature for truths that reason has already established, then the whole doctrine must be rejected as contrary to experience. The fact that Descartes had studied anatomy and that many of his followers were engaged in experimental investigations was proof that even those who accepted the doctrine of innate ideas were unable to hold consistently to its principles.

Locke went even further and denied that we possess any innate knowledge at all. Since truth, therefore, cannot be deduced from maxims "stamped upon the mind of man," Locke asks:

> Whence comes [the mind] by that vast store which the busy and boundless fancy of man has painted on it with an almost endless variety? Whence has it all the materials of reason and knowledge? To this I answer in one word, from experience: in that all our knowledge is founded, and from that it ultimately derives itself.[5]

The mind of the child at birth is like a sheet of blank paper, a *tabula rasa*. Experience writes upon this sheet, and the letters upon it are put there by experience alone. Furthermore, since no person is able to know more than he has experienced, the ultimate reality that is the sum of all possible experience is beyond personal knowledge. We know only the relations of our ideas to one another, and not that which lies beyond them. Our knowledge of external objects is derived through sensation; by reflection we discover the operations of our own minds. Human knowledge can go no further than sensation and reflection.

> . . . All those sublime thoughts which tower above the clouds, and reach as high as heaven itself, take their rise and footing here: in all that

great extent wherein the mind wanders, in those remote speculations it may seem to be elevated with, it stirs not one jot beyond those ideas which sense or reflection has offered for its contemplation.[6]

Thus, just as rationalism had reached the point of being able to offer absolute truth "in all matters whatsoever," Locke appeared on the scene declaring that the quest for certainty in most areas of knowledge is vain. Only in the realms of mathematics and morality is certainty possible. In other fields of inquiry man must rest content with probable knowledge. Finite creature that he is, "furnished with powers and faculties very well fitted to some purpose, but very disproportionate to the vast and unlimited extent of things," [7] man would do well to avoid rash claims to powers of mind he does not possess. It is better that he should understand that "scarcely anyone ever miscarried for want of knowledge" who sought sincerely to know his duty. "The candle that is set up within us shines bright enough for all our purposes."

How did Locke justify his belief that morals are, like mathematical truths, universal and eternal? There would appear to be little connection between the two. Certainty in mathematics is possible because mathematics deals only with abstract ideas to which precise definitions have been given. Morality, on the other hand, deals with the actual experiences of life, where the meaning attached to various practices varies widely. Revelation affords one answer to the question "What is good?" But Locke's ethical doctrines are not based on revelation, although he does admit that most people have neither the leisure nor the ability to analyze moral behavior and must, therefore, be guided in their conduct by the revealed will of God. How, then, does he support his statement that moral truths are possibly as certain and demonstrable as those of mathematics? The answer is that he does not himself attempt to formulate a science of morality. Aaron believes that

> Locke's failure to provide the system he visualized lies in an inner contradiction in his thoughts, a contradiction which becomes plain when we read the various statements he makes from time to time about morality. As was often the case elsewhere, so here in morals he could feel the force of more than one tendency. Two theories compete with each other in his mind. Both are retained; yet their retention means that a consistent moral theory becomes difficult to find. The first is hedonism, which, in Locke's writings, assumes the form that the good is whatever produces pleasure, so that our judgment about good and evil ultimately rests on our feeling of pleasure and pain. The second is rationalism, the view that reason alone can determine what is truly good.[8]

In this matter, as in others, Locke appears to waver between a developed rationalism that he could not wholly accept and a nascent empiricism that he could not fully comprehend. His empiricism is shown in his utilitarianism; he could demonstrate that some acts afford pleasure under certain conditions, whereas others cause pain. His rationalism is revealed in his belief that reason operates according to nature's laws. Those laws constitute "an external immutable standard of Right."

Since this is precisely what the medieval theologians had said, what is novel in Locke's approach to moral truth? What could his empiricism contribute to those eternal truths given man in revealed religion, which Locke himself devoutly accepted? Simply this: Locke denied that anyone has the right to decide for all others the rules of conduct to be followed forever. No man's reason can be trusted that far, just as no group of men can bind their descendants to a political constitution that seemed to them reasonable at the time it was adopted. Along with the other seventeenth-century philosophers, Locke was struggling not so much against the old order, much of which was an ineradicable part of his being, as against the shackles imposed by that order. He wanted freedom. He claimed for himself and for all men the right to see and to hear and to have an open mind. He maintained that the law of nature is "nowhere to be found but in the minds of men." He trusted mankind to temper freedom with moderation. As C. H. Driver says, Locke set forth

> . . . a policy and a method for man to pursue. Even though his natural reason—the candle of the Lord—may flicker and go dim, yet man may feel his way to something of order and something of attainment by empirical investigation alone. . . . It is a universe of wonder and mystery, says Locke, but by its very nature demands effort and adventure. Passive acquiescence in received opinions is utterly foreign to the whole conception.[9]

HUMAN NATURE

Locke was able to espouse individual freedom because he had confidence in his fellow man. He asked, as Hobbes had done, how man would appear in a state of nature where none of the restraints imposed by organized society exist. Hobbes had given a very dark picture of the situation which would there be found. "I put for a generall inclination of mankind," he said, "a perpetuall and restless desire of Power after Power, that ceaseth onely in Death." If men were free to do as they pleased, there would be a constant war of each against all, since in all men are found the three principal causes of quarrel—competition, diffidence, and glory. The first causes men to use violence to "make themselves Masters of other men's persons, wives, children, and cattell; the second, to defend them; the third, for trifles, as a word, a smile, a different opinion." Since men are by nature so equal that "the weakest has strength enough to kill the strongest, either by secret machination, or by confederacy with others, that are in the same danger with himselfe," the life of man in a state of nature would be "solitary, poore, nasty, brutish, and short." [10] We are reminded of St. Augustine's statement, "A man living according to man . . . is like the devil."

Locke's conception of the state of nature is far different. Men would be free "to order their actions and dispose of their possessions and persons as they think fit . . . without asking leave, or depending upon the will of any other man." Men, therefore, are born for freedom, and nothing in human nature makes it necessary for them to forfeit that natural right. If they lived naturally, they would live according to the law of nature—that is, according to the Law of God.

In the state of nature men would, moreover, be equal, not in capabilities, for in that respect some are superior to others, but in the sense that no one among them would have the right to exercise arbitrary power over another. Furthermore, they would be social. Men seek naturally the company of their fellows. "God hath woven into the principles of human nature tenderness for offspring," says Locke, and in another place he observes that "truth and keeping of faith belong to men as men."

Finally, men are by nature rational. There are individual variations in the ability to make rational judgments, but collectively men are capable of acting in accordance with the law of nature. Since Locke, like the other philosophers of his time, assumed that human nature does not change, his description of man in a state of nature amounts to a definition of basic personality traits. According to Locke, therefore, all men are born free, equal (see p. 353), social, and rational; and if their natures remained uncorrupted, they would live happily and in peace.

The law of nature confers certain rights and imposes certain duties. The rights that Locke most frequently mentions are those to life, liberty, and property; the duties are those demanded by respect for the rights of others. The two are inseparable; no one can justly claim his inherent natural rights who neglects his natural responsibilities.

Individual rights are not, therefore, inalienable. A man who attempts "to get another man into his absolute power" forfeits his right to life. "For I have reason to conclude," says Locke, "that he who would get me into his power without my consent, would use me as he pleased when he had got me there, and destroy me, too, when he had a fancy to it; for nobody can desire to have me in his absolute power, unless it be to compel me by force to that which is against the right of my freedom, i.e., make me a slave." Likewise a thief enters into a state of war with the person whose property he unjustly seizes and thus forfeits his right to life itself. In fact, anyone who violates the law of nature ceases to have its protection. Locke did not show why in the state of nature one man should seek to enslave another or seize his property; he merely pointed out that those who do so act break a natural bond with others and enter into a state of war with them.

Thus, in his theory of human nature, Locke steered a course between the Scylla of inalienable rights and the Charybdis of inherent depravity. Unrestricted freedom is no more natural than is complete submission. Men are disposed by nature to be rational and just, and the kind of social order which Locke preferred is possible because, in his opinion, most men actually are rational and just. He never said that the voice of the people is the voice of God, but he did suggest that the natural impulses of the average person are to be trusted. Unless this was his view of human nature, it is difficult to explain his faith in liberalism.

POLITICS

Locke's main contribution to political theory was made in his *Two Treatises of Government*. The first of these treatises attempted to show that the theory of divine rights and absolute powers of kings is based on false principles. Locke directed his attention against Sir Robert Filmer's *Patriarchia,* a rather awkward attempt to show that monarchs inherit from Adam a just claim to absolute powers. His criticism of Filmer is interesting today mainly as a reminder of the fact that as late as the seventeenth century the people of England were being constantly urged by ecclesiastics and other men of learning to submit without question to the will of the Lord's Anointed who happened at the moment to occupy the throne. Filmer was saying what men who discussed politics openly were expected to say. For daring to criticize the king, Algernon Sidney was executed in 1683 for treason.

In the second treatise Locke gave his positive views on the "true original [origin], extent, and end of civil government." In this treatise he interpreted the political trends of his age and gave clarity and logical support to some basic principles of modern democracy. Locke is sometimes accused of seeking only to justify the Revolution of 1688 and to make good King William's title "in the consent of the people." It is obvious, however, that he was also attempting to put an end to the old conception of Divine Rights.

It must not be supposed that Locke was a democrat in the modern sense of the term. He apparently shared with other liberals in his time a distrust of universal or manhood suffrage. He did not believe that men are equal in all respects.

> Though I have said above "That all men by nature are equal," I cannot be supposed to understand all sorts of "equality." Age or virtue may give men a just precedency. Excellency of parts and merit may place others above the common level. Birth may subject some, and alliance or benefits others, to pay an observance to those to whom Nature, gratitude, or other respects, may have made it due; and yet all this consists with . . . that equal right that every man hath to his natural freedom, without being subjected to the will or authority of any other man.[11]

It is probably going too far to call Locke, as Lord Acton did, "the philosopher of government by the gentry," but at least it can be said that he did not work actively to expand the limited democracy which existed in Great Britain in his day.

SOCIAL CONTRACT

The idea that the civil state is created by a social contract is a very old one. It appears in the writings of the Epicureans, the Roman jurists, the medieval scholars, Grotius, Hooker, Hobbes, and many others who preceded Locke, just as it is found in Rousseau and many other later political theorists. It has many shades of meaning and has served many purposes. Precisely what it meant to Locke is not altogether clear. There is some evidence that he regarded it as a historical fact as well as an expository device. If he did believe that civil society actually developed by means of a social contract from a state of nature, then he differed in this respect from many social-contract theorists and most other seventeenth- and eighteenth-century writers. Certain it is that he attempted to base his political system on natural law revealed by the light of reason. In doing so he found it necessary to ask how men would act toward one another if there were no political institutions. His political theory begins with a blank page comparable to the *tabula rasa* of his theory of knowledge. Starting from a real or imagined "state of nature," he sought to discover what takes place when this state is transformed into a civil society. He came to the conclusion, reached by many others, that society as we know it is a kind of social contract.

Government is created, says Locke, by the consent of the governed and exists only to promote their welfare. These two points must be kept distinct, since an efficient government is not necessarily a lawful one. Most rulers claim to act "for the public good," and paternalistic governments and benevolent despotisms are sometimes remarkably successful in providing for the general welfare. From Locke's point of view, however, a monarch who takes the position "I am the state" is a despot, no matter how wisely and well he may rule, since only a servant of the people exercising authority "by their consent" can lawfully govern them.

As Laski says:

> The theory of consent is vital because without the provision of channels for its administrative expression, men tend to become the creatures of a power ignorant at once and careless of their wills. Active consent on the part of the mass of men emphasizes the contingent nature of all power and is essential to the full realization of freedom; and the purpose of the State, in any sense save the mere satisfaction of material appetite, remains, without it, unfilled. The concept of natural right is most closely related to this position.[12]

Locke left somewhat vague, however, the means by which consent is expressed. What he seemed to have in mind is a constitutional type of civil society where there is freedom of speech, where laws are made by representatives of the people, and where the executive exercises only delegated powers. He says that

> . . . there remains still in the people a supreme power to remove or alter the legislative when they find the legislative act contrary to the trust reposed in them. . . . And thus the community perpetually retains a supreme power of saving themselves from the attempts and designs of anybody . . . so foolish and wicked as to lay and carry on designs against the liberties and properties of the subject.[13]

What actually does a man give up when he accepts membership in civil society? Certainly not the rights which he possesses under the law of nature to life, liberty, and property; civil society is created to protect these rights. He gives up only the right to interpret and to execute the law of nature himself.

> The . . . power . . . of doing whatsoever he thought fit for the preservation of himself and the rest of mankind, he gives up to be regulated by laws made by the society, so far forth as the preservation of himself and the rest of that society shall require; which laws of the society in many things confine the liberty he had by the law of Nature.
>
> Secondly, the power of punishing he wholly gives up, and engages his natural force which he might before employ in the execution of the law of Nature, by his own single authority as he thought fit, to assist the executive power of the society as the law thereof shall require. For being now in a new state wherein he is to enjoy many conveniences from the labour, assistance, and society of others in the same community, as well as protection from its whole strength, he is to part also with as much of his natural liberty, in providing for himself, as the good, prosperity, and safety of the society shall require, which is not only necessary but just, since the other members of the society do the like.[14]

Once an individual has "by actual agreement and any express declaration given his consent to be [a member] of any commonweal, [he] is perpetually and indispensably obliged to be and remain unalterably a subject to it, and can never be again in the liberty of the state of nature; unless, by any calamity, the government he was under comes to be dissolved, or else by some public act cuts him off from being any longer a member of it." However, if consent has been expressed only tacitly by physical presence and ownership of property, a person is at liberty to "go and incorporate himself into any other commonwealth, or to agree with others to begin a new one in any part of the world they can find free and unpossessed." [15] What Locke seems to mean here is that once the social contract has been entered into and a legal government established, the individual must accept its authority or, in some circumstances, leave. "There remains still in the People a supreme power to remove or alter the Legislative," but until such a time as that authority may be actually acted upon in a legitimate manner, the obligation to obey the magistrates is binding.

POPULAR SOVEREIGNTY

The supreme power remaining in the hands of the people raises a thorny problem. Locke avoided, perhaps intentionally, the use of the word "sovereignty." His numerous references to the "supreme power" of the people make it clear that he believed that sovereignty resides in them. He failed to show, however, in what manner and in what circumstances that power is exercised. The Constitution of the United States sets up specific safeguards against the usurpation by the government of the sovereign power of the people, but government is not limited in Locke's political system by positive law. Subject to the risk of being overthrown, it may do what it pleases. The sovereignty of the people seems to consist, therefore, only in their right to rebel against a government which acts contrary to "the trust that went along with it in its first institution." The people may alter it or replace it by another; otherwise their sovereign powers are in abeyance.

Locke was searching for safeguards against arbitrary personal authority, such as James II had claimed. Locke found a guarantee of the liberties of the people in their right to dispossess James and to replace him by a king of their own choice. Unlimited popular sovereignty would appear, therefore, to be Locke's refutation to a claim to arbitrary personal sovereignty. Willmoore Kendall asks, if the popular sovereignty "which Locke claims for his community is not unlimited sovereignty, where would one turn, in the literature of politics, to find a sovereignty which *is* unlimited?"[16] Obviously Locke believed that government is limited by its moral obligation to dispense justice according to the law of nature. If it fails in its trust, the people can revolt. Does he offer no other means by which popular sovereignty can be expressed? Gough is of the opinion that he does not.

> Locke makes a passing reference to democratic government as a theoretical possibility, but he evidently did not think it worth serious consideration. The power of the people, in his system, is exercised at the foundation of the state, but after that it remains dormant unless a revolution becomes necessary, for the established government is sacrosanct so long as it fulfils its trust. Locke accepted, in fact, the political outlook normal in his day, but his concept of trusteeship served to reinforce the notion that governments are not arbitrary and irresponsible organs of power, but have a responsibility to promote the public welfare.[17]

MAJORITY RULE

At any time in any state there are likely to be people who are opposed to the existing government and who would like, consequently, to alter or replace it. How is it decided that a revolution is, or is not, justified? The argument that the people hold ultimate authority in the state means very little unless there is some provision for the settling of differences of opinion among them. The good of certain members of society is sometimes gained at the expense of other members. Moreover, although Locke appears not to have questioned the existence of a body of common interests, it is conceivable that there is in reality no general good but only numerous aggregates of individual goods. People rarely speak with one voice; consequently a theory of government which attaches importance to popular opinion must answer the question "Whose voice is entitled to be heard?"

Locke makes a forthright statement on this point: "When any number of men have . . . consented to make one community or government, they are thereby presently incorporated, and make one body politic, wherein the majority have a right to act and conclude the rest." [18]

Kendall believes that Locke's faith in majority rule rests on a "latent premise" that "the chances are at least 50+ out of 100 that the average man is rational and just." [19] He says:

> Did Locke really mean that the majority has a right to (e.g.) maintain in power a government which oppresses or treats unjustly the "rest"? Did he really believe that it is the fact of majority support which *makes* right in politics? The correct reply to these questions is: Obviously not; Locke could never have committed himself to the moral relativism implied in the proposition that majorities make right—as anyone can see from reading the first three pages of the *Second Treatise*. Here is a writer who believed, with a passion which has rarely been equalled in the history of political theory, not only in the moral law but also in the possibility of applying moral law to the problems of politics!
>
> What, then, is the key to the riddle of the *Second Treatise*? It is, in the opinion of the present writer, to be found in the fact that, while the proposition "right is that which the majority wills" is by no means identical with the proposition "the majority always wills that which is right," the two propositions nevertheless come to precisely the same thing when considered as first principles of politics—since it follows from both that a good political system is one which lodges ultimate power in the hands of the majority.[20]

Gough raises some doubts regarding this interpretation:

> I am not sure how far Locke would have accepted Mr. Kendall's statement as an amplification of his unwritten thoughts, but I suspect that some of the logical difficulties which critics like Mr. Kendall, and others before him, have found in the *Treatise* arise simply because Locke did not notice them, and that he would have been surprised at the ingenuity expended in trying to reconcile them.[21]

Locke's position on majority rule would have been considerably clarified, for example, had he stated more explicitly his views on the extent of suffrage. Whatever his opinion on this point, however, it is probably safe to say that he believed in majority rule, not because majorities are always right but because majorities are self-corrective.

TOLERATION

Locke's plea for freedom in religion is entirely consistent with his staunch support of individual liberty in general. He would deny toleration to only two groups: to those who owe allegiance to a foreign power (he names Catholics and Mohammedans as examples) and to atheists. In the case of the former, Locke is concerned with the danger of conspiracy, not the threat of heresy. As for atheists, he maintains that those who "deny the being of God" cannot be expected to keep "the promises, covenants, and oaths, which are the bonds of human society." The magistrates may employ civil power to control faith and forms of worship, therefore, only where the security of the state is involved. The state may punish those who hold, in the name of religion, antisocial opinions or who violate for any reason "those moral rules which are necessary to the preservation of civil society." In all other respects, the state has nothing to do with religious matters.

In arguing for the separation of church and state, Locke declares that the civil government is concerned only with "men's civil interest" and has "nothing to do with the world to come." A church he defines as "a voluntary society of men, joining themselves together of their own accord in order to the public worshipping of God, in such a manner as they judge acceptable to him, and [as they deem] effectual to the salvation of their souls." [22] He pointed out that any people forced to religious conformity are in effect commanded "to offend God," since only voluntary obedience to His will can please Him. Nor has the magistrate "any power to forbid the use of such rites and ceremonies as are already received, approved, and practised by any Church; because, if he did so, he would destroy the Church itself: the end of whose institution is only to worship God with freedom after its own manner." The church and the state, therefore, have different ends and operate by means of different principles. The use of civil power to regulate religion is certain, Locke declares, to be ineffective.

Another of Locke's arguments has been summarized by Aaron as follows:

> In the second place, it is most unlikely that any church or any individual man possesses the full truth about human life and destiny. And this very limitation makes intolerance at once justifiable. For when two men genuinely disagree after a sincere search for truth, what possible justification can there be for intolerance and persecution on the part of one of these men? Surely no man has a right to persecute another because this other fails to see eye to eye with him. The persecuted party may be nearer the truth than the persecuting. All over Europe in Locke's day the differing sects persecuted each other. Not more than one of them could possess the

full truth, and the extreme probability was that none of them possessed it fully. And yet one had the incongruous spectacle of men "punished in Denmark for not being Lutherans, in Geneva for not being Calvinists, and in Vienna for not being Papists." It will be time enough to be intolerant when the full truth is known.[23]

PROPERTY

Locke's theory of property* is of interest mainly as a link between the communal ideals of the medieval world and the socialism of the modern world. Locke did not think of himself, of course, as a socialist. In fact, his reputation as an individualist is based to a considerable extent on his vigorous defense of property rights against arbitrary acts of government. He regarded the right of property as one of those natural rights which men have in a state of nature and which they create civil societies to protect. He never explicitly recognized the right of eminent domain. Sir Frederick Pollock says in this connection: "We cannot suppose that he would have actually denied the moral right of the State to take private property for public purposes on payment of just compensation, but he may have thought it so liable to abuse as to be best kept in the background." [24]

Locke was personally identified with the aristocratic and propertied class in England, and his theory of politics is based upon distrust of government interference with private rights, among which the right to possessions is mentioned repeatedly. Nevertheless, he was not by modern standards a "rugged individualist," and socialism has found support in his doctrine that a person is entitled to exclusive possession of only those goods "with which he has mixed his labour."

The medieval conceptions of property with which Locke had to reckon and from which he never succeeded wholly in freeing himself have been stated as follows:

> In the Middle Ages the stage was not set for the obtrusion of individualistic notions into the social theory of property. The ways of thought, rather than the activities of the folk, were against it. Then, as now, men were disposed to use a strong arm, cunning mind, or strategic position to help themselves and to do as they pleased with their own; and doubtless a multitude of facts could be assembled in support of a doctrine of privacy of ownership. But . . . good Christians were severally members one of another; the community was a single organic whole.
> . . . In the explanations set down in books, the idea of trusteeship permeated all the institutions of secular ownership. The fief gave support to

---

* Although Locke sometimes employed the term "property" to refer to "life, liberty, and estate" and writes of "that property which men have in their persons as well as goods," he also used it to mean material possessions; it is in the latter sense that it is treated here.

the warrior in return for his service of protection; feudal tenure was conditional and contingent; in its terms "liberties" were always associated with responsibilities. The village commons and the open-field system were as much the genuine property of the village folk as the common altar and common prayer. . . . Even after obligations began to wane and men of property began to talk glibly of their individual own, the communal idea lingered on. The most reputable of religious and political writers defended the right of the indigent to help themselves to the necessities of life. When eventually there came to be a state, there was set down as among the first of its functions provisions for "the peace, riches, and public conveniences of the whole people." [25]

In his attempt to support the sanctity of private property, Locke could not afford to ignore, even had he chosen to do so, the traditional communal conceptions that had developed from the belief that God had given the world to all mankind. He admitted that "the earth and all that is therein is given to men for the support and comfort of their being . . . and nobody has originally a private dominion, exclusive of the rest of mankind in any of them, as they are in their natural state." [26] He was speaking, of course, of conditions found in a state of nature and not of those that prevail in civil societies.

Private property is a fact in human history that, however it may be regarded, cannot be denied. Realistic thinkers have, therefore, been concerned more with property rights than with utopian dreams of universal communism. Locke was fully conscious of the necessity for some restraints in the use of private property. He could not have been ignorant of those which ancient and medieval theorists had offered in the just price, the prohibition against usury, the limitations on the ends served by the use of property, and other restrictive principles derived from natural law. Under the secular influences of the seventeenth century, however, these notions no longer suited the temper of the times, and they did not suit Locke. Consequently, in his search for the nature of private property, he made no attempt to deal with earlier ideas on the subject but instead went back to the emergence of private possessions from those things given by God "to mankind in common." His theory has been briefly summarized by Aaron:

> Locke's theory of property runs as follows. In the first place, each man possesses himself, his own person, absolutely. But in addition he also possesses anything "with which he has mixed his labour." "Whatsoever," Locke explains, "he removes out of the state that Nature hath provided and left it in, he hath mixed his labour with, and joined to it something that is his own and thereby makes it his property." "Though the water running in the fountain is every one's, [he continues] yet who can doubt but that in the pitcher is his only who drew it out." Thus it is labour which creates property. It is labour also which gives value to most things. "It is labour indeed that puts the difference of value on everything. . . . of

the products of the earth useful to the life of man, nine-tenths are the effects of labour." Locke here suggested a labour theory of value which was to be extensively developed by later thinkers, particularly by socialist writers.[27]

Unfortunately, Locke's theory of property was never fully developed. The statement that whatever a person "hath mixed his labour with and joined it to something that is his own" becomes "his property" may have some meaning in a primitive economy; in a modern industrial society it is wholly ambiguous. The same can be said of Locke's labor theory of value. Locke saw that a man should not be allowed to "engross as much as he will," but he did not show how greed should be checked. He deplored waste, and he thought that any person who allowed spoilage to occur because he held more goods than he could use should be punished. However, he saw no objection to the conversion of goods into money, which, since it does not spoil, may be held in any quantity. In fact, he believed that the convention of money amounts to a tacit agreement among men "to a disproportionate and unequal possession of the earth."

Locke was not an advocate of a *laissez-faire* economic policy; he supported the regulation of trade and regarded the preservation of property as "the great and chief end . . . of men's uniting into commonwealths, and putting themselves under government." Just how far government controls should go he did not say, but he did point out that "the price of the hire of money" cannot be regulated by law. In one connection he put a higher value on property, which he never clearly defined, than on life and liberty: a person made captive in an unjust war forfeits his right to live but not his goods, since these belong to his children "to keep them from perishing." He believed that property plays an important part in the development of personality and that the entire society gains by an individual's solicitude for his own possessions.

That Locke's theory of property is incomplete and, as he left it, inconsistent and illogical, many critics have pointed out. Yet Driver calls it "one of the most fascinating parts of Locke's political speculation," and Gough says that "we may feel that Locke reached the right conclusions, even though his reasoning was faulty and his route muddled, and we may be thankful that his sane moderation, even if it was based on too sanguine a belief in the reasonableness of mankind, has characterized much of our constitutional development." [28]

EDUCATION

Even had Locke not been a teacher, his theory of knowledge would have caused him to attach great importance to education. "Of all the men we meet with," he says, "nine parts of ten are what they are, good or evil, useful or not, by their education." His most important work on this subject, *Some Thoughts*

Concerning Education, grew out of a request from a friend, Edward Clark, for help in the training of a son. Although Locke organized and expanded the ideas contained in his advice to Clark, he never attempted to formulate a complete theory of education. A posthumous publication on education, *Conduct of the Understanding,* was intended by Locke to be a chapter for the *Essay* and was evidently still unfinished at the time of his death.

Nevertheless, despite his failure to deal with education as exhaustively as he did with epistemology and with politics, Locke made a substantial contribution to educational theory. Many of his ideas, regarded at the time as radical, are commonplaces today partly because of his influence. He was extremely critical of certain methods followed in his day and did not hesitate to speak out against them. He spared neither Westminster, one of England's leading preparatory schools, nor Oxford, whose walls sheltered him for more than thirty years.

Locke's discussion of education is concerned almost wholly with the training of members of the upper social classes. He dismissed the masses by saying that they lacked the leisure to pursue education. A child of humble birth had time to learn only "the business of his particular calling in the commonwealth and . . . religion, which is his calling as he is a man in the world." For the masses, therefore, Locke expressed the hope that they might be taught religion and a trade. He did not foresee the time when labor-saving devices might make it possible for a large portion of mankind to enjoy the education which he envisaged for gentlemen. Consequently, the principles that he advanced for the education of the privileged few may apply today to the many. Especially is this true of his statement of the aims of education.

AIMS OF EDUCATION

"A sound mind in a sound body, is a short but full description of a happy state in this world: he that has these two, has little more to wish for; and he that wants either of them, will be but little the better for any thing else." With this statement Locke began his discussion of education. His individualism is clearly apparent: the end of education is the individual, not society. Education should make people happy. They cannot be happy if they lack the physical strength to meet the ordinary demands of life; consequently, Locke recommended "plenty of open air, exercise, and sleep; plain diet, no wine or strong drink, and very little or no physic; not too warm and strait clothing." Some of his prescriptions for physical conditioning must be rejected, and altogether his methods of building a sound body are of little interest today. When, however, he turns to an analysis of a sound mind and the means by which it is developed, his insights become timely and illuminating.

A sound mind, according to Locke, is not merely a well-informed mind; it is a mind strong and free. "As the strength of the body lies chiefly in being able to endure hardships, so also does that of the mind." The person who possesses a sound mind cannot be a victim either of his own appetites or of external circumstances. He is in command of his rational faculties, and therein alone is freedom found. Until the child has learned to exercise rational judgment, he must depend for freedom on the guidance of his parents.

> . . . we are born free, as we are born rational; not that we have actually the exercise of either: age that brings one, brings with it the other too. And thus we see how natural freedom and subjection to parents may consist together, and are both founded on the same principle. A child is free by his father's title, by his father's understanding, which is to govern him till he hath it of his own.[29]

Education, therefore, should make men free—free from the leaden weight of physical bodies too frail to withstand the ordinary strains of life, and free from the ignorance and fears of minds too weak to make rational judgments, man's supreme achievement.

More specifically, Locke gives four aims of education, listed in the order of their importance. "I place Virtue as the first and most necessary of those endowments that belong to a Man or a Gentleman," Locke declares. Next comes wisdom, the practical judgment that enables a person to manage his worldly affairs "ably and with foresight." The third aim of education is good breeding, which gives the youth a knowledge of manners and of men and thus enables him to avoid thinking meanly either of himself or of his fellows. Lack of good breeding is revealed in "sheepish bashfulness," in "misbecoming negligence and disrespect in carriage," in "excess of ceremony," and in similar defects. Good breeding is shown in a "disposition of mind not to offend others" and an "acceptable and agreeable way of expressing that disposition." Last in the list Locke places learning, saying,

> You will wonder, perhaps, that I put learning last, especially if I tell you I think it the least part. This may seem strange in the mouth of a bookish man . . . [but] when I consider what a-do is made about a little Latin and Greek, how many years are spent in it, and what a noise and business it makes to no purpose, I can hardly forbear thinking that the parents of children still live in fear of the school-master's rod.[30]

Then follows this interesting addition:

> I have one more thing to add, which as soon as I mention I shall run the danger to be suspected to have forgot what I am about, and what I have written above concerning education, which has all tended towards a gentleman's calling, with which a trade seems wholly to be inconsistent. And yet I cannot forbear to say, I would have him *learn a trade, a manual trade;* nay, two or three, but one more particularly.[31]

Locke evidently intended the trade to be an avocation to which one would be able to turn for relaxation, physical exercise, and recreation.

METHODS AND SUBJECT MATTER

In his discussion of methods, Locke stated a number of ideas that have become identified in modern times with progressive education. He showed no reverence for the old, established practices but was concerned only with the full development of the individual. He believed that pupils are better off with tutors than in organized classes, since learning is a matter of personal growth and not something to be imparted. "I can no more know anything by another man's understanding," he says, "than I can see by another man's eyes." He insisted that in the absence of a desire to know, little learning could take place. He felt that the dreary language exercises to which he himself had been subjected were a waste of time. Foreign languages, including Latin, should begin, he thought, with conversation.

Since Locke saw no reason to study languages at all except as they were needed as tools, he felt that most students should be spared Greek and Hebrew, and given instead arithmetic, geometry, geography, history, astronomy, ethics, law, and "Natural Philosophy." Like Plato, he was able to say little in favor of poetry. "For it is very seldom seen," he says, "that any one discovers mines of gold or silver in Parnassus. 'Tis a pleasant air, but a barren soil." He doubted that music justifies the time that has to be devoted to it, and he noted also that it puts one "in such odd company." He considered travel advantageous for the young in enabling them the more easily to learn a foreign language, and helpful to the mature in bringing them into contact with scholars abroad.

PERSONAL EXAMPLE

Above all, Locke insisted on the importance of example in shaping the mind and character of youth. He warned parents against doing anything that they would not have their children imitate, and says of companions:

> Having named company, I am almost ready to throw away my pen, and trouble you no farther on this subject. For since that does more than all precepts, rules, and instructions, methinks 'tis almost wholly in vain to make a long discourse of other things, and to talk of that almost to no purpose.[32]

Locke's personal life affords a superb example of his own conception of an educated gentleman:

> In an age of excitement and prejudice, he set men the example of thinking calmly and clearly. When philosophy was almost synonymous with the arid discussion of scholastic subtleties, he wrote so as to interest statesmen and men of the world. At a time when the chains of dogma were far tighter, and the penalties of attempting to loosen them far more stringent, than it is now easy to conceive, he raised questions which stirred the very depths of human thought. And all this he did in a spirit so candid, so tol-

erant, so liberal, and so unselfish, that he seemed to be writing not for his own party or his own times, but for the future of knowledge and of mankind. To sound every question to the bottom, never to allow our convictions to outstrip our evidence, to throw aside all prejudices and all interests in the pursuit of truth, but to hold the truth, when found, in all charity and with all consideration towards those who have been less fortunate than we—these are the lessons which, faithfully transmitted through two centuries by those who had eyes to see and ears to hear, he has bequeathed to us and our posterity.[33]

LOCKE'S CHARACTER AND INFLUENCE

In philosophy John Locke was an empiricist; in ethics, a utilitarian; in religion, a Latitudinarian; in politics, an individualist; in education, a progressive; and in economics, an exponent of the labor theory of value. Thus he was a radical who risked his reputation and even his life in support of dangerous ideas. But he was at the same time a rationalist, an absolutist respecting morals, an orthodox Christian, and a conservative in politics, education, and economics. He was even a timid man who feared for his life and exercised care in publishing his thoughts. It is clear, therefore, that he cannot be easily and precisely labeled.

A deeply pious man, Locke was disturbed by the theological controversies of his day, for he saw in them the sources of strife and bloodshed. Religious convictions ought to be expressed, he felt, in ways that enable all men to secure for themselves the blessings of freedom and property. It seemed to Locke that if religion were pruned of theological growths that add nothing of value to its spiritual and ethical content, it would lead to recognition of the brotherhood of man and inspire the toleration so necessary for peace. In no way does religion of this kind, he maintained, conflict with science, when science is confined to what is provable by experience.

Locke despised extremes, including those to which logic leads; his willingness to stop short of conclusions to which he appears to have been committed by his reasoning is quite apparent. He was a practical man, seeking solutions to the political, economic, educational, religious, and moral problems of his time. He sensed the importance of certain radical ideas that were then transforming society, and by supporting some of these and opposing others he helped to decide the course of history. He said what people were prepared to believe, and for this reason, as well as for the soundness of what he said, his influence in the British Isles, on the continent, and in America was tremendous. Such documents as the Virginia Bill of Rights and the Declaration of Independence show the indebtedness of the American colonists to him.

John Locke's ambition in life was to gain, as he said, "a true knowledge of things." His intellectual experience should prove helpful to those who share that ambition.

15 · GIAMBATTISTA VICO

(1668-1744)

> ... *the place in which he cried was a wilderness that gave no answer. But the crowd and the wilderness add nothing to and take nothing from the intrinsic character of a thought.*
>
> —BENEDETTO CROCE

Giambattista (John Baptist) Vico was born in Naples on June 23, 1668. In his *Autobiography* he says that his mother was an uneducated woman of "melancholy temper" and that he inherited her temperament rather than that of his father, Antonio Vico, keeper of a small bookshop and, according to the son, a man of "cheerful disposition." Young Vico was no ordinary child. Although a serious head injury, which he received as the result of a fall from a ladder at the age of seven, kept him out of school for three years, he found the pace set by his classmates so slow that he withdrew from school to pursue his education privately, seeking the guidance of such teachers as from time to time he found inspiring.

One of his early teachers was Father Ricci, a Jesuit, who proved to him that metaphysics need not be so dull as the scholastic philosophers made it appear. Vico soon found, however, that he was no more able to accept the rationalism which dominated seventeenth-century thought in Europe than the scholasticism which had preceded it. The philosophy of the Cartesian school probably made a deeper impression on him than he ever realized, but he was too independent a thinker to become a disciple of Descartes and eventually rebelled against the most influential philosopher of the day.

As a youth Vico happened to hear in the Royal University a lecture on law that won him over completely for the time being to jurisprudence. His father had long wanted him to enter the legal profession, as in the Naples of that time a man of ability might hope to gain fame and fortune at the bar. Young Vico began his studies with diligence and made such progress that within a few months he was able successfully to defend his father in court. Although both the judge and the opposing counsel praised his handling of the case, Vico viewed with dismay the prospect of spending his life in the courtroom, and his legal career ended with his initial success. Thenceforth his life was dedicated to philosophy, if, indeed, it had not been so dedicated from childhood.

Unfortunately, the study of philosophy requires both leisure and financial means, and Vico was poor. By rare good fortune, however, he met with an experience that enabled him to pursue his studies in favorable circumstances. In his *Autobiography* (written throughout in the third person) he tells of this happy event.

> At this time his health, already delicate, was endangered by consumption, and the family fortunes had been severely reduced. Yet he had an ardent desire for leisure to continue his studies, and his spirit felt a deep abhorrence for the clamor of the law courts. It was therefore a happy occasion when in a bookstore he had a conversation on the right method of teaching jurisprudence with Monsignor Geronimo Rocca, Bishop of Ischia and a distinguished jurist, as may be seen from his works. For the Monsignor was so well satisfied with his views as to urge him to go as tutor to his nephews in a castle of the Cilento, beautifully situated and enjoying a perfect climate. It belonged to the Monsignor's brother, Don Domenico Rocca, in whom he was to find a most kindly Maecenas, who shared his taste in poetry. He was assured that he would be treated in every way as a son of the family, and so it proved in fact. The good air would restore his health, and he would have all the leisure he needed for study. So it happened that living in the castle for nine years he made the greatest progress in his studies.[1]

During this period Vico read such works as a serious-minded young man with ample leisure and a capacity for self-education might be expected to read: the poetry, philosophy, and history of early as well as of contemporary writers. He became thoroughly versed in the ancient classics and probed deeply into the myths and legends of Greece and Rome. He deliberately sought to improve his style of writing, both in prose and in poetry, and developed an ability to express himself that was to serve him well in later years, when an occasional composition written on commission afforded a badly needed supplement to his slender income from teaching.

A poem written in 1692 reveals Vico's intellectual struggles during these formative years. His "Feelings of One in Despair" is overburdened with youthful indulgence in despair but expresses, despite its affectations, the sentiments of a sensitive spirit and foreshadows some of the ideas that were to appear later. In this poem Vico expressed the belief that nations pass through a pattern of development corresponding to the life cycle of organisms and declared that his own time was one of senility and decay.

> For now the iron age draws to its fall,
> The Fates for our destruction are arrayed;
> Our ills like to our crimes are grown so great
> Beyond the altitude of earlier times;
> . . . Under the weight of novel maladies
> We groan and weaken, pallid, frail and bowed,
> And our life's wings flit swifter to the tomb.[2]

Young Vico was convinced that the times were out of joint, and he felt as his own the burdens under which the people struggled. He expressed envy of those who in their ignorance were unmindful of the ills that beset mankind, and in a pastoral image described their happy lot.

> Oh! blest, and in your innocence content,
> Ye nymphs and shepherds, who for all your toils
> Can you find your peace again in rustic fare,
> Apples or milk. To whom nor frost nor heat
> Is other than delight, the shade of boughs,
> Or homely consecration of the hearth;
> Who need no other joys than your rude loves,
> Or pleasant weariness of rustic chase.[3]

But he realized that such innocence and contentment were not for him, and he ended the poem with a statement of resignation to his destiny and even with a youthful challenge to Fate to lay on the anguish.

Since throughout life Vico was never able to earn more than a bare living and died without having gained the recognition to which he was undoubtedly entitled, it might appear that Fate accepted his challenge. Instead of a chair in jurisprudence at the University, which he had every right to expect, he held for forty-two years (1699-1741) a post as teacher of rhetoric to youths preparing for higher studies, a position which paid so little that he had to supplement his income by writing orations, inscriptions, panegyrics, biographies, and histories for those who had money but lacked literary skill.

Even his domestic life was marred by tragedy. A devoted father, he was saddened by having a defective daughter and by the misdeeds of a son who became so vicious that the police had finally to be called to take him into custody. Vico's compassionate nature is revealed by his action on this occasion. When he heard the officers coming up the stairs in answer to his summons, he ran to his son saying, "Save yourself, my son." Nevertheless the boy spent a long time in jail. Fortunately, two other children, a daughter talented in poetry and a son who took over Vico's job when he was no longer able to work, were a great joy to him.

Vico's failure to gain recognition in his own day is difficult to understand. Montesquieu visited Italy in 1728 but, although he certainly must have known of Vico's work, he failed to get in touch with that person among his contemporaries whose ideas were nearest to his own. Newton showed no interest in a copy of one of Vico's books that was sent to him. With respect to his masterpiece, Vico tells us:

> In this city I know that it has fallen on barren ground. I avoid all places of resort where I might meet any to whom I have sent it, and if I do unavoidably come upon them I pass by with a hasty salutation. As they never give me any recognition that they have received my book, I am confirmed in my belief that here it has gone forth in a veritable desert.[4]

Nevertheless, despite his failure to gain recognition, Vico never doubted the value of his work. The faith in himself so evident in his youth was not shaken by the neglect and adverse criticism of some of the scholars whose approval he so much desired. He had hitched his wagon to a star, and if others were unable to go along with him, the fault was theirs. Although he was often disappointed, he was never defeated. The strength which came from within his own spirit was inexhaustible. In a sonnet he says:

> I draw within myself again, and pressed
> By heavy cares, return to where I stood:
> My fate and not my fault I do lament.[5]

Vico continued to study and to write as long as he had the strength. When finally he grew too old to teach, he had the satisfaction of seeing his son Gennaro installed in the University in his stead. He spent his last days "sitting silently in a corner of his house and taking very little food." At the age of seventy-six he died peacefully, a good Catholic to the end.

MAJOR WORKS

By far the most important work of Vico is *The New Science*.[6] He himself regarded this famous work on what he called the "Common Nature of Nations" as his supreme achievement and often expressed the wish that only this single book might survive him, since it contained all that he had accomplished. It was first published in 1725, when he was fifty-seven years of age, but the ideas that it presents had long stirred in the author's mind; many of them are found in a germinal form in his earlier works. These ideas developed slowly, and Vico declared that he felt a great sense of relief when finally he was able to nurture them to maturity. When he had published *The New Science,* he wrote to a friend saying:

> Since I have completed my great work, I feel that I have become a new man. I am no longer tempted to declaim against the bad taste of the age,

because in denying me the place which I sought [the chair of jurisprudence at the University] it has given me time to compose my "New Science." Shall I say it? I perhaps deceive myself, although most unwilling to do so; the composition of that work has animated me with a heroic spirit, which places me above the fear of death and the calumnies of my rivals. I feel that I am seated upon a rock of adamant, when I think of that law of God which does justice to genius by the esteem of the wise.[7]

The task of publishing the book which he had labored so long to write was for Vico a formidable one. He had to meet the cost of printing himself, and he sold a ring in order to obtain the necessary funds. Since the amount raised in this way was inadequate, he had to condense the book in order to bring the cost of its publication within his means. As his earlier years were devoted to preparation for the composition of this great work, so were his later years spent in revising and extending it. As a consequence, the later editions, especially the third, which was published in the year of his death (1744), contain elaborations and expositions not found in the original work. The English translation of Fisch and Bergin is made from the third edition.

Vico's *Autobiography,* written in 1725 and first published in 1728, grew out of the proposal of Count Gian Artico de Porcía to the scholars of Italy "to write their autobiographies for the edification of young students and with a view to the reform of school curricula and methods." From among the autobiographies submitted, Porcía chose for publication that of Vico, saying:

Since we are not yet in position to publish the entire work [which had been planned to contain works by various authors], we content ourselves with offering a model in the autobiography of Signor Don Giovanni Battista Vico, the celebrated Neapolitan scholar, which better than any other so far received conforms to the plan we have in mind. This autobiography will serve as a norm for anyone who, by imitating both Signor Vico's generosity and his manner of laying before the public the detail of his studies, will lend a hand to the completion of this useful enterprise.[8]

The book records the author's intellectual growth rather than the events of his life, his thoughts rather than his acts. Vico stated his aim in these words:

We shall not here feign what René Descartes craftily feigned as to the method of his studies simply in order to exalt his own philosophy and mathematics and degrade all the other studies included in divine and human erudition. Rather, with the candor proper to a historian, we shall narrate plainly and step by step the entire series of Vico's studies, in order that the proper and natural causes of his particular development as a man of letters may be known.[9]

In the *Autobiography* Vico describes his intellectual struggles: how he rejected Stoicism because it seeks "to mortify the senses and chains man to fate," and Epicureanism because it "exalts the senses and abandons man to chance"; how the metaphysics of Aristotle had proved to be of no avail to him in his study of moral philosophy; how the "Chrysippean logic" of scholasticism had been beyond his grasp; how Plato had inspired him, Tacitus had informed him, Bacon had guided him, and how, finally, Grotius had helped him to discover the universal law of the nations. The book reveals Vico's supreme confidence in himself. He admits his gift of genius and declares that he was born for the glory of Naples and of all Italy; he congratulates himself on the success of his lectures; he believes that because of *The New Science* it will be said of him as it was of Socrates:

> I would not shun his death to win his fame;
> I'd yield to odium, if absolved when dust.[10]

In the *Autobiography* Vico writes simply. Perhaps he gave heed to Count Porcía's desire that the intellectual autobiographies submitted to him be written in such fashion "as to promote a new method in the studies of the young, which would make their progress more certain and efficacious." No such criterion was imposed on his composition of *The New Science,* and it must be admitted that this book is not easy reading. Clear expression inevitably involves selection and exclusion as well as vision, and Vico attempted in this one work to compress the intellectual accomplishments of a lifetime spent in earnest study. The book is not lacking in unity—in fact Vico may be criticized for following too closely a single track; but, although he holds to the course as his thought darts here and there, it is easy for the reader to get lost. Vico will not make the common nature of the nations appear simpler than it really is. Consequently, as Vaughan says:

> Despite the richness of its matter, despite the poetic phrases which condense whole pages of argument as in a flash of lightning, the book remains a jungle: resembling nothing so much as "the vast forest of the earth" in which [Vico] conceives primitive man to have roamed, when he was yet only a step above the beasts, before the first dawn of awe and shame had given him the rude beginnings of settled home, of family affections and of worship.[11]

Vico's poems, orations, panegyrics, inscriptions, letters, lectures, and treatises should be studied if one is fully to comprehend the thought of the man who is one of Italy's most distinguished philosophers, but *The New Science* contains his main contributions to social thought.

METHOD OF THE NEW SCIENCE

Pontius Pilate is said once to have asked in jest, "What is truth?" Men of serious mind and earnest purpose, however, are not willing to dismiss this question lightly. Descartes had found one answer in flight from skepticism. By pushing doubt to its limit he had reached something that could not be doubted—namely, the indubitable consciousness of self-existence. Here was a criterion of truth, the Cartesians believed, which would make possible the discovery of every law of nature. It established mathematical truths, and these in turn disclosed the mathematical order in the universe. By tuning the human mind to natural order by the precise tools of mathematics, they believed that nature would stand revealed in all its simplicity and beauty. Alexander Pope expressed the sentiment of his age when he said:

> Nature and Nature's laws lay hid in night:
> God said, Let Newton be! and all was light.

Vico greatly feared that Descartes' science would abandon to lore and idle speculation what today we call human culture. Descartes had spoken out boldly against history, language, literature, and other subjects dealing with human experience, claiming that science has nothing to do with "whatever depends on experience alone."

What man most needs to know, Vico maintained, is himself, and Descartes had diverted attention away from human experience to cold abstractions about nature. Vico believed that the proper study of mankind is man, although he did not state his belief in these words, and, like other humanists, he was troubled by the materialistic turn that science had taken. What really matters, he declared, is to free man through knowledge of himself from "the impulses, yearnings, and blank misgivings of a creature moving about in worlds not realized." What Descartes had actually developed, Vico believed, was a mathematical manner of reasoning adequate for physics when linked with experimentation but quite inadequate for philology. By philology Vico meant the science not merely of words but of language, literature, history, politics, customs—in short, the science of human culture.

Vico emphatically insisted that social and cultural phenomena are proper subjects of scientific investigation. He claimed, furthermore, that Descartes had failed to understand the use of science in those areas of inquiry which matter most to mankind simply because he failed to understand the nature of science and supposed that his own limited method was the whole method of scientific inquiry.

Vico could not see how the Cartesians could claim to have delivered man from skepticism. He admitted that knowledge removes doubt, but he insisted that the method of Descartes affords only the certitude of consciousness, not knowledge. Vico denied that knowing and being conscious of—however clearly and distinctly an idea appears in consciousness—are the same. One can be certain of the existence of self, of God, and of the material universe, but certainty is a state of mind, not of fact. Vico had no doubt about the certainties established by individual and common consciousness, but he maintained that these certainties lie outside the domain of science. He believed that scientific knowledge goes just so far and no further, and that beyond science lies a vast realm in which faith holds sway. The distinction he made between truth and certainty may be expressed in terms of the difference between intuitive awareness and knowledge established by reason and experience.

> Men who do not know the truth of things try to reach certainty about them, so that, if they cannot satisfy their intellects by science, their wills at least may rest on conscience.[12]

Having put science in its place, however, Vico identified himself with science and built his theory of the common nature of nations on the solid foundations of observation and logical analysis.

The Cartesians were right, Vico said, in their assertion that scientific knowledge is formed of clear and distinct ideas. But he asked why some ideas are clear and distinct and others are not. The answer was not far to seek: we know clearly and distinctly what we have made, and that only. Consequently, the criterion of truth is to have made it. Man grasps mathematical truths with certainty because they are of his own making. Two plus two equals four because the symbols on each side of the equation are synonyms: four is simply another way of saying two plus two. Similarly all mathematical truths are tautological. A geometrical system—intricate, harmonious, perfect—is but an elaboration into a variety of expressions of one or more initial assumptions. It is a human construct, grasped with certainty because it is not immersed in corporeal matter.

For the same reason, ideas gained through experimentation are clear and distinct, though perhaps in less degree. The experimental method provides conditions of control under which a certain event can be made to occur. In modern terms, one can know that the bite of a mosquito will, under certain conditions, result in malaria fever because one has caused the fever to occur by exposing an individual to the bite of a mosquito. One knows what one has made, no more, no less. That is to say, one never really knows until one has found the cause which adequately explains the matter.

The bearing of this position on social science is immediately obvious. Human causes are comprehensible to the finite mind. This being so, the value of the study of history, language, literature, and customs, which the rationalists had questioned, becomes clear.

> Whoever reflects on this cannot but marvel that the philosophers should have bent all their energies to the study of the world of nature, which, since God made it, He alone knows; and that they should have neglected the study of the world of nations or civil world, which, since men had made it, men could hope to know.[13]

Vico went on to point out that language was created by men to afford expression to their thoughts and emotions and that the meaning of words cannot be understood apart from the life situations in which the words are found. The study of language, therefore, makes it possible for modern men to recreate the institutions of the early societies and thus to comprehend the history of man. If language originates in experience, as Vico believed, it follows that from a study of the roots of the speech of ancient men and from their legends and myths can be gained an understanding of their behavior and their collective wisdom. Far from being uncertain knowledge, as Descartes had believed, this is the most certain *knowledge*—as distinguished from consciousness—of which man is capable. In language, myths, fables, legends, laws, and customs, the mind of universal man is revealed, and it can be known as the awful forces of nature can never be.

Vico's *New Science* attempted to prove that a scientific methodology rooted securely in the convertibility of the true with the created could yield a larger and more certain knowledge of universal man than can ever be had of nature. His application of this method to the data available to him—history, language, law, and literature—resulted in a science of social origins, social organization, and social change.

It must be remembered that Vico died more than two centuries ago. Unlike Descartes, he did not write for his own age. Perhaps he wrote for ours, and if we bring up to date his ideas on the nature and function of social science, this is what he said:

1. There are three ways of knowing: through experience, through reason, and through intuition. Through experience and reason man attains scientific knowledge; through intuition, those certainties which are established in consciousness.

2. Man can have scientific knowledge, as contrasted with intuitive knowledge, only of that which he has made. Fragments of natural phenomena may be grasped by the forceps of man's own making—concepts, operations—and made part of his comprehensible experience, but human culture, which is wholly the work of man, can be known as nature cannot be known by the finite mind.

3. Since social science deals with phenomena created wholly by man, it attains positive truths. The measure of these truths is awareness, since they are within the grasp of the human mind, and consensus, since no one familiar with the evidence can doubt them.

4. The warmth of meaningful human experience gives social science a claim on the attention of men far different from the prospect of cold and forbidding groping in the infinitude of nature. It affords the security of knowing existence rather than the restless discontent and everlasting reaching out of those who seek the laws of nature.

5. Social science discloses the path along which man has moved and his position at any particular moment in time, and it affords a grand and distant vision

of what lies ahead. Prediction takes many forms, and there are questions which social science does not answer. Will a marriage be successful? What will be the price of pork? Who can say? Does this mean that social science must be content with probability? Not at all. Probability is a weak and sickly form of prediction, a poor specimen of the same sort of thing. According to Vico, social science yields positive knowledge of the future, because it discovers the causes which adequately explain the past and the present. Among these causes is the human will. Nothing comparable to human volition appears in natural phenomena to disturb its uniformity and orderly sequence. Consequently prediction in social science differs from that in natural science not in degree but in kind. Vico was convinced that the kind of prediction of which social science is capable is more meaningful, more satisfying, and more certain than that offered by natural science.

That Vico took a stand against the materialism of his age is obvious, as is the fact that he searched for scientific knowledge in an area which Descartes had declared to be barren. His was a voice crying in the wilderness, but it had been heard before. The admitted sources of his inspiration are revealing of his intellectual leanings. He acknowledges indebtedness to four men: to Plato, for his teachings on divine providence, moderation, and immortality, and for his portrayal of man as he should be; to Tacitus, for his history of man; to Bacon, for his understanding of the unity in history and of the proper uses of philosophy; and to Grotius, for his insight into the true principles of universal law. Whatever Vico may have borrowed from these four men, however, he recast in a mold peculiarly his own anything he may have selected, and what emerges is a philosophy of history, although Vico did not call it that, and a science of human culture.

LAW OF THE THREE AGES

An important part of Vico's social science is his theory of social change. For most of his data, Vico turned to the Homeric and Hellenic ages of Greece and to the early Roman periods. It is strange that he should have made so little use of other sources of information, but since he believed that all nations pass through essentially the same stages of development, he regarded as universally applicable the principles derived from Greco-Roman history.

His religious scruples required that he recognize sacred history not only as accurate in the minutest details but also as requiring no interpretation. Accordingly, he distinguished between the Jews, whose history is recorded in the Scriptures, and the gentiles, whose history is found in profane sources, and he repeatedly states that what he is saying about the history of mankind is applicable only to the gentiles.

AGE OF THE GODS

The first age through which a nation passes, as it slowly emerges from bestiality, Vico calls the "Age of the Gods." This is the state of nature, says Vico, so dear to those who call it the Golden Age. He sees it in a far different light. It is not an age in which kindly and innocent people take their ease in the enjoyment of nature's bounty and live out their days in contentment. On the contrary, it is an age in which men live in a state of "superstitious fanaticism."

In this age human nature is bestial, reasoning power is weak, and imagination is strong. Customs are "tinged with religion and piety." Government is theocratic, and law is assumed to be the will of the gods. Speech is rude, and the characters used in writing are pictorial. Jurisprudence is "mystic theology," punishment is of "cyclopean cruelty," authority is divine and absolute, and revelation takes the place of reason.

This is the stage in a nation's history, according to Vico, when man has not learned to restrain imagination by reason; when the presence of the divine is felt as a terrifying and mysterious force; when brute mating has yielded to the slowly dawning awareness of family bonds, but family institutions are still "monastic, cyclopean, and monarchic"; when speech is the poetry of natural sounds and writing the hieroglyphics of religious superstition; when man is immersed in the senses, buffeted by the passions, and buried in the body; when only the strong can protect the weak from the violent. It can be seen how far Vico differs in his conception of primitive society both from those who deplore the decline from a Golden Age and from those who assume that in the primitive state man is intellectually capable of creating social order by means of a contract.

AGE OF THE HEROES

There is no sudden transition from one age to another, as can be seen in the histories of Greece and Rome, where,

> even as the mighty current of a kingly river retains far out to sea the momentum of its flow and the sweetness of its waters, the age of the gods continued to run its course, for that religious way of thinking must still have persisted by which whatever men themselves did was attributed to the agency of the gods.[14]

Nevertheless, the "Age of the Gods" is eventually succeeded by the "Age of the Heroes." In this age human nature is heroic, law is based on force, and right is decided with a spear. Government is aristocratic. Conventional symbols with little or no sacred meaning are used in writing. Jurisprudence is a matter of correct form. Authority rests on "the solemn formulae of the laws." Reason is the pronouncement of experts.

In summarizing Vico's portrayal of social organization in Greece and Rome in the age of the heroes, Fisch and Bergin say:

> To secure themselves against mutinies of their serfs as well as against outlaw invasions, the fathers formed mutual alliances, patrician orders, "heroic states," with the fathers as citizens and the serfs as plebs. The heroic state was not a monarchy like the earlier family state, for its king was simply one of the fathers, the magistrate of the order; often, in fact, there were two or more such magistrates. It was not a democracy, for the "people" was simply the patrician order, exclusive of the plebs; the only freedom, the only rights, were those of the patricians; the fatherland was the land of the fathers. It was in fact a feudal aristocracy. . . .
>
> The whole life of these heroic states centered in the conflict between patricians and plebeians. The two classes, as Vico put it, had two eternal contrary properties, the plebeians wishing always to change the state, and the nobles to preserve it as it was. The patricians were better organized; they owned the land; they had the arms and the military discipline; they had a monopoly of public office and knowledge of law; they alone knew how to ascertain the will and win the favor of the gods; the solemn rites of marriage and burial were theirs alone; and they were bound by oath to keep the plebs in subjection.[15]

The age of the heroes is characterized by the appearance of strong men who claim divine origin and inspiration, by the law of force exercised in the name of the gods, by government of the aristocrats, by the use of heroic blazonings to symbolize authority and prestige. In this age the exploits of a whole people are attributed to some hero—*e.g.,* Greek wisdom to Homer, Greek courage to Achilles, and Greek sagacity to Odysseus. Jurisprudence rests on form—using the proper words, observing the proprieties at the bar, knowing "how to draw up pleas at law and articles." The government justifies its action by reasons of state which are naturally comprehensible not to all men but only to "the few experts in government who are able to discern what is necessary for the preservation of mankind." In other words, feudal government is under obligation not to consult with the people but only to persuade them that whatever is being done by the government is for their benefit.

Vico finds much to his liking in heroic society, but he realizes that the feudal heroes must yield sooner or later to the demand of the plebs for the natural rights of man. No matter how strong the walls which the aristocrats build to protect their position, the incessant pressure of the masses will finally breach them, and the nobles will be tumbled from their high seats of authority.

> [The heroic commonwealths of Greece and Rome] remained aristocratic as long as the fathers preserved this authority of ownership within their reigning orders, and until the plebs of the heroic peoples had obtained from the fathers themselves laws extending to them the certain own-

ership of the fields, the right to solemn nuptials, the sovereign powers, the priesthoods and thereby the science of the laws.¹⁶

When the masses come into possession of the full rights and powers of citizens, the age of heroes is ended. When men are weak, they will accept the restraints of feudal organization, but their natural yearning for freedom and equality is strong even in bondage, and they will not tolerate masters when they have the strength to overcome them.

AGE OF MEN

In the "Age of Men," which follows the heroic age, human nature is intelligent and modest. Custom is formed by "one's own sense of civil duty." Law is directed by human reason. Government is designed to ensure equality; at first it may be of the free popular type but it must become monarchical if it is to endure long. Language is articulate speech, and the characters used in writing are merely conventional signs, such as the letters of the alphabet. Jurisprudence "benignly bends the rule of law to all the requirements of the equity of the causes." Authority is based on the trust of the people in their leaders. Judgment is rendered on the basis of all the facts in each case and is, consequently, always "extraordinary." Sovereignty is in the people, but every citizen does not have an equal voice in the government. Vico says that in the popular commonwealth of Rome "the industrious and not the lazy, the frugal and not the prodigal, the provident and not the idle, the magnanimous and not the faint-hearted—in a word, the rich with some virtue or semblance thereof, and not the poor with their many shameless vices—were considered the best for governing."

DECADENCE AND REFLUX

Unfortunately the age of men breeds ills which destroy it. Popular states become corrupt. The unchecked liberty of free people, the "worst of all tyrannies," leads to anarchy. Philosophy turns to skepticism, and eloquence becomes an instrument of power. When liberty becomes license, when so many laws are passed that none of them is respected, when the rich grow richer and the poor grow poorer because no one is in position to bridle the passions that are running free, when the people are stunned by the realization of their inability to govern themselves—perhaps then

> Some Caesar rises up who proves capable of protecting society from the worst effects of its own evil passions, and of satisfying in some tolerable measure its legitimate desires, and he succeeds in substituting his own will for the law which democratic license had rendered vain. The corruption of a nation may advance so far, however, that no remedy can be found within itself, but must come from without; and in such a case a nation is either subdued by a foreign enemy or sinks into barbarism.¹⁷

SOCIAL PROGRESS

In stating his cyclical theory of social change, Vico did not rule out the possibility of progress. His principles disclose a universal pattern of change, but he recognized the fact that a nation's culture is not lost as a result of its political disintegration and that a new nation, drawing from the heritage of the old, may begin its development on a higher plane. He pointed out that "all the wisdom of Greece shone forth at Rome in the splendor of the Roman language." Consequently, although the picture of the future that might be drawn from Vico's principles is certainly not "tinged with glowing colors," it need not be viewed as darkly pessimistic. Flint interprets Vico's position on this point as follows:

> He held that ancient Egypt, Greece, and Rome alike passed through a cycle of three stages, but he nowhere represented these three histories as precisely alike. He fully recognized that each nation had its own individuality; that the events and the personages of one nation were not repetitions of those of another, but had each a special character of its own. . . . He deemed feudalism sufficiently like the heroic age of Greece to be accounted a second heroic age, but he was not ignorant that these two ages had great differences. He thought Dante might be regarded as another Homer, but he did not imagine that all that he had affirmed about Homer he could reaffirm about Dante. He held that the ethnic religions arose, flourished, and decayed, but also that Christianity as a revealed religion was not subject to this law. . . . His belief in cycles or *ricorsi* was, indeed, inconsistent with a belief in continuous progress in a straight line, but not with advance on the whole, not with a gradually ascending spiral movement; and still less did it imply that any cycle was perfectly like another, and that history merely repeated itself.[18]

THE UNITY OF CULTURE

In his recognition of the fact that the component parts of the culture of a people fit together more or less harmoniously to form a pattern, and in his use of that fact, Vico was far ahead of his time. Even now, despite the prodigious labors of such scholars as Sorokin, Max Weber, and Pareto, to mention only a few, the nature of cultural unity has not been fully revealed. Vico realized, however, the essential nature of cultural integration: the interdependence of law, government, language, art, literature, jurisprudence, philosophy, religion, and various other elements of culture in a specific society. The following passage, which sums up an analysis which he made of Greek philosophy, illustrates Vico's recognition of the unity in culture.

> From all the above we conclude that these principles of metaphysics, logic and morals issued from the market place of Athens. From Solon's

advice to the Athenians, "Know thyself" . . . came forth the popular commonwealths, from the popular commonwealths the laws, and from the laws emerged philosophy; and Solon, who had been wise in vulgar wisdom, came to be held wise in esoteric wisdom. This may serve as . . . a last reproof . . . against Polybius, who said that if there were philosophers in the world there would be no need of religions. For [the fact is that] if there had not been religions and hence commonwealths, there would have been no philosophers in the world, and if human affairs had not been thus guided by divine providence there would have been no idea of either science or virtue.[19]

This observation is very similar to Max Weber's discovery, from his monumental study of the relationship between religious and economic institutions, that the two are so closely linked that modern capitalism, for example, may be said to have taken root in the Protestant ethic and to have been sustained by it.

THE VULGAR WISDOM

Vico realized, furthermore, that the unity in culture is basically a matter of common mentality, which he called the "vulgar wisdom." By this he meant the collective thought of the whole people. Men share and express in their thoughts and behavior the mentality of their society. Primitive people, however widely separated in time and space, are much alike, as are enlightened people, whatever the age or country in which they live. Greek mentality in the primitive period, for example, was much like Roman mentality in a similar stage of Rome's development, and the savage Greek had less in common with the enlightened Greek than he had with the savage Roman. Similarly, feudal societies have the same basic mentality, and consequently the same basic institutions, wherever they are found.

This idea furnishes the key to Vico's science of the common nature of nations. He reached one level of abstraction in his awareness of cultural integration. To realize that laws make morals and morals make laws, that the arts and sciences thrive in a time of military glory because the strength and vigor of the soldiers is matched by that of the civilians, that religion affects thought and behavior in business and politics as these in turn affect religion, and that all other parts of culture are similarly interdependent—this was an important achievement. But Vico did not stop there; he went on to develop, on a higher level of abstraction, the theory that the parts of culture change together in a definite and universal pattern. An insight into the popular wisdom of a people affords, therefore, not only a comprehensive view of a society at a specific time but also a revelation of its stage of development. This popular wisdom can be discerned only in the actions and expressed ideas of individuals, but Vico was fully persuaded that the wisdom is that of the whole people. He illustrated this point by a detailed study of the Greek poet Homer.

THE TRUE HOMER

From his study of the *Iliad* and the *Odyssey* Vico came to the conclusion that these are but "two great treasure stores of the customs of early Greece." They contain nothing, he says, not found in the Greek society of the time, and far from being, as Plato supposed, the creative works of a man of genius, they are but mirrors of social life and thought in Greece's heroic age. The qualities attributed to Homer—comparisons wild and savage, descriptions of battles and deaths cruel and fearful, expressions of passion in a style clear and splendid—are the properties of an age of "vigorous memory, robust imagination and sublime invention."

Almost all the cities of Greece claimed to be Homer's birthplace, because in reality they were; "the Greek peoples were themselves Homer." The time during which Homer was supposed to have lived is much disputed, because he truly lived "on the lips and in the memories of the peoples of Greece throughout the whole period from the Trojan War down to the time of Numa, a span of 460 years." Homer's reputed blindness was introduced because of the popular opinion that "the blind have marvelously retentive memories." All this, Vico says, "does not make Homer any less the father and prince of sublime poets," but it does make it clear that the accomplishments attributed to him were those of the people rather than of the man.

The "Homeric question" raised by Vico has been much debated, and although there is not now, nor is there likely ever to be, complete agreement as to its answer, the discussion which it prompted has been of inestimable value. The source of the inspiration of creative artists is an intriguing subject. Sometimes the voice of the people, whoever the spokesman, is heard, and folk literature belongs to all the people in a sense in which Milton's *Paradise Lost,* for example, does not.

THE EFFECT OF INTEGRATION ON CHANGE

It follows from the nature of the integration of culture that a change in any one part will affect all the others. The political triumph of the plebeians at the end of Rome's heroic age resulted in a change in philosophy, religion, manners, morals, family relationships, language, literature, property rights, conceptions of justice, and all other elements of the culture. Although he insisted that these elements change together, Vico did not say that they change at the same rate. He did maintain, however, that a society cannot embrace a belief or practice entirely foreign to its dominant mentality. Nations in contact may borrow from one another, but savages borrow from savages, feudal societies from feudal societies, and enlightened peoples from those of similar mental development. The ethics of Aristotle can mean no more to savages than the superstitions of savages mean to the informed.

Vico did not attempt to cope with—if, indeed, he recognized—the problem of inharmonious and destructive elements in a culture, but he saw clearly the spider-web nature of its structure, with every thread connected with every other thread in such a way that a dislocation at one point would bring about a compensatory change in every part of the system.

HUMAN NATURE

Vico attempted to go no further back in time than the Deluge. He began his history with the descendants of Ham, Japheth, and Shem, whom he portrays as wandering on the face of the earth more like beasts than men.

> By fleeing from the wild beasts with which the great forest must have abounded, and by pursuing women, who in that state must have been wild, indocile and shy, they became separated from each other in their search for food and water. Mothers abandoned their children, who in time must have come to grow up without hearing a human voice, much less learning any human custom, and thus descended to a state truly bestial and savage.[20]

From this primitive state man slowly advanced by means of religion and marriage. Endowed by nature with imagination, he came to fear the divine power revealed in the thunderbolts. Then the unnatural practice of promiscuity that he had followed before religion awakened within him a sense of shame gave way to marriage, "the first kind of friendship in the world." The humanity of man appeared, therefore, only after man had become aware of religious and family obligations. Without religion and family life he is only another animal. Since the natural inclination to worship and to form permanent family ties is universal among men, no force other than the inherent demands of man's own nature is required to create civilization.

INFLUENCE OF FAMILY LIFE

Vico observed that all nations, "barbarous as well as civilized," contract solemn marriages. All animals mate, but only the human being is capable of the religious awe which leads to marriage. Love for a mate quickens a sentiment of affection that embraces not only children but also friends. "Piety and marriage," says Vico, "form the school wherein are learned the first rudiments of all the great virtues."

The family feeling extends beyond the simple household, and even beyond the clan and the tribe. The shared affections of the home arouse and sustain the moral sentiments that maintain society.

> . . . in the bestial state [man] desires only his own welfare; having taken wife and begotten children, he desires his own welfare along with

that of his family; having entered upon civil life, he desires his own welfare along with that of his city; when its rule is extended over several peoples, he desires his welfare along with that of the nation; when the nations are united by wars, treaties of peace, alliances and commerce, he desires his own welfare along with that of the entire human race.[21]

THE SOCIAL NATURE OF MAN

Man is by nature social, not in the sense of possessing a herding instinct but because it is natural for him to follow the customs of his own society. He is molded, consequently, by his social environment. Primitive man is strong in imagination and weak in reason. Heroic man is "boorish, crude, harsh, wild, proud, difficult and obstinate." Only in an enlightened society is man able to achieve the rational powers of which he is capable.

Man is not by nature unjust, but he becomes unjust when he lives in a society where justice does not prevail. His natural desire for equality may yield under social pressure to an unnatural urge to strive for superiority. Even the restraint of custom may be removed by social experience, so that the natural inclination to conform gives way to the unnatural desire found among men to put themselves above the laws.

Only in a very limited sense may it be said that human nature does not change. On the contrary, the individual reflects in his personality the dominant characteristics of his time. "The nature of peoples," says Vico, "is first crude, then severe, then benign, then delicate, and finally dissolute." Hard times produce hard men, as corrupt and decadent conditions produce men lacking in integrity. Man's social nature is, therefore, a source both of strength and of weakness: it enables him to conform, to swim with the tide, and thus makes organized society possible; but at the same time it makes difficult the escape from forces carrying a society to destruction.

FREEDOM OF WILL

When carried to its logical extreme, this line of reasoning leads to a complete denial of human freedom in any form. Vico saw, however, no necessity for rejecting experience for the sake of logic. He observed evidence of human choice. In fact he regarded freedom of action as so evident that he based his science on the assumption that man is active and creative rather than passive and impotent. Human plans often miscarry, and rarely are the ends gained that had been anticipated, but Vico was persuaded that history is made by men. It is made, however, in accordance with a design foreordained. Divine Providence has so created the human mind as to ensure the preservation of the human race and the orderly course of human action.

> It is true that men have themselves made this world of nations . . . but this world without doubt has issued from a mind often diverse, at times

> quite contrary and always superior to the particular ends that men had proposed to themselves; which narrow ends, made means to serve wider ends, it has always employed to preserve the human race upon this earth. Men mean to gratify their bestial lust and abandon their offspring, and they inaugurate the chastity of marriage from which the families arise. The fathers mean to exercise without restraint their paternal power over their clients, and they subject them to the civil powers from which the cities arise. The reigning orders of nobles mean to abuse their lordly freedom over the plebeians, and they are obliged to submit to the laws which establish popular liberty. The free peoples mean to shake off the yoke of their laws, and they become subject to monarchs. The monarchs mean to strengthen their own positions by debasing their subjects with all the vices of dissoluteness, and they dispose them to endure slavery at the hands of stronger nations. The nations mean to dissolve themselves, and their remnants flee for safety to the wilderness, whence, like the phoenix, they rise again. That which did all this was mind, for men did it with intelligence; it was not fate, for they did it by choice; not chance, for the results of their always so acting are perpetually the same.[22]

Vico's faith in mankind was securely rooted in his faith in God. Although the individual is shaped by the cultural influences to which he is subjected, and inhibited in his conduct by the demands of conformity, collectively men are free to work out their destiny, limited only by the divine plan. As Vaughan points out, "for the fulfillment of divine purpose, nothing more is needed than the natural instincts of man, acting on and, in turn, acted on by the purely natural operation of circumstance and physical conditions." [23]

In this way Vico was able to reconcile freedom with necessity and thus surmount the most important barrier to a science of society.

> Human choice, by its nature most uncertain, is made certain and determined by the common sense of men with respect to human needs. . . . Common sense is judgment without reflection, shared by an entire class, an entire people, an entire nation, or the whole human race.[24]

ECONOMIC INSTITUTIONS

Vico observed that in the feudal or heroic ages of Greece and Rome wealth was in land, and that those who had possession of the fields were socially far removed from the landless. Through ownership of the land the feudal lord was able to control those who tilled it, and the peasant was in reality a vassal who voluntarily accepted slavery for the sake of security. Hence there was a rule in ancient civil law providing that "no one may acquire by a person not under his power." Under feudal economy the barter of possessions did not apply to real estate. The landowner kept possession of his fields as long as possible, for "it is characteristic of the strong not to relinquish through laziness what they have acquired by courage. Rather do they yield, from necessity or for utility, as little as they can and bit by bit." [25] The acquisition of land by those who till it destroys the feudal system, since the power of the feudal lords is broken when they no longer have vassals under their absolute control.

LAND TENURE

There are, says Vico, three types of land tenure. The first is the *bonitary,* which is occupation by vassals of land that they do not own and that they use subject to such restrictions and obligations as may be imposed upon them by the owners. The second is the *quiritary,* which exists when property is acquired through force of arms and through civil transfer and is held by armed might or by the power of civil law. This type of tenure is represented, though not exactly, by the modern freehold, which gives title in fee simple to the owner. Under feudal conditions this kind of ownership is optimum, since the owner acknowledges no encumbrance of any kind on his property. When the Roman plebs claimed and received under the *Law of the Twelve Tables* the right to marry, they were really demanding the right of citizens to quiritary tenure of land, so that they would be able to transmit their real property to their heirs.

The third type of tenure is *eminent domain,* which is found where all property actually belongs to the state. The power to tax implies the power to regulate and even to confiscate; consequently sovereignty resides in the state whenever the state has the authority to impose taxes.

> This is at bottom the reason why sovereign civil powers may dispose of whatever belongs to their subjects: their persons as well as their acquisitions, their works and their labors, and impose thereon tribute or taxes, whenever they have to exercise that dominion over their lands which, from different points of view but with the same meaning in substance, moral theologians and writers on public law now call eminent domain, just as they now speak of the laws concerning this domain as the fundamental laws of the realm. Since this dominion is over the lands themselves, sovereigns naturally may not exercise it save to preserve the substance of their states, on whose stability or collapse hinges the stability or ruin of all the private interests of their peoples.[26]

Vico gave the ancient Romans credit for having established these three types of ownership of land. He shows how, in "the world's first agrarian law," the heads of large households granted bonitary ownership to their vassals, and how in the long struggle between nobles and plebeians the rights of quiritary possession were not only widely distributed among the people but were also subordinated to the authority of the state. Apparently Vico assumed that this authority would be exercised to protect rather than to destroy private property. The protection of law, he says, made any Roman citizen who possessed land, after a government by law had been established, the owner and recognized master of his estate. Even though his private patrimony was really only a segment of the public patrimony, it lost its distinct designation and reverted to the public treasury only in default of a private owner. Lacking an heir because of failure to marry and bear children, an owner forfeited his right to determine his successor, and his estate became public property. Vico regarded this as a clear confirmation of the rights of the state with respect to property held by individuals, as they were established under the provisions of the *Lex Papia Poppaea*.

GOVERNMENT AND LAW

CRITICISM OF SOCIAL-CONTRACT THEORIES

Vico vigorously attacked the belief, commonly accepted in his day, that government was logically founded in a voluntary agreement. Hobbes and Locke had portrayed a state of nature from which mankind had passed into a state of society by means of a social contract. Hobbes had declared that man was able to escape from an existence "nasty, brutish, and short" only by giving up, for the sake of peace, some of his natural rights. Vico criticized both the historical accuracy and the logical necessity of this theory. The state was formed, he says, not out of individuals, but out of family groups. In that primitive time when man dwelt in isolation from his fellows, the only basis of social order was the law of the jungle. Primitive man was incapable of the kind of reason required to enable him to see the advantages of government. According to Vico, the only force that can tame a savage people is religion, which in turn leads to family discipline. Let us reflect, says Vico, on the long period of "cyclopean family discipline" required to bring the men of the gentile world to the point of giving up their "feral native liberty" and obeying naturally the laws of civil states. Reason cannot subdue the fierce passions; it can function only after they have been brought under control. Religion alone is able to make men reasonable. The social-contract theorists falsely assumed that primitive man possessed the rational powers of the men of their own enlightened age; Hobbes, the cultivated philosopher, endowed savages with his own informed intellect.

ORIGIN OF GOVERNMENT

In contrast to this view, Vico held that the real origin of government is found in man's basic nature rather than in his sophisticated reason. Government is necessary because it is natural. Communion with his fellows is one of man's most urgent needs, once he has attained through piety and a sense of shame the capacity for moral virtue. This need is a result neither of gregariousness nor of practical judgment regarding the material advantages of cooperation. Governments arise because men seek to realize themselves, and because they are so constituted in mind and body that self-realization is possible only in the state. The organization of a society into a state with a sovereign civil power is an inevitable outcome of man's struggle to satisfy the imperative demands of his own nature.

FORMS OF GOVERNMENT

The form of government found in a nation at any one time depends upon that nation's level of development. In the most primitive stage of man's existence, government is a theocracy. Men live in superstitious terror and rely upon oracles for the commandments of the gods. Vico had little to say about government in this stage but turned instead to the three simple patterns of government which appear as civil society takes shape under human effort: aristocracy, the free popular commonwealth, and monarchy. The first is found in the heroic age, and the other two are found in the age of men.

Aristocracy is a natural outcome of the submission of the weak to the strong for the sake of protection against the violent. "Men come naturally," says Vico, "to the feudal system when the helpless seek the altars of the strong to save themselves from Hobbes' violent men." Feudal aristocracy lasts as long as the nobles are able to retain possession of the fields—*i.e.,* as long as they control the nation's wealth—but sooner or later the masses force the enactment of laws that enable them to acquire property. With the power of wealth in their hands, they force the aristocrats to give over the reins of government. Then the government becomes a free popular commonwealth.

This type of government is by its very nature unstable. With legislative power in their hands, the people pass so many laws that confusion and a general lack of respect for law result. They are incapable of grasping universals and find it necessary, therefore, to pass "new laws every day for particular occasions." The masses are easily seduced by ambitious leaders, who exploit the power in the hands of the people for their own selfish ends. The free popular commonwealth is destroyed by "factions, seditions, and civil wars," and a monarchy is created to restore order.

> Since in the free commonwealths all look out for their own private interests, into the service of which they press their public arms at the risk of ruin to their nations, to preserve the latter from destruction a single man must arise, as Augustus did at Rome, and take all public concerns by force of arms into his own hands, leaving his subjects free to look after their private affairs and after just so much public business, and of just such kinds, as the monarch may entrust to them. Thus are the peoples saved when they would otherwise rush to their own destruction.[27]

Vico regarded monarchy as "the form of government best adapted to human nature when reason is fully developed." The happiest fate for a people "rotting from civil illness," if they cannot agree upon a monarch, is to be conquered by a strong nation able to govern them. Otherwise, they will revert to barbarism, the "last remedy of Providence."

CYCLE OF CHANGE

No form of government, not even the brutal and savage type of barbarism, endures. Sooner or later a few survivors from even the most degenerate system will gradually develop religion and morality, and a new cycle will begin.

Vico denied the theory, expressed by Bodin and many others before him, that the order of change in government is from monarchy to tyranny, and then to a popular commonwealth, which in turn yields to an aristocracy. The order, he believed, is just the reverse of that. The true aristocrats were the feudal lords, who owned all the wealth, made all the laws, declared justice, and provided such security as lay within their power. Feudalism inevitably breaks down when wealth is distributed and the people gain the right to make laws, to demand justice, and to take measures to protect themselves from their enemies.

The free popular commonwealth is the least secure of governments, since it depends for its existence on a degree of self-discipline of which the fickle masses are incapable. The monarchy lasts as long as the people are contented, for without "universal satisfaction and content of the people, monarchic states are neither lasting nor secure." When discord arises, and no cure can be provided by the government, the state is overcome from without and loses its independence.

> . . . since peoples so far corrupted had already become naturally slaves of their unrestrained passions—of luxury, effeminacy, avarice, envy, pride, and vanity—and in pursuit of the pleasures of their dissolute life were falling back into all the vices characteristic of the most abject slaves (having become liars, tricksters, calumniators, thieves, cowards and pretenders), providence decrees that they become slaves by the natural law of nations . . . and that they become subject to better nations which, having conquered them by arms, preserve them as subject provinces. Herein two great lights of natural order shine forth. First, that he who cannot govern himself must let himself be governed by another who can. Second, that the world is always governed by those who are naturally fittest.[28]

SOURCE OF LAWS

The laws of a people, like the form of its government, reveal the common mentality. The belief expressed by some earlier writers that the Romans had borrowed their *Law of the Twelve Tables* from the Greeks was to Vico untenable. He praised this earliest Roman legislation but attributed its excellence to the superiority of the ancient Romans. A nation in one stage of its development, he insisted, could not possibly take over the laws of another nation in a different stage. The *Law of the Twelve Tables* reflected customs prevailing in Rome at the time they were written down and not those found in Athens in the heyday of Greece's splendor. Vico asked how nations could be different and yet be ordered by the same laws. With remarkable insight, he recognized the fact that laws are defined not by words but by practices, that they are not promulgated by men of vision or power but slowly shaped by human experience. The laws of inheritance, for example, record rather than establish rights. "Legitimate succession," says Vico, "must naturally have been observed by all the first nations before they had any notions of testaments." [29]

NATURE OF LAWS

The meaning of a law is not fixed, Vico declared, since in so far as it functions as a guide to conduct it must be interpreted in such a way as to induce right behavior. Men are not equally capable of understanding the law, but only men of limited ideas, says Vico, attach to the words in which laws are stated an express meaning.

> Golden is the definition which Ulpian assigns to civil equality: "a kind of probable judgment, not naturally known to all men . . . but to those few who, being eminently endowed with prudence, experience, or learning have come to know what things are necessary for the conservation of human society." . . . Intelligent men take for law whatever impartial utility dictates in each case.[30]

By nature men are impelled to conform. They live by law not because of fear but because of fellow-feeling. It is natural, and for that reason pleasant, to observe natural customs—man is not unjust by nature but only weak. Law supports man and enables him to realize his deep yearning to live justly. Law grows out of human needs and serves not only to restrain action but also to guide it into satisfying forms of self-expression.

PENAL JUSTICE

In his discussion of the right of society to punish its recalcitrant members, Vico stated his position regarding the ends which punishment may reasonably be expected to serve. He believed that the only adequate penalty is that which produces remorse. Conscience is the most effective monitor of conduct, but conscience may lose its edge. In that case it must be sharpened by social pressure. Crimes result from ignorance, weakness, or brutishness. For a misdeed growing out of ignorance, such social action is necessary as will bring about on the part of the offender a consciousness of the significance of his act. The conscience of the weak cannot stand alone and must be supported by the external voice of justice. As for the brutish, reform is likely to be extremely difficult or impossible. Crimes resulting from brutishness must, therefore, be met with restrictive and exemplary punishment. Vico insists, however, that this type of punishment be employed only where the welfare of the whole society is at stake.

VICO'S MAJOR CONTRIBUTIONS TO SOCIAL THOUGHT

Vico packed into a single volume the fruits of all his intellectual labors. It is not surprising, therefore, that *The New Science* is condensed and terse to the point of being cryptic. What astounds the reader is the extent of Vico's contributions to living social thought. A brief summary of a few of his more important ideas follows.

1. Human history is made by mankind. Divine providence acts *upon* humanity only *through* humanity and never through the exercise of arbitrary will or power. The bearing of this conception on the modern idea of progress, which means movement in a desirable direction through human action, is evident.

2. Since the criterion of truth is to have made it, social science affords not mere probability but the most certain knowledge of which man is capable. The impulses, yearnings, and "blank misgivings of a creature moving about in worlds not realized" are not less, but more, understandable than are the laws of nature.

3. The common nature of nations is a psychological unity which is reflected in the laws, customs, governments, language symbols, truth systems, and religions of a people and in types of personality. All the component parts of a culture articulate the mental state of its members.

4. The course of nations, and thus the history of mankind, is the progression of the mental state through three stages, which may be called the Age of Gods, the Age of Heroes, and the Age of Men. This cyclical pattern of social change means the inevitable decadence of any specific culture but not a reversion of all mankind to barbarism. New nations emerge as old nations decay, and the historical cycles may form an ascending spiral.

5. The law of the "Three Ages" describes and explains the dynamic relationship of society, culture, and personality. Vico maintained that personality is the expression in individual behavior of the culture of a society. He saw that society, culture, and personality change together, and he believed that he had discovered the law governing that change.

Vico was a bold and an independent thinker. As if to refute his own argument that personality is determined by culture, he disregarded prevailing opinion. As a critic of rationalism he might have gained a following, because he said what many people were prepared to hear, but when he ventured opinions about the nature of social science out of harmony with trends in empiricism, a rising tide of positivism engulfed him. He saw evidence in history of human progress, but he offered a cyclical view of social change to a society eager to embrace the idea of continuous improvement. At a time when people were fascinated by the promises of individualism, he reduced the stature of the individual by showing the role of culture in shaping human personality. He failed to keep step with the leading figures of his age in his analysis of such topics as land tenure, government, and law. For these reasons, as well, no doubt, as for others, the wilderness in which he cried, as Croce says, gave no answer. Nevertheless, with truly remarkable insight Vico anticipated some modern developments in social thought.

16 · AUGUSTE COMTE

(1798-1857)

> *The future progress of Sociology can never offer so many difficulties as this original formation of it; for it furnishes both the method by which the details of the past may serve as indications of the future, and the general conclusions which afford universal guidance in special researches.*
> —AUGUSTE COMTE

The problem of preserving order in society without sacrificing progress was to the nineteenth century what the problem of reconciling religion and science had been to the seventeenth. Each period wrestled valiantly with its main social problem without finding an entirely satisfactory solution. The later problem was in many respects the more difficult. Social order demands stability, whereas social progress depends upon change. Consequently, an inherent contradiction exists between the two which not even the modern concept of a moving equilibrium can wholly resolve. They may be, and often are, opposed to one another.

The French Revolution (1789-1795), for example, shattered a social order based upon the divine right of kings, the special privileges of the nobility, the authority and wealth of the Catholic Church, and the ignorance of the masses. As a result of the Revolution, the King lost his autocratic powers and finally his head, the nobles had to give up their feudal rights, the Catholic Church was forced to relinquish most of its property and much of its civil authority, and the masses, no longer cowed, raised their voices to claim liberty, equality, and fraternity. All this meant progress, but it also meant social chaos. Then, with the shadow of anarchy over the land, a young man named Napoleon, born in Corsica of obscure parents, seized political control of France and proceeded to restore order. By preserving for the people some of the advantages they had gained from the Revolution, he was able to make himself dictator. Thus, for a few years the French had order but not peace.

Another example of the opposition between order and progress is afforded by the policies and actions of Great Britain. The rise of nationalism in the nineteenth century posed a serious threat of international anarchy. Nothing less than a strong power acting to preserve order among the nations was required. Britain undertook the responsibility of maintaining on the continent of Europe a balance of power. She ruled the seas and used her forces to suppress all rebellions that threatened international order.

The practical British avoided violence as much as possible and yielded to the demands for self-government of some of their colonies in time to salvage from the Empire a British Commonwealth of Nations; but in certain other colonies—for example India and Africa—they resorted to strong measures to maintain the established order. The price demanded by Britain for this service was high, even if no other strong nation on earth at that time would have settled for less. Nevertheless, the price was paid, though not equally by all or willingly by some, and thus progress toward the achievement of self-government for all peoples, so clearly demanded by the humanitarian and liberal ideas of the century, was tempered by restraints imposed by Britain to preserve order among the nations.

A third example is found in the veritable flood of proposals for social reform that the century produced. The tide of liberalism was running strong, the idea of progress was well established and widely accepted, and the future of mankind looked exceedingly bright. Serious and well-meaning persons declared that now all that was required to have both order and progress was a general acceptance of their particular plan of reform. There was no dearth of socialistic schemes. They were proposed by such men as Robert Owen, Ruskin, and Kingsley in England; Fourier, Saint-Simon, Blanc, and Comte in France.

These schemes aimed at social progress, but they promised social order as well. Realists were little impressed by the claims of the idealists that love and sympathy would produce order in society. They called this "sentimental nonsense" and saw no reason to believe that mankind was prepared, for the sake of order, to practice the Golden Rule. They could not see how the call to fight for progress could at the same time be a soothing refrain inspiring universal love. They saw that progress means the transformation of old institutions, centers of power, and modes of thought; and they shuddered when they contemplated the wrecking of the old social order that this transformation would make necessary.

Thus it is that, wherever one turns in the social thought of this interesting century, one is confronted with the problem, sometimes ignored and sometimes bravely faced, of preserving social order amidst tremendous social change. Many solutions were offered to this problem, among them the following: "Progress is the development of Order." To Auguste Comte, the author of this maxim, who founded a science that has endured and a religion that failed to take deep roots, we now turn.

BIOGRAPHICAL SKETCH

Auguste Comte was born at Montpellier in 1798. Early in life he gave evidence of two distinctive traits: a remarkable intellectual ability and a disposition to dissent from established authority. His parents were ardent Royalists; he became a Republican. They were devout Catholics; he became a severe critic of Catholicism. At the Polytechnic School in Paris, where he distinguished himself as a student, he took an active part in an attempt to have one of the professors dismissed; this resulted in his own dismissal and in the temporary closing of the school. That he was precocious is obvious. At thirteen he rejected the political and religious convictions of his family. At fourteen he wanted to reconstruct society. At sixteen he gave lectures in mathematics. In various ways he showed early in life that he was a bold and an independent thinker.

Comte was only twenty years of age when he first met Saint-Simon. He was immediately attracted to the famous French socialist and worked closely with him for about six years. But since Saint-Simon was unsystematic in his thinking, whereas Comte was precise and logical, a break between them was inevitable. It came in 1824, when Comte claimed that his ideas were being used by Saint-Simon's followers without acknowledgment. The break was violent and final. Thereafter Comte usually spoke of his former master and friend only with contempt.

This experience must have been greatly disturbing to Comte. Shortly afterward he made an unfortunate marriage which somehow endured for seventeen years before it was terminated by separation. Not long after his marriage Comte undertook to give a series of lectures, which he hoped would gain him recognition. The strain was too much for him, and he had a mental breakdown which lasted for more than a year. While he was convalescing under his wife's care, he became so despondent that he attempted to drown himself in the Seine. Finally, however, he recovered completely, and was able to work zealously at the task he had staked out for himself until death claimed him.

In several early pamphlets, Comte had shown an interest in social reorganization. In 1819 he wrote that politics should take rank as a positive science. A year later he declared that science and industry were destined to replace theology and war. In 1822 he actually drew up "A Plan of the Scientific Operations Necessary for Reorganising Society." But he soon discovered that a systematic examination of the entire structure of scientific knowledge was needed to provide a theoretical framework for social policy. Consequently, in 1826, he outlined a plan for this vast undertaking, and in 1830 the first volume of his *Positive Philosophy* was published. Twelve years later he brought out the sixth and last volume of this work. He then turned back to his plan for the reconstruction of humanity and, between 1851 and 1854, published the four volumes of his *Positive Polity*.

Since the influence of Clotilde de Vaux is very evident in this last work, and since many rumors have been spread about Comte and Madame de Vaux, a brief statement of their relations is enlightening. The following is from Richmond L. Hawkins:

> Far from being a siren, Clotilde de Vaux was a very ordinary and a very unhappy woman. Born in Paris on April 3, 1815, at the age of twenty she married Amédée de Vaux, who shortly after became tax-collector at Méru (Oise). In 1839 Amédée stole the money in his office, falsified his books, and set fire to the building in which the office was located. Her husband a fugitive from justice, Clotilde returned to her parents in Paris. The laws of France prevented her from securing a divorce, and so she tried courageously, but in vain, to earn a living with her pen. In April, 1844, she became acquainted with Auguste Comte, who was not only a cerebral prodigy, but also an extremely sensual man. Comte fell in love with Clotilde immediately, and his love changed his manner of living and caused a complete revolution in his mode of thought. A remarkable correspondence between them began on April 30, 1845, and ended on March 8, 1846, a month before Clotilde's death from pulmonary tuberculosis. This correspondence shows that, thanks to her determined resistance, the relations between the philosopher and his "incomparable angel" never went beyond a kiss and her deification by him. She never loved Comte, and never lived under the same roof with him. . . . [His adoration of her reveals] a morbid love on Comte's part, to be sure, but a love that will go down in history as the only one which enabled a lover, during his lifetime, to compel his followers to worship his beloved. If Clotilde de Vaux could have returned to earth and seen that Comte had made her the goddess of a new religion, she would surely have been filled with amazement.[1]

Comte's public life was not less tempestuous than his private. After his dismissal from college he earned a bare living by giving private instruction, until the publication of the first part of his *Positive Philosophy* gained for him a post as examiner of candidates applying to the Polytechnic School for admission. This job gave him official recognition and some little addition to the meager income he derived from his lectures. As his fame spread, friends and followers began to contribute to his support. In 1845, for example, John Stuart Mill raised in England about twelve hundred dollars for him. Comte regarded the contributions he received as support to the cause for which he stood and complained that they were too small. He was even more irritated by the failure of his doctrines to inspire the religious revolution he had anticipated. His disciples were few, and when cancer brought about his death in 1857, his dream of a Positive

Society virtually died with him. But his labor was not lost, and social science is what it is today partly because Auguste Comte lived and devoted his life to help create it.

BASIC WRITINGS

Comte's major works are, as we have seen, the *Positive Philosophy,* published in six volumes, between 1830 and 1842, and the *Positive Polity,* published in four volumes, between 1851 and 1854. His verbose style—he admits that he followed the practice of "re-writing nothing"—would have created a severe barrier to general knowledge of his ideas in English-speaking countries had it not been for an excellent liberal translation and condensation of his earlier and more abstruse work made by Harriet Martineau.* In 1853 this talented Englishwoman brought out a translation in which the 4700 pages of the *Positive Philosophy* were reduced to less than one thousand. She declared that she had left out nothing essential, and Comte was so pleased with her book that he had it, rather than his own work, listed in the "Positive Library" that he had recommended to his followers. Unfortunately no similar abridgement of the *Positive Polity* has been made, although a number of Comte's supporters did collaborate in an English translation of this entire work.†

UNITY IN COMTE'S WORK

There has been considerable controversy regarding the unity in Comte's life and work. Some of those who warmly supported his *Philosophy* were equally heated in their condemnation of the *Polity*. John Stuart Mill was one of those who believed that Comte went seriously astray after his first great philosophical work, and attempted some explanation of his decline.

> It should be known that . . . even before completing his first great treatise, M. Comte adopted a rule, to which he very rarely made any exception: to abstain systematically, not only from newspapers or periodical publications, even scientific, but from all reading whatever, except a few favorite poets, in the ancient and modern European languages. This abstinence he practised for the sake of mental health. . . . We are far from thinking that the practice has nothing whatever to recommend it. . . .

---

* First published in three volumes (Bohn edition) but since reprinted. The Martineau version was translated into French by Jules Rig, 2 vols., Baillière et Fils, Paris, 1881. All references to the *Positive Philosophy* in this chapter are from Harriet Martineau, *The Positive Philosophy of Auguste Comte* (2 vols., 3d ed., London: Kegan Paul, 1893).

† John H. Bridges (Vol. I), Frederic Harrison (Vol. II), Edward S. Beesly (Vol. III), and Richard Congreve (Vol. IV), *Comte's Positive Polity* (London: Longmans, Green & Co., 1875–1877).

> [When a man of Comte's ability] has laboriously and conscientiously laid in beforehand . . . an ample stock of materials, he may be justified in thinking that he will contribute most to the mental wealth of mankind by occupying himself solely in working upon these, without distracting his attention by continually taking in more matter, or keeping a communication open with other independent intellects. The practice, therefore, may be legitimate; but no one should adopt it without being aware of what he loses by it. . . .
>
> When once he has persuaded himself that he can work out the final truth on any subject, exclusively from his own sources, he is apt to lose all measure or standard by which to be apprised when he is departing from common sense. Living only with his own thoughts, he gradually forgets the aspect they present to minds of a different mould from his own; he looks at his conclusions only from the point of view which suggested them, and from which they naturally appear perfect. . . . The natural result of the position is a gigantic self-confidence, not to say self-conceit. That of M. Comte is colossal. Except here and there in an entirely self-taught thinker, who has no high standard with which to compare himself, we have met with nothing approaching it. As his thoughts grew more extravagant, his self-confidence grew more outrageous. The height it ultimately attained must be seen, in his writings, to be believed.[2]

On the contrary, Comte himself declared that his work is all of one piece, and he attached as an appendix to the fourth volume of the *Polity* some of his early essays to prove the point. In introducing these essays he says:

> All but those who grasp the necessary connexion between the philosophic basis and the religious superstructure must regard the two portions of my career as divergent. The fact, therefore, that my second life simply realised the aim which I proposed to myself in early life requires to be made clear. This the present Appendix is calculated to do, since it proves, that from the outset, I endeavoured to found that new Spiritual Power, of which I now lay the basis. . . . I devoted the first half of my career to constructing, out of the materials supplied by the sciences, a truly Positive Philosophy, this being the only possible basis of a universal religion. The theoretic foundation being thus laid, the residue of my life was with good reason devoted to that Social Aim which at first I had imagined was accessible without any intellectual preparation.[3]

Comte's self-evaluation on this point has been shared by most of those who have given careful study to his life and work. For example, Professor Lévy-Bruhl, in one of the most penetrating studies of Comte yet published, declares:

> His whole life was the methodical execution of his programme. . . . He had but one system, not two. From the *Opuscules* of his twentieth year to the *Synthèse* of his last year, it is the development of one and the same conception.[4]

Hawkins shares this opinion. He says:

> Comte's thought evolved, it is true, between 1822 and 1857, but in a manner prescribed by the *Plan*. Although it is certain that, because of the influence of Clotilde de Vaux, Comte's thought and writing assume a mystical tinge, there is no inconsistency or contradiction in his two "careers." [5]

Barnes and Becker refer to Comte's *Polity* as "a detailed expansion of his theoretical doctrines and their practical application to the construction of a 'positive' or scientifically designed commonwealth." Disagreeing with those who regard the *Philosophy* as Comte's only important contribution to knowledge, they say: "Though the *Polity* is verbose, prolix, involved, and repetitious, nearly all his chief postulates are developed in it with far greater maturity and richness of detail than in the *Philosophy*." [6]

Comte's minor works are numerous, beginning with *Separation of Opinions from Aspirations* (1819) and ending with the first volume of the *Synthèse Subjective* (1856). In addition, Comte carried on an extensive correspondence with various persons interested in his theories, and many of his own letters and of those he received from his correspondents have been preserved. The writings which Comte left to posterity are, therefore, voluminous. Whatever may have been Comte's faults, he did not fail to commit to writing a substantial body of ideas by which he may be judged.

COMTE'S POSITIVISM

The varieties of positivism are many, and of Comte himself it has been said: "The father of positivism was the least positive of men." Yet Comte called himself a positivist, and some of his ideas constitute the hard core of positive principles. On the other hand, he expressed in the name of positivism many ideas which are not accepted by most persons who regard themselves as positivists. Comte's positivism is a highly abstract concept. As is the case with all such abstractions—*e.g.,* religion, democracy, the mores—it means so much that its meaning cannot be neat.

One meaning which Comte attached to the term *positive* is "scientific." He assumed that the whole universe is ordered by "invariable natural laws" and that these laws can be known only by the methods of science. All the knowledge within human grasp is, therefore, reached in the same manner. The various sciences are related as branches of a single trunk; the tree of knowledge is a single growth.

Positivism, or science, does not attempt to go beyond phenomena, since only phenomena can be known. Comte did not deny the existence of an unknown, even an unknowable, reality. He was, says Bridges, well aware of the mystery that lay beyond the world of phenomena. He felt it at every step, as the sailor is aware of the unfathomable ocean across which he steers his path. But since it is not given to man to penetrate that mystery, he has to turn his activities to the region where they will bear fruit. . . . The ultimate source of gravitation, the ultimate constitution of matter, the full and final explanation of heat, electricity, chemical affinity—these things are for ever hid from us; not less darkly are the origins of life and the first promptings of love. The *why* and *whence* of these things we cannot know; enough for us to see something of the *how* —of the laws of their working.[7]

Comte denied, therefore, that positivism is atheistic, since it is in no way concerned with the supernatural. He also claimed that it is not fatalistic, since it asserts that the external order is modifiable; or optimistic, since it lacks the theological roots of optimism; or materialistic, since it subordinates material to intellectual forces. Positivism is concerned with the *real* rather than the fanciful, with *useful* knowledge rather than all knowledge, with facts that are *certain* to the degree that prevision is possible. It is concerned with *precise* knowledge rather than vague impressions, with ever-changing *organic* truth rather than the eternal verities, with the *relative* rather than the absolute. Finally, positivism is *sympathetic,* in that it binds in one fellowship all those who share its spirit and methods. In short, positivism (science) is a mode of thought which can be universally accepted.

POSITIVISM AS A RELIGION

If Comte had stopped at this point, he would have identified himself with all those who for several centuries had been working to increase scientific knowledge. In fact, because of his rare ability to organize and systematize the findings of his predecessors in science, he was entitled to recognition as one of the leading scientists of his age. Likewise, if he had confined himself to making inductions and deductions from experience, a task for which he showed in the *Positive Philosophy* a genuine talent, he might have retained the warm support of men like John Stuart Mill and gained that of others who were repelled by his later speculations.

But Comte was not content to be merely a scientist. He had early set for himself another, and from his point of view a far higher, aim: the complete reorganization of society on positive principles, with science enthroned. Only when this had been accomplished, he believed, would egoism be subordinated to altruism. Only then would social progress based on social order and guided by love be made certain for all mankind. Positivism was, therefore, a religion *for* humanity. From the Positivist Society, founded in Paris in March 1848, comes the following succinct statement of this aspect of positivism.

Positivism is a scientific doctrine which aims at continuous increase of the material, intellectual, and moral well-being of all human societies, and in particular of the societies or nations of Europe. It seeks to effect this object by special modes of instruction and education. Positivism has three divisions:—

1. Philosophy of the Sciences, summed up in the conclusion that mankind must rely solely on its own exertions for the amelioration of its lot. The sciences co-ordinated in this philosophy are: mathematics . . . astronomy, physics, chemistry . . . biology, sociology . . . and ethics. . . .

2. Scientific religion and ethics. Positive religion has nothing to do with any supernatural or extra-terrestrial being; it is the Religion of Humanity. The moral code of Positivism may be summed up thus: physical, intellectual, and moral amelioration with the view of becoming more and more fit for the service of others. . . .

3. Positive politics, aiming at the suppression of war and the formation of the Commonwealth of European States. . . .

In this transformation of society Positivism repudiates all violent procedure. It acts by demonstration and persuasion, not by compulsion. Its device is: Love the Principle; Order the Basis; Progress the End. Morally its formula is: Live for Others.[8]

It was this part of positivism that saddened Mill to the point that he was prepared, so he tells us, to weep "at this melancholy decadence of a great intellect." As Comte's mysticism increased, and his readiness to issue pontifical statements revealed a distrust of the freedom of speculation that is the breath of science, the religious aspects of positivism came to predominate over its scientific aspects in the thoughts of Comte's disciples. The Positivism of Comte is both science and religion. Comte believed that the two are inseparable. The modern world has generally accepted the science and drawn a veil over the religion of positivism.

SOCIOLOGY

Comte coined the word *sociology,* but that fact is of itself of little importance; perhaps some other word would have served as well. In his early works he had used the expression "social physics" to distinguish the science of social organisms from biology, the science of individual organisms. It was not until 1838, in the forty-seventh lecture of Volume IV of the *Positive Philosophy,* that he adopted *sociology* in place of the earlier term. Far more important than the name, however, is what it stands for. What, to Comte, is sociology?

OBJECTIVE INVESTIGATION OF SOCIAL PHENOMENA

In the first place, sociology meant to him the science that came into existence when the spirit of inquiry which had proved so rewarding in the investigation of natural phenomena was adopted by those seeking knowledge about social phenomena. It is misleading to say that Comte assumed that the tools used in studying nature are adequate for the study of society. Just as astronomy employs not only the tools of mathematics but also those required by the properties of its peculiar phenomena, and biology could not advance beyond the physical sciences until it discovered special means of dealing with living matter, so is sociology required by the peculiar characteristics of the phenomena with which it is concerned to employ methods not used by biology. Repeatedly Comte calls attention to the great complexity of social phenomena. The methods of observation, experimentation, and comparison are not less valuable in sociology than in other sciences, but sociology requires an additional method, the historical. It is this method, above all others, according to Comte, that enables sociology to make its most important contributions to knowledge.

What the sciences have in common is not a set of identical instruments with which they work; it is rather an identical spirit of objective investigation of phenomena. The science of sociology demands, Comte believed, not less than other sciences, the emancipation of the intellect from outmoded theological and metaphysical conceptions. It requires, as do all other sciences, a stern discipline of feeling. In observing the legs of a creature, the biologist, *as a scientist,* does not weep because there are so many; he merely counts them. So does the sociologist, if he is faithful to the spirit of science, weigh social facts without permitting his observation to be distorted by emotional indulgence.

AN ABSTRACT SCIENCE

Sociology is also, according to Comte, an abstract science. In that portion of his work in which he was concerned with the nature of science rather than with its ends—wherever, that is, he was concerned with prevision instead of action—Comte disregarded the concrete sciences. He declared that science consists of laws and not of facts, and he was seeking above all else to discover "the laws which regulate phenomena in all conceivable cases." He did not deny the value of the concrete sciences. In giving his attention, for example, to biology rather than to botany or zoology, and to chemistry rather than to mineralogy, Comte explains that he did so not because the concrete sciences are less important but because progress in them depends upon that made in the abstract sciences. It is the function of the concrete sciences to apply to objects or beings the basic laws discovered by the abstract sciences; without abstract science there can be no concrete science worthy of the name.

Consequently, Comte's sociology is an abstract science of society; it is not merely a science of politics, economics, jurisprudence, or any other segment of social phenomena. It is a science that searches for the fundamental laws of society upon which all social science is based.

There are, from this point of view, only two major divisions of sociology:

social statics and social dynamics. The former is concerned with the structure of society; the latter, with its development. Without abstract laws of social order and of social progress, the concrete social sciences would be as retarded as the physical sciences would be without the law of gravitation. Comte did not claim that sociology would ever be able to achieve the abstractness of the physical sciences. Human beings are too immersed in concrete experiences to push beyond social facts to social laws. For this reason sociology appeared to him likely always to be less positive, less precise, and less abstract than the other fundamental sciences. Comte was, however, optimistic about its possibilities.

> Yet we cannot but feel, after this review of its spirit, its function, and its resources, that the abundance of its means of investigation may establish it in a higher position of rationality than the present state of the human mind might seem to promise. The unity of the subject, notwithstanding its prodigious extent, the conspicuous interconnection of its various aspects, its characteristic advance from the most general to more and more special researches, and finally the more frequent and important use of *a priori* considerations through suggestions furnished by the anterior sciences . . . may authorize the highest hopes of the speculative dignity of the science.[9]

AN INTEGRATIVE SCIENCE

In scope and complexity, the abstract sciences can be arranged, according to Comte, in a hierarchy. At the bottom of the ladder—or, more accurately at its base—is mathematics, the simplest, the most general, and the most abstract of the sciences. Mathematics affords both a standard of precise knowledge and a solid body of basic laws. Astronomy, the next in order of the sciences, builds upon the foundation mathematics has established but adds certain laws derived from its own more complex phenomena. Then come physics, chemistry, biology, and, finally, sociology, in that order.*

> . . . this classification marks, with precision, the relative perfection of the different sciences, which consists in the degree of precision of knowledge and in the relation of its different branches. It is easy to see that the more general, simple, and abstract any phenomena are, the less they depend on others, and the more precise they are in themselves, and the more clear in their relations with each other. Thus, organic phenomena are less exact and systematic than inorganic; and of these again terrestrial are less exact and systematic than those of astronomy. This fact is completely accounted for by the gradation we have laid down; and we shall see as we proceed that the possibility of applying mathematical analysis to

---

* Toward the end of his life Comte placed another science, morals, at the top of his hierarchy of the abstract sciences, but since he never completed a detailed and systematic formulation of his ethical theory, we may, at this point, disregard this addition. It will be discussed briefly in connection with his religion of humanity.

the study of phenomena is exactly in proportion to the rank which they hold in the scale of the whole.¹⁰

Standing at the top of the hierarchy of fundamental sciences, sociology surveys a vast domain. It was not to Comte the mistress of the sciences; it was only the most inclusive. Since society is made up of living beings whose bodies are formed from the matter of the universe, sociology begins with the laws of the sciences lower in the scale.

> Social life cannot be understood without first understanding the medium in which it is developed, and the beings who manifest it. We shall make no progress, therefore, in the final science [sociology] until we have sufficient abstract knowledge of the outer world and of individual life to define the influence of these laws on the special laws of social phenomena.¹¹

Consequently, the laws of number, gravitation, equilibrium, heat, chemical affinity, growth, and other laws of the less complex sciences provide the solid foundation upon which sociology rests. At the same time, sociology is in a position to discover the manner in which all the sciences are related. This unique advantage has enabled sociology, Comte believed, to discover the organic unity of the sciences and to create by a synthesis of all the sciences a single, positive system.

A PREDICTIVE SCIENCE

Sociology was to Comte a predictive science; otherwise it could not claim to be a science at all. The measure of all science is prevision. Scientific laws enable the outcome of certain combinations, the issue of certain processes, to be known in advance. It is the function of sociology to discover the future of society by close scrutiny of its present state. To understand the present, however, we must know the past. The dead govern the living. The men and women of any society are not only flesh and bone, subject to the laws of matter, but they are also bearers of a social heritage, and thus subject to the laws of history. It does not follow from this fact that a fatalistic view must be taken. The dead hand of the past is heavy only when its existence is unknown. Abstract conceptions, such as liberty of conscience, equality, and sovereignty of the people, have, in fact, been reified, just as material objects have been deified. It is only when the theological and metaphysical roots of certain ideas are exposed that the present can be really understood and the future correctly predicted.

Sociology is, Comte says, the least precise of the fundamental sciences, but that is not at all to say that it is the least certain. He is emphatic on that point.

> We must beware of confounding the degree of precision which we are able to attain in regard to any science with the certainty of the science it-

self. The certainty of science and our precision in the knowledge of it are two very different things which have been too often confounded. . . . A very absurd proposition may be very precise; as if we should say, for instance, that the sum of the angles of a triangle is equal to three right angles; and a very certain proposition may be wanting in precision in our statement of it; as, for instance, when we assert that every man will die.[12]

Comte's position can be stated as follows—physics can say: *this* rock, if released, will fall at a certain rate of speed and strike with a certain force; sociology can say: at some unknown time and under conditions which cannot now be foreseen, *this* man will die. The physicist may be annoyed at the sociologist's prediction, but the fact remains that the law of gravitation is not more certain than the law of death. Furthermore, the physicist is not expected to predict the number and exact sizes of the pieces into which the rock will break when it strikes and the exact location of each piece when finally it comes to rest, but it is just that kind of prediction that is most demanded of the sociologist.

A PLAN OF ACTION

Although Comte pursued knowledge of social phenomena in the true spirit and with the methods of science, it cannot be denied that he also launched sociology as a program of social reconstruction and moral awakening. Many persons today believe that sociology suffers as a science by its proximity to man's interests and passions. Knowledge about man merges with plans to improve his condition. Behind the determination of all scientists to know the truth is the faith that knowledge serves the highest ends of man, but those who study nature can divorce their attention from human welfare as those who study man cannot. It can be said of Comte that he was first a scientist and only later a man of action or, perhaps more accurately, that he became a scientist in order to prepare himself for the task of reconstructing society. In his attempt to make sociology an abstract science, he clearly recognized the need for a theoretical framework within which concrete experience can be understood. But sociology is concerned with action as well as with knowledge. Comte never doubted that science exists for man and not man for science. He saw that scientific knowledge enables man to chart a course to a destination he may want to reach.

He believed also that man's ends are moral ends. That is not to say, however, that they lie beyond and above science. Comte saw no necessary conflict between science and religion. They are separated by a gulf only where the positive spirit prevails in the former and the theological and metaphysical spirit in the latter. Comte believed that religion need not be theological and metaphysical, and that a positive (scientific) religion was not only possible but also urgently required to provide a substantial base for morality. It is easy to say that science provides the means and religion the ends of human action, but Comte saw that this distinction between means and ends is a highly artificial abstraction from the whole context of social experience. He saw the confusion that arises when men justify action by metaphysical conceptions charged with emotional force, such as conscience, liberty, and equality. He believed that sociology could relieve this confusion by establishing the functional interaction of means and ends, the essential unity in knowledge and action, the identity of the science of humanity with the religion of humanity. Comte's views on this point have been stated by E. L. Thorndike as follows:

> We should regard nothing as outside the scope of science, and every regularity or law that science can discover in the consequence of events is a step towards the only freedom that is of use to men and an aid to the good life. If values do not reside in the orderly world of Nature, but depend on chance or caprice, it would be vain to try to increase them. The world needs, not only the vision and valuation of great sages, the practical psychology of men of affairs, but also scientific method to test the worth of the prophets' dreams, and scientific humanists to inform and advise its men of affairs, not only about what is, but also about what is right and good.[13]

HUMAN NATURE

Throughout his sociological work Comte was concerned with "man in society." Although he readily admitted that sociology requires a knowledge of the individual, he believed that it must look first to biology for that knowledge. He explained that sociology could not come into existence until biology, including physiology and psychology, had made sufficient advances to discover the fundamental laws of human nature. He pointed out that Montesquieu and Condorcet had caught a dim vision of sociology but had been unable to see it clearly because of the immaturity of biology in their day. Montesquieu had observed, for example, that human laws are "the necessary relations following from the nature of things," a penetrating view of the unity in social phenomena; but he mistook secondary factors for primary, as his exaggeration of the influence of climate proves. Condorcet "lost himself in wanderings after an indefinite perfectibility" of man, partly because "a great deficiency remained in the imperfect state of biological knowledge." Comte believed that he was able to succeed where they failed because biological laws inaccessible to them were available to him. This does not mean that biology affords an adequate explanation of man. Comte's sociology of human nature is not a projection of the biological laws of the individual into the social order; rather it accepts as data what biology can reveal about *Homo* the animal and proceeds to formulate a theory of man the human being.

MAN AS A SOCIAL ANIMAL

The recognition of man as a social animal has appeared often in the preceding pages of this book, but it should be noted that this observation has various meanings. Comte emphatically declared that "man's social tendencies" are now proved to be inherent in his nature and not the result of utilitarian considerations. Man seeks the company of his fellows spontaneously and without regard to any advantages he may gain through them. In fact, Comte argued, private and group interests often conflict, and the individual may well lose more through association than he gains. "It is thus evident," he continued, "that the social state would never have existed if its rise had depended on a conviction of its individual utility."

Furthermore, it is fellow feeling, not reason, which brings human beings together. As the first essential idea of man's true nature, we must recognize "the preponderance of the affective over the intellectual faculties." Man is so constituted organically that intellectual activity, "if ever so little protracted beyond a certain degree, occasions in most men a fatigue which soon becomes utterly insupportable."

> Whatever the intrinsic pleasure of intellectual labour, it is certain that it cannot be sustained in full energy except for the purpose of directing a course of action prompted by some kind of passion. . . . We act from affection; we think in order to act. . . . The real unity of life depends invariably upon affection of one kind or other.[14]

Comte was far from taking the extreme view that rationality enables the individual conveniently to find reasons for doing what he wants to do. The intellect and the heart work harmoniously to guide action, or at least they would do so if the positive spirit prevailed. It is one of the virtues of positivism that it brings "Reason into complete harmony with Feeling without impairing the activity of either."[15] Social order is possible only because man's affective faculties give direction to his intellectual activities and prevent random and meaningless speculation.

EGOISM AND ALTRUISM

To say, however, that social life is possible because man is capable of fellow feeling is not to deny the existence of another side of his affective nature: his self-love. Comte did not deny or minimize the importance of the egoistic quality in human nature. The Golden Rule bids man to love his neighbor *as himself,* and Comte declares: "Our moral nature would . . . be destroyed, and not improved, if it were possible to repress our personal instincts, since our social affections, deprived of necessary direction, would degenerate into a vague and useless charity, destitute of all practical efficacy."[16] Comte assumed, therefore, the persistence of a strong feeling of self-interest. In fact, his emphasis on altruism arises from his observation that egoism is a basic human trait so pronounced as to be self-evident. What most needs to be pointed out, he declared, is that altruism is another side of man's nature. Self-realization and social order are compatible precisely because they both result from a proper subordination of egoism to altruism. Subordination of egoism, however, does not mean its suppression:

> Summing up its conception of sound morality in the expression "Live for Others," Positivism sanctions a reasonable measure of satisfaction to the self-regarding instincts on the ground that they are indispensable to our material existence, the basis on which all our higher attributes are founded. Consequently it censures all practices, however respectable the motives inspiring them, which by excessive austerity diminish our energies and render us less fit for the service of others. By giving a social purpose to self-regarding measures it at once ennobles and controls them, steering clear of undue attention to them on the one hand, and of dangerous neglect on the other.[17]

IMMUTABILITY

In contrast to the view commonly held in his day that human nature is indefinitely perfectible, Comte maintained that, although the nature of man evolves under certain conditions, it is everywhere basically the same and always develops in the same manner. Comte's law of the three stages requires this postulate, since if human nature were subject to random variation under the forces of circumstance, his theory of natural progress could not be supported. As Lévy-Bruhl says:

> The various physical, moral and intellectual faculties, must be found the same at all the degrees of historical evolution, and always similarly coordinated among themselves. The development which they receive in the social state can never change their nature, nor consequently destroy or create any one of them, nor even intervene in the order of their importance.[18]

It is precisely because the basic nature of man is universal and immutable that "the general direction of human evolution, its rate of progress, and its necessary order" can be predicted. The direction is from animality to humanity:

> In Man's social infancy, the instincts of subsistence are so preponderant, that the sexual instinct itself, notwithstanding its primitive strength, is at first controlled by them: the domestic affections are then much less pronounced; and the social affections are restricted to an almost imperceptible fraction of humanity, beyond which everything is foreign, and even hostile: and the malignant passions are certainly, next to the animal

> appetites, the mainspring of human existence. It is unquestionable that civilization leads us on to a further and further development of our noblest dispositions and our most generous feelings, which are the only possible basis of human association, and which receive, by means of that association, a more and more special culture.[19]

When such factors as climate and race are disregarded and only universal causes are taken into account, the rate of progress is "in proportion to the combined influence of the chief natural conditions relating to the human organism first, and next to its medium." The human organism is so constituted that mere physical activity may be satisfying, as with savages and children; it is only as man develops an inborn capacity for boredom that he feels the need to exercise his highest faculties. His rate of progress depends upon the extent to which he is driven by *ennui* to develop intellectually and morally.

The brevity of human life is a great handicap to man. "We have hardly thirty years," says Comte, ". . . to devote to other purposes than preparation for life or for death; and this is a very insufficient balance between what man can devise and what he can execute." Population density also has an effect on personal development, because it creates "new wants and new difficulties" and affords "a growing ascendency to those intellectual and moral forces which are suppressed among a scanty population."

The order of development is from bondage to the appetites and passions to the freedom that the exercise of the intellect affords. This order is found in social as well as in personal development.

> It is only through the more and more marked influence of the reason over the general conduct of Man and of society, that the gradual march of our race has attained that regularity and persevering continuity which distinguish it so radically from the desultory and barren expansion of even the highest of the animal orders, which share, and with enhanced strength, the appetites, the passions, and even the primary sentiments of Man.[20]

It is, however, the law of the succession of the three states which best describes the order of the development of the individual. Where personal development occurs at all, the order is invariable: from a primitive, theological state through a transient, metaphysical state to a positive state.

INEQUALITY

Finally, Comte declared that men are not equal. Although recognizing the utility of the dogma of equality in breaking up old political systems, he was persuaded that this dogma is an obstacle to an effective reorganization of society.

> Since the abolition of slavery, there has been no denial, from any quarter, of the right of every man (innocent of strong anti-social conduct) to expect from all others the fulfilment of the conditions necessary to the natural development of his personal activity, suitably directed; but beyond that undisputed right, men cannot be made, because they are not, equal, nor even equivalent; and they cannot therefore possess, in a state of association, any identical rights beyond the great original one. The simple physical inequalities which fix the attention of superficial observers are much less marked than intellectual and moral differences; and the progress of civilization tends to increase these more important differences, as much as to lessen the inferior kind; and, applied to any assemblage of persons thus developed, the dogma of equality becomes anarchical, and directly hostile to its original destination.[21]

Comte blamed this dogma for that false claim to liberty of conscience which induces men, regardless of their competence, to express opinions on all matters whatever. "There is no liberty of conscience," he says, "in astronomy, in physics, in chemistry, even in physiology, in the sense that everyone would think it absurd not to accept in confidence the principles established in those sciences by competent persons. If it is otherwise in politics, the reason is merely because, the old doctrines having gone by and the new ones not being yet formed, there are not properly, during the interval, any established opinions." [22] Although Mill confessed to some lack of sympathy with Comte on this point, he summarized Comte's views well:

> . . . when every man is encouraged to believe himself a competent judge of the most difficult social questions, he cannot be prevented from thinking himself competent also to the most important public duties, and the baneful competition for power and official functions spreads constantly downwards to a lower and lower grade of intelligence. In M. Comte's opinion, the peculiarly complicated nature of sociological studies, and the great amount of previous knowledge and intellectual discipline requisite for them, together with the serious consequences that may be produced by even temporary errors on such subjects, render it necessary, in the case of ethics and politics, still more than of mathematics and physics, that whatever legal liberty may exist of questioning and discussing, the opinions of mankind should really be formed for them by an exceedingly small number of minds of the highest class, trained to the task by the most thorough and laborious mental preparation; and that the questioning of their conclusions by any one not of an equivalent grade of intellect and instruction, should be accounted equally presumptuous, and more blamable, than the attempts occasionally made by sciolists to refute the Newtonian astronomy.[23]

These views of human nature form the basis of Comte's social theories.

SOCIAL ORGANIZATION

In his theory of social organization, Comte developed a logical system in which elements of both the actual and the ideal appear. He did not draw a sharp line between things as they are and things as he believed they ought to be—that is, between the social structure which as a scientist he was attempting to comprehend and that which as a reformer he was seeking to create. He did not neglect the existing state of society, but neither did he abstain from contemplating the social organization that he firmly believed would at some time in the future be realized.

SOCIAL STATICS

Comte believed that social phenomena can be studied from two points of view, the static and the dynamic. Social statics is the branch of sociology that studies society in cross section. It seeks to discover "the laws of action and reaction of the different parts of the social system—apart, for the occasion, from the fundamental movement which is always gradually modifying them." It corresponds to the study of anatomy in biology and of equilibrium in physics. It is concerned with what Comte called the *consensus* of the social organism, by which he meant the harmony in the interdependent parts. He pointed out that

> there must always be a spontaneous harmony between the whole and the parts of the social system, the elements of which must inevitably be, sooner or later, combined in a mode entirely conformable to their nature. It is evident that not only must political institutions and social manners on the one hand, and manners and ideas on the other, be always mutually connected; but, further, that this consolidated whole must always be connected, by its nature, with the corresponding state of the integral development of humanity, considered in all its aspects, of intellectual, moral, and physical activity.[24]

It is the aim of social statics to investigate this harmony and discover the conditions of social stability. Since Comte believed that he lived in a time when social balance was seriously disturbed, this meant to him a study of the conditions necessary for the restoration of that balance. Social statics is not, therefore, limited to a study of the consensus existing at any particular time and place; it is concerned also with "the radical consensus proper to the social organism." Comte was mindful of the truly remarkable consensus established by Catholicism, which had integrated music, art, science, and industry in one great religious system and had thus provided the moral basis for effective political organization.

> The grand social characteristic of Catholicism was that by constituting a moral power, wholly independent of the political, it infused morality into

political government. . . . It was under Catholicism that the speculative class began to assume the character assigned to it by the immutable laws of human nature, neither engrossing political sway, as in theocracies, nor remaining outside of the social organization, as under the Greek *regime*. Henceforth its post was one of calm and enlightened, but not indifferent observation of practical life, in which it could interpose only in an indirect manner by its moral influence. . . .

Morally regarded, there can be no doubt that this modification of the social organism developed among even the lowest ranks of the nations concerned in it a sense of dignity and elevation before almost unknown; for the universal morality, thus established by general conviction outside of and above the political sphere of action authorized the meanest Christian to adduce, on occasion, to the most powerful noble, the inflexible prescriptions of that common doctrine which was the basis of obedience and respect; an obedience and respect which were now due to the function, and no longer to the person; so that submission might henceforth cease to be servile, and remonstrance to be hostile. In a purely political view, this happy regeneration realized the great Utopia of the Greek philosophers, in all that was useful and reasonable, while excluding its follies and extravagances; since it constituted, in the midst of an order founded upon birth, fortune, or military valour, an immense and powerful class in which intellectual and moral superiority was openly entitled to ascendancy.[25]

Medieval Catholicism, therefore, afforded Comte a historical example of a high degree of consensus. It is the business of social statics to probe into such systems and to discover the sources of their strength. Comte was convinced that the principles of consensus are the same whether the social system be theological and metaphysical in character or positive. In fact, positivism as a system of social organization bears close resemblance to a Catholicism stripped of its nonpositive elements, if one could imagine such a thing.

THE SOCIAL ORGANISM

It is in his discussion of social statics that Comte most clearly revealed his organismic conception of society. Although he repeatedly warned against a "servile analogy" between the social and the individual organism, he pointed out that there is a real correspondence between the two. Society possesses the attributes of vitality and of growth. Its parts are similar to those of the individual organism: families are the cells, social forces form the tissues, and cities or states are the organs. In society, as in the individual, there is specialization and a division of labor. The distribution of functions is made possible in both instances by a combination of efforts. Both are characterized by consensus, the only difference being that the individual organism is more sensitive and more easily destroyed than is the social organism by the failure of one of its parts to function properly.

Comte's opposition to individualism is evident. Society represents an advance beyond the individual in distribution of functions and combination of efforts. It is capable of great improvement, whereas man's essential nature remains unchanged. Just as a part of an organic body is only matter when detached, so as a distinct entity is man apart from society only an abstraction. "Man indeed, as an individual, cannot properly be said to exist, except in the too abstract brain of modern metaphysicians."

POLITICAL ORGANIZATION

Social unity is not merely a matter of specialization of parts and distribution of functions; even more does it require a combination of efforts. Consequently, government is necessary. Comte declared that "society without a government is no less impossible than a government without society." Lévy-Bruhl points out that to Comte

> Government is not a simple institution of police, a guarantee of public order, nor, as was said in the eighteenth century, a necessary evil which will reduce itself to a minimum with progress, or even will tend to disappear. On the contrary, the more a society is developed, the more indispensable the function of government becomes in it, the more importance it assumes. Progress in the future will make a more and more considerable place for it in social life. Although it does not itself realise any determined social progress, government necessarily contributes to whatever progress society can make.[26]

This important function of government, which is nothing less than that of representing the highest and noblest sentiments of the whole society, makes the promotion of the material prosperity of the people only a minor part of the responsibility of government. Intellectual anarchy and the destruction of public morality are fatal to social order and to social progress. Consequently, it is the duty of government to guide thought and regulate morals. To the government should be given, therefore, all the forces which society can command; material, intellectual, and moral.

The actual organization of such a government, with its two main divisions of the temporal and the spiritual powers, is described by Comte in great detail. The following summary is from Mill:

> A few words will sufficiently express the outline of his scheme. A corporation of philosophers, receiving a modest support from the state, surrounded by reverence, but peremptorily excluded not only from all political power or employment, but from all riches, and all occupations except their own, are to have the entire direction of education; together with, not only the right and duty of advising and reproving all persons respecting both their public and their private life but also a control (whether authoritative or only moral is not defined) over the speculative

class itself, to prevent them from wasting time and ingenuity on inquiries and speculations of no value to mankind (among which he includes many now in high estimation), and compel them to employ all their powers on the investigations which may be judged, at the time, to be the most urgently important to the general welfare. The temporal government which is to coexist with this spiritual authority, consists of an aristocracy of capitalists, whose dignity and authority are to be in the ratio of the degree of generality of their conceptions and operations—bankers at the summit, merchants next, then manufacturers, and agriculturists at the bottom of the scale. No representative system, or other popular organization, by way of counterpoise to this governing power, is ever contemplated.[27]

Arguments in favor of government by experts with unlimited power assume that the experts will not abuse their powers and that people do not set a very high value on individual liberty. Since Comte dealt in some detail with the second of these assumptions, we may conclude this discussion with his own statements on this point.

> . . . there is a much stronger inclination to obedience in the generality of men than it is customary in our day to suppose. If men were as rebellious as they are at present represented, it would be difficult to understand how they could ever have been disciplined: and it is certain that we are all more or less disposed to respect any superiority, especially any intellectual or moral elevation, in our neighbours, independently of any view to our own advantage: and this instinct of submission is, in truth, only too often lavished on deceptive appearances. However excessive the desire of command may be in our revolutionary day, there can be no one who, in his secret mind, has not often felt, more or less vividly, how sweet it is to obey when he can have the rare privilege of consigning the burdensome responsibility of his general self-conduct to wise and trustworthy guidance: and probably the sense of this is strongest in those who are best fitted for command. In the midst of political convulsions, when the spirit of revolutionary destruction is abroad, the mass of the people manifest scrupulous obedience towards the intellectual and moral guides from whom they accept direction, and upon whom they may even press a temporary dictatorship, in their primary and urgent need of a preponderant authority. Thus do individual dispositions show themselves to be in harmony with the course of social relations as a whole, in teaching us that political subordination is as inevitable, generally speaking, as it is indispensable.[28]

SOCIAL CHANGE

Comte's theory of social change offers a general account of human progress arrived at inductively from the study of history, but it does not stop there: it depicts the future of mankind. It shows not only whence man came and by what means he advanced but also whither he is going and what is most needed to help him reach his destination. Comte's science of social dynamics does not stop with the discovery of laws: it puts them to work. His idea of progress is not merely an explanation: it is a justification and a hope. His law of the three stages is not simply a scientific fact to be grasped intellectually: it is a principle to be felt and lived by.

SOCIAL DYNAMICS

Comte spoke of the statical view of society as basic, but it is obvious that he regarded the dynamic as both more important and more interesting. Social dynamics studies the development of mankind. It is the science of "the necessary and continuous movement of humanity." Comte declared that it is easy to establish that "the successive modifications of society have always taken place in a determinate order." This order is not absolute, since determinism, like free will, is a metaphysical and not a positive concept. Nevertheless, certain uniformities and necessary sequences can be discovered; there is continuity in the development of social states.

> The true general spirit of social dynamics then consists in conceiving of each of these consecutive social states as the necessary result of the preceding, and the indispensable mover of the following, according to the axiom of Leibnitz—*the present is big with the future*. In this view, the object of science is to discover the laws which govern this continuity, and the aggregate of which determines the course of human development. In short, social dynamics studies the laws of succession, while social statics inquires into those of coexistence; so that the use of the first is to furnish the true theory of progress to political practice, while the second performs the same service in regard to order.[29]

Social dynamics derives its basic data from history and is, therefore, a science of history. It begins with history and not with metaphysical speculations about social origins; from Comte's point of view, science does not answer questions about origins. Social dynamics does not, however, end with the past or even with the present. The principles that explain the past also reveal the future of mankind. Social dynamics shows, Comte declared, that the dead ever govern the living and that man is ever becoming more religious.

The knowledge that the course of the future is silently ordered by the past, and that the intellectual change revealed in history is not mere fluctuation but progressive development of man's spiritual and moral faculties, affords a basis for predicting with confidence the shape of things to come. Social dynamics is concerned, therefore, not only with discovering the laws of progress but also with projecting their operation far into the future. Comte scorned utopian dreams based on nothing more substantial than arbitrary hopes, but his own dream of reconstructed humanity was ever before him. The science of social dynamics enabled him to convert that dream into a positive social ideal founded on what he regarded to be the observed laws of progress.

THE IDEA OF PROGRESS

Cyclical theories of social change and doctrines of decline from a Golden Age are at least as old as the records of the thought of man, but the idea of progress is a modern conception—no older, in fact, than modern science. It was grasped imperfectly by certain ancient writers—Lucretius, for example—and by medieval philosophers, such as Roger Bacon, who belonged in spirit to a future age rather than the one into which they were born. As we know it today, it is a part of the faith of mankind in modern science, and it had to await the advancement of scientific knowledge before it could develop. It assumes that such knowledge can and will be put to use by man to improve his lot. It is, therefore, both an interpretation of history and an ethical ideal. Also, it has many meanings. The idea of progress did not originate with Comte, and the value of his contributions to it may be disputed, but it does constitute an important part of his social theory.

The intellectual and moral development of mankind was to Comte the most important characteristic of progress. The improvement of man's material condition is secondary to his escape from ignorance and superstition and his growth in sociability. Progress is "in its essence identical with order, and may be looked upon as order made manifest." [30] Social order is possible because man is capable of intellectual and moral progress, because he alone of all animals can be guided by the principle of love to live for others. Progress means growth in religious feeling and subordination of egoism to altruism. "All systematic study of human progress must then consist in the development of its one law—Man is ever becoming more religious." [31]

Comte did not, to be sure, neglect the material aspects of progress. He pointed out that

> material progress, long by an inevitable necessity the exclusive object of man's care, furnishes him with the basis on which he is able to build all higher improvements, physical, intellectual, and ultimately moral.[32]
>
> . . . we may say that the one great object of life, personal or social, is to become more perfect in every way; in our external condition first, but also and more especially in our own nature. The first kind of progress we share in common with the higher animals; all of which make some efforts to improve their material position. It is of course the least elevated stage of progress, but being the easiest it is the point from which we start towards the higher stages. A nation that has made no efforts to improve itself materially will take but little interest in moral or mental improve-

ment. This is the only ground on which enlightened men can feel much pleasure in the material progress of our own times. It stirs up influences that tend to the nobler kinds of progress; influences which would meet with even greater opposition than they do were not the temptations presented to the coarser natures by material prosperity so irresistible. Owing to the mental and moral anarchy in which we live, systematic efforts to gain the higher degrees of progress have been as yet impossible; and this explains, though it does not justify, the exaggerated importance attributed nowadays to material improvements.[33]

Social progress continues as generations come and go and as nations rise and fall; mankind is one, and the products of human activity accumulate. The individual in an advanced society, however, has *at birth* no advantage over his barbarian ancestors. He possesses the same primitive instincts that they inherited. Although the kind of society in which he lives greatly influences, if it does not actually determine, his personal development, every person starts life on the bottom rung of the ladder leading from bestiality to humanity. Progress has nothing to do with increase in human happiness across the generations.

> We have nothing to do here with the metaphysical controversy about the absolute happiness of Man at different stages of civilization. As the happiness of every man depends on the harmony between the development of his various faculties and the entire system of the circumstances which govern his life . . . the chimerical notion of unlimited perfectibility is thus at once excluded.[34]

Finally, Comte regarded progress, as he defined it, as inevitable—that is, it is as probable as the working out of any natural law.

> The law of human progress dominates all; men are only its instruments. Although this force springs from ourselves, it is no more possible for us to withdraw from its influences or control its action than to change at our pleasure the original impulse which causes our planet to revolve about the sun.[35]

This is not to say that human activity is futile. As Lévy-Bruhl says,

> There is . . . no contradiction in affirming the reality of these laws [of social progress] and in considering at the same time the intervention of human activity in social phenomena as efficacious. . . . It belongs to social science to determine the limits of the useful action of man upon social phenomena. These limits are narrow enough. Man can only modify, from the static point of view, the intensity, and from the dynamic point of view, the speed of social phenomena. To suppose the contrary would be to deny the very existence of these laws. . . . The statesman, infatuated with his power, will perhaps find this a very humble part to play. But,

LAW OF THE THREE STAGES

even within these limits, human intervention could still be of capital importance provided that it were directed by science.[36]

The Law of the Three Stages is not only Comte's most characteristic contribution to sociology but also his earliest. In 1822, when he was only twenty-four, he stated that law in the following form:

> From the nature of the human intellect each branch of knowledge, in its development, is necessarily obliged to pass through three different theoretical states: the theological or fictitious state; the metaphysical or abstract state; lastly, the scientific or positive state.[37]

Whether Comte regarded this only as a hypothesis, which his scientific studies later confirmed, may be disputed; but there can be little doubt that this law is the key principle in his sociological system. It describes the necessary order of mental development of the individual, of independent societies, and, finally, of all humanity. This law plays so important a part in Comte's social theories that his statement of it merits close scrutiny.

> From the study of the development of human intelligence, in all directions, and through all times, the discovery arises of a great fundamental law to which it is necessarily subject and which has a solid foundation of proof, both in the facts of our organization and in our historical experience. The law is this:—that each of our leading conceptions,—each branch of our knowledge,—passes successively through three different theoretical conditions: the Theological or fictitious; the Metaphysical, or abstract, and the Scientific, or positive. . . .
>
> In the theological state, the human mind, seeking the essential nature of beings, the first and final causes (the origin and purpose) of all effects,—in short, Absolute knowledge,—supposes all phenomena to be produced by the immediate action of supernatural beings.
>
> In the metaphysical state, which is only a modification of the first, the mind supposes, instead of supernatural beings, abstract forces, veritable entities (that is, personified abstractions) inherent in all beings and capable of producing all phenomena. . . .
>
> In the final, the positive state, the mind has given over the vain search after Absolute notions, the origin and destination of the universe, and the causes of phenomena, and applies itself to the study of their laws,—that is, their invariable relations of succession and resemblance. Reasoning and observation, duly combined, are the means of this knowledge. What is now understood when we speak of an explanation of facts is simply the establishment of a connection between single phenomena and some general facts, the number of which continually diminishes with the progress of science.[38]

The theological stage is seen in the thinking of children and primitives about the phenomena of nature. They attribute whatever happens to gods, who display the human emotions and the arbitrary will which they discover in themselves. This first awakening of the human mind to speculative thought marks a great advance over sheer animal existence. It begins with *fetichism,* which regards all objects in nature as animate. Fetichism prepares the way for *polytheism,* a much more general and abstract theological conception, and this leads finally to *monotheism,* which is belief in a single abstract will expressing all the attributes of deity.

The metaphysical stage follows naturally from the theological, since it requires only the dropping of the idea of a supernatural *personal* will. It possesses no well-defined characteristics, since it is merely a "mongrel and transitional" link between the two more significant stages. Mill described it as follows:

> The mode of thought which M. Comte terms Metaphysical, accounts for phenomena by ascribing them, not to volitions either sublunary or celestial, but to realized abstractions. In this stage it is no longer a god that causes and directs each of the various agencies of nature; it is a power, or a force, or an occult quality, considered as real existences, inherent in but distinct from the concrete bodies in which they reside, and which they in a manner animate. Instead of Dryads presiding over trees, producing and regulating their phenomena, every plant or animal has now a Vegetative Soul. . . . At a later period the Vegetative Soul has become a Plastic Force, and still later a Vital Principle.[39]

In the metaphysical stage men do not deify objects, but they do reify and personify abstractions. Descartes' *cogito ergo sum* might have afforded Comte a good example. What Descartes really discovered was that thinking exists, but unwittingly he assumed the existence of a concrete entity, the self, which thinks. In the metaphysical stage men do not recognize their assumptions. They imagine that they are making deductions from eternal truths, when really they are neglecting in their reasoning what most needs to be examined. They imagine that freedom, equality, and sovereignty actually exist, whereas really these are human constructs with many meanings.

The final stage, the *positive,* is reached when the quest for certainty is abandoned and men accept the scientific laws derived from experience as the highest form of knowledge within human grasp.

Comte did not fail to observe, as some of his critics have claimed, that these three ways of thinking may coexist in the same mind or the same society and are not always successive.

> During the whole of our survey of the sciences, I have endeavoured to keep in view the great fact that all the three states, theological, metaphysical, and positive, may and do exist at the same time in the same mind

in regard to different sciences. I must once more recall this consideration, and insist upon it; because in the forgetfulness of it lies the only real objection that can be brought against the grand law of the three states. It must be steadily kept in view that the same mind may be in the positive stage with regard to the most simple and general sciences; in the metaphysical with regard to the more complex and special; and in the theological with regard to social science, which is so complex and special as to have hitherto taken no scientific form at all.[40]

Nevertheless, Comte maintained that this law of human progress is clearly demonstrated in the development of the individual and in the history of Western civilization. In 1839 he wrote:

> Seventeen years of continuous meditation on this great subject, discussed under all its aspects, and subjected to all possible tests, authorise me to affirm beforehand, without the slightest scientific hesitation, that we shall always see confirmed this historical proposition, which now seems to me as fully demonstrated as any of the general facts actually admitted in the other parts of natural philosophy.[41]

THE FAMILY

Comte's admiration for Catholic institutions, as obvious as his distaste for Catholic dogma, is clearly shown in his views on family institutions. The positivist concepts of the family are basically the same as those of Catholicism. The importance of the family, the blessings of marriage and parenthood, the different but complementary natures of men and women, the personal and social significance of the affections and disciplines of the home, the exclusive and indissoluble nature of marriage—these and other similarities are apparent. That is not to say, however, that the two systems are identical, as a brief survey of the positivist system will show.

MARRIAGE

According to Comte, marriage is not only a "universal natural disposition" but also a universal social necessity. By marriage the man and the woman grow from egoism to altruism, a condition indispensable to social order. He believed that only priests should be compelled to marry, since they need, more than others, from whom less is demanded, the stimulating influence of affection; but apparently he assumed that most people will marry voluntarily, especially when the blessings of marriage are revealed to them. He made entirely secondary in its meaning to women the family function of procreation:

> Vast as is the moral importance of maternity, yet the position of wife has always been considered even more characteristic of woman's nature;

as shown by the fact that the words woman and wife are in many languages synonymous. Marriage is not always followed by children; and besides this, a bad wife is very seldom indeed a good mother. The first aspect then under which Positivism considers woman is simply as the companion of man, irrespective of her maternal duties. Viewed thus, marriage is the most elementary and yet the most perfect mode of social life. It is the only association in which entire identity of interests is possible. In this union . . . the noblest aim of human life is realised, as far as it ever can be . . . that is to say, in the subjection of self-interest to social feeling.42

DIVORCE

Since one of the most important personal benefits derived from marriage is a feeling of security in the affections of husband or wife, the full meaning of marriage can be realized only when it is accepted as both exclusive and indissoluble. Mindful of the unhappy situation of Madame Clotilde de Vaux, Comte did not make the prohibition against divorce absolute: it was to be allowed if a spouse had committed an offense punishable by a penalty amounting to social death. Also, he was willing to accept the principle of legal separation where there were good and sufficient causes. With these minor exceptions, however, the marriage vows once made are irrevocable. Under no conditions, Comte stated, should remarriage be regarded as acceptable. Perpetual widowhood is the moral duty of one separated from a former spouse. "Constant adoration of one whom Death has implanted more visibly and deeply on the memory leads all high natures and philosophic natures especially, to give themselves more unreservedly to the service of humanity." 43

FAMILY ORGANIZATION

According to Comte, the family creates an atmosphere of love and trust necessary for socialization. It is in the family that the child first gets some dim awareness of the meaning of sympathy, and it is here that men and women are made to realize that they are part of the endless stream of life.

> The first germ of social feeling is seen in the affection of the child for its parents. Filial love is the starting-point of our moral education: from it springs the instinct of continuity, and consequently of reverence for our ancestors. It is the first tie by which the new being feels himself bound to the whole past history of man. Brotherly love comes next, implanting the instinct of solidarity, that is to say of union with our contemporaries: and thus we have already a sort of outline of social existence. With maturity new phases of feeling are developed. . . . This second stage in moral education begins with conjugal affection, the most important of all, in which perfect fullness of devotion is secured by the reciprocity and indissolubility of the bond. It is the highest type of all sympathetic in-

stincts, and has appropriated to itself in a special sense the name of Love. From this most perfect of unions proceeds the last in the series of domestic sympathies, parental love. It completes the training by which Nature prepares us for universal sympathy: for it teaches us to care for our successors; and thus it binds us to the future, as filial love has bound us to the past.[44]

The subordination of wives to their husbands appeared to Comte to be both natural and necessary. A woman's place is in the home; it is through the influence of her affections in the home that her force in society is exercised. Children should be taught to venerate their superiors as well as to obey them. Since benevolence grows out of veneration, people are able finally to live for others because they have learned to venerate humanity.

Children are entitled to an education and to a material start in life; beyond that, any property that the family possesses should be shared with others. Domestics should be regarded as members of the family, so that with the children of the household they can feel veneration for those whose benevolence they enjoy. Also, the custom of adoption should be encouraged, since in this way homes without children can be made complete, and children without homes can enjoy the warmth of domestic love.

THE STATUS OF WOMEN

The influence of Clotilde de Vaux cast a sentimental glow over Comte's attitude toward women. That he adored womankind as few men have is plain to see, even if his adoration did take a peculiarly Comtean form. Yet by modern standards some of his views are patronizing if not actually insulting to women. He speaks of them as living in "a kind of state of continuous childhood." Superior to men in sympathy and sociability, women are portrayed in his writings as inferior to men in practical activity and intellect. No woman should be required, or even permitted, to work outside the home for a living. A female is entitled from birth to death to support from a father, a husband, a male relative, or, lacking any of these, the state. She should at no time in life have the responsibility of managing property. Those qualities which constitute feminine strength and the social usefulness of women are destroyed, Comte declared, when women participate in political activities, attempt to control wealth, or work outside the home. Men are by nature fitted for public life; women, for domestic life.

> Different as the two sexes are by nature, and increased as that difference is by the diversity which happily exists in their social position, each is consequently necessary to the moral development of the other. In practical energy and in the mental capacity connected with it, man is evidently superior to woman. Woman's strength, on the other hand, lies in feeling. She excels man in love, as man excels her in all kinds of force. It is

impossible to conceive of a closer union than that which binds these two beings to the mutual service and perfection of each other, saving them from all danger of rivalry. The voluntary character too of this union gives it a still further charm, when the choice has been on both sides a happy one. In the Positive theory, then, of marriage, its principal object is considered to be that of completing and confirming the education of the heart by calling out the purest and strongest of human sympathies.[45]

As Comte became in the last years of his life more and more absorbed in the Religion of Humanity, his worship of Clotilde de Vaux, and through her of all womankind, almost shifted the burden of reconstructing humanity to women, since he portrayed the positivist thinking of the male as paling into insignificance in comparison with the positivist feeling of the female.

THE RELIGION OF HUMANITY

Comte's religion can easily be made to appear a repudiation of his science. He declared that there are no absolutes; yet his *humanity* is a supreme reality not unlike the gods of other religions. He warned against transposing ideas into beings or things; yet his Great Being (Humanity) is a deification of an abstract concept.

Two facts about Comte's religion are clear: (1) despite its initial appeal to a small group of Oxford scholars and a few others, it did not take hold and has today only a few small groups of adherents; and (2) Comte's social theories cannot be examined in isolation from his Religion of Humanity.

THE ETHICAL BASIS

The problem of social order is the central theme in Comte's thought: how to transform society so that egoism will be universally subordinated to altruism and all men everywhere will work harmoniously to realize the benefits of social progress. Comte believed that political unity is possible only after intellectual unity had been established, and that a practical universal ethic, universally accepted, is a *sine qua non* of social order.

Comte offered positivism as an intellectual and an ethical solution to the fundamental social problem. Positivism affords a solution to the problem of the conflict between science and religion: a scientific religion and a religious science. It provides a final solution to the old problem of progress and order: progress is the development of social order through a universal religion. It draws men together in the name of humanity, with love as a principle, order a basis, and progress an end, to forget self and to live for others.

> Such . . . is the essential character of the system of life which Positivism offers for the definite acceptance of society; a system which reg-

ulates the whole course of our private and public existence, by bringing Feeling, Reason, and Activity into permanent harmony. In this final synthesis, all essential conditions are far more perfectly fulfilled than in any other. Each special element of our nature is more fully developed, and at the same time the general working of the whole is more coherent. Greater distinctness is given to the truth that the affective element predominates in our nature. Life in all its actions and thoughts is brought under the control and inspiring charm of Social Sympathy.[46]

THE RELIGIOUS SYSTEM

The Religion of Humanity is not, however, primarily a system of ethics. In his later works Comte added Morals as a seventh science crowning the hierarchy of the abstract sciences. It is concerned with man as a product of humanity, and it could not come into existence until sociology had discovered that man is not merely an animal. It would link man to the world through humanity. However, even this science, which Comte never fully described, is not identical with his religious system. The Religion of Humanity embraces all scientific knowledge, but it includes feeling and will as well as intellectual activity; it is a religion.

Comte's full definition of religion, as he understands it, occupies hundreds of pages in his books—if, indeed, all that he says about positivism is not to be interpreted as his view of the nature and meaning of religion. He did, however, specifically declare that religion is "that state of complete harmony peculiar to human life, in its collective as well as in its individual form," and that its constituent elements are a doctrine, a system of worship, and a government.

According to Comte, individual and collective harmony—that is, man's peace with himself and with his fellows—is possible only if feeling, thought, and will are concentrated on a definite purpose. The Religion of Humanity offers a purpose: Live for Others. Its doctrine establishes humanity as the object of worship, defines sin as selfishness and salvation as social service, and sets forth the principle that the good that men do lives after them and gives them immortality. The Positive system of worship is described by Comte in great detail. It includes many features of other religions, including sacraments and prayer. Positive prayer was not to be a petition but "a solemn out-pouring, whether in private or in public, of men's nobler feelings, inspiring them with larger and more comprehensive thoughts." [47]

THE ORGANIZATION

The government of the Religion of Humanity was to be vested in a priesthood composed not of theologians but of scientists and artists. Hawkins describes the nature and activities of this body as follows:

> The positive priests were to be . . . very powerful. They were to preach, conduct public worship, administer the sacraments, give counsel

to the faithful, teach science, act as arbiters in industrial and international conflicts, and turn public opinion into channels which would best serve mankind. They were to be a body of scholars, physicians, poets, artists, and even dancers and singers.

The training of the priests was to be long and strenuous. From the age of twenty-eight to thirty-five, the candidate was to study under the older members of the faculties of the positivist schools, and from thirty-five to forty-two, he was to serve as vicar and pass through an apprenticeship of teaching and giving advice. At the age of forty-two he was to be admitted to the priesthood. Priests were to receive no salary and hold no political office. They were to be obliged to marry in order that they might come under the salutary influence of woman.

At the head of the universal priesthood was to be the High Priest of Humanity, who was to reside in Paris, the Holy City of positivism. This supreme pontiff was to have the power to ordain, transfer, suspend, or dismiss priests.[48]

Since the priests would have no temporal power, they would be able to employ only moral force to gain obedience. With the masses on their side, this force would be sufficient to bring any recalcitrant into line. Their control over education would ensure the preparation of young people for life in a positivist society. The priests would be more concerned with the discipline of the intellect than with its stimulation. A positivist library consisting of a hundred volumes was to be established. Comte actually prepared a list of one hundred and fifty volumes from which the selection was to be made and suggested that all other books be destroyed.

CRITICISM

The failure of the Religion of Humanity to gain general support is not hard to understand. It asks more in the name of religion than people are willing to give, and it offers less in return than they demand from religion. It sacrifices the individual to humanity and takes from him the freedom that gives life personal meaning. Thomas Henry Huxley described it as "Catholicism minus Christianity," [49] and, as if that were not ridicule enough, added that he would as soon worship a wilderness of apes as humanity.

COMTE'S CHARACTER AND INFLUENCE

Auguste Comte was a man of large vision, but, although his mental powers were great, he did not always succeed in reaching his goals. He sought to create a science of social phenomena; he emerged with a plan of social action. He attempted to erect a verifiable system of scientific ideas that no clear-headed person could reject; he produced finally a curious medley of religious ideas that caused even a stanch supporter like John Stuart Mill to declare him "morality-intoxicated" and to forsake him. He led people to expect from him a science of religion; he gave them, as his crowning achievement, a religion of science.

It is easy to believe that there were two Comtes, the one a brilliant scientist and the other a religious mystic of little distinction. Nevertheless, the fact that his science embraced his religion is itself evidence of a unity in Comte's work.

Comte's faults were grievous, but he appeared at the crucial moment in history when the social sciences were beginning to develop. His philosophy of the sciences encouraged belief that the methods that had proved so fruitful in dealing with natural phenomena could be applied with similar results to social phenomena. His law of the three stages made manifest "the gradual ascendancy of the faculties of humanity over those of animality" and showed how the spirit of positivism opens wide the way to human progress as he defined it. Indeed, the hopeful mood so apparent in the social thought of the late nineteenth century was a reflection of the faith in social science that Auguste Comte helped to create.

17 · SOCIAL PHILOSOPHY AND SOCIAL SCIENCE

Since this book is itself a summary of social thought selected from the long period of time between Hammurabi and Comte, no attempt will be made to summarize the ideas presented in the foregoing pages. And no judgment will be made as to their value, although in their selection a judgment was obviously made as to what was considered to be timely and important. Since, however, the question must surely have arisen as to whether social thought is speculative social philosophy or empirical social science, the answer can now be given: it is both.

In the middle of the nineteenth century Auguste Comte stood at a crossways which, like others before him, he mistook for a junction. Science and religion seemed to him, as reason and faith had seemed to Thomas Aquinas, to have come together, never again to separate. As Comte looked back, he saw the perilous ways of theology and metaphysics; but ahead glittered the well-lighted avenue of positivism. He was confident that all sensible and informed people would gladly abandon the dangerous paths of philosophical speculation about social matters and set out together to reach a common destination.

A more adequate knowledge of the history of ideas might have tempered Comte's enthusiasm. Had he been better acquainted with mankind's quest through the ages for meaningful social knowledge, he might have learned that men seek various goals in life and follow devious routes. He did not realize that the way he pointed out had been seen before and had been rejected by those who had conceptions different from his of the meaning of human life and, consequently, of the nature of human progress.

The old proverb that nothing is new obviously applies to social thought. This is not to say that ideas do not change with time. The Platonism revived by Augustine was different from that which long before had developed in the Academy. The Aristotelianism into which Thomas Aquinas breathed new life was transformed into something different by the warmth of his religious zeal. Lucretius caught a glimpse of human progress, but the vision he saw was not the one that fascinated Comte. Ikhnaton declared that there was but one God, yet the Hebrews gave monotheism to mankind. All societies have doctrines of class, but nowhere, not even in India, has anything exactly like the caste system described in the sacred literature of the Hindus ever appeared. The new science of Giambattista Vico was different in important respects from the new science of Ibn Khaldun. Comte's altruism was similar in form to Micah's, but the Golden Rule did not mean to the French positivist what it had meant to the Hebrew prophet.

Although it is true that there is nothing new under the sun, it is equally true that nothing under the sun abides. Every day is a new day. Old ideas reappear, but they are never clothed in exactly the same fashion. They may even look strange until they are recognized against the background of the truth system that had provided an earlier setting.

Three broad systems of truth criteria appear in history. These may be called the systems of authority, reason, and experience. They were known to Plato, expressly recognized by Vico, and described by Comte. These systems change with time; they are not mutually exclusive; and even though one of them usually dominates the thought of an individual or a society, the others are not entirely absent. A brief review of these systems, as they have influenced social thought, may be helpful.

Wherever the criterion of truth is identical with the authority for morality, there are no social truths except moral truths. At various times and places the answers to fundamental social questions have been found in religious dogmas. Sacred books and their interpreters prescribe all rules of conduct regarded as necessary; nothing more is required except acceptance on faith of the truths thus revealed. This type of truth system was dominant in most of the ancient civilizations and has continued to influence profoundly the social thought of peoples whose mentality has been little affected by science. It found eloquent expression in the Hebrew prophets, and, after being pushed into the background by Greek and Roman philosophers, reappeared with tremendous vitality in medieval Christendom.

In the fifth and fourth centuries B.C., the Greek philosophers dethroned the Olympian gods by an appeal to reason. The faith of Plato and Aristotle in human reason was equal to that which the Homeric Greeks had placed in oracles and which, much earlier, Ikhnaton had reposed in Aton, the sun-god. Greek rationalism suffered from misuse by the Romans and neglect by the early Christians. It was restored to prominence by Thomas Aquinas, found its most complete, and perhaps ultimate, expression in Cartesianism, and then yielded to the truth system of science.

Since the seventeenth century the scientific spirit has dominated thought in the Western world. We have seen that, three centuries earlier, Ibn Khaldun had sought for social truths in experience and had formulated a science of history. The men and women of the Renaissance and the Reformation had sipped the heady wine of experience and found it good. Then came the great natural scientists who established, by an appeal to the senses, truths about nature that could be demonstrated to any competent observer. As knowledge derived from experience accumulated, social thinkers began to adopt the criteria of science. Machiavelli described the rules of politics as he saw them, not as he thought they ought to be. John Locke's theories of human nature, politics, property, and education were products of empiricism. Although Auguste Comte turned from science to social reform, positivism as a religion emerged from positivism as a science. The modern social sciences derived their initial character and their appeal from the application to social phenomena of the truth criteria which had created natural science.

Optimism came easy in the nineteenth century. As nature's secrets were laid bare, nature's laws were made to serve human ends. In this atmosphere of great achievements and glowing prospects, it is not to be supposed that social scientists were content merely to describe. They were inspired, equally with the natural scientists, by that idea of progress which John B. Bury has called "the animating and controlling" idea of modern Western thought. Most of them believed that the social sciences needed only to fall into step with the natural sciences in order to join in the march of progress. They declared that the social sciences lagged only because superstitions, fears, and blank misgivings yet lingered where science had not cleared away the mist. Comte was not alone in the view that human control over human destiny awaited only the universal adoption of the method and the spirit of science. He merely expressed what most educated people were beginning to believe. The idea spread that what was demanded was that speculative social philosophy give way to empirical social science.

Social thought did, in fact, take a decided turn in the nineteenth century toward empiricism and scientific objectivity. A problem soon arose, however, which can best be stated as a question: Is it the function of social science only to discover and to describe, or should it seek to define ends as well as to describe means? Without ever actually recognizing that problem, and completely unaware of its implications, Comte offered one solution to it in his religion of humanity. His way out of the dilemma is much too easy to be realistic, as its rejection proves. A clearer conception of the nature of this basic problem might have enabled Comte to propose something more acceptable. As it was, he wholly neglected the possibility that a fundamental difference exists between social science and natural science.

An illustration clarifies this point. The law of gravitation describes a natural relationship existing between physical objects. Its truth—that is, its accuracy as a description—is a matter of great concern, but natural science is not required to decide whether or not the observed order *ought* to exist. It can be known and used, but it cannot be changed; the heavenly bodies are held in place by a force greater than any power man has yet learned to command. In human relations, however, nothing approaching the inflexibility of the law of gravitation has been found. Morality is at the heart of every social question, and uniformity in social phenomena is no proof of naturalness or, in that sense, of rightness. In nature whatever *is* is natural, and therefore right. In society it is not so easy to define the natural, and consequently the right. Certainly whatever social situation exists can be changed by human will and effort to something different.

Does this mean that social science is confronted not only with the task of discovering uniformities in social phenomena but also with the obligation of defining justice in social experience? There is difference of opinion on this question. Nevertheless, the readiness not merely to improve old social institutions but to efface those which cannot be reconciled with human dignity and reasonable human aspirations is more pronounced now than ever before. The "law" of slavery, long accepted as a part of nature, was discovered to be no law at all but only a human practice that could be ended by human means. Perhaps the "law" of war may prove to be a similar practice.

The development of social science since Comte provides the theme for an exciting story of bold thought and solid achievement, but that story is only an episode in the account of man's age-long effort to discover how best to live with his fellow man.

NOTES

SUGGESTED READINGS

INDEX

NOTES

CHAPTER 1

1. Lines from Schiller quoted from Howard Becker and Harry Elmer Barnes, *Social Thought from Lore to Science* (2 vols.; 2d ed.; Washington: Harren Press, 1952), I, 10.
2. G. D. H. Cole in J. J. Rousseau, *The Social Contract and Discourses*, trans. G. D. H. Cole (London: J. M. Dent & Sons, 1913), p. vii.

CHAPTER 2

1. Robert W. Rogers, *History of Babylonia and Assyria* (New York: Eaton and Mains, 1900), I, 84.
2. Also known as Xisuthros and as Ziusudra.
3. From "The Epic of Gilgameth," trans. E. A. Speiser, in James B. Pritchard (ed.), *Ancient Near Eastern Texts* (Princeton: Princeton University Press, 1950), p. 72.
4. Quoted from G. Maspero, *The Struggle of the Nations* (New York: D. Appleton and Company, 1897), pp. 43-44.
5. Epilogue, xxv, 7-19.
6. Ltr. VII, in L. W. King, *The Letters and Inscriptions of Hammurabi* (London: Luzac and Company, 1900), III, 190-191.
7. From "Gilgamesh and Agga," trans. S. N. Kramer, in Pritchard, *op. cit.*, pp. 44-45.
8. Code of Hammurabi, 196, 197, 200.
9. *Ibid.*, 218.
10. *Ibid.*, 143.
11. *Early History of Assyria* (London: Chatto and Windus, 1928), p. 338.
12. C. H. W. Johns, *Babylonian and Assyrian Laws, Contracts and Letters* (New York: Charles Scribner's Sons, 1904), p. 229.
13. "Lamentation over the Destruction of Ur," trans. S. N. Kramer, in Pritchard, *op. cit.*, pp. 455-463.
14. Leonard W. King, *A History of Babylon* (London: Chatto and Windus, 1915), pp. 163-164.
15. From "Hymn to Ishtar," trans. Ferris J. Stephens, in Pritchard, *op. cit.*, p. 383.
16. Johns, *op. cit.*, p. 336.
17. From "The Legend of Sargon," trans. E. A. Speiser, in Pritchard, *op. cit.*, p. 119.
18. Johns, *op. cit.*, p. 42.
19. A. H. Sayce, *Religions of Ancient Egypt and Babylonia* (Edinburgh: T. and T. Clark, 1902), p. 303.
20. G. Maspero, *Dawn of Civilization* (London: Society for Promoting Christian Knowledge, 1901), pp. 643-644.
21. From "The Creation Epic," trans. E. A. Speiser, in Pritchard, *op. cit.*, p. 68.
22. From "The Creation of Man by the Mother Goddess," trans. E. A. Speiser, in Pritchard, *op. cit.*, p. 99.
23. Sayce, *op. cit.*, p. 294.
24. From "The Epic of Gilgameth," trans. E. A. Speiser, in Pritchard, *op. cit.*, p. 79.
25. *Ibid.*, p. 90.
26. From "Akkadian Observations on Life and the World Order," trans. Robert H. Pfeiffer, in Pritchard, *op. cit.*, p. 435.

CHAPTER 3

1. M. Rostovtzeff, *A History of the Ancient World* (Oxford: Clarendon Press, 1926), I, 95.
2. James H. Breasted, *A History of the Ancient Egyptians* (New York: Charles Scribner's Sons, 1911), p. 129. Quoted with permission of Charles Scribner's Sons.
3. George Steindorff and Keith C. Seele, *When Egypt Ruled the East* (Chicago: The University of Chicago Press, 1947), p. 24.
4. Breasted, *op. cit.*, p. 244.
5. A. H. Sayce, *The Religions of Ancient Egypt and Babylonia* (Edinburgh: T. and T. Clark, 1902), pp. 29-30.
6. Adolf Erman, *Life in Ancient Egypt*, trans. H. M. Tirard (New York: Macmillan and Company, 1894), p. 3.
7. Adolph Erman, *The Literature of the Ancient Egyptians* (London: Methuen & Co., 1927), p. 67.
8. James H. Breasted, *Ancient Records of Egypt* (Chicago: The University of Chicago Press, 1906), III, 176-181.
9. Steindorff and Seele, *op. cit.*, pp. 85-86.
10. Breasted, *Ancient Records*, II, 270-271.
11. James H. Breasted, *Dawn of Conscience* (New York: Charles Scribner's Sons, 1934), p. 214. Quoted with permission of Charles Scribner's Sons.
12. "Egyptian Instructions," trans. John A. Wilson, in James B. Pritchard (ed.), *Ancient Near Eastern Texts* (Princeton: Princeton University Press, 1950), p. 415.
13. Breasted, *Ancient Records*, II, 269.
14. *Ibid.*, I, 152.
15. "Instruction of Amen-em-opet," trans. John A. Wilson, in Pritchard, *op. cit.*, p. 421.
16. "Instruction for Kagemni," quoted from Erman, *The Literature of the Ancient Egyptians*, p. 66.
17. Breasted, *Dawn of Conscience*, pp. 144-145.
18. "Instructions for King Meri-ka-re," trans. John A. Wilson, in Pritchard, *op. cit.*, p. 415.
19. *Ibid.*, p. 415.
20. "The Eloquent Peasant," in E. A. W. Budge, *The Literature of the Ancient Egyptians* (London: J. M. Dent & Sons, 1914), p. 176.
21. Erman, *Life in Ancient Egypt*, pp. 425-445.
22. W. M. Flinders Petrie, *Social Life in Ancient Egypt* (New York: Houghton Mifflin Company, 1923), p. 78.
23. *Ibid.*, p. 21.
24. *Ibid.*, p. 27.
25. Quoted from Erman, *Life in Ancient Egypt*, p. 445.
26. Budge, *op. cit.*, p. 251.
27. From "Songs of the Common People," trans. John A. Wilson, in Pritchard, *op. cit.*, p. 469.
28. From "The Tradition of Seven Lean Years in Egypt," trans. John A. Wilson, in Pritchard, *op. cit.*, p. 31.
29. Breasted, *Ancient Records*, III, 90.
30. *Life in Ancient Egypt*, pp. 439-440.
31. *Ibid.*, pp. 193-194.
32. Margaret A. Murray, *The Splendour That Was Egypt* (New York: Philosophical Library, 1949), p. 100.
33. Budge, *op. cit.*, p. 227.
34. See Erman, *Life in Ancient Egypt*, pp. 153-154, and Murray, *op. cit.*, pp. 101-104.
35. William F. Edgerton, "Notes on Egyptian Marriage," *Studies in Ancient Oriental Civilization* (Chicago: The University of Chicago Press, 1931), I, i, 25.
36. Quoted from Will Durant, *The Story of Civilization* (New York: Simon and Schuster, 1935), I, 165.
37. Quoted from Erman, *The Literature of the Ancient Egyptians*, pp. 239-240.
38. Quoted from Robert Briffault, *The Mothers* (New York: The Macmillan Company, 1931), p. 276.
39. Murray, *op. cit.*, pp. 103-104.
40. *Dawn of Conscience*, p. 120.
41. Breasted, *Ancient Records*, I, 86-87.
42. C. P. Tiele, "The Egyptian Religion," *Religious Systems of the World*

(New York: The Macmillan Co., 1901), p. 3.
43. *The Development of Religion and Thought in Ancient Egypt* (New York: Charles Scribner's Sons, 1912), p. 247. Quoted with permission of Charles Scribner's Sons.
44. Durant, *op. cit.,* p. 199.
45. From "Heroic Tales," trans. John A. Wilson, in Pritchard, *op. cit.,* p. 12.
46. Quoted from Breasted, *The Development of Religion and Thought in Ancient Egypt,* p. 18.
47. E. A. Wallis Budge, *The Book of the Dead* (New York: G. P. Putnam's Sons, 1913), I, 56.
48. *Ibid.,* I, 106-107.
49. "Hymn to Aton," in Arthur Weigall, *The Life and Times of Akhnaton* (London: Thornton Butterworth, Ltd., 1923), p. 132.
50. Quoted from Murray, *op. cit.,* p. 210.
51. *Dawn of Conscience,* p. 45.
52. *Op. cit.,* pp. 144-46.
53. *Dawn of Conscience,* p. 320.
54. Murray, *op. cit.,* p. 306.
55. From "The Good Fortune of the Dead," trans. John A. Wilson, in Pritchard, *op. cit.,* pp. 33-34.
56. Breasted, *Ancient Records,* IV, 205.
57. From "Egyptian Didactic Tales," trans. John A. Wilson, in Pritchard, *op. cit.,* p. 406.
58. *Dawn of Conscience,* p. 215.
59. *Ibid.,* p. 417.
60. James Baikie, *The Amarna Age* (New York: The Macmillan Company, 1926), p. 458.
61. *Op. cit.,* p. 251. All Egyptologists do not share this high regard for Ikhnaton. For example, see Margaret A. Murray's *Egyptian Religious Poetry* (London: John Murray, 1949), pp. 29-30.
62. *A Study of History* (6 vols., London: Oxford University Press, 1939), IV, 81.

CHAPTER 4

1. Thomas Watters, *Laotzu* (London: Williams and Norgate, 1870), pp. 12-13.
2. *Book of History,* I, 1, in F. Max Müller (ed), *Sacred Books of the East,* trans. James Legge (Oxford: Clarendon Press, 1879-82).
3. Friedrich Hirth, *The Ancient History of China* (New York: Columbia University Press, 1908), p. 56.
4. *Ibid,* p. 57.
5. H. G. Creel, *Confucius* (New York: John Day Co., 1949), pp. 20-21.
6. *The Analects,* trans. William E. Soothill (London: Oxford University Press, 1937), p. xxii.
7. *Op. cit.,* pp. 51-52.
8. Quoted from *The Chinese Classics,* trans. James Legge (London: Trübner and Co., 1861-72), I, 87.
9. *Sacred Books of the East,* III, 285.
10. *Sacred Books of the East,* XVI, xv.
11. *Doctrine of the Mean,* XX, 8, from Legge, *op. cit.,* I, 270-271.
12. Edward H. Parker, *Ancient China Simplified* (London: Chapman and Hall, 1908), p. 312.
13. Leonard S. Hsü, *The Political Philosophy of Confucianism* (New York: E. P. Dutton & Co., 1932), p. 172.
14. *Analects,* XII, 7, from *The Sayings of Confucius,* trans. Lionel Giles, (London: John Murray, 1907).
15. *Book of History,* V, xx, 4, in *Sacred Books of the East,* III, 229.
16. *Analects,* XVI, 2, from Soothill, *op. cit.*
17. *Great Learning,* X, 5, from Legge, *op. cit.,* I, 239.
18. *Book of History,* III, iii, 2, in *Sacred Books of the East,* III, 79.
19. *Analects,* XIII, 6 and XIII, 4, from *Chinese Philosophy in Classical Times,* trans. E. R. Hughes (London: J. M. Dent & Sons, 1942).
20. *The Great Learning,* I, 4, from Legge, *op. cit.,* I, 222-223.
21. *Op. cit.,* p. 112.
22. *Op. cit.,* p. 125.
23. Marcel Granet, *Chinese Civilization* (New York: Alfred A. Knopf, 1930), p. 311.
24. Quoted from E. R. Hughes, *op. cit.,* p. 35.
25. *Op. cit.,* IV, i, 165-166.
26. *Op. cit.,* p. 158.
27. Quoted from Legge, *Chinese Classics,* IV, i, 166.
28. *Book of Rituals,* III, ii, 2.

29. *Book of Rituals,* IX, 10. The Mother of Mencius quotes this passage to her son when he is torn between the desire to go out into the world to serve humanity and his feeling of responsibility to her.
30. *Analects,* XVII, 25. Quoted from Giles, *op. cit.,* p. 108.
31. *Book of History,* V, viii, 2-3.
32. *Ibid.,* V, ix, 3.
33. *Analects,* II, 7.
34. *Analects,* II, 7, from Giles, *op. cit.,* p. 54.
35. *Doctrine of the Mean,* XVIII, 1.
36. *Analects,* IV, 18, from Soothill, *op. cit.*
37. *Analects,* IV, 15.
38. Chang Wing-tsit, "The Story of Chinese Philosophy" in Charles A. Moore, Ed., *Philosophy—East and West* (Princeton: Princeton University Press, 1944), pp. 28-29.
39. *Book of Mencius,* VI, i, 6-7, from Legge, *op. cit.,* II, 278-279.
40. *Analects,* II, 4, from Soothill, *op. cit.*
41. *Analects,* XVII, 2.
42. *Analects,* XVII, 8, from Soothill, *op. cit.*
43. *Analects,* VII, 7.
44. *Analects,* XI, 3.
45. *Analects,* XV, 30.
46. *Analects,* XV, 23, from Soothill, *op. cit.*
47. *Analects,* XIV, 36.
48. *Analects,* VII, 15, from Soothill, *op. cit.*
49. Creel, *op. cit.,* p. 289.
50. *The Wisdom of Confucius* (New York: Random House, 1938), p. 6.
51. Quoted from E. R. Hughes (ed.), *op cit.,* p. 29.

CHAPTER 5

1. Quoted from E. J. Rapson, *Ancient India* (Cambridge: University Press, 1914), p. 1.
2. Gertrude E. Sen, *The Pageant of India's History* (New York: Longmans, Green and Co., 1948), p. 56.
3. *The World's Great Classics* (New York: Colonial Press, 1900), XL, 155.
4. Quoted from Will Durant, *The Story of Civilization* (New York: Simon and Schuster, 1935), I, 410.
5. *The World's Great Classics,* XXXVIII, 167.
6. Durant, *op. cit.,* p. 561.
7. *Svetasvatara-Upanishad,* I, 1. The translations are those found in F. Max Müller (ed.), *Sacred Books of the East* (Oxford: Clarendon Press, 1884-86) unless otherwise shown. *Brahman* in the text is shown here as *Brahma.* There is considerable variation in the spelling of some of the most important Hindu terms. In some instances the difference is merely one of preference or represents a change in meaning with the passage of time. In others, different conceptions are expressed by similar, but not identical, terms. For example, either *Brahman* or *Brahmin* may be used to refer to a member of the sacerdotal caste. On the other hand, *Brahman* and *Brahma* both refer to God, but they are distinctly different concepts. Also, in later writings the term *Brahmā* (masculine in form while *Brahma* is neuter) came to represent the Trinity of personal Creator including Vishnu and Shiva. These differences are important in Hindu theology, but they are extremely difficult to recognize by those unfamiliar with Hindu metaphysics and mythology. Since the diacritical marks used by scholars are meaningless to most of those for whom this book is intended, they have been omitted. Likewise, parenthetical elements introduced by some translators to clarify the original text are not placed in parentheses but appear as part of the text. For the sake of consistency, and in order to avoid confusion between a human being and the divine being, *Brahman* refers in this book to a human member of the priestly caste, and *Brahma* refers to God; quotations have been modified, when necessary, to maintain this distinction.
8. *Mundaka-Upanishad,* I, i, 7 and *Atharva Veda,* XIII, iv, 3.

9. *Op. cit.*, p. 514.
10. *Khandogya-Upanishad*, VI, ii, 3.
11. *The Ramayana and the Mahabharata*, condensed into English verse by Romesh C. Dutt (London: J. M. Dent & Sons, 1910) III, viii.
12. *Mundaka-Upanishad*, III, ii, 8.
13. *Khandogya-Upanishad*, V, x, 7.
14. *Sacred Books of the East*, I, 314.
15. *Laws of Manu*, IV, 240-242.
16. Quoted from Selwyn G. Champion, *The Eleven Religions* (New York: E. P. Dutton & Co., 1945), p. xviii.
17. *The Song Celestial*, trans. Sir Edwin Arnold (London: Trübner and Co., n. d.), Book II.
18. *Laws of Manu*, XII, 38.
19. *Maitrayana-Brahmana Upanishad,* IV, 2.
20. *Khandogya-Upanishad*, VII, xix, 1.
21. *Laws of Manu*, VII, 110, 103.
22. S. Radhakrishnan, *Indian Philosophy* (London: George Allen and Unwin, Ltd., 1948), I, 112-113.
23. *Laws of Manu*, X, 80.
24. *Ibid.,* IV, 258.
25. *Ibid.,* I, 96.
26. *Ibid.,* X, 3.
27. *Ibid.,* I, 89.
28. *Ibid.,* IX, 320.
29. *Ibid.,* I, 90.
30. *Ibid.,* IX, 333.
31. *Ibid.,* X, 4.
32. *Ibid.,* VIII, 414.
33. *Op. cit.*, p. 42.
34. *Laws of Manu*, XI, 181.
35. *Op. cit.*, Book XVIII.
36. *Laws of Manu*, IX, 96.
37. *Ibid.,* III, 34.
38. *Op. cit.*, I, vi.
39. *Laws of Manu*, X, 5.
40. Quoted from Durant, *op. cit.*, p. 493.
41. *Laws of Manu*, IX, 3.
42. *Ibid.,* IX, 65.
43. *Brihadaranyaka Upanishad*, I, iv. 1.
44. *Laws of Manu*, III, 60-62.
45. *Ramayana,* Dutt's version, III, i.
46. M. Hiriyanna, *The Essentials of Indian Philosophy* (London: George Allen & Unwin, 1949), pp. 27-28.

CHAPTER 6

1. Quoted from Charles C. Butterworth, *The Literary Lineage of the King James Bible* (Philadelphia: University of Pennsylvania Press, 1941), p. 5.
2. R. H. Kennett, *Ancient Hebrew Social Life and Custom* (London: Oxford University Press, for the British Academy, 1933), pp. 76-77.
3. *Op. cit.*, p. 8.
4. *Ibid.,* p. 10.
5. From S. E. Dwight, *The Hebrew Wife* (New York: Leavitt, Lord & Co., 1836), p. 102.
6. Quoted from Cecil Roth, *The Jewish Contribution to Civilization* (New York: Harper & Bros., 1940), p. 21.

CHAPTER 7

1. George W. Botsford and Charles A. Robinson, *Hellenic History* (New York: The Macmillan Company, 1948), p. 236. Copyright 1948. Quoted with permission of the Macmillan Company.
2. Arnold J. Toynbee, *A Study of History* (New York: Oxford University Press, 1947), p. 296.
3. *Laches,* 186. Jowett's translation of the works of Plato is used unless otherwise indicated, and the references are to the pages of Stephens given in the margin of the translation.
4. Diogenes Laertius, *Lives of Eminent Philosophers,* trans. R. D. Hicks (New York: G. P. Putnam's Sons, 1925), I, 153.
5. *Ibid.,* I, 155.
6. *Apology,* 30.
7. *Phaedo,* 116-118.
8. Diogenes Laertius, *op. cit.,* I, 315.
9. Sir Richard Burton, *The Kasidah of Haji Abdu El-Yezdi* (Philadelphia: David McKay Co., 1931), p. 43.
10. *Protagoras,* 352.
11. *Apology,* 30-31.
12. *The Philosophy of Plato* (New York: Charles Scribner's Sons, 1939), p. 385. Quoted with permission of Charles Scribner's Sons.
13. *Protagoras,* 322.
14. *Laws* VII, 792.
15. *Republic* VII, 514-515.
16. *Laws* X, 903.

17. *Republic* VIII, 561.
18. *Republic* III, 415.
19. *Republic* V, 457.
20. *Republic* V, 461.
21. *Republic* V, 460.
22. *Republic* V, 456.
23. *Laws* VII, 806.
24. *Laws* VI, 772.
25. Sir Richard Livingstone, *Plato and Modern Education* (New York: The Macmillan Company, 1944), p. 12. Copyright 1944. Quoted with permission of The Macmillan Company.
26. *Laws* III, 689.
27. *Protagoras*, 314.
28. *Laws* II, 653.
29. *Laws* VII, 808.
30. Quoted from Livingstone, *op. cit.*, p. 36.
31. *Republic* V, 473.
32. *Laws* V, 737-738.
33. Botsford and Robinson, *op. cit.*, p. 160.
34. *Republic* V, 466.
35. *Laws* V, 739.
36. *Statesman*, 303.
37. *Laws* VI, 757.
38. *Republic* VIII, 562-563.
39. *Republic* VIII, 566-569.
40. *Statesman*, 269.
41. *Statesman*, 271.
42. *Laws* IV, 713.
43. Raphael Demos, *op. cit.*, pp. 102-103. It is important not to attribute to Plato certain ideas about the nature of God that came to prevail in the Christian churches. Yet, as Demos points out, "In the complexity of the Platonic doctrine, with its fusion of the ideas of transcendence and immanence, of finitude, or moral perfection, and of rationality, the ensuing religious schools found a rich storehouse from which to replenish themselves" (p. 125).
44. *Laws,* VII, 803.

CHAPTER 8

1. *Nicomachean Ethics,* 1177b-78a. Hereafter this work will be referred to simply as the *Ethics*. References are to pages in the Bekker edition of Aristotle, since this work is widely used to locate passages in Aristotle's writings. The translations are those given in W. D. Ross, ed. *The Works of Aristotle* (11 vols., Oxford: The Clarendon Press, 1908-1931), unless otherwise indicated.
2. Quoted from Preserved Smith, *A History of Modern Culture* (New York: Henry Holt & Company, 1930), I, 147.
3. Quoted from S. H. Butcher, *Harvard Lectures on Greek Subjects* (New York: The Macmillan Co., 1904), p. 98.
4. Quoted from Thomas Davidson, *Aristotle* (New York: Charles Scribner's Sons, 1905), p. 153.
5. Will Durant, *Story of Philosophy* (New York: Simon and Schuster, Inc., 1927), p. 58.
6. See Werner Jaeger, *Aristotle,* trans. Richard Robinson (Oxford: Clarendon Press, 1934).
7. Ernest Barker, *The Politics of Aristotle* . (Oxford: Clarendon Press, 1946), p. 353.
8. Quoted from Durant, *op. cit.,* p. 64.
9. *Ibid.,* p. 71.
10. *Metaphysics,* 981a.
11. *Posterior Analytics,* 71a.
12. Quoted from George H. Lewes, *Biographical History of Philosophy* (New York: D. Appleton & Co., 1875), p. 261.
13. *Ethics,* 1103a.
14. *Ethics,* 1169b.
15. Quoted from Thomas Davidson, *op. cit.,* p. 9.
16. *Ethics,* 1094b-95a.
17. Edwin Wallace, *Outlines of the Philosophy of Aristotle* (Cambridge: University Press, 1927), p. 108.
18. *Ethics,* 1097b-1098a. From *The Nicomachean Ethics,* trans. J. E. C. Welldon (London: Macmillan and Company, 1892).
19. *Ethics,* 1176b-1177a. From Welldon's translation.
20. Werner Jaeger, *Paideia: the Ideals of Greek Culture,* trans. Gilbert Highet from Second German Edition (Oxford: Basil Blackwell, 1939), p. 3.

21. *Ethics*, 1178*b*-1179*a*. From Welldon's translation.
22. *Ethics*, 1106*b*. From Welldon's translation.
23. *Ethics*, 1104*a*. From Welldon's translation.
24. Arthur W. Rogers, *A Student's History of Philosophy* (New York: The Macmillan Co., 1923), p. 115.
25. *Ethics*, 1106*b*. From Welldon's translation.
26. *Ethics*, 1094*b*. From Welldon's translation.
27. *Op. cit.*, pp. xlvii-xlviii.
28. *Politics*, 1283*a*.
29. *Politics*, 1254*a*-55*a*.
30. *Life and Education in Early Societies* (New York: The Macmillan Co., 1949), p. 419. Copyright 1949. Quoted with permission of The Macmillan Company.
31. Quoted from Davidson, *op. cit.*, p. 3.
32. *Politics*, 1253*a*.
33. *Ibid.*, 1295*b*.
34. *Ibid.*, 1296*a*.
35. *Ibid.*, 1295*a*.
36. *Op cit.*, p. 10.
37. Quoted from *European Morals*, in Davidson, *op. cit.*, p. 172.
38. *Ethics*, 1161*a*. From Welldon's translation.

CHAPTER 9

1. Samuel Dill, *Roman Society from Nero to Marcus Aurelius* (New York: The Macmillan Company, 1905), p. 330.
2. *Thoughts of the Emperor M. Aurelius Antoninus*, trans. George Long (New York: F. M. Lupton Publishing House, n. d.), p. 80.
3. *De Beneficiis*, trans. John W. Basmore (London: William Heinemann, 1935), III, 31.
4. Cicero, *Letters to Atticus*, trans. E. O. Windstedt (London: William Heinemann, 1944), I, 77.
5. Seneca, *Epistulae Morales*, trans. Richard M. Gummere (London: William Heinemann, 1934), I, 459.
6. Lucretius, *Of the Nature of Things*, trans. William E. Leonard (New York: E. P. Dutton and Company, 1950), pp. 103-104.
7. Cicero, *De Legibus*, trans. Clinton Walker Keyes (London: William Heinemann, 1943), p. 321.
8. Seneca, *Epistulae Morales*, I, 277.
9. Cicero, *De Finibus*, trans. H. Rackham (London: William Heinemann, 1931), p. 467.
10. Seneca, *Epistulae Morales*, I, 63-64.
11. Cicero, *The Letters to His Friends*, trans. W. Glynn Williams (London: William Heinemann, 1929), III, 195.
12. Seneca, *Epistulae Morales*, XV, 9.
13. Dill, *op. cit.*, pp. 499-500.
14. Cicero, *De Finibus*, p. 15.
15. *De Re Publica*, trans. Clinton Walker Keyes (London: William Heinemann, 1943), pp. 15-16.
16. Seneca, *Epistulae Morales*, I, 157.
17. *Ibid.*, pp. 187-193.
18. Polybius, *The Histories*, trans. W. R. Paton (London: William Heinemann, 1922), II, 293.
19. *De Re Publica*, p. 71, 105.
20. *The Histories*, III, 309-311.
21. *De Re Publica*, p. 169.
22. *Ibid.*, pp. 221-223.
23. *De Legibus*, p. 505.
24. C. W. Keyes, "Original Elements in Cicero's Ideal Constitution," *American Journal of Philology*, XLII (1921), pp. 309-323.
25. *The Histories*, III, 293.
26. *Of the Nature of Things*, p. 231.
27. *De Re Publica*, p. 65.
28. Cicero, *De Officiis*, trans. Walter Miller (London: William Heinemann, 1947), p. 61.
29. *De Re Publica*, p. 49.
30. *Ibid.*, p. 213.
31. *Epistulae Morales*, II, 397.
32. *The Twelve Tables*, in *Remains of Old Latin*, trans. and ed. by E. H. Warmington (4 vols.; London: William Heinemann, 1938), III, 463.
33. *Ibid.*, p. 505.
34. Quoted from Maurice Pellison, *Roman Life in Pliny's Time* (Philadelphia: George W. Jacobs & Co., 1897), pp. 45-46.
35. *Op. cit.*, p. 445.
36. *The Histories*, I, 249.
37. *Of the Nature of Things*, p. 242.
38. *De Re Publica*, p. 237.

39. *De Legibus,* p. 415.
40. *Epistulae Morales,* p. 411.
41. *Moral Essays,* trans. John W. Basmore (London: William Heinemann, 1928), I, 89.
42. *The Histories,* I, 221.
43. *Of the Nature of Things,* pp. 229-230.
44. *De Officiis,* p. 57.
45. *Moral Essays,* III, 155-157.
46. M. Rostovtzeff, *The Social and Economic History of the Roman Empire* (Oxford: The Clarendon Press, 1926), p. 486.
47. *Of the Nature of Things,* p. 205.
48. *Ibid.,* pp. 219-220.
49. *Ibid.,* pp. 228-229.
50. *Ibid.,* pp. 244-246.
51. *The Histories,* III, 275-277.
52. *Ibid.,* p. 289.
53. Sallust, Florus, and Velleius Paterculus, *Historical Works,* trans. J. S. Watson (London: G. Bell, 1881), pp. 287-88.
54. *Epistulae Morales,* II, 407-409.
55. *Quaestiones Naturales,* quoted from George H. Hildebrand, *The Idea of Progress* (Berkeley: University of California Press, 1949), p. 106.

CHAPTER 10

1. Preface to his Commentary on Ezekiel, quoted from *The City of God,* trans. John Healy (Edinburgh: John Grant, 1909), I, vii.
2. *The City of God,* trans. Marcus Dods (New York: Random House, Inc., 1950), XVIII, 41.
3. *Select Letters,* trans. James H. Baxter in Loeb Classical Library (New York: G. P. Putnam's Sons, 1930), p. 527.
4. *The Confessions,* trans. E. B. Pusey, Everyman Edition (New York: E. P. Dutton & Co., 1950), IV, 12.
5. *Ibid.,* X, 38.
6. *Ibid.,* I, 4 and 1.
7. Quoted from Pierre De Labriolle, *History and Literature of Christianity,* trans. Herbert Wilson (New York: Alfred A. Knopf, 1925), p. 411.
8. W. Cunningham, *S. Austin* (London: C. J. Clay & Sons, 1886), p. 115.
9. *City of God,* XV, 1.
10. *Ibid.,* XVIII, 54.
11. P. A. Sorokin, *The Crisis of Our Age* (New York: E. P. Dutton & Co., 1941), p. 112.
12. *City of God,* XI, 26.
13. *Confessions,* VI, 7.
14. *Confessions,* VII, 16.
15. See Angel C. Vega, *Saint Augustine His Philosophy,* trans. Denis J. Kavanagh (Phila.; The Peter Reilly Company, 1931), pp. 62-114, for numerous quotations from Augustine on this point.
16. *Crisis of Our Age,* p. 111.
17. *Confessions* vii, 23.
18. G. Papini, *Saint Augustine,* trans. M. P. Agnetti (New York: Harcourt, Brace and Co., Inc., 1930), pp. 213-214. Copyright 1930. Quoted with permission of Harcourt, Brace and Co., Inc.
19. Quoted from Meyrick H. Carré, *Realists and Nominalists* (Oxford: Clarendon Press, 1946), p. 19.
20. *De. Trin.,* XII, xv, 25.
21. W. Windelband, *A History of Philosophy,* trans. James H. Tufts (New York: The Macmillan Co., 1901), p. 276.
22. *City of God,* XIV, 4.
23. *City of God,* XIII, 14.
24. *Ibid.,* XIV, 3.
25. *Loc. cit.*
26. Windelband, *op. cit.,* p. 284.
27. *Confessions,* I, 6.
28. Tennyson, *In Memoriam.*
29. *City of God,* XIX, 24.
30. See Joseph McCabe, *St. Augustine and His Age* (New York: G. P. Putnam's Sons, 1903), p. 401.
31. *City of God,* XIX, 15.
32. *Ibid.,* XIX, 15.
33. Phyllis Doyle, *A History of Political Thought* (New York: Henry Holt & Co., 1932), pp. 64-65.
34. *City of God,* XIX, 17, 12.
35. *Ibid.,* XIX, 12.
36. Ernst Troeltsch, *The Social Teaching of the Christian Churches,* trans. Olive Wyon (London: George Allen and Unwin, 1949), I, 129-130.
37. *Confessions,* VIII, 7.
38. Papini, *op. cit.,* p. 131.
39. Mary E. Keenan, *The Life and Times of St. Augustine as Revealed in His Letters* (Washington: The

Catholic University, 1935), p. 176.
40. *City of God,* XIX, 14.
41. *Confessions,* IX, 19.
42. *Op. cit.,* pp. 114-115.
43. *City of God,* XII, 14.
44. *Ibid.,* XIII, 10.

CHAPTER 11

1. Meyrick H. Carré, *Realists and Nominalists* (New York: Clarendon Press, 1946), p. 66.
2. R. W. Vaughan, *The Life and Labours of Saint Thomas of Aquin* (London: Burns and Oates, 1890), pp. 543-544.
3. M. C. D'Arcy, *Thomas Aquinas* (London: Ernest Benn, Ltd., 1930), pp. 49-50.
4. G. P. Benkert, *Thomistic Conception of an International Society* (Washington: Catholic University Press, 1942).
5. *Op. cit.,* p 30.
6. Quoted from Will Durant, *The Age of Faith* (New York: Simon and Schuster, 1950), p. 962.
7. Quoted from Benkert, *op. cit.,* p. 59.
8. F. J. C. Hearnshaw, ed., *Mediaeval Contributions to Modern Civilisation* (New York: Barnes and Noble, 1949), p. 264.
9. *The Everlasting Conflict.* An address delivered at the 185th Commencement of Columbia University, June 6, 1939. Quoted from Benkert, *op. cit.,* p. 117.
10. In F. J. C. Hearnshaw, ed., *Social and Political Ideas of Some Great Mediaeval Thinkers* (New York: Barnes and Noble, 1928), pp. 95, 96.
11. Hearnshaw, *Mediaeval Contributions,* p. 263.
12. Bede Jarrett, *Social Theories of the Middle Ages* (Boston: Little, Brown & Co., 1926), p. 126.
13. Quoted from Jarrett, *op. cit.,* p. 154.
14. Ernst Troeltsch, *The Social Teaching of the Christian Churches,* trans. Olive Wyon (New York: The Macmillan Company, 1949), I, 320.
15. Anthony L. Ostheimer, *The Family* (Washington: Catholic University Press, 1939), p. 15.
16. *Ibid.,* pp. 35-37.
17. Quoted from Jarrett, *op. cit.,* pp. 70-84.
18. Ostheimer, *op. cit.,* p. 63.
19. *Ibid.,* pp. 82-83.
20. *Ibid.,* p. 95.
21. Canon 1366, Par. 2.

CHAPTER 12

1. Quoted from Bernard Lewis, *The Arabs in History* (London: The Anchor Press, 1950), pp. 9-10.
2. Will Durant, *The Age of Faith* (New York: Simon and Schuster, 1950), p. 174.
3. Quoted from Selwyn G. Champion, *The Eleven Religions* (New York: E. P. Dutton, 1945), p. 173.
4. *Ibid.,* p. 177.
5. Robert Flint, *History of the Philosophy of History* (New York: Charles Scribner's Sons, 1894), p. 161.
6. *Ibn Khaldun* (New York: Columbia University Press, 1930), pp. 41-46.
7. Arnold J. Toynbee, *A Study of History* (London: Oxford University Press, 1934), III, 321-322.
8. *A Systematic Source Book in Rural Sociology* (Minneapolis: University of Minnesota Press, 1930), I, 54.
9. *Op. cit.,* p. 87.
10. *Op. cit.,* p. 160.
11. Quoted from Charles Issawi, *An Arab Philosophy of History* (London: John Murray, 1950), xi.
12. Mohammad A. Enan, *Ibn Khaldun* (Lahore: Sh. Muhammad Ashraf, 1941), p. 54.
13. *Les Prolegomenes d'Ibn Khaldoun,* Traduits en Français et Commentes par M. de Slane (Paris: Imprimerie Imperiale, 1863-1868).
14. Published as *An Arab Philosophy of History* (London: John Murray, 1950), 190 pp.
15. See especially Sorokin, Zimmerman, and Galpin, *op. cit.,* I, 55-68.
16. *Prolegomena,* p. 26. Unless otherwise indicated, the quotations from the *Prolegomena* given in this chapter are from Issawi's translation.
17. *Prolegomena,* p. 166.
18. *Ibid.,* p. 68.
19. *Op. cit.,* p. 475.
20. *Prolegomena,* pp. 51-52.

21. *Op. cit.*, III, 324.
22. Quoted from Flint, *op. cit.*, p. 167.
23. *Op. cit.*, p. 32.
24. *Prolegomena*, pp. 114-115.
25. *Ibid.*, p. 110.
26. *Ibid.*, p. 59.
27. Quoted from H. A. R. Gibb, "The Islamic Background of Ibn Khaldun's Political Theory," *Bulletin of the School of Oriental Studies* (University of London), VII, 23-31.
28. Erwin I. J. Rosenthal, "Ibn Khaldun: A North African Muslim Thinker of the Fourteenth Century", *Bulletin of the John Rylands Library*, XXIV, 307-320.
29. *Prolegomena*, pp. 122-125.
30. *Ibid.*, p. 88.
31. *Ibid.*, p. 69.
32. Quoted from Mohammad A. Nashat, "Ibn Khaldoun, Pioneer Economist," *L'Egypte Contemporaine*, May 1944, pp. 377-490.
33. *Prolegomena*, p. 79.
34. *Op. cit.*, p. 317.
35. Quoted from Nashat, *op. cit.*, p. 383.
36. *Prolegomena*, pp. 117-118.
37. Quoted from Sorokin, Zimmerman and Galpin, *op. cit.*, I, 64. By permission of the University of Minnesota Press.
38. *Ibid.*, I, 67-68. By permission of the University of Minnesota Press.
39. *Op. cit.*, p. 31.
40. *Op. cit.*, p. 476.

CHAPTER 13

1. F. J. C. Hearnshaw, *The Social and Political Ideas of Some Great Thinkers of the Renaissance and the Reformation* (New York: Barnes & Noble, 1949), pp. 12-13.
2. Edith H. Sichel, *The Renaissance.* Quoted from E. M. W. Tillyard, *The English Renaissance* (Baltimore: The Johns Hopkins Press, 1952), p. 6.
3. *The Age of the Reformation* (New York: Henry Holt & Co., 1920), pp. 612, 674-675.
4. II, 691.
5. Quoted from J. H. Randall, *The Making of the Modern Mind* (Boston: Houghton Mifflin Co., 1926), p. 166.
6. *Ibid.*, p. 167.
7. *Praise of Folly*, trans. John Wilson (Oxford: Clarendon Press, 1931), p. 117.
8. *Ibid.*, pp. 31-32.
9. Quoted from A. K. Rogers, *A Student's History of Philosophy* (New York: The Macmillan Co., 1923), p. 205.
10. *Ibid.*, p. 242.
11. *Op. cit.*, p. 698.
12. E. M. W. Tillyard, *op. cit.*, p. 18.
13. *Ibid.*, p. 19.
14. *Cambridge Modern History*, I, 533.
15. *The Essays of Montaigne*, trans. E. J. Trechmann (London: Oxford University Press, 1927), I, 540.
16. *The Prince*, trans. Luigi Ricci (New York: Random House, 1940), p. 64.
17. Quoted from *Cambridge Modern History*, I, 203.
18. *Introduction to Machiavelli* in Tudor Translations, I, xvii. Quoted from J. P. Lichtenberger, *Development of Social Theory* (New York: The Century Co., 1923), p. 127.
19. Quoted from Tillyard, *op. cit.*, p. 20
20. *Discourse*, III, 41. Quoted from W. A. Dunning, *A History of Political Theories, Ancient and Medieval* (New York: Macmillan Co., 1919), p. 300.
21. *King Richard II*, Act. II, Scene 1.
22. *Institutes*, Book IV, Chap. xx, par. 25. Quoted from Dunning, *Political Theories from Luther to Montesquieu* (New York: The Macmillan Co., 1919), p. 29.
23. Quoted from Preserved Smith, *op. cit.*, pp. 594 ff.
24. Quoted from J. W. Allen, *A History of Political Thought in the Sixteenth Century* (London: Methuen & Co., 1928), p. 56.
25. Quoted from Hearnshaw, *op. cit.*, p. 188.
26. *Ibid.*, p. 211.
27. *Ibid.*, p. 215.
28. *The Prince*, ch. XVIII.
29. *Discourses*, III, xli.
30. Smith, *op. cit.*, p. 516.
31. Talcott Parsons, "Max Weber's Sociological Analysis of Capitalism and Modern Institutions," in H. E. Barnes, Ed., *An Introduction to*

the *History of Sociology* (Chicago: University of Chicago Press, 1948), p. 297.
32. André Gide, *The Living Thoughts of Montaigne* (New York: Longmans, Green & Co., 1939), p. 12.
33. Quoted from F. J. C. Hearnshaw, *The Social and Political Ideas of Some Great Thinkers of the Renaissance and the Reformation* (New York: Barnes & Noble, 1949), p. 128.
34. *Table Talk,* quoted from Bernard J. Stern, *The Family Past and Present* (New York: D. Appleton-Century Co., 1938), p. 131.
35. *Op. cit.,* p. 408.
36. Canon X of the Doctrine on the Sacrament of Matrimony.
37. *Op. cit.,* p. 507.
38. Stern, *op. cit.,* p. 129.
39. *Op. cit.,* p. 511.

CHAPTER 14

1. Preserved Smith, *History of Modern Culture* (New York: Henry Holt, 1930), I, 145-146.
2. *Principia,* Book III.
3. *Ethics,* I, Prop. xxix.
4. *Ethics,* I, Prop. xxxii, Corollary I.
5. *Essay Concerning Human Understanding,* Bk. II, Ch. i, Par. 2.
6. *Essay,* II, i, 24.
7. *Journal,* March 6, 1677.
8. R. I. Aaron, *John Locke* (New York: Oxford Univ. Press, 1937), pp. 257-258.
9. F. J. C. Hearnshaw, *The Social and Political Ideas of Some English Thinkers of the Augustan Age* (New York: Barnes & Noble, 1923), p. 83.
10. *Leviathan,* Part I, ch. 13.
11. Quoted from Willmoore Kendall, *John Locke and the Doctrine of Majority Rule* (Urbana: University of Illinois Press, 1941), XXVI, 121.
12. Harold J. Laski, *Political Thought in England* (New York: Henry Holt, 1919), pp. 59-60.
13. *Second Treatise of Government,* Par. 149.
14. *Ibid.,* Pars. 129-130.
15. *Ibid.,* Par. 121.
16. *Op. cit.,* p. 106.
17. J. W. Gough, *John Locke's Political Philosophy* (London: Oxford University Press, 1950), p. 115.
18. *Second Treatise,* Par. 95.
19. *Op. cit.,* p. 134.
20. *Ibid.,* p. 133.
21. *Op. cit.,* p. 43.
22. The first *Letter Concerning Toleration,* p. 13.
23. *Op. cit.,* p. 298.
24. *Essays in the Law* (London: Macmillan & Co., 1922), p. 91.
25. Walton H. Hamilton, "Property According to Locke," *Yale Law Journal,* XLI (1932-33), pp. 864-80.
26. *Second Treatise,* Par. 26.
27. *Op. cit.,* pp. 279-280.
28. *Op. cit.,* p. 92.
29. *Second Treatise,* 61.
30. *Some Thoughts Concerning Education,* Par. 147.
31. *Ibid.,* Par. 201.
32. *Ibid.,* Par. 70.
33. Thomas Fowler, *Locke* (New York: Harper & Bros., English Men of Letters Series), pp. 199-200.

CHAPTER 15

1. *The Autobiography of Giambattista Vico,* trans. Max H. Fisch and Thomas G. Bergin (Ithaca: Cornell Univ. Press, 1944), pp. 118-119.
2. Quoted from H. P. Adams, *The Life and Writings of G. Vico* (London: George Allen and Unwin, 1935), pp. 223-226.
3. *Ibid.*
4. *Ibid.,* p. 145.
5. Quoted from Benedetto Croce, *The Philosophy of G. Vico* (London: Howard Latimer, 1913), p. 263.
6. English translation by Max H. Fisch and Thomas G. Bergin (Ithaca: Cornell Univ. Press, 1948). All quotations in this book from the *Autobiography* and *The New Science* are from the Fisch and Bergin translations unless otherwise noted.
7. Quoted from Robert Flint, *Vico* (Philadelphia: J. B. Lippincott & Co., 1884), p. 35.
8. Quoted from Fisch and Bergin, *Autobiography,* p. 6.

9. *Autobiography*, p. 113.
10. *Ibid.*, p. 200.
11. C. E. Vaughan, *Studies in the History of Political Philosophy Before and After Rousseau* (Manchester: Univ. of Manchester Press, 1925), p. 207.
12. *The New Science,* Par. 137.
13. *Ibid.,* Par. 331.
14. *Ibid.,* Par. 629.
15. Introduction to *Autobiography*, p. 51.
16. *New Science,* Par. 1006.
17. Flint, *op. cit.,* pp. 224-225.
18. *Ibid.,* pp. 227-228.
19. *New Science,* Par. 1043.
20. *Ibid.,* Par. 369.
21. *Ibid.,* Par. 341.
22. *Ibid.,* Par. 1108.
23. *Op. cit.,* p. 247.
24. *New Science,* Par. 141-142.
25. *Ibid.,* Par. 261.
26. *Ibid.,* Par. 602.
27. *Ibid.,* Par. 1008.
28. *Ibid.,* Par. 1105.
29. *Ibid.,* Par. 992.
30. *Ibid.,* Par. 320-323.

CHAPTER 16

1. *Positivism in the United States* (Cambridge: Harvard University Press, 1938), pp. 54-55. Reprinted by permission of the publishers. Copyright 1938 by The President and Fellows of Harvard College.
2. John Stuart Mill, *The Positive Philosophy of Auguste Comte* (New York: Henry Holt & Co., 1887), pp. 115-118.
3. *Polity,* IV, General Appendix, i-ii.
4. L. Lévy-Bruhl, *The Philosophy of Auguste Comte,* trans. Kathleen de Beaumont Klein (New York: G. P. Putnam's Sons, 1903), p. viii.
5. Richmond L. Hawkins, *Auguste Comte and the United States* (Cambridge: Harvard University Press, 1936), p. 93. Reprinted by permission of the publishers. Copyright 1936 by The President and Fellows of Harvard College.
6. Harry Elmer Barnes and Howard Becker, *Social Thought from Lore to Science* (2 vols., New York: D. C. Heath & Co., 1938), I, 568-569.
7. John H. Bridges, *Illustrations of Positivism* (Chicago: The Open Court Publishing Co., 1915), p. 281.
8. *Ibid.,* pp. 222-223.
9. *Philosophy,* II, 104.
10. *Ibid.,* I, 24.
11. *Polity,* I, 32-33.
12. *Philosophy,* I, 24.
13. Quoted from F. S. Marvin, *Comte* (New York: John Wiley & Sons, 1937), p. 196.
14. *Polity,* I, 554-555.
15. *Polity,* I, 177.
16. *Philosophy,* II, 108.
17. *Positive Catechism,* quoted from Bridges, *op. cit.,* p. 122.
18. *Op. cit.,* p. 245.
19. *Philosophy,* II, 125.
20. *Ibid.,* II, 130.
21. *Ibid.,* II, 14.
22. Quoted from Mill, *op. cit.,* p. 69.
23. *Ibid.,* p. 70.
24. *Philosophy,* II, 65.
25. *Ibid.,* II, 218-220.
26. *Op. cit.,* p. 257.
27. *Auguste Comte and Positivism,* 1866 Ed., p. 122.
28. *Philosophy,* II, 122-123.
29. *Philosophy,* II, 69-70.
30. *Polity,* I, 84.
31. *Ibid.,* III, 8-9.
32. *Ibid.,* II, 147.
33. *Ibid.,* I, 84.
34. *Philosophy,* II, 72-73.
35. Quoted from Wilfred H. Schoff, "A Neglected Chapter in the Life of Comte," *The American Academy of Political and Social Science* 186 (Nov. 17, 1896), p. 67.
36. *Op. cit.,* pp. 269-270.
37. Quoted from Bridges, *op. cit.,* p. 90.
38. *Philosophy,* I, 1-2.
39. *Positive Philosophy of Auguste Comte,* p. 12.
40. *Philosophy,* II, 143-144.
41. Quoted from Lévy-Bruhl, *op. cit.,* p. 46.
42. *Polity,* I, 188.
43. *Ibid.,* I, 192.
44. *Ibid.,* I, 75-76.
45. *Ibid.,* I, 188-189.
46. *Ibid.,* I, 257.
47. *Ibid.,* I, 209.
48. *Positivism in the United States,* p. 139.
49. *Fortnightly Review,* Feb. 1, 1869 and June 1, 1869.

SUGGESTED READINGS

CHAPTER 1. INTRODUCTION

Among the general surveys of the subjects covered by this book the following works might be used for supplementary reading.

HARRY ELMER BARNES and HOWARD BECKER, *Social Thought from Lore to Science* (2 vols.; Boston: Heath, 1938). This work, a new, expanded edition of which is available in both one-volume and two-volume format as Becker and Barnes, same title (Washington: Harren Press, 1952), emphasizes sociological concepts and offers a comprehensive "history and interpretation of man's ideas about life with his fellows" from ancient to modern times.
WILL DURANT, *The Story of Civilization* (6 vols.; New York: Simon and Schuster, 1935–). Five volumes of this survey of human culture have been published: Vol. I, *Our Oriental Heritage;* Vol. II, *The Life of Greece;* Vol. III, *Caesar and Christ;* Vol. IV, *The Age of Faith;* and Vol. V, *The Renaissance.* When completed, this series will offer a history of the life and thought of mankind.
PRESERVED SMITH, *A History of Modern Culture* (2 vols.; New York: Holt, 1930–1934), is a survey of exciting events and ideas between the Copernican revolution (1543) and the American Revolution (1776).
Encyclopedia of the Social Sciences (15 vols.; New York: Macmillan, 1930) is a general reference work in the social sciences.
Special Topics. The following works are authoritative in their respective fields: William A. Dunning, *A History of Political Theories* (3 vols.; New York: Macmillan, 1919–1936); C. H. McIlwain, *The Growth of Political Thought* (London: Macmillan, 1932); P. A. Sorokin, *Social and Cultural Dynamics* (4 vols.; New York: American Book, 1937–1941); and Ernst Troeltsch, *The Social Teaching of the Christian Churches* (2 vols.; London: Allen and Unwin, 1931).
F. J. C. Hearnshaw (ed.), *Social and Political Ideas* (New York: Barnes and Noble). The following volumes in this series will be of especial interest: *Mediaeval Contributions to Modern Civilization* (1949); *The Social and Political Ideas of Some Great Mediaeval Thinkers* (1950); *The Social and Political Ideas of Some Great Thinkers of the Renaissance and the Reformation* (1949); *The Social and Political Ideas of Some Great Thinkers of the Sixteenth and Seventeenth Centuries* (1949); *The Social and Political Ideas of*

Some English Thinkers of the Augustan Age (1950), Chaps. 1, 2, and 4; *The Social and Political Ideas of Some Great French Thinkers of the Age of Reason* (1950), Chaps. 1 and 5; *The Social and Political Ideas of Some Representative Thinkers of the Age of Reaction and Reconstruction* (1949), Chaps. 1 and 7.

CHAPTER 2. BABYLONIA

The Code of Hammurabi. A number of translations of this famous code have been made. James B. Pritchard (ed.), *Ancient Near Eastern Texts* (Princeton: Princeton University Press, 1950), pp. 163–180, contains the entire code. Earlier translations, with some sections missing, will be found in Robert F. Harper, *The Code of Hammurabi* (Chicago: University of Chicago Press, (1904); W. W. Davies, *The Codes of Hammurabi and Moses* (Cincinnati: Jennings and Graham, 1905); C. H. W. Johns, *The Oldest Code of Laws in the World* (Edinburgh: Clark, 1903); and in a number of other books.

James B. Pritchard (ed.), *Ancient Near Eastern Texts* (Princeton: Princeton University Press, 1950), pp. 159–163, has fragments of the *Lipit-Ishtar Law-code* and *The Laws of Eshnunna*.

Pritchard, *op. cit.,* pp. 72–98, also contains the *Epic of Gilgamesh.* The *Epic* should be read not only for its antiquity and literary qualities, but also for its revelation of many aspects of Babylonian life and thought.

C. H. W. Johns, *The Relation between the Laws of Babylonia and the Laws of the Hebrew Peoples* (London: Oxford University Press, 1917), has an interesting comparison of Babylonian and Hebrew legislation.

Edward Chiera, *They Wrote on Clay* (Chicago: University of Chicago Press, 1938), tells the story of the discovery of Babylonian civilization through archaeological explorations.

Seton Lloyd, *Twin Rivers* (London: Oxford University Press, 1947), Chaps. 2 and 3, presents a brief history of Babylonia.

L. W. King, *A History of Babylonia* (London: Chatto and Windus, 1915), has a more detailed account.

CHAPTER 3. ANCIENT EGYPT

Egyptian Stories. Among the numerous Egyptian tales the following are recommended: "The Tale of the Two Brothers," "The Story of the Educated Peasant," "The Story of Sinuhe," and "The Shipwrecked Sailor." They can be found in E. A. Wallis Budge, *Literature of the Ancient Egyptians* (London: Dent, 1914), pp. 67–94, 169–213; in *The World's Great Classics* (New York: Colonial Press, 1901), XLII, 173–187; and in James B. Pritchard (ed.), *Ancient Near Eastern Texts* (Princeton: Princeton University Press, 1950), pp. 18–23.

"Wisdom" Literature. The "wisdom" literature of ancient Egypt consists of numerous short proverbs, precepts, fables, instructions, and various other types

of didactic writing. See, for example, Budge, *op. cit.,* pp. 224–240; Adolph Erman, *Literature of the Ancient Egyptians* (London: Methuen, 1927), pp. 54–85, 234–242; and Pritchard, *op. cit.,* pp. 412–432.
Egyptian Religion. Egyptian religious beliefs are found in Budge, *op. cit.,* pp. 3–131; Erman, *op. cit.,* pp. 283–287; Pritchard, *op. cit.,* pp. 383–392; and, especially the hymns to the sun-god, in James H. Breasted, *Dawn of Conscience* (New York: Scribner, 1934), pp. 281–289. The "Legend of the Destruction of Mankind," in Budge, *op. cit.,* pp. 14ff., is a good version of the Egyptian account of the Deluge. The most popular study of Egyptian religious thought is James H. Breasted, *Dawn of Conscience* (New York: Scribner, 1934). See also Breasted, *Development of Religion and Thought in Ancient Egypt* (New York: Scribner, 1912) and A. H. Sayce, *Religions of Ancient Egypt and Babylonia* (Edinburgh: Clark, 1902).
Secular Writing. Egyptian secular writing should not be neglected. Good accounts are found in Erman, *op. cit.,* pp. 243–253; and Pritchard, *op. cit.,* pp. 467–470.
Social Life. Social life in ancient Egypt is described in W. M. Flinders Petrie, *Social Life in Ancient Egypt* (Boston: Houghton Mifflin, 1923) and in Adolph Erman, *Life in Ancient Egypt* (London: Macmillan, 1894).
Of a large number of books on Egyptian life and thought which have been published recently, the following are recommended: Margaret A. Murray, *The Splendour That Was Egypt* (New York: Philosophical Library, 1949); George Steindorff and Keith C. Seele, *When Egypt Ruled the East* (Chicago: University of Chicago Press, 1947); Leonard Cottrell, *The Lost Pharaohs* (New York: Philosophical Library, 1951); Margaret A. Murray, *Egyptian Religious Poetry* (London: John Murray, 1949).

CHAPTER 4. CONFUCIUS AND THE CHINESE CLASSICS

The Chinese Classics. Translations made by James Legge and published as *The Chinese Classics* (8 vols., London: Trübner, 1861–1872) are still the standard renditions in English of the Chinese classics. They were reprinted under the same title (8 vols.; Oxford, 1893–1895) and are included in part in F. Max Müller (ed.), *Sacred Books of the East* (50 vols.; Oxford: Clarendon, 1879–1882), Vols. III, XVI, XXVII, and XXVIII. An inexpensive edition of selections from the Confucian classics will be found in Lin Yutang, *The Wisdom of Confucius* (Modern Library, 1938). Everyman's Library also has an edition of Chinese philosophy, translated and edited by E. R. Hughes (London, 1937), which contains selections from the classics. Readings in the Chinese classics should be guided by specific interests, but the *Book of Poetry* has a wide appeal. *The Doctrine of the Mean* (Legge, I, 246–298) might be studied for comparison with Aristotle's treatment of the same subject. *The Great Learning* (Legge, I, 219–245) is a short political work which declares the practice of virtue to be the only way to create a good society.

448 · Suggested Readings

Analects of Confucius. Portions of the *Analects* are available in a number of English translations. Among them are the following: *The Analects of Confucius,* trans. William E. Soothill (London: Oxford University Press, 1937); *The Sayings of Confucius,* introduction and notes by Lionel Giles (London: John Murray, 1945); *Analects of Confucius,* trans. Arthur Waley (London: Allen and Unwin, 1949); *The Sayings of Confucius,* trans. Leonard A. Lyall (New York: Longmans, Green, 1925); and Tehyi Hsieh (ed.), *Confucius Said It First* (Boston: Chinese Service Bureau, 1936).

Philosophy of Confucius. A number of books dealing with specific topics in Confucian philosophy have been published. Among these are: Miles M. Dawson, *The Ethics of Confucius* (New York: Putnam, 1915); Leonard S. Hsü, *The Political Philosophy of Confucianism* (New York: Dutton, 1932); Elbert D. Thomas, *Chinese Political Thought* (New York: Prentice-Hall, 1927).

H. G. CREEL, *Confucius* (New York: John Day, 1949), gives a stimulating introduction to the life and thought of the Chinese sage.

"Confucianism," *Encyclopedia of the Social Sciences* (New York: Macmillan, 1930), provides an introduction to this philosophy.

Additional Reading. For further study, the works of Max Weber, M. Granet, and F. S. C. Northrop are suggested. Portions of Max Weber's important sociological studies of the Orient have recently appeared in *The Religion of China,* trans. Hans H. Gerth (Glencoe, Ill.: Free Press, 1951). See especially Chap. 6, "The Confucian Life Orientation." *From Max Weber: Essays in Sociology,* trans. H. H. Gerth and C. Wright Mills (New York: Oxford University Press, 1946), contains the important essay, "The Chinese Literati," which is found also in *The Religion of China.* Marcel Granet wrote a number of penetrating books on China, of which *La Pensée chinoise* (Paris, 1934) is the most important. Available in English is his *Chinese Civilization,* trans. Kathleen E. Innes and Mabel R. Brailsford (London: Routledge and Keegan Paul, 1950). F. S. C. Northrop, *The Meeting of East and West* (New York: Macmillan, 1946), analyzes the basic contrasts between Eastern and Western ways of thinking and suggests means of achieving better understanding.

CHAPTER 5. ANCIENT INDIA

The Ramayana, the Mahabharata, and the Bhagavad-Gita. Selections from the *Ramayana* and the *Mahabharata* will be found in a number of collections. The *Bhagavad-Gita* is in Vol. VIII of F. Max Müller (ed.), *Sacred Books of the East* (50 vols.; Oxford: Clarendon, 1879–1882). It was also published as *The Song Celestial,* trans. Sir Edwin Arnold (London: Trübner, n.d.). Everyman's Library contains Romesh C. Dutt's condensed version of these poems. See also *The Bhagavad-Gita,* trans. Arthur W. Ryder (Chicago: Chicago University Press, 1929).

The Vedas. Some of the Vedic hymns appear in Vol. XXXIII of *Sacred Books of* the East, op. cit., and in *Hindu Scriptures,* ed. by Nicol Macnicol (Everyman's Library, 1948). The Rig-Veda is generally considered to be the most interesting of the Vedas.

The Upanishads. For selections from the *Upanishads,* see *Hindu Scriptures, op. cit.,* pp. 43–221; *Sacred Books of the East, op. cit.,* Vols. I and XV; and especially a little book, *The Ten Principal Upanishads,* trans. Shree P. Swami and W. B. Yeats (New York: Macmillan, 1937).

Hindu Law Codes. Of especial importance to students of social thought are the ancient law codes of the Hindus. Selections from these codes will be found in Vols. II, XIV, and XXV of the *Sacred Books of the East.* For a commentary on the laws of Manu, see Kewal Motwani, *Manu, A Study of Hindu Social Theory* (Madras: Ganesh and Company, 1934).

S. RADHAKRISHNAN, *Indian Philosophy* (London: Allen & Unwin, 1948), I, 21–267, gives an introduction to Upanishadic philosophy.

J. M. MACFIE, *Myths and Legends of India* (Edinburgh: Clark, 1924), has a prose presentation of "parables and legends which should enable the reader to appreciate what constitutes the most vital, and in some respects, the most salutary influences of Hinduism."

"Brahmanism and Hinduism," *Encyclopedia of the Social Sciences* (New York: Macmillan, 1930), provides a general survey of ancient Hindu thought.

Additional Reading. For further study, Max Weber's analysis of Hinduism, perhaps available in translation in mimeographed form from Prof. Don Martindale, University of Minnesota, Department of Sociology, should be read. See also "The Brahman and the Castes," in *From Max Weber: Essays in Sociology,* trans. Hans H. Gerth and C. Wright Mills (Glencoe, Ill.: Free Press, 1951), Chap. 16.

CHAPTER 6. THE HEBREWS OF THE OLD TESTAMENT

The Old Testament is so well known that no specific references are necessary. For supplementary reading the following books are suggested:

MADELEINE S. MILLER and J. LANE MILLER, *Encyclopedia of Bible Life* (New York: Harper, 1944), Chap. 1, Agriculture; Chap. 11, Homes; Chap. 17, Professions and Trades; and Chap. 19, Social Structure.

ABRAM L. SACHAR, *A History of the Jews* (New York: Knopf, 1948), pp. 3–123.

MAX RADIN, *The Life of the People in Biblical Times* (Philadelphia: The Jewish Publication Society of America, 1943).

CHARLES C. BUTTERWORTH, *The Literary Lineage of the King James Bible* (Philadelphia: University of Pennsylvania Press, 1933).

R. H. KENNETT, *Ancient Hebrew Social Life and Custom* (London: Oxford, 1933).

LOUIS WALLIS, *Sociological Study of the Bible* (Chicago: University of Chicago Press, 1912).

"Judaism," *Encyclopedia of the Social Sciences* (New York: Macmillan, 1930).
MAX WEBER, *Ancient Judaism,* trans. Hans H. Gerth and Don Martindale (Glencoe, Ill.: Free Press, 1952).

CHAPTER 7. PLATO

The Dialogues of Plato, translated by B. Jowett, has for more than half a century been the popular rendition of Plato for English readers. It has appeared, in whole or in part, in numerous printings made by several publishers. The edition of Jowett's translation published in a two-volume format as *The Dialogues of Plato* (New York: Random House, 1937) contains the complete text as well as marginal notes. Inexpensive publications of selections from Plato are *The Philosophy of Plato* (Modern Library), *The Republic* (Modern Library), *Ion, and Four Other Dialogues* (Everyman's Library), *The Republic* (Everyman's Library), and *Socratic Discourses of Plato and Xenophon* (Everyman's Library). The following reading is suggested: *Lysis; Meno; Phaedo;* Books I, IV, and V, of the *Republic;* Book III of the *Laws;* and the *Statesman.*

Plato's Thought. For a general discussion of Plato's thought see A. E. Taylor, *Plato: The Man and His Work* (New York: Dial Press, 1927); and Raphael Demos, *The Philosophy of Plato* (New York: Scribner, 1939), especially Chaps. 16–19.

Greek Educational Ideals. Sir Richard Livingstone has written a number of books dealing with the educational ideals of the Greeks. His *Plato and Modern Education* (New York: Macmillan, 1944) gives a short summary of Plato's contributions to modern education. See also R. L. Nettleship, *The Theory of Education in Plato's Republic* (Oxford: Clarendon, 1935).

THOMAS WOODY, *Life and Education in Early Societies* (New York: Macmillan, 1949), Chaps. 10, 14, 15.

GEORGE W. BOTSFORD and CHARLES A. ROBINSON, *Hellenic History* (New York: Macmillan, 1948), especially "Athens and the Triumph of Democracy"; and R. L. Nettleship, *Lectures on the Republic of Plato* (London: Macmillan, 1937).

"Greek Culture and Thought," *Encyclopedia of the Social Sciences* (New York: Macmillan, 1930), is a good introduction to Greek social thought. See also "Plato and Platonism" in this encyclopedia.

CHAPTER 8. ARISTOTLE

J. A. SMITH and W. D. ROSS (eds.), *The Works of Aristotle* (11 vols.; Oxford: Clarendon, 1908–1931), is a standard edition of Aristotle's complete works. Collections of his most important works are: *The Basic Works of Aristotle,* ed., Richard McKeon (New York: Random House, 1941) and *Aristotle,* trans. and ed., Philip Wheelwright (New York: Odyssey, 1951). All of the *Ethics* and the *Politics* should be read, but if selections from either, or from both, must be made, the summaries contained in *The Nicomachean Ethics of Aristotle,* trans. J. E. C. Welldon (London: Macmillan, 1892), and in *The Politics of Aristotle,* trans. J. E. C. Welldon (London: Macmillan, 1888), will help the reader to locate specific ideas in these books. Inexpensive editions of Aristotle are: *Politics* (Everyman's Library), *Nicomachean Ethics* (Everyman's Library), *Introduction to Aristotle* (Modern Library), and *Politics* (Modern Library).

WERNER JAEGER, *Aristotle* (Oxford: Clarendon Press, 1934), Chap. 15, Aristotle's Place in History.

WILL DURANT, *Story of Philosophy* (New York: Simon and Schuster, 1926), Chap. 2, Aristotle and Greek Science.

Aristotle's Theories of Education. A collection of Aristotle's theories of education, based on extracts from the *Ethics* and *Politics,* will be found in *Aristotle on Education,* trans. and ed., John Burnet (Cambridge: Cambridge University Press, 1905).

Greek Social Life. See J. P. Mahaffy, *Social Life in Greece* (London: Macmillan, 1913), and T. G. Tucker, *Life in Ancient Athens* (New York: Macmillan, 1929).

"Aristotle," *Encyclopedia of the Social Sciences* (New York: Macmillan, 1930).

CHAPTER 9. ROME

Lucretius. Lucretius is such pleasant reading that all of the *De Rerum Natura* should be read. Everyman's Library has an inexpensive edition: *Of the Nature of Things,* trans. William E. Leonard, 1950. If time is limited, read Book V for Lucretius' views on social origins and social change.

"The Twelve Tables," *Remains of Old Latin,* trans. E. H. Warmington (Loeb Classical Library), III, 425–515.

Polybius. From *The Histories* of Polybius (Loeb Classical Library), read Book I, 1–6, and Book VI, 2–18.

Cicero. Books II and III of Cicero's *De Legibus* (Loeb Classical Library) are important. See also Cicero's *De Officiis,* Book I; *De Finibus,* Book V; *De Re Publica,* Book III (Loeb Classical Library).

Seneca. "On the Philosopher's Mean," "On Practising What You Preach," "On Master and Slave," "On Choosing Our Teachers," "On the Supreme Good," "On Liberal and Vocational Studies," and "On the Happy Life," in Seneca's *Epistulae Morales* (Loeb Classical Library) should be read.

Roman Manners and Customs. For a picture of manners and customs in Rome, see Maurice Pellison, *Roman Life in Pliny's Time* (Philadelphia: Jacobs, 1897); J. Carcopino, *Daily Life in Ancient Rome* (New Haven: Yale University Press, 1940); V. Chapot, *The Roman World* (New York: Knopf, 1928); and S. Dill, *Roman Society from Nero to Marcus Aurelius* (London: Macmillan, 1937).

"The Roman World," *Encyclopedia of the Social Sciences* (New York: 1930).

CHAPTER 10. AUGUSTINE

Writings of St. Augustine. The *Confessions* should be read as a whole. It is available in a translation by W. Watts (2 vols.; London: Heinemann, 1912) and in both Modern Library and Everyman's Library. Books III and IV describe Augustine's troubled youth, and Books VIII and IX, his conversion. In the *City of God,* trans. Marcus Dods (Modern Library, 1950) or trans. J. Healey (2 vols.; Edinburgh: Grant, 1908), read Books II, XI, XIII, and XIX.

MEYRICK H. CARRÉ, *Realists and Nominalists* (Oxford: Clarendon, 1946), Chap. 1, has an analysis of Augustine's method.

JOHN N. FIGGIS, *The Political Aspects of S. Augustine's "City of God"* (London: Longmans, 1921), Chap. 3, has an analysis of Augustine's political theories.

GIOVANNI PAPINI'S *Saint Augustine,* trans. Mary P. Agnetti (New York: Harcourt, Brace, 1930), gives a sympathetic account of Augustine's life and thought.

MARY E. KEENAN, *The Life and Times of St. Augustine as Revealed in His Letters* (Washington: Catholic University, 1935), discusses some of the conditions which faced Augustine.

"Augustine," *Encyclopedia of the Social Sciences* (New York: Macmillan, 1930).

CHAPTER 11. THOMAS AQUINAS

Introduction. M. C. D'Arcy, *Selected Writings of St. Thomas Aquinas* (Everyman's Library); Anton C. Pegis, *Introduction to Saint Thomas Aquinas* (Modern Library, 1948).

Treatise on Government. De Regimine Principum, *The Governance of Rulers,* trans. Gerald B. Phelan (London: Sheed and Ward, for the Institute of Mediaeval Studies, 1938). See especially Chaps. 1, 2, 10, and 15.

Thomism. For a discussion of various aspects of Thomism, see: Mortimer J. Adler, *St. Thomas and the Gentiles* (Milwaukee: Marquette Press, 1938); Winston Ashley, *Theory of Natural Slavery in Aristotle and St. Thomas* (Notre Dame: University Press, 1941); Frederick E. Flynn, *Wealth and Money in Thomas Aquinas* (Notre Dame: University Press, 1942); Anthony L. Ostheimer, *The Family, a Thomistic Study* (Washington: Catholic University Press, 1939); G. F. Benkert, *Thomistic Conception of International Security* (Washington: Catholic University Press, 1942).

Life and Thought of Thomas Aquinas. The life and thought of Thomas Aquinas are presented in M. C. D'Arcy, *Thomas Aquinas* (London: Benn, 1934); Étienne Gilson, *The Philosophy of Thomas Aquinas* (London: Herder, 1937); and Jacques Maritain, *The Angelic Doctor* (New York: Dial Press, 1931).

Catholic Social Theory. A number of books on Catholic social theory have been written. Among them are: Melvin J. Williams, *Catholic Social Thought* (New York: Ronald, 1950), and Wilhelm Schwer, *Catholic Social Theory* (St. Louis: Herder, 1940).

"Aquinas" and "The Universal Church," *Encyclopedia of the Social Sciences* (New York: Macmillan, 1930), are good introductory essays.

CHAPTER 12. IBN KHALDUN

Prolegomena of Ibn Khaldun. The French translation of the *Prolegomena* is available in only a few libraries in the United States; no complete English translation of this work has been made. However, *An Arab Philosophy of History,* trans. Charles Issawi (London: Murray, 1950), contains an excellent selection and arrangement of Ibn Khaldun's most important ideas. Issawi's book can be obtained in the United States from Transatlantic Arts, Hollywood, Fla. A German translation of selected portions of the *Prolegomena* has been published as *Ibn Khaldun: Ausgewählte Abschnitte aus der Muqaddima,* trans. from Arabic by Annemarie Schimmel (Tubingen: Mohr, 1951).

MOHAMMAD ABDULLAH ENAN, *Ibn Khaldun* (Lahore: Sh. Muhammad Ashraf, 1941), presents an account of the life and thought of Ibn Khaldun, with generous quotations from his works.

NATHANIEL SCHMIDT, *Ibn Khaldun* (New York: Columbia University Press, 1930).

MOHAMMAD ALY NASHAT, "Ibn Khaldun, Pioneer Economist," *L'Egypte Contemporaine,* XXXV (May, 1944), 377–490.

History of the Arabs. Recent histories of the Arabs are Philip K. Hitti, *History of the Arabs* (New York: Macmillan, 1951), and Bernard Lewis, *The Arabs in History* (London: Hutchinson's University Library, 1950).

Nomadic Conquests. The subject of conquests by nomads is treated in two articles by Howard Becker, "Pastoral Nomadism and Social Change," *Sociology and Social Research,* XV (May–June, 1931), 417–427; and "Conquest by Pastoral Nomads," *Sociology and Social Research,* XV (July–August, 1931), 511–526.

CHAPTER 13. RENAISSANCE AND REFORMATION

"Renaissance and Reformation" and "Humanism," *Encyclopedia of the Social Sciences* (New York: Macmillan, 1930).

Erasmus. Erasmus' *In Praise of Folly* (London: Allen and Unwin, 1937; and Princeton: Princeton University Press, 1941) and *The Education of a Christian Prince* (New York: Columbia University Press, 1936).

Montaigne. Selections from Montaigne in *The Living Thought of Montaigne* (New York: Longmans, Green, 1939).

Machiavelli. Machiavelli, *The Prince and the Discourses* (Modern Library).
Luther. Luther's thought can be studied in Preserved Smith, *The Life and Letters of Martin Luther* (Boston: Houghton Mifflin, 1911), and in A. C. McGiffert, *Martin Luther, the Man and His Work* (New York: Century, 1911).
Calvin. A good biography of Calvin is Williston Walker, *John Calvin* (New York: Putnam, 1906). Ernst Troeltsch has written an interesting article, "Calvin and Calvinism," *Hibbert Journal,* VIII, 102-121.
PRESERVED SMITH, *The Age of the Reformation* (New York: Holt, 1920) is the standard history of the period.
F. J. C. HEARNSHAW (ed.), *The Social and Political Ideas of Some Great Thinkers of the Renaissance and the Reformation* (New York: Barnes and Noble, 1949). Read "Sir Thomas More," "Desiderius Erasmus," "Martin Luther," and "John Calvin."

CHAPTER 14. JOHN LOCKE

Locke's Writings. Of Civil Government (Everyman's Library), Chaps. 2, 3, 5, 6, 7, and 19 of the Second Treatise. In these chapters Locke gives his views on nature, war, slavery, property, paternal power, civil society, and the dissolution of government. *An Essay Concerning Human Understanding* (Everyman's Library), Book II, Chap. 1; Book IV, Chaps. 5 and 18, contains Locke's views on the origin of ideas, the nature of truth, and the provinces of faith and reason. *A Letter Concerning Toleration* (New York: Appleton-Century, 1937), and *Some Thoughts Concerning Education* (Cambridge: Cambridge University Press, 1902).
THOMAS FOWLER, *Locke* (New York: Harper, 1880, English Men of Letters Series), has a short presentation of the life and thought of Locke. A more detailed biography is R. I. Aaron, *John Locke* (London: Oxford, 1937).
J. W. GOUGH, *John Locke's Political Philosophy* (Oxford: Clarendon Press, (1950), presents the political thought of Locke.
"Locke," *Encyclopedia of the Social Sciences* (New York: Macmillan, 1930).

CHAPTER 15. GIAMBATTISTA VICO

Vico's Writings. Autobiography, trans. M. H. Fisch and T. G. Bergin (Ithaca: Cornell University Press, 1944), is short (only about 100 pages) and should be read for the self-portrait of the man. In their introduction to the *Autobiography* (pp. 1-107), Fisch and Bergin give a sketch of Vico's life and influence and describe briefly his two major works. In *New Science,* trans. M. H. Fisch and T. G. Bergin (Ithaca: Cornell University Press, 1948), read pars. 119-360, for a statement of principles; pars. 502-519, for the origin of marriage and of moral virtue; pars. 582-618, for the origin of commonwealths; pars. 780-904, for a theory concerning the Greek Homer; pars. 915-

1045, for a theory of social change; and pars. 1097–1112, for some concluding remarks.

ROBERT FLINT, *Vico* (Edinburgh: Blackwood, 1884), was, until recently, the main source of information in English about Vico. In this book Chap. 4 presents a general estimate of Vico, and Chap. 9, an analysis of Vico's new science.

BENEDETTO CROCE, *Philosophy of Vico,* trans. R. G. Collingwood (London: Howard Latimer, 1913), is generally regarded as the best analysis of Vico's philosophy yet published in English. Chapters 11 and 18 analyze Vico's theory of historical reflux, and Chaps. 19 and 20 present an evaluation of Vico.

C. E. VAUGHAN, *Studies in the History of Political Philosophy* (Manchester: Manchester University Press, 1925), I, 207–253.

HENRY P. ADAMS, *The Life and Writings of Giambattista Vico* (London: Allen and Unwin, 1935), contains a biography and an analysis of some of Vico's main ideas.

CHAPTER 16. AUGUSTE COMTE

Comte's Writings. Positive Philosophy, trans. Harriet Martineau (2 vols.; London: Kegan Paul, 1893), I, Chaps. 1 and 2; II, Chaps. 1, 3–6, and 13. This suggested reading contains a statement of aim, the law of the three stages, the hierarchy of the sciences, the need for a science of social physics, the characteristics of the positive method in its application to social phenomena, the relation of sociology to the other sciences, the theory of social statics, the theory of social dynamics, and a final estimate of the positive method. *Positive Polity,* trans. John H. Bridges (London: Longmans, Green, 1875), I, Chaps. 1, 2, 4, and 6. These chapters contain Comte's discussion of the practical character of positivism, the social aspects of positivism, the influence of positivism on women, and the religion of humanity.

L. LÉVY-BRUHL, *The Philosophy of Auguste Comte,* trans. Kathleen de Beaumont-Klein (New York: Putnam, 1903), I, Chap. 2; III, Chap. 2; IV, Chap. 3.

JOHN STUART MILL, *Auguste Comte and Positivism* (Philadelphia: Lippincott, 1866), especially Part II, is devoted to an unsympathetic but keen analysis of Comte's religion of humanity.

"Comte" and "Positivism," *Encyclopedia of the Social Sciences* (New York: Macmillan, 1930). A chapter on Comte will be found in most books dealing with the history of social thought.

Additional Reading. For further study of Comte, the following books might be consulted: F. S. Marvin, *Comte* (London: Chapman and Hall, 1937); Edward Caird, *Social Philosophy and Religion of Comte* (New York: Macmillan, 1885); Richmond L. Hawkins, *Auguste Comte and the United States* (Cambridge, Mass.: Harvard University Press, 1936), and Richmond L. Hawkins, *Positivism in the United States* (Cambridge, Mass.: Harvard University Press, 1938).

CHAPTER 17. SOCIAL PHILOSOPHY AND SOCIAL SCIENCE

P. A. SOROKIN, *Social and Cultural Dynamics* (New York: American Book, 1937), II, 3–123.

ÉTIENNE H. GILSON, *Reason and Revelation in the Middle Ages* (New York: Scribner, 1938).

A. N. WHITEHEAD, *Science and the Modern World* (New York: Macmillan, 1928), pp. 1–28.

INDEX

Aaron, R. I., 350, 358-359, 360-361
Abelard, 260, 261, 262
Adam (*see* original sin)
adultery, in Babylonia, 33
Aeschylus, 157
afterlife (*see* immortality)
agriculture
  in Ancient Egypt, 57-59
  in Babylonia, 31
  among Hebrews, 142-143
  Khaldun's views on, 306-307
Akkad, 14, 15
Albertus Magnus, 9, 263
Alexander, 46, 158, 181, 182, 184
Alfred the Great, 260
Al-Gazzali, 289
Allen, J. W., 271, 330-331, 338
altruism, Comte's views on, 406-407
Ambrose, 234, 235
Amenhotep III, 46, 62
Ammonites, 127, 286
Amorite migration, 14
Amos, 134, 136, 137
Analects of Confucius, 2, 81, 82
ancestors (*see* piety, filial)
Ancient Egypt, 42-74
  agriculture in, 55-57
  and Babylonia, 73-74
  documents of, 46-49
  economy of, 54-59
  ethics in, 70-73
  family in, 59-64
  government of, 49-53
  history of, 44-46
  justice in, 52-54
  law in, 49-53
  property in, 54-55
  religion in, 65-69
  slavery in, 54
  social classes in, 55-57

Ancient India, 102-124
  caste in, 113-119
  and Chinese social thought, 123-124
  ethics in, 110-113
  family in, 119-122
  historical background of, 102-103
  literature of, 104-107
  marriage in, 119-121
  religion of, 107-113
  social classes in, 113-119
Anselm, 260, 261
Antiochus, 214
Apocrypha, 129-130
Apuleius, 209
Aquinas, Thomas, 1, 2, 3, 4, 9, 10, 155, 156, 178, 205, 258, 260-282, 333
  biographical sketch of, 262-264
  on children, 280
  on economics, 272-277
  on education, 280-281
  on family, 277-281
  on government, 271-272
  on "just price," 276-277
  on marriage, 278-279
  methods of, 266-268
  on natural law, 270-271
  on politics, 268-272
  problems of, 266-268
  on property, 273, 274-275
  on society, 269
  on state, 270
  on status of women, 279-280
  on usury, 275-276
  works of, 265-266, 268
Arabs, 285, 286-287
Aramaeans, 286
aristocracy, 174, 201
  Roman views on, 219
Aristophanes, 157
Aristotelianism, 204-205

458 · Index

Aristotle, 2, 3, 6, 10, 155, 156, 157, 174, 179-205, 213, 261-267 *passim*, 273, 280
  biographical sketch of, 181-182
  and causation, 187-188
  on children, 203-204
  on citizenship, 199-200
  on democracy, 202
  and doctrine of mean, 194-197
  on ethics, 191-197
  on family, 203-204
  on government, 201-202
  on human nature, 188-189
  and induction, 186-187
  on man, 189-191
  on marriage, 203-204
  method of, 185-188
  on political change, 202-203
  on politics, 197-203
  on slavery, 199-200
  on social classes, 188
  on state, 200-201
  on status of women, 204
  and syllogism, 186
  works of, 182-185
Aryans, 11, 103, 117, 118
asceticism, Confucius and, 99
Assyrians, 41
Atharva-veda, 104
Augustine, 1, 3, 4, 9, 10, 132, 155, 156, 178, 205, 233-259, 265
  biographical sketch of, 234-241
  on family, 253-256
  on human nature, 246-248
  influence of, 258-259
  on marriage, 254-255
  method of, 241-246
  on origin of state, 249-250
  on peace, 252-253
  on politics, 249-253
  on property, 251-252
  on slavery, 250-251
  on social change, 256-268
  on status of women, 255-256
Aurelius (*see* Marcus Aurelius)
authority, during Renaissance and Reformation, 318-319
Aveling, F., 271
Averroës, 261, 262
Averroists, 268
Avicenna, 261

Babylonia, 8, 11, 13-41, 43-44, 73-74, 128

Babylonia—*Continued*
  achievements of, 40-41
  agriculture in, 31-32
  and Ancient Egypt, 43-44, 73-74
  economy of, 27-31
  epics of, 17-18
  family in, 32-36
  government in, 20-27
  and Hebrews, 128
  history of, 13-15
  industry in, 28-29
  justice in, 19-20
  language of, 128
  law in, 20-27
  legal documents in, 19-20
  myths of, 17-18
  religion in, 37-40
  slavery in, 30-31
  social classes in, 30-31
  trade in, 28-29
Bacon, Francis, 320, 321, 342
Bacon, Roger, 321
Baikie, James, 72
Barker, Ernest, 198
Barnes, Harry Elmer, 398
Becker, Howard, 104*n*., 300, 398
Benkert, G. P., 266
Bergin, Thomas G., 377
Berossus, 17
Bhagavad-Gita, 10, 102, 106, 108, 111, 118-119
Bible (*see* New Testament; Old Testament)
biographical data, and social thought, 5
biology, 4
Blanc, Jean Joseph Charles Louis, 393
Boccaccio, 315, 319
Bodin, Jean, 284, 329, 335, 336
Book of the Dead, 48, 66, 70
Boyle, Robert, 349
Brahe, Tycho, 321
Brahma, 108
Brahmanism, 107-113 *passim*, 120
Brahmans, 114-115
Breasted, James H., 44, 46, 51, 53, 64, 65-66, 70, 72
Bridges, John H., 398-399
Britain
  international policies of, 393
  political revolution in, 344-345
Bruno, Giordano, 284
Buddhism, 107, 120
Budge, E. A. W., 48
Bury, John B., 428
Butler, Nicholas Murray, 271

Cabot, John, 315
Calvin, John, 2, 284, 318, 319, 325-338
    passim
Canaanites, 127
capitalism, 333-334
Carlyle, Thomas, 1
Carré, Meyrick H., 261-262
Carter, Howard, 73
caste, in India, 6-7, 113-119, 120-121
    (*see also* social class)
Cato, 209, 215
causation, Aristotle's views of, 186-187
Chaldea, 13
Champollion, J. F., 73
Charlemagne, 260
Cheops (*see* Khufu)
children
    Aquinas' views on, 280
    Aristotle's views on, 203-204
    Augustine's views on, 256
    Chinese attitude toward, 91-92
    Hebrew attitude toward, 147-148
    Plato's views on, 168-169
China, 75-101, 123-124
    family in, 86, 88-93
    government in, 85-88
    historical sketch of, 76-79
    and Indian social thought, 123-124
    justice in, 85
    marriage in, 90-91
    social order in, 83-85   334
    (*see also* Confucius)
Chou Dynasty, 77-79
Christianity, 234, 239 (*see also* church)
church, 234, 239
    Anglican, 344
    Augustine's views on, 250
    growth of, 249
    and state, 330-331
    and Western civilization, 260-262
    (*see also* Aquinas; Augustine; Reformation; religion)
church fathers, 234, 253-254
Cicero, 155, 207, 209, 211-212, 213-226
    passim, 249, 250
citizenship, Aristotle's views on, 199-200
City of God, Augustine's, 239-240, 257, 258
city states
    in Babylonia, 14
    Greek, 198-199
classes (*see* social classes)
Cleopatra, 46, 49
climate, and civilization, 14

code
    of Hammurabi, 19-20, 22-27, 27-41
        passim, 139
    Lipit-Ishtar, 20
    of Manu, 106-107
    Mosaic, 139
    Roman (*see* Twelve Tables)
    (*see also* law)
Code of Manu, 106-107
coinage, Babylonian, 28
Colbert, Jean Baptiste, 335
Columbus, Christopher, 315, 321
Comte, Auguste, 5, 6, 9, 10, 283, 284, 295n., 392-425
    biographical sketch of, 394-396
    on divorce, 420
    on family, 419-422
    on human nature, 405-409
    influence of, 424-425
    on marriage, 419-420
    on political organization, 412-413
    positivism of, 398-400
    on religion, 422-424
    on social change, 413-419
    on social organization, 410-413
    on status of women, 421-422
    writings of, 396-398
Condorcet, Marie Jean Antoine, 405
Confessions, Augustine's, 10, 235, 238-239, 265
Confucian classics, 81-83
Confucianism, 99-101
Confucius, 2, 8, 10, 11, 12, 75-101, 123-124
    biographical sketch of, 79-81
    and Christian ethics, 98-99
    classics of, 81-93
    on education, 97-98
    on family, 88-93
    on filial piety, 93-95
    and Golden Rule, 98-99
    on government, 85-88
    and Indian social thought, 123-124
    on justice, 85
    on social order, 83-85
    on superior man, 95-101
consensus, 410
contracts, in Babylonia, 27-28 (*see also* law)
Copernicus, 343, 347
Coptic writing, 47
Cortes, Hernan, 316
Council of Trent, 129
Creation Epic, Babylonian, 38-39
Creel, H. G., 78, 80-81, 89

Croce, Benedetto, 366
Crusades, 260, 261, 272-273, 315
Cudworth, Ralph, 178
culture, unity of, Vico's views on, 379-382
cuneiform, 14, 15-17
Cunningham, W., 240, 257
cyclical theory
   Comte's views on, 415-419
   Khaldun's, 309
   Vico's, 375-379, 388
   (*see also* Golden Age)

D'Arcy, M. C., 265, 267
David, 127, 128, 132, 133, 135, 136
Davidson, Thomas, 203
death
   Augustine's views on, 258
   Egyptian attitude toward, 65
   (*see also* immortality)
deities
   of Ancient Egypt, 65
   of Babylonia, 36, 37-38
   Lucretius' view of, 210
   (*see also* God; religion)
deluge myth, 17
democracy
   Aristotle's views on, 199, 202
   Plato's views on, 167, 174-175
   Roman views on, 219
   (*see also* sovereignty)
Democritus, 2, 157
Demos, Raphael, 165, 176
demotic script, 47
Descartes, René, 242, 342, 346, 347-349, 372-375, 418
determinism (*see* freedom of will)
Diaz, Bartolomeu, 321
Dill, Samuel, 212-213, 219
Diogenes Laertius, 182, 183
divine right, in Babylonia, 20-21 (*see also* ruler)
divorce
   in Babylonia, 36
   in China, 90
   Comte's views on, 420
   (*see also* marriage; polygamy)
documents (*see* writings)
Donatists, 236
Doyle, Phyllis, 251-252
Drake, Francis, 316
Dravidians, 102-103, 117
Driver, C. H., 351, 361

Duns Scotus, Joannes, 267
Durant, Will, 181, 287

economics
   Khaldun's views on, 304-308
   during Renaissance, 332-336
   Vico's views on, 384-386
economy
   of Ancient Egypt, 54-59
   of Babylonia, 27-32
   of Hebrews, 141-145
   of Rome, 231-232
Edomites, 127, 286
education, 7
   in Ancient Egypt, 56-57
   Aquinas' views on, 280-281
   Aristotle's views on, 191
   in Babylonia, 35
   Confucius' views on, 97-98
   among Hebrews, 148
   Locke's views on, 361-365
   Plato's views on, 170-171
egoism, Comte's views on, 406-407
Egypt (*see* Ancient Egypt)
Emerson, Ralph Waldo, 109
Empedocles, 180
empiricism, 241
Enan, Mohammad A., 297n.
endogamy, among Hebrews, 148-149
England (*see* Britain)
environment, Aristotle's views on, 190-191 (*see also* natural environment)
Epic of Gilgamesh, 16, 18, 22, 36, 39
epics
   of Ancient Egypt, 48
   Babylonian, 22
   Hindu, 105-106
   (*see also* literature; myths; religion; writings)
Epicureanism, Vico and, 371
Epicurus, 210, 213, 216
Erasmus, 284, 320, 323, 324, 337-338
Erigena, Scotus, 260, 261, 267
Erman, Adolph, 48, 59
ethics
   in Ancient Egypt, 70-73
   in Ancient India, 110-113
   Confucian vs. Christian, 98-99
   and politics during Renaissance, 331-332
   Roman view of, 213-219
   (*see also* Golden Rule; morality)
Ethics, Aristotle's, 183-184

Eudemus, 205
eugenics, Aristotle's views on, 190
Euphrates River, 13
Euripedes, 157
exogamy, among Hebrews, 149-151
experience, Renaissance view of, 320-321

fables, 17
faith
   Aquinas' views on, 267
   Augustine's view of, 242-243
family
   in Ancient Egypt, 59-64
   in Ancient India, 119-122
   Aquinas' views on, 277-281
   Aristotle's views on, 203-204
   Augustine's views on, 253-256
   in Babylonia, 32-36
   Comte's views on, 419-422
   Confucius' views on, 86, 88-93
   among Hebrews, 135, 145-152
   Plato's views on, 168-170
   during Renaissance and Reformation, 336-340
   in Rome, 222-226
   Vico's views on, 382-383
   (see also marriage; women)
family institutions, 7
feudalism, 272-273, 384-385
   in China, 76
filial piety, in China, 93-95
Filmer, Robert, 353
Fisch, Max H., 377
Flint, Robert, 292, 295n., 379
folk tales, 17
Fourier, François Marie Charles, 393
freedom
   Augustine's view of, 248
   Plato's views on, 166, 167
   Vico's views on, 383-384
French Revolution, 392

Galen, 2
Galileo, 2, 284, 321, 342, 347
Galpin, C. J., 292
Gama, Vascoda, 315, 321
Gandhi, Mohandas K., 117-118
Gautama, 107
Gemeinschaft, 300, 312
Genghis Khan (see Jenghiz Khan)
Gesellschaft, 300, 312
Gibb, H. A. R., 287, 311
Gibbon, Edward, 240

Gide, André, 224, 337
Gilgamesh (see Epic of Gilgamesh)
God
   Augustine's view of, 242
   Hindu view of, 288-289
   Plato's views on, 175-176
   (see also deity; monotheism; religion)
Goethe, Johann Wolfgang, 162-163, 181
Golden Age
   Augustine's views on, 249
   Seneca's theory of, 230-231
   Vico's views on, 376
   (see also cyclical theory)
Golden Mean, 2, 3
Golden Rule
   in Ancient India, 111
   Augustine and, 250
   in China, 98-99
   Comte's views on, 406-407
   Confucius' views on, 84-85, 93
   nineteenth-century views on, 393
   (see also ethics)
Gough, J. W., 356, 357, 361
government
   in Ancient Egypt, 49-53
   Aquinas' views on, 271-272
   in Babylonia, 20-27
   of Hebrews, 135-138
   Polybius' views on, 229
   Roman views of, 219-221
   Vico's views on, 386-390
   (see also ruler; social contract; state)
grace, doctrine of, 247-248, 259
Granet, Marcel, 89, 90, 100
Greece, 155-156
   historical background of, 157-158
   (see also Aristotle; Plato)
Gregory the Great, 234
Grotius, Hugo, 354
Gumplowicz, Ludwik, 308

Hammurabi, 19-22, 128
   Age of, 17
   Code of, 19-20, 22-27, 27-41 *passim,* 139
Hannibal, 207
happiness
   Aristotle's views on, 192-193
   Roman views of, 213-214, 216-217
Harnack, Adolf, 236
Hatshepsut, 46
Hawkins, Richmond L., 395, 398, 423-424
Hegira, 287

Hebrews, 2, 3, 9, 12, 127-129
  agriculture among, 142-143
  children among, 147-149
  economy of, 141-145
  family life among, 135, 145-152
  government of, 135-138
  heritage of, 152-153
  justice among, 139-141
  kingship and, 135-136
  law among, 138-141
  marriage among, 146-147
  and monotheism, 152-153
  as nation, 136
  occupations of, 141-142
  polygyny among, 146
  property among, 144
  slavery among, 143
  social order among, 136-137
  usury among, 145
  views of
    on human nature, 132-135
    on labor, 143
    on wealth, 144-145
Heraclitus, 157
heredity, Aristotle's views on, 190-191
Herodotus, 43, 44, 61, 67, 69
hieratic script, 47
hieroglyphs, 47
Hinduism (*see* Brahmanism)
Hindus, 9, 11 (*see also* Ancient India)
Hippocrates, 157
history
  Khaldun's views on, 294-296
  social thought and, 3-4, 5
Hobbes, Thomas, 6, 8, 9, 297, 347, 351-352, 354, 386
Homer, Vico's study of, 381
Horace, 207, 209
Hughes, E. R., 88-89
human nature
  Aristotle's views on, 188-189
  Comte's views on, 405-409
  Confucius' views on, 96-97
  Hebrew view of, 132-135
  Hindu view of, 111-113
  Khaldun's views on, 296-297
  Locke's views on, 351-353
  Plato's views on, 165-168
  Roman view of, 213-219
  social thought and, 6-7
  Vico's views on, 382-384
humanism
  Greek, 179-180
  Renaissance, 322-324
Huxley, Thomas Henry, 424

Ikhnaton, 46, 48, 50, 62, 68, 72-73
immortality
  Augustine's views on, 258
  Babylonian conception of, 39
  Egyptian view of, 68-70
  Roman view of, 218-219
  (*see also* death; reincarnation)
incest
  Hebrew conception of, 149-151
  Plato's views on, 169
India (*see* Ancient India)
induction, Aristotle's use of, 186-187
industry
  in Babylonia, 28-29
  Khaldun's views on, 306-307
inequality, social, Comte's views on, 408-409
institutions, and social thought, 7 (*see also* family; religion; *and other institutions*)
interest (*see* loans; usury)
irrigation
  in Ancient Egypt, 44
  in Babylonia, 14, 19
Isaiah, 133, 134
Islam (*see* Moslem civilization)
Israelites, 286 (*see also* Hebrews)
Issawi, Charles, 295n., 297n.

Jaeger, Werner, 184
Jainism, 108
James, William, 205
Janet, Paul, 240
Jenghiz Khan, 289
Jeremiah, 133, 134, 136
Jerome, 9, 130, 234, 254
Jerusalem, 127
Jews (*see* Hebrews)
Joachim of Floris, 260
Jones, William, 104
Josephus, 45
Judaic-Christian tradition, 12 (*see also* Hebrews)
judges, Hebrew, 140-141
Julius Ceasar, 49, 207, 209
"just price," 3, 276-277
justice
  in Ancient Egypt, 52-54
  in Ancient India (*see also* karma)
  in Babylonia, 22-27
  Confucius' views on, 85
  among Hebrews, 139-141
  Vico's views on, 389-390

Justinian, 261
Juvenal, 207, 209, 215

Kant, Immanuel, 241
karma, 7, 109-110
Kassites, 41
Keenan, Mary E., 255
Kendall, Willmoore, 357
Kennett, R. H., 144, 147, 148
Kepler, Johannes, 321, 342
Keyes, C. W., 220
Khaldun, Ibn, 2, 5, 10, 283-284, 285-312
   biographical sketch of, 289-292
   on economics, 304-308
   on history, 294-296
   on human nature, 296-297
   on occupations, 305-307
   on physical environment, 298-299
   on politics, 301-304
   on profit motive, 304-305
   on religion, 295-296
   science of, 311-312
   on science, 295-296
   on social change, 308-311
   on social environment, 299
   on social institutions, 307
   on social solidarity, 297-298
   on society, 296-301
   on state, 301-304
   works of, 292-294
Khufu, 44
King, Leonard W., 30
king
   in Ancient Egypt, 49-50, 51-52
   Aristotle's views on, 201
   divine right of, 353*ff.*
   Plato's views on, 174
   Roman views on, 219
   (*see also* ruler; sovereignty)
Kingsley, Charles, 393
Koran, 288, 295-296
Kshatriya, 115-116

labor
   in Babylonia, 29
   Hebrew attitude toward, 143
   (*see also* slavery)
land tenure
   among Hebrews, 144
   Vico's views on, 385-386
   (*see also* property)
language, 7
   Babylonian, 16

Laotse, 76, 79
Laski, Harold, 354
law
   in Ancient Egypt, 49-53
   in Babylonia, 20-27
   Confucius' views on, 85
   among Hebrews, 138-141
   natural (*see* natural law)
   Roman (*see* Twelve Tables)
   Vico's views on, 386-390
   (*see also* code)
Laws, Cicero's, 211
Laws of Eshnunna, 20, 29
Laws of Manu, 106-107
Laws, Plato's, 172, 177*ff.*
legal documents, Babylonian, 19-20
Legge, James, 82, 83, 90
Leibnitz, Gottfried Wilhelm, 342
Leviathan state, 6
levirate, 150
Lévy-Bruhl, L., 397, 407, 412, 416-417
Lewis, Bernard, 292
lex talionis, 22, 23, 139-141
literature
   of Ancient Egypt, 48
   of Ancient India, 104-107
   of Hebrews (*see* Old Testament)
   (*see also* epics; myths; writings)
Livingstone, Richard, 170
Livy, 209
loans, in Babylonia, 28-29 (*see also* usury)
Locke, John, 2, 8, 9, 10, 283-284, 342-365, 386
   biographical sketch of, 345-347
   on education, 361-365
   on human nature, 351-353
   influence of, 365
   method of, 349-351
   on morality, 350
   on politics, 353-359
   on popular sovereignty, 356-357
   on property, 359-361
   on religious toleration, 358-359
   on slavery, 351
   and social contract, 354-356
logic (*see* reason; syllogism)
Lollards, 317
Lowes, John Livingston, 131
Lucretius, 155, 207, 209, 210-211, 215, 216, 217, 218, 221, 225-226, 227-229
Luther, Martin, 2, 284, 317-318, 325, 327, 329, 330, 333, 335, 336, 337, 338, 339
Lycurgus, 184

464 · Index

Machiavelli, Niccolo, 8, 9, 284, 324, 325, 326, 327, 331-332
Magellan, Fernando, 316, 321
Magna Carta, 260
Mahabharata, 105, 108
Maimonides, 260
man, Aristotle's views on, 189-191 (*see also* human nature)
Manetho, 45
Manichaeism, 235, 236, 238
Manu, 106-107, 112, 119, 121
manus, 222, 223
Marcus Aurelius, 209, 213, 265
Maritain, Jacques, 281
Marlowe, Christopher, 323-324
marriage
   in Ancient Egypt, 61-63
   Aquinas' views on, 278-279
   Aristotle's views on, 203-204
   Augustine's views on, 254-255
   in Babylonia, 32-34
   consanguinity and, 150
   among Hebrews, 146-147
   Reformation views on, 338-339
   in Rome, 223-224
   (*see also* endogamy; exogamy; divorce; family; incest; polygamy; polygyny; women)
Martel, Charles, 285
Martial, 209
Martineau, Harriet, 396
Maspero, G., 63
matriarchy, in Ancient Egypt, 60-61
Matthews, W. R., 331
Mayas, 14
medieval social thought, 155-156 (*see also* Aquinas; Augustine)
Melancthon, Philipp, 328, 335
Mencius, 82, 87, 96
Menes, 44
mercantilism, 334-335
Mesopotamia, 13
metaphysics, 183
Micah, 133, 134
Middle Ages, 313-314 (*see also* medieval social thought)
Mill, John Stuart, 395, 396-397, 399, 400, 412-413, 418, 424
Mishna, 130
Moabites, 127, 128, 286
Mohammed, 287-288
Mohammedanism, 288-289
monarchy, Polybius' views on, 229 (*see also* king; ruler; sovereignty)

money
   in Ancient Egypt, 54-55
   in Babylonia, 28
monogamy
   in Ancient Egypt, 62-63
   in Rome, 226
   (*see also* marriage)
monotheism
   in Ancient Egypt, 67-68
   Hebrews and, 152-153
Montaigne, Michel Eyquem de, 284, 323, 324, 325, 337
Montesquieu, 9, 368-369, 405
moral growth, Confucius' views on, 96
morality, Locke's views on, 350 (*see also* ethics)
More, Henry, 178
More, Thomas, 284, 323, 327, 334-335, 336, 337-338
Moses, 139
Moslem civilization, 285-289
Müller, Max, 63
Murray, Margaret A., 42*n*., 63
mysticism, 243-244
   of Augustine, 244, 246
   Khaldun and, 295-296
myths, Babylonian, 17-18, 22 (*see also* epics; literature; religion)

Napoleon, 392
nationalism
   of Cicero, 222
   during Renaissance and Reformation, 327-328
natural environment, 13
   of Ancient Egypt, 44
   of Hebrews, 126
   Khaldun's views on, 298-299
   of Rome, 207
natural law, Aquinas' views on, 270-271
natural resources, and civilization, 14
natural sciences, 4
nature, Augustine's views of, 244-245
   (*see also* human nature; natural environment)
Nebuchadnezzar, 41, 128
Neoplatonism, 178, 244
Nero, 212, 214
New Science, 10
New Testament, 129
Newton, Isaac, 342, 369
Nicomachean Ethics, 183-184, 192-193
Nile River, 43, 58

Index · 465

nomadism, 299-301
nominalism, 262
norms (*see* social norms)
Northrop, F. C. S., 100

occupations, among Hebrews, 141-142
  (*see also* agriculture; industry; trade)
Octavius Caesar, 46
offenses, legal, in Babylonia, 25 (*see also* punishment)
Old Testament, 9, 12, 129-132
oligarchy, 174
  Polybius' views on, 229
Organon, Aristotle's, 183
original sin, 249, 254
  Augustine's views of, 246-247
Ostheimer, Anthony L., 278-279, 280
outcastes, 117-118
Ovid, 207, 209, 215
Owen, Robert, 393

Palestine, 125-127 (*see also* Hebrews)
Papini, G., 244
parents, attitude toward, in China, 93-95 (*see also* children)
Pareto, Vilfredo, 379
Pascal, Blaise, 342
Pelagians, 236
Pentateuch, 139
Pericles, 157
personality, caste and, 117-118
Petrarch, 315, 318
Petrie, Flinders, 56
Petronius, 209
pharaoh (*see* king)
Philo, 240
physical environment (*see* natural environment)
Pizarro, Francisco, 316
Plato, 1, 2, 3, 5, 6, 9, 155, 156, 157-178, 179, 181, 184, 204, 205, 213, 240, 261
  approach of, to knowledge, 162-164
  biographical sketch of, 162
  dialogues of, 163, 164-165
  on education, 170-171
  on family, 168-170
  on freedom, 166, 167
  on human nature, 165-168
  on slavery, 168
  on social change, 175-177
  on social stratification, 167, 173

Plato—*Continued*
  on state, 166, 168, 172-175
  on status of women, 169-170
Platonism, 177-178
Pliny, 209
Plotinus, 178, 241
Plutarch, 209
polis, 198-199
political change, Aristotle's views on, 202-203 (*see also* social change)
political organization, 7
  Comte's views on, 412-413 (*see also* politics)
Politics, Aristotle's, 184-185, 205
politics
  Aquinas' views on, 268-272
  Aristotle's views on, 197-203
  Augustine's views of, 249-253
  Khaldun's views on, 301-304
  Locke's views on, 353-359
  and theology, 4
Pollock, Frederick, 359
polyandry, in Ancient India, 121
Polybius, 155, 210, 216, 219, 221, 225, 229
polygamy, Luther's views on, 339
polygyny
  in Ancient India, 121-122
  among Hebrews, 146
polytheism, in Ancient Egypt, 65-67
Pope, Alexander, 372
Porcia, Gian Artico de, 370
positivism, 398-400
prices, in Babylonia, 29 (*see also* "just price")
profit motive, Khaldun's views on, 304-305 (*see also* trade; usury)
progress
  Comte's views on, 415-417
  Plato's views on, 175-176
Prolegomena, 10, 293-294
property
  in Ancient Egypt, 54-55
  Aquinas' views on, 273, 274-275
  Augustine's views on, 251-252
  in Babylonia, 33
  among Hebrews, 144
  Locke's views on, 359-361
  (*see also* land tenure)
Protestantism (*see* Reformation)
Protrepticus, 184
Pseudepigrapha, 129, 130
Ptah-hotep, 42, 44, 61, 62, 64
Ptolemy, 46

punishment
  in Babylonia, 24-25
  among Hebrews, 139
Pyramid Texts, 44, 48

Rabelais, 323
Radhakrishnan, S., 114
Ramayana, 105, 110, 115, 120
Ramses, 46, 49, 71
rationalism, 241
  Cartesian, 347-349, 373-375
reason
  Aquinas' views on, 267
  Augustine's view of, 242-243
  faith and, 267
  Plato's views on, 163-164, 165
  Reformation views on, 319-320
  Roman view of, 217
  (*see also* rationalism)
redemption, Hebrew concept of, 138
reform, social, 393
Reformation, 317-318
  and authority, 318-319
  church and state during, 330-331
  and experience, 319-320
  family during, 336-340
  nationalism during, 327-328
  and reason, 319-320
  views during
    on human nature, 322-326
    on politics, 326-332
  (*see also* Renaissance)
reincarnation, 7, 68-69
  Hindu view of, 109-110
  (*see also* death; immortality)
religion, 7
  in Ancient Egypt, 65-69
  in Ancient India, 107-113
  in Babylonia, 20-22, 37-40
  Comte's views on, 398-400, 422-424
  of Hebrews, 127-153 *passim*
  Khaldun's views on, 295-296, 302-303
  Locke's views on, 358-359
  positivism as, 398-400, 422-424
  in Rome, 233
  and social thought, 4
  and state, 302-303
  Vico's views on, 386
  (*see also* church; epics; myths; Reformation)
Renaissance, 5, 314-317
  and authority, 318-319
  economics during, 332-336
  and experience, 320-321

Renaissance—*Continued*
  humanism of, 322-324
  nationalism during, 327-328
  and reason, 319-320
  science during, 340-341
  status of women during, 337-338
  views during
    on human nature, 322-326
    on marriage, 338-339
    on politics, 326-332
  (*see also* Reformation)
Republic, Cicero's, 211
Republic, Plato's, 164*ff.*, 172*ff.*, 177*ff.*, 201, 205
retaliation (*see* lex talionis)
Retractations, Augustine's, 240-241, 258
Rig-veda, 104, 108
rituals, Mohammedan, 288-289 (*see also* religion)
Rogers, Arthur W., 196
Rome, 155-156
  Augustine and, 233
  Christianity in, 239
  decline and fall of, 231-232
  economy of, 231-232
  family in, 222-226
  government of, 219-221
  historical background of, 206-208
  law in (*see* Twelve Tables)
  marriage in, 223-224
  religion in, 233-234
  social change in, 226-231
  status of women in, 224-225
Rosenthal, Erwin I. J., 297*n.*, 302-303, 307
Rosetta Stone, 47, 73
Rostovtzeff, M., 43, 227
ruler
  Confucius' views of, 86-87
  of Hebrews, 135-136
  Khaldun's views on, 305-306
  Reformation views on, 328-330
  (*see also* government; king; sovereignty; state; tyrant)
Ruskin, John, 393

Sachar, Abram, 127*n.*
St. Augustine (*see* Augustine)
St. Dominic, 260
St. Francis, 260
Saint-Simon, Claude Henri, 393, 394
salvation, Christian doctrine of, 6
Sama-veda, 104
Sappho, 157

Sarton, George, 292
Saul, 127
Savonarola, Girolamo, 319
Sayce, A. H., 47
Schmidt, Nathaniel, 291, 295n., 300
Scholasticism, 267
Schopenhauer, Arthur, 105
science, 2-6
　emergence of, 343-344
　Khaldun's views on, 295-296, 311-312
　Renaissance and, 321, 340-341
　Vico and, 371-375
　(see also rationalism; reason)
Scipio Africanus, 210
sedentary societies, 299-301
Seele, Keith C., 42n.
self-expression, 7
Semites (see Hebrews)
Sen, Gertrude E., 105, 118
Seneca, 155, 207, 209, 212-213, 215-219 passim, 222, 225, 226, 230-231, 240
Servetus, Michael, 319
Shakespeare, William, 2-3, 4, 5, 162
Shang Dynasty, 75-77
Sidney, Algernon, 353
Sikhism, 108
sin, original, 249, 254
　Augustine's views of, 246-247
slavery
　in Ancient Egypt, 54
　Aristotle's views on, 199-200
　Augustine's views on, 250-251
　in Babylonia, 30-31
　among Hebrews, 143
　Locke's views on, 351
　Plato's views on, 168
　Roman view on, 217
　(see also labor)
Smith, Preserved, 316-317, 320-321, 340
Smith, Sidney, 27
social change
　Augustine's views on, 256-258
　Comte's views on, 413-419
　Khaldun's views on, 308-311
　in Rome, 226-231
　social organization and, 7-8
　Vico's views on, 375-379
　(see also political change)
social classes
　in Ancient Egypt, 55-57
　in Ancient India, 113-119
　Aristotle's views on, 188
　in Babylonia, 30
　Plato's views on, 167, 173

social contract
　Locke and, 354-356
　Vico's views on, 386
social dynamics, 402, 414-415
social environment, Khaldun's views on, 299
social equality, Confucius' views on, 83-84
social institutions, 7
　Khaldun's views on, 307
social justice, in Babylonia, 25-27 (see also justice)
social mobility, in Babylonia, 33-34 (see also social classes)
social norms, of Hebrews, 137
social order
　Confucius' view of, 83-85
　among Hebrews, 136-137
social organization
　Comte's views on, 410-413
　and social change, 7-8
social science, 2-3, 4 (see also sociology)
social solidarity, Khaldun's views on, 297-298
social statics, 402, 410
social status, in Babylonia, and legal obligations, 24 (see also social classes)
social thought, and social history, 3-4
social values, 8
society
　Aquinas' views on, 269
　Khaldun's views on, 296-301
　nomadic vs. sedentary, 299-301
　Plato's views on, 167-168
sociology, 4
　Comte's conception of, 400-405
Socrates, 157, 158-161, 164
Socratic method, 164-165
Solomon, 136
Solon, 157
Sophists, 164
Sophocles, 157, 172
Sorokin, Pitirim A., 241, 243-244, 292, 300, 379
sororate, 150
soul, Hindu view of, 110
sovereignty
　Hebrew views on, 135-136
　popular, Locke's views on, 356-358
　Vico's views on, 376-378
Spinoza, Baruch, 342
state
　Aquinas' views on, 270

state—*Continued*
  Aristotle's views on, 184, 197-198, 200-201
  Augustine's views on, 249-250
  church and, 330-331
  Plato's views on, 166, 168, 172-175
  Reformation views on, 330-331
  (*see also* citizenship; government; ruler; sovereignty)
Steindorff, George, 42*n*.
Stoicism, Vico and, 370-371
Stoics, 240, 249 (*see also* Zeno)
stratification (*see* social classes)
Strato, 205
Sudra, 117
Sufism, 289
Summa Theologica, 10, 260, 265
syllogism, 186

tabula rasa, 349, 354
Tacitus, 209
Tagore, Rabindranath, 121, 122
Talmud, 130
Teachings of Ptah-hotep, 44
Tertullian, 119, 254
theology, 4 (*see also* religion)
Theophrastus, 205
Thomism, 266, 281-282
Thorndike, E. L., 405
Thutmose III, 45, 46, 51
Tigris River, 13
Tillyard, E. M. W., 322
timocracy, 174
toleration, Locke's views on, 358-359
Tönnies, Ferdinand, 300, 312
Torah, 139
Toynbee, Arnold J., 73, 100, 158, 292, 295*n*., 297*n*., 298, 300
trade
  in Babylonia, 28-29
  Khaldun's views on, 305-306
  (*see also* capitalism; mercantilism; profit motive; usury)
Troeltsch, Ernst, 254, 276-277
Tutankh-Amon, 46
Twelve Tables, 209-210, 221, 223, 224, 225, 385, 388, 389
Tyndale, William, 328
tyrant, Plato's views on, 175 (*see also* king; ruler)

Ulpian, 223
Universal History, Khaldun's, 293

Upanishads, 104-105, 108, 110-111, 112
usury
  Aquinas' views on, 275-276
  Hebrew view of, 140, 145
  during Renaissance, 335-336
  (*see also* profit motive; trade)

Vaisya, 116-117
values, social, 8
Vaughan, R. W., 264, 371
Vaux, Clothilde de, 5, 395, 420, 421, 422
Vedas, 2, 104, 112
Vesalius, 321, 343
Vico, Giambattista, 2, 6, 8, 9, 10, 283, 284, 366-391
  biographical sketch of, 366-369
  contributions of, 390-391
  on economics, 384-386
  on family life, 382-383
  on freedom of will, 383-384
  on government, 386-390
  on Homer, 381
  on human nature, 382-384
  on justice, 389-390
  on law, 386-390
  on religion, 386
  and science, 371-375
  on social change, 375-379
  on social nature of man, 383
  on unity of culture, 379-382
  writings of, 369-371
Vinci, Leonardo da, 5, 315, 316-317
Virgil, 207, 209
virtue
  Aristotle's views on, 194
  Confucius' views on, 99
  Hindu view of, 110-111
vizier, in Ancient Egypt, 50-51
"vulgar wisdom," 380-381

wages, in Babylonia, 29 (*see also* "just price"; labor)
Waldensians, 317
Wallace, Edwin, 191
water
  and Babylonian civilization, 13
  and Egyptian civilization, 43
Watters, Thomas, 76
wealth, Hebrew attitude toward, 144-145
Weber, Max, 100, 318, 334, 379, 380
Western civilization
  Arabs and, 285-286
  Hebrew contributions to, 152-153
  medieval society and, 260-261

Westminster Confession, 130
Whitehead, Alfred North, 178
Wilde, Oscar, 1
William the Conqueror, 260
Wilson, Epiphanius, 105
Wilson, Woodrow, 153
Windelband, Wilhelm, 236, 247-248
women, status of
  in Ancient Egypt, 61, 63-64
  in Ancient India, 119-121
  Aquinas' views on, 279-280
  Aristotle's views on, 204
  Augustine's views on, 255-256
  in Babylonia, 26, 34-36
  in China, 91
  Comte's views on, 421-422
  Plato's views on, 169-170
  during Renaissance, 337-338
  in Rome, 224-225
  (*see also* marriage; matriarchy)
Woody, Thomas, 200
writing
  in Ancient Egypt, 47
  in Babylonia, 14, 15-17

writing—*Continued*
  in China, 75
  cuneiform, 14, 15-17
writings
  of Ancient Egypt, 46-49
  of Aquinas, 265-266, 268
  of Aristotle, 182-185
  of Augustine, 237-241
  of Comte, 396-398
  of Khaldun, 292-294
  of Locke, 347
  Roman, 208-213
  of Vico, 369-371
Wycliffe, John, 130

Yajur-veda, 104
Young, Robert, 73
Yutang, Lin, 100

Zeno, 2, 213
Zimmerman, Carle, 292
Zwingli, Ulrich, 318, 335

the practice of putting notes at the end of a book and re-number for each chapter

poetic language

the culture of the great (oriental) ancient empires cannot be understood outside the framework provided by cultural anthropology

HM 19 .C36 1954
Chambliss, Rollin.
Social thought, from
 Hammurabi to Comte

DATE DUE